Uncle John's FACTASTIC BATHROOM READER®

By the Bathroom Readers' Institute

Bathroom Readers' Press
Ashland, Oregon

Thank You!

The Bathroom Readers' Institute sincerely thanks the people whose advice and assistance made this book possible.

Gordon Javna

John Dollison

Jay Newman

Brian Boone

Trina Janssen

Kim Griswell

Thom Little

Tom Deja

Michael Brunsfeld

Brandon Hartley

Jack Mingo

Megan Todd

Pablo Goldstein

Jeff Giles

Hannah L. Bingham

Jahnna Beecham

Tracy Vonder Brink

Aaron Guzman

Jill Bellrose

Julie McLaughlin

Andy Sohn

Patrick Merrell

Dan Mansfield

JoAnn and Melinda

Jennifer, Mana, and Lilian

David Hoye

Blake Mitchum

Peter Norton

Mighty John Marshall

Rusty von Dyl

Raincoast Books

Media Masters

Publishers Group West

Maggie, Sam & Gid

Q. Duck

Dirt Boots

Ricky Meatball

Porter's Ghost

Thomas Crapper

*　　*　　*

"Having a baby changes the way you view your in-laws. I love it when they come to visit. They hold the baby and I go out."
—**Matthew Broderick**

Contents

Because the BRI understands your reading needs, we've divided the contents by length as well as subject.

Short—a quick read

Medium—2 to 3 pages

Long—for those extended visits, when something a little more involved is required

* Extended—for those leg-numbing experiences

*　　　*　　　*

SOY VEY!

Even the most devoted soy lover might gag at the thought of eating these food items.

- **Natto:** This traditional Japanese breakfast food of fermented soybeans has a dis-stink-tive odor. It's been described as smelling like a public urinal. But despite the aroma, natto was a vital source of nutrition for people in feudal Japan. It is rich in protein, high in vitamin K2 (for bones and teeth), and loaded with healthy bacteria. For modern Japanese, natto's health benefits still outweigh the nasty smell…though its slippery texture looks to some like "soybeans held together by snot."

- **Kitto Katsu:** Nestlé's Japanese version of the Kit Kat bar, flavored with soy sauce.

- **Vegan Fish:** This San Francisco restaurant was pescetarian—catering to people who eat seafood but no other meats. One of their weirdest menu items: vegan "fish" and chips—fermented soybean cakes that are flavored with ginger, then rolled in rice flour and sesame seeds, deep-fried, and served with french fries, cole slaw, and vegan tartar sauce. Want to try it yourself? Too late! The restaurant closed in 2014.

- **Soy Sauce Sorbet:** It takes only four ingredients to make this low-fat "treat"—water, sugar, soy sauce, and orange zest. Optional ingredient: a few teaspoons of vodka—not to make it alcoholic, but to prevent the frozen dessert from freezing solid.

- **Stik Tahu:** These crunchy fried tofu snacks come in a bag with the name of the chain store that sells them printed in giant letters across the front of the package: POO.

- **Nodogoshi Nama:** A soy-based beer substitute that avoids Japan's high beer taxes by using soy protein instead of malted grain, the primary ingredient in beer. This non-beer, or "third beer," as such beverages are called in Japan, has a taste that's been described as light and crisp but not at all beerlike. That's putting it gently—"Green vegetable smell… with a touch of toothpaste," one reviewer posted online. "Pretty dirty soda aftertaste, avoid!"

Uncle John's 28th Fact-troduction

W elcome one and all to our 28th annual edition—*Uncle John's FACTASTIC Bathroom Reader!* Happy to have you with us. Now, in keeping with the book's theme, let me start off this year's introduction with a VSF (Very Special Fact):

The most valuable bathtub in the world is valued at $5 million. It is solid gold.

That was our very first "running foot"—the little fact that ran underneath the very first article in the very first *Uncle John's Bathroom Reader*, published way back in 1988.

And the fact that we're still around 28 years later is a testament to the power of great facts. They truly are the building blocks of *Uncle John's Bathroom Reader*, the atoms that bind this whole series together. You'll find thousands of facts throughout this book on everything from anatomy to baseball to ballet to whatever else piques our curiosity.

And to pique *your* curiosity, we thought we'd do something a little different this year and riffle through the manuscript and find some fascinating facts to share right here. (Because, after all, I'm not just the boss of the Bathroom Readers' Institute, I'm also a fan.) So here goes.

• Flipping to "3-D Printing" on page 191, you'll read that **NASA uses 3-D printers to make pizzas for astronauts.**

• From page 177, "The Only Two States": **The only two states where you can't pump your own gas are New Jersey and Oregon.** (Another fun fact: Uncle John's never pumped gas—he grew up in New Jersey and now lives in Oregon.)

• Trivia quiz: **What ubiquitous piece of technology was patented in the 1960s as an "X/Y Position Indicator"?** (Answer on next page.)

• **The guy who invented the game Operation was so broke late in his life that he couldn't afford an...operation.** More ironies on page 114.

• For history buffs, on page 131 is the inspiring story of **J. E. Hanger— the first Civil War soldier to lose a leg—who invented the modern prosthetic limb.**

• **Why did author Peter Benchley become a shark conservationist late in life? He regretted the fact that his bestselling 1975 novel** *Jaws* **made people afraid of sharks.** More authors who regretted their books on page 154.

• In "Weird Baby Facts" on page 80, it says that **babies in the womb are covered with hair. (And they pee.)**

• **A common paint color called "Mummy Brown" was made from real powdered Egyptian mummies.** More "True Colors" on page 91.

• I love the pages of slang in this book. Here's one from page 305: **During the Civil War, soldiers from Georgia were called "goober grabbers."**

• From "Tunnel Vision" on page 234, **only 45 percent of the London Underground is actually underground.**

I could keep going, but I have to stop before I run out of room, even though I haven't even scratched the surface of what you'll find in *FACTASTIC*. And rest assured that, as in any great Uncle John's tome, there's much more than fascinating facts. We've amassed our usual array of odd news, wordplay, science, quotations, how-to tips, and all sorts of other goodies.

As our regular readers have no doubt noticed, this book has a new look—it's larger than past annual editions, and we've even updated the style. Our goal was to cram even more great bathroom reading onto every page without making it look too daunting. What that means for you: your new *Bathroom Reader* has a lot more facts than previous editions!

I'll end this introduction with one final fact: this book could not have been made without the unwavering dedication of our unwavering staff. Great job, team! Keep not wavering. As for you, dear reader, it's time for me to shut up and for you to embark on your…FACTASTIC Journey.

As always: Go with the Flow!

—**Uncle John, Felix the dog, and the BRI staff**

Answer to the trivia quiz on the previous page: It's the computer mouse. (More office origins on page 27.)

You're My Inspiration

It's always interesting to find out where the architects of pop culture get their ideas. Some of these may surprise you.

CHEWBACCA. When *Star Wars* concept artist Ralph McQuarrie showed George Lucas his early sketches of Han Solo's companion, Lucas didn't think the character looked alien enough. He showed McQuarrie an illustration of a tall, furry beast from a 1975 short story called "And Seven Times Never Kill Man." That beast ended up as the basis for Chewbacca. The short story's author: George R. R. Martin, who would later create *Game of Thrones*.

THE MINIONS. The unintelligible little creatures from the *Despicable Me* movies are a combination of the Oompa-Loompas from *Willy Wonka & the Chocolate Factory* (the 1971 Gene Wilder version) and the Jawas from *Star Wars*.

FLO, THE PROGRESSIVE GIRL. Played since 2008 by comedian Stephanie Courtney, the Progressive Insurance spokeslady was based on a 1960s Comet Cleanser ad campaign that featured Josephine the Plumber, played by actress Jane Withers.

PAVEL CHEKOV. Two TV shows debuted on NBC in 1966: *The Monkees*, which was a huge hit, and *Star Trek*, which had trouble finding viewers. So for *Trek*'s second season, a new character was added—a Russian ensign played by Walter Koenig. His purpose: to appeal to teenagers, just like *The Monkees*' Davy Jones. Both characters are young, foreign, and have a "floppy Beatles moptop."

POKÉMON. In this video game, first created for the Nintendo Game Boy in 1995, players have to train species of Pokémons to fight other Pokémon teams. The game was conceived by Satoshi Tajiri in 1989. His inspiration: as a kid he used to collect insects. The name is a contraction of *Poketto Monsuta*—"Pocket Monsters."

E.T. THE EXTRA-TERRESTRIAL. Director Steven Spielberg told his design team that he wanted an alien that 1) no one had ever seen before, and 2) "only a mother could love." Result: E.T.'s body is based on a snapping turtle embryo, his behind was inspired by Donald Duck, and his facial features are a combination of author Ernest Hemingway, poet Carl Sandburg, and Albert Einstein.

The brain is the fattiest organ in the human body—it's about 60% fat.

Flubbed Headlines

These are 100% honest-to-goodness headlines.
Can you figure out what they were trying to say?

**Astronaut Welcomes
Baby from Space**

Parking Lot Floods
When Man Bursts

**Elderly Woman
Found Using GPS**

Indiana Guardsman Gets 2
Years in Ohio Bomb Case

*Bans on Children Aim
to Stop Swine Flu Spread*

Road Rage Leads Police to
Murder Victim's Boyfriend

VIDEO: QUEEN VISITS
IRISH NATIONAL STUD

MYSTIC EVACUATED;
COWS DIE

**28M Gallons of Sewage
into Mianus**

Most Doctors Agree
Breathing Regularly Is
Good for You

**Editor's Wife Rented to 2
Suspects, FBI Says**

Scientists Decode Why
Humans Are Intelligent
Than Chimps

*Lawmakers Disagree Over
Why They Can't Agree*

Navy SEALs Responsible for
Getting Osama Bin Laden to
Be Honored at 9/11 Museum

**For Most, Water Is a
Good Hydrating Drink**

*State Population to Double
by 2040; Babies to Blame*

BISHOPS AGREE
SEX ABUSE RULES

Authorities Pursue Man
Running with Scissors

**Sultan Woman with Dog's Head
Taken to Hospital**

REPORTERS RETURN TO
TIBET AFTER RIOTING

Barbershop Singers Bring
Joy to School for Deaf

HAY NOT PLEASED WITH
SLUMPING PP

**Solar System Plagued
Again by Thieves**

Big Rig Carrying Fruit
Crashes on 210 Freeway,
Creates Jam

The U.S. Supreme Court receives 10,000 petitions per year but hears only about 80 cases.

Fruity Geography

*We've treated you to a lot of food name origins over the years.
Here are a few we missed—of the fruity variety.*

P **EACH.** The English word *peach* is, surprisingly enough, derived
from an ancient Greek name for Persia. The Greeks called the
peach the *Persikon malon*, meaning "Persian apple," or simply
Persikos. Reason: It was the Persians who first introduced the fruit—
which actually originated in China—to Europe. The Greek name
evolved over the centuries, becoming *pesca* in Latin, and then *pesche* in
Old French, before arriving in English as *peach* around 1400.

ANJOU PEAR. These creamy pears, sometimes called *beurré d'Anjou*,
meaning "butter of Anjou" in French, are named after the northwest
French province of Anjou. But this is believed to be a mistake. Botanists
say Anjou pears were bred from the European pear (from which the
world's most popular pear cultivars were derived) in the early 1800s,
probably in Belgium. When they were first exported to the U.K. and the
U.S. in the 1840s, someone named them Anjou—and nobody knows
quite why…but that's what they've been called ever since.

FUJI APPLE. In the late 1930s, botanists at the Tohoku Research
Station in Fujisaki, Japan, began work on creating an apple that was
sweet, crisp, and didn't spoil quickly. It took more than 20 years, but
in 1962, the TRS's Fuji apple—as in "Fujisaki"—went to market
worldwide. A cross of two American varieties, the Ralls-Genet and the
Red Delicious, Fuji apples are very sweet, extra crisp, and are notable
for yellow, green, orange, and red stripes. The Fuji is one of the top 10
best-selling apple varieties in the U.S.…but it's still the #1 seller in Japan.

CURRANT. This raisin variety got its name from the Greek city of
Corinth. In the 13th century, raisins from the Mediterranean region
started becoming popular in England. In the 14th century, a special kind
of raisin made from very small seedless grapes started selling under the
name *reisin de Corauntz*, meaning "raisin of Corinth," after the city in
southern Greece, where these raisins were produced. By 1500, *reisin* had
been dropped, and *Corauntz* had evolved into *currant*—still our name
for the tiny raisin today. (Extra fact: *Currant* is also the name of a genus
of berries, including the black currant, red currant, and white currant.
The berry got that name in the late 1500s—because it resembled the
grape-derived currant.)

Better Than Gold

"Worth its weight in gold" is used to describe very valuable items. But based on weight, gold—worth around $40 a gram—is far from the most valuable commodity around.

CASH. According to the U.S. Bureau of Engraving, all American bills weigh a gram. That means a $50 bill is worth $50 a gram…more than gold.

RHINO HORN. Rhinos are endangered, but their horns are an ingredient in traditional folk medicines in Vietnam, China, and other Asian countries. A gram of powdered rhino horn sells for about $55.

TOMATOES. Genetically modified foods, particularly tomatoes, are trademarked by the agribusiness companies that develop them, such as DuPont and Monsanto. A pound of GMO tomato seeds can run as high as $18,000—more than a pound of gold.

HONEY. Elvish honey can be collected only from a deep cave in northeastern Turkey. Professional climbers have to extract it, meaning that a 4.5-ounce jar costs € 5,000, or $6,800—around $53 a gram.

PLUTONIUM. The active ingredient in nuclear warheads. Price: about $4,000 per gram.

RHODIUM. Listed on the periodic table of elements as a transitional metal, rhodium is rare, but it is a useful substance in pollution prevention. Used to manufacture three-way catalytic converters in car engines, it costs about $45 per gram.

ILLEGAL DRUGS. In terms of their weight, street drugs are very expensive. One 250-microgram dose of LSD costs about $10. That's $3,000 a gram. (Cocaine is a relative bargain at $150 per gram.)

TAAFFEITE. This beautiful purple gem is thought to be a million times rarer than diamonds. It's suitably expensive: as much as $20,000 per gram.

TRITIUM. This green-glowing mineral used to light up glow-in-the-dark exit signs is extremely rare and costs $30,000 per gram.

MELANIN. This organic material determines skin tone in humans. But it's also a natural source of ink, harvested from cuttlefish, who use it to camouflage themselves and avoid predators. Current market price: about $360 a gram.

Barbie's first outfit: A black-and-white striped swimsuit.

"OW!"

A few weird, strange, odd—and sometimes just funny—painful news stories.

VICTIM: In July 2013, a 15-year-old boy in Columbus, Ohio, built himself a homemade blowgun using instructions he found on the Internet. Once finished, he gave it a test run.

OW! Before he could blow the roughly three-inch-long, needlelike dart out of the gun, the boy took a deep breath…and inhaled the dart into his windpipe, where it became lodged. The boy went to his parents, but, afraid to tell them about the blowgun, he said only that he'd suddenly started coughing and wheezing. His parents took him to a hospital, where—about three hours later—an X-ray finally revealed the truth, and the boy was forced admit what had happened. Doctors were able to remove the dart (by inserting a tubelike device, fitted with tiny forceps, into the boy's windpipe via his mouth—ow!—again), noting that the boy would be fine and would not suffer any permanent damage.

VICTIM: A 44-year-old New Zealand woman was smooching with her husband one night in 2010 when he gave her a hickey on the right side of her neck.

OW! A few days later, the woman had a stroke—caused by the hickey. Dr. Teddy Wu of Auckland's Middlemore Hospital made the surprising diagnosis after he examined the woman and noticed the fading bruise left by the hickey. Further examination found that the hickey had damaged an artery in the woman's neck, which in turn had caused a blood clot to form. The clot, said Dr. Wu, had then traveled from the woman's neck to her heart, where it caused the stroke, resulting in the partial paralysis of the left side of her body. Thankfully, after treatment with anticoagulants, the woman made a full recovery. According to Dr. Wu, whose report was published in the *New Zealand Medical Journal*, it was the only case of a hickey causing a stroke ever recorded.

VICTIM: In 2010 actor Channing Tatum was in Scotland working on the film *The Eagle*. In one of Tatum's scenes, his character, a Roman centurion named Marcus Flavius Aquila, wades, fights, and lies down in a river. Because it was a very cold river, and because the scene took many hours to film, Tatum wore a partial wetsuit under his clothes. To help keep the actor warm, an assistant would regularly take a pot of boiling water, mix in some cold river water, and pour the mixture into the wetsuit. But this one time…

Mothers over age 40 are twice as likely as younger mothers to have a left-handed baby.

OW! ...the assistant forgot to mix cold water into the pot. Tatum immediately pulled the wetsuit away from his body, but that only allowed the boiling water to travel further down into the suit. Too far down: Not only was he seriously burned over his stomach, but the scalding water, according to Tatum, "pretty much burnt all the skin off my [you-know-what]." The actor was rushed to a hospital, where he was administered painkillers and treated for the severe burns. "It was by far the most painful and excruciatingly dark situation I've ever got myself into," Tatum later told the *Sunday Times*. Remarkably, though, he made a quick and full recovery and was back on the set in just a few days.

VICTIM: In June 2015, Fiona Crabb of Manchester, England, arrived home at about 10:00 p.m. after work. She reached for the front door handle to her apartment...and couldn't let go.

OW! Crabb shouted for help until her husband woke up and they called emergency services, who thought she was joking. She wasn't—but the two teenage boys she says she saw running off laughing after she reached for the door handle were. The pranksters, still unidentified, had left superglue on the handle. Paramedics, firefighters, and other emergency personnel arrived. Various methods were used to free Crabb, including WD-40, vegetable oil, and even Coca-Cola. Four hours later, an emergency responder cut the door handle out of the door, and Crabb was taken to a hospital, where the knob was removed after doctors used a special solution to dissolve the glue. Crabb was left with painful burns on her hand that took weeks to heal.

VICTIM: In December 2013, a 30-year-old man was asked to leave Fiddler's Pub in the town of Northampton, England, for being too intoxicated. The man left, but then walked around to the rear of the building and tried to reenter the pub by climbing over a tall metal fence near the back door. Some time later, someone heard the man calling for help.

OW! The man had made it up the fence, but had then fallen and skewered his lower leg, near his ankle, on one of the decorative metal spikes on top of the fence. When pub employees found him, he was hanging upside-down from his skewered foot. Rescue workers had to delicately cut the fence into several pieces to free him, after which he was taken to a local hospital and treated. The rescue workers said the man was so drunk that he didn't feel any pain from the injury, and described him as being in "good spirits" during the ordeal. (We're pretty sure he experienced the "OW!" the next day.)

INSULT TO INJURY: The man needn't have climbed the fence: there was a gate, and it was open. According to one of the pub's bouncers, "He could have just walked through it."

Mr. and Mrs. Gross-Pantti

Will these couples, taken from actual newspaper wedding announcements, be hyphenating their married names? Doubtful…but we wish they would.

Elizabeth MacDonald + Joel Berger = **MacDonald-Berger**

Edna Gowen + Jason Getter = **Gowen-Getter**

Joe Looney + Shelby Warde = **Looney-Warde**

William Best + Jennifer Lay = **Best-Lay**

Daniel Hardy + Rachel Harr = **Hardy-Harr**

Lauren Partee + William Moore = **Partee-Moore**

Keiran Rump + John Orefice = **Rump-Orefice**

Amy Moore + Anthony Bacon = **Moore-Bacon**

Marissa Sawyer + Robert Hiney = **Sawyer-Hiney**

James Rather + Lydia Grim = **Rather-Grim**

Allie Miller + Matthew Bruski = **Miller-Bruski**

Kara Gorey + John Butcher = **Gorey-Butcher**

Elizabeth House + Christopher Reckker = **House-Reckker**

Annette King + Brian Sizer = **King-Sizer**

Jennifer Coody + Jason Head = **Coody-Head**

Crystal Butts + Levi McCracken = **Butts-McCracken**

Sarah Flem + Michael Greene = **Flem-Greene**

Paul Flynt + Loural Stone = **Flynt-Stone**

Morgan Ruff + Jason Goings = **Ruff-Goings**

Justin Funk + Mara Kee = **Funk-Kee**

Amanda Sharp + James Payne = **Sharp-Payne**

Brynn Stolen + Jason Ford = **Stolen-Ford**

Crystal Jaeger + Andrew Meister = **Jaeger-Meister**

Kimberley Yuhasz + Colin Gass = **Yuhasz-Gass**

Brooke Gross + Kevin Pantti = **Gross-Pantti**

Lindsay Broeker + Brandon Nuckles = **Broeker-Nuckles**

Let's hope it's this one! The average American buys less than one book a year.

Borrowed Words

English has been acquiring words from other languages since the fifth century. We've published examples of these "loan words" before. Here are some gnu ones…and the languages they came from.

Chimpanzee (from Tshiluba, spoken in the Democratic Republic of the Congo)

Slalom (from Norwegian)

Dinghy (from Hindi, spoken in India)

Alpaca (from Aymaran, spoken in parts of Bolivia, Peru, and Chile)

Kangaroo (from Guugu-Yimidhirr, spoken in northwest Australia)

Shawl (from Persian)

Tattoo (from Tahitian, spoken on the Pacific island of Tahiti)

Mammoth (from Russian)

Kiwi, mako (from Maori, spoken in New Zealand)

Bog (from Scottish Gaelic)

Stucco (from Italian; it means "plaster.")

Cocaine, condor, guano, puma, quinine (from Quechua, spoken in Peru, Ecuador, and Bolivia)

Vigilante (from Spanish)

Meerkat (from Afrikaans)

Taboo (from Tongan, spoken on the Pacific island of Tonga)

Safari (from Swahili, spoken in Kenya, Uganda, Tanzania, and the island of Zanzibar)

Hoi polloi (from Greek, where it means "the majority." In English it means "rabble.")

Cashew, cayenne, cougar, piranha, tapioca (from Tupi, spoken in Amazon regions of Peru and Brazil)

Gnu (from Hottentot, spoken in southern Africa)

Boomerang, dingo, koala (from Dharug, an extinct language once spoken in southeast Australia)

Impala (from Zulu, spoken in South Africa)

Petunia (from Guarani, spoken in Paraguay and Brazil)

Wanderlust (from German)

Poncho (from Araucanian, spoken in parts of Chile)

Ombudsman (from Swedish)

Cooties (from Malay, where *kutu* means "lice")

(Re)Name That Stadium

Most professional sports stadiums used to be named after the teams that played there (Dodger Stadium, Tiger Stadium) or a person (Wrigley Field, Joe Robbie Stadium). But over the last 20 years or so, teams have developed a source of revenue by selling "naming rights" to their stadiums for millions of dollars. A corporation gets a stadium named after itself as a form of advertising...but what happens when that company goes out of business?

ENRON FIELD: In 1999, shortly before the brand-new Ballpark at Union Station was scheduled to open for Houston Astros games, energy conglomerate Enron Corporation paid the team $100 million for the right to name the stadium Enron Field for 30 years. Then, two years later, Enron was exposed in one of the biggest accounting scandals in history. Financial statements were faked, shareholders were defrauded, and several executives were jailed. The company's share price collapsed and Enron went bankrupt. To avoid being associated with the most loathed company in America, the Astros bought back the rights from Enron for just $2.1 million in early 2002. Naming rights were immediately sold to Minute Maid, a Houston-based subsidiary of Coca-Cola. The price: same as Enron paid, $100 million over 30 years.

THE TWA DOME: Eight years after the NFL's St. Louis Cardinals moved to Phoenix, St. Louis got a new football team in 1995, when the city successfully lured the Los Angeles Rams with a brand-new domed stadium. The costs associated with getting the Rams were offset by selling the naming rights of the complex to St. Louis–based Trans World Airlines for $1.3 million per year. Just one year later, TWA began a rapid decline precipitated by Chapter 11 bankruptcy restructuring and the crash of TWA flight 800, caused by a fuel tank explosion. TWA filed for a third (and final) bankruptcy in 2001. TWA's assets were acquired by American Airlines, but the company did not assume naming rights in St. Louis. Since 2002, the St. Louis facility has been called the Edward Jones Dome, after the investment company.

ARCO ARENA: The first team in the NBA to sell naming rights to its home arena was the Sacramento Kings. In 1988, the Sacramento Sports Arena became ARCO Arena, after the oil and gasoline company. The agreement expired in February 2011, and the rights were snatched up

---

It takes 5.4 gallons of water to produce a single head of broccoli.

by a company called Power Balance—a manufacturer of bracelets that used "holographic technology" to make the wearer better at sports by "resonating and responding to the natural energy field of the body." In other words—and according to multiple independent studies—hogwash. Less than a year after Power Balance bought the naming rights to the Sacramento arena, the company paid $57 million to settle a false advertising claims lawsuit and filed for Chapter 11 bankruptcy. As of 2012, the Kings play in the Sleep Train Arena, named for a locally headquartered mattress store chain.

ADELPHIA COLISEUM: The Tennessee Titans (formerly the Houston Oilers) started playing in Nashville in 1999 in the brand-new Adelphia Coliseum. The naming rights were held by Adelphia Communications, at the time the fifth-largest cable TV provider in the U.S....but the company was virtually unknown in Nashville. Adelphia shelled out $30 million for a 15-year contract, using the naming rights to advertise and position itself against the Nashville area's dominant telecommunications company, BellSouth. The first sign of trouble came in 2002, when Adelphia failed to pay the stadium owners a quarterly payment of $500,000. A few weeks later, Adelphia filed for bankruptcy when an internal accounting scandal broke. The name Adelphia was dropped from the stadium, which was known as just the Coliseum for the next four years. In 2006, Nashville-based lumber company Louisiana Pacific picked up the rights—and the Titans now play on LP Field.

PSINET STADIUM: When the Internet became available for use outside of research institutions and the military in the late 1980s, PSINet was established as one of the very first online service providers, right alongside companies like CompuServe, Prodigy, and America Online. In 1995, just six years after its founding, PSINet was earning $33 million annually. But while it was growing, it wasn't growing as fast—or earning the name recognition—as its competitors. To increase brand awareness, in 1999 the company bought the naming rights to the new Baltimore Ravens football stadium, less than 50 miles from PSINet corporate headquarters in northern Virginia. Within the year, the company had invested $1.4 billion to expand its services and build a fiber-optic network. Unfortunately, the moves were too aggressive...and used up too many financial resources (money) that the company didn't have. PSINet filed for bankruptcy in 2002. The stadium was known as Ravens Stadium for a year, and in 2003 the naming rights were sold to M&T Bank (based in Buffalo, New York), which still owns them.

If an atom were the size of an Olympic stadium, its nucleus would be about the size of a quarter.

The Blessed Breakfast Taco of Beeville, Texas

If you're not a believer in the old saying, "The Lord works in mysterious ways," take a look at some of the places He (and the Virgin Mary) have been sighted lately.

THE HOLY SOCK OF ORPINGTON

Location: Hanging on a clothesline in England

Background: In December 2011, Sarah Crane left her wet laundry sitting in the laundry basket overnight. The following morning, when she went to hang it up to dry, she noticed one particular damp, crumpled sock with wrinkles and water stains that formed an image. "I called my boyfriend over straight away. We both could clearly see the face of Jesus," she told England's *Daily Record* newspaper.

What Happened: Crane and her boyfriend thought about creating a shrine for the sock, but when they moved it, some of the wrinkles disappeared and the face became harder to see. "It's not quite good enough to donate to our local church, but our friends have all been around to see it. We think it's a sign," she says, "but for what we don't know."

THE GLOWING MADONNA OF BELGIUM

Location: In the home of an elderly couple in the village of Jalhay

Background: The couple had owned the 12-inch statue of the Virgin Mary for more than 15 years when, in 2014, it suddenly—and inexplicably—began glowing. In the weeks that followed, thousands of people made pilgrimages to Jalhay to see the statue, including 500 in a single day in March 2014. Four people say they have been cured of physical disabilities after praying to it.

What Happened: When interest in the statue showed no signs of abating, the bishop called for an investigation, and the statue was examined by scientists from the University of Liege. So what causes the statue to give off its strange light? Glow-in-the-dark paint.

Update: No one knows who applied the paint (a prankster may be to blame), but that hasn't stopped the faithful from coming; today the statue is displayed in a nearby church, where crowds can visit it without disturbing the owners.

Gluttons for punishment? More than 50% of female lawyers are married to other lawyers.

THE SACRED STAIN OF ADLINGTON, ENGLAND

Location: On a T-shirt

Background: Musician Terry O'Neill, 45, says he was "not a nice person" before he became born-again in the late 1990s. Since then he's turned his life around, and to celebrate, in 2013 he paid the Psycho Monkey tattoo parlor nearly $1,500 to cover his entire back with a giant portrait of Jesus. (The inking took 14 hours; O'Neill refused all pain-relieving gel during the process. "I thought that would be cheating a bit with me being a Christian. Jesus went through a lot more," he said.)

What Happened: To protect O'Neill's clothes from being stained by ink and blood while the tattoo was healing, the parlor gave him a T-shirt to wear home. It wasn't until he got home and took the T-shirt off that he discovered the face of Christ, imprinted on the inside of the T-shirt. "It was amazing. It's like the shroud [of Turin]. My family and friends' jaws dropped when they saw it," O'Neill told England's *Metro* newspaper.

Update: The folks at Psycho Monkey say it certainly isn't unusual for ink from a fresh tattoo to leave stains (that's what the T-shirt is *for*, after all) or for the stains to be in the image of the tattoo. But they framed the T-shirt anyway. Today it hangs in the tattoo parlor.

THE HOLY PIEROGI OF ECORSE, MICHIGAN

Location: St. Andre Bessette Church

Background: The church was having its annual festival in September 2014 when a parishioner approached chairman Robert Heller, who was making tacos in a food booth. "They came up to me and said, 'Jesus loves Polish food more than Mexican food' and I asked why," he told WXYZ TV News. The parishioner showed him the pierogi. "You can definitely see the face of Jesus," Heller said.

What Happened: The pierogi was immediately locked away in the church freezer, where it will stay until someone figures out what to do with it.

THE CHOCOLATE MADONNA OF FOUNTAIN VALLEY, CALIFORNIA

Location: Under a vat of chocolate

Background: Kitchen worker Cruz Jacinto, 27, had just clocked in for her shift at the Bodega Chocolate store in August 2006 when she noticed a peculiar two-inch chunk of dark chocolate drippings beneath the vat. She pulled out a picture of the Virgin of Guadalupe that she keeps with her at all times and compared it with the chocolate. The chunk, she said, was the spitting image of the Madonna and Child.

What Happened: A glass table was set up near the front door of the store, and the figurine was set out among the candles, roses, and other gifts left by the faithful. "Just look at her. It's love and sweetness, like the chocolate," Jacinto told the *Orange County Register*.

Update: Bodega Chocolate went out of business in 2010; the whereabouts of the Chocolate Madonna are unknown.

THE BLESSED BREAKFAST TACO OF BEEVILLE, TEXAS

Location: Scorched into a tortilla

Background: 80-year-old Texan Ernesto Garza was halfway through his bacon-and-egg taco one morning in August 2012 when he suddenly recognized the face of Jesus in the burn marks of the tortilla.

What Happened: Garza gazed at the taco for about five minutes, then wrapped the miracle in aluminum foil and put it in the fridge. He plans to frame it and hang it on the wall, just as soon as he figures out a way to preserve it without refrigeration. "It's a blessing from God," he said.

THE CHICKEN DINNER REDEEMER (MAYBE) OF POCONO SUMMIT, PENNSYLVANIA

Location: Fried into a homemade breaded chicken breast

Background: In November 2014, Ernesto Hernandez was sitting down to a delicious chicken dinner prepared by his wife. He cut off a bite-size piece from a chicken breast, and just as he was about to pop it in his mouth, he saw the face of a bearded man seared into the fried bread crumbs. Which bearded man? "It looks like Jesus. I'm not saying it's Jesus. It's definitely a bearded man," he told a reporter.

What Happened: Hernandez put the miraculous morsel in the refrigerator overnight. (It shrank a bit, but the face was still visible.) At last report he and his wife were trying to figure out a way to preserve it permanently. "If I could convey a message to people, it would be, 'pay attention, there are signs everywhere,'" he said.

THE SACRED SEAT CUSHION OF COVENTRY

Location: On a chair in the Coventry Irish Society, England

Background: During Holy Week in March 2013, Irish Society counselor Katie Keogh was taking a call at her desk when she looked over and saw what appeared to be eyes, a nose, a mouth, and a beard squashed into the folds of the green seat cushion on the chair opposite hers. "I had to do a double take," she told the *Coventry Telegraph*. "I thought it looked like any face at first, but when I looked closely I realized it was the face of Jesus."

What Happened: The society brought in a priest to bless the cushion, but there are no plans to preserve it forever. "Someone's going to have to sit on it sometime," Keough said, "and when it's moved, I'm sure the face will disappear."

Ancient Egyptian royalty wore fake metal beards to imitate the god Osiris.

Life in a Democrazy

Here are four odd stories from the halls of U.S. state legislatures.

LIKE, MEOW, DUDE. In 2015 Nevada state senator Tick Segerblom proposed a bill legalizing medical marijuana…for dogs and cats. Segerblom acknowledged that there are no formal studies proving the medical benefits of getting your furry friends high, but said a veterinarian told him it could potentially ease the suffering of pets with debilitating illnesses. When asked if pot might be harmful to pets, he said, "You don't know until you try."

A WHEEL BIG PROBLEM. In 2013 Washington state representative Ed Orcutt replied to an e-mail sent from a bike shop owner protesting a $25 tax on new bicycles over $500. Defending the tax, Orcutt claimed that cyclists cost the state money: "The act of riding a bike results in greater emissions of carbon dioxide from the rider. Since CO_2 is deemed to be a greenhouse gas and a pollutant, bicyclists are actually polluting when they ride." After a public outcry, Orcutt backpedaled, saying he meant that cyclists "have a lower footprint but not a zero footprint" but that his e-mail was "poorly worded."

SIXTY SHADES OF DUMB. During an Iowa House debate on collective bargaining for teachers, State Rep. Ross Paustian was photographed holding a book called *Sex After Sixty*. Hundreds of the Republican's constituents complained to his office, but Paustian said it was an innocent mistake. He wasn't reading the book, he explained, but merely "holding it for a friend," fellow lawmaker Robert Bacon.

HAWKISH BEHAVIOR. In 2015 a fourth-grade class from Hampton Falls, New Hampshire, worked with their teacher to draft a new law that would make the red-tailed hawk New Hampshire's "state raptor." The bill had already made it through two subcommittees when the students went on a field trip to the state capitol building to watch the final floor vote. When they arrived in the assembly hall, the lawmakers applauded them…and then lambasted the bill. "This hawk grasps its prey with its talons and then uses its razor-sharp beak to basically tear it apart limb by limb," said Rep. Warren Groen. "It would serve as a much better mascot for Planned Parenthood." Rep. John Burt added, "If we keep bringing more of these bills…we'll be picking a state hot dog next." Then the civic-minded students got to watch their beloved House Bill 373 lose by a 160-133 vote.

Office Origins

The stories behind the stuff you use at work every day.

THE COMPUTER MOUSE

In the 1960s, computers still operated by having users enter long lines of code, which could be why they were used primarily at academic and research facilities. A Stanford Research Institute engineer named Douglas Engelbart thought computers would be a lot easier to use if they were more interactive. While sitting in a meeting one day, he thought about creating a small wheeled object that would move across a table, and its movements would translate to moving a cursor across the screen. He wasn't the first to come up with the idea, but he and fellow engineer Bill English incorporated technology from some other SRI prototypes into his design (including a foot-pedaled cursor controller) and created a handheld wooden box with two wheels on the bottom and a button on the top. After writing software that made the computer able to recognize the device, they wired it into the computer, and as Engelbart wheeled the box around his desk, the cursor on his screen moved accordingly. Engelbart patented it as an "X/Y Position Indicator," but his coworkers thought it looked like a mouse. So that became its name.

BINDER CLIPS

In the early 20th century, here's how you bundled a large stack of papers together: punch holes into the left side of each sheet, thread twine between the holes, and bind them together like a book. It was secure, but annoying if you had to remove a page. You'd have to unthread the stack, remove the page, and then rethread it. Sixteen-year-old Louis Baltzley saw his father—an inventor who often had to revise patent applications—do it hundreds of times. In 1911, he had an idea. Inspired by surgical clamps, he made a hinged metal clamp. It could bind a stack of pages, but if one had to be removed, he simply opened the clamp. More than 100 years later, the design of the binder clip is largely unchanged.

PAPER SHREDDERS

In 1935 Adolf Ehinger ran a small machine repair shop in his home town of Balingen, Germany. At night, he secretly printed anti-Nazi pamphlets. One day a neighbor discovered what Ehinger was doing and threatened to report him to the authorities. Ehinger had to get rid of the incriminating evidence. Taking inspiration from a hand-cranked pasta maker, which turns sheets of dough into pasta, Ehinger built a hand-cranked wooden shredder that turned paper into thin strips. It worked. After attaching an electric motor to it in 1936, Ehinger got a patent and took his *aktenvernichter* (literally "paper shredder") to office product trade shows…where no company was interested in mass-producing it. But as World War II picked up, so did the need for secrecy, and Ehinger's company, EBA Maschinenfabrik, sold thousands of shredders to government offices around the world. Today "information destruction" is a multimillion-dollar industry, and shredders have become essential equipment for almost every business.

PHOTOCOPIERS

Chester Carlson graduated with a physics degree in 1930—at the beginning of the Great Depression. Jobs were scarce then, and the only work he could find was as a clerk in the patent department of Bell Labs in New York. The job—hand-copying patent applications, along with their included sketches and charts—exacerbated the arthritis in his hands, so Carlson set out to create an automatic document-copying technique. He set up shop on his kitchen table in Queens and started experimenting with *photoconductivity*, charging metal plates with static electricity to make chemical powders cling to the plate and then applying heat (from his stove) to transfer an image to paper. In 1938, Carlson made a glass slide with the date on it, rubbed cotton against a sulfur-coated zinc plate, and then pressed the slide to the plate. He held the slide up to a light, dusted it with chemical powders, then pressed the slide to paper on the heated plate. The image transferred. In 1945, after GE and IBM turned it down, the Haloid Company bought Carlson's technology. They called the process *xerography*, Greek for "dry writing," and named the machine that performed it a *Xerox*. Xerox machines sold moderately in the 1950s, but sales soared when the first fully automated push-button model was introduced in 1960. By 1968, the Xerox Corporation was selling $1 billion worth of copiers a year.

LASER PRINTERS

After Xerox debuted the photocopier, a Xerox employee named Gary Starkweather wondered if the technology could be used to print documents directly from the company's mainframe computer. He worked for two years, from 1967 to 1969, modifying a Xerox copier, replacing its photographic machinery with a mirrored eight-sided drum and a laser. The laser's light bounced off the spinning drum, burning images onto the paper as it moved through the machine. Starkweather had invented what he called the Scanned Laser Output Terminal (SLOT), but it was used only internally at Xerox until 1977. That year, the company debuted the Xerox 9700 laser printer commercially. It's now the standard method of printing in offices (and homes) around the world.

Welcome to Transylvania, USA

Want to impress your friends with tales of travels to exotic lands?
Tell them you've been to one of these places. (But you'll
have to tell them your camera was out of order.)

WARSAW, VIRGINIA (pop. 1,512)

If you thought this town was probably founded by home-sick Poles, guess again. From 1692 until 1831, the village was known as Richmond Courthouse. That September, however, the villagers were so moved by Poland's doomed struggle for independence during the Polish-Russian War (1830–31) that they voted to rename their village in honor of the Polish capital after it fell to the Russians.

MOSCOW, IDAHO (pop. 23,800)

When the first farmers arrived in this part of the Idaho panhandle in the early 1870s, their pigs fed so well on camas bulbs and other local plants that the farmers called it "Hog Heaven." Would you settle in a place called Hog Heaven? The name soon gave way to "Paradise Valley." Then in 1877, postmaster Samuel Neff, a native of Moscow, Pennsylvania, and onetime resident of Moscow, Iowa—and a man apparently lacking in imagination—gave the settlement its current name while filling out the papers for its first post office.

DAMASCUS, OREGON (pop. 10,539)

Damascus, Syria, is one of the oldest continuously occupied cities in the world. Oregon's Damascus, on the other hand, is one of the state's newest cities. It voted to incorporate in 2004 to avoid being annexed by the nearby city of Portland. It nearly became one of Oregon's shortest-lived cities in 2013, when disputes over taxes and land use planning prompted angry residents to put a measure on the ballot dissolving the city government and returning control to the county. Nearly two-thirds of its citizens voted to kill their own city, but the measure fell 700 votes short of passage, so Damascus is still a city…for now.

TRANSYLVANIA, LOUISIANA (pop. 743)

Like Moscow, Idaho, Transylvania is only indirectly named for its European namesake. The town was founded in the early 1800s by a real estate speculator named Dr. W. L. Richards, an alumnus of Transylvania

---

Bigger faces? A standard American washcloth is 1 inch larger per side than a British washcloth.

University, the oldest college in Kentucky. The school in turn was named for the Transylvania Colony, which comprised much of modern-day Kentucky and part of Tennessee. The "colony," founded with help from Daniel Boone in 1775, faded away just one year after it was organized, when the Continental Congress declined to recognize it.

PARIS, TEXAS (pop. 25,171)

This community was founded in 1844 when a farmer, storekeeper, and postmaster named George W. Wright donated 50 acres of land to establish the town. No word on whether he'd ever been to Paris, but he liked the association with the French capital enough to name his general store after it. Since it was the most prominent business in town, the town was named Paris as well. It's one of more than a dozen U.S. cities and towns named Paris, and like a lot of the others, it has its own Eiffel Tower replica. The 70-foot tower in Paris, Texas, is topped off with a cowboy hat, partly as a statement of Texas pride, but also to make sure that it's a few inches taller than the Eiffel Tower in Paris, Tennessee.

SINGAPORE, MICHIGAN (pop. 0)

If you want to visit Singapore in Southeast Asia, all you need is a plane ticket, but if you want to see the one in Michigan, you'd better bring a shovel. This former mill town on the shores of Lake Michigan boomed in the early 1870s following the Great Chicago Fire (and the fires that destroyed Peshtigo, Wisconsin, and Holland and Manistee, Michigan). So much forestland around Singapore was chopped down to provide lumber for rebuilding that the town no longer had a physical barrier between it and the sand dunes along the lakeshore, nor did it have any protection from the high winds that blow in off the lake. Its timber resources exhausted, Singapore was abandoned by 1875, and within a few decades was completely buried in sand.

EAST BERLIN, PENNSYLVANIA (pop. 1,521)

John Frankenberger, a German immigrant, named the tiny settlement after his hometown in 1764. But Pennsylvania already had a town called Berlin, 100 miles to the west, so Frankenberger's town became East Berlin. It was perhaps the only place so named until 1949, when Soviet dictator Joseph Stalin split East Germany off from Germany proper and made Soviet-occupied East Berlin the capital. Pennsylvania's East Berliners joked (perhaps not really believing) that one day their city would once again be the world's only East Berlin, something that came true with the reunification of Germany in October 1990. (When Joseph Stalin's daughter, Svetlana Alliluyeva, defected to the West in 1970, she chose East Berlin, Pennsylvania, as the place to burn her Soviet passport.)

Aerial Archaeology

If you had to list the tools an archaeologist uses, you'd probably include a pick, a shovel, and maybe a trowel, a brush, or even a dental pick. Here's one to add to your list: an airplane.

BACKGROUND

In 1899 Italian archaeologist Giacomo Boni was leading an excavation project at the Roman Forum, the massive collection of structures that made up the center of ancient Rome, when he decided to augment the slow, painstaking work on the ground with something new: he took photographs of the site from a hot-air balloon, floating 250 feet off the ground. The photos gave Boni a perspective nobody had ever seen before. The entire site—about seven acres—was laid out below him, much the way you'd see the site on a map.

Within a decade, aerial photography was being used at ancient sites around the world, and a whole new field of study—aerial archaeology—was born. The field has expanded exponentially in the century since because of advances in both flight and imaging technology, and today is considered a major part of archaeology in general. And while it is most often used to expand understanding about already known sites, it's used to discover new ones, too. Here are the stories of a few of those discoveries, with some insights into the tools and tricks of the trade developed in the years since Boni's humble balloon flight.

THE BIG CIRCLES

In 1920, British air force pilot and archaeology enthusiast Lionel Rees was flying over a vast, remote desert region in what is now Jordan when he saw what seemed to be three large circles drawn on the empty desert below him. They were enormous—one was more than 1,200 feet in diameter—and they were so close to perfectly round that Rees felt they *had* to be man-made. He took photographs from his plane and wrote about the circles in archaeology journals. Amazingly, though, they were largely ignored for decades and have only been formally studied in the last 20 years, during which time several more "Big Circles," as they are known today, have been discovered in Jordan, Syria, and Turkey. Ranging from 700 to 1,400 feet in diameter, the circles are actually made from low rock walls, a few feet high and a few feet thick, constructed at least 2,000 years ago—possibly much longer. Nobody has any idea who made them or what purpose they served. And nobody had any idea they were there until Rees spotted them from his airplane in 1920.

Metal miscellany: When placed in mercury, lead floats, but tungsten sinks.

Studies of the circles—and searches for more—are ongoing.

WOODHENGE

In 1925 another British air force pilot, Gilbert Insall, was flying over southern England—not far from the famous ancient ruin Stonehenge—when he spotted an odd pattern of crops in the farmland below. It was the discovery of what aerial archaeologists now call "cropmarks." Simple explanation: the buried remains of ancient ruins can affect crops planted above them, creating discernible patterns in those crops. For example, the remains of a square structure lying beneath a wheat field can result in a square pattern in the field by stunting the growth of the plants directly above them. And while such patterns may be difficult to make out from the ground, they're often easy to see from an airplane. In this instance, Insall took photographs of the odd patterns he saw and showed them to local archaeologists, who were intrigued enough to start a dig at the site. A few years later, it was announced that Insall had discovered an ancient Stonehenge-like ruin, built around 2200–2300 BC. Instead of the rings of stone pillars Stonehenge is famous for, however, this site had rings of wooden poles—168 in total—hence the name "Woodhenge." (Bonus: In 1928 Insall discovered another ancient ruin, this one more than 5,000 years old.)

THE APULIA SETTLEMENTS

During World War II, progress in both flight and photographic technology resulted in extensive use of aerial photography to gather intelligence. When the war ended, many people with years of experience studying such photography applied their skills to aerial archaeology. One of the most notable: John Bradford, who, as a British intelligence officer, was stationed in the Apulia region of southeastern Italy. (The region includes the "heel" of the boot of Italy.) After the war, Bradford started studying aerial photographs of Apulia that he'd taken both during the war and after. Through careful study of cropmarks in the photos, Bradford was able to discern the ruins of several previously unknown ancient human settlements in Apulia, some more than 8,000 years old, and all of them holding a wealth of information about Italy's earliest civilizations. How many ancient settlements did Bradford discover? More than 200. Many of the sites are still being studied today.

THE RADAR RIVERS

In November 1981, NASA's first space shuttle, *Columbia*, was on its second mission when it took images of a large area of the eastern Sahara using its Shuttle Imaging Radar system (SIR-A). Because the area was covered in exceptionally dry sand, which the SIR-A system was able to penetrate to a depth of almost 20 feet, the images that came back revealed the world beneath the sand—and those images stunned scientists around the world. Reason: they revealed the presence of major river systems, long since dried up—and that the famously barren region was once a lush, watery wilderness. The discovery of the ancient rivers, which researchers came to call the "Radar Rivers," was of special interest to archaeologists because ancient civilizations settled near fresh water systems. Excavations at locations along the heretofore unknown rivers have since revealed hundreds of ancient human settlements, some dating back tens of thousands of years. Ancient tools, such as stone axes—some dating back *hundreds* of thousands of years—have been discovered along the rivers as well.

A LOST MAYAN CITY

In the early 1980s, the husband-and-wife archaeology team of Arlen and Diane Chase started doing on-the-ground work at the ancient Mayan settlement of Caracol in Belize. In 2009 the Chases heard about LIDAR (an acronym for "light detection and ranging") imaging technology. LIDAR uses lasers to develop extremely high-resolution, three-dimensional topographic maps of large swaths of land. The technology was of special interest to the Chases because it can "see" through dense vegetation, such as the jungle they had been fighting for more than two decades. In 2009 they arranged for a LIDAR-equipped two-engine plane to fly over the site. After just 24 hours of back-and-forth flying over the treetops, the system produced a map that told the Chases more about the site than they had learned in the previous 24 years. "I'm pretty sure we uttered some expletives," Diane Chase told the BBC. The images revealed thousands of ancient structures that the Chases had no idea existed, as well as roads, waterways, and farmland. Without realizing it, the Chases had been studying the remains of an enormous Mayan city—roughly 80 square miles in size.

*　　　*　　　*

JUDGE NOT

In 2009 Supreme Court judge David Souter announced his retirement. Souter lives on a farm in rural New Hampshire, and one day, while on a drive, he stopped at a small roadside diner. A couple noticed him and asked, "Aren't you a Supreme Court justice?" He confirmed that he was. Then they asked, "Are you Justice Scalia?" Not wanting to embarrass them, Souter said that yes, he was Justice Antonin Scalia. The couple then asked what his favorite part of working on the Supreme Court. His reply: "The great honor of getting to work with Justice David Souter."

Original name of the Elks Lodge: the Jolly Corks. It began in 1868 as a drinking club.

Canned Laughter

Real jokes pulled from actual restroom walls.

THE WORLD IS FLAT
—Class of 1492

Tolkien is hobbit-forming.

Many are cold,
but few are frozen.

**We've been having
a bad spell of wether.**

Laugh and the world laughs
with you. Snore and
you sleep alone.

QUESTION EVERYTHING
Why?

**Join the army and see
the next world.**

JESUS SAVES STAMPS

I hate Rachel Prejudice.

**Be kind to the unkind people,
they need it the most.**
Go home, Mom. You're drunk.

A miss is as good as a male.

**24 hours in a day
24 beers in a case
Coincidence??**

SATIN RULES!!!
Well, it's a nice fabric and all, but
I don't know if it rules.

Vu Ja De: The strange
feeling that you've never
been here before.

**What if the hokey pokey really
is what it's all about?**

WWJD?
He wouldn't vandalize
bathroom walls.

DYSLEXICS UNTIE!

Help Wanted: Telepath
(You know where to apply)

**He who laughs last
doesn't get the joke.**

———————————
You have to draw the line
somewhere.

*RELEASE ALL POLITICAL
PRISONERS!!!*
Especially the slutty ones

Haikus are easy
But sometimes they don't
make sense
Refrigerator

I HATE GRILS
It's *Girls*, stupid.
What about us grils???

Avoid life.
It'll kill you in the end.

Horseshoe crabs are more closely related to spiders than they are to other crabs.

I Spy...at the Movies

You probably remember the kids' game "I Spy, with My Little Eye…"
Filmmakers have been playing it for years. Here are some in-jokes
and gags you can look for the next time you see these movies.

HARRY POTTER AND THE DEATHLY HALLOWS, PART 1 (2010)

I Spy... A seminude poster of star Daniel Radcliffe

Where to Find It: In the diner scene when Harry and his friends get attacked, there's a poster on the wall for Peter Shaffer's play *Equus*, which Radcliffe controversially appeared in…naked. Who put the poster on the set? According to Radcliffe, he did: "It's my own little in-joke to myself."

FROZEN (2013)

I Spy... A tribute to the man who penned the original fairy tale

Where to Find It: In the names of the characters Hans, Kristof, Anna, and Sven. If you say those names out loud, it sounds a bit like "Hans Christian Andersen." In the 19th century, the Danish author wrote several fairy tales, including *The Little Mermaid*, *The Ugly Duckling*, and *The Snow Queen*, on which *Frozen* is based.

INVASION OF THE BODY SNATCHERS (1978)

I Spy... The star of the original *Body Snatchers* movie

Where to Find Him: When Matthew and Elizabeth (Donald Sutherland and Brooke Adams) are driving, an older man runs into their car yelling, "They're coming!" That was Kevin McCarthy, star of the 1956 *Invasion of the Body Snatchers*, who just happened to be filming another project nearby. Sutherland thought it would be neat if McCarthy re-created the final scene from the original film, so he did.

STAR WARS (1977)

I Spy... A dinosaur from a Disney movie

Where to Find It: When C-3PO is on the desert planet Tatooine, he walks past a massive skeleton lying in the sand (called a Greater Krayt Dragon). That's a prop from the 1975 Disney movie *One of Our Dinosaurs Is Missing*—a farce about a skeleton that was stolen from a museum. In 2002, when George Lucas and company returned to Tunisia, Africa, to film *Attack of the Clones*, they discovered that the skeleton was still there. (It has since been scavenged by *Star Wars* collectors.)

Not quite as catchy as 007: James Bond creator Ian Fleming's secret agent number was 17F.

BIRDMAN (2014)

I Spy... The carpet from *The Shining*

Where to Find It: The orange carpet in the theater where *Birdman* is set has the same hexagonal pattern as the carpet in the Overlook Hotel, where *The Shining* takes place. That's no coincidence. Both films are about men in mental decline who see visions. The carpet was director Alejandro Inarritu's nod to Stanley Kubrick's 1980 horror classic.

WILD (2014)

I Spy... *Wild* author Cheryl Strayed (and her daughter)

Where to Find Them: At the beginning of the film—a true story of a depressed woman who hiked the Pacific Crest Trail in 1995—Strayed has a cameo role as a woman who drops off Reese Witherspoon (who plays Strayed in the movie) at the trailhead. In flashback scenes, the young Cheryl was played by Strayed's six-year-old daughter, Bobbi.

FARGO (1996)

I Spy... Actor Bruce Campbell

Where to Find Him: In the kidnappers' cabin, Gaear Grimsrud (Peter Stormare) is watching a soap opera on a fuzzy TV screen starring a young Bruce Campbell. "I tried to get in the movie," recalled Campbell, "but there were no roles. I gave them [directors Joel and Ethan Coen] this footage to use as a joke, and they used it. It's from an old soap opera from the '80s in Detroit that I did. Now I can say I've been in an Academy Award–winning movie!"

IRON MAN (2008)

I Spy... A reference to *The Big Lebowski*

Where to Find It: On a computer screen. In *Iron Man*, Jeff Bridges played Obadiah Stane—a corporate bad guy who couldn't be more different from slacker Jeff "the Dude" Lebowski, also played by Bridges. When Pepper Potts (Gwyneth Paltrow) is looking at secret documents on Stane's computer, there's a shipping invoice for a vessel called the "MSC Lebowski." The port of origin is listed as Long Beach, where the Dude and his beloved rug once lived.

TRON (1982)

I Spy... Pac-Man

Where to Find Him: Bad guy Sark (David Warner) is yelling "Get them!" at a computer screen. In the middle of the screen is a large yellow pattern surrounded by blue dots. If you look closely, among the blue dots is a tiny yellow Pac-Man chomping in place. If you listen closely, you can hear his trademark "waka-waka" sound.

Rise and shine! Most preschoolers learn more easily in the morning than in the afternoon.

The Dog Ate My...

Ever tell your teacher the dog ate your homework? These folks probably wish their dogs had eaten their homework...instead of what they did eat. (But don't worry—all the pilfering pooches below made full recoveries.)

DOG: Kia, a five-year-old boxer owned by Marc Laird, who plays for England's Southend United soccer team

DOGGONE IT: Laird spends a lot of time on the road, and when he returns home, his five-year-old boxer, Kia, goes nuts the minute he walks in the door. But when Laird got home in December 2012, Kia "just wagged her tail a little and then wandered back to lie down," he said. He knew right away that Kia was sick, but he had to head straight back to London for another game, so he asked his partner, Lindsey Crowe, to take the dog to the animal hospital. The vet took X-rays, which revealed what appeared to be a large wad of aluminum foil in Kia's stomach. But when the vet operated to remove it, the "foil" turned out to be 10 Brillo pads—wads of steel wool impregnated with dish soap. Kia apparently gobbled them up after Crowe left a kitchen cupboard open while cleaning the oven. "Brillo pads are pretty unusual," says veterinarian Claire Nichols, who performed the surgery. "You would have thought it would be horrible to get past the teeth."

DOG: Pepsi, a Staffordshire bull terrier puppy owned by Steven and Cathy Vance, who live outside Belfast, Northern Ireland

DOGGONE IT: When Pepsi started yelping and limping following a walk in 2002, Steve and Cathy assumed she'd injured her leg and took her to the vet. A physical exam failed to identify the trouble, so veterinarian Stephen McLean ordered X-rays. Those revealed a 12-inch-long metal object inside the puppy. But it wasn't until McLean performed surgery and saw the words "Made in England" stamped on a black plastic handle that he realized what the object was—a screwdriver. "It was almost the entire length of the dog's body," McLean said. "We didn't think something that long could fit into an 18-inch-long puppy." Adding to the mystery of how Pepsi could swallow such a big screwdriver is the question of *whose* screwdriver it was in the first place. "We haven't a clue where it came from. It's certainly not ours," Cathy Vance told reporters.

DOG: Boo, a six-month-old mutt owned by the Bryson family of Dundee, Scotland

---

That wasp's nest might not be abandoned. Wasp queens and their eggs hibernate for the winter.

DOGGONE IT: One afternoon in September 2013, the youngest member of the Bryson family, seven-year-old Reese, accidentally dropped a bag of dog biscuits on the floor. Boo instantly ran over and gobbled them up. But because they landed next to a piece of fake dog doo that Reese likes to leave on furniture or the floor to freak out her mom, Boo ate the faux doo, too. The Brysons hoped Boo would poop it out again (just like the genuine article), but she didn't. Instead, she started vomiting. They rushed Boo to the vet, who removed the object in emergency surgery. "Needless to say," Shelly Bryson told the Glasgow *Herald*, "we won't be having any joke dog poo in our house again."

DOG: Elsie, a St. Bernard puppy owned by Jane Scarola of Fort Lauderdale, Florida

DOGGONE IT: In September 2005, Elsie became agitated and shaky, so Scarola took her to the vet. When a physical exam failed to reveal anything amiss, veterinarian Jon-Paul Carew ordered X-rays. Only then did Scarola realize what had become of her 13-inch serrated carving knife, which had gone missing *four days* earlier. Not only had Elsie swallowed it whole, she'd done so without injuring herself seriously or showing any sign of distress for four days. "I was just flabbergasted when I saw the X-rays. I thought it was some kind of joke," said Dr. Carew, who removed the knife in emergency surgery. Scarola had the knife framed and gave it to Dr. Carew to hang in his waiting room.

DOG: Frieda, a bug-obsessed dog owned by Deborah Carlson of Pullman, Washington

DOGGONE IT: Carlson didn't know that Frieda's fixation with eating bugs extended to the artificial variety…until she was preparing to leave on a fishing trip in September 2010 and Frieda knocked some fishing tackle off the kitchen counter. As Carlson cleaned up the mess, she noticed that all 16 of her brand new "flies"—fishhooks tied with feathers, thread, and other materials to look like bugs—were nowhere to be found. Carlson immediately took Frieda to the local veterinary college for X-rays, and sure enough, 15 of the flies showed up on the X-rays (the 16th was never found). Somehow they had made it all the way into Frieda's intestines without snagging on anything, so Carlson decided to wait and see if the flies would make it the rest of the way and pass naturally…and all 15 did. "It's just amazing that none got stuck in her stomach or throat, and these were barbed," Carlson told the *Lewiston Morning Tribune*. "It's just one more thing to go in her little scrapbook."

Parenthood

Having kids is easy; raising them is hard.

"Having a baby is like getting a tattoo on your face. You need to be certain it's what you want before you commit."
—**Elizabeth Gilbert**

"You know your children are grow-ing up when they stop asking you where they came from and refuse to tell you where they're going."
—**P. J. O'Rourke**

"Parenthood doesn't improve one's character, it exposes it."
—**Leslie A. Gordon**

"Always be nice to your children because they are the ones who will choose your rest home."
—**Phyllis Diller**

"It is amazing how quickly the kids learn to drive a car, yet are unable to understand the lawn-mower, snowblower, or vacuum cleaner."
—**Ben Bergor**

"I always wondered why babies spend so much time sucking their thumbs. Then I tasted baby food."
—**Robert Orben**

"Saturday mornings are a great opportunity for kids to sneak into your bed, fall back asleep, and kick you in the face."
—**Dan Pearce**

"A person soon learns how little he knows when a child begins to ask questions."
—**Richard L. Evans**

"Diaper backward spells repaid. Think about it."
—**Marshall McLuhan**

"Don't try to make children grow up to be like you, or they may do it."
—**Russell Baker**

"Always kiss your children good night, even if they're already asleep."
—**H. Jackson Brown Jr.**

"People who say they sleep like a baby usually don't have one."
—**Leo J. Burke**

"Families with babies and families without are so sorry for each other."
—**Ed Howe**

"You know your life has changed when going to the grocery store by yourself is a vacation."
—**Louis C.K.**

"There should be a children's song: 'If you're happy and you know it, keep it to yourself and let your dad sleep.'"
—**Jim Gaffigan**

Research shows: Men are more attracted to women whose bone structure resembles their mother's.

Wacky Celebrity Beliefs

Stars believe in just as many strange things as normal people do.
Maybe even more.

Celebrity: Rudolph Valentino
Belief: Imagine attending a séance where a major Hollywood star was not only the host but also the medium. That could've happened in the 1920s, because actor Rudolph Valentino (*The Sheik, Blood and Sand*) genuinely believed he could communicate with the dead. He and his wife held séances where Valentino performed "automatic writing"—a psychic activity in which a spirit sends written messages from beyond the grave by moving the medium's pen-holding hand over paper. The spirit guiding Valentino was a Native American named Black Feather, who was not only Valentino's spirit guide but also his muse: in 1923 Valentino published a book of poetry titled *Day Dreams* that he claimed Black Feather had directed him to write.

Celebrity: Randy Quaid
Belief: "I am being embezzled by this monstrous ring of accountants, estate planners, and lawyers who are trying to kill my career and, I believe, murder me in order to gain control of my royalties," complained actor Randy Quaid, just after he and his wife fled to Canada in 2010. Quaid insisted that they were forced to leave the U.S. because they were being persecuted by a group they called the "Star Whackers." (U.S. authorities suspect that the Quaids ran to avoid charges of burglary and vandalism relating to their house in Santa Barbara, California.) According to Quaid, the Star Whackers set up the deaths of some celebrities to collect insurance money and threatened others, hoping to squeeze cash from them. Quaid cited the deaths of actors Heath Ledger and David Carradine, telling reporters, "I believe these actors were whacked, and I believe many others, such as Britney Spears, Lindsay Lohan, and Mel Gibson, are being played to get at their money."

Celebrity: Joan Rivers
Belief: In 1987 the comedienne bought an apartment in New York City. Before long, she started noticing eerie cold spots in the apartment. Then her dog refused to cross the threshold, and a member of

---

Hot stuff: Microwave oven inventor Percy Spencer had only a third-grade education.

the building's staff told her why: "Mrs. Spencer," supposedly the niece of financier J. P. Morgan, had lived and died in Rivers apartment and was haunting the building. Rivers hired a voodoo priestess named Sallie Glassman, who performed a ritual to cleanse the apartment and then went door-to-door to do all the other apartments in the building. They remained quiet for several months…until Rivers began to notice cold spots again. Then Rivers stumbled on an old portrait of Mrs. Spencer in the basement. She had the portrait cleaned and hung it in the lobby, which apparently placated the ghost, because after that, Rivers referred to Mrs. Spencer as "a comforting, protecting presence."

Celebrity: Dan Aykroyd

Belief: Aykroyd is self-described as the "MUFON consultant for Hollywood." MUFON is the Mutual UFO Network. It investigates UFO sightings, abductions, cattle mutilations, or anything having to do with UFOs. Aykroyd says he's seen UFOs four times and once had a run-in with the Men in Black (the shady characters, possibly government agents, whose job it is to cover up UFO contact). In 2005 Aykroyd was the subject of a documentary, *Dan Aykroyd Unplugged on UFOs*, where for an hour and 20 minutes he expounded on UFO history and theories, showed clips of UFOs, and shared his personal experiences. "There should be no debate anymore," says Aykroyd. "UFOs exist; they are intelligently manufactured and guided technology from somewhere else, not this planet."

Celebrity: Jesse Ventura

Belief: In 2003, after leaving office as governor of Minnesota, the wrestler-turned-politician plunged headlong into conspiracy theories. He wrote three books on the subject, and from 2009 to 2013, he hosted *Conspiracy Theory with Jesse Ventura*, a show on TruTV that explored conspiracies of all kinds—government, alien, time travel, lizard peo-ple—anything that featured a purported cover-up. In 2010 the show aired an episode called, "Police State" that suggested FEMA was build-ing "concentration camps" in case martial law had to be declared after a disaster. From that point on, said Ventura, TruTV (owned by Time Warner) set out to destroy the show because the network was uncom-fortable with the truths he was revealing. "It's clear," he said, "they're doing everything they can to make it a failure so they don't have to renew it." (They didn't.)

*   *   *

"Every man prefers belief to the exercise of judgment.

—**Seneca**

Mcflops

*Not every McDonald's product can be as successful as the Big Mac
or the McRib. Here are some that were McDuds.*

A **RF!** Ray Kroc, the man who made McDonald's an international behemoth, didn't want his restaurants to serve hot dogs.
Ever. "There's no telling what's inside a hot dog's skin, and our
standard of quality just wouldn't permit that kind of item," he wrote in
his 1977 memoir. Nevertheless, in the 1990s, a handful of franchises in
the Midwest and the U.K. tried putting McHotDogs on the menu. Kroc
was right—they flopped.

OINK! Predating the present-day bacon craze by nearly 20 years,
in 1992 McDonald's locations in Australia briefly served the Bacon
Bacon McBacon—a double cheeseburger topped with BBQ sauce and a
whopping five slices of bacon. And in case that's not bacon-y enough for
you, the bun was dipped in pork drippings.

MOO! In 1980, McDonald's tried to class up its act with a slightly
more upscale "Dinner Menu," available only after 4:00 p.m. The
centerpiece was the Chopped Beefsteak Sandwich, which turned out to
be fancy-sounding jargon for a long hamburger patty ("The big taste of
beefsteak!") served on a French roll "with slivers of onion" and topped
with steak sauce. Diners weren't fooled; it flopped.

BOO-HOO! A fancy long hamburger couldn't be served with mere
fries, so as part of its 1980 Dinner Menu, McDonald's offered Onion
Nuggets—chopped, battered, and deep-fried onion balls.

MOO! MOO! In 2013 company analysts targeted the one part of the
day when business was way down: between mealtimes. To get people to
eat snacks at McDonald's, the company marketed Son of Mac. It had
the same flavors and ingredients as a Big Mac—including the special
sauce—but didn't make it as a Snac, and it had just two buns (not
three) and one beef patty (not two). Son of Mac was discontinued.

MAMA MIA! By 1991, McDonald's was having trouble attracting
customers during dinner hours and introduced a series of non-burger
dinner choices: this time with a pasta-based menu. Among the choices:
lasagna, spaghetti, fettuccine Alfredo (as well as roasted chicken and
mashed potatoes). Each pasta dish came with a bowl of cooked vegetables. Who goes to McDonalds for Italian food? Not surprisingly, the
concept flopped.

Divorce Facts

Like it or not, it's a part of modern life.

About 70% of couples who got married in the 1990s are still married, and if trends hold, 75% of those who married in the 2000s will make it till death do they part.

• State with the highest divorce rate: Nevada, where 14.6% of the population is divorced. State with the fewest divorces: New Jersey, at 8.6%.

• Average length of a marriage ending in divorce: eight years.

• A divorce is a legal petition to dissolve a marriage. What's an annulment? It's the *cancellation* of a marriage. From a legal standpoint, an annulled marriage doesn't exist and never did. Some grounds for annulment: invalidity due to bigamy, incest, or mental illness at the time of marriage, or if one of the spouses was drunk, underage, or coerced.

• Oldest couple to divorce: a 99-year-old Italian man and his 96-year-old wife. They married in 1934, but he filed for divorce in 2011 when he found love letters that she'd written to another man in the 1940s.

• The divorce rate for second marriages (both spouses) is 90% higher than for first marriages.

• Most expensive celebrity divorce: Mel Gibson's. The day after Gibson was arrested for drunk driving in 2006, his wife, Robyn, filed for separation. When they divorced in 2009 after 26 years of marriage, she received half of Gibson's fortune—about $425 million.

• Shortest celebrity marriage: in 1983, Zsa Zsa Gabor married lawyer Felipe DeAlba. The marriage was called off the next day when Gabor discovered her previous divorce had never been finalized. The couple never "re"-married. Length of marriage (which was Gabor's eighth overall): about 24 hours.

• At the time Russian businessman Dmitry Rybolovlev divorced his wife, Elena, in 2014, he was ranked #146 on *Forbes'* magazine's list of billionaires. Not anymore. Elena got about half of his fortune, or $4.5 billion, the largest divorce settlement in world history.

• Only two nations where divorce is illegal: the Philippines and Vatican City.

Hot heads: 99% of Finnish people use a sauna once a week.

King of the Wild Frontier...World

Davy Crockett "killed him a bear when he was only three." Fess Parker, the man who played him for years on TV, meanwhile, could never get a theme park honoring Crockett off the ground.

THE WESTERN MARCH HAD JUST BEGUN

In the 1950s, Westerns dominated television. There were dozens of them, and top-rated shows like *Gunsmoke*, *Wanted: Dead or Alive*, and *Maverick* made stars out of James Arness, Steve McQueen, and James Garner, to name just a few. But the one Western star who became a pop culture phenomenon was Fess Parker, thanks to his portrayal of frontiersman Davy Crockett from 1954 to 1955 in a series of episodes of the *Disneyland* program.

The Walt Disney Company licensed the sale of hundreds of "Davy Crockett" products—from toys and games to books, records ("The Ballad of Davy Crockett" was a #1 hit in 1955), lamps, lunchboxes, cameras, clothing, bubble gum cards, comic books, cookie jars, and, of course, coonskin caps. On opening day at Disneyland in July 1955, Parker appeared in a live broadcast as Crockett, riding into the park's Frontierland area on horseback, and sang a tribute to Crockett's rifle ("Ol' Betsy"). That wouldn't be the last time the actor was involved with a new theme park.

HIS POLITICKIN' WAS DONE

After the Crockett series ended, Parker starred in several Disney films, including *Westward Ho, the Wagons!* and *Old Yeller*. But he hung up his coonskin cap in 1958 after butting heads with the Disney Company over a restrictive contract that prevented him from accepting roles in two classic movies—*The Searchers* and *Bus Stop*. A few years after leaving Disney, Parker agreed to play another folk hero, Daniel Boone, in a long-running NBC show produced by rival studio 20th Century Fox.

By the late 1960s, Parker had become a wealthy real estate baron to boot. He was an obvious choice to become the face of (and an investor in) a new theme park devoted to key figures in American history. In 1968, the actor and a group of backers announced their plans for Fess Parker's Frontier World, an extravagant park located in Boone County, Kentucky.

The project seemed like a sure bet, especially after Parker came on board. How could they lose with a tourist destination devoted to America's heroes located smack dab in the middle of the county named for Daniel Boone himself? Parker, perhaps eager to get even with Disney by opening his own theme park, bought 1,500 acres for the project.

WHILE HE WAS HANDLING THIS RISKY CHORE

The concept for Frontier World was even more ambitious than Disneyland. Parker and his crew drew up plans for a 140-acre theme park with additional areas set aside for large commercial and residential developments. By comparison, the original Disneyland was only 85 acres.

Like Disneyland, Frontier World would have been broken up into a series of themed "lands." Visitors would enter through a full-scale replica of the *Mayflower*, the ship that brought the Pilgrims to the New World. On the other side of the park, the planners hoped to construct a true re-creation of the Pilgrims' Plymouth Colony, "a land," according to one account, "as fresh and primeval as the Pilgrims found in 1620."

PACKED HIS GEAR AND HIS TRUSTY GRIN

Frontier World's other areas would have transported visitors to the American frontier, the Salem witch trials, the gold rush, the world of the future, and the *Adventures of Huckleberry Finn*. And it's no coincidence that two of the attractions at Frontier World were going to be very similar to two at Disneyland—Tomorrowland and Mark Twain's Riverboat. The rides themselves would have also rivaled their cutting-edge counterparts in Anaheim. Blueprints were created for a Rocky Mountain–themed roller coaster (similar to the Matterhorn), a water attraction with animatronic pirates (similar to the Pirates of the Caribbean), a time machine ride, and the "Salem Witch Whirl-Through."

Another idea included a full-scale showboat for live concerts. Parker and his crew also planned to hire actors to roam through the lands portraying folk heroes like Boone and Crockett, in addition to fictional ones like Yankee Doodle and Casey Jones.

A GRINNIN' TO FOLLOW THE SUN

Much like Davy Crockett, who was famously killed at the Alamo, Frontier World died a tragic death. While Parker and his cronies had created a great idea for a theme park, their plans were far too complex and ambitious. So was their proposed timeline. After announcing the project in September 1968, they hoped to complete construction the following year. Around that same time, plans were announced for Kings

Island, another theme park in Mason, Ohio, less than a two-hour drive from the spot selected for Frontier World. Parker's investors jumped ship.

But that wasn't quite the death knell for the project. A few years later, the concept was briefly resurrected, and Parker hoped to move Frontier World to a different location: California. In 1972, the actor hired an architect to begin drafting blueprints for an improved version of the park, slated for a 452-acre plot of land that he owned in Santa Clara. However, after Parker joined forces with the Marriott Corporation, the concept was reworked into something much more realistic—a toned-down theme park called Great America.

In June 1973 Parker agreed to sell out to Marriott. Marriott wanted only the land under the park, but Parker insisted they buy everything—the property and his interest in the park. Great America opened its gates in May 1976, and it's still operating. The actor turned his attention to the Fess Parker Winery, which is also in California and still in business today. Guests at the 1,500-acre complex will find a visitors' center and a tasting room filled with bottles whose labels bear Davy Crockett's distinctive coonskin cap.

HE LOST HIS LOVE AND HIS GRIEF WAS GALL

Years later, Parker admitted that his plans for Frontier World were "cockamamie." As he told a journalist: "I get a little queasy every time I think about it because that land that I forced Marriott to take became the center of Silicon Valley. I had 352 acres, free and clear. Money in my pocket. I describe that year as the year I was certifiably insane. I made a whole bunch of stupid mistakes."

Parker also later patched things up with Disney. He was honored as a "Disney Legend" by the company in 1991. Over a decade later, in December 2004, Parker received a further tribute, this time ironically at Disneyland. During a ceremony marking the 50th anniversary debut of his first TV series, the actor (who died in 2010) was photographed holding up a sign for the Davy Crockett Coonskin Cap Company. The inscription reads "Fess Parker—Proprietor." It can still be found in a window over the Bonanza Outfitters shop in the park's Frontierland.

* * *

OOPS!

In 1979 a Japanese politician named Nitaro Ito was lagging behind in his campaign to win a seat in the house of representatives. He thought he could gain some sympathy votes if he staged a knife attack on himself, but while doing so, he accidentally nicked an artery in his thigh and died.

The Weird World of Crime

Calling all cars: two albino zebras have been spotted paddling a stolen pancake down Main Street! Be on the lookout!

NOW YOU SEE IT...

In 2015 a 26-year-old woman (name withheld—probably out of embarrassment) was walking down College Street in Charlotte, North Carolina, when a man approached her and offered to show her a magic trick. She agreed, and then he asked if she had any cash, assuring her she would get it back. He must have been a pretty good magician, because she never saw her $1,600 again.

BAD SANTA

In December 2014, a resident in Cornwall, England, called police to report a stolen Christmas tree. Oddly, a man was seen running away, but police only described the Christmas tree on their Facebook page: "It is described as around six feet tall, with lots of green branches and prickly bits." Despite receiving several leads (a few of them were even serious), police were unable to locate the tree.

IF YOU CAN'T BEAT IT, EAT IT

• In 2014 Kenneth Desormes, 40, got pulled over for speeding on Interstate 95 in New York. He appeared intoxicated, so he was taken to the police station for a Breathalyzer test. When an officer held up the printout to show Desormes the results—a 0.13 percent blood alcohol level, well over the legal limit of 0.08—Desormes grabbed the piece of paper and ate it. Amazingly, his cunning plan didn't work: he was charged with DUI...*and* criminal tampering.

• On a train traveling through Mumbai, India, a man grabbed a necklace from a female passenger and tried to run away but was quickly apprehended. There's nothing weird about a "grab-and-run" jewelry theft. Unfortunately, it's pretty common. What's weird is what happened next. When confronted, the crook swallowed the evidence and then denied he'd done anything wrong. So the police were called. They took him to a hospital to be X-rayed, but the X-ray failed to reveal the chain. "See?" he said. "I told you." Then doctors ran an ultrasound...and the gold chain showed up clear as day. To recover the stolen chain, the cops

Africa's true size is far larger than how it's depicted on most maps.

fed the thief bananas—96 of them over a period of 24 hours—until the gold chain showed up again.

TAKE IT E-Z

Semitrailer driver Pablo Ortega, 45, was hauling a load of candy to New York City in 2015, but he had a scam going to help him avoid the $95 toll (the fee for commercial 18-wheelers) to cross the George Washington Bridge. Just before he arrived at the EZ-Pass lane, Ortega flipped a switch on his dashboard to activate a "James Bond–style device" that rotates his front bumper upwards 90 degrees so the license plate isn't readable by the EZ-Pass camera. (He also greased his back license plate so it wouldn't be readable.) But an astute police officer stationed at the busy toll booth saw the bumper rotating as the truck approached. Ortega was stopped and cited, and the illegal device was confiscated. He said the device cost him $2,500—it's not known whether he'd already used it enough times to recoup his investment.

'TIL LIFE DO YOU PART

San Diego Superior Court Judge Patricia Cookson officiated the wedding of Danne Desbrow and Destiny Winters. What's weird about that? Desbrow had shackles around his ankles—because a few minutes earlier, Judge Cookson had sentenced him to life in prison for first-degree murder. (She did have the good sense to have the victim's family escorted out of the courtroom first.) Desbrow and Winters were high school sweethearts but lost contact for nearly 20 years until Desbrow went on trial in 2013 for a 2003 murder. He claimed it was self-defense, but the jury found him guilty. During the two-month trial, the lovebirds rekindled their romance; Desbrow proposed, and Winters said yes. And they asked Judge Cookson to officiate—no matter the trial's outcome. The judge agreed and even baked a cake especially for the occasion. But instead of going on a honeymoon, Desbrow went to prison, and Winters went home.

COLD COMFORTS

How cold was it during the January 2014 "polar vortex"? It was so cold that the Chicago Zoo had to put its polar bears and penguins *inside*. And in Kentucky it was so cold that an escaped prisoner decided to go back to prison just so he could warm up. The ex-ex-con, Robert Vick, had run away from the minimum-security Blackburn Correctional Complex where he was serving a six-year sentence for burglary and possession of a forged instrument. But he picked a bad day to escape: the temperature in Lexington was only 3°F, and the windchill made it seem like -17°F. (Kentuckians aren't used to those kinds of temperatures.) So Vick, who had no money and spent the night in an abandoned house, went to a motel the next morning—but not to check in. "He walked in and told me to call the law on him. He was frozen," said manager Maurice King. "I don't think the police even believed me. I had to call again." Vick was scheduled to go before a parole board in only two months, but instead he had another five years tacked on to his sentence.

MIDNIGHT SPECIAL

The front desk clerk at the Old Towne Inn in Manassas, Virginia, got a 2:00 a.m. call for room service. Sensing something was amiss (it was a bit late for dinner), the clerk checked the register and discovered that room was supposed to be empty. So instead of sending food, the clerk sent the cops. An officer knocked, and 30-year-old Vinod Adhikary answered. He was drunk and hungry, and seemed surprised that his cunning plan of breaking into a hotel to get a free meal didn't work. He did, however, end up getting room service…in jail.

UNWITTING ACCOMPLICE

In 2013 a Jackson County Mental Health caseworker (name not released) was driving a patient named Nicholas York, 35, around Medford, Oregon, to do some errands. York had been kicked out of a motel the night before, so the caseworker was taking him to check into another one. (York was in town receiving treatment for an undisclosed mental health condition.) On the way to the motel, York said he needed to withdraw some money from Chase Bank. The caseworker pulled into the parking lot and waited in the car while York went inside. A few minutes later, York walked out, got back in the car, and the two men drove away. Strangely, the bank workers came outside and were watching them. The caseworker waved as he pulled onto the street and headed for the motel. A few minutes after he dropped off York, the caseworker received a phone call: the bank had been robbed, and the robbers had driven away in a Jackson County Mental Health vehicle! The confused caseworker led police to the motel, where they found York and all the money. He had no weapon; he'd simply demanded some cash, and the teller gave it to him. York was arrested without incident.

PIPE DREAMS

In the midst of a bitter divorce in 2013, Randolph Smith of Vero Beach, Florida, came up with a unique way to annoy his soon-to-be ex-wife. When she arrived home one afternoon, she discovered a pipe bomb on the kitchen table, with a note that read: "This is a explosive. It's a bomb." And written directly on the table: "Boom!" His wife quickly called 911. The police determined the pipe bomb was fake, and then tracked down Smith at a nearby Burger King. When asked what he was thinking, he explained, "She pissed me off. What? Is that illegal?" (Yes.)

$occer Jersey$

Like NASCAR drivers in the U.S., soccer teams, or "football clubs" in the rest of the world, wear jerseys adorned with advertisements for their sponsors, which could be a shoe maker, a brewery, an airline, or something weirder...like one of these.

- In 1990 a Belgian vodka producer sponsored the British soccer team Scarborough F.C. The company makes Black Death vodka. Its logo—a skull and crossbones—appeared on the team's jerseys, along with the company's slogan, "Drink in Peace."

- An antismoking foundation paid to sponsor West Bromwich Albion (U.K.) in 1985. The image on players' jerseys was the familiar "no smoking" sign. (Oddly, though, smoking was allowed in the team's stadium.)

- From 2003 to 2006, Columbia Pictures sponsored Spanish team Atletico Madrid. Every few weeks, jerseys would change, advertising a different movie. Among the movies advertised: *White Chicks, Hitch, Spider-Man 2, Resident Evil 2,* and *Spanglish.*

- Atletico Madrid is sponsored by the tourism board of Azerbaijan. Their jerseys state, "Azerbaijan: Land of Fire."

- Spanish club Getafe landed a sponsorship deal with Burger King in 2009. When players lifted their shirts to wipe the sweat off their faces, they revealed the image of Burger King's creepy King mascot, which was printed upside-down on the inside of the jersey.

- In 2012 British team Burnley's sponsor was Totally Wicked, a maker of e-cigarettes and "e-cigarette juice." The jerseys bore the company logo—an alien/devil hybrid wearing sunglasses and smoking an e-cigarette.

- In 2010 England's Middlesbrough F.C. offered one-month jersey sponsorships, which were cheaper than a full-season deal. Sponsors not only included major brands like Jaguar and Carlsburg Beer, but also Deepdale Solutions, a local, family-owned construction company.

- The Greek minor league team Voukefalas received sponsorship from Soula. What's Soula? A brothel.

- The Washington Freedom played in the short-lived Women's Professional Soccer League until entrepreneur Dan Borislow bought the team in 2011 and renamed it "magicJack" after the telephony-via-Internet gadget he invented. (A year later, the league folded.)

Ask the Experts

Everyone's got a question they'd like answered—basic stuff like "Why is the sky blue?" Here are a few questions, with answers from the world's top trivia experts.

UN-SUN HERO

Q: *How does sunscreen protect your skin, and what does "SPF" mean?*

A: "There are two basic types of sunscreen lotions on the market: products that penetrate the outermost layer of skin to absorb ultraviolet rays, and products that coat the surface of the skin as a physical barrier to ultraviolet rays. Both are rated with sun protection factor (SPF), which lets the consumer know how much protection the product provides against ultraviolet radiation. The SPF of a product is the ratio of the time required for a person's protected skin to redden. For example, SPF 15 means that a person whose unprotected skin would redden in 10 minutes can apply the product and stay in the sun 15 times longer, or 150 minutes, before he or she gets a sunburn." (From *How Things Are Made* by Sharon Rose and Neil Schlager)

HEY, WATCH WHERE YOU POINT THAT THING!

Q: *Can bees sting each other?*

A: "Yes. There are about 20,000 species of bee in the world, but let's look at honeybees. Although some species are stingerless, female bees typically have a stinger to defend their colony against enemies that might steal their honey or even eat the bees themselves. Male bees do not have a stinger and do nothing in the colony, except a few of them will mate with the queen bee.

"Honeybees will attack worker bees from other colonies if they try to enter, but a queen honeybee will only sting and kill other rival queens. A newly emerged queen will search the colony for cells where other queens are developing and when she finds them she will sting and kill them." (Dr. George McGavin, from *Can a Bee Sting a Bee?*, compiled by Gemma Elwin Harris)

...AND EVERYTHING NICE

Q: *What's the difference between an herb and a spice?*

A: "There's no hard and fast definition of either. The following are general guidelines, however, used to distinguish between the two. Herbs are the aromatic leaves of plants and come primarily from temperate

On Venus, the sun rises in the west and sets in the east.

regions of the world. Spices consist of the seeds, buds, fruit or flower parts, and bark or roots of aromatic *and* pungent plants, usually from tropical regions." (From *Why Does Popcorn Pop?* by Don Voorhees)

NOT QUITE THE QUEEN'S ENGLISH

Q: *Avast, me hearties, why do pirates talk the way they talk? Yarrrr.*

A: "The linguist Molly Babel points out that our current associations of pirate speech came about largely through film, and that one of the primary influences was the native West Country English dialect of Robert Newton, who played the main characters in several early pirate movies: *Treasure Island* in 1950, *Blackbeard the Pirate* in 1952, and *Long John Silver* in 1954. Two examples: 'flay your shriveled tongue' and 'scurvy dog.' So influential was Newton and his interpretation that a variation of West Country English became standard for subsequent portrayals of pirates on stage and screen. 'Speakers of the West Country regional dialect tend to emphasize their r's, unlike other British regions,' said Babel. They tend to replace the verbs 'is' and 'are' with 'be,' and indeed, use the word 'arrr' in place of 'yes.'" (From Gretchen McCulloch's "Lex-i-con Valley" blog, *Slate.com*)

TO KEEP DORITOS AND TACO BELL IN BUSINESS

Q: *Why do people who use marijuana get "the munchies"?*

A: "Scientists have finally worked out why people get the munchies when they're stoned. It turns out the munchies aren't anything to do with your stomach at all—instead, the dope turns off a signal in your brain which tells you, 'You're full, stop eating,' the journal *Nature* reported. Hence, you can eat an entire KFC bucket and have a packet of graham crackers for dessert. In their study, scientists led by Tamas Horvath of Yale University focused on molecules called *receptors* that cannabinoids bind to and activate in the brains of both mice and men. They expected to find that when cannabinoids did so, the receptors sent out a signal quieting nearby neurons that suppress appetite. That could lead to the munchies. To their surprise, Horvath said, they found that activating the cannabinoid receptors in mice's brains instead increased, not decreased, the activity of appetite-suppressing neurons. The reason they did not suppress appetite was that the neurons, instead of emitting their usual appetite-killing neurochemicals, emitted completely different ones. Called *endorphins*, they traveled to the brain's appetite-control region, the hypothalamus, stimulating the mice's desire to eat. 'Neurons that normally shut down eating instead promoted it, even when the mice were full,' Horvath said. 'Marijuana fools the brain's feeding system.' Basically, there's nothing you can do about it. So, you know, tuck in, bro." (Rob Waugh, *Metro* UK)

Sh-Boom, Kaboom!

Fear of nuclear war was so pervasive during the 1950s and 1960s that the A-bomb became a subject of pop culture. Here are some real songs of the Atomic Age.

"A Mushroom Cloud"
Sammy Salvo
(1961)

"My Radiation Baby (My Teenage Fallout Queen)"
George McKelvey
(1964)

"Atom Bomb"
Glenn Barber
(1955)

"A-Bomb Bop"
Mike Fernandez
(1959)

"Crawl Out Through the Fallout"
Sheldon Allman
(1960)

"Atom Bomb Baby"
The Five Stars
(1957)

"Guided Missiles"
The Cuff Links
(1956)

"When That Hell Bomb Falls"
Fred Kirby (1950)

"Leave De Atom Alone"
Josephine Premice
(1958)

"(My) Fallout Filly (With the Atomic Kiss)"
Chris Cerf (1961)

"Old Man Atom"
Sam Hinton (1950)

"Radioactive Mama"
Sheldon Allman
(1960)

"Uranium Rock"
Warren Smith
(1958)

"Atomic Love"
Thelma Farmer
(1953)

"When the Atom Bomb Fell"
Karl & Harty
(1946)

"Uranium Fever"
Elton Britt (1955)

"Atomic Nightmare"
The Talbot Brothers (1957)

"Fifty Megatons"
Sonny Russell
(1963)

"You Hit Me Baby Like an Atomic Bomb"
Fay Simmons
(1954)

"Atomic Telephone"
Spirit of Memphis Quartet (1952)

"Rock and Roll Atom"
Red McCoy with the Sons of the Soil
(1959)

"Great Atomic Power"
The Louvin Brothers (1952)

"The Duck and Cover Song"
"Two Ton" Baker
(1953)

"The Song of the Atom Bomb"
Dexter Logan and Darrell Edwards
(1952)

"Tic, Tic, Tic"
Doris Day
(1949)

"Watch World War Three (On Pay TV)"
The Crown City Four (1960)

"Your Atom Bomb Heart"
Hank King with Bud Williams
(1955)

Flamin' Hot Cheetos were invented in 1976 by a janitor at a Cheetos factory.

How to Behave on a Bicycle

The first practical "safety" bicycles were introduced in the mid-1880s, and by the turn of the century, millions of people—male and female—were riding them. Which raised an interesting question: how were proper ladies and gentlemen to behave on bicycles? A few tips from The Manners & Customs of Polite Society, *written by Maude C. Cooke in 1896.*

FOR THE LADIES

F "It is distinctly understood in the first place that 'cycling' is the correct word; the up-to-date woman dares not speak of 'bicycling' nor of 'wheeling.'"

"The maiden who is a stickler for form, does all her cycling in the hours which come before noon—unless there be a special meet, a bicycle tea, for instance, or a spin by moonlight."

"The unmarried woman who cycles must be chaperoned by a married lady—as every one rides nowadays, this is an affair easily managed. Neither must the married woman ride alone; failing a male escort, she is followed by a groom or a maid."

"Society insists on an upright position, with, of course, no attempt at racing pace. It also frowns upon constant ringing of the bell—that will do for the vulgar herd who delight in noise."

"Don't buy a bicycle with down-curve handles. It is impossible to sit erect and hold that kind of a handle."

FOR THE GENTLEMEN

"The man's duty to the woman who rides might be made the text for a long sermon; but long sermons are never popular; therefore, it may be better to state briefly that he must always be on the alert to assist his fair companion in every way in his power—he must be clever enough to repair any slight damage to her machine which may occur en route, he must assist her in mounting and dismounting, pick her up if she has a tumble, and make himself generally useful and incidentally ornamental and agreeable."

"Very gallant escorts use a tow rope when accompanying a lady on a

---

The nectar of citrus flowers contains caffeine. Studies show that bees prefer it over caffeine-free nectar.

wheeling spin....One end is attached to the lady's wheel at the lamp bracket or brake rod by a spring swivel, and the other end is hooked to the escort's handle bar in such a way that he can set it free in a moment, if necessary. When he has finished towing he drops back to the lady's side, hanging the loose end of the cord over her shoulder, to be ready for the next hill. A gentle pull that is a bagatelle to a strong rider is of great assistance to a weak one up hill or against a strong wind."

"In meeting a party of cyclists who are known to each other and desire to stop for a parley, it is considered the proper thing for the men of the party to dismount while in conversation with the ladies."

"Gentlemen: don't try to raise your hat to the passing 'bloomer' until you become an expert in guiding your wheel....From five to six lessons are always considered necessary before one can master even the details of riding."

AND DON'T FORGET

"Every bicyclist in the land will rise up and call the inventor of the ammonia gun for dogs blessed. Nothing is more annoying to the rider than to have a mongrel dog barking at his pedals and scurrying across his pathway in such close proximity to the front wheel as to be a constant reminder of a possible 'header.' The gun is calculated to make an annoying dog sneeze and sniff away all future ambitions to investigate the pace of a rider. It is said to be a perfect instrument in every way."

"Don't believe the farmer boy who says that it is 'two miles to the next town.' It may be two, four, six or twelve."

"Don't absent yourself from church to go wheeling, as you and your bicycle are welcome at most houses of worship."

"Don't go out on a bicycle wearing a tail coat unless you enjoy making a ridiculous show of yourself."

"Don't ride ten miles at a scorching pace, then drink cold water and lie around on the grass, unless you are tired of life."

*   *   *

Random Bicycle Fact: The first person to bike around the world was Fred Birchmore in 1935. He rode 25,000 miles and went through seven sets of tires.

His best years: Italian dictator Benito Mussolini didn't speak until age three.

People in Your Body

How many parts of the human anatomy are named after somebody? Surprisingly, there are dozens—from the Achilles tendon (in your lower calf) to the zonule of Zinn (connective fibers behind the lens of your eye). We researched a few that might be familiar.

FALLOPIAN TUBES. The thin tubes that carry an egg from the ovaries to the uterus—and their function—were discovered in 1561 by Italian physician Gabriele Falloppio. (He also conducted the first clinical trial of condoms in 1546—he made them himself out of thin linen, but they were designed to prevent syphilis, not pregnancy.)

ISLETS OF LANGERHANS. While studying and dissecting a human pancreas in 1869, German pathologist Paul Langerhans (who was just 22 years old) found small clumps of clear cells within the body of the organ, which he described as "islets," another word for islands. Those cells make up just 1 percent of the pancreas but are responsible for the organ's most notable function: creating and secreting insulin. Langerhans also discovered Langerhans cells, skin cells that aid in immune response.

EUSTACHIAN TUBES. When your ears "pop" at high elevations or in an airplane, you're actually just widening the auditory tubes in your middle ear, which equalizes pressure between your ears and the surrounding atmosphere. Called your Eustachian tubes, they're named for Bartolomeo Eustachi, a 16th-century Italian scientist who specialized in the ear. In 1552 he wrote of the pressurizing tubes in his book *Anatomical Engravings*—but he didn't publish the book for fear of being excommunicated from the Catholic Church. It was published in 1714, and the auditory tubes he discovered were named in his honor.

G-SPOT. Ernst Gräfenberg was a gynecologist and medical school professor in Berlin in the early 20th century. He studied and discovered many elements of how eggs are implanted, and he invented the IUD birth control device. In a 1950 paper on female sexuality, Gräfenberg wrote that "an erotic zone always could be demonstrated on the anterior wall of the vagina along the course of the urethra." Gräfenberg had discovered the "G-spot"…but it wasn't named after him until 1981, more than 20 years after his death. An article in *Journal of Sex Research* by a team of sexuality researchers coined the term. Only thing: despite the claims of sex researchers, the existence of the G-spot has never actually been proved scientifically.

First in Death

Most of us will never make it into the record books. That's not the case for these unlucky people, though. Making history was the last thing they ever did.

ACTON BEALE (1991–2011)
Claim to Fame: First confirmed "planking" fatality
Deadly Details: Planking was a fad that began in England in 1997 and, thanks to Facebook and other social media websites, spread around the world in 2007. It wasn't particularly challenging: all you had to do was lie face down someplace unusual—in a tree, in a field, atop a foosball table, etc.—with your arms by your sides and stiff as a board (hence the name). Then you took a picture and posted it online. It wasn't particularly dangerous, either...unless the person happened to plank in a place that wasn't safe. That was Acton Beale's mistake: he chose a balcony on the *seventh floor* of a building in Brisbane, Australia. He was positioning himself on the balcony railing when he fell to his death. To date he's the only reported planking fatality.

VLADIMIR LIKHONOS (1984–2009)
Claim to Fame: First person killed by exploding bubble gum
Deadly Details: Likhonos lived in the city of Konotop, in northeast Ukraine. He studied chemistry at a regional campus of the Kiev Polytechnic Institute, and like a lot of chemistry students, he liked to fool around with explosive chemicals. One afternoon in December 2009, he had 3.5 ounces of an unidentified explosive powder sitting on his desk in a small plastic bag. Next to the bag he had a saucer of citric acid, a common food additive, also in powder form. Family members say Likhonos liked to dip his bubble gum in the citric acid to give it a sour taste. On this particular day, however, he dipped his bubble gum in the wrong powder. As soon as he popped the gum in his mouth, it exploded. He suffered horrific injuries to his face and lower jaw and died a short time later.

DICK WERTHEIM (1923–1983)
Claim to Fame: First U.S. Open tennis ball–related fatality
Deadly Details: Wertheim wasn't a tennis player, he was a *linesman*—a referee who officiates at matches. In September 1983 he was doing just that, officiating as the center linesman at the boys' singles final when Sweden's Stefan Edberg hit an errant serve that struck Wertheim in the groin. Reeling from the impact, he fell backward and struck his head on

---

An average dairy cow weighs 1,200 pounds, about half as much as a MINI Cooper.

the hard court surface. He never regained consciousness and died one week later.

PHILIP QUINN (1980–2004)

Claim to Fame: First death by lava lamp

Deadly Details: A lava lamp has a lightbulb in its base that melts the wax in the lamp's sealed glass container. That turns the wax into molten blobs that float in the clear liquid also in the container. Quinn's lightbulb may have been burned out, or maybe he just thought it was taking too long to melt the wax, because he decided to heat his lava lamp on the stove.

Did we mention that it was a sealed glass container? When the liquid inside came to a boil, the lamp exploded, sending shards of glass flying. The medical examiner believes Quinn must have been standing in front of the stove when it blew up, because one of the shards struck his chest, piercing his heart. He stumbled into his bedroom and died before he could call 911 for help. Family members found his body later that evening.

ALAN STACEY (1933–1960)

Claim to Fame: First Formula One driver killed by a bird

Deadly Details: The 26-year-old Stacey was only a few years into his career, with just six championship races under his belt, when he entered his seventh, the Belgian Grand Prix, in June 1960. He was in sixth place in the 25th lap of the race and approaching a turn at 120 mph when a bird flew into his path and struck him in the face, causing him to lose control of his car and crash in a nearby field. By the time the paramedics got to him, he was already dead from a broken neck; investigators never determined whether it was the crash or the bird that caused the fatal injury.

SINGRAI SOREN (1975–2010)

Claim to Fame: First person slashed to death by a chicken

Deadly Details: Soren, who hailed from West Bengal, India, had just won a cockfight with his prizefighting rooster when he decided to go for two in a row instead of letting the bird rest before its next fight. That's how he learned that even chickens have their limit: when he tried to shove the tired bird back into the ring, it attacked *him*, slashing his throat with the razor blades that Soren had tied to its legs. The slash severed Soren's jugular vein, and he bled to death.

Update: Just one month later, a man named Jose Luis Ochoa, 35, died in Tulare County, California, when his fighting rooster slashed him on his right calf during a police raid on an illegal cockfight. The slash severed an artery, and though Ochoa was rushed to the hospital, he died before doctors could save him.

Brazilian artist Adriana Bertini's medium: condoms. She makes dresses out of them.

Vote for Me!

*Every so often a political candidate comes along and makes you think that maybe—
just maybe—there's hope for humanity. HA HA HA HA HA!
Just kidding! But for our entertainment, there are
always bizarre candidates like these.*

Candidate: Matayoshi Mitsuo
Background: He's a Protestant preacher from the city of
Ginowan, in Japan's Okinawa Prefecture.
Vote for Me! In 1997 Matayoshi announced that he was running for
mayor of Ginowan but made it clear that the campaign was just a small
part of a greater plan by which he would ascend through Japan's political
hierarchy—from mayor, to governor, all the way to prime minister. And
after that he would become secretary-general of the United Nations,
a post from which he would rule the entire world as "the Only God
Matayoshi Mitsuo Jesus Christ," or just "Matayoshi Jesus" for short.
This, he promised, would bring peace and prosperity to the world.
Matayoshi—somehow!—didn't win…but that hasn't discouraged him
from running for various political seats in Japan almost every year since.
While campaigning, he's regularly urged his political opponents to
kill themselves via the traditional Japanese disemboweling technique
known as *hari-kari*. (Amazingly, Matayoshi has never won an election.)

Candidate: Robert "Prince Mongo" Hodges
Background: Hodges is a former pizza parlor and nightclub owner in
Memphis, Tennessee.
Vote for Me! Hodges has run for mayor of Memphis in every election
since late 1991, under what he says is his real name: "Prince Mongo."
He claims he was born 300 years ago on the planet Zambodia, which
he says is located nine light-years from Earth. His mission: he was sent
here to help Earthlings find enlightenment (and to Memphis specifically
because the rulers of Zambodia felt it was the place on Earth most in
need of assistance). Mongo is known for wearing a blond wig, a long,
colorful robe, and old-fashioned aviator goggles; his program for enlightenment includes hanging criminals, flushing "political turds"—his
description of Memphis's political leaders—and issuing Uzi submachine
guns to all Memphis citizens who want one so they can protect themselves from criminals. (Mongo netted almost 3,000 votes in his first
mayoral race and still gets several hundred every time he runs.)

University of Washington study findings: Rats "laugh" when they are tickled.

Candidate: Huh Kyung-young

Background: The South Korean businessman ran for president of his country in 1997 and again in 2007, when he got almost 100,000 votes.

Vote for Me! Huh was known as an eccentric, but when he ran for the South Korean presidency again in 2012, the 62-year-old upped the ante by proclaiming that he could perform miracle cures of diseases by gazing into people's eyes and rearranging their chromosomes. He also claimed he has an IQ of 430. As for his political platform, Huh said that if elected, he would give 100 million won ($90,000) to every newlywed couple in the country and move the United Nations headquarters from New York to the demilitarized zone between North and South Korea. When asked how he would pay for his proposals, he said, "I have all the solutions in my head. Remember, my IQ is 430." (Huh received zero votes in the 2012 election. After being convicted of defamation in 2009, he was officially barred from running. He ran anyway.)

Candidate: Jonathon "the Impaler" Sharkey

Background: He's a musician, composer, and part-time professional wrestler from New Jersey.

Vote for Me! Sharkey started running for Congress in 1999—first in New Jersey, then in Indiana the following year, and in Florida the year after that. Since 2004, he has run in every U.S. presidential election. Sharkey also claims to be a vampire and drinks human, cow, or pig blood a couple times a week. He registers as a candidate under the name Jonathan "the Impaler" Sharkey, after his hero, Vlad "the Impaler" Dracula, the 15th-century Romanian prince who was the inspiration for Bram Stoker's 1897 novel, *Dracula*. Among his political positions, Sharkey, who calls himself a "right-wing vampire," advocates hiring the Sicilian Mafia to battle drug dealers in the United States. He promises that under his watch, murderers and rapists will be publicly impaled on spikes on the Capitol lawn in Washington, D.C. Bonus: He'll do the impaling himself.

Candidate: Toyama Koichi

Background: Toyama was a Tokyo street musician and political activist when, in 2007, at the age of 36, he decided to run for governor of Tokyo prefecture.

Vote for Me! To garner support for his campaign, Toyama made a YouTube video in which the bald-headed, black-shirted candidate glared into the camera and told prospective voters, "I despise each and every one of you!" and encouraged them not to vote in the election. "I do not have a single constructive proposal," he said, and then called Japan a "detestable" nation that "must be destroyed." (Toyama received more than 15,000 votes.)

"Hooch" derives from Alaska's Hoochinoo Indians, who sold cheap liquor to US soldiers in the 1800s.

Sleepwalking in the U.K.

Time for some strange stories about sleepwalking. For reasons we can't explain, they all occurred in the British Isles.

YAWN ON THE LAWN

A One night in March 2005, Rebekah Armstrong of London awoke around 2:00 a.m. to the sound of a motor outside her home. She immediately noticed that her husband, 34-year-old Ian Armstrong, wasn't beside her in bed, so she went looking for him. A few minutes later she found him in their yard, mowing the lawn...in his sleep. He was also naked. "I dread to think how long he'd been there," she told the *Sun* newspaper the next day, "but he'd nearly finished." She was afraid to wake him in the middle of the task, so she unplugged the electric mower and left her naked husband walking back and forth across their lawn in the middle of the night pushing the now-quiet mower—and went back to bed. Ian climbed back into bed some time later. The next morning, Rebekah told reporters, she had to point out her husband's dirty, grass-stained feet to convince him that he'd actually mowed the lawn in his sleep.

WINDOW DRESSING

Rachel Ward, 18, of Horsham, West Sussex, went to bed around 9:30 one evening in May 2009. A few hours later, her parents heard her screaming for help and found her in a daze outside their home. The teen, who had no memory of how she'd gotten there, had apparently gotten up from bed, walked in her sleep across the bedroom, crawled out the second-story window, and fallen 25 feet to the ground below. Divots in the ground (she landed on a narrow strip of grass just a few feet from the asphalt driveway) indicated she'd landed on her feet. Amazingly, X-rays showed no broken bones. (When her parents found her, Rachel was wearing a "jumper"—the British term for a sweater—which she hadn't been wearing when she went to bed. She apparently put it on in her sleep before taking that leap.)

HIGH THERE!

In June 2005, a 15-year-old girl in London got up in the middle of the night, walked in her sleep from her home to a nearby building site,

Some 19th-century parenting manuals advised that toilet training begin almost immediately after birth.

climbed 130 feet into the air on the arm of a crane, then walked across a narrow steel beam to a large concrete block that served as a counterweight for the crane arm. A passerby saw the girl and immediately called emergency services. Police feared the girl was suicidal, but when a rescue worker made it up the crane and reached her, she was curled up on the concrete block…fast asleep. The worker gently woke her up, ready to grab her in case she was startled, then got her to use her cell phone to call her parents. They kept the girl calm while a rescue ladder was sent to the scene, and after a delicate two-hour rescue operation, she was lowered to safety. After being checked out in a local hospital (she was fine), the girl was sent home. Her parents told police she was a regular sleepwalker.

IT'ZZZZZZZZZ ART

By day, Lee Hadwin is a nurse in Wales. By night, he's a sleep artist. When he awakes each morning he finds that during the night he's made as many as 10 elaborately detailed pencil drawings. His subjects range from humans to landscapes to fantastical creatures to intricate abstract designs. Yet, despite this, Hadwin claims to lack both an aptitude and interest in art. "It is the most extraordinary feeling to wake up and find myself surrounded by artworks and have no recollection of having drawn them," he told the *Daily Mail*. Hadwin's problem began when he was four (he drew on walls). As a teenager on a sleepover, he drew all over a friend's kitchen. Since his 20s, he's left art supplies scattered around the house for himself. He's agreed to have himself filmed for a documentary (while he sleeps) and to be observed by the Edinburgh Sleep Centre (while he sleeps).

ZZZ...OW...ZZZ...OW...ZZZ...OW...

Morag Fisher, 40, was staying at the home of a friend in Long Eaton, near Nottingham in central England, when she got up in the middle of the night and went on one of her regular sleepwalks. In her own home, such nighttime excursions ended with Fisher simply returning to her bed. But because she was staying at a friend's house…things didn't end well. The sleepwalking woman fell down a set of steep stairs and broke her jaw, nose, both cheekbones, one eye socket, a couple of ribs, and both wrists, and damaged vertebrae in her neck and back. Fisher's friend, 39-year-old Carl Muggleton, found her in a pool of blood at the bottom of the staircase and, fearing she was dead, called emergency services. Fisher had to undergo multiple surgeries, but she made what doctors called a remarkable recovery and was able to return home in less than two weeks. Bonus: Fisher slept through the entire ordeal and didn't wake up until she was in the ambulance. (There are now baby gates at the top of the stairs in both Fisher's and Muggleton's homes.)

Hey, Nice Mudflaps!

Early automobiles were boring black boxes, devoid of personality…until all this stuff came along to spice things up. So honk if you like car-accessory origins!

FUZZY DICE

During World War II, American fighter pilots glued ordinary game dice to their instrument panels, arranged so that seven dots, or "pips," were visible—a lucky 7. It was a good-luck charm for the dangerous combat missions they flew. After the war, thousands of former fighter pilots and airplane mechanics got caught up in America's burgeoning car culture—in particular, building and customizing hot rods. One small customization was a holdover from the war: hanging a pair of plastic dice over the rearview mirror. Mark Shepherd was aware of the fad—he'd been a radar and electronics technician in the navy during World War II. While working at Texas Instruments in 1952 (where he helped develop the integrated circuit and eventually became CEO), he asked a toy maker to create some dice for him, but extra-large and plush, so that they were soft like a stuffed animal instead of hard plastic. Shepherd gave them as a good-luck gift to a friend who was into hot rods and drag racing, and it caught on.

BUMPER STICKERS

Forest Gill ran a silk-screen printing business in Kansas City in the late 1930s, manufacturing canvas awnings for local businesses with their name printed on them. In 1946 he heard about new "DayGlo" inks developed by a printing company in Cleveland—bright colors that glowed in the daytime and also didn't fade or run when exposed to rain. Gill started offering them on his awnings, but around the same time, he became aware of another new technology—thin cardboard with a paper backing that, when peeled off, exposed pressure-sensitive adhesive tape. That gave him an idea. He combined the DayGlo inks with the sticker board to create a brightly colored card with a message on it that people could stick to their cars. He got the idea from a Tennessee tourist attraction called Rock City. Cars would get a free piece of cardboard that read "See Rock City," which an employee would tie to the bumper with wire. The signs could be seen on cars all over the South and Midwest. Gill presented his idea to the Nationwide Advertising Specialty Company, which in turn sold his "bumper stickers"—the perfect inexpensive souvenir for car owners in the 1950s—to tourist destinations nationwide (including Rock City).

Adolf Hitler was a proponent of natural remedies—notably, leeches and enemas.

SEXY LADY MUDFLAPS

California-based long-haul trucker Stewart Allen liked to decorate the inside of his rig with pictures of his wife, Rachel Ann Allen. His favorite: a photo of her sitting on the beach, wearing a swimsuit, hair flapping in the wind. But when a new boss at his trucking company told him to stop decorating his truck with personal items, inspiration struck. He turned the photo into a silhouette and had a metal fabricator create a chrome version, which he had the fabricator affix to a sheet of rubber. Result: his wife's figure on mudflaps, which were far less likely to be noticed by his boss. In 1967 Allen's friend Bill Zinda asked if he could reproduce and sell the mudflaps as part of a line of truck accessories. Allen agreed, and those mudflaps depicting Rachel Ann became very popular as trucking culture captivated America in the 1970s. Neither man had bothered to trademark the image, though, so Zinda's sexy lady mudflaps were widely copied. The trademark for the original image is now owned by fashion designer Ed Allen—Stewart and Rachel Ann's son. In 2009 he released a line of T-shirts showing off his mother's figure.

THE "FRONT-END BRA"

Bill Colgan ran Colgan Custom Manufacturing in Burbank, California, in the 1950s, designing custom upholstery for boats and cars. In 1960 three German engineers who worked at a nearby Lockheed plant asked Colgan to make a custom cover for the front end of each of their Porsches. For reference, they gave Colgan what they'd been using to protect their cars: Porsche road-test covers made of canvas, with wooden slats, hooks, and rubber bands sewn in. Six weeks later, Colgan had crafted 12 covers out of vinyl and leather, and lined with felt. Colgan called it a "bra" because it fit tightly around the front of a car, and to him it looked like a brassiere. The engineers referred Colgan to Porsche, which contracted him to make 150 more, and then hundreds more. By 1975 Colgan was manufacturing thousands of bras a year for various makes and models. As Porsche had used the cover to road-test new cars without damaging the front end, Colgan's bra promised to protect the bumper and hood from scratches and paint wear. (It's also a way to conceal front-end damage.) Only thing: according to some auto experts, bras have big downsides—they catch air (which slows down the car) and retain moisture (which actually *accelerates* the paint's decay).

*   *   *

"I know a lot about cars, man. I can look at any car's headlights and tell you exactly which way it's coming."

—**Mitch Hedberg**

Every year, Americans spend about $330 million on Halloween costumes—for their pets.

The Peary Dinner

On November 11, 1909, a banquet was held in New York City honoring Admiral Robert E. Peary, recent "discoverer" of the North Pole. Here's the actual (and bizarre) Arctic Circle–inspired menu.

• **BLUE POINT OYSTERS.** An oyster once harvested in Long Island, New York. (Not anymore—they've been near-extinct since the 1910s.)

• **PETITE BOUCHEE WALRUS.** Thin slices of fermented walrus meat.

• **VELOUTE PTARMIGAN AUX CROUTINS.** A soup made by mixing cream with stock made from the ptarmigan—a game bird with red, gristly meat—served like French onion soup, with a big slice of toast on top.)

• **SUPREME DE NARWHAL, VERONIQUE.** A boneless slice of narwhal meat, served with its layer of blubber intact. The large fillets of the dark gray "unicorn of the sea" were served in cream sauce and garnished with raisins.

• **MIGNON DE MUSK OX, VICTORIA POMMES PARISIENNES.** Musk ox looks like beef, but reportedly tastes like horse. "Victoria," a style popular in the early 20th century, meant that the fillet was served with a black truffle sauce and lobster chunks (and potatoes in clarified butter).

• **MOUSSE DE PEMMICAN, KOSSUTH EPINARDS AUX FLEURONS.** Pemmican is a jerkylike preparation of dried and spiced meat. This one was reindeer meat, ground and whipped into a mousse and served in the Hungarian "Kossuth style"—with sour cream, paprika, and spinach.

• **SORBET "NORTH POLE."** In fine dining, sorbets are fruit-flavored ices, eaten as a palate cleanser between courses. At this dinner, the ices were flavored with mint and sea salt.

• **PERDEUX ROTI, BARDE AUX FEUILLES DE VIGNE COEUR DE ROMAINE EN SALADE.** Each diner was served a roasted, whole partridge, wrapped in grape leaves and stuffed with juniper berries, and served with a romaine salad.

• **BISCUIT GLACÉ KNICKERBOCKER CORBEILLE DE MIGNARDISES.** Glacé is a French frozen dessert, similar to ice cream, but much, much richer, made with cream and meringue instead of cream or milk. That gives the dish a nougatlike taste and consistency. Here, it was served like the now-forgotten Knickerbocker cocktail—with rum, raspberries, oranges, lemons, and lime. (And a biscuit—a cookie—on the side.)

Random fact: About half of people who are allergic to latex are also allergic to bananas.

"Do You Know Who I Am?!"

You can't really blame celebrities for trying to use their fame to receive special treatment or to get out of trouble when they're behaving badly—but as these stories prove, it doesn't always work.

STAR: Christina Aguilera, pop singer

STORY: In December 2014, Aguilera celebrated her 34th birthday with some friends at Disneyland's California Adventure. According to the gossip website TMZ, a "theme park source" reported that Aguilera, who got her start as a *Mickey Mouse Club* Mousketeer, wanted to get her picture taken with Mickey Mouse. But the performer inside the costume was going on break; a park staffer told Aguilera that Mickey would return in 30 minutes. Angry, Aguilera called Mickey Mouse an "*sshole" and then shouted, "Don't you know who I am?" As Mickey retreated, Aguilera's bodyguard started "hurling threats" at the giant mouse. Security guards were dispatched, but by the time they arrived, the singer and her entourage had moved on.

AFTERMATH: Aguilera's publicist said she had "no comment." The pop star later posted a photo of her group—all wearing mouse ears—along with the caption: "Fun birthday celebration at the happiest place on earth #disneyland." (Mickey is nowhere to be seen.)

STAR: Gloria James, mother of NBA superstar LeBron James

STORY: Being the mother of the most famous basketball player in the world has made Gloria James a celebrity in her own right. And her story is inspiring: after having LeBron when she was 16 years old, she raised him alone. And LeBron credits his success to her.

But she might have let that "star power" go to her head in 2011 after a night of clubbing with friends at the Fontainebleau Hotel in Miami Beach. (LeBron was playing for the Heat at the time.) At around 4:00 a.m., a hotel parking valet named Rockfeller Sorel retrieved James's SUV and—as is the policy—waited inside the car with the engine running until she was ready to get in. But James continued talking to her friends outside the hotel...for 30 minutes. Finally, Sorel shut off the car and handed the keys to the valet station cashier. At that point, James, 43, confronted Sorel: "Where are my f*cking keys?" He tried telling her, but she started insulting him with racial epithets. An altercation ensued, and police were called. According to their report: "All the while the victim tried to explain...Then for no apparent reason James struck the victim with an open hand across the right side of his face and in the process causing herself to lose her balance and fall to the ground." (Surveillance video backs up that story.) James was arrested for battery and disorderly intoxication. Sorel later said, "I'm very, very humiliated because she told me, 'Do you know who I am?' when she slapped me."

AFTERMATH: James made a deal to avoid jail time—20 hours of community service and a $1,000 donation to a Haitian charity. (Sorel is from Haiti.) But the deal didn't satisfy Sorel. He sued her in civil court, claiming that the incident and subsequent media attention left him "emotionally scarred." In December 2012, the case was settled before going to trial, and although the terms weren't disclosed, it's a good bet that the valet received a sizable payoff from the mom of one of the richest athletes on the planet.

STAR: Reese Witherspoon, actress

STORY: In 2013 Witherspoon and her husband Jim Toth went out to dinner in Atlanta. Witherspoon later admitted that they probably drank "one too many glasses of wine." While Toth was driving them home, a police officer saw the car weaving, pulled them over, and gave Toth a sobriety test...which he failed. He was placed under arrest. At that point, according to the police report, Witherspoon, 37, "began to hang out the window and say that she did not believe that I was a real police officer." Then she got out of the car and refused to get back in, repeatedly shouting, "I am an American citizen!" The officer told her she was under arrest.

That's when she yelled, "Do you know my name?"

"No, ma'am," replied the officer.

The Oscar winner replied, "You're about to find out who I am!"

"That's fine," said the officer. "I'm not really worried about you, ma'am." Witherspoon was put in handcuffs and started yelling that she was pregnant. She was charged with disorderly conduct.

AFTERMATH: Witherspoon, who was promoting a movie, canceled talk show appearances and kept a low profile for a few days. When she did make a statement, she said, "I'm deeply embarrassed. I have no idea what I was thinking that night. I saw him arrest my husband and I just panicked. I said all kinds of crazy things to the officer. I even told him I was pregnant. I am not pregnant."

*   *   *

Man plans and God laughs. —**Yiddish proverb**

Welcome to No-Man's-Land

Is it possible that there's any place on earth that still isn't claimed by a country? Believe it or not, yes. In fact, there are quite a few.

BIR TAWIL

B

Location: An 800-square-mile patch of barren desert, midway between the Nile River and the Red Sea on the disputed border of Egypt and Sudan.

Details: Egypt recognizes the 22nd parallel, a straight line running east to west, as the border between the two countries. That line, first used in 1899, places Bir Tawil south of Egypt, in Sudan. Sudan recognizes a different border, though. It uses an irregular administrative boundary dating to 1902 that briefly dips below the 22nd parallel and then rises on its way to the Red Sea. That line places Bir Tawil north of Sudan, in Egypt. Drawing the border two different ways allows both countries to lay claim to a more valuable plot of land north of the 22nd parallel—the Hala'ib Triangle, which is 10 times larger, contains arable land, and borders the Red Sea.

What Happened: Egypt and Sudan are working to resolve their border dispute. For now, Egypt administers Bir Tawil but leaves it off official maps. But that hasn't stopped other people from trying to claim it: in 2010 a 30-year-old Egyptian named Kareem Hamdy claimed it as a nation for displaced people. He never actually went to Bir Tawil, but in June 2014 a Virginia man named Jeremiah Heaton made the 14-hour trek across the desert and planted a flag in the sand, proclaiming the area the Kingdom of North Sudan to "fulfill his six-year-old daughter's wish to become a princess." Neither claim is ever likely to be recognized: under international law, only countries, not people, can assert sovereignty over territory.

SIGA

Location: On the west bank of the Danube River, which serves as the international border between Serbia and Croatia.

Details: Both Serbia and Croatia recognize the Danube as the border between their two countries. Problem: Serbia (on the east side of the river) uses the modern *channel* or flow of the Danube, which is comparatively straight, and Croatia (on the west side) recognizes the course of the Danube as it was in the 19th century, when it meandered all over the place. Result: Croatia claims some 40 square miles of territory, or "pockets" of land, east of the Danube, on the Serbian side. Serbia also claims this territory.

By comparison, less than four square miles *west* of the Danube (the Croatian side) used to be on the *east* side. The largest such parcel is a 2.5-square-mile pocket of land called Siga. Croatia doesn't claim Siga as its territory…and, since it's on the wrong side of the river, neither does Serbia. Three smaller unnamed pockets of land on the western bank of the river have received the same treatment: neither side recognizes them as its own territory.

MARIE BYRD LAND

Location: A 620,000-square-mile wedge-shaped portion of western Antarctica, between the areas claimed by Chile and New Zealand

Details: By the time the Antarctic Treaty was signed in 1959, seven countries (Argentina, Australia, Chile, France, New Zealand, Norway, and the United Kingdom) had laid claim to vast stretches of Antarctica. But Marie Byrd Land, which is larger than Alaska, was so remote and inaccessible—even by Antarctic standards—that it had not yet been claimed.

What Happened: The Antarctic Treaty froze (so to speak) existing claims and prevented any new ones from being made. That meant that Marie Byrd Land, which American explorer Admiral Richard Byrd named in honor of his wife, will never belong to anyone—at least not as long as the Antarctic Treaty is in effect.

SEBORGA

Location: In northwest Italy, near the border with France

Details: You'll have to decide for yourself whether Seborga is unclaimed territory or not. As far as the Italian government is concerned, it is and always has been part of Italy. But in the early 1960s the town's florist, a man named Giorgio Carbone, found documents in the Vatican archives that he said proved the town had *never* been part of Italy. The documents showed that the town had belonged to an order of monks from AD 954 until 1729, when the monks sold the town to the kingdom of Sardinia (part of modern-day Italy). But, Carbone argued, that transaction was never officially recorded, which meant that Seborga never became part of Sardinia. Thus, when Sardinia united with other Italian states to form the Kingdom of Italy in the early 1860s, Seborga was left out of the union and was in territorial limbo for more than 130 years.

Carbone's claims haven't won much support in Italian legal or historical circles, but that didn't stop all but four of Seborga's 308 citizens from voting to affirm the town's independence from Italy in 1995 and proclaiming Prince Giorgio I its head of state.

What Happened: Whatever objection the mayor of Seborga may have had to sharing power with an upstart florist-prince evaporated when it became clear just how good declaring independence was for business. Before 1995, Seborga was just another sleepy town; today it receives as many as 100,000 visitors a year who pump millions into the local economy, snapping up Seborgan flags, passports, license plates, and other souvenirs. If nothing else, independence is certainly a clever marketing gimmick, and the locals hope that one day Seborga will achieve the same official status as the Republic of San Marino, another city-state in northern Italy that the Italian government *admits* has never been part of Italy.

THE BOTTOM OF THE OCEAN

Location: Any part of any ocean floor at least 200 nautical miles from the shores of any country

Details: According to international law, the territory of any coastal nation extends 12 nautical miles from its shore, and an *exclusive economic zone*, in which the country has sole rights to fishing and other natural resources, extends out to 200 miles from shore. Anything beyond that is considered international waters or "the high seas," and those belong to no one.

*   *   *

PUNS.COM

- **Q:** Why shouldn't you leave your cat alone with your computer?
  A: Because cats are notorious hackers.

- **Announcement:** Whoever stole my copy of Microsoft Office will be punished severely. You have my Word.

- **Q:** What do you call it when a northern European transfers a digital image of a bird to his computer?
  A: Scandinavian.

- When choosing a browser company to work for, it's probably better to try Safari or Firefox because everyone knows Chrome doesn't pay.

- **Q:** What's the number-one video site for sheep?
  A: EweTube.

- A spammer spammed one too many people and his computer exploded. He was blown to Kingdom.com.

The first artificial Christmas trees were made of dyed goose feathers.

Uncle John's Stall of Fame

Uncle John is amazed—and pleased—by the unusual ways people get involved with bathrooms, toilets, and so on. That's why he created the "Stall of Fame."

Honoree: A man living in Palo Alto, California, in 2013
Notable Achievement: Making a splash by getting rid of a really old pot (yes, *that* kind of pot)
True Story: For decades the city of Palo Alto, 32 miles south of San Francisco, had a program where residents can turn in an old, inefficient toilet and receive a rebate toward the purchase of a new high-efficiency model. They've gotten plenty of old commodes over the years, but it wasn't until March 2013 that they got one *this* old, or this inefficient: a man (he asked to remain anonymous) turned in a toilet that was manufactured in 1928, which made it 85 years old and the oldest ever traded in. It used *12 gallons*, or about 100 pounds of water, every time it was flushed. "When I discovered that newer, higher-efficiency toilets were both reliable and only used 1.28 gallons per flush, I finally decided to make the switch," he told the *San Jose Mercury News*. The city gave the man $125 toward the purchase of a new toilet, which could save him as much as 43,000 gallons of water per year—enough to fill a swimming pool. (The man can flush his new toilet nine times and still not use as much water as he did flushing the old toilet once.)

Honorees: Todd Bermann and Allen Klevens, two friends who live in Southern California
Notable Achievement: Making a visit to the bowl at the Hollywood Bowl a little more pleasant
True Story: The Hollywood Bowl isn't a bowling alley—it's a 1920s outdoor amphitheater in Los Angeles that seats 18,000 people. It's a great place to see an outdoor concert…but if you're a woman and you've had to make a pit stop during intermission, you know that the women's restrooms are not nearly as great as the rest of the place. The largest ladies room has 68 toilet stalls arranged in long rows. When it's crowded and you *really have to go*, finding an available toilet among all the occupied stalls can be quite a challenge. "They used to have to push on the doors to see if anybody was inside or peek through a crack or look under the stall door for feet," operations manager Christine Whitman told the

---

They're not synonymous: Cement is one of the ingredients used to make concrete.

Los Angeles Times in 2014. The Bowl had to station an attendant at the entrance to encourage women to go deeper into the restroom and look for unoccupied stalls way in the back.

Stage manager Todd Bermann was asked if he could figure out a solution to the problem. He and his friend Allen Klevens came up with a system of LED lights installed in the ceiling in front of each stall. The light glows red when the door is latched shut and the stall is occupied, and green when the door is open and the stall is available. Now instead of pushing on one door after another and peeking in, women simply look down the rows of stalls to see which lights are green, then head straight for an unoccupied stall. The Hollywood Bowl estimates that the lights have improved traffic flow in the restrooms by 100 percent.

Update: Klevens and Bermann have founded a company called Tooshlights to market their system to other venues. The company's slogan: "Know Where to Go." Next up: a smartphone app that allows patrons to see which stalls are free before they even get to the restroom.

Honorees: A team of sanitation workers in Union City, California

Notable Achievement: Helping a resident realize her pipe dream of recovering a precious family heirloom

True Story: Mehvish Tapal and her husband Munazzar live in Union City along with their three-year-old son Maaz. In late 2014 Mehvish and Maaz were watching the 2003 movie *Finding Nemo*, about a fish in a dentist's office aquarium who escapes down a drain and makes his way to the ocean. Unfortunately, Maaz got a little too into the movie: before Mehvish knew it, the boy had run into the bathroom and flushed a diamond and sapphire ring down the toilet. "He kept saying, 'Nemo will find the ring!'" Mehvish later told newspaper reporters. "I freaked out and called a plumber, but he said it was likely long gone into the city drain."

The ring was a precious heirloom that had been in the family for more than 50 years. (It had belonged to Mehvish's mother-in-law; she gave it to Mehvish as a gift when she became pregnant with Maaz.) So rather than accept the loss, as many people would have done, Mehvish called the sanitation department and asked for help. In the weeks that followed, the workers came out several times to flush out the sewer lines near the house and look for the ring. Their odds weren't much better than finding a needle in a very disgusting haystack—the sanitation department says it had recovered just two valuable objects in the past 20 years—but about a week before Thanksgiving, they recovered the ring from a sewer pipe down the street from the Tapals' house. "It's in pristine condition. Just needs a little cleaning," a very grateful Mehvish told reporters. "It's a real miracle."

Famed trial lawyer Clarence Darrow was a law school dropout.

Beatles Firsts

It's been decades since they broke up, but bands are still catching up to the ways the Fab Four pioneered and shaped pop music.

LONG SINGLES. Up until the late 1960s, pop music radio stations adhered to strict playlists and wouldn't play songs much longer than three minutes. The Beatles' 1968 song "Hey Jude" is over seven minutes long, but because it was a Beatles song, it got airplay in its uncut version. Not only did it open the door for songs longer than three minutes to get on the radio (or songs *much* longer, such as "American Pie" and "Stairway to Heaven"), but it hit #1 and was the Beatles' most successful single.

COHESIVE ALBUMS. Before the Beatles, albums by pop acts were merely collections of songs. Typically, a band would perform a few songs at a recording session. Their record company would release some as singles and then compile a bunch onto an album. The band would have little input into the order of the songs, or even the choice of what went on the album, or what was released as a single. That all changed with 1967's *Sgt. Pepper's Lonely Hearts Club Band*. Working with producer George Martin, the Fab Four created an album that, from start to finish, presented a related group of songs: a concert performed by the fictional group "Sgt. Pepper's Lonely Hearts Club Band." Some music historians cite this as not just the first sequenced album but also the first concept album.

VANITY LABELS. It became common in the 1980s and 1990s for record labels to give top-selling acts a "vanity imprint"—basically their own record label, through which they could develop new artists and get a cut of the profits. Some examples: Interscope Records established Aftermath Entertainment for Dr. Dre, Capitol made Grand Royal for the Beastie Boys, and Warner Bros. created Maverick Records for Madonna. The first time this was done was when EMI helped the Beatles create Apple Records—a music label and studio over which they had full reign. Among the acts that got a break on the early Apple Records: Badfinger, Mary Hopkin, Billy Preston, and James Taylor.

STADIUM SHOWS. The Beatles were the first "supergroup," so it's understandable that they brought rock music into sports stadiums. Before the Beatles, rock 'n' roll concerts were relatively small affairs, booked into concert halls, amphitheaters, auditoriums, armories, and

---

Eeew! Polymorphonuclear cells are better known as pus cells. Eeew!

gymnasiums. But by 1965, the only way the Beatles could meet the demand for tickets was to play huge facilities. The first time a band played a stadium was on August 15, 1965, when the Beatles played at Shea Stadium in Queens, New York, to 55,000 fans. The show brought in $300,000—at the time the most ever for a rock concert…or any performance in the history of show business.

HEAVY METAL. The band that pioneered one of the most innocent kinds of music also pioneered one of the darkest. Music historians cite the 1968 *White Album* track "Helter Skelter" as the first example of what would later be called "heavy metal." Predating Black Sabbath and Led Zeppelin, "Helter Skelter" used heavily distorted guitar chords and hard-charging drums—so hard that the song ends with Ringo Starr screaming, "I've got blisters on me fingers!" Also, predating the controversies that would surround heavy metal and the supposedly evil influence it had on fans, "Helter Skelter" famously inspired mass murderer Charles Manson.

INCLUDING LYRICS. Lyrics are commonplace in CD booklets, as they were for decades before, printed on record album jackets or included as an insert inside the sleeve. The first album to print lyrics to the songs—in this case, directly on the jacket—was *Sgt. Pepper's Lonely Hearts Club Band*.

BACKWARD LYRICS. In the 1980s, rumors that some heavy metal albums contained secret messages that could only be heard by spinning an album backward on a turntable and listening very, very closely created panic among parents. Dozens of bands have included backward voices, but only to add a weird-sounding audio component. The Beatles' 1966 song "Rain" is the first song with "backward tracking"—vocal tracks inserted backward. (Lennon and McCartney were fans of electronic music composer Karlheinz Stockhausen, whose music inspired them to experiment with tape loops.)

SOME OTHER FAB FOUR FIRSTS

• The Beatles' 1964 hit "I Feel Fine" contains the first recorded example of intentional feedback.

• The 1968 album *The Beatles* (otherwise known as *The White Album*) was the first double album by a rock band.

• In 1966 the Beatles began experimenting with LSD and other psyche-delic drugs. Foreshadowing the late '60s psychedelic rock movement, music historians cite the *Revolver* tracks "Tomorrow Never Knows," "She Said, She Said," and "I'm Only Sleeping" as the first examples of psychedelic rock, because of the use of bizarre lyrics, droning sounds, tape loops, and guitar distortion.

"Sure Hits" That Missed

Have you ever watched a hit TV show and thought, "Anyone could come up with something like this?" Like so many things that look easy, coming up with a hit TV show is anything but.

THE MICHAEL J. FOX SHOW

In the summer of 2012 agents representing Michael J. Fox told the Big Four broadcast networks that Fox was working on a new TV series. This would mark Fox's first regular television series since he left *Spin City* in 2000 because of Parkinson's disease. Predictably, a bidding war developed. ABC, which had aired *Spin City*, offered Fox the plum time slot after the megahit *Modern Family*. NBC went bigger, promising a full 22-episode season without a pilot episode or audience testing, and won the show. *The Michael J. Fox Show* debuted in September 2013 to 7.5 million viewers. But neither the premise (Fox plays a news anchor with Parkinson's) nor the writing was very funny and most of those viewers didn't come back—by episode 14, fewer than 2 million people were watching. Contractually obligated to air all 22 episodes of a show with dramatically low ratings, NBC opted to buy out Fox's contract and pulled the show off the air for good in January 2014.

EXTREME

ABC thought it couldn't miss with the action-adventure show *Extreme*, filmed on high peaks in the Rocky Mountains. James Brolin starred as the leader of a search-and-rescue crew. The network was so sure *Extreme* would be a hit that it decided to debut it in the most visible spot possible: immediately following the 1995 Super Bowl. It then moved to its regular slot, Thursdays at 8:00 p.m.—opposite NBC's ultra-popular "Must See TV" lineup, which included *Mad About You* and *Friends*. That was extreme-ly bad luck. Result: The show's life was extreme-ly short—only seven episodes aired. However, *Extreme* did make TV history—it taught the networks to shy away from using the post–Super Bowl slot to debut new, untested shows. Only Fox's *Family Guy* and CBS's *Undercover Boss* have since premiered postgame.

AMAZING STORIES

A popular format in the 1950s and 1960s, the anthology series had disappeared from network TV by the 1980s. NBC decided to revive it with *Amazing Stories* in 1985, and brought out the big guns to do it. Steven Spielberg served as executive producer and agreed to direct several episodes. Like the classic TV anthology shows *The Twilight Zone* and

A study of 6,000 stock market "expert" predictions found that only 47.4% turned out to be accurate.

The Outer Limits, each episode of *Amazing Stories* was a self-contained story focusing on new characters, played by new actors, and written and directed by new people. (Among the directors: Clint Eastwood and Martin Scorsese.) Sometimes it would be a comic episode, sometimes science fiction, sometimes even a cartoon. NBC had such faith that people would tune in that they committed to airing *Amazing Stories* for two full years and scheduled it against CBS's top-rated *60 Minutes*. Bad idea. *Amazing Stories* earned only middling ratings, in part because it couldn't defeat *60 Minutes*. Some TV writers think the format was what ultimately sank the show—audiences, unfamiliar with the anthology concept, were confused each time they tuned in.

JOANIE LOVES CHACHI

Who was the breakout character on ABC's nostalgic 1974–84 sitcom *Happy Days*? Fonzie, of course. But he didn't get the spinoff—Joanie Cunningham (Erin Moran) and her boyfriend Chachi (Scott Baio) did. The premise: they move from Milwaukee to Chicago, where they try to make it in the music industry. *Happy Days* creator Garry Marshall helped create and produce *Joanie Loves Chachi* and imported several *Happy Days* writers onto the new series, set to debut in the middle of the 1981–82 season. Airing immediately following *Happy Days* for just four weeks, the show was a hit, finishing the season at #17 in the ratings—one spot higher than *Happy Days*. When it returned in the fall, however, all the veteran *Happy Days* writers returned to that show, and ABC moved *Joanie Loves Chachi* to Thursday nights against CBS's *Magnum, P.I.* Total run of *Joanie Loves Chachi*: 17 episodes.

BIONIC WOMAN

The hottest new show of the 2006–07 TV season was NBC's *Heroes*, a science-fiction show about a group of people who suddenly develop superpowers. NBC took the success of that show to mean that viewers wanted more science-fiction. So in 2007 it debuted a remake of the 1970s series *Bionic Woman*. The network poured a lot of money into the show—the pilot cost $7.4 million, and episodes were budgeted at $6 million. (For comparison, most high-profile dramas top out at $1 million an episode.) Starring a British actress named Michelle Ryan in the title role, the first episode was viewed by a whopping 14 million people, and then the ratings began to drop. Some critics said it was too edgy; others said it wasn't edgy enough. Whatever the reason, by the eighth episode the audience had dwindled to less than half. That was about the time that a writers' strike ended production on the show. When the strike was settled the following spring, NBC opted to cancel the show, and production never resumed.

It takes 1.1 gallons of water to produce a single almond, and 4.9 gallons to produce a walnut.

Secede!

You probably know that the American Civil War was sparked when 11 of the 15 slave states tried to secede from the Union. Here are some modern secessionist movements you've probably never heard of.

THE REPUBLIC OF KUGELMUGEL

Seceded From: Austria

Details: In the 1970s an Austrian artist named Edwin Lipburger built himself a spherical three-story house. Spheres are a more "natural" shape than box-shaped houses, he explained, and therefore better to live in. The local government disagreed and refused to grant him the necessary permits for the giant ball, so he seceded from Austria and built it anyway. He named his new country Kugelmugel, which translates roughly as "Ball Hill," and gave himself an address on what he called "Anti-Fascism Square."

The authorities might well have ignored Lipburger and let him live in his spherical nation if he had simply left it at that, but when he stopped paying taxes (Austria was now a "foreign country," he said) and began selling Republic of Kugelmugel postage stamps, he ended up serving a stretch in prison.

Outcome: Not a very long stretch, though. Lipburger was just 10 weeks into his prison sentence when the president of Austria granted him a full pardon. Now in his late 70s, Lipburger lives in "exile" in Austria proper; his house has been moved from its original location in the province of Lower Austria to a riverfront park in Vienna, where it is a popular tourist attraction.

AKHZIV LAND

Seceded From: Israel

Details: In the early 1950s, Eli Avivi, a Tel Aviv man in his 20s, visited his sister in a village in northern Israel, close to the Lebanese border. While Avivi was there, he hiked over to the Mediterranean coast. There he fell in love with an isolated stretch of shoreline called Akhziv, 10 miles north of the port city of Acre. Why return home? Avivi stayed put. He moved into an old abandoned house just off the beach and built guest cabins for visitors, which he rented out to tourists for years without incident. But he didn't own the land, and in 1970 government officials finally obtained a court order to evict him.

Avivi refused to leave, even after the government bulldozed some of the cabins. The eviction was later thrown out of court, but the experience made him so angry that he declared independence for his "State of Akhziv Land" and made himself president. He ran afoul of the authorities again when he started issuing his own visas and marriage licenses, but that case was also thrown out of court.

Outcome: President Avivi still lives in Akhziv Land today and still rents out cabins. He has reached an accommodation of sorts with the government and says that he has obtained a 99-year lease for the property. The Ministry of Tourism has even erected signs pointing the way—to "Eli Avivi," not "Akhziv Land." (As far as the ministry is concerned, the resort is part of Israel.)

THE PRINCIPALITY OF WY

Seceded From: Mosman, a suburb of Sydney, Australia

Details: Paul Delprat, the principal of an art school, lives with his wife Susan and their kids in Mosman. In 1993 he and his wife asked the local council for permission to build a paved road to his property, permitting vehicle access to his home for the first time. The request got mired in red tape, and 11 years later, the road still wasn't approved. "We thought, look, this is crazy," he told a reporter in 2010. "All councils provide is roads and take away your rubbish so we thought, 'We'll secede'—and we did."

Outcome: On November 15, 2004, the Delprats declared independence and formed the Principality of Wy (named after a local landmark, Wyargine Point). Delprat, who proclaimed himself a prince, says he's stopped paying local taxes (other than for garbage collection) but continues to pay provincial and national taxes, since he hasn't seceded from the state of New South Wales or from Australia. Any other money he pays to the Mosman city council, he says, is a "gift." That's fine with the council: as long as he keeps paying what's owed, they don't care what he calls it.

Update: In 2013 Prince Paul marked 20 years of waiting for approval to build a road to his home, something he says must be "the longest-running development application in the world." At this rate the project may never be completed, but even if it is, the Principality of Wy will endure. "I will maintain it as a beacon of hope to all those oppressed by bureaucracy," says His Majesty.

THE PRINCIPALITY OF DUBELDEKA

Seceded From: The town of Mittagong, approximately 80 miles south of Sydney, Australia

Details: The Land Down Under has what must be the largest number of secessionist micronations in the world. They have become a popular form of protest against bureaucratic stubbornness and inefficiency. In this case the owners of the 134-year-old Braemar Lodge were startled to learn in 2000 that the local government was planning to dig up their property and run a sewer pipe through the middle of it, which would have been terrible for business. Owners Vasudeo and Doreen Khandekar protested the decision with letters, phone calls, and visits to government officials. When that failed, they staged a sit-in to block the bulldozers and also seceded from Mittagong, founding the Principality of Dubeldeka. The new country's motto: "Tenacity is our virtue."

Outcome: Their tenacity paid off. The government finally agreed to move the sewer pipe, and at last report both Braemar Lodge and the Principality of Dubeldeka were still in business. If you ever happen to visit, be sure to ask Prince Vasudeo or Princess Doreen to stamp your passport.

THE REPUBLIC OF WHANGAMOMONA

Seceded From: New Zealand

Details: In 1989 the national government redrew regional council boundaries, moving the township of Whangamomona (pronounced FONG-ah-MOE-mah-nah) from Taranaki to Manawatu-Wanganui. That shouldn't have been a big deal for the community of 40 people, but it meant that Whangamomona's rugby players would have to play on the same team as their longtime rivals in Manawatu-Wanganui...and *that* was more than the locals could bear. Result: on November 1, 1989, they voted to sever all ties with New Zealand. (New Zealand, of course, ignored them.)

Outcome: What started out as a half-serious protest against needless government meddling into local affairs soon turned into an excuse to throw a party and attract trainloads of tourists to the area on "Republic Day." Today it's celebrated every other year in January, when the weather is better than in November. Electing a president for the republic is a big part of the festivities; so is whip-cracking, sheep running, and "possum skinning." Past presidents include a goat named Billy Gumboot and a poodle named Tai. Current president: Murtle the Turtle (a car mechanic, not a turtle), who defeated Mike the Wizard in a landslide in 2011.

*   *   *

THE SPEED (BUMP) OF LIGHT

Light travels at 186,000 miles per second—about 671,000,000 miles per hour. That's a scientific fact. But not always. In 1998 scientists at Harvard University shot laser light through supercooled atomic gas and slowed it down to a speed of 38 mph, the slowest light speed ever recorded.

President Gerald Ford's son Steven was an actor on the TV soap *The Young and the Restless.*

9 Weird Facts About Babies

Babies: they're even weirder than you thought.

1 **They can't taste salt.** Babies are born with a well-developed sense of taste—but not for salt. Studies show that babies can't taste salt until they're about four months old. They can taste other flavors as well as adults can, especially sweet, bitter, and sour flavors (which might explain all the "baby tastes lemon" videos on YouTube)—and maybe even better: some studies indicate that babies actually have more taste buds than adults do.

2. They don't shed tears. Babies cry an awful lot—but they can't shed tears: they don't have functional tear ducts until they're between three and twelve weeks old. (They can, however, produce "basal tears"—the nonemotional tears we produce constantly to keep our eyes moist.)

3. They have no kneecaps. Really! Well…sort of. If you X-ray a baby's legs, you likely won't see anything where the kneecaps should be, or if you do, it'll just be small, smudgy spots. Reason: all bones start off as cartilage, and they harden, or *ossify*, over time. Kneecaps take an especially long time to form—from three to five years—and because cartilage doesn't show up on X-rays, babies appear to have no kneecaps. That lack of hard kneecaps is a good thing, because the spongy tissue serves to absorb some of the abuse toddlers take during their crawling months and from their frequent falls.

4. They have more bones than adults do. Way more—about 300, compared to our paltry 206. The reason is related to why they lack real kneecaps: some of a baby's separate bones fuse together into single bones as they ossify in the months and years after birth. Example: the skull starts off as several separate bones that fuse together into one large bone by about the age of two.

5. They menstruate. While still in the womb, babies are exposed to high levels of the female hormone estrogen. At birth, when the baby becomes "disconnected" from mom, as it were, those estrogen levels fall rapidly and in girls can cause what is known as *pseudomenstruation*, similar to menstruation in young and adult women. (Sharp drops in estrogen and related hormones are in fact what triggers menstruation in adult women.) Mothers unaware of this phenomenon often freak out when they see a little blood in their babies' diapers—but it's very common and happens in about a quarter of all female babies, usually in the first seven days of life.

6. They lactate. The drop in hormone levels that causes psueudomenstruation can also cause *galactorrhea*, a phenomenon in which newborns develop tiny breast buds—and actually lactate, producing tiny amounts of milk from their nipples. And it can happen in boys as well as girls. Like pseudomenstruation, it's not dangerous or uncommon, occurring in about 5 percent of all newborns, and can persist for up to two months. (In old European folklore, milk from the breasts of newborn babies was referred to as "witch's milk" and was thought to have magical powers.)

7. They pee. Babies start urinating in the womb just a few months after conception. Where does it go? They drink it! More precisely, the urine mixes with the amniotic fluid surrounding the baby in the uterus. And by the third trimester of pregnancy, a fetus swallows about a liter of amniotic fluid every day. Since a fetus does not need hydration or nutrition in the womb—that comes from mom via the umbilical cord— experts say this serves mostly as practice for swallowing and digestion. This means that every last one of us spent several months of our lives drinking our own pee. (Fetal *pooping* is rare…but it does happen sometimes. And that's all we're going to say about that.)

8. They remember what they taste. As we told you earlier, newborn babies cannot taste salt, but they can taste other flavors—and they can taste those flavors while they're still in the womb, starting from about four or five months into pregnancy. Amniotic fluid is believed to be affected by the food the expectant mother eats, which, in turn, is believed to affect a baby's flavor preferences after birth. If a pregnant mom eats a lot of garlicky foods, for example, the baby will taste that in her amniotic fluid in the womb—and will have a good chance of being drawn to garlic-flavored foods after birth.

9. They're covered in hair. Sometimes babies are born with just a few tufts of hair on the top of their heads, or a fine "peach fuzz" all over their tiny domes. This isn't what we're talking about. As it develops in the womb, a baby's entire body becomes covered in a thin layer of hair called *lanugo*. Child development experts say that the hair helps regulate a body's temperature, in utero. So, if your baby is born looking like a werewolf-in-training, don't worry—it's perfectly normal. The hair will gently fall out on its own over the first few weeks of the newborn's life. If your baby wasn't born covered in lanugo, well, it already fell off toward the end of gestation, and the baby ate it.

Take a Hint

Whether you call them "everyday shortcuts" or "life hacks, these simple household tips are bound to make you ask "why didn't I think of that?" (And they're very entertaining.)

Place a coin inside the bottom hem of a tie to keep it from flying around and smacking you in the face on a windy day.

• Throw wrinkled shirts in the dryer with a few ice cubes for 10 minutes on high to steam away the wrinkles.

• To help remove deodorant stains on your shirt, rub a dryer sheet on the stain before washing it.

• To keep canvas shoes dry in the rain, rub beeswax over them and blow dry until the wax melts. That will create a waterproof seal.

• Cheetos are delicious, but the sticky orange fingers you get after handling them are a pain. Use chopsticks instead to keep your fingers clean.

• Keep pizza hot on the ride home by putting the pizza box on your car seat and turning on the seat warmer.

• Do you bang your fingers with a hammer every time you nail something into a wall? Use a fine-tooth comb to keep the nail in place and keep your fingers safe.

• Scratches in wood can be fixed by rubbing a de-shelled walnut over the area.

• Putting a dry tea bag in your shoes overnight will absorb funky odors. (But remember to throw away the bags when you're done.)

• For an effective way to clean a dirty toilet, drop in a couple of denture tablets. After 20 minutes, scrub the toilet bowl and flush.

• Spraying nonstick cooking spray on shovels will keep them ice-free while you're shoveling snow.

• Price tag stickers are usually a nightmare to remove. Once you've picked away most of the tag, slather peanut butter over the site and wipe with a cloth to remove any remaining glue residue.

• Running a slightly damp rubber glove over furniture will pick up pet hair quickly and easily.

• After sweeping up the remnants of a broken glass, press a slice of bread over the area. Any remaining glass bits will stick to the bread.

87% of U.S. parents give their kids Easter baskets. 81% will steal candy from it.

What's the Word?

The English language has been evolving and de-volving for centuries. Often, interesting words or phrases come along—and then, sadly, disappear. Here are a few actual words that went the way of the cicisbeo.

UHTCEARE ("OOT-key-ARE-ay")
Meaning: Pre-dawn worry
Details: This Old English word is found in only one existing piece of writing—a 10th-century poem called "The Wife's Lament". Translated literally, *uht* meant the very early morning period just before sunrise, and *ceara* meant "care," "worry," or "anxiety." More expansively, *uhtceare* is described as meaning "lying in bed before dawn unable to go back to sleep due to worrying about things." How widely this word was used is unknown (some experts believe the poet may have made it up), but it has become a favorite of etymologists because it's something almost everybody has experienced at one time or another, and there's no other word to describe it.

NUDIUSTERTIAN ("noo-dee-uhs-TUR-shuhn")
Meaning: Relating to the day before yesterday
Details: Older versions of the *Oxford English Dictionary* (OED) listed this word even though they acknowledged that it may have been used properly just once—by the person believed to have coined it, Nathaniel Ward, a Puritan clergyman and colonial American pamphleteer. Ward, who was prone to making up words, used it in his celebrated work, *The Simple Cobler of Aggawam in America*, written in 1647. According to the OED, the word was derived from the Latin *nudestarianus*, which means "today the third day." Ward used it in the sense of "very recent," writing about "the nudiustertian fashion of the Court," meaning dress that just came into fashion—that is, "the day before yesterday."

CICISBEO ("chi-chiz-BAY-oh")
Meaning: A married woman's male companion
Details: In the 18th and 19th centuries it was common for Italian noblewomen to have a special arrangement with their husbands, who were often much older. The wife was allowed to have a *cicisbeo* (called a *cavalier servente* in Italian—literally "servant knight"), which was basically a male escort. A woman's cicisbeo would accompany her to public events and might also be her lover. The word made its way to the English language in the early 1700s. One of its most famous uses came

---

If Earth were the size of a grape, the Moon would be roughly a foot away and the size of a raisin.

in 1819, in a letter from the English poet Lord Byron to a friend. Byron, writing from Ravenna, Italy, tells his friend that he has become a *cicisbeo* to a 19-year-old woman who had recently married a man 40 years her senior. (The origin of the word *cicisbeo* is unknown. Some etymologists believe it may have been onomatopoeic, simply meant to mimic the sound of a whisper.)

GANDER MONTH

Meaning: The month after a woman gives birth

Details: This phrase was used in England and its colonies from the early 17th century until the late 19th century. It described the weeks after childbirth during which a new mother would convalesce, getting her strength back and taking care of her infant. And because the wife was laying low…the husband was free to sleep with other women. Really. How common this practice was is uncertain, but it was apparently common enough to garner this term, which appears in several writings from the era. It was said to be taken from the way a male goose, or *gander*, wanders about when the female is brooding over her eggs.

Bonus: A husband who was active during gander month was known as a "gander-mooner."

ULTRACREPIDARIAN

Meaning: Someone who gives advice or opinions on subjects beyond his or her knowledge

Details: Coined by English essayist William Hazlitt in an 1819 letter to William Gifford, editor of the *Quarterly Review*, in which he told Gifford, "You have been well called an Ultra-Crepidarian critic." (Zinger!) The word's root comes from a story by the ancient Roman scholar Pliny the Elder about a Greek artist named Apelles, who had the habit of hiding near his paintings and listening to people's comments about them. When a cobbler noted that the sole of a shoe had not been painted correctly, Apelles fixed it—after which the puffed up cobbler proceeded to give his opinion about other parts of the painting. Apelles replied, *Ne sutor ultra crepidam*, meaning "Shoemaker, not beyond the sandal."

MORE WEIRD WORDS

• **Nugatory:** Meaningless, of little or no consequence. First recorded in 1603, from the Latin *nugari*, meaning "trifles." Sample use: "Given the scope of the problem, the government's measures were nugatory."

• **Panjandrum:** A pompous or pretentious important person. This 19th-century word was taken directly from the "Great Panjandrum," a figure in an English nonsense poem written by Samuel Foote in 1754. Sample use: "That DMV guy is such a panjandrum."

Stolen! Returned!

"We'll take 'Things that were stolen and later returned' for $200, Alex."
What? Someone stole the $200? Don't worry. If the thief follows
the examples these folks set, they'll bring it back someday.

STOLEN! In 1999 an undetermined amount of money went missing from the cash register at Gibb's sports bar in Beatrice, Nebraska. Owners Pam and Gibb Hedges never figured out where the money went.

RETURNED! Fifteen years later, in July 2014, the Hedges, who had sold the bar two years earlier, got a letter in the mail—with a check for $200 inside. "I worked for you back in 1999 or 2000," the letter said. "Not only was I a flaky employee, I also stole from the drawer when I worked." The sender, identified in news reports only as a woman in her 30s, said the $200 was an estimate of how much she had stolen. She also apologized, adding, "I have my life back on track now, and I regret everything I did." The Hedges called the return of the money "courageous" and said they hoped to meet their former employee someday.

STOLEN! In 1983 someone broke into the Middle Mart convenience store in Hastings, Michigan, and stole $800 from the cash register.

RETURNED! Thirty years later, in 2013, the sheriff's department in Hastings received an anonymous letter confessing to the crime. "I did a very bad thing that I am shamed of," the letter said, adding (as written), "I was a foolishstupid man when I did that and i amsorrie." Inside the envelope was $1,200 in cash: the $400 extra was for interest, the repentant thief said. Sheriff Bob Baker was able to track down the former owner of the store, who'd sold it in 1988—and had long since forgotten about the theft. "He was shocked just as much as everybody else was," Baker said of the former owner's reaction, "because this just does not happen every day."

STOLEN! In January 2014, a pickup truck was stolen from a parking spot near a home in Bridport, England. The truck belonged to 62-year-old Matt Hart, and most distressingly for him, inside the truck was a red terra-cotta urn holding the ashes of his mother, who had recently died at the age of 98. Hart had left the urn in the truck because he was leaving early the next morning to scatter the ashes in the small town in Scotland where his mother had once lived.

RET·URN·ED! News of the theft made headlines all over the U.K.,

---

In Japan, only major streets are named. The rest are numbered...and not always in order.

and Hart started a Facebook campaign to get the ashes returned...and it worked. Two weeks later, one of Hart's neighbors excitedly knocked on his door to tell him the urn had been found on the ground right in the middle of the parking space from which the truck had been stolen. (The identity of the thief is still unknown.)

STOLEN! One night in 1976, someone climbed the flagpole atop the Weston Observatory, a historic observation tower in Manchester, New Hampshire, and stole the specially made bicentennial flag from the pole. The theft caused outrage in the town, which was in the midst of patriotic fervor in the much-ballyhooed bicentennial year.

RETURNED! Nearly 40 years later, the Manchester Historic Association got a package in the mail with the flag inside. "I regretted having done this for many years and apologize for my selfishness," a note in the package said. The note was signed "a flawed son of Manchester." (Interestingly, the package had been mailed from somewhere in Nevada.)

STOLEN! In 1958 two potted hydrangea flower plants were taken from Centennial Park, a large park in Nashville, Tennessee.

RETURNED! In May 2012—54 years later—72-year-old Bill Teitleff showed up at the park with two pots of hydrangeas and confessed to the long-forgotten theft. Teitleff explained that he'd stolen the potted flowers when he was 18 because he didn't have any money and couldn't afford to buy his mother a Mother's Day present. And in a way, he was actually returning the same flowers he stole more than five decades earlier. The two potted hydrangeas he brought with him had been grown from the root stock of the very flowers Teitleff stole in 1958, which his mother had planted in the family's backyard, and still flourished after all those years. Park officials happily accepted the two hydrangeas and forgave Teitleff for the theft.

STOLEN! One night in October 2014, Aaron Wiener noticed that the Tuscan kale he'd planted in the front yard of his home in Washington, D.C., was gone. All that remained of the two-foot-tall vegetable was a small stump and some leaves that had fallen off during the theft.

RETURNED! The kale was never recovered...but the story doesn't end there. About two weeks after the thief absconded with the kale, Wiener came home to discover a piece of cardboard underneath a flowerpot on his porch. It was a $25 gift card to a local hardware store. Along with it was a note that read,

> To: Wonderful gardener
> From: A remorseful kale thief (I was drunk, and I'm very sorry.)

Wiener used the gift card to purchase another kale plant.

As a child, Charles Lindbergh was afraid of heights.

At Your Service

While watching an episode of Downton Abbey, *Uncle John marveled at how many servants required to run an English estate during the Edwardian Age. What's the difference between, say, a lady's maid and a parlor maid, or a footman and a butler? And what does a "footman" actually do? Here are some answers.*

YOU RANG?
A servant's duties typically varied from estate to estate. Larger houses had large staffs; smaller houses had fewer servants, so positions were often combined. Payment for each position also varied, but those listed here—from 1900—are fairly average for the late 19th and early 20th centuries. You will note that the wages seem extremely low, even adjusted for inflation. How could anyone live on such little money? Well, the reason these grand houses could operate in such lavish fashion is that labor was cheap…plus servants' housing, food, and clothing were provided by the master.

BUTLER: In a great house, the butler was the head of the staff, the highest-ranking servant, and always male. He also oversaw the duties and activities of the male staff but reported to the lady of the house. In addition to coordinating the duties and goings-on at the great house, he was in charge of the pantry, the wine cellar, making sure the dining room was properly set up, and the hiring and firing of lower-level staff. Salary: £50 per year ($6,800 in today's money), plus tips he received from the vendors who stocked the house with food and sundries.

HOUSEKEEPER: The highest-ranking female servant. She was responsible for the appearance of the house, maintaining furnishings, and directing the duties of female staff members. (The housekeeper was always addressed as "Mrs." even if she wasn't married.) Salary: £45 per year ($6,100)—£5 less than the butler.

COOK: The cook was in charge of food preparation and menu planning, as well as overseeing the kitchen staff. She (it was almost always a woman) reported to the housekeeper, but food ordering was done with the butler. Salary: £30 per year ($4,000).

LADY'S MAID AND VALET: They were the private, personal servants of the lady and master of the house, respectively. They each assisted their charge with dressing, cared for their clothes, packed for trips, and served as companions. Because the job was fairly intimate,

---

The average office worker walks 46 miles a year scanning, photocopying, printing, and faxing.

the lady and master would hire their lady's maid and valet themselves, rather than have the butler or housekeeper do it. Salary: £20 to £30 per year ($2,700 to $4,000).

FIRST FOOTMAN: While the first footman had specific duties—accompanying the lady of the house on shopping trips, serving meals in the dining room, assisting the butler—his main duty was to be tall. The first footman stood by, tall and proud, during formal dinners to show off the house's dignity and grandeur. In fact, the taller the first footman, the more his potential earnings. Salary: £30 a year or more ($4,000), depending on his height and posture.

SECOND FOOTMAN: An apprentice to the first footman, he opened doors, served meals, and assisted the lady, master, butler, and first footman as needed. Salary: £25 a year ($3,400), although some could earn more if they were the same height as the first footman.

CHAMBERMAIDS: They were the maids who cleaned the private chambers of the family who lived in the great house. Because they cleaned the family's bedrooms and their intimate quarters, they had to be more discreet and were paid a little better. Salary: £20 a year ($2,700).

PARLOR MAIDS: These maids cleaned public gathering spaces, such as sitting rooms, drawing rooms, and parlors. Salary: £15 ($2,100).

NURSES: They tended to the family's babies and young children, similar to what a nanny would do today. They weren't much older than the children—they could be as young as 12 years old. Salary: £10 a year ($1,400).

SCULLERY MAIDS: The youngest and lowest-ranked female servants, they reported to the kitchen assistant. They didn't eat at the servants' dining table because one of their tasks was to stay in the kitchen during staff meals to watch the family meal on the stove or in the oven. They also had to perform lowly kitchen duties, such as washing dishes, scouring flours, plucking fowl, and scaling fish. Salary: £13 a year ($1,800).

HALL BOY: The lowest-ranked male servant. A hall boy may never have even seen a member of the family who lived in the great house. The hall boy was a child or young teenager, a servant to the servants, doing things like emptying servants' chamber pots or cleaning their boots. Salary: £7 per year ($960), although many rose through the ranks to better-paying positions, such as valet or even butler.

A Slice of Heaven

Fascinating facts about the best food on Earth—pizza.

The first pizza in the U.S. was sold in Lombardi's, an Italian restaurant in New York's Little Italy. Cost: 5¢.

• A medium pizza in the U.S. almost always has a diameter of 12 inches. A large pizza in Australia almost always has a diameter of 11 inches.

• The U.S. pizza takeout business is a $38 billion industry.

• About 350 pieces of by-the-slice pizza are consumed by Americans every second. That's 21,000 slices a minute, or 1.26 million slices an hour.

• In 2012 Papa John's ordering website was shut down by a hacking group. Reason: one of the hackers had ordered a pizza from his local Papa John's, and it arrived two hours late.

• Frozen pizzas came on the market in 1957. One of the first brands was "Pizza." (The company was owned by a man named Anthony J. Pizza.)

• On an average day, one in eight Americans will eat pizza. More than 25 percent of boys age 6 to 19 eat pizza every day.

• Most popular pizza topping in the U.S.: pepperoni. It's on a third of all pizzas ordered.

• In the 1980s, Domino's Pizza famously offered a "30 minute guarantee" on delivery orders. They ended the practice in 1993 after losing a $79 million lawsuit from a woman who suffered spinal injuries after being struck by a speeding Domino's driver's car.

• More pizzas are ordered on Saturday than on Mondays, Tuesdays, and Wednesdays combined.

• Leavened bread wasn't developed until about the year 1000. Before that the food called "pizza" was a thin, crispy flatbread topped with olives and vegetables—but no tomato sauce. It was also served topped with raisins, apricots, figs, and honey.

• The word *pizza* comes from the ancient Greek word *pikte*, or pastry. It came to Latin as *picta*, and to Italian as *pizza*. Pita bread has the same etymology.

• The average adult American consumes 744 calories per pizza-eating session and eats 46 slices a year. An estimated 93 percent of adults regularly eat pizza. Some scientists believe that 34 percent of the average American adult's body fat is directly pizza-related.

Tiny roundworms called *nematodes* make up about 90% of all life on the ocean floor.

Dumb Jocks

Playing sports is hard. Talking is harderer.

"I've been consistent in patches this season."
—**Theo Walcott, soccer player**

"They were numerically outnumbered."
—**Garry Birtles, soccer player**

"We may make a lot, but we spend a lot, too."
—**Patrick Ewing, NBA player, defending players' salaries**

"How can I play baseball if I'm stupid? If I was stupid I wouldn't have pitched in the World Series. I'd be playing ball in Mexico or Yugoslavia or on Pluto."
—**Joaquín Andújar, MLB player**

"I'm not talented enough to run and smile at the same time."
—**Emil Zatopek, runner, on why he frowns during races**

"It was six of a half and one dozen of the other."
—**Danny Higginbotham, soccer player**

"I view this situation as one big lie…that I repeated a lot of times."
—**Lance Armstrong, cyclist, coming clean about his doping scandal**

"What I was always good at was letting things go through, like, through one ear and out the other, so to say."
—**Ryan Lochte, swimmer**

"I PRAISE YOU 24/7!!!!!! AND THIS HOW YOU DO ME!!!!! YOU EXPECT ME TO LEARN FROM THIS??? HOW??!! ILL NEVER FORGET THIS!! EVER!!! THX THO…"
—**Steve Johnson, NFL player, who, after dropping a pass, went on Twitter to blame God**

"I was dizzy from the middle of the first set and then I saw Snoopy and I thought, 'Wow Snoopy, that's weird.'"
—**Frank Dancevic, tennis player, after collapsing from the heat**

"People say I'll be drafted in the first round, maybe even higher."
—**Craig Heyward, college football player**

"If you don't believe you can win, there is no point in getting out of bed at the end of the day."
—**Neville Southall, soccer player**

True Colors

Here's something to think about next time you open a box of crayons. We take it for granted that the pigments used to color our clothes, dishes, and art supplies are clean and safe—but as these colors of the past reveal, that's not necessarily so.

Color: Mummy Brown

Made From: Actual mummies

How Did That Become a Thing? Long before there were art stores, the most reliable source of powdered chemicals of all kinds was the apothecary. Europeans had gotten it into their heads that Egyptian mummies were powerful medicine, and from the 1300s to the early 20th century, ground mummies were prescribed for everything from headaches to gout to epilepsy. Adventurous artists discovered that when mixed with oil paint, powdered flesh from mummies made an excellent light brown color. It was used extensively from the 1700s into the mid-1920s.

True Colors: Despite the belief that mummies were indestructible, it turned out that flesh in paint tended to shrink and crack with time. But the thing that really doomed Mummy Brown was the dwindling supply of mummies. By 1964, it was officially as dead as a pharaoh; an article in *Time* magazine quoted a representative of a major art supply house as saying, "We may still have a few limbs lying around somewhere, but not enough to make any more paint."

Color: Chrome Yellow

Made From: Lead chromate

How Did That Become a Thing? In the 1790s, French chemist Nicolas Vauquelin identified a new element in the mineral lead chromate, which had been discovered 35 years earlier in Siberian caves. The new element, dubbed "chromium," was used to make a rich yellow paint that covered other colors in one coat. It was not only bright—it was also cheap to make, leading it to become a favorite of Vincent van Gogh. Unfortunately, van Gogh had a peculiar habit: he liked to nibble on his paints. In fact, he liked Chrome Yellow so much that he once emptied a tube of it into his mouth. Many of the symptoms of insanity the artist exhibited, including the halos around lights that appeared in his paintings, can be caused or exacerbated by heavy metal poisoning.

True Colors: Unfortunately, Chrome Yellow was not only toxic but also unstable. When exposed to sunlight, it tended to fade and turn brown or green; exposure to sulfur (an ingredient in some paints) hastened that process. In fact, many of van Gogh's paintings have been affected. Although artists can still buy leaded paints, Chrome Yellow has been largely supplanted by the safer, more permanent Cadmium Yellow.

Color: Royal Purple

Made From: Sea snails

How Did That Become a Thing? When Cleopatra became fond of a very expensive purple dye, she started a long tradition. The color was expensive because making it was difficult and unpleasant. You started by crushing the mucus out of 250,000 sea snails (known as the spiny dye murex) and soaking it for weeks in stale urine. Worse, a quarter million snails could make only half an ounce of dye—enough to color a single toga, a piece of tapestry, or a ceremonial flag or two. The stench was so bad that dyers were required to do their work far outside the city walls. The nauseating smell clung to them even after washing; in fact, the Talmud granted an automatic divorce to women whose husbands became dyers. Yet all that trouble and expense—and even the smell—only made it more attractive to those who wanted to show off their money and power.

True Colors: You'd think that overharvesting of that sea snail would kill the dye. It didn't. Neither did the horrible stench that clung to the fabric. The hue remained a status symbol worn by the royal and the wealthy for many centuries. And it might still be stinking up the place if an 18-year-old chemist named William Perkin hadn't accidentally invented the first synthetic dye in 1856. The color of Perkin's dye was a rich purple he called "mauve." It was also inexpensive, which made it accessible to almost anybody…and that's what killed Royal Purple.

Color: Emerald Green/Paris Green

Active Ingredient: Arsenic

How Did That Become a Thing? Until 1775, green paint was commonly made from copper carbonate—the rust you see on copper building trim and the Statue of Liberty. That year Carl Scheele, the brilliant Swedish chemist who discovered chlorine, invented a beautifully bright green pigment from an arsenic compound. He called it Scheele's Green, and it quickly replaced the older paints. Unfortunately, nobody was yet aware of how poisonous arsenic was, and Scheele—who had a habit of sniffing and tasting his discoveries—succumbed to heavy metal poisoning from exposure to arsenic, mercury, lead, and other chemicals, and he died in 1786. In 1814 a slightly improved version of his recipe became commercially available as Paris Green or Emerald Green. These arsenic-based pigments became popular among artists and manufacturers of cloths, candles, wallpaper, printing ink, and even candies. Of course, in the 1800s, sudden unexplained deaths weren't unusual, so the Paris Green deaths weren't immediately recognized. Especially dangerous was its use in wall paint and wallpaper: when moisture degraded the pigment, it released deadly arsine gas. (Napoleon, who died in a bright green room with mildew on the walls, was found to have an unusually high amount of arsenic in his hair and bones.)

True Colors: In the 1890s, Italian authorities became aware of a disturbing trend: more than 1,000 apparently healthy children had died mysteriously in recent years. A chemist investigated their homes and discovered that virtually all of them played in rooms with mildew and Emerald Green wallpaper. Arsine gas, heavier than air, tended to stay close to the floor, where kids sat and played. Countrywide removal of the green wallpaper prevented further deaths.

Color: Uranium Yellow

Active Ingredient: Uranium oxide ore

How Did That Become a Thing? Unlike equally dangerous radium, which was used in paint on clocks and airplane dials because it glowed, uranium ore's appeal was its bright yellow-orange color. Used in art-works as far back as ancient Roman times, uranium-based pigment is so bright that it almost seems lit from within. Added to glass water pitchers or kids' marbles, uranium glows with a ghostly translucent yellow or green, and in pottery glazes, a festive yellow or orange. One popular example: Between 1938 and 1943, and then again from 1959 to 1972, the manufacturer of a popular line of ceramic dinnerware called Fiesta used a glaze that contained trace amounts of uranium oxide pigments in its "Fiesta Red" orange-red plates and bowls.

True Colors: Slowing sales—not fear of radiation—caused the manufacturer to discontinue the entire Fiesta line by 1973, including Fiesta Red. When the line was reintroduced in 1986, new glazes were used that did not contain uranium oxide. But because uranium oxide has a half-life of 4.5 billion years, if you hold a Geiger counter up to a vintage Fiesta Red plate or bowl, the radiation can still be detected. Because of this, the Environmental Protection Agency cautions collectors of vintage orange-red Fiesta ware against using them to serve food or drink, and to dispose of any cracked or broken pieces.

*　　*　　*

POP CULTURE QUIZ

Q: What is the "Corellian Engineering Corporation YT series YT-1300 Transport" better known as?

A: The *Millennium Falcon*, Han Solo's ship from *Star Wars*.

Genetically, men and women differ about as much as men and chimps: 1 to 2%.

Who Put the Blue in Bluetooth?

We've told you the stories behind the names of several tech businesses before—Apple, Yahoo!, Amazon, and the like. Here are a few more—for your high-tech bathroom-reading pleasure.

S KYPE. Skype, the online video-phone service, was developed using specialized network technology known as *P2P*, or "peer-to-peer," technology. That meant that the communication work was handled by Skype users' computers (using Skype software) rather than having a middleman—such as a big phone or Internet company—do the work. (Since Microsoft bought Skype in 2010, things have changed—but that's how Skype originally worked.) The name first proposed for the service: "Sky Peer-to-Peer," "sky" being a metaphor for communication signals that travel through the air. "Sky Peer-to-Peer" was shortened to "Skyper," but Internet domain names associated with that name—such as *skyper.com*—were already taken, so it was shortened again, to "Skype."

TiVo. TiVo's digital television recording technology was developed by Silicon Valley tech veterans Mike Ramsay and Jim Barton in 1997, and they hired the San Francisco husband-and-wife design team Michael Cronan and Karin Hibma to come up with a name for it. More than 1,600 names were considered, including "Bongo" (because the up and down buttons on a TV remote could be said to resemble bongo drums) and "Lasso" (because you could "lasso" or capture shows you wanted to watch whenever you wanted to watch them). In the end, however, "TiVo" won out, partly because it had "TV" in it and partly because Cronan liked the way the "i" and "o" in the name related to the I/O acronym for the "input/output" jacks on a TV.

YELP. Two former PayPal employees, Jeremy Stoppelman and Russel Simmons, left the Internet payment processor in 2004 to start a network that would allow people to refer each other to local businesses via email—an idea that came about when Stoppelman caught the flu and needed a recommendation for a doctor. As the site was developed, the founders, along with investor David Galbraith, decided that their project should be a website where people could recommend or *not* recommend businesses by rating them and leaving reviews. It was Galbraith who came up with the site's name: Yelp. Because it had so many business listings, Galbraith conceived of their site as an Internet version of the Yellow Pages. He formed the word Yelp by combining "yel" from "yellow" and "p" from "pages."

BING. Microsoft wanted a catchy one-syllable name for its Google-like web search engine and came up with "Bang"…but then went with "Bing" instead. Why? According to Microsoft advertising guru David Webster: "'I banged it' is very different than 'I binged it.'" Besides, says Webster, "Bing" was reminiscent of "bingo"—and represented the "sound of found." (Microsoft engineers reportedly joke that the name is an acronym for "Bing Is Not Google." Critics like to make that joke, too.)

ETSY. Etsy is an e-commerce website (similar to Amazon) founded in 2005 that specializes in vintage and handmade items. For years, nobody knew where the name came from—because founder Robert Kalin refused to tell anyone. Kalin finally revealed in a 2010 interview with *Reader's Digest* that the name was basically gibberish. "I wanted a nonsense word because I wanted to build the brand from scratch," Kalin said. "I was watching [filmmaker Federico] Fellini's 8½ and writing down what I was hearing. In Italian, you say 'etsi' a lot. It means 'oh, yes.'" And so "Etsy" it was.

BLUETOOTH. In 1996 Intel engineer Jim Kardach was one of a group of people from several companies—including Swedish telecommunications giant Ericsson, and its Finnish counterpart, Nokia—trying to develop a way to use short-range radio waves to link computers to cell phones without any cables. At the same time, Kardach happened to be reading about King Harald Bluetooth, the 10th-century Danish king best known for uniting the various warring factions of Denmark. Kardach got the idea that this was similar to the work he and the other computer engineers were doing: trying to "unite" different devices—as well as the competing companies that produced them—by creating a wireless technology that worked across the industry. So he called the technology "Bluetooth" after King Harald. (That weird Bluetooth logo is actually the runic symbol for Harald's initials, HB.) Interestingly, Bluetooth was only meant to be a code name for the project while it was still in development. When it came time to trademark the technology in 1997, they didn't have anything better…and the rest is wireless (and funny-looking earpiece) history.

*　　*　　*

"If you can't make it good, at least make it look good." **—Bill Gates**

The Hit Parade

A few years ago, a radio disc jockey told Uncle John that he had to meet a fellow record fanatic called "Mighty John" Marshall. It was a match made in heaven. Here, courtesy of the two Johns, are some music trivia tidbits. (Shameless plug: check out Mighty John's website—Moneymusic.com.)

• **VICE VICE BABY.** "It's All in the Game" has been recorded by dozens of performers, including Van Morrison, Elton John, George Benson, Ricky Nelson, and Merle Haggard, to name a few. But the best-known version was by Tommy Edwards, hitting #1 on the Billboard Hot 100 chart in 1958. And part of the credit goes to Charles Dawes, vice president of the United States under Calvin Coolidge. In 1911, years before he became vice-president, Dawes wrote a composition called "Melody in A Major." In 1951 Dawes's melody was given words and a rock 'n' roll beat. It comes in at #38 on Billboard's All-Time Top 100.

• **AMERICAN BANNED-STAND.** There were two records that Dick Clark refused to play on American Bandstand. In 1959 Lloyd Price hit #1 with "Stagger Lee," but because the lyrics dealt with violence and murder, Clark refused to air it until a toned-down version was issued. In 1960 Chubby Checker (given his stage name by Clark's wife, Barbara, who thought he looked like Fats Domino) had a monster hit with "The Twist." But Checker's record was a cover of the original version, written and recorded by Hank Ballard, which was too raunchy and suggestive for Clark's taste, so he played Checker's "cleaned-up" version on Bandstand—and that's the version that lives in rock 'n' roll history.

• **STRIPES AND STARS.** "The Twist" was the most popular dance craze of the early 1960s. In New York City the place to twist was the Peppermint Lounge, where you could see celebrities from Jackie Kennedy to John Wayne. The house band at the Peppermint Lounge: Joey Dee and the Starliters. Members at one time or other included Felix Cavaliere, who would find fame as the lead singer of the Young Rascals; Jimmy James, who would later change his name to Jimi Hendrix; and a young guitar player named Joe Pesci, who became an actor, starring in such movies as My Cousin Vinny, Home Alone, and Goodfellas.

• **GIRLS! GIRLS! GIRLS!** In 1964 Elvis Presley starred in the movie Kissin' Cousins. It was a typical Elvis formula movie—lots of songs, lots of pretty girls. (The only unique aspect of this film was that Elvis played two roles: Cousin Josh and Cousin Jodie.) Among the

One bushel of corn can sweeten more than 400 cans of soda.

pretty girls were Yvonne Craig, who would later star as TV's Batgirl; a young Teri Garr, who would later be nominated for Best Supporting Actress for *Tootsie*; and Maureen Reagan, whose father would later be elected president of the United States.

• **CRASH COURSE.** On February 2, 1959, three of the headliners of the "Winter Dance Party" tour, Buddy Holly, Ritchie Valens, and the Big Bopper, took a plane from Clear Lake, Iowa, to Fargo, North Dakota. What's often forgotten about the tour is the fourth headliner— Dion and the Belmonts. Dion didn't have the $36 to take the plane ride with the others, who died in the most famous rock 'n' roll tragedy in history. Dion would go on to have one of the most successful solo careers in rock 'n' roll. It all began in 1961 when he warned listeners to "keep away from Runaround Sue." Dion married his high school girlfriend, Susan Butterfield, in 1963. (They're still married.) She's been telling people that she's the real Sue for more than 40 years…although Dion claims the song's real inspiration was a girl named Roberta.

• **YOU DON'T KNOW BO.** He was born Ellas Bates, wrote songs under the name Ellas McDaniels, and recorded as Bo Diddley. His influence on rock 'n' roll stars seems endless, including the Who and Eric Clapton. Diddley performed his first hit, "Bo Diddley," on the *Ed Sullivan Show* in 1955. Sullivan wasn't impressed, but the young viewers were: the song became a hit. And that makes Bo Diddley the only recording artist to sell a million copies of a record on which the title and the performer's name are the same.

• **HOUND DOG.** Elvis Presley's biggest hit (and the song he said was his personal favorite) was "Don't Be Cruel." The song was first offered to another recording artist signed to RCA at the time, but the songwriter, Otis Blackwell, wanted it to go to Elvis. He knew that he'd make more money if Elvis recorded it instead of an unknown. And that other young singer was gracious and consented to having "Don't Be Cruel" given to Elvis. But don't feel bad. The "unknown" singer became almost as famous. His name: Frankie Valli.

• **WHODUNNIT?** In the mid-1960s, Bobby Fuller was on the verge of becoming a star when he mysteriously died. He was found outside his apartment in Hollywood in a car he'd just purchased. Some reports say he committed suicide. But then why would he buy a new car the day before? There were some bruises on his body, but he had no broken bones. The closest cause of death the coroner could determine was inhalation of gasoline. There were also rumors of mob ties and a police cover-up. If that's true, his big hit is one of the biggest ironies in rock history. That song: "I Fought the Law (And the Law Won)."

In Spanish, *armadillo* translates to "little armored one."

Nailed It

These real nail polish names are funny. (But we still can't tell what colors they are.)

Trophy Wife	Lemon Shark	No Prenup
Sand in My Suit	East Hampton Cottage	Raisinnuts
Ballet Slippers	Going Incognito	Fishnet Stockings
Whack	Brown Bag	Stockholm Syndrome
Two-Hour Lunch	Prune Danish	Tomorrow
Vodka & Caviar	I Only Eat Salads	Bitter Buddhist
Freaky Like Freud	Snappy Socialite	Vegas Post Apocalyptic
Let's Talk	What's My Name?	Cut the Mullet
Lose Your Lingerie	Mr. Sandman	Feathers and Flesh
Loophole	Rent	Psycho Candy
Uh, as If!	Cougar Attack	Eternal Optimist
Russian to a Party	Friar, Friar, Pants on Fire	Lonesome Dove
Need a Vacation	Using My Maiden Name	Did You Ear about van Gogh?
Fondola Gondola	Tenderoni	Butler Please
I'm with the Lifeguard	Fauntleroy	Shattered Souls
Plastic Beach	Russian Navy	Conga Line
Suzi Sells Sushi by the Seashore	Pillow Pie	Dirty Baby
Chubby Cheeks	Bond with Whomever	Detox!
Are Mermaids Real?	Ants in My Pants	Another Polish Joke!

The Czech Republic's Ceský Krumlov castle is protected by a moat filled with bears.

Animals Under the Influence

It turns out that humans aren't the only animal species that can develop a taste for alcohol.

WASTED WASPS

In September 2013, the British Red Cross issued a warning that the previous year's long, cold winter and late spring led to record numbers of "jobless" worker wasps around the British Isles. For much of the year, the wasps are hard at work bringing nectar to the queen of the hive. But by the fall, the queen has stopped laying eggs and no longer needs nectar. What do the worker wasps do once their work is done? According to Red Cross spokesperson Joe Mulligan, "All they are doing now is feasting on fermenting fruit and getting 'drunk,'" which makes them more aggressive than they are the rest of the year.

INEBRIATED ELEPHANTS

Visitors to African safari parks have long been told that the elephants there can get drunk on the rotten fermenting fruit of the marula tree. But a 2006 study published in the journal *Physical and Biochemical Zoology* laid that myth to rest. The amount of alcohol in each piece of fruit is so minuscule that it's impossible for the elephants to eat enough of them at one "sitting" (it would take 1,400 or more) to become intoxicated.

Fruit is one thing, but *beer* is another—villagers in northeast India learned this the hard way while brewing the potent rice beer they use in religious festivals each fall. The beer is typically stored in plastic or earthenware barrels in and around the villagers' huts, and wild elephants in the surrounding forests have developed a taste for it. Drunk-and-disorderly behavior is not uncommon. One example: in 2010 a herd of elephants got liquored up on the stuff and went on a four-day rampage, destroying more than 50 homes and trampling three people to death as they staggered through one village after another in search of more beer. **Sobering Thought:** In 2007, and again in 2010, groups of drunken elephants died after they uprooted utility poles and were electrocuted. Indian officials warn that as civilization continues to encroach on elephant habitats, the problem will only get worse. "It's great to have such a huge number of elephants," Pradyut Bordoloi, former environment minister for Assam state, told the Associated Press, "but the increasing man–elephant conflict…is giving us nightmares."

MESSED-UP MOOSE

In September 2008, a 68-year-old Swedish woman named Agneta Westlund went walking with her dog in the woods near the village of Loftahammer. When she didn't return home, her husband went out looking for her and found her dead body. That was *his* story, but when the police found evidence of a struggle on the body, they arrested him on suspicion of murder. The husband, Ingemar Westlund, spent 10 days in jail before the case against him was dropped. Forensic analysis of Agneta Westlund's body found moose hair and saliva on her clothes. Moose normally avoid contact with humans, but police suspect that the animal in question, who remains at large, may have become more aggressive after getting drunk on fermenting apples in the area.

SLOSHED SHREWS

When the sugary nectar of the bertam palm's flowers comes in contact with wild yeast, the yeast converts the sugar to alcohol, carbon dioxide, and other compounds. Result: a natural nectar "beer" that contains 3.8 percent alcohol by volume and even has a head of foam, just like a glass of beer. (Bud Light, by comparison, contains 4.2 percent alcohol.)

Nectar beer is the pen-tailed tree shrew's primary source of food. It spends two hours a night—*every* night—"bar hopping" from one flower to the next and downing all the nectar it can find. In the process it helps fertilize the bertam palms by carrying their pollen from one plant to the next. The shrew may be the only pollinator in nature that is rewarded for its efforts with beer.

Sobering Thought: Pound for pound, the rat-sized animals drink the equivalent of nine to twelve beers every night, enough to put the average human in the hospital. But the shrews never show signs of drunkenness, nor do they appear hung over the morning after. Biologist Frank Wiens, who studies pen-tailed shrews, speculates that they developed their superior ability to metabolize alcohol as a matter of survival. "Inebriation would increase the risk for these small animals to be killed by a predator," he says.

BLOTTO BATS

Bats in the Central American nation of Belize gorge on rotten fruit and, like the pen-tailed tree shrews, are remarkably adept at "holding their liquor." We know this thanks to Canadian zoologist Brock Fenton. In 2009 Fenton and his colleagues captured more than 106 bats from six different species in northern Belize. A control group was fed sugar water;

the rest were fed a solution of 1.5 percent alcohol in sugar water. Then the researchers had the bats fly an obstacle course and also studied their echolocation calls, checking for signs of "slurred speech."

The drunkest bats had blood alcohol levels of 0.3 percent—nearly four times the legal limit for motor vehicle drivers in the United States—but they navigated the obstacle course as easily as the teetotalers, and their echolocation calls were indistinguishable from the sober bats. Whether the findings apply to bat species in the rest of the Americas remains to be seen. "We'd like to find a company that sells alcoholic refreshments who will sponsor an expanded study," Fenton says.

BOOZY BEARS

In August 2004, a black bear wandered into a campsite at Baker Lake Resort in northwestern Washington in search of food and (it turns out) something to wash it down with. By the time Department of Fish and Wildlife agents found the bear passed out drunk on the lawn of the resort, it had downed a case and a half of Rainier Beer. The bear also found a few six-packs of Busch beer at another campsite, but it drank just one can of the stuff before moving on. "He didn't like Busch and consumed, as near as we can tell, about 36 cans of Rainier," Sergeant Bill Heinick told USA *Today.* "This is a new one on me. I've known them to get into cans, but nothing like this. And it definitely had a preference." (When the bear regained consciousness, Heinick and the other agents removed it from the resort by catching it in a humane trap they baited with doughnuts, honey…and two cans of Rainier.)

HONORABLE MENTION: SWINO THE PIG

In September 2013, a group of campers at a rest stop near the De Grey River in Australia failed to secure their beer before turning in. Later that night they were awakened by "scrunching" sounds that turned out to be a feral pig (later nicknamed "Swino") chomping on their beer cans. The campers had left three six-packs out where Swino could get at them, and the scrunching didn't stop until he'd downed them all. Not long after Swino finished his 18th beer, he picked—and lost—a fight with a nearby cow. "There were some other people camped right on the river and they saw him running around their vehicle being chased by the cow," one of the campers told a reporter. "It was going around and around and then it went into the river and swam across." Swino was later found passed out drunk beneath a large log on the other side of the river. Swino made headlines again a month later, when he was hit by a truck and killed while trying to cross a road. (No word on whether alcohol was involved in that incident.)

Let's roll! In Operation Desert Storm, some U.S. tanks were camouflaged with toilet paper.

Follow the Leader

Some thoughts on what it takes to be a good boss.

"Leadership is a potent combination of strategy and character. But if you must be without one, be without the strategy."
—**Norman Schwarzkopf**

"To do great things is difficult; but to command great things is more difficult."
—**Friedrich Nietzsche**

"A boss creates fear, a leader confidence. A boss fixes blame, a leader corrects mistakes. A boss knows all, a leader asks questions. A boss makes work drudgery, a leader makes it interesting."
—**Russell H. Ewing**

"Leadership at one time meant muscle; but today it means getting along with people."
—**Mohandas Gandhi**

"Set exorbitant standards, and give your people hell when they don't live up to them. There is nothing so demoralizing as a boss who tolerates second-rate work."
—**David Ogilvy**

"It's hard to lead a cavalry charge if you think you look funny on a horse."
—**Adlai E. Stevenson II**

"The worst mistake a boss can make is not to say 'well done.'"
—**John Ashcroft**

"The leadership instinct you are born with is the backbone. You develop the funny bone and the wishbone that go with it."
—**Elaine Agather**

"You don't have to hold a position in order to be a leader."
—**Henry Ford**

"The leader has to be practical and a realist, yet must talk the language of the visionary and the idealist."
—**Eric Hoffer**

"A good leader is a person who takes a little more than his share of the blame and a little less than his share of the credit."
—**John C. Maxwell**

"You do not lead by hitting people over the head. That's assault, not leadership."
—**Dwight D. Eisenhower**

"A leader is best when people barely know he exists, when his work is done, his aim fulfilled, they will say: We did it ourselves."
—**Lao Tzu**

Most ducks have a 360-degree field of vision.

You Swallowed What?

One of the first things your mother told you was, "Don't put that in your mouth." Why? Because you might end up like these people.

IT ONLY HURTS WHEN I LAUGH

In 2012 a 30-year-old woman in Atlanta, Georgia, was demonstrating to friends that she had no gag reflex. How? By sticking a butter knife into her mouth and down her throat, kind of like a sword swallower. When she unexpectedly let out a small laugh, the knife slipped from her fingers…and she swallowed it. The woman was rushed to Emory University School of Medicine, where an X-ray revealed that the knife had gone all the way down the woman's esophagus and partway into her stomach. Fortunately, doctors were able to remove the knife using an endoscopy tube fitted with forceps. Remarkably, the woman wasn't injured by her knife-swallowing trick.

FORK IT OVER

Lee Gardner, 40, of South Yorkshire, England, was taken to the hospital in 2012 after he started vomiting. He was especially concerned because there was some blood in the vomit. A doctor performed an endoscopy with a camera-equipped endoscope and, during the procedure, asked Gardner if he'd swallowed anything unusual. Gardner said no. The doctor replied, "I can see the prongs of what appears to be a fork." That's when Gardner remembered that he *had*, in fact, swallowed something unusual—a plastic fork. But it had happened ten years earlier. Gardner said he went to the hospital at the time, but was told the fork would pass through his system safely—and because he had experienced no problems afterward, he'd simply forgotten about it. But after sitting in his stomach for ten years, the doctors told him, the fork's prongs had perforated his stomach lining, causing an ulcer, which had subsequently burst. Surgeons performed a 45-minute operation to remove the fork from Gardner's stomach. He made a full recovery.

WHAT'S FOR DINNER?

In 2013 an eight-year-old boy was taken to an emergency room in Darwin, Australia, with complaints of a stomachache. An X-ray, however, revealed there was something else going on: the boy's appendix was extremely enlarged and appeared to have several small metal objects lodged in it. Doctors performed an emergency appendectomy, and were shocked to discover 57 small metal pellets in the boy's appendix. It

---

National Doughnut Day, the first Friday in June, was created by the Salvation Army in 1938.

turned out that the boy's father regularly hunted geese with a shotgun, and the birds were cooked and eaten as a regular part of the family's diet. But they never bothered to remove the shotgun pellets from the meat. The boy and his sister, the father said, regularly played a game of eating the pellets in the goose meat "to make them disappear." Most of them were passed naturally via the bowel, but for some reason, over many months or possibly years, some of them accumulated inside the boy's appendix. Thankfully, he recovered just fine (and we're guessing dad now removes the pellets from the goose before dinner).

YOU LOSE

In March 2014, Radu Calincescu of Bacau, Romania, went to the local emergency room complaining of a severe pain in his chest. Doctors did an X-ray...and discovered a fork in Calincescu's esophagus. Asked how it got there, the 25-year-old admitted that he'd bet his friends he could swallow a fork without being hurt. (He lost.) He added that he'd been drinking at the time.

THE PEN-ULTIMATE SWALLOWING

In October 2011, the *British Medical Journal* reported the case of a 76-year-old woman who was taken to an emergency room in Exeter, England, after experiencing intestinal discomfort and rapid weight loss. Doctors performed a CT scan, and were surprised to see a rod-shaped object in the woman's stomach. They asked if she had swallowed something odd, and she at first said no. Then she remembered that she *had* once swallowed something odd: a felt-tipped pen. (She was using the pen to probe one of her tonsils, she said, when she accidentally swallowed it.) When had that happened? *Twenty-five years earlier.* Her doctor at the time didn't believe her story about swallowing the pen, especially after it failed to show up on an X-ray. The woman said she forgot all about it, because the pen hadn't given her any problems until then. Using an endoscope, doctors were able to remove the pen through the woman's mouth, and she felt better after just a couple of days.

Bonus Fact: The doctor who didn't believe the woman's story about swallowing the pen was the woman's husband. The BMJ report made a note of the doctor/husband's dismissal of his wife's story, saying that "occasionally it may be worth believing the patient's account, however unlikely it may be."

Bonus Fact II: After 25 years in the woman's stomach, the pen was in remarkably good shape. How good? It still worked.

Lights, Camera, Ouch!

The stories of some actors who really suffered for their art.

LEONARDO DiCAPRIO. During the filming of a scene in *Django Unchained* (2012) where slave owner Candie (DiCaprio) reveals that he knows Django (Jamie Foxx) is trying to free Django's wife, DiCaprio slammed his hand so hard on a table that he accidentally smashed a crystal glass. But DiCaprio didn't stop his fiery monologue even as his hand started to visibly bleed. The scene made it into the film.

VIGGO MORTENSEN. In a scene from *The Lord of the Rings: The Two Towers*, Aragorn (Mortensen), Legolas, and Gimli arrive at a flaming pyre in search of lost hobbits Merry and Pippin. When Gimli finds a burned belt belonging to one of the hobbits, Aragorn becomes so enraged that he kicks a helmet and drops to his knees, howling in emotional pain. Even though Mortensen is a fine actor, there was very little acting in that scene—he actually broke two of his toes with that kick.

BRAD PITT. In the 2004 film *Troy*, Brad Pitt played Achilles, the legendary warrior of ancient Greece. While filming a battle scene, Pitt landed awkwardly and hurt himself. In possibly the most ironic injury in film history, Pitt, while playing Achilles, injured his Achilles tendon. (The take used in *Troy* is the one where Pitt got hurt, and you can really see the pain on his face.)

MALCOLM McDOWELL. In one of the most famous scenes in *A Clockwork Orange*, Alex (McDowell) is brainwashed by having his eyes clamped open to force him to watch violent images until he's ill. A doctor periodically steps into the scene to place eyedrops in McDowell's eyes. Turns out that one of the clamps scratched McDowell's corneas, and the "doctor" was a real doctor, who made sure the temporary blindness McDowell suffered didn't become permanent.

ELLEN BURSTYN. In a scene in *The Exorcist*, the demon possessing young Regan (Linda Blair) forces the girl to pick up and throw her own mother—portrayed by Burstyn—across a room. As the crew strapped Burstyn into a flying harness for the scene, they accidentally dropped her. She landed on her tailbone and suffered permanent damage to her spine.

The seagulls in the film *The Birds* were fed whiskey-soaked wheat to keep them from flying too much.

Quotes About Goats

These proverbs date back to a time when the world was more agrarian, but we think they still make a lot of sense...even if they are all about goats.

"The more the billy goat stinks, the more the nanny goat loves him."
Belgium

"If you put a silk dress on a goat, he's still a goat."
Ireland

"It's out of ignorance that a goat will attend a leopard's party."
Africa

"The goat must browse where she is tied."
Romania

"When you give a friend a goat, you have to let go of the leash."
Kenya

"It don't take a genius to spot a goat in a flock of sheep."
Old West

"He who lets the goat be placed on his shoulders will soon have to carry the cow."
Italy

"Where there are no sheep they call the goat princess."
Turkey

"A man accused of stealing a goat should not entertain his visitors with goat meat."
West Africa

"Look for a black goat while it is still daytime."
Nigeria

"You are correct, but the goat is mine."
Corsica

"The goat that has many owners will be left to die in the sun."
Haiti

"Don't approach a goat from the front, a horse from the back, or a fool from any side."
Russia

"Even an old goat likes to lick salt."
Hungary

"By candlelight a goat looks like a lady."
France

"If wisdom were measured by the size of the beard, the goat would be a philosopher."
Denmark

"A man and a goat may be friends, but don't expect the goat to pay the first visit."
West Africa

"If you're short of trouble, take a goat."
Finland

The ancient Egyptians used fly swatters made from giraffe tails.

New Money

Short on cash? Try making your own! Here are some modern currency systems that could provide an alternative to the regular old dollar.

CRYPTOCURRENCY. This digital currency was first developed for secure Internet transactions in 2009. It doesn't exist in a physical form and isn't issued by a government or backed by a central bank or a gold standard. This means it can be used across nations or continents. To fight devaluation, only certain amounts of currency are issued, and their use is tracked by a public ledger. Some examples of e-money: Mastercoin, Doge, Ripple, and, the first and best known, Bitcoin. In early 2014, Bitcoin peaked at a value of $1,200 for 1 bitcoin (current value: less than 20 percent of that…and falling). According to experts, it's mostly used to purchase black-market goods anonymously.

CORPORATE COIN. Like some other conservative politicians, U.S. senator Rand Paul (R-KY) opposes government regulation of currency. In 2015 he suggested major corporations issue their own currency, backed by company stock. This would allow them to eliminate credit card companies and fees, be more profitable, and stimulate the economy. He theorized that in this system, "Wal-Coin," for example, could be used as store credit or exchanged for Walmart stock.

BERKSHARES. The Berkshires is a hilly region of Massachusetts and Connecticut with its own money. Launched in 2006 to help the local economy, more than 350 businesses accept BerkShares, which are dispensed at local banks. One BerkShare equals $1, although to stimulate its use, the cost was lowered to 95¢. BerkShares come in various denominations and feature portraits of Berkshires-born notables, such as W. E. B. Du Bois (on the 5-note) and Norman Rockwell (on the 50).

CANADIAN TIRE MONEY. Once an auto parts store, Canadian Tire is now a 490-store chain and Canada's biggest retailer. In the 1950s, the company introduced a loyalty program, giving customers "Canadian Tire money" (or CTM) coupons in 5-cent, 10-cent, 25-cent, 50-cent, and $1 denominations to exchange for merchandise. Since then, more than $1 billion in CTM has been issued. (And it's printed at the Royal Canadian Mint—the same place real Canadian currency is printed.) Today more than 700 other Canadian businesses accept Canadian Tire money. Reason: the owners and employees of those stores will just end up using it at Canadian Tire anyway.

According to a Government Study

The federal government spends billions of dollars on research each year, and we have the moon landings, the Internet, fuel-efficient cars, and other benefits to show for it. But not every federally funded study passes the sniff test, as these examples demonstrate.

S **tudy:** "Water Pipe Tobacco Smoking Among University Students in Jordan"

Purpose: "Assess the prevalence of water pipe tobacco smoking among university students in Jordan"

Methodology: "A trained interviewer administered a questionnaire among 548 randomly selected students at four prominent universities in Jordan."

Findings: 1) "Water pipe smoking is highly prevalent in Jordan. 61.1% of respondents reported using a water pipe at least once in their lives and 42.7% reported using at least monthly."

2) "Water pipe tobacco smoking...remains relatively constant across most sociodemographic variables, including age, nationality, university level, marital status, and housing status."

3) "Those who believe water pipe tobacco smoking to be less harmful and/or addictive are generally more likely to use a water pipe to smoke tobacco."

Cost to American taxpayers: $170,000

Study: "The Urine Nutrient Reclamation Project"

Purpose: Test the effectiveness of human urine as fertilizer for agricultural crops, in what its sponsor, the Rich Earth Institute (REI) of Brattleboro, Vermont, says is "the first legally authorized and publicly documented community-scale urine reuse project in the United States."

Methodology: "Since 2012 we have been collecting urine from over 170 volunteer participants in and around Brattleboro, Vermont. After sanitizing the urine, we apply it to farmland that is producing hay. Throughout the process we collect detailed data on the effect of urine fertilizer on the quantity and quality of the hay harvest and on the properties of the soil."

Findings: 1) "Urine-treated fields were twice as productive as unfertilized fields."

2) Urine-treated fields have an unpleasant smell, "but only for about an hour after application." "Any ammonia-based fertilizer smells," say the researchers.

3) "The 'ick' factor of collecting urine is a potential barrier for people to adopt new urine diverting technologies."

Cost to American taxpayers: $15,000

Study: "The Electoral Implications of Candidate Ambiguity"

Purpose: To answer the question "Why do candidates employ ambiguity, and what are the consequences?"

Methodology: An Internet polling firm asked a representative sample of U.S. voters to choose between two candidates—one who gave vague answers to policy questions and one who gave precise answers.

Findings: 1) "Candidates regularly employ ambiguity in primaries and general elections."

2) "Ambiguity can help candidates gain support from members of their own party without costing them votes from members of the opposition."

3) "Candidates may portray their own ambiguity as a virtue—as proof of their commitment to bipartisanship, flexibility, and thoughtfulness."

Cost to American taxpayers: $216,884

Study: "Patterns of Brain Activation When Mothers View Their Own Child and Dog"

Purpose: To "investigate differences in how important brain structures are activated when women view images of their children and their own dogs."

Methodology: "We examined functional magnetic resonance imaging (fMRI) brain activation patterns as mothers viewed images of their own child and dog, and an unfamiliar child and dog."

Findings: "Although there are similarities in the perceived emotional experience and brain function associated with the mother-child and mother-dog bond, there are also key differences that my reflect variance in the evolutionary course and function of these relationships."

Cost to American taxpayers: $371,026

*　　*　　*

COACHES SAY THE DARNDEST THINGS

Q: "What do you think of your team's execution?"

A: "I'm in favor of it."

—John McKay, NFL coach, after his team finished the season winless

The Mad Potter of Biloxi

If you have any droopy, squashed, or otherwise odd-looking ceramic pots lying around the house, they may be worth a lot more than you realize. George Ohr made thousands of them in his lifetime; today they're worth a fortune. Many are still out there, waiting to be discovered.

THE DRIFTER

George E. Ohr was born in Biloxi, Mississippi, in 1857. As was the custom in those days, as soon as this son of a blacksmith was old enough, he went to work as an apprentice in his father's trade. But blacksmithing wasn't for him. Neither was tinkering, working on the docks, seafaring, or any of the 16 other jobs he tried from age 14 to 22. It wasn't until a friend, Joseph Meyer, talked him into accepting a $10-a-week apprenticeship in his family's pottery studio that Ohr finally found something he wanted to do. "When I found the potter's wheel I felt it all over, like a wild duck in water," he said.

Ohr stuck with the apprenticeship for two years—a record for him. When he felt he'd learned everything he could from the Meyers, he hopped a boxcar and spent another two years traveling through 16 eastern states, visiting local pottery studios, museums, county fairs, and anyplace else he could meet potters and study their work. He returned to New Orleans in 1882 and the following year built his own studio in Biloxi.

MOONLIGHTING

Ohr supported himself and, after he married in 1886, his growing family of 10 children—Ella, Asa, Leo, Clo, Lio, Oto, Flo, Zio, Ojo and Geo, only five of whom lived to adulthood—by selling bowls, pitchers, mugs, jugs, and other wares door to door from a handcart. (If the man of the house was around, he also sold bawdy, anatomically suggestive pots and "brothel tokens"—ceramic coins decorated with risqué images of rabbits, jackasses, screws, and other double entendres.) When he wasn't busy earning a living, he explored the artistic side of pottery. Working with unusually moist, sandy clay he dug from the banks of a nearby river, Ohr taught himself to make the walls of his clay pots wafer-thin and to fire them in a way that prevented them from cracking in the heat. No one quite knows how he did it; more than a century later, potters struggle to reproduce his results.

In 1555 Nostradamus published his famous book of prophecies...and a cookbook.

CRACK POT

Ohr's "mud babies," as he called his artistic pieces, were wildly uncon-ventional. He folded, dented, ruffled, and crumpled the clay, giving his pots a very asymmetrical and offbeat appearance. Some pots drooped, as if they had melted in the sun, and others looked squashed, as if they'd been vandalized by a prankster. Others had long, winding, snakelike handles. Many pieces were purely artistic—some vases couldn't hold flowers, and some pitchers and mugs couldn't hold water. Others were as tiny as shot glasses.

Ohr's choices of glazes and colors were also unconventional for the time: he mixed bright reds with dull grays, olive drab with sunny orange, and vivid blues with mustard yellows. He invented many glazes himself, and kept the formulas secret. After 1903 he used no glazes at all. "God put no color or quality in souls," he said.

Just as wild as the pots was the way Ohr promoted them. He lived in the age of P. T. Barnum, and he displayed a similar flair for bombast. He grew a mustache that was 18 inches long from tip to tip, and he often wore it folded over his ears, with the tips tied together behind his head. He added a five-story pagoda-style tower to his pottery shop and covered it with signs that read "GREATEST POTTER ON EARTH" and "GET A BILOXI SOUVENIR BEFORE THE POTTER DIES, OR GETS A REPUTATION." He may have even given himself the nickname "Mad Potter of Biloxi," rather than waiting for the locals to bestow it upon him. "You think I'm crazy, don't you?" he once asked a reporter. "I found out a long time ago that it paid me to act this way."

POT HOLDER

And yet for all of Ohr's efforts, his pots didn't sell well at all. This was partly because they were so strange-looking: few people would have been willing to buy such oddities under the best of circumstances. But it also appears that Ohr could not bring himself to part with his creations. He charged $25 a pot, the equivalent of more than $500 today, and on those rare occasions when he actually managed to sell one, he'd often chase after the customer and try to buy the pot back. When much of downtown Biloxi was destroyed in a fire in 1894, Ohr's studio was destroyed with it. But he couldn't even bring himself to part with the charred, ruined pots that he rescued from the ashes. They were his "killed babies," he said, and he couldn't let them go. After the fire he went back to making new pots, and he couldn't part with those, either.

NO SALE

As conflicted as Ohr was about selling his creations, he still got discour-aged when people showed no interest in buying them. It grated on him that he wasn't taken seriously as an artist. For every critic who admired his work, there were dozens who dismissed his pots as "monkey jars" that "lacked proportion" and were "distorted," "conceited," and "quaint."

When Ohr sent examples of his work to museums, they were either put in storage or refused outright; when he sent eight pots to the Smithsonian Museum in 1899, they sat ignored on a shelf for 50 years. Once, when he'd suffered one rejection too many, Ohr took a bunch of his pots out into some nearby woods and buried them there. As far as anyone knows, those pots are still out there.

END OF THE ROAD

By 1910 Ohr had become so frustrated at not being taken seriously that he closed up shop and never made another pot. He turned his studio over to his sons, and after they packed up some 7,000 unsold pots and put them in a shed out back, they turned the studio into the Ohr Boys Auto Repairing Shop.

For the last eight years of his life, Ohr told anyone who'd listen that one day he'd be recognized as "the greatest art potter on earth." But when he died from throat cancer in 1918 at the age of 60, the only people who hadn't already forgotten him were the ones who were still laughing at him.

Ironically, it was the act of *closing* his pottery studio that ensured that one day his prediction would come true—that he would indeed become one of America's most famous potters.

How? Part II of the story is on page 283.

*   *   *

SAVED BY THE COWELL

On a 2007 episode of the U.K.'s X *Factor*, a singing contestant named Jacqui Gray, 46, auditioned in front of Simon Cowell and Sharon Osbourne, but the judges weren't impressed with her "weird" voice. "Something happens to your throat when you sing," Cowell told Gray. "It is quite raspy. It sounds as if you have someone else in there, like you were choking on something." Osbourne agreed and told Gray that she should get it checked out. So Gray went to a throat specialist the next day…and found out she had a potentially fatal lung infection. It's incurable, but thanks to the judges, it was caught in time to get her on a treatment regimen. "Without going on the show," Gray said, "I wouldn't have even thought about going to the doctor about it. Simon Cowell and Sharon Osbourne saved my life."

Q. Why did Maryland create an "Oyster Navy" in 1868? A. To combat "oyster pirates" from Virginia.

Ironic, Isn't It?

There's something about a good irony that's so satisfying to read about. Perhaps it's because you're witnessing a cosmic joke being played out...on someone else.

IRONY THAT WON'T STAY DOWN

More than 100 food-safety experts who attended the 2014 Food Safety Summit in Baltimore, Maryland, got sick from food poisoning after eating the food in the convention center.

IRONY THAT DOES NOT COMPUTE

• Ben Bernanke applied for a loan to refinance his mortgage, but the bank's computerized approval system denied the loan because he'd recently changed jobs, which automatically puts up a "red flag." The job Bernanke left: he was the chairman of the Federal Reserve, the central banking system for the United States, which determines interest rates for banks.

• In February 2015, 800 graduate school applicants received acceptance e-mails from Carnegie Mellon University in Pittsburgh, Pennsylvania, a school "recognized around the world as a leader in all facets of computer science." Later that day, those same applicants received a second e-mail informing them that the first e-mail was a mistake. A school spokesperson blamed the goof on a "computer error."

STUPID @$%& IRONY

One of the most frustrating things in life: struggling to open stubborn plastic packaging. But now there's an As Seen on TV product called OpenX, with a "dual blade opener" that cuts plastic "like butter" so you can "stop struggling with stubborn plastic packages!" Only problem: you might need an OpenX to open OpenX because it comes in one of those "stubborn plastic packages."

ACCIDENTAL IRONY

• A newspaper truck for the *Republican*, based in Massachusetts, crashed into a home in 2010. Printed in big letters on the side of the truck were the words "Where News Hits Home."

• In 2014 a semitrailer driver for Halfords, a U.K.-based auto parts retailer, was driving through London when his 17-foot-tall trailer became wedged underneath a 15-foot bridge. Printed on the back of the trailer was the slogan "We Fit." (They didn't.) Underneath that was

---

When you get angry, your body releases a painkiller called *norepinephrine*.

another slogan: "We Go the Extra Mile," which prompted a London Fire Brigade official to quip, "Going the 'extra mile' might have been the better option rather than trying to fit under a bridge."

HISTORICAL IRONIES

• In the ninth century, Chinese alchemists were trying to create an "elixir of immortality" but instead ended up inventing gunpowder.

• Who invented the fire hydrant? No one knows for sure because the patent was destroyed in a fire at the U.S. Patent Office in 1986.

OPERATIONAL IRONY

In 1964 a University of Illinois industrial design student named John Spinello got an assignment: create an electronic game in which players try to insert a metal rod into a hole without setting off a buzzer. He got to work and decided on a surgery theme. Good news: Spinello got an A! Bad news: he sold the rights of the game for $500 to the Milton Bradley Company, which turned it into Operation. Spinello's invention became one of the 20th century's most popular board games, but Spinello never made another cent off it. That could be why, in 2014, the 77-year-old couldn't come up with the $25,000 he needed for…an operation. (He had dental problems that required oral surgery.) Thanks to a crowd-funding site started by fans of Operation, along with a generous offer by Hasbro to purchase Spinello's original prototype (Hasbro bought Milton Bradley in 1984), he was able to pay for his operation.

THE GREAT CHICAGO FIRONY

In 2015 a Chicago building caught fire. More than 150 firefighters battled the blaze, but they couldn't save the structure because of a lack of water nearby. The building, by the way, housed a factory that manufactures fire extinguishers.

IRONY CUT SHORT

A British Royal Marine named Andy Grant had a tattoo on his leg that read "You'll Never Walk Alone," which is the motto of his favorite soccer team, Liverpool FC. Sadly, while serving in Afghanistan in 2009, Grant stepped on an IED that exploded, causing him to lose part of his leg. When his surgeon removed the bandage, Grant discovered that he'd lost part of the tattoo as well. Now it reads "You'll Never Walk."

Update: Not only did Grant walk again thanks to a prosthetic lower leg, but he's become a Paralympic athlete and has won several races. He now works as a motivational speaker. "The tattoo is bizarre and I just laugh about it," he said, adding that, ironically, the injury has "given me more of a life than I probably would have had."

Uncle John's Page of Lists

Some random bits from the BRI's bottomless trivia files.

10 Women Once "Involved" with Warren Beatty
1. Cher
2. Joan Collins
3. Jackie Onassis
4. Goldie Hawn
5. Diana Ross
6. Mary Tyler More
7. Jane Fonda
8. Elizabeth Taylor
9. Barbra Streisand
10. Madonna

3 Former Dentists
1. Zane Grey, author
2. Doc Holliday, gunslinger
3. Thomas Welch, grape juice magnate

5 Toilet Paper Brands Around the World
1. Delica (Greece)
2. Belana (Bulgaria)
3. Kittensoft (Ireland)
4. Tenderly (Italy)
5. Crepto (Hungary)

4 Most Popular U.S. "Official State Birds"
1. Cardinal (7 states)
2. Meadowlark (6)
3. Mockingbird (5)
4. Robin (3)

Johnny Cash's To-Do List (undated)
1. Not smoke
2. Kiss June [his wife, June Carter]
3. Not kiss anyone else
4. Cough
5. Pee
6. Eat
7. Not eat too much
8. Worry
9. Go see Mama
10. Practice piano
Note: Not write notes

First 5 Atari 2600 Games (Sept. 1977)
1. *Air-Sea Battle*
2. *Basic Math*
3. *Blackjack*
4. *Combat*
5. *Indy 500*

8 Words Scripps Nat'l Spelling Bee Contestants Missed
1. Rhytidome
2. Ochidore
3. Prosopopoeia
4. Schwarmerei
5. Maecenas
6. Gnathonic
7. Coryza
8. Terribilita

10 Nicknames Made Up by George W. Bush
1. Dick Cheney: "Big Time"
2. Vladimir Putin: "Pootie-Poot"
3. Barbara Boxer: "Ali"
4. John McCain: "Hogan"
5. Silvio Berlusconi: "Shoes"
6. Barney Frank: "Sabertooth"
7. Chris Christie: "Big Boy"
8. John Boehner: "Boner"
9. Barack Obama: "Rock"
10. Karl Rove: "Turd Blossom"

The first place potatoes were planted in the U.S.: New Hampshire (1719).

Strange Medical Conditions

It's time to play "Stump the Doctors." That sounds like fun, except that these medical conditions are real, as are the people who suffer from them. Okay, so no laughing. Instead, we invite you to marvel with us at how bizarre the human body can be.

SUBJECT: A 49-year-old man in Brazil

CONDITION: "Pathological generosity"

STORY: In August 2013, the medical journal *Neurocase* published a report by Brazilian doctors about a 49-year-old man, referred to only as "Mr. A," who had undergone a bizarre personality change after suffering a stroke. The change: he could not stop himself from giving things to people. That included buying candy, food, and gifts to give to kids on the street and giving away his money to people he hardly knew. The man was so prone to "pathological generosity," the report said, that over the course of just a few years his behavior put a serious financial strain on his family, especially after it caused him to lose his job as a manager at a large corporation. The doctors said they believed the bizarre symptoms were caused by damage the stroke did to an area of the man's brain (the *subcortical region* of the frontal lobe—for you neuroscientists playing along at home) that is known to take part in the regulation of human behavior. They added that Mr. A's was the only known case of "pathological generosity" ever recorded.

SUBJECT: A 19-year-old Iranian man

CONDITION: "Hairy eyeball"

STORY: In 2013 researchers from Iran's Tabriz University of Medical Sciences reported that they had treated a man who was born with a tiny whitish growth on his right eyeball. For many years it hadn't bothered him, nor had it affected his vision. But it had grown in size, reaching about a quarter-inch in diameter, and it had started to become annoying—especially after several black hairs started to grow out of it. Luckily, those hairs actually helped doctors diagnose the growth: it was a *limbal dermoid*, a very rare type of tumor that has the bizarre characteristics of being able to grow things like hair, cartilage, bone—and even sweat glands. More good luck: such tumors aren't cancerous. Doctors successfully removed the tumor from the man's eye without causing any lasting damage, and the man resumed his life...minus one hairy eyeball.

SUBJECT: Shanya Isom, 30, of Memphis, Tennessee
CONDITION: Unknown condition affecting hair follicles
STORY: In September 2009, Isom, a student at the University of Memphis, had an allergic reaction to the steroids she was given to treat an asthma attack. Initially, the reaction caused her skin to itch all over her body…but then it got much worse: she started growing oddly shaped, stiff, sharp black growths all over her body. Two years later, after seeing dozens of doctors, all to no avail, she sought treatment at Johns Hopkins Medical Center in Baltimore. There, doctors finally figured out what was happening. Isom's hair follicles were producing 12 times the number of cells they normally do, and they weren't producing hair cells—they were making nail cells, like the ones produced for fingernails and toenails. She was basically growing sharp black fingernails all over her body. The doctors informed Isom that she was the only person ever known to have such a condition…and they had no idea what was causing it. They were able to alleviate her symptoms to a degree, but unfortunately, she continues to suffer from the condition today.

SUBJECT: Natalie Adler, 27, of Melbourne, Australia
CONDITION: Unknown condition affecting the eyes
STORY: One morning in 2004, Adler, then 17, woke up and couldn't open her eyes. The condition lasted for three entire days…and then she could open her eyes again. Three days after that, she couldn't open her eyes, and three days after *that*, she could. Mind-bogglingly, that's been happening ever since. (For the three days her eyes are shut, Adler is legally blind, able to see only through a tiny slit in her left eye.) She went to numerous doctors in both Australia and the U.S., but none could determine what was causing her bizarre symptoms. At first, most of them told Adler the problem was in her head, but they don't any more, because over the years, additional symptoms have appeared. They include headaches, nausea, stiffness in the neck and arms, and, most alarmingly, paralysis of Adler's stomach muscles, which has resulted in her having to be fed through tubes permanently inserted into her stomach. As of 2014, Adler has been seen by more than 40 specialists—and they still don't know what's going on. The latest guess: Adler is suffering from a previously unknown genetic disorder. Tests are ongoing.

SUBJECT: Alexandra Allen, 17, of Mapleton, Utah
CONDITION: An allergy to water
STORY: When she was 12 years old, Alexandra was on vacation and went for a swim in a pool. She woke up in the middle of the night, most of her body covered in incredibly itchy hives. Her doctor initially diagnosed her as having a chlorine allergy and told her to stay out of

pools. But it got worse as she got older—almost all physical contact with water was causing her skin to break out in hives and welts. Although the human body is about two-thirds water, it's still possible to be allergic to water (at least on the skin). Allen is one of a handful of cases of water allergy, or *aquagenic urticaria* on record. Allen has to avoid being submerged in it, and can only take brief, cold showers. The main treatment? A topical application of capsaicin, the active ingredient in chili peppers.

SUBJECT: Graham Harrison of Exeter, England

CONDITION: Cotard's syndrome

STORY: In 2004 Harrison, 48, went to a doctor with an odd complaint: he was dead. He explained that he'd attempted to commit suicide several months earlier (he took an electrical appliance with him into a bath), and while he *seemed* to have survived, he was convinced he had, in fact, killed his brain. Harrison recognized that he could walk and talk, but he was still convinced his brain had ceased to function. His rationale: he had lost all sensation, he said, including the ability to smell, to taste, and to feel pleasure. He was so convinced he was dead that he saw no point in eating. (His family had to make sure he ate food and took his medications.) Finally in 2013, after nine years of suffering with the symptoms, doctors finally diagnosed Harrison's condition as Cotard's syndrome, also known as "walking corpse syndrome," an extremely rare psychological disorder, the cause of which is unknown. People with Cotard's sincerely believe they are, basically, zombies. After the diagnosis, Harrison was able to return to the land of the living: "I don't feel that brain-dead any more," he told *New Scientist* magazine. "Things just feel a bit bizarre sometimes."

UPDATE: In the course of being treated, Harrison underwent brain scans, and they were, according to his doctors, *surprising*: Harrison's brain showed a level of activity similar to someone in a vegetative state. "I've been analyzing scans for 15 years," said Dr. Steven Laureys. "I've never seen anyone who was on his feet, who was interacting with people, with such an abnormal scan result."

*　　*　　*

DUMB CROOK

During a traffic stop in Lincoln, Nebraska, police searched the car of Jordan Meier, 21. An officer looked under the driver's seat and found a sour cream container with "Not Weed" written on the lid. Guess what was inside. Meier was arrested for DUI and possession of marijuana.

Why are they called "turtle" doves? It's from the Latin word *turtur,* meaning "dove."

Take My Advice

Some sage words of counsel from the advice books of yesteryear.

SMOKE SCREEN

"Don't buy cigars from mysterious-looking foreigners, who say they have just done a neat little job of smuggling from Havana, and are willing to let you in on a good thing. They may even flatter you by telling you that you look trustworthy. They really mean that you look easy. It's your move."

—The College Freshman's Don't Book (1910)

KID STUFF

"There always are and always will be children to be taken care of. There is no way in which a girl can help her country better than by fitting herself to undertake the care of children."

—Official Handbook of the Girl Scouts (1925)

GOOD DEED FOR THE DAY

"Kill a mad dog at once. Wrap a handkerchief around your hand to prevent the dog's teeth from entering the flesh and grasp a club of some kind. If you can stop the dog with a stick you should hit him hard over the head with it, or kick him under the jaw. A handkerchief held in front of you in your outstretched hands will generally cause the dog to stop to paw it before he attempts to bite you. This will give you an opportunity to kick him under the lower jaw. Another way suggested is to wrap a coat around the left arm and let the dog bite it; then with the other hand seize the dog's throat and choke him."

—The Boy Scout's Handbook (1911)

THE FACTS OF LIFE

"Whenever you are curious about the wonderful experience which we call 'birth,' think of it reverently, and go at once for information to your father or mother; if you lack these, to some high-minded friend much older than you. Otherwise, enclose a stamped envelope addressed to yourself in a letter to the Y.M.C.A. or the Y.W.C.A. or the Federal Bureau of Information, Washington, D.C., asking the title of the best book for a boy or a girl of your age, about the Beginnings of Life. Never listen to explanations from the ignorant or the vulgar. Impure thoughts on this subject lead to the ruin of both body and spirit."

—Manners and Conduct in School and Out (1921)

Ben Franklin's cure for flatulence: dried rhubarb and rose oil dissolved in wine. (Let us know if it works.)

HEALTH AND BEAUTY TIPS

• "To persons whose hair is in a declining state, the frequent and regular use of oil or bear's grease is often of much service, as it is calculated to assist in supplying that nourishment which is so necessary."

• "Nobody needs to have an offensive breath…A bit of charcoal held in the mouth…two or three times in a week, and slowly chewed, has a wonderful power to preserve the teeth and purify the breath…If these hints induce only one person to take better care of the teeth, I shall be more than rewarded for the trouble of writing."
—*Polite Manual for Young Ladies* (1847)

BOTTOMS UP

"Never eat or drink anything HOT…If you drink tea (which we do not recommend), let it be the best of black tea, and not strong. Coffee, if drunk at all, should be diluted with twice its quantity of boiled milk, and well sweetened with white sugar."
—*Pocket Manual of Republican Etiquette* (1887)

MISCELLANEOUS

"Novel-reading strengthens the passions, weakens the virtues, and diminishes the power of self-control. Multitudes may date their ruin from the commencement of this kind of reading; and many more, who have been rescued from the snare, will regret, to the end of their days, its influence in the early formation of their character. It is, too, a great waste of time…If you wish to become weak-headed, nervous, and good for nothing, read novels."
—*Polite Manual for Young Ladies* (1849)

"Gentlefolk have 'friends' stopping with them, never 'company.' Servants have and keep 'company.'"
—*The Complete Bachelor: Manners for Men* (1896)

DON'T EVEN THINK ABOUT IT

"A lady should never look up in a waiter's face while giving an order, refusing wine, or thanking him for any special service. This savors of familiarity, and should be avoided. A man, however, that is attentive will see that a lady has none of these things to do."
—*The Manners and Customs of Polite Society* (1896)

"It is not polite for married ladies to talk, in the presence of gentlemen, of the difficulty they have in procuring domestics, and how good-for-nothing they are when procured."
—*The Ladies' Book of Etiquette, and Manual of Politeness* (1860)

Name-Changers, Game-Changers

What's in a name? A lot—at least to the multitude of people who've changed theirs. They do it for all sorts of reasons: social, political, religious—or simply because they don't like the ones their parents gave them. These athletes had interesting reasons, too.

RON ARTEST

In 2004 Ron Artest of the Indiana Pacers got into a fistfight with opposing players during a game against the Detroit Pistons. Then he took the fight into the stands, where he brawled with Pistons fans. The NBA suspended him for the rest of the season and the playoffs, a total of 86 games. It was the longest suspension for on-court actions in league history. When Artest returned to the NBA, he continued to start fights, which was probably one of the reasons he bounced from team to team. Things came to a head when he was charged with misdemeanor domestic violence during a stint with the Sacramento Kings. After being forced to undergo counseling as part of his plea bargain, Artest voluntarily sought out additional therapy and gradually began to turn his life around—a life that began in the violent, poverty-stricken Queensbridge projects of New York. In 2009 the champion L.A. Lakers shocked the NBA by signing the volatile small forward, but Artest's clutch three-pointer that clinched the Lakers' win in the NBA Finals silenced all doubt. Artest thanked his therapist on live TV as tears streamed down his face. After the victory, he auctioned off his championship ring and donated the proceeds—more than $500,000—to youth charities across America. Then in 2011, he left the old "Ron Artest" behind for good by changing his name to Metta World Peace—*Metta* being a Buddhist word for "loving kindness and friendliness for others." Now retired from the NBA, Mr. Peace has continued his mental health activism and writes children's books.

CHAD JOHNSON

During Johnson's years with the Cincinnati Bengals, the wide receiver who wore #85 became known for his touchdown dances and for antagonizing head coaches and NFL executives. In a 2006 preseason game, Johnson took the field in a jersey with "OCHO CINCO" on the back...only to have it ripped off by teammate Carson Palmer to reveal "Johnson" underneath. Johnson later told reporters he did it in

---

Largest primate ever: *Gigantopithecus,* **a prehistoric ape from China. It stood 12 feet tall.**

honor of Hispanic Heritage Month (although technically, *ocho cinco* translates to "eight five" not "eighty-five"). The NFL wasn't amused and fined him $5,000. Nevertheless, in 2008 Johnson made the nickname permanent and had his name legally changed to Chad Ochocinco. But because Reebok had already printed thousands of JOHNSON jerseys (100,000, actually) before his paperwork was filed, Johnson was contractually obligated to wear his old uniform for the 2008 season. And if he refused, he would have been forced to buy out Reebok's entire stock of Johnson jerseys at a cost of $4 million. By 2012, the Bengals were sick of Ochocinco…and so was he. When he signed with the Miami Dolphins that season, the wide receiver went to a Florida courthouse and reclaimed the name Johnson.

SHARMON SHAH

Believe it or not, NBA Hall of Famer Kareem Abdul-Jabbar, born Lew Alcindor, isn't the only athlete who converted to Islam and changed his name to Abdul-Jabbar. Just before Sharmon Shah entered the 1996 NFL Draft, the UCLA Bruins running back converted to Islam and took the name Karim Abdul-Jabbar. This didn't go over too well with *Kareem* Abdul-Jabbar. He filed a lawsuit claiming there were too many similarities, including the same jersey number (#33), for it to be a coincidence. While Karim testified in court that his imam gave him the name and that he'd chosen #33 to honor Dallas Cowboys running back Tony Dorsett, not Kareem, the courts ruled in Kareem's favor. The football player legally changed his name to Abdul-Karim al-Jabbar in 2000, his final year in the NFL.

JOE THEISMANN

While Theismann never changed his name, he did alter the pronunciation. In 1970, his senior year at Notre Dame, the quarterback was named a finalist for the Heisman Trophy. That's when the school's sports information director suggested that he change the pronunciation of his name from "Thees-man" to "Thighs-man"—to rhyme with "Heisman" as a publicity stunt. He didn't win the award, but the new name stuck, and it's what he was called throughout his NFL career. (Back home, though, friends and family still call him Joe "Thees-man.")

*   *   *

"My father was a proctologist, and my mother was an abstract artist. That's how I view the world."

—Sandra Bernhard

Famous... and Adopted

Being adopted used to be a real stigma. These people didn't let the stigma stop them. They went on to fame and fortune.

STEVE JOBS. Jobs's biological parents were Syrian-American Abdul Fattah Jandali and Swiss-American Joanne Schieble, who met when they were students at the University of Wisconsin. When Schieble became pregnant, her conservative father refused to allow her to marry Jandali, and she went to California to have the baby and give it up for adoption. Jobs, born in February 1955, was subsequently adopted by Paul and Clara Jobs, a middle-class couple in San Francisco. (They had been married for nine years; Clara was unable to have children.) Ironically, just months after she gave up her baby, Schieble's father died—and she and Jandali were soon married. They had a daughter, Mona, who went on to become the novelist Mona Simpson. Jobs eventually tracked down his mother and sister but never established contact with his father.

RAY LIOTTA. The *Goodfellas* star was born to an unmarried couple in Newark, New Jersey, in 1954 and lived with his biological parents until he was six months old, before being given up for adoption when the couple realized that they couldn't afford to raise him. Shortly thereafter, he was adopted by Alfred and Mary Liotta, who owned an auto parts store in Newark. Liotta has said in interviews that he grew up knowing he was adopted and was angry about it for many years, feeling he'd been abandoned. But he claims he overcame those feelings when, in 1997, he tracked down his birth mother and found out that he had one full sister, five half-sisters, and one half-brother. "Man," he said, "I'm so glad I was adopted."

KRISTIN CHENOWETH. The actress best known for her roles on NBC's *West Wing* and ABC's *Pushing Daisies* was adopted five days after her birth in 1968 by Junie and Jerry Chenoweth, a chemical engineer, in Broken Arrow, Oklahoma. Chenoweth has said that she never felt a need to meet her biological mother—who was a 21-year-old flight attendant when she gave her up for adoption—but that she may have met her once anyway. "I was doing an event and a woman came up to me," Chenoweth told *Prevention* magazine in 2012. The woman told

---

Collectively, Americans spend about $300 billion per year on lawsuits.

her, "I've been following your career and I am so proud of you. I just want you to know that someone is always thinking of you." After the woman left, Chenoweth's manager told her, "That woman looked like you. You looked like her." (The woman was even about the same height as Chenoweth—and Chenoweth is four feet eleven inches tall.)

MELISSA GILBERT. The *Little House on the Prairie* star was adopted by Hollywood actors Paul Gilbert and Barbara Cowan in 1964—when she was one day old. Gilbert wrote in her 2009 autobiography that she was surprised to find out much later that her parents had no plan to adopt until just before the adoption took place. "I got a phone call that there was a baby available and did I want it," Gilbert says her mother told her. "I called your dad. He was on the road and he said, 'Yes, that's the one. Go get it.'" (The Gilberts later adopted another child, Jonathan Gilbert, who played Willie Olson on *Little House on the Prairie*.)

ERIC CLAPTON. He was born in England in 1945 to 16-year-old Patricia Clapton and a 25-year-old Canadian soldier. The soldier—who was already married—returned to Canada at the end of World War II, leaving Patricia on her own. Because she was so young, and because of the powerful stigma attached to unwed mothers at the time, she gave birth in secret—in a back room of her parents' home—and disappeared from the scene, leaving her parents to raise the boy as their son. Clapton didn't find out that his "parents" were actually his grandparents, and his "older brother" Adrian was actually his uncle, until he was eight. Patricia arrived back on the scene when Clapton was nine (she had married another Canadian soldier) and was portrayed in public as his older sister. Clapton wrote in his 2007 autobiography that the difficulties surrounding the issues relating to his mother were what led him to music. "Music became a healer for me," he wrote. "I found that it could wipe away all the emotions of fear and confusion relating to my family."

FRANCES McDORMAND. McDormand, best known for her Academy Award–winning role in the 1996 Coen brothers' film *Fargo*, was born in Chicago in 1957 and was adopted by Canadian-born American couple Vernon and Noreen McDormand at 18 months old. (McDormand has said that she doesn't know who her biological parents are.) Vernon was a pastor, and the family moved often, from congregation to congregation around the American Bible Belt, before settling down in southwest Pennsylvania in the early 1970s. The McDormands had no children of their own but fostered several children over the years and adopted some, too. "They take in strays," McDormand said in a 2003 interview. "They also have nine cats."

Plastic-bodied cars aren't new; the Ford Motor Company made the first one in 1941.

The Nuclear Option

Don't have a meltdown—here's some atomic trivia about nuclear power.

IT DOESN'T CREATE AIR POLLUTION... How much do properly-functioning nuclear reactors pollute the air? Not at all. They emit no greenhouse gases, and emissions from the process of creating nuclear energy are comparable to that of wind power. Coal ash, however, contains small amounts of radiation-emitting uranium. In fact, coal power puts more radiation into the air than nuclear power does (along with seven million tons of greenhouse gases annually).

...BUT IT DOES PRODUCE TOXIC WASTE. Nuclear power may not produce greenhouse gases, but it does produce toxic waste. American nuclear power plants produce more than 2,000 cubic meters of waste each year in the form of spent, irradiated uranium fuel. Power plants must shut down every 18 months or so for the safe and complete removal of that waste, which is then transported to Grundy County, Illinois—home of the Morris Operation, the only high-level radioactive storage site in the United States.

IT EMITS VERY LITTLE RADIATION. Here's how a power plant works. Several tons of enriched uranium are split in the plant's core, creating a chain reaction that generates heat. It heats water, which then creates steam, and the steam drives a turbine to make electricity. But all the radiation is encased inside the energy-creating chambers. The area around the plant is no more radioactive than most other places. Standing outside a nuclear plant every day for four years would result in as much radiation absorption as one chest X-ray.

IT'S NOT A RENEWABLE ENERGY SOURCE. There is a finite supply of uranium on Earth, most of which comes from mines in Kazakhstan, Australia, and Canada. Uranium is so rare that it has to be carefully separated from ore known to contain the element. The rest of that ore is thrown away—about 40 pounds of waste for every pound of usable uranium.

IT IS "CLEAN" ENERGY. Only 20 percent of power generated in the United States is nuclear, but 70 percent of clean electricity is nuclear-derived. Along with wind, solar, geothermal, and hydroelectric power, nuclear power is technically considered "clean" energy because it doesn't pump any toxic greenhouse gases into the atmosphere.

IT'S NOT THAT WIDELY USED. There are 437 nuclear power plants in operation worldwide, providing 11 percent of the world's electricity. The biggest users: France (80 percent of its electricity is nuclear-generated), South Korea (30 percent), and Japan (25 percent). The last new power plant in the United States was opened in 1996 (although it had begun construction in 1972).

IT'S DESTROYING THE OCEANS. In 2014, three years after the Fukushima disaster, Japanese officials admitted that radioactive water leaking from the power plant was entering the Pacific Ocean at a rate of 300 tons a day. Scientists also believe the discovery of fish bleeding from their gills and eyeballs found in waters off western Canada could be related to exposure to Fukushima-contaminated water.

IT USED TO BE MORE POPULAR. The peak period for nuclear energy was the early 1970s. From 1970 to 1975, 45 plants were built in the United States. During several energy crises, nuclear power was widely seen as a clean, safe way to end American dependence on foreign oil. The 1979 partial meltdown at Three Mile Island in Pennsylvania brought an end to those good feelings.

IT MAY BE ON THE WAY OUT. Properly functioning nuclear plants are one thing, of course, but plants melting down are another. After an earthquake led to the meltdown in Japan's Fukushima plant in 2011, the governments of Italy and Switzerland announced plans to close nuclear power facilities there. In Germany, 25,000 people marched in 21 cities, demanding an end to nuclear power entirely. Chancellor Angela Merkel agreed and put into motion a plan to make Germany nuclear-free by 2022.

IT WAS TARNISHED BY THE SIMPSONS. When *The Simpsons* debuted in 1990, nuclear power was a controversial topic. The Soviet Union's Chernobyl disaster—the latest and most devastating in a line of nuclear events, which included the Three Mile Island disaster and the release of nuclear meltdown film *The China Syndrome*—had occurred only four years earlier. *The Simpsons* satirized the nuclear industry by making the workers at the Springfield Nuclear Power Plant dumb and incompetent, and showing the plant as responsible for acid rain and three-eyed fish. After the U.S. Council for Energy Awareness (a nuclear industry group) sent a letter to the show's producers expressing "horror" at the depiction, producer Sam Simon agreed to tour the San Onofre plant in San Clemente, California, and the show subsequently cut back on anti-nuclear sentiment. (The San Onofre plant was shut down in 2013 after it was deemed "unsafe" to the eight million people who lived within a 50-mile radius.)

Facebook Scams

There are more than 1.2 billion Facebook users, so it should come as no surprise that some are less than honest. They invade your timeline and your e-mail inbox, and they'll even "private message" you. Here are some scams you won't "like."

F**ACEBOOK "WORK FROM HOME PROGRAM"**
What It Says: "If you spend much time online and have been wanting to work from home, you might be in luck. Facebook has now released a 'Work from Home Program' that will allow people to work from the comfort of their own homes."

But Really: Facebook only posts job openings on its careers page, and you actually have to apply, go through the interview process, and then go to work in one of the company's corporate offices.

If You Click It: The link takes you to what looks like an official Facebook page—but it isn't. You are then informed that you must purchase a $4 "Facebook Millionaire Kit." Four bucks might not seem like much...until you notice the fine print: After one week, you'll automatically be charged $94 a month for "continued access." (And your Facebook job will never materialize.)

"WAT ARE U DOING IN THIS VIDEO"

What It Says: A private message, possibly from a friend's account, reads, "Hey [Name of user], wat are u doing in this video lol! Search ur name and skip to 1:53. Type in browser with no spaces->"

But Really: Your friend's account has been compromised.

If You Copy/Paste It: The URL takes you to a fake Facebook page that asks for your account login name and password and then tells you to install a special app. The personal information you provide allows scammers to lock you out of your own account and take control. And the app you installed accesses your friends list and sends private messages containing the scam to everyone you know.

"TERMS OF SERVICE VIOLATION"

What It Says: "Your account is reported to have violated the policies that are considered annoying or insulting to Facebook users. We will disable your account within 24 hours if you do not do the reconfirmation. If you still want to use Facebook, please confirm your account below."

But Really: Facebook already has your information. You gave it to them when you set up your account. If you really were in violation of their terms of service, they'd automatically suspend your account without requiring you to send them your personal details.

If You Copy/Paste It: The page to "confirm" your account asks for your name, e-mail address, Facebook account name and security question, and the first six numbers on your credit card. That gives the scammers access to take over your account, use your credit card, and potentially steal your identity.

"PRIVACY ALERT NOTICE"

What It Says: "In response to the new Facebook guidelines, I hereby declare that my copyright is attached to all of my personal details, illustrations, comics, paintings, professional photos and videos, etc. (as a result of the Berner Convention). For commercial use of the above my written consent is needed at all times!"

But Really: Facebook doesn't own *any* of your media, period. And there's no such thing as the "Berner Convention." When you join Facebook, you do grant the company permission to use and share what you post, depending on your privacy settings, but posting a bogus copyright claim on your wall doesn't change the terms of that agreement. If you're ever uncomfortable with the possibility of Facebook sharing your media, you can simply edit your privacy and application settings or delete your account. (Once your account is deleted, any permissions you granted to Facebook end.)

If You Post It: The "Privacy Alert" has been around since 2012 and has been widely debunked. It's harmless…but if you put it on your wall, your friends will know you fell for it.

"SHOCKING MERMAID/ALIEN/ACCIDENT VIDEO"

What It Says: "I am shocked!!! I'm NEVER texting AGAIN since I found this out. Video here." Or "Breaking News: [UNCUT VIDEO] RARE! Mermaid found inside a shark!"

But Really: No such video exists.

If You Click It: Some fake videos require you to install a plug-in before you can watch the video, and the plug-in embeds malware in your computer. Other scams require you to complete surveys that ask for your user names and passwords, or financial accounts before you're "granted access" to the video. If you think no one would fall for such obvious scams, think again: in only two days in January 2015, a bogus video link that required a "Flash update" infected more than 110,000 Facebook users' computers with malware—malware that allowed the scammers to take over the victims' computers. So be careful what you click on…or you just might click your life away.

Bombed on Broadway

If your play manages to get to Broadway, you've already achieved a huge accomplishment in the world of theater. But, um, then you've got to deliver. These folks didn't.

DUDE: THE HIGHWAY LIFE (1972)

This was a much ballyhooed musical production by Gerome Ragni and Galt MacDermot, two of the creators of the 1967 hit *Hair*. The story revolves around Dude, a young man who battles a series of temptations from a Satan-like character named Zero. The plot was so convoluted and confusing that the actors threatened to walk out while the show was in rehearsal. Also during rehearsals, the show's producers decided that the dude playing Dude, a 23-year-old white actor named Kevin Geer, couldn't sing well enough to play the role. So they replaced him…with an 11-year-old African American actor (Ralph Carter, who went on to play the little brother in the 1970s sitcom *Good Times*). That meant all the character's adult-centered dialogue had to be rewritten. By the time the play started previews, the production was such a shambles that both the director and choreographer quit and had to be replaced. When the show finally opened, critics hated it. So did audiences. *Dude* was gone after just 16 performances.

RACHAEL LILY ROSENBLOOM (AND DON'T YOU EVER FORGET IT) (1973)

This play was the brainchild of 25-year-old actor, singer, and composer Paul Jabara. At the time he was known only for his performances in the musicals *Hair* and the London production of *Jesus Christ Superstar*, but he convinced music business legends Robert Stigwood (the Bee Gees' manager) and Ahmet Ertegün (the founder of Atlantic Records) to invest $500,000 in this Broadway musical. It was a campy, over-the-top disco-themed extravaganza with a story line that traces the life of Rachael Lily Rosenbloom, a Brooklyn fish market worker who becomes a famous Hollywood gossip columnist and later an Oscar-nominated actress. After just eight previews—and a string of mocking reviews, such as the one by *New York Times* critic Frank Rich, who called it a "musical fantasy of surpassing lavishness that made no sense, at any level, from beginning to end"—the show was closed before it even had an official opening night. Stigwood and Ertegün lost their entire $500,000 investment.

How do they know? Male cats tend to be southpaws, whereas female cats are usually righties.

MOOSE MURDERS (1983)

This "whodunit" by playwright Arthur Bicknell was about a group of people who get stuck in the "Wild Moose Lodge" in New York's Adirondack Mountains during a storm. Then they start getting murdered...by someone wearing a moose costume. Notable characters: a wheelchair-bound quadriplegic man entirely wrapped in gauze, and a hippie teenager named Stinky who is obsessed with trying to sleep with his mother. The only reason the play made it to Broadway was that the producers convinced longtime Hollywood star Eve Arden (*Our Miss Brooks*) to play the lead. But the play was so...stinky that Arden quit after the first preview. *Moose Murders* received some of the most scathing reviews in Broadway history. *New York Post* critic Clive Barnes wrote that it was "so indescribably bad that I do not intend to waste anyone's time by describing it." The *New Yorker's* Brendan Gill said the play "would insult the intelligence of an audience consisting entirely of amoebas." And *New York Magazine* said it seemed as if the play was staged by "a blind director repeatedly kicked in the groin." *Moose Murders* was canceled after one performance.

Bonus fact: In 2013 Bicknell published a book entitled *Moose Murdered: Or How I Learned to Stop Worrying and Love My Broadway Bomb*, the behind-the-scenes story of the flopped play. And...it got great reviews.

INTO THE LIGHT (1986)

This was a musical written by unknown playwright Jeff Tambornino. Plot: a nuclear physicist becomes obsessed with verifying—or debunking—the veracity of the shroud of Turin, the purported burial cloth of Jesus Christ. Alienated from his wife and his son, the physicist copes with his obsession by inventing an imaginary friend—a mime. How did Tambornino manage to get a story like that to Broadway? He got actor Dean Jones, the star of two Disney hit movies—*That Darn Cat!* (1965) and *The Love Bug* (1969)—to play the lead. (Jones had recently become a born-again Christian and liked the pro-Christianity message of the play.) The show, which was advertised as "futuristic," featured generous use of a fog machine and lasers, as well as dancing nuns. And remember—it was a musical, so it had Jones, as the nuclear physicist, singing about molecules, quarks, antimatter, and other physics-related things. *Into the Light* fizzled out after six performances. The show's producers reportedly lost around $3 million.

*　　*　　*

"If all else fails, immortality can always be assured by spectacular error."

—**John Kenneth Galbraith**

The Kingdom of Bhutan has issued stamps that are scented, made of silk, and contain 3-D images.

Life and Limb

*Throughout most of history, if you lost a limb, the replacement of choice
was a wooden peg (which only looked cool if you were a pirate).
But that all changed after a young soldier lost a leg in the
Civil War and refused to take his injury lying down.*

WALKING TALL

W "You'll dance again, but it's going to take a year." That's
the kind of thing that Dr. Mac Hanger III tells a lot of
his patients. As one of the world's leading prosthetists, it's his job to
fit amputees with new limbs and help them acclimate to them. For
example: Hanger helped several maimed victims of the 2013 Boston
Marathon bombings get their lives back.

Losing a limb once meant losing your quality of life, but that's not
so anymore. "People really become different people," Hanger says. "You
lose a leg, but you gain a lot of wisdom and strength." He should know,
because that's exactly what happened to his great-great-grandfather, J. E.
Hanger. And that's how the modern prosthetics industry was born.

CASUALTY OF WAR

On June 3, 1861, the first land battle of the Civil War took place in
Philippi, Virginia. Early that morning, an 18-year-old Confederate
soldier named James Edward Hanger was standing guard outside a stable
where his fellow soldiers were sleeping. Private Hanger had enlisted
only two days earlier. He'd dropped out of engineering school to join his
brothers in the Confederate Army. But his career as a soldier would be
short-lived. Just after dawn, Hanger heard gunfire, so he ran inside the
stable to get his horse. Just then a six-pound cannonball tore through
the barn and struck his left leg.

With only a bit of skin keeping his lower leg attached, Hanger
crawled to a corner of the barn to hide…and passed out. The next thing
he knew, Union soldiers had him on a table, and he was writhing in
pain. Unable to save the leg, two field surgeons spent an hour with a
jagged saw cutting through Hanger's skin, muscle, and bone a few inches
above his knee. The surgeon then cauterized the wound with a hot iron.
The excruciating amputation saved Hanger's life. But what kind of life
would that be?

Private Hanger spent the next two months as a prisoner of war in
a Union hospital. "I cannot look back upon those days in the hospital
without a shudder," he later said. "In the twinkling of an eye, life's

fondest hopes seemed dead. I was the prey of despair. What could the world hold for a maimed, crippled man?" In those days most amputees, unable to work, ended up begging on the streets.

After a prisoner exchange, the teenager was relieved of duty. He arrived home in Churchill, Virginia, fitted with a heavy wooden pegleg that was painful to wear and difficult to get around in. He hobbled upstairs to his room and asked his parents to leave him alone. But Hanger didn't spend his time wallowing in self-pity. The former engineering student studied his wooden "Yankee leg" and quickly realized that its main problem was that it had little in common with a real leg. So Hanger decided to make one himself.

WHEN LIFE GIVES YOU LEMONS...

Three months after retreating to his room, Hanger walked down the stairs without the aid of crutches. His family was astonished. Gone was the pegleg; in its place was the world's first articulated prosthetic limb. Hanger made his contraption out of oak barrel staves—the narrow strips of wood that form the sides of a barrel—which were more flexible than a solid piece of hardwood. Then he'd added hinged joints at the ankle and the knee. This not only made walking easier, but also sitting down and getting up. Hanger even carved himself a wooden foot so he could wear two shoes again. Best of all: the artificial limb weighed only about five pounds. All of a sudden, a new world opened up for Hanger. And it was about to open up for a lot of other wounded veterans as well.

Hanger had the dubious distinction of being the Civil War's first amputee, but he was far from the last. By the time the conflict ended four years later, at least 60,000 other soldiers had suffered similar fates. Now that Hanger was back on his "feet," the 18-year-old decided to open his own prosthetics business, and two years later he patented his first "Hanger Leg." Rival inventors were attempting to create artificial limbs as well, but thanks to Hanger's superior design, in 1864 the Association for the Relief of Maimed Soldiers chose his company to supply prosthetics for wounded men. He was awarded a grant of $20,000 and got to work. By the time the war ended, thousands of amputee soldiers were sporting Hanger prosthetics.

STAND AND DELIVER

Hanger was just getting started: he married in 1873 and would father eight children. By 1888 his company had grown so large that he moved its headquarters to Washington, D.C., and then expanded into other cities. Hanger died in 1919. Today, Hanger Orthopedic Group, Inc. is a billion-dollar corporation that employs nearly 5,000 people and fits about a million people with new limbs every year.

A Helena, Montana, law prohibits dancing on a saloon table unless you're wearing 3 lbs. 2 oz. of clothing.

LASTING LEG-ACY

A lot has changed since Hanger's first articulated leg, but the goal of prosthesis design remains the same: to mimic natural movement as much as possible. The biggest difference with today's limbs is what they're made of. In fact, modern prosthetics look like something out of a superhero movie. Patients are fitted with space-age materials that are lighter and stronger than ever before. Robotic knees can anticipate where the wearer wants to go and help them go there. The next step in prosthetics, already underway, is hooking up people's artificial hands to their brains so they can open and close their fingers just by thinking about it. And stroke victims who have lost the use of their limbs are fitted with prosthetic exoskeletons that respond to their brain activity. This technology isn't cheap—a new limb will run you from $6,000 to upward of $70,000 for the really fancy ones. (Hopefully, as the technology improves, getting a new limb won't cost an arm and a leg.)

Mac Hanger III is proud that, thanks to modern technology, an amputee can come to his office with just a stump and leave with a new limb that same day. "As they get up on a prosthesis," he says, "particularly these new ones with more responsive technology, you can see hope return to their eyes."

*　　*　　*

WEIRD BROWSER EXTENSIONS

Add these programs to your browser. (It'll make surfing the web more fun.)

Twivo. This blocks mentions of your favorite shows on Twitter so you don't get them "spoiled" before you get around to watching them.

Millennials Begone. This extension replaces all instances of the word "millennials" with "pesky whipper-snappers."

Mustachio. It adds a large, cartoonish handlebar mustache to the faces of every photo you see.

nCage. It replaces all images with ones of actor Nicolas Cage.

Jailbreak the Patriarchy. It "gender-swaps" words. "He" becomes "she," "father" becomes "mother," etc.

AbeVigosaStatus. It keeps open a little window that tells you whether *Barney Miller* actor Abe Vigoda is alive or not. (As of press time, he is.)

Downworthy. This reduces hyperbolic Internet headlines into simple English. For example, "will blow your mind" is changed to "might mildly entertain you for a moment."

Upside Down. It makes everything upside-down.

Weird Animal News

This year's edition features incontinent crows, amorous eagles, bitey ants, and a crazy duck. Proceed with caution.

ROAD KILLER

R Motorists in Spring Hill, Tennessee, met with a gruesome sight on a Saturday afternoon in March 2015: dozens of dead birds littered a short section of North Field Lane. Feathers, blood, and wings were strewn all over the place; many of the birds had been cut in half. Who or what was responsible? Was it an airborne pathogen? An out-of-control drone? No, it was pizza delivery driver Russell Thomas. He was making a delivery in his brand-new white Kia when a flock of birds swooped down and flew head-on into his car. Carnage ensued, but Thomas still had a pizza to deliver, so he fled the grisly scene (which only became grislier as other drivers flattened more of the dead birds). Tennessee wildlife officials closed off the area for a short time and took samples for testing, but as of last report, they couldn't explain the birds' odd behavior. And neither can Thomas: "I was just a guy delivering pizzas and a freak thing happened!"

FERAL CROWS

In January 2015, hundreds of crows took up residence in the trees around the Monroe County Courthouse in Bloomington, Indiana, and started pooping all over the parking meters. Authorities tried using decoy owls to scare the crows away, but that didn't work, nor were the crows scared by the sounds of predator birds emitted over loudspeakers. The crows just kept on pooping. It got so bad that people had to park elsewhere to avoid the disgusting meters, which started eating into the city's revenue. Then parking enforcement manager Raye Ann Cox got an idea to recycle old road signs into barriers that could shield the parking meters. Result: each meter now has its own metal "umbrella." Sorry, crows.

FIXING NEMO

What would you do if your pet goldfish got cancer? Flush it? Not Janie Gordon. The Scottish woman paid £500 ($750) for a team of doctors (yes, a team) to remove cancerous tumors from her two goldfish: Star, who had a tumor on his eye, and Nemo, who had one on his back. "The difficult surgery," said a veterinarian spokesperson, "involved an exotic consultant surgeon, a vet keeping the goldfish under anesthetic, and a nurse monitoring their heart rates." Both operations were a success, and Star and Nemo are doing fine. When asked why she would pay so much, Gordon explained, "My daughter would have been distraught if anything had happened to the goldfish." (Her daughter, by the way, is 21 years old.)

QUACKTASTROPHE

Ducks are horrible pets, so says actress Angie Harmon (*Law and Order, Rizzoli & Isles*). One Easter morning, she let her kids take in three orphaned ducklings because they were "cute." But as Harmon soon learned, "They grow up and they become attack ducks." Technically, only one became an attack duck because the other two flew the coop. But the remaining duck, Dr. Nibbles, wouldn't even let the family go into the backyard without attacking them. One time Dr. Nibbles even tore Harmon's clothes off: "I was in a nightgown," she says, "and by the time I made it back to the house, I was in nothing. Like, nude. Naked!" (No word on Dr. Nibbles's fate.)

HE'S AN ANTEATER

Ever wonder what it's like to be a spiny anteater? Noting that the creatures can feed for up to 10 minutes while getting bitten by thousands of ants, a 27-year-old nature lover and thrill seeker named Andrew Ulces decided to try it...and film it for his YouTube channel. His only protection: a pair of nose plugs and earplugs. With cameras rolling, he lay down on the dirt with his face right on top of a ground nest and then started beating the dirt to upset the ants. Within seconds, his arms and head were covered by the biting insects. Ulces screamed in agony. His 10 minute attempt was cut short by about 9 minutes and 30 seconds when, still screaming, he ran away and jumped in a lake.

THE EAGLES' GREATEST HITS

In November 2014, a typical day at a Seattle, Washington, park turned odd when several people noticed something unusual—two bald eagles flying overhead appeared to be attacking each other. All of a sudden, the birds became entangled and spiraled down to the ground...together. They landed hard on an asphalt path—then they were motionless. A crowd gathered, but no one wanted to get too close to the two full-sized raptors. Seattle police officer Vanessa Flick saw the crowd and investigated, but she didn't know what to do either. A bird watcher at the scene said the two eagles "must be performing some kind of mating ritual." (He was right.) Officer Flick called animal control, but before they arrived, the two "erotically entwined" eagles got up and flew away...together. The crowd cheered.

Who Is "András Tamás?"

World War II ended in 1945…so how long do you think it took for the last prisoner of war to return home? A lot longer than you'd think.

THE PATIENT

In the summer of 1998 a Russian doctor (unnamed in news reports) examined an elderly patient at a hospital in Kazan, a city 450 miles east of Moscow. The man, who was admitted under the name András Tamás, had been an inmate in a psychiatric hospital in Kotelnich, 225 miles to the north. He was in Kazan for medical treatment because he was suffering from high blood pressure and had already lost his right leg to poor circulation.

Tamás was diagnosed as schizophrenic, and when the doctor examined him, he began mumbling. The attendants at the psychiatric hospital in Kotelnich had never been able to make sense of his mumbling. They assumed it was incoherent babble and part of his mental illness. But this doctor noticed something they had not: Tamás was speaking Magyar, or Hungarian, a language unrelated to Russian. The doctor was familiar with it because he was of Slovak heritage and had grown up near the Hungarian border. Tamás apparently spoke almost no Russian and didn't seem to understand the language very well either. The doctor suspected that he was a Hungarian citizen. But if that was true, what was he doing in a Russian psychiatric hospital?

LOST

Tamás, it turned out, had been an inmate at the Kotelnich facility for more than 50 years. After the passage of so much time, it's not even clear how many people even remembered that he was from Hungary. A check of archival records there filled out some of his biographical details: he'd been a private in the Hungarian army during World War II and had been captured by the Red Army in 1945. He spent two years in a prisoner-of-war camp east of Leningrad. When that camp closed in 1947, he and the rest of the POWs were loaded onto a train to be sent east to another camp in Siberia. The others made it, but Tamás never did. On the way to Siberia, he began to show signs of "severe psychosis," one report read, so the guards took him off the train at Kotelnich and left him at the psychiatric hospital there. He'd been a patient at the facility ever since.

WHAT'S MY NAME?

One thing the records did *not* reveal was Tamás's real name—something investigators discovered when they alerted the Hungarian authorities that a POW named András Tamás had slipped through the cracks and was still in Russia. The Hungarians couldn't find anyone by that name who was unaccounted for. And after more than half a century locked in a mental institution, "Tamás" could no longer remember his name.

In fact, he had trouble communicating anything at all: he was the only patient in the psychiatric hospital who spoke Hungarian, so no one could understand what he was saying. He'd never learned more than a few words of Russian, so he couldn't understand what other people were saying to him either. The man hadn't even been allowed to write: when hospital administrators saw him writing in a language they couldn't understand, they became suspicious and forbade him from writing again. What few books and newspapers were available to the patients were all in Russian. So were the radio and television programs. The man spent more than 50 years, from his late teens to his early 70s, completely cut off from the only language he understood and from anyone he could communicate with.

DISCHARGED

If you've ever applied for a passport, you know it seems like it takes forever to get one. And that's when the government knows who you are. How long would it take if they *don't* know who you are? In this case it took two years. In the summer of 2000 the man was issued a passport, released from the psychiatric hospital in Kotelnich, and allowed to return to Hungary, where he began a lengthy rehabilitation at the Psychiatric and Neurological Institute in Budapest. He was also fitted with a prosthetic leg (the first thing he asked for), a new set of dentures, and a hearing aid.

While the mysterious man recovered, a team of doctors and officials from the ministry of defense tried to figure out who he was. Now that the man was surrounded by people with whom he could communicate, the language skills he hadn't used since the late 1940s began to return. So did his memories: he was able to tell interviewers the town where he'd been born, where he went to school, and where he worked as a blacksmith's apprentice before being drafted into the army at the age of 19. He had a thorough knowledge of artillery pieces, indicating that he had likely served in an artillery unit. But for some reason he refused to describe his unit's insignia, which would have told interviewers which regiment he served in. And after years of not being allowed to write anything down, he still refused to do so.

These and other clues led the investigators to the region around the

---

The first letter from North America was sent from Hernán Cortéz to King Carlos I of Spain (1519).

city of Nyiregyhaza, 145 miles northeast of Budapest, and from there to the nearby village of Sulyanbokor. At long last they were able to identify the man by name: he was András *Toma*—not András Tamás. They were also able to track down his surviving family members—a half-brother named Janos and a half-sister named Anna. In September 2000, Toma traveled from Budapest to Sulyanbokor to be reunited with his half-siblings after 56 years apart.

Technically, since Toma had never been discharged from the military, he was still a soldier in the army and had in fact been serving continuously since 1944. The ministry of defense decided to honor him by promoting him to the rank of sergeant major before discharging him from the army (honorably) in a formal public ceremony. They also paid his salary for all the years he'd been away.

ONE OF A KIND

After Toma's visit with his family was over, he returned to the Psychiatric and Neurological Institute in Budapest to continue with his rehabilitation. His schizophrenia was mild enough that he didn't need to be institutionalized, and after his treatment was finished, he went to live with his half-sister Anna in Sulyanbokor. His remaining years were peaceful and likely filled with conversation, since he had a half-century's worth of catching up to do. He died in March 2004.

Toma's story ended happily enough, but the investigators who helped him get home were haunted by the possibility that there might be others like him languishing in psychiatric hospitals in Russia. A team of investigators searched other psychiatric facilities for other World War II POWs who might have fallen through the cracks. And that's where this story gets its second happy ending: at last report, they hadn't found any.

*　　*　　*

HYPOCRITE ALERT!

A 12-year-old Tampa, Florida, boy named T. J. Guerrero made the evening news in 2013 because of his lemonade stand. Reason: he was giving most of the proceeds to a local animal shelter. Everyone from city officials to the *New York Times* lauded the boy's efforts…everyone except his neighbor, Doug Wilkey. The 61-year-old actually tried to get the lemonade stand shut down because T. J. didn't have a license to operate the "illegal business." A two-year legal battle ensued, which brought even more attention (and donations) to the lemonade stand. Then an anonymous tipster suggested city officials check into *Wilkey*'s business practices. Lo and behold, it turned out that he was operating a financial services business out of his home…without a license.

Eight out of ten blind people suffer from insomnia. (Their circadian light/dark cycle is disrupted.)

Rest in Pieces

When people pass away and their remains are buried, we say that they are being "laid to rest." Unfortunately, that's not always the case.

JUAN PERÓN (1895–1974)

Claim to Fame: Three-term president of Argentina and husband of Evita Perón, subject of the Andrew Lloyd Webber musical *Evita*

Not-So-Final Resting Place: The Perón family crypt in La Chacarita Cemetery in Buenos Aires

Going to Pieces: On June 10, 1987, vandals broke into the crypt and made off with the hands from Perón's corpse, along with his hat and sword. Soon afterward, the leaders of Perón's Justicialista Party received a ransom letter demanding $8 million for their return, but the party refused to pay—and neither the hands, nor the hat, nor the sword were ever recovered. In 2006 Perón's body—sans hands—was moved to a new crypt in his former summer home, which is now a museum.

THE MARQUIS DE SADE (1740–1814)

Claim to Fame: French aristocrat infamous for his wild sex life and erotic writings (The word "sadistic" is derived from his name)

Not-So-Final Resting Place: The graveyard of the insane asylum in France, where he was confined for the last 11 years of his life

Going to Pieces: A few years after Sade was laid to rest, the grounds of the asylum were renovated, and in the process, his grave was exhumed. The doctor at the asylum, L. J. Ramon, took the opportunity to remove Sade's skull in order to study it. Ramon was a *phrenologist*, and believed that bumps and other features on a person's skull could provide insights into their personality. (He reported that Sade's skull showed "no excess in erotic impulses" and was "similar to that of a Father in the Church.")

Some time after that, Johann Spurzheim, one of the pioneers of phrenology, asked to borrow the skull and do his own analysis. Spurzheim promised to return it, but never did. The skull is believed to have been in his possession when he contracted typhoid and died in Boston in 1832. What happened to the skull after that is a mystery. All that survives today is a plaster cast Ramon made of the skull while it was still in his possession. Today the cast is part of the collection of a Paris anthropological museum called the Museum of Man. It's rarely on public display, but don't worry: Sade's descendant, Count Hugues de Sade, sells bronze replicas of the cast for $3,100 a pop. (He's also negotiating with Victoria's Secret to offer a line of Marquis de Sade lingerie.)

Athlete featured most often on the Wheaties box: Michael Jordan (18 times). Tiger Woods is #2.

JOHN MILTON (1608–1674)

Claim to Fame: English poet best known for his poem *Paradise Lost*

Not-So-Final Resting Place: Beneath the floor of St. Giles Cripplegate Church in London

Going to Pieces: Legend had it that Milton was buried in a vault beneath the church clerk's desk, but a century later the marker was lost, the desk had been moved, and no one knew for sure where the grave was anymore. When the church underwent renovation in the 1790s, authorities searched for his coffin and found one that they believed to be his. The discovery generated considerable interest, and the following morning, a few locals, including the church warden, a surgeon, a pawn-broker, and a coffin maker, went to the church and pried open Milton's coffin to get a look at the body before it was reinterred. But while they were looking, the raiders succumbed to temptation…and stole several pieces of the corpse, including some of the hair and most of the teeth, as souvenirs. Philip Neve, a barrister and admirer of Milton, was so disgusted by the desecration when he learned about it that he tried to buy back the pilfered parts so they could be reinterred with the rest of Milton's remains—but all he managed to find was a portion of the hair and a single tooth. The rest of the teeth, plus whatever else was taken, were never returned.

LUDWIG VON BEETHOVEN (1740–1814)

Claim to Fame: German composer

Not-So-Final Resting Place: Währing cemetery, northwest of Vienna, Austria

Going to Pieces: In 1863 Beethoven's body was exhumed and moved to a sturdier burial vault. While this was in progress, his skull was removed from the coffin so that it could be measured, photographed, and cast in plaster. No one knew it at the time, but a physician named Romeo Seligmann apparently pocketed two large pieces of Beethoven's skull along with eleven smaller ones. The theft wasn't discovered until 1888, when Beethoven was exhumed a second time to be moved to another cemetery, and his skull was found to be missing the pieces. The skeletal shards passed from one relative to another until 2005, when Seligmann's great-great-nephew donated them to the Center for Beethoven Studies at San Jose State University in California. The school has no plans to reunite them with the rest of Beethoven's remains.

Note: Beethoven's ear bones never even made it to his grave; a pathologist removed them from his skull during the autopsy, in hopes of using them to diagnose the cause of the composer's deafness. He never returned them; they have not been seen since.

Not-So-Easy Riders

A rider is the part of a performer's contract that includes a list of backstage demands. The promoter must provide these items, or the artist might not go on. Here are some real excerpts from real riders.

LADY GAGA: On her "Monster Ball" tour, she wanted her dressing room decorated with David Bowie, Queen, and Elton John posters, plus a "mannequin with puffy pink pubic hair."

ADELE: Even if you won free tickets to her concert, you'd still have to pay. Adele requires that fans picking up tickets they've won must make a $20 donation to Sands, a British infant-welfare charity. (She also wants a few packs of Marlboro Lights backstage.)

BEYONCÉ: Promoters must provide titanium drinking straws with which Beyoncé can drink a special alkaline water served at 69°F. Also: red toilet paper.

KANYE WEST: The chauffeur who drives him to the concert venue must wear 100 percent cotton clothes. "No man-made fibers."

SLAYER: The band requires "one hundred snow-white goats for slaughter," "a butcher to slaughter the goats," and "freezer bags and coolers to preserve the goat meat." (We assume they're kidding.)

BOYZ II MEN: When the singing group performs their hit "I'll Make Love to You," they hand out long-stemmed red roses to ladies in the audience. Promoters must provide the trio with six dozen roses free of thorns and leaves, separated into three equal bunches—one for each member of Boyz II Men. The contract rider includes a drawing to make sure promoters know what a long-stemmed red rose looks like.

ROLLING STONES: A backstage room for their snooker table.

MICHAEL BUBLÉ: The pop crooner is Canadian, which might explain why he asks for a "local team hockey puck" in his dressing room.

CARROT TOP: Backstage food and beverages are fine, but "please no carrot cake. It's still not funny."

HANSON: 1990s sibling performers aren't little kids anymore. Their rider requires that their dressing room have a cold case of beer—specifically, "Corona, Newcastle, Coors, or Fat Tire Pale Ale." But that's only if the group is playing an acoustic show. Oddly, if it's a traditional, plugged-in rock show, Hanson wants just a half-gallon of soy milk.

RUFUS WAINWRIGHT: "Hip gay magazines."

DANIEL TOSH: The comedian performs a lot on college campuses, which is why he asks to be provided with "a book you think Daniel might like to read."

MÖTLEY CRÜE: Several band members are recovering alcoholics, so they want a schedule for local AA meetings. Their rider also calls for a submachine gun and a jar of Grey Poupon mustard.

BRITNEY SPEARS: When the pop star played London in 2011, she asked for McDonald's hamburgers without the buns and a framed picture of Princess Diana.

GUNS N' ROSES: Singer Axl Rose demands a square watermelon, which is very hard to find outside of Japan.

EMINEM: Before a 2011 concert in Northern Ireland, he asked that promoters build a koi-filled wooden pond for him backstage.

BRANDON FLOWERS: The lead singer of the alternative rock band the Killers embarked on a solo tour in 2010. His rider included a precise schedule of jams for different days of the week. Sundays and Tuesdays it was strawberry jam; Mondays and Thursdays, apricot; and red raspberry was served on Wednesdays, Fridays, and Saturdays.

REO SPEEDWAGON: Apparently not partying quite as hard as they did in the 1980s, the arena rockers' rider requests Honey Maid Graham Crackers.

KANSAS: Also not partying quite as hard as they did in the 1980s, these arena rockers' rider requests a quart of prune juice.

JACK WHITE: The blues rocker requires guacamole backstage, specifically guacamole prepared fresh and with a recipe he provides. "Avocados cut in half the long way, remove the pit and dice into large cubes with a butter knife. 3 or 4 slits down, 3 or 4 across. You'll scoop out the chunks with a spoon, careful to maintain the avocado in fairly large chunks. We want it chunky."

Research shows: Partners with similar genes are more likely to have a happy marriage.

Choose Your Words Carefully

Uncle John can never remember without looking it up that Washington, D.C., is the capital, and the building where Congress meets is the Capitol. Here are some more word pairs that drive him crazy.

FLAUNT...OR...FLOUT?

• To *flaunt* something is to display it ostentatiously. When people flaunt their wealth, they are showing off to impress others or make them envious.

• To *flout* something, such as a rule or a law, means to openly disregard it, often in a mocking or contemptuous fashion.

PRESCRIBE...or...PROSCRIBE?

• *Prescribe* means to authorize or establish something as a rule or a guide, such as when a doctor prescribes medication to a patient.

• *Proscribe* means to forbid, denounce, or condemn. Example: Smoking is proscribed in most government buildings; if you want to smoke, you have to step outside.

ENORMITY...or...ENORMOUSNESS?

• *Enormity* refers to the large scale of something evil or morally wrong, such as the enormity of a murderer's crimes.

• If you're describing the giant size of something in a context where no negative moral judgment is implied, believe it or not, the correct word to use is *enormousness* (or, if that sounds too weird, *immensity*). Though it's common for people to use the word *enormity* in a neutral context—"the *enormity* of the task at hand," for example—purists consider this usage to be incorrect.

COMPLIMENT...or...COMPLEMENT?

• *Compliment* means to express praise or admiration.

• *Complement* means to add to something in a way that improves it, such as when an attractive scarf or necktie *complements* an outfit.

AUGER...or...AUGUR?

• An *auger* is a tool similar to a drill that is used to bore holes in wood, ice, dirt, or some other substance.

That's a relief! Lightning on Saturn is only cloud-to-cloud, never cloud-to-ground.

- *Augurs* were ancient Roman priests who studied natural phenomena (especially the flight of birds) for signs indicating whether the gods approved or disapproved of human activities. If such signs did not *augur well* for an upcoming battle, election, or some other planned action, it could be delayed or canceled until the gods were in a better mood.

ENSURE...or...INSURE?

- *Ensure* and *insure* are largely interchangeable. Both mean "to make certain that something will happen." Putting on a coat can both ensure *and* insure that you will be warm when you go outside.

- The words are not interchangeable where insurance policies are concerned: people can buy *insurance*, but they can't buy *ensurance*.

PRECIPITATE...or...PRECIPITOUS

- *Precipitate* can mean to cause something to happen suddenly or prematurely—the spilled drink precipitated a barroom brawl. It can also refer to rain.

- *Precipitous*, on the other hand, means steep. Example: In 2008 there was a precipitous drop in U.S. home sales.

DISCREET...or...DISCRETE

- When someone is *discreet*, they are being cautious and showing good judgment.

- When something is *discrete*, it is separate and distinct from other things. The individual pieces of a jigsaw puzzle, for example, are discrete objects that are placed together to complete the puzzle.

ADVERSE...or...AVERSE

- *Adverse* means "harmful, unfavorable, or inhibiting success," and is applied to situations or conditions. Prolonged drought, for example, has an *adverse* effect on crop yields.

- *Averse* means "opposing or having a strong dislike," and usually describes someone's attitude. A person's shyness makes them *averse* to reading their own writing aloud. (Note: Because the Latin origin of *averse* means "turn from," purists prefer "averse from," but "averse to" is more commonly used.)

COUNCIL...or...COUNSEL

- A *council* is a group of people who serve as administrators or advisors.

- To *counsel* someone means to give them advice or to recommend a course of action. In the legal profession, attorneys on opposing sides of a court case are called *counsels* for the prosecution and for the defense. The advice given can also be referred to as counsel.

Huh? Jelly doughnuts have fewer calories and less fat than plain glazed doughnuts.

The Department of Silly Measurements

You've heard of a "New York minute" and a "stone's throw"…but how about a "potrzebie"? Here are a few more strange units of measurement (and one very serious one) that you may not be familiar with.

THE SHEPPEY

Description: The shortest distance from which sheep can appear picturesque—or about ⅞ of a mile.

Explanation: Invented by Douglas Adams, author of the *Hitchhiker's Guide to the Galaxy* series, and British television producer John Lloyd, in their book *The Meaning of Liff*, a collection of fake—and funny—definitions of actual place names. (Liff is a village in Scotland.) They named the sheppey after the Isle of Sheppey, which lies off England's southeast coast and is famous for its picturesque sheep.

THE GARN

Description: A measure of space sickness, with one garn being the highest level of space sickness possible.

Explanation: Named after U.S. senator Jake Garn of Utah, who became the first sitting member of Congress in space, when he flew aboard the space shuttle *Discovery* in 1985. Garn, who had very little training prior to the mission, became violently ill from of the effects of weightlessness during the flight—so ill that people around NASA derisively created the *garn* measurement from his name. "Most guys will get maybe to a tenth garn, if that high," NASA scientist Robert E. Stevenson said in a 1998 interview. "The mark of being totally sick and totally incompetent is one garn."

THE SAGAN

Description: The sagan is a measure of quantity equal to billions and billions (or just a lot) of something.

Explanation: Invented as a humorous tribute to famed astronomer and writer Carl Sagan, who became a target of comedians in the 1980s for his frequent use of the phrase "billions and billions" to describe the vast number of stars, galaxies, black holes, and other cosmic objects in his television shows and documentaries. Sagan denies ever using the phrase, although he did use the word "billions" (and "millions" and "trillions") a lot. The joke started in February 1980, when Johnny Carson did a sketch impersonating Sagan, wearing a thick silver wig and corduroy jacket and used the phrase "billions and billions" several times, putting a comedic emphasis on the "b" in "billions". The *sagan* was invented with that in mind, and it became popular by the early 1990s. Sagan himself must have thought it was funny: his last book, published in 1997, is titled *Billions and Billions*.

THE POTRZEBIE

Description: A measurement of length equal to the thickness of issue #26 of *Mad* magazine (November 1955), or 2.263348517438173216473 millimeters.

Explanation: The *potrzebie* was invented for a piece in the June 1957 issue of *Mad* magazine, titled "The Potrzebie System of Weights and Measures," written by 19-year-old Donald E. Knuth (who, incidentally, went on to become a world-renowned computer scientist). Knuth got "potrzebie" from the magazine itself. *Mad*'s founder, Harvey Kurtzman, discovered it in 1954, in the Polish language section of an instruction sheet in a bottle of aspirin. (It's a form of the Polish word *potrzeba*, meaning "a need.") He liked the word so much, he used it in the magazine numerous times. (In the June 1954 issue, for example, an airplane in the background of a comic is seen pulling a banner with the word "Potrzebie" printed on it.) Knuth took the word, invented his potrzebie measurement system—and the rest is *Mad* history.

THE BARN

Description: A unit of area used in nuclear physics equal to 10^{-28} square meters, which is really, *really* small. It's a serious unit of measure with a funny story behind it.

Explanation: In 1942 physicists at Indiana's Purdue University were working on the Manhattan Project (the World War II project that led to the development of the atomic bomb) and needed a secret code word for the area of a uranium nucleus. The number is incredibly important in nuclear physics because it's fundamental to the math involved in creating nuclear reactions. They wanted a code name for it so they could write and talk about it without the risk of giving vital information to the enemy. At some point the physicists focused on the phrase "as big as a barn"—because uranium nuclei, while incredibly tiny, are actually huge compared to the nuclei of other elements. So the area of a uranium nucleus became known as a *barn*. The name stuck…and the barn is still a fundamental part of nuclear physics today.

Bonus: A millibarn, or thousandth of a barn, is called a *skilodge*. And a microbarn, or a millionth of a barn, is an *outhouse*. (Really.)

Return to Sender

Usually it's pieces of mail that are stamped "return to sender," but sometimes it seems like it's the mail carriers and postal employees who should be sent back from whence they came.

Mail Carrier: Joseph Brucato, a Brooklyn, N.Y., mailman

Accused of: Turning his apartment into a dead letter office (for letters that weren't really dead)

Details: Brucato came under suspicion in September 2014 when his supervisor noticed piles of undelivered mail in his car. (Brucato used a government vehicle on his route and wasn't authorized to carry mail in his own car.) More undelivered mail was found stuffed into Brucato's locker, and when postal inspectors searched his apartment, they found another 40,000 pieces of mail, some of it dating back to 2005. It took five postal agents five hours to remove all 2,500 pounds of mail from the apartment. They hauled away so much stuff that one neighbor thought Brucato was moving "and the post office was helping him out by lending him a truck," his landlord told the *New York Post*.

Canceled! Brucato was suspended without pay, arrested, and charged in connection with hoarding the mail. He was released on his own recognizance and told to "abstain from excessive alcohol consumption." If convicted, he faces up to five years in federal prison. (In 1989 a Pensacola, Florida, mail carrier was sentenced to a year in prison after 500,000 pieces of mail were found in his home and in the surrounding woods.)

Post Office Employee: Philip Dorsey III, chairman of the "Stamp Destruction Committee" for the Pittsburgh (Pennsylvania) General Mail Facility, and James Gall Jr., the facility's marketing manager

Accused of: Delivering old stamps—lots of them—to themselves

Details: When the price of a first-class stamp rose from 25¢ to 29¢ in 1991, demand for 25¢ stamps plummeted. Dorsey was in charge of destroying the unwanted stamps, but after an audit uncovered some irregularities, postal inspectors decided to search both men's homes. Result: they recovered $500,000 worth of 25¢ stamps that had supposedly been destroyed. A spokesperson for the Postal Inspection Service called the incident "by far the biggest theft by postal employees we've ever seen."

Canceled! Dorsey and nine other postal employees were fired, three

---

Sugar dust is combustible. In large quantities (like in a sugar factory), it can explode.

more were suspended, and Postmaster Donald Fischer was forced into retirement. (Gall chose to resign rather than be fired.) Dorsey was sentenced to 27 months in federal prison; Gall got 18 months.

Note: That incident wasn't the only scandal on Fischer's watch. In 1990 mail carriers continued to deliver mail to the mailbox of two elderly sisters, Evelyn and Clementine Rochester, long after they'd stopped bringing it inside. The mail piled up on the Rochesters' front porch for *seven months* before someone finally thought to call the police; that's when the decomposing remains of both sisters were found inside the house. The coroner was unable to determine a cause of death for either woman, but he did estimate the *date* of death to be late January 1990. How did he know? The oldest letters on the porch were postmarked January 29.

Mail Carrier: Thomas Myers, a mail carrier in Denison, Iowa

Accused of: Crashing his postal truck into a parked car, then leaving the scene of his "special delivery"

Details: In December 2005, Myers was delivering mail when he hit a parked car hard enough to do $5,000 in damage to the two vehicles. Rather than report the incident to police—as required by law—or notify his supervisors, Myers just finished his route. (That same morning, he'd been reprimanded for sleeping on the job. Myers blamed his sleepiness on medication.)

Canceled! Myers was convicted of failing to maintain control of his vehicle and was fired from his job. He got his job back three weeks later when his union filed a grievance, but a judge denied his claim for unemployment on grounds that he was "careless and had jeopardized the lives of others by continuing to drive after his accident."

Mail Carrier: An unnamed (but not un-photographed) mail carrier in Portland, Oregon

Accused of: Delivering a "parcel" of a personal nature to one of the homes along his delivery route

Details: Portland resident Don Derfler happened to be at home and (unfortunately) looking out the window in April 2011 when he saw the mail carrier walk into his neighbor's yard. Rather than deliver the mail, however, the carrier dropped something else off: "He started pulling down his pants and defecating," Derfler told a TV news reporter. "At that point I grabbed my camera and started to take pictures." The pictures soon found their way to TV and the Internet; by dinnertime the post office had quite a stink on its hands.

Canceled! The mail carrier was placed on unpaid leave while an investigation was conducted. Result: the carrier was...allowed to keep his job. (He was, however, transferred to a different route.)

Mail Carrier: Walter Earl Morrison, 20, a UPS worker assigned to the company's Phoenix Sky Harbor facility in Arizona
Accused of: Trading a rock he did not own for some plant matter he was not legally allowed to possess
Details: In 2014 Morrison was unloading packages from a cargo plane when he saw one that looked like it might contain some money. He took it and stuffed it under his shirt. Later, when he opened the package, he was disappointed to find out that it contained not cash but a gemstone of some kind. Morrison wasn't sure if it was real or not, but figured it had to be worth something, so he traded it for enough marijuana to make two joints.—about $20 worth.
Canceled: The gemstone did turn out to real. It was a diamond worth $160,000. When something that valuable goes missing, the police get right on the case, and with a little help from package-tracking technology they soon arrested Morrison, recovered the diamond, and returned it to its rightful owner. At last report Morrison was out of a job and awaiting trial on felony theft charges. (No word on whether he'll be charged with possessing the two joints.)

Mail Carrier: An unnamed "rogue postal employee" assigned to a delivery route in Dallas County, Texas
Accused of: Unauthorized use of the "Return to Sender" stamp
Details: The mail carrier apparently lacked either the interest, the energy, or the inclination to deliver all of the mail on his route: beginning in December 2013 the carrier would deliver *some* of the letters and packages, then stamp the rest "Return to Sender" and go home early. The post office might never have admitted the problem existed had some of the returned mail not been voter registration cards from the Dallas County Elections Office, causing nearly 400 registered voters to be stricken from the rolls. When voters were turned away from early voting in the 2014 Texas primary, they complained to the elections office, who complained to the post office. Only then did the post office fess up about what had happened.
Canceled! Because it considered the matter a "personnel issue," the post office would only say that the mail carrier had been fired and three other employees suspended. How long the mail was not delivered they would not say. (The elections office had to hire extra staff to sort through 90,000 voter registration cards and make sure no one else had been improperly stricken from the voter rolls.)

Ain't I Great?

Celebrities talk about their favorite subject: themselves.

"My music has shaken hands with the world—it's a beautiful disease, and I'm glad I got it."
—**R. Kelly**

"I think that's part of the reason I'm here. Not just because I'm talented, but because God has a purpose for me to just help people."
—**Justin Bieber**

"My hero is me."
—**Gene Simmons**

"Even as a kid I always had eyes on me, like bees on honey. I was always outrageous and I was always very smart."
—**Lady Gaga**

"Part of the beauty of me is that I'm very rich."
—**Donald Trump**

"I'm like a vessel, and God has chosen me to be the voice and the connector."
—**Kanye West**

"We are bigger than Jesus. We will be as big as the Beatles, if not bigger."
—**Liam Gallagher of Oasis**

"I feel safe wearing white because, deep down inside, I'm an angel."
—**P. Diddy**

"My baby is already more famous than you will ever be."
—**Kim Kardashian**

"Your father's the biggest movie star in the world, and you're struggling in this extreme shadow."
—**Will Smith, on what it's like to be his son Jaden**

"I'm tired of pretending I'm not special—of pretending I'm not a total bitchin' rock star from Mars. People can't figure me out. You can't process me with a normal brain."
—**Charlie Sheen**

"I'm a walking art piece, just a ball of creativity."
—**Chris Brown**

"I have a high self opinion. I don't need to hide that. I don't need to be self-depreciating."
—**Adam Levine**

"I am God, and my lawyers are my 12 disciples."
—**Courtney Love**

"Sometimes I wish I was the weather. You'd bring me up in conversation forever. And when it rained, I'd be the talk of the day."
—**John Mayer**

Weird Body Parts of the Rich & Famous

What do Mark Wahlberg and the three-nippled bandicoot of Borneo have in common? Both have three nipples. (That's probably where the similarity ends, though.) Wahlberg has a small extra—or supernumerary—one, a few inches below his left nipple. "I won't get that thing removed," he told Rolling Stone *magazine. "It's my prized possession." Here are a few more stars with anatomical oddities.*

DENZEL WASHINGTON: In 2004 a photo of Washington gesturing to fellow star Meryl Streep went viral online—because something looked freakishly wrong with the pinky finger on his right hand: it was bent at a 45-degree angle. The star explained in subsequent interviews that he broke the finger playing football as a young man, and it had never been completely fixed. Most of the time it's straight, and fairly normal looking—which is why you don't see it oddly bent in movies—but it pops out sometimes, like it did just before someone snapped that photo. (Washington says his kids sometimes ask him to show their friends his "magic finger.")

MATTHEW PERRY: Look closely in *Friends* episodes, or in Perry's films and interviews, and you'll notice that the middle finger on his right hand looks kind of like part of it has been lopped off. That's because it was. Perry lost part of the body part as a little boy when his grandfather accidentally slammed the finger in a car door.

JENNIFER GARNER: Garner has a condition known as *brachymetatarsia*, in which one or more of the long bones in the foot are abnormally short, making the foot look somewhat disfigured. The condition usually affects the fourth metatarsal (and it's more common in women than men), but in Garner's case, it's the fifth metatarsal—the baby toe—on her right foot. Result: Her baby toe sits well behind her other toes, and above the base of the toe next to it.

TAYE DIGGS: The *Private Practice* star doesn't have any odd anatomical features today, but he used to. In a 2012 interview he revealed that he was born with twelve fingers—six on each hand. Doctors asked his mother if she wanted the extra digits to stay or go—and she chose to have them removed. Diggs said it was too bad, explaining "I could have been really handy." (Get it? *Handy?*)

Too bad you can't sue: On average, 54% of the money awarded by courts goes to cover legal fees.

KE$HA: When the pop singer most famous for the song "TiK ToK" was born, she had a hint of a vestigial tail. She told the magazine *Heat* that it "was a tiny tail, about a quarter of an inch. Then they chopped it off."

STEPHEN COLBERT: The talk show host had surgery to remove a tumor in his right ear when he was a kid, and it left him not only deaf in that ear but also with the ear noticeably disfigured—it sticks out much farther than his left ear. On a 2012 episode of the *Late Show with David Letterman*, Colbert demonstrated a "stupid human trick" in which he folded his ear in on itself, then freed it by winking. (Stupid…but funny.)

VINCE VAUGHN: Vaughn mangled his right thumb in a car wreck when he was 17. "I had the skin ripped off the back part of my thumb," he explained in a 2007 interview with the U.K. tabloid, the *Sun*. "The length of my thumb is the same but the back pad got ripped off." He added that the thumb now looks like a "penis with a fingernail."

DAN AYKROYD: The comedian and actor has a condition called *syndactyly*. That means he has webbed toes.

KATE BOSWORTH: The star of *Blue Crush* and *Superman Returns* has a rare condition called *heterochromia*. That means her eyes are two different colors: her left eye is blue, and her right eye is brown.

KAROLINA KURKOVA: Images of the Czech supermodel often show her with a normal belly button—but that's the result of some careful image altering. In fact, Kurkova has no navel because of surgery she had when she was an infant; she has just a small, smooth indent where her navel used to be.

MEGAN FOX: The *Transformers* star has what's medically known as *brachydactyly type D*, a genetic trait colloquially known as "clubbed thumb," resulting in one or both thumbs being abnormally short and wide, with short and wide nails. Or, as Fox told Jay Leno in 2012, her thumbs are "weird and really fat." She added that she blames her condition on her mom who ate lots of mercury-laden tuna when she was pregnant with her. (We're pretty sure she was joking.)

HARRY STYLES: Mark Wahlberg may have three nipples, but that's nothing compared to One Direction sensation Harry Styles, who has *four* nipples. Styles has small extra nipples below both his left and right nipples. "I must have been a twin," he said in April 2014, "but the other one went away…and left its nipples behind."

Arthur Conan Doyle, creator of the rational detective Sherlock Holmes, was a devoted spiritualist.

"Don't Buy My Book"

Just as Uncle John would rather not discuss his 1985 publication
"My Secret Life as a Fonzie Impersonator," here are the stories
of some famous authors who came to hate their own books.

VIRGIL. The ancient Roman poet's epic poem *Aeneid*, written between 29 and 19 BC, recounts the travels and deeds of the hero Aeneas. It is considered one of the most influential works of literature ever written—and we're lucky it made it past Virgil himself. Reason: the story was meant to be a serious history of the Romans, but in his final years, Virgil came to believe that he'd gotten much of it wrong, and he tried to fix it. On his deathbed, in 19 BC, feeling he had failed in his attempt to repair the work, he demanded that the manuscript be burned. Fortunately, that demand was refused—some say by Roman emperor Augustus himself—and the rest is literature history.

NATHANIEL HAWTHORNE. In 1828 Hawthorne, then 24 years old, paid a Boston printer $100 to publish his first novel, *Fanshawe*, based on his years as a student at Bowdoin College in Maine. The book, which was published anonymously, didn't do well. Dejected, Hawthorne burned all the unsold copies. Years later, after the success of such works as *The Scarlet Letter* (1850) and *The House of the Seven Gables* (1851), Hawthorne came to be embarrassed by his early work. He swore his friends to secrecy about its authorship and never even told his wife about the book. (She found out about it only after he died.) Hawthorne tried to track down every copy of the book—so he could destroy them— but he failed, and *Fanshawe*, now considered the first in what later became the "campus novel" genre, is still available today.

FRANZ KAFKA. Kafka is considered one of the most influential writers in modern history, which makes it all the more remarkable that most of his work was published against his wishes. By the time Kafka died in 1924, at the age of 40, only a small number of his writings had been published, and he left all his unpublished manuscripts—thousands of pages worth—to his best friend, Max Brod. In his will, Kafka instructed Brod to destroy every last scrap of them. Thankfully, Brod ignored his friend's wishes and started making plans to have the works published—which is the only reason the world is now familiar with such Kafka masterpieces as *The Trial*, *The Castle*, *Amerika*, and several collections of short stories, personal diaries, and letters. (Scholars believe Kafka, who suffered from depression for much of his adult life, burned most of his writings himself—perhaps as much as 90 percent of his total output—before leaving what remained to Brod.)

STANISLAW LEM. Polish science-fiction master Lem is best known for his 1961 novel *Solaris*, which has been adapted into film several times. *The Astronauts*, written 10 years earlier, was his first novel, and although it made him famous, Lem came to hate it. It was written during an era of oppressive Soviet rule. To get it past the censors, Lem was forced to make hundreds of revisions, and the book became overtly pro-communist. (It takes place in a fictional 2003, when communism has conquered the world and made everyone happy and free.) "Today," Lem wrote years later, "I am of the opinion that my first novels lack any value (despite the fact that I gained world acclaim through their numerous editions)." About *The Astronauts* in particular, he wrote, "I am disgusted by this book." By the 1970s, Lem refused to allow further reprints of the book, and it is difficult to find copies today.

PETER BENCHLEY. The 1975 film version of Benchley's novel *Jaws*, about a shark that terrorizes a resort town, became so famous that the book is often overlooked. It was a huge success, spending 44 weeks on the best-seller list and selling more than five million copies before the film was even released. (It went on to sell more than 20 million copies in all.) But Benchley, while not disowning the book outright, later came to regret it because it gave sharks a reputation as wanton killers. "Knowing what I know now, I could never write that book today," Benchley said shortly before his death in 2006. "Sharks don't target human beings, and they certainly don't hold grudges." The regret spurred Benchley to become a dedicated ocean conservationist for the last decade of his life, and he even wrote several books about sharks in hopes of educating people about the mysterious—and not savage—beasts.

STEPHEN KING. The plot of King's novel *Rage*, which was first published in 1977 under the pseudonym Richard Bachman, centers around the story of an angry high school student who shoots a teacher to death. The book was reprinted in 1985 in *The Bachman Books*, a collection of four novels King wrote using the Bachman pseudonym. And King *really* came to regret writing the book when, in 1997, a 14-year-old student in a Kentucky high school shot eight of his fellow students, killing three of them. The student had a copy of *Rage* in his locker. It was the fourth occurrence of a student who was known to have read the book and taken part in a high school gun incident, though this was the only one that ended in deaths. The 1997 incident, King later said, "was enough for me. I asked my publisher to take the damned thing out of print. They concurred."

More than 60% of your body weight is water. Your blood makes up another 7%.

The Lost Leonardo

Only 15 paintings by the Italian Renaissance master Leonardo da Vinci are known to exist. But what if there were more…and what if Leonardo's greatest work—one that's been presumed destroyed since 1563—was safely hidden, just waiting to be discovered? Start looking.

THE BIG PICTURE

In 1503 the Republic of Florence (now part of Italy) commissioned Leonardo da Vinci to paint a mural in the Palazzo Vecchio ("Old Palace"), which housed the city-state's government. The mural was to be painted on a wall of the palace's Hall of the Five Hundred, the room where the city's 500-member grand council conducted its affairs. The city fathers wanted scenes of Florence's military triumphing over its enemies, so Leonardo painted the Battle of Anghiari, in which Florence and its allies defeated Milan in June 1440.

Typically, murals on walls were painted using the *fresco* technique: dry pigments were mixed with water and brushed into wet plaster as the wall was being built. Frescoes can be spectacular, but they come at a cost: the artist must paint quickly, before the plaster dries, and he cannot revise his work because once the pigments have soaked into the plaster, they can't be removed or painted over. And the choice of colors is limited, because lime contained in the plaster bleaches many types of pigments. Only pigments that are resistant to chemical bleaching can be used.

SOMETHING NEW

Leonardo didn't want these restrictions, so he decided to experiment with a new and untested technique of mural painting. He used oil paints, which are normally used on canvas, and got them to stick to the wall by treating the plaster surface with a preparation containing some kind of waxy substance, probably beeswax.

The oil paints went on well enough, but they didn't dry quickly enough to prevent dripping (perhaps because Leonardo used too much wax), so he brought in *braziers* (charcoal stoves) to get the paint to dry more quickly. Bad idea: instead of drying the paint, the heat melted the wax, causing even more damage. Leonardo was so discouraged that he abandoned the project entirely. Instead of getting a battle scene playing out across the entire expanse of wall, all the city fathers got for their money was the centerpiece: a 15-by-20-foot depiction of a few soldiers on horseback fighting over a battle flag, and a few others battling it out on foot.

ANATOMICALLY CORRECT

For all its flaws, the drippy, melted, and unfinished painting was a sight to behold, thanks to Leonardo's obsession with presenting human and animal anatomy as accurately as possible. Over the course of his lifetime, Leonardo dissected more than 30 executed criminals and medical cadavers, plus countless frogs, pigs, dogs, cows, horses, bears, and other animals. When he performed his dissections, he took exhaustive notes and made minutely detailed sketches of what his scalpel revealed so that he could use them in his art. His sketches of the human body are considered the first medically accurate drawings ever made.

All this attention to detail paid off: many Renaissance artists considered *The Battle of Anghiari* Leonardo's finest painting, quite a compliment considering that he also painted *The Last Supper* and the *Mona Lisa*. For decades afterward, people made special trips to the Palazzo Vecchio just to look at the mural, both to study the poses of the soldiers and the expressions on their faces, and especially to look at the horses. The startling realism of the giant creatures was so inspiring to other artists that many of them made copies of the scene, no doubt hoping that some of Leonardo's genius would rub off. The most famous copy—actually believed to be a copy of a copy—is a drawing made by the Flemish painter Peter Paul Rubens in 1603. Today it hangs in the Louvre.

GOING...GOING...GONE?

It's a good thing that Rubens and others made copies, because they may be the only surviving record of what Leonardo's version looked like. When the Hall of the Five Hundred was enlarged and remodeled in 1563 by an architect and painter named Giorgio Vasari, the walls were painted with new battle scenes, this time with frescoes painted by Vasari. In the process, every trace of Leonardo's masterpiece vanished. No record of what happened to *The Battle of Anghiari* survives—for that matter, no one even knows for certain on which wall it was painted. It was assumed that the painting was destroyed during the renovations.

BEHIND THE SCENES

In the late 1960s, an Italian art historian and da Vinci expert named Carlo Pedretti proposed a different theory: maybe *The Battle of Anghiari* was still intact and still in the Hall of the Five Hundred, only covered up (and, hopefully, preserved) during the renovations of 1563. In his 1968 book *The Unpublished Leonardo*, Pedretti cites the examples of two churches and one courtroom in Florence that Vasari was hired to renovate in the 1500s. In all three cases, rather than destroy the existing artwork, Vasari protected existing frescoes by building new walls just an inch or so in front of the old ones. He likely made no secret of what he was doing, but he apparently made no record of it either, and over the centuries, all knowledge of the inner walls and the artwork they still concealed was forgotten. The frescoes remained safely hidden away for hundreds of years until they were rediscovered during new renovations in the 1800s.

Was it possible that Vasari had done the same thing with *The Battle of Anghiari?* Pedretti thought so. In the mid-1970s he conducted a study of the Hall of the Five Hundred. Based on historical evidence and a thorough physical examination of the hall, he concluded that *The Battle of Anghiari* had been painted on the east wall of the room, where a Vasari fresco commemorating the Battle of Marciano of 1554 is today.

THE VASARI CODE?

It was during that same survey of the hall that an assistant of Pedretti's named Maurizio Seracini noticed something unusual: near the top of the Battle of Marciano fresco, some 40 feet up, where no one at ground level would ever see it, the words *cerca trova* ("seek, and you shall find") are painted in tiny, faint lettering on a small green battle flag. These are the only words painted on any of the Vasari frescoes in the Hall of the Five Hundred.

Seracini believes the words are a message from Vasari: that the Leonardo painting is behind the Battle of Marciano fresco, right where Pedretti theorized it would be. But neither of the men could do much about it in the 1970s because the Vasari frescoes are themselves Renaissance masterpieces, and at the time, there was no technology available that would have allowed them to look behind the Vasari without damaging it. In 1977 their work came to a halt.

By the year 2000, new technologies such as laser scanning, thermal imaging, and ground-penetrating radar (and computers powerful enough to process the resulting data) made it possible for Seracini to resume the search. It was suddenly possible for him to see where doors and windows had been bricked up during the 1563 renovation and the original height of the ceiling before it was raised. In 2002 something even more significant was discovered: the existence of a half-inch air gap behind the east wall, and the presence of another, older wall right behind it—just as Pedretti had predicted there would be.

SO CLOSE...

Once again, Seracini bumped up against the limits of technology. His devices enabled him to detect the presence of the hidden wall, but there was no way for him to tell what, if anything, was painted on it. It wasn't until 2005, when some physicists at a scientific conference told him that it should be possible to build a "gun" that shoots gamma rays (similar to X-rays) onto the hidden wall without damaging either Vasari's fresco or Leonardo's mural, if it really is painted on the wall beneath. The subatomic particles that bounce back, called neutrons, could then be analyzed for signatures of specific paints and pigments that Leonardo is known to have used. Bonus: the gamma ray gun offered the possibility of even producing an image of any artwork painted on the inner wall.

But there was a catch: no such gun existed as yet, and it was estimated that developing one was going to cost more than $2 million, money that Seracini did not have and was unable to raise. Even worse, though the gamma ray technology was demonstrably safe and harmless to both paintings and humans, shooting a ray gun at a Renaissance masterpiece certainly didn't *sound* harmless, and the Florence authorities balked at the idea.

HOLE IN THE WALL

Having exhausted all noninvasive technology options, in 2011 Seracini decided to use *minimally* invasive techniques instead. Working with restorationists who were repairing damage to the Vasari fresco, he sought permission to drill tiny holes into areas of the fresco where no original paint remains, thereby sparing the work from damage. The holes would be barely a tenth of an inch in diameter, just large enough for a medical device called an *endoscope* to be poked through the holes to see what's painted on the inner wall.

Seracini wanted permission to drill 14 holes but only received permission to drill seven. In the end, he only drilled six. None of the holes were located in areas that he felt offered the most promise, and only two even made it into the air gap between the two walls. Of these two, only one produced any evidence at all, but the evidence was compelling nonetheless: tiny samples of paint taken from the inner wall showed evidence of two pigments, one brown and one black, that Leonardo is known to have used in his painting. When compared with similar pigment used by Leonardo to paint both the *Mona Lisa* and a painting of St. John the Baptist, the sample of black pigment was found to contain the same proportions of iron and manganese oxide.

THE END?

And that's where the hunt for the lost Leonardo stands today. Drilling holes into the Vasari fresco, even into cracks and other places where there isn't any original paint remaining, proved so controversial that the hunt for the lost Leonardo was suspended in September 2012, perhaps for good. Unless Seracini comes up with the money for the gamma ray gun and gets permission to use it, that may be as close as we ever get to finding out if the painting really is where he thinks it is. More than 30 years into the search, he isn't giving up: "I still have the same passion. I don't want to quit now," he says. "I'm so close."

The West African saw-scaled viper is responsible for more human deaths than any other snake.

For Your Infra-Mation

When you open your garage or change your TV channels with a remote control, you are using a ray of invisible light called infrared.

NOW YOU SEE IT...

By 1782 the British astronomer Sir William Herschel was already famous for his discovery of the planet Uranus. Eighteen years later he turned his attention to the study of light. Shining a focused beam of sunlight through a glass prism, he saw, as Sir Isaac Newton had first noticed a century before, that the beam separated into the familiar spectrum of seven colors we see in a rainbow: red, orange, yellow, green, blue, indigo, and violet. What Herschel wondered was: did each different band of color shining through the prism also emit a different temperature?

To find out, Herschel conducted an experiment. First, he painted the bulbs of thermometers black so they would absorb more heat. Then he placed one thermometer on each color of the spectrum. He discovered that each color did indeed have its own temperature, and the closer he got to the color red, the hotter it was. He then set a thermometer just beyond the red beam where there appeared to be no light at all. Herschel was amazed to find that this area had the highest temperature of all. After more tests, Herschel concluded there must be a band of light the human eye could not see. He called it infrared—*infra* being Latin for "below." But after Herschel's discovery of the temperature of light waves, it took more than 150 years for science to make use of this knowledge. Here are a few of its modern uses.

• **DOCTOR'S ORDERS.** In 1961 British doctors found that breast cancer tumors were warmer than the rest of the body. This led to the development of the infrared camera, or *thermograph*, which can detect changes in body temperature. The thermograph (it looks like a hand-held camcorder) is now widely used for diagnosing cancers and allergies, spotting bruises hidden below the skin, and measuring the depth of burns. It can also detect certain types of strokes before they occur. During the 2009 swine flu pandemic, thermographs were used by airport security to detect passengers who were carrying the H1N1 virus.

• **LIGHTEN UP.** The uses for infrared light aren't limited to medical diagnosis. The military uses night-vision goggles to observe people and animals in low-light situations without being detected. Police and SWAT units use infrared for surveillance and tracking a target in

Official government documents were once bound with actual red tape.

absolute darkness. Firefighters use infrared goggles to see in thick smoke, which helps them rescue people and find the source of the fire. Traffic cops use infrared-sensitive cameras to catch speeding motorists who have no idea they've been photographed until they get the ticket in the mail.

• **LITTLE PRINTS.** Forensics detectives examine crime scenes with infrared cameras to see heat "fingerprints" left by people, plants, animals, and electrical devices. Infrared devices can detect when a computer that's been shut down was last used. An infrared camera can even detect soil, blood, and fluids for hours after they have been removed.

• **GROWTH INDUSTRY.** Farmers use infrared photography to detect disease and insect infestation in crops. The Drug Enforcement Agency uses it to find illegal drug farms from the air. Marijuana plants are often hidden under other crops like corn, and at first glance are undetectable. But infrared imagery can clearly show the marijuana as a different color from the corn, making it relatively easy to sort out illegal drug growers from regular farmers.

• **REVENGE!** When Renoir created his famous 1881 painting of a gathering of his friends called *Luncheon of the Boating Party*, he originally painted Charles Ephrussi—wealthy editor of the *Gazette des Beaux Arts*—looking directly at the viewer. But after an argument with Ephrussi, Renoir altered his painting to have the man's face turned away. How do art historians know this? Infrared photography revealed the original painting beneath the visible layer.

• **THE HEAT IS ON.** Infrared cameras detect heat leaks in homes, check for overheating in electrical instruments, and detect motion in burglar alarms. They have even been used to ensure that clothing designed for polar climates is free of any heat leaks. There are infrared saunas and ovens, and even infrared thermometers that measure thermal radiation emitted by the eardrum. Many household emergency kits include a lightweight silver "space" blanket that will keep the user warm by reflecting infrared radiation.

• **THE OUTER LIMITS.** Were Herschel alive today, the great astronomer would probably be most pleased by how his discovery has influenced the study of the universe. Astronomers now use infrared radio telescopes to peer into deep space and see what Herschel never could. Infrared rays can pass through gas and space dust, allowing cosmologists to see the formation of stars and galaxies. NASA used infrared measurements to determine whether the atmosphere on Mars would be safe enough for astronauts to land by parachute. (It's not: the air is too thin.)

Geardos & Woobies

Colorful language from our Armed Forces.

Chicken Guts (Civil War): The gold braiding on an officer's cuffs

Army Strawberries (WWII): Prunes

Speed Bumps/Crunchies (Afghanistan/Iraq): Tank drivers' term for foot soldiers

Beetle-headed (Revolutionary War): Stupid

Tonkin Gulf Yacht Club (Vietnam): U.S. Navy ships operating off the coast of Vietnam

Bubble Dancing (WWII): Washing dishes

CHU (Afghanistan/Iraq): Containerized housing unit, made from a shipping container; groups of them are called CHU Farms

Wet CHU (Afghanistan/Iraq): A CHU built for VIPs—it has its own bathroom

Waste of a Uniform/Oxygen Thief (Afghanistan/Iraq): A soldier who's absolutely useless

Sneaky Petes (Vietnam): U.S. Army Special Forces

Varsity/Jedi/Snake Eaters (Afghanistan/Iraq): U.S. Army Special Forces

Seeing the Elephant (Civil War): Experiencing battle

Break Starch (Vietnam): Put on a set of freshly washed and starched fatigues for the first time

Brass Hat (WWI): A high-ranking officer—they had gold-colored decorations on their caps

Geardo (Afghanistan/Iraq): A soldier who spends too much money on fancy military gear; rhymes with "weirdo"

Yankee Peas (Revolutionary War): Buckshot

Canteen medals (WWI): Food stains on the front of a uniform shirt

Bohica (Vietnam): An undesirable assignment—short for "bend over, here it comes again"

Bedpan Commando (WWII): Medical corpsman

Rest Camp (WWI): Cemetery

Snot Locker (Vietnam): Nose

Mitt Flopper (WWII): A yes man—they're always saluting

Christians in Action (Afghanistan/Iraq): The CIA

More people live in California than in all of Canada.

Shoddy (Civil War): Cheap fabric made from waste wool; uniforms made of shoddy fell apart quickly, and the term eventually came to apply to anything poorly made

Pals Battalions (WWI): Soldiers from the same town who trained together and served in the same units

Bumblebees (Civil War): Flying bullets—they make a buzzing sound as they whiz past your head

Whiskey Tango Foxtrot (Afghanistan/Iraq): The phonetic alphabet equivalent of "WTF?!"

Cold Meat Ticket (WWI): The British equivalent of a dog tag; soldiers were issued two: if they died in battle, one was removed and the other remained with the body so that it could be identified

Penguin/Dodo (WWII): A Army Air Corps cadet who hasn't learned how to fly

Moaning Minnie (WWI): Noisy shells fired from a German trench mortar called a *minenwerfer*

Land Ship (WWI): A tank

Wallpapered (Civil War): Drunk

Comic books (Vietnam): Maps

DBIED (Afghanistan/Iraq): Donkey-borne improvised explosive device

Corn Plaster Commando (WWII): An infantryman

Woobie (Afghanistan/Iraq): An insulated blanket that doubles as a poncho liner—"without it, you woobie cold"

Snoop and Poop (Vietnam): A search-and-destroy mission

Pump Ship (WWI): To pee

40 Dead Men (Civil War): A box of 40 cartridges

Cook-off (Vietnam): A machine gun so hot that it ignites the powder in a cartridge and the gun fires even if the trigger isn't pulled

Hospital Rat (Civil War): A soldier who is faking illness or injury to avoid combat

Chin-strapped (WWI): So exhausted that the only thing holding you up is the chinstrap on your helmet

*　　*　　*

"It's a short time on this planet. It's a date, and then a hyphen, and then another date. And we're the hyphen."

—**Craig Ferguson**

According to research, listening to sad songs can improve your mood.

The Magic Kingdoms

Random facts about the happiest places on Earth: Disneyland and Walt Disney World.

• Walt Disney hated seeing chewing gum on the ground, so he prohibited Disneyland and Disney World from selling it.

• In fact, Disney didn't want any garbage on the ground at all. So before Disneyland opened, he had planners study families at other parks. They found that if people had to walk more than 30 feet to find a trash can, they just threw the garbage on the ground. Result: you're never more than 30 feet from a trash can in Disney parks.

• Only times Disneyland has shut down unexpectedly: the national day of mourning for President John F. Kennedy (1963), after the Northridge earthquake (1994), and on September 11, 2001.

• About 21,000 people work at Disneyland; about 50,000 work at Disney World.

• Number of visitors to Disney World per day in 1971: 10,000. Today: about 50,000.

• Ever hear a Disney park employee say "Code V" into a walkie-talkie? They're letting a cleanup crew know that a park guest has vomited.

• Opening day adult admission at Disneyland in 1955: $1. At Disney World: $3.50 (1971). The rides cost extra. Today tickets are all-inclusive, and both parks charge the same admission: $99.

• Average number of sunglasses turned in to Disney World's lost and found every day: 200.

• Mission Space, a space simulator at Disney World, requires more computing power than NASA needed to operate the space shuttle.

• One of Disneyland's earliest attractions (1956–60): the "Bathroom of the Future," an exhibit sponsored by bathroom fixture manufacturer Crane Plumbing. It envisioned gold-plated bathtubs and bidets.

• Lots of kids have been to Disneyland, but three were actually born there.

• Sleeping Beauty's Castle displays a traditional family crest just above the drawbridge. That's the Disney family crest.

• The "Pirates of the Caribbean" ride at Disneyland contains a real human skull.

Why do sausages curl when you cook them? The casing shrinks when exposed to heat.

Only in Canada

Here are a few really weird news stories…
that could only have happened in Canada.

SNOWED IN

Nelson Rubia of St. Jude's, Newfoundland, got his snowmobile back from the mechanic in March 2015 and decided to take it for a test ride…only it hadn't been completely repaired. As Rubia attempted to cross a highway, the throttle got stuck and the snowmobile picked up speed. Rubia was thrown from the vehicle, and the snowmobile took off on its own, heading west down the Trans-Canada Highway, bouncing off the snowbanks on either ride of the road. Rubia, uninjured, called the police for help. They were unable to stop the snowmobile, which traveled 15 miles before it hit a snowbank, flipped onto its side, and died.

LIE-BRARY

Lucy Maud Montgomery's 1908 novel *Anne of Green Gables* is about a plucky 11-year-old redheaded orphan named Anne who charms a stuffy town on Prince Edward Island. It's a Canadian classic, and dozens of printings of the book, as well as numerous film and TV adaptations, have depicted Anne exactly the way she's referred to in the original: as an 11-year-old redhead. In 2013 a company called CreateSpace caused a minor uproar when it published a new version of *Anne of Green Gables* with a cover depicting not a redheaded child but a sexy blonde in her 20s.

GRIN AND BEAR IT

In March 2014, cab driver Mohammed Naim had just dropped off a passenger in a Toronto suburb when he spotted a bear. He immediately locked himself in his cab and called police. They quickly arrived on the scene and tracked the bear tracks…to the home of the man Naim had just dropped off. Bear attack in progress? Nope—what Naim thought was a bear was actually a 150-pound very shaggy dog of the Newfoundland breed. The dog's name: Bear.

LANGUAGE BARRIER

Canada is a bilingual nation, at least legally. Only 22 percent of the general population speaks French, but public signage must be presented in both English and French, a law fiercely enforced by the Office de Langue Francaise (French Language Office). In November 2014, the comedian Sugar Sammy paid for a series of ads in the Montreal Metro subway system that read, "For Christmas, I'd like a complaint from the Office de

La Langue Francaise." Because he didn't include the French translation, he got his wish. Sid Lee, the advertising firm responsible for the ads, was required to black out most of the sign's text so that it read, *Pour Noel, j'ai eu une plainte de l'Office de Langue Francaise.* Translation: "For Christmas I got a complaint from the Office de la Langue Francaise."

FOOT IN MOUTH

The signature cocktail of the Downtown Hotel in Dawson City, Yukon, is the Sourtoe. It's a tourist tradition to try the drink—a shot of whiskey with a leathery, black mummified toe in it. It started in 1973; the first toe was the detached frostbitten toe of a 19th-century fur trapper. Customers aren't supposed to consume the toe—only to let it touch their lips (the alcohol reportedly keeps it sterile), but some people have accidentally swallowed the toe. If it happens, the Downtown Hotel charges $500. The hotel has gone through two dozen old toes in the past 40 years and was down to its last toe. In 2013 a man named Josh (from New Orleans) came into the bar, drank a shot with the toe in it, swallowed the toe, slapped $500 on the bar, and left. The hotel is now running this print ad: "Got frostbite? The Downtown Hotel in Dawson City, Yukon, is currently seeking toes for its World Famous Sourtoe Cocktail."

FORT STONEWALLED

When the 2014 winter began, Yann Lefebvre of Beaconsfield, Quebec, promised his four kids that he would build them "the fort of all forts." He did. It was the size of a small house, with two snow couches and a snow coffee table inside. Neighborhood kids loved it, until the city government told Lefebvre in January 2015 that he'd have to remove it. Reason: it was blocking snowplow paths. "We're not against snow forts," Mayor Georges Bourelle told reporters, adding that technically, it was built on city property. Lefebvre had a party, during which he and friends tore it down and rebuilt it farther back from the road. (They invited the mayor, but he didn't show.)

ODD CANADIAN TAX RULES

• Benefits paid to Canadian war veterans aren't taxed, but benefits paid by Germany to former members of the Nazi Party living in Canada are.

• All cosmetic procedures are taxed, including nose jobs, botox, breast enhancement, and teeth whitening. Exceptions: "congenital abnormality, a personal injury, or disfiguring disease."

• When Canadians buy a new car, there's a hidden $100 fee buried in the cost—a tax on automobile air conditioners. (Hearses, ambulances, and motor homes are exempt.)

Aunt Gladys the Great

Uncle John's great-aunt Gladys likes to make people think she has psychic powers, but does she really? See if you can figure out what she's up to—is she a psychic, or just a trickster?

ONE...TWO...THREE...

O"It's a good thing that you're well behaved," Aunt Gladys said to me on my last visit. "With my psychic powers I can control your behavior and make you do anything I want. But since I like you, I won't use my power to make you do anything embarrassing…like maybe run up and down the street in your underpants."

"Listening to you talk about your psychic powers is about all the embarrassment I can take," I laughed.

"You don't believe me? Okay, smart guy," she said as she laid out 25 matchsticks in a neat row on the kitchen table in front of me. "Here's what we'll do: You pick up one, two, or three matches, it doesn't matter which," she said. "Then it's my turn. I'll pick up one, two, or three matches, whichever I choose. We'll take turns until all the matches are gone. The loser is the person who gets stuck with the last match. And I'll use my psychic powers to stick you with the losing matchstick every time!"

We played the game just as Aunt Gladys instructed. Each time I went first and picked up one, two, or three matches. Then Aunt Gladys picked up one, two, or three matches, the two of us taking turns until all the matches were gone. But every time, no matter what I tried, she stuck me with the last match! How did she do that?

MULTIPLICATION

"My psychic powers don't just work on humans, they also work on matches," Aunt Gladys said to me as she cleared away all but five of the matches and lined them up in a row, like this:

"I can turn these five matches into fifteen," she said. "And I'll do it without breaking them in half to make more matches." Then she did it, right before my very eyes.

"Now that's what I call match *shtick*," I said. How did she do it?

SUBTRACTION

"And now I will turn the thirteen into eight, using only this napkin," she said with a flourish, picking a white napkin up from the table. Impossible, I thought, but sure enough, Aunt Gladys turned the thirteen into eight. How did she do it?

CONNECTING THE DOTS

"I can also use my psychic powers to communicate with inanimate objects, such as these dominoes," Aunt Gladys said as she reached into her junk drawer and pulled out a complete set of 28 dominoes. She proceeded to dump them out on the table, turning them so that all the dominoes were facedown. Then she mixed up all the dominoes around with her hands so that neither of us could tell (or remember) which dominoes were which.

"I'm going to go into the next room and close the door," she said. "While I'm in there, I want you to turn the dominoes faceup and match them together to form one long row. If a domino has three dots at one end, for example, match it with another domino that has three dots at one end, and so on, until you've created a single row of dominoes matched end to end. Let me know when you're finished, and I'll use my psychic powers to hold a domino séance and ask the spirits how many dots are at each end of the row." With that, she left the room and closed the door behind her.

I did as she instructed—I turned over the dominoes and matched them together into one long row. When I was done, I saw that at one end of the row there was one dot, and at the other end there were four.

"I'm finished!" I told her.

"O, Spirit of the Dominoes," I heard Aunt Gladys say from the next room, with the door still closed, "how many dots are there at each end of the row?" She paused a moment, then said, "The dominoes have spoken. They say there is one dot at one end of the row, and four dots at the other end." She was correct! How did she do that?

Psychics will know this without being told...but for the rest of us: The answers to Aunt Gladys's puzzles are on page 509.

They Cheated!

Bamboozlers! Deceivers! Scammers! Double-crossers! Anytime there's a sports competition, you can be sure that somebody's trying to figure out an angle— some way to win without doing the work. Here are three such scoundrels.

SYLVESTER CARMOUCHE

Background: Carmouche was a jockey who raced out of the Delta Downs Racetrack in southwestern Louisiana. On January 11, 1990, he saddled up a below-average horse named Landing Officer for a race. It was extremely foggy that day; spectators could barely see the horses as they raced ghostlike past the grandstand.

Suspicious Activity: Carmouche and Landing Officer won the race by an incredible 24 lengths (192 feet), coming in just a second off the course's record time. But something seemed fishy. Officials reviewed video of the race and could only see eight horses running—and there were nine horses in the race.

Busted: Shortly after leaving the starting gate, Carmouche had pulled his horse up and stopped racing…and waited in a patch of heavy fog where nobody could see him. Then, when he heard the other horses coming around, he sprinted to the finish line way ahead of the pack, making it look like he'd won by a huge margin.

Outcome: Carmouche was banned from racing in Louisiana for 10 years but was reinstated in 1998 and earned more than $11 million in winnings before retiring in 2013. He never admitted to the cheating stunt, insisting that the horse had simply been very fast that day.

PAUL TORMANEN

Background: Tormanen, of Lee's Summit, Missouri, was an angler who regularly competed in professional fishing competitions and earned almost $60,000 in prize money between 2003 and 2005. In November 2005, he entered the Red River Bassmaster Central Open tournament near Natchitoches, Louisiana.

Suspicious Activity: Three days before the tournament began, another fisherman, Sam Huckabee, was practicing for the competition when he found a large live bass tied to a stump in a small lake in the contest zone. Sensing something fishy going on, the angler notified Bassmaster officials.

Busted: On the second day of the competition, Tormanen brought the fish he had supposedly caught to the weigh-in…and was arrested on

Wombat poop is cube-shaped.

the spot. How did they nab him? Acting on Huckabee's tip, Bassmaster called Louisiana Wildlife and Fisheries officials. They found Huckabee's fish, along with several others, and marked them by clipping their fins. When Tormanen showed up with the fish—boom.

Outcome: Tormanen admitted that he'd caught the fish in the days before the event and then planted them so that he could "catch" them during the event. Tormanen later pleaded guilty to contest fraud, was given a suspended jail sentence, fined $588, and banned from Bassmaster fishing events for life.

HARLEQUIN FOOTBALL CLUB

Background: The Harlequins are an English rugby team. In April 2009, they were playing Leinster, an Irish team, in the Heineken Cup, one of the sport's most prestigious tournaments. Late in the game, the Harlequins, down by one point, were desperate to get their star player, Nick Evans, back on the field—but they couldn't. Evans had left the game earlier because of an injury and, per the rules, wasn't allowed back in the game…unless somebody on the team experienced an injury that caused bleeding.

Suspicious Activity: With less than four minutes remaining, Harlequin player Tom Williams stumbled off the field with blood running from his mouth, and Evans was allowed back in the match. Leinster ended up winning 6–5, but the team complained to the league about the Harlequins' stunt anyway, and an investigation was launched.

Busted: The league made a determination that Williams had somehow faked the bleeding injury, and he was banned from rugby for a year. Williams didn't appreciate being the fall guy—so he started talking. Not only had he been instructed to fake an injury, he told investigators, but he'd been given a capsule filled with fake blood and told to bite it open to make it look like he was bleeding, just so Evans could reenter the game. And, he said, the team's director, rugby legend Dean Richards, had orchestrated the ruse.

Outcome: "Bloodgate," as it was called in the British press, became the biggest scandal in rugby history. The Harlequins were fined £258,000 (almost $400,000), and Richards was banned from the sport for three years. Two other team staff members were banned as well. (The investigation also found that the Harlequins had pulled off the fake blood cheating maneuver at least four times in previous matches.)

*　　*　　*

"Conscience is the inner voice that warns us somebody may be looking."

—H. L. Mencken

Love sick: Millions of bacteria are transferred in one kiss.

Want More Coffee?

Is it good for you? Is it bad for you? It's good and bad.

IT'S GOOD! A Dutch study found that people who drink two to four cups of coffee a day have a 20 percent lower risk of developing heart disease than those who drink no coffee.

IT'S BAD! The caffeine in coffee increases the activity of *catecholamines*, which are stress hormones.

IT'S GOOD! According to a Finnish study, people in their 40s and 50s who drink between three and five cups of coffee per day have a 65 percent lower chance of developing dementia and Alzheimer's disease later in life. (No such connection was found with tea.)

IT'S BAD! Caffeine stimulates the production of *cortisol*, which leads to general inflammation.

IT'S GOOD! In a study of women by the Harvard School of Public Health, those who drank four or more cups of coffee a day were 25 percent less likely to develop endometrial cancer, compared to women who drank no coffee.

IT'S BAD! Caffeine addiction decreases insulin sensitivity. Insulin is the hormone that processes carbohydrates and turns them into energy. Coffee makes it slightly harder for your body to process carbs.

IT'S GOOD! More than 1,000 different antioxidants (natural compounds that prevent diseases from taking root) have been isolated in unroasted coffee beans. A few hundred more develop during roasting.

IT'S BAD! Coffee is well known to cause stomachaches, and it can also lead to *dysbiosis*, or an imbalance of gut flora—the bacteria in your stomach that help digest food.

IT'S GOOD! *The Archives of Internal Medicine* published a study that found a decreased risk of cirrhosis among heavy drinkers who also drink coffee. Those who drank one cup regularly had 20 percent less risk. Those who drank four: 80 percent.

IT'S BAD! Coffee is a diuretic, which means it increases urine production. But when you excrete more urine, you also excrete more of minerals the body needs, particularly calcium, magnesium, and potassium.

Try it: Holding your pen a little more loosely will make your handwriting neater.

Mistakes Were Made

Here's what happens when companies and organizations get into trouble and then try to "PR" their way out of it.

FACE TO FACE

F In October 2014, the Swiss retailer Migros had to issue an apology after a customer in a railway station café discovered the face of Adolf Hitler printed on one of the company's dairy creamer packets. In Switzerland, the lids of the single-serving packets are decorated with sports cars, animals, landscapes, and other innocuous images; customers collect them. In this instance a series featuring 55 vintage cigar labels included one with Hitler's face on it and another with Italian dictator Benito Mussolini's.

Migros pulled the creamers from café shelves and apologized for not noticing them earlier. (Peter Waelchli, an executive with the company that supplied the images, defended the Hitler and Mussolini lids as "unproblematic" but conceded they might be disturbing to "certain people." Migros says it has severed all business ties with Waelchli's firm, which was facing bankruptcy without the Migros account.)

GLASS HOUSES

In 2015 Lego introduced a new character in its Mixels line of monster toys: "Turg," a yellow, one-eyed creature with a long red tongue. "Part frog, part chicken, part back-of-the-bus window-licker, Turg has the longest tongue of them all," the company said. No word on whether the higher-ups at Lego realized it, but "window-licker" is a derogatory term for children with learning disabilities, something that quickly became apparent when disabled people and their advocates took to social media to voice their complaints. "As a disabled person, I thought I was beyond insults but this is awful," one person tweeted. Lego pulled the offensive term from its website, apologized, and said that it was reviewing its procedures "to make sure this doesn't happen again."

THE OSCARS

Fresh on the heels of the 2014 scandal that denied critical medical care to veterans and forced the resignation of Secretary of Veterans Affairs Eric Shinseki, the VA became embroiled in another controversy when the *Philadelphia Inquirer* obtained internal training materials that belittled veterans. In an 18-page slide show titled "What to Say to Oscar the Grouch—Dealing with Veterans During Town Hall Claims Clinics,"

If your dog's paws smell like corn chips, that's a condition known as "Frito feet."

pictures of the *Sesame Street* monster who lives in a trash can were used with captions like "Don't Get in the Swamp with the Alligator" and "100% GROUCHY, DEAL WITH IT."

When contacted by the *Inquirer*, the Philadelphia VA office, which had presented the slide show to employees the week before, said it regretted any misunderstanding and had discontinued use of the slide show. "The training provided was not intended to equate veterans with this character," spokesperson Marisa Prugsawan told the paper. (The incoming VA secretary, Robert McDonald, ordered a nationwide review of training materials to ensure they're in keeping with "the kind of open culture we want in the new VA.")

COMING CLEAN

In August 2013, health officials in New Brunswick, Canada, publicly apologized after it was discovered that a women's clinic at the Miramichi Regional Hospital had been using unsterilized forceps on patients for 14 years. (The officials were careful to note that while the offending forceps *were* sterilized at the end of each day, between individual biopsies they were merely *disinfected*, which kills 99.99 percent of blood-borne pathogens…but not all of them. Sterilization kills 100 percent and has been the clinical standard in North America for more than 50 years.)

Nearly 2,500 patients who had biopsies performed at the clinic between 1999 and 2013 were offered blood tests to check for HIV, hepatitis B, and hepatitis C. Dr. Gordon Dow, an infectious disease specialist, said that while he expected some patients to test positive for the diseases "based on their prevalence in the general population," the likelihood that they contracted their diseases from the forceps was "very, very small…None of those people would have acquired their infection" from the forceps, he reassured the public.

SHE THREW THE BOTTLES, HE THREW THE BOOK

After two years of putting up with the same motorist tossing an empty iced tea bottle into his yard nearly every day, in July 2011 a Leavenworth, Kansas, homeowner named Gary Bukaty put a stop to the maddening behavior by photographing the tosser in the act and giving the photo to police. That's how Carole Green of Bonner Springs found herself in front of a judge, charged with four misdemeanor counts of littering. Perhaps hoping to get off easy, Green admitted guilt and apologized to Bukaty, explaining that she bore him no ill will: his yard just happened to be where she finished drinking her tea each day. She also explained that if she had it to do over again, "of course I wouldn't do it." (Apology accepted…but the judge still fined Green $1,200 plus court costs.)

Lincoln, Starring Liam Neeson

Some roles are so closely associated with a specific actor that it's hard to imagine he or she wasn't the first choice. But it happens all the time. Can you imagine, for example…

JOHN KRASINSKI AS STAR-LORD (*Guardians of the Galaxy,* 2014). More than 25 movies based on Marvel comics had been released since 2000, and the comics publisher had to dig a little deeper into its archives for new movie ideas. Result: *Guardians of the Galaxy,* a funny, quirky story about a ragtag team of intergalactic superheroes. For the lead role of Star-Lord, Marvel wanted a comic actor and offered it to Joseph Gordon-Levitt. But he passed on the role, so it came down to two stars of quirky sitcoms—John Krasinski (*The Office*) and Chris Pratt (*Parks and Recreation*). Pratt was chosen because he's more muscular. It was the second time that Krasinski was the runner-up for a Marvel movie—he lost the lead in *Captain America* to Chris Evans. (Same reason.)

JON HAMM AS NICK DUNNE (*Gone Girl,* 2014). Director David Fincher offered the role to his first choice: Hamm, star of the period TV drama *Mad Men.* Hamm was shooting the last few episodes of the series, and he was looking forward to launching a film career, so he accepted the part. Only problem: *Mad Men* creator and producer Matthew Weiner wouldn't rearrange the show's shooting schedule to accommodate Hamm's, so Ben Affleck got the role instead.

JULIANNE HOUGH AS AMY DUNNE (*Gone Girl,* 2014). After informing *Gone Girl's* producer, Reese Witherspoon, that she wasn't right for the role of the calculating, sociopathic killer, director David Fincher nearly cast Hough—best known as one of the professional dance partners on *Dancing with the Stars.* She's had a couple of parts in big movies (*Footloose, Rock of Ages*), but Fincher ultimately decided she was too inexperienced for such a complex role. British actress Rosamund Pike was ultimately cast, and she received an Oscar nomination for Best Actress.

HENRY CAVILL AS JAMES BOND (*Casino Royale,* 2006). After a half-decade break, the James Bond movie series geared up for a revival in 2005. First order of business: finding a new actor to play the role vacated by Pierce Brosnan. Dozens of British actors were rumored to be in the running for the role of 007, including Henry Cavill, who'd had roles in just four films at the time. Producers narrowed down the search to two actors: Cavill and British star Daniel Craig. At the time of casting, Cavill was 23 and Craig was 38. Producers decided they wanted an older Bond, and Cavill looked too young, so Craig got the part.

VANESSA WILLIAMS AS LETICIA (*Monster's Ball*, 2001). Williams is a very successful singer and actress, but she's still probably best known for having to resign her Miss America title in 1984 when graphic nude pictures of her surfaced. Ironically, she turned down the role of Leticia in *Monster's Ball* because of its extensive nudity and graphic sex scenes. "I just had a baby, and I was like, 'I am not getting naked in front of a crew of people at this time!,'" Williams said in an interview with Oprah Winfrey. The role of a depressed woman who strikes up a romance with a prison guard after her husband is executed for murder went to Halle Berry...who won an Oscar for the part.

LIAM NEESON AS ABRAHAM LINCOLN (*Lincoln*, 2012). Steven Spielberg spent years planning his biopic of Lincoln, focusing on the passage of the constitutional amendment that would abolish slavery. He hired noted historian Doris Kearns Goodwin as a consultant and Pulitzer Prize–winning playwright Tony Kushner to write the script. For smaller roles, he cast Oscar-winning actors such as Tommy Lee Jones and Sally Field. And for the daunting lead role, Spielberg chose Neeson, with whom he'd worked on *Schindler's List*. The cast got together to read the script in early 2009, but Neeson's state of mind was not good—his wife had tragically died a month before, and he didn't feel up to the role. "We started reading, and then I see 'Lincoln:' where I have to start speaking, and I had a thunderbolt moment. I've passed my sell-by date. I don't want to play this Lincoln. I can't be him." Neeson gave up the role, and Spielberg took three years to finish the film. *Lincoln* was released in 2012 starring Daniel Day-Lewis as Lincoln, for which he won his third Oscar for Best Actor.

JACK NICHOLSON AS MICHAEL CORLEONE (*The Godfather*, 1972). It's the defining role of Al Pacino's career. He played it three times over three movies, tracking Michael Corleone's journey from innocent to Mafia crime boss. But in 1972, Pacino was relatively unknown, and director Francis Ford Coppola wanted an established star for the lead role. Coppola offered the part to Nicholson, but Nicholson turned it down. He felt that an Italian-American actor should play such a quintessentially Italian-American character.

The Unfriendly Skies

If you're reading this on an airplane, we hope you can take comfort in the thought that even if your flight isn't perfect, you'll probably have a better experience than the folks on these flights did.

NUTS

One afternoon in December 2014, Korean Air flight 86 was on the runway waiting to take off from New York's JFK International Airport when it suddenly turned and taxied back to the gate. Often in such cases, the problem is mechanical, but this time it was macadamical: someone made the mistake of serving first-class passenger Heather Cho a bag of macadamia nuts. Company regulations require that passengers in first class be served nuts on *plates*—and Cho, the daughter of Korean Air chairman Cho Yang-ho and the airline's senior vice president—was so angered by the poor service that she ordered the pilot to taxi back to the gate so the offending crew member could be thrown off the plane. Flight 86 was delayed only 11 minutes, but the Korean press made such a stink about Cho's nepotistic "nut rage" that her father had to publicly apologize for "not raising her better." Then he had to fire her. Found guilty of violating Korea's Air Safety Law, which prohibits interfering with a flight crew, Cho was sentenced to one year in prison; the airline could pay up to $2 million in fines.

SHE SAID, SHE SAID

In March 2011, a California woman named Irum Abbasi was in her seat on a Southwest Airlines flight from San Diego to San Jose. Abbasi was talking on her cell phone, and because the plane was about to leave the gate, she ended the call, saying, "I've got to go." But a flight attendant thought she heard Abbasi say, "It's a go." That sounded suspicious, and Abbasi, an observant Muslim, was wearing a *hijab*, the traditional Islamic head scarf. The flight attendant alerted the TSA; three agents escorted Abbasi off the plane. After a quick interview and a partial pat-down, the agents concluded Abbasi was *not* a security risk but still wouldn't let her back on the plane—she made the flight crew "uncomfortable," they said. Abbasi was bumped to another flight, arrived in San Jose four hours late, and missed her meeting. At last report she was suing Southwest for discrimination plus "breach of contract, negligence, and intentional infliction of emotional distress." "This time they said they weren't comfortable with the head scarf. Next time, they won't be comfortable with my accent or my South Asian heritage," she said.

In 2011 thousands of turtle doves fell from the sky in Italy. Cause of death: indigestion, from overeating.

PIT STOPPED

In June 2014, Jennifer Devereaux and her three-year-old daughter were passengers on a JetBlue flight to Boston that was delayed for 30 minutes on the tarmac at JFK. The three-year-old had to go the bathroom, but the flight attendant wouldn't let her get up—FAA rules require passengers to remain in their seats after an airplane has left the gate, except in an emergency, and the flight attendant didn't feel it was an emergency.

Sure enough, a few minutes later the girl had an accident in her seat. When Devereaux got up to clean up the mess, the flight attendant reported her to the pilot, who returned to the gate so the "disobedient passenger" could be removed. So many outraged passengers came to Devereaux's defense that she and her daughter were allowed to remain on the plane. She later filed a complaint with the airline. After an investigation, JetBlue apologized and offered to donate $5,000 to the charity of her choice. Devereaux says she's satisfied: "It's about human decency," she told WBZ-TV. "My daughter was sitting in a pool of urine and I couldn't do anything about it. As a mom it just broke my heart."

HELLO? HELLO?

In 2010 a blind woman named Jessica Cabot boarded a United Airlines flight from British Columbia to Florida. She had to switch planes at Chicago's O'Hare Airport, and the flight attendants told her they would escort her off the plane as soon as everyone else had exited. "That's what they tell me every time, so I didn't think much about it," Cabot told Canada's CBC News. This time, however, after the last person left the plane, she heard the cabin door being sealed shut, followed by…silence. Cabot spent a terrifying ten minutes alone inside the locked and empty plane before a maintenance crew member found her and helped her off the plane. "They told me they had done their sweep of the plane and I was a tiny girl," the 5'3" Cabot told the *Vancouver Sun*. "Does that mean if you're short they're not responsible?" (She flew home on Delta.)

TOO FRIENDLY

When a passenger complained to US Airways via Twitter about a flight delay in April 2014, the airline tweeted back, "Please provide feedback to our Customer Relations team." In place of a link to Customer Relations, however, was a photo of a naked woman using a toy airplane in a way not intended by its maker. The airline quickly deleted the tweet and apologized to its 428,000 Twitter followers. An investigation found that another Twitter user had tweeted the offending image to the airline and when an employee tried to flag it as inappropriate, they accidentally included it in the reply to the passenger with the flight delay. So…was the employee fired? Nope: "It was an honest mistake," said a US Airways spokesperson.

The Only Two States...

What makes your state special? Possibly something
that makes one other state special, too.

...where you may not pump your own gas: Oregon and New Jersey.

...where casinos are legal statewide: Nevada and Louisiana.

...where you can't buy alcohol on Election Day: Kentucky and South Carolina (but sales in Kentucky resume after the polls close at 6:00 p.m.).

...where condemned death row inmates may be executed by firing squad: Utah and Oklahoma.

...where cheating on a standardized test is against the law: Oregon and Delaware.

...that don't allow religious exemptions for vaccinations: Mississippi and West Virginia.

...where it's never gotten really, *really* hot. Alaska and Rhode Island. Alaska is too far north (the temperature in Ft. Yukon, Alaska, reached 100°F exactly once, in 1915) and Rhode Island has a coastal, windy climate (Providence's hottest day on record: 104°F in August 1975).

...where farming is still the #1 profession: North and South Dakota.

...that Franklin Roosevelt didn't carry in the 1936 presidential election: Maine and Vermont.

...that were once sovereign nations: Vermont (1777–91) and Texas (1836–45).

...that prosecute 16- and 17-year-old criminal offenders as adults: New York and North Carolina.

...that require carbon monoxide detectors in public schools: Maryland and Connecticut.

...where dogs must be leashed when they're out of your home: Michigan and Pennsylvania.

...where the most popular red wine isn't Cabernet Sauvignon: Washington (red blends) and Oregon (Pinot Noir)

...of the greenery was thought to soothe their voices—hence the name "green room."

How to Use Your Watch as a Compass

Until you download that compass app for your smartphone, here's a simple trick to help you find your way around the woods.

WHAT YOU'LL NEED

W

An analog watch (the kind with hour and minute hands) set to the correct time.

A pen, pencil, or twig and a clear view of the sun.

WHAT TO DO

Poke the pen upright into the ground so that it casts a shadow.

Set the watch on the ground in the shadow cast by the pen.

Rotate the watch until the hour hand lines up with the shadow and points at the sun. (The shadow is cast directly away from the sun, so aligning the hour hand with it also aligns it with the sun.)

Note the angle formed by the hour hand and the 12 o'clock mark on the face of the watch. Now divide it in half to find the midpoint. Example: if it's 8:00, the hour hand points to the 8. The midpoint between the 8 and the 12 is the 10 on the watch face.

The line created by the midpoint number (10 in the example) and the number opposite it on the watch face (4) form a north-south line. If you're not sure which is which, remember that the sun is in the east before noon and in the west after noon. In this case the 10 points north and the 4 south, which means that east (and the sun) is at 1, and west is at 7.

TIPS AND TRICKS

Daylight Saving Time? From March to November, your watch is set an hour ahead, so find the north-south line by bisecting the angle created by the hour hand and *1 o'clock* instead of 12 o'clock.

South of the equator? Point the 12 at the sun instead of the hour hand and bisect the angle they create to find the north-south line.

Wearing a digital watch? A carefully drawn picture of a clock with the hour hand pointing to the correct time works just as well.

Weird Energy

Coal is sooty. Petroleum is becoming depleted. Fracking for natural gas is controversial. Wind and solar technology isn't developed enough to satisfy our energy demands. Isn't anybody coming up with new energy alternatives? Oddly enough…yes.

BODY HEAT

Cremation is an increasingly popular way of dealing with the dead—it's cheaper and more ecologically sound than traditional burials. In a typical crematorium, the furnace reaches a temperature of about 1,800°F. The deceased's body is reduced to ashes, but that's not the whole story. All the organic matter in the body, which is mostly water, vaporizes and becomes gaseous. Most nations require that the gases be treated before they're released. So the gases are passed through a cold water chamber, which cools them to 350°F, and then a filter traps any gassified toxins—primarily the mercury in tooth fillings. The gas is released into the air, but the water in the cooling chamber is now very hot and nonpotable because it had cremation gases passed through it. Solution: more than half of Denmark's crematoria send the water into municipal heating systems. It was a controversial plan, but the Danish Council of Ethics (a board of scientists and clergy) approved it, as did the International Cremation Federation. The key was that the energy is being donated—if the water were being sold, it would violate a 1937 treaty that bars crematoria from selling "residue of cremation." The plan went into effect in 2012, and the idea is spreading to other European nations. A low-income housing project in Paris, for example, is now heated with crematorium water, and a crematorium in England is using its wastewater to heat…itself.

SOLAR WIND

The sun is always going to shine (or at least it will for another billion years or so), which means solar power has the potential to be an infinitely renewable resource. But the sun provides another source of potential harnessable power in the form of solar wind. Solar wind is a high-powered stream of charged particles constantly shooting out of the sun. Brooks Harrop and Dirk Schulze-Makuch of Washington State University are the leading researchers on the idea, and they believe that a sun-orbiting satellite could be used to capture those beams of energy. Using onboard batteries (solar-powered) to run an electric charge through a copper wire, the satellite would generate a magnetic field that would in turn attract solar wind particles. The energy could then be

Gold has been discovered on every continent on Earth.

zapped to a receiver on Earth via an infrared laser. While all this sounds like science fiction, the principles are scientifically sound. The main problem Harrop and Schulze are trying to solve is how to aim and shoot a laser beam from the sun to the earth—a distance of nearly 100 million miles—without losing much energy. Harrop and Schulze think their technology could at least be used to beam solar wind energy to other satellites and spacecraft. How much energy could solar wind ultimately provide? One hundred billion times the planet's current power needs.

SEWAGE

You are practicing good hygiene when you flush your toilet. You're right to want to dispose of your body's waste products as quickly and efficiently as possible. But your poop might have incredible economic and environmental value. Feces are a key resource in obtaining methane, a natural gas that could be used for heat and energy like, well, natural gas. Park Spark in Cambridge, Massachusetts, along with Norcal Waste in San Francisco, is testing out pilot programs designed to extract as much usable methane as possible from (for now) dog poop. The companies provide dog owners with biodegradable dog waste bags. The doggies provide the waste, the owners fill the bags, and then the energy companies feed the bags into a machine called a "digester," where microorganisms process (okay, eat) the dog poop. The byproduct: methane.

ALGAE

One of the main obstacles in developing alternate energy sources is that alternatives are more expensive than oil. The fact that algae-based energy could be as cheap as petroleum might make it one of the more viable long-term options. Currently, crude oil is pumped out of seabeds, where it was created from heat and pressure, transforming algae and other microorganisms over the course of millions of years. Scientists at the U.S. Department of Energy's Pacific Northwest National Laboratory in Washington state have devised a way to re-create and speed up the process of turning algae into oil. If they scale it up to mass production, the lab estimates that it could sell this biofuel for about $2 a gallon. Other benefits: the technology that converts algae into petroleum creates fertilizer that can be used to make more energy in the form of natural gas. The big negative: real estate. To produce enough energy to meet current U.S. needs, we'd need an area the size of Maryland for algae production.

*   *   *

No one knows the story of tomorrow's dawn. —**African proverb**

In 2011 the U.S. Treasury had an operating cash balance of $73.7 billion. Apple's was $76.4 billion.

Mock 'n' Roll

"Tribute bands" perform the songs of a specific band and even dress like them. (Famous example: Beatlemania.) Can you guess which bands these tribute bands are paying tribute to? (Answers on page 510.)

1. Bricks in the Wall

2. No Way Sis

3. Bjorn Again

4. Rubber Souldiers

5. The Dayglo Pirates

6. Katchafire

7. Alcoholica

8. Mojo Risin

9. All Summer Long

10. The Landsharks

11. Separate Ways

12. To Hell and Back

13. Zoso

14. Strutter

15. Hell's Belles

16. West End Girls

17. Paradise City

18. Sticky Fingers

19. Even Better Than the Real Thing

20. Uncle John's Band

21. Nearvana

22. Tragedy

a) The Beach Boys

b) Led Zeppelin

c) AC/DC

d) The Beatles

e) Bob Marley & the Wailers

f) Pink Floyd

g) Guns n' Roses

h) Journey

i) KISS

j) Jethro Tull

k) Rolling Stones

l) Pet Shop Boys

m) Oasis

n) ABBA

o) Grateful Dead

p) Metallica

q) The Doors

r) Jimmy Buffett

s) Meat Loaf

t) U2

u) Nirvana

v) The Bee Gees

It took the *Apollo 11* crew just over four days to get to the moon.

Roll Models

Something everyone thinks about as they get close to retiring is "What am I going to do with all that free time?" Some people move to the country, others travel the world. Still others make a difference right where they are.

HIGH ROLLERS

One of the perks that come with working in a swanky, well-run high-rise office building in cities like Seattle, Washington, is that you almost never run out of toilet paper. The janitors see to it. Each night they replace the old toilet paper rolls with new ones, whether the old rolls are used up or not. And what happens to the rolls that get replaced? In the old days, the janitors just threw them out, something that drove Allison Delong, the manager of several buildings in Seattle in the 1990s, crazy. She hated to see all that toilet paper going to waste, but what was she going to do with all those partially used rolls?

The problem continued until Allison's father, Leon Delong, retired in 1999 and found himself with more free time than he knew what to do with. When Allison told him about all the toilet paper rolls that were being thrown away, he offered to collect them and donate them to area food banks. She instructed the janitors in her buildings to set the rolls aside, and every other week Leon would load them into his pickup truck and deliver them to the food banks. They packaged the rolls in groups of three or four and put them out for people who didn't have enough money to buy toilet paper. "Putting out Leon's toilet paper is like putting out T-bone steaks," food bank manager Anthony Brown told the *Seattle Times*. "If we don't hold some of it back, it's gone in an hour."

ON A ROLL

Seattle's "Toilet Paper Guy," as Leon came to be known, added one building after another to his paper route (so to speak) until he was collecting rolls from about a quarter of all the high-rent office buildings in Seattle. He collected some 2,000–3,000 rolls every other week—enough to fill the bed of his pickup truck three times. He kept at it for 15 years, until a bout with pneumonia over the holidays in 2014 forced him to hand over the route to other volunteers. By then he'd saved what he estimates as around one million rolls of toilet paper from the trash and made them available to people in need. "I'm amazed how much this mattered to people," he told the *Seattle Times* in 2014. "To me, it was just a nice thing to do. Now it's my claim to fame. You know, I'm sort of proud of it."

According to one estimate, a third of male fish in British waters are changing sex due to pollution.

Common Medical Maladies Explained

We've all heard people complain about such medical conditions as a "charley horse," "post-nasal drip," or "diddler's toe" (okay, maybe not that last one). Perhaps you've even been a sufferer—but never understood exactly what you were suffering from. Well, here are some quick descriptions.

CHARLEY HORSE. This is a common term for a muscle spasm—when a muscle tightly and painfully contracts. It can occur in any muscle, but it's mostly associated with muscles of the calves and thighs. While the spasm of a charley horse normally only lasts a short time, from a few seconds to a couple of minutes, the residual pain can last for hours or, in extreme cases, days. Common causes include dehydration, overuse of the affected muscle, not stretching before exercise, and exercising in very hot or cold temperatures. Treatments include stretching, massage, heat, and, in more severe cases, antispasmodic medications. People most affected: athletes, the elderly, the obese—and infants. (Note: another name for a painful muscle spasm: a *cramp*.)

PULLED MUSCLE. Also known as a strained muscle, wherein a muscle—or tendons attached to that muscle—is damaged by being overstretched, causing muscle and tendon fiber to tear. Result: severe pain and, in some cases, bruising. Pulled muscles can be caused by overuse, such as lifting very heavy objects, or accidents, such as falls. Commonly strained muscles and tendons include those in the lower back, neck, and shoulders. One you've probably heard of from the sports world: a pulled hamstring. (*Hamstring* properly refers to the tendons at the back of the knee, but it also commonly refers to large muscles and tendons in the back of the thigh and lower buttocks.)

SPRAIN. A sprain is basically the same as a strain—but it refers to overstretched and damaged *ligaments* rather than muscles and tendons. Ligaments are always associated with a joint—they're the tough, sinewy tissues that connect bones to each other at joints—and in severe cases, sprains can include damage to the joint and bones related to the affected ligaments. (Especially severe sprains often result in *avulsion fractures*, in which a ligament is pulled so hard that it breaks off a piece of the bone it is attached to.) Recommended treatment for sprains and strains: the

---

Gotcha! A swimming polar bear can jump eight feet out of the water to surprise a seal.

RICE method—rest, ice, compression, and elevation of the injured area. More serious sprains and strains may require surgery.

PSORIASIS. Taken from a Greek word meaning "itching condition," psoriasis is a skin disorder characterized by itchy and often painful lesions on the skin. There are five main types, the most common being *plaque psoriasis*, which appears as red patches covered with a scaly white buildup; the most commonly affected areas are the back, the scalp, the knees, and the elbows. The cause of psoriasis is unknown. What is known: there's a genetic component to the disease, as it's often hereditary; it's an *autoimmune* disorder, meaning it involves a malfunction of the body's immune system (not unlike multiple sclerosis and lupus); and it can be set off by *triggers*—meaning that factors such as stress, injury, and infection can cause a breakout of psoriasis. The disorder affects roughly 3 percent of the world's population, or 125 million people. The worst type, *erythrodermic psoriasis*, can spread over most of the body and disrupt the victim's ability to regulate temperature—thereby making it potentially fatal.

GERD. *Gastroesophageal reflux disease*, also known as acid reflux, is a chronic condition in which digestive stomach acids regularly make their way up into the esophagus. Because the lining of the esophagus has little protection against those stomach acids, they can damage the esophageal lining, thereby causing pain, most often felt as heartburn. Sometimes the pain is so intense that it can be mistaken for a heart attack. The most common causes of GERD are problems with the *esophageal sphincter*, which normally acts as a barrier and keeps stomach contents from entering the esophagus. Malfunction of the sphincter (yes, your body has more than one sphincter) can itself be caused by many different things, including injury, obesity, and overproduction of stomach acids. Treatments include dietary changes, medication, and surgery.

TINNITUS. According to the American Tinnitus Association, 50 million people in the U.S. experience varying degrees of tinnitus—16 million severely enough to seek medical attention and 2 million so severely that it prevents them from performing normal daily activities. Tinnitus is the "ringing in the ears" condition wherein one perceives sound that is not being produced outside the ears. The sound can manifest in many different ways—as a high-pitched ringing, a raspy buzz, beeping and ticking, or even a loud roar. For most sufferers, tinnitus is simply annoying, but severe cases can lead to loss of sleep, anxiety, and severe depression. Experts stress that it is not a disease—it is a symptom of something else. In some cases, that something else can be determined: for example excessive wax buildup in the ears, damage to the ear due to medical conditions, such as tumors, or listening to loud music for too long. But in many cases, there is no known cause.

POST-NASAL DRIP. Glands in the back of your nose regularly produce mucus that drips into your throat, mixes with saliva, and is swallowed. (That mucus serves the important purpose of trapping any toxins you might inhale, preventing them from making their way to the lungs.) Normally you don't notice this, but sometimes the glands produce too much mucus, or mucus that is especially thick, causing annoying sensations in the back of the throat related to post-nasal drip. Excessive or thick mucus production can be caused by cold, flu, allergies, sinus infections, and drug side effects. Post-nasal drip usually has minor symptoms, such as throat irritation, but it can occasionally lead to serious conditions, including chronic cough and sore throat, swollen tonsils, difficulty breathing, and vomiting. Treatment usually involves medications, such as antibiotics, to reduce mucus output.

DEVIATED SEPTUM. The *nasal septum* is a structure made of thin bone and cartilage that divides your nose into two nostrils. A *deviated septum* is simply a septum that is out of its normal position, either pushed to one side or running in a slanted or crooked line. It can be congenital, meaning the septum may be misplaced at birth, but more often it is caused by trauma—such as getting punched in the nose. Some studies indicate that as much as 80 percent of the population has some degree of septum deviation, but only people with significantly deviated septums experience symptoms. Those symptoms can include dry and crusty nostrils, nosebleeds, nasal infections, and sleep disorders, including excessive snoring and sleep apnea. The only treatment for a deviated septum: surgery.

DIABETES. More than 28 million Americans suffer from diabetes, but what is it, exactly? There are three forms: type 1, type 2, and gestational. Type 1 diabetes is usually diagnosed during childhood or adolescence, brought on when a person's pancreas stops making insulin, the hormone that regulates the absorption of carbohydrates. People with type 1 diabetes are treated with multiple daily insulin injections. Type 2 diabetics still make insulin, but their bodies have difficulty absorbing it. (The extra fat associated with being overweight prevents insulin from being effective). It's treated with medications that help make the body less resistant, but sometimes insulin shots are administered. More than 95 percent of diabetics have type 2 diabetes. Gestational diabetes is similar to type 2, in that the body has insulin absorption issues. The difference is that it's temporary—it occurs only while a woman is pregnant. Once she delivers, the disease goes away.

Birds do not have bladders. (When they gotta go, they just go.)

The Dark Side

If "Have a nice day!" makes you gag, this page is for you.

"It's always darkest before it turns absolutely pitch black."
—**Paul Newman**

"The glass is always half-empty. And cracked. And I just cut my lip on it. And chipped a tooth."
—**Janeane Garofalo**

"Always borrow money from a pessimist. He won't expect it back."
—**Oscar Wilde**

"Live every day as if it were your last, because one of these days it will be."
—**Jeremy Schwartz**

"I don't know, I don't care, and it doesn't make any difference."
—**Jack Kerouac**

"A journey of a thousand miles begins with a single step. Of course, so does falling down a flight of stairs."
—**Jewish proverb**

"Your phone doesn't suck. Your life sucks around the phone."
—**Louis CK**

"I like pessimists. They're always the ones who bring life jackets for the boat."
—**Lisa Kleypas**

"I love mankind. It's people I can't stand."
—**Charles M. Schulz**

"Sometimes that light at the end of a tunnel is a train."
—**Charles Barkley**

"If all the world's a stage, I want to operate the trapdoor."
—**Paul Beatty**

"The world is a grindstone and life is your nose."
—**Fred Allen**

"Life is one long process of getting tired."
—**Samuel Butler**

"In the depths of my heart I can't help being convinced that my dear fellow-men, with a few exceptions, are worthless."
—**Sigmund Freud**

"Wise men say that time is like a river. I say time is like a river of sh*t...and as you float down that river in your little canoe, your paddles are getting smaller and smaller."
—**Lewis Black**

"Cheer up, the worst is yet to come."
—**Philander C. Johnson**

Pigs can run at the rate of about 11 miles per hour. Housecats: 30 miles per hour.

Who *Blarted*?

Some so-called comedies are so bad they're not even funny…but the scathing reviews are. Case in point: the 2015 stinker Paul Blart: Mall Cop 2.

"Paul Blart (Kevin James) is an idiot. He's also gluttonous, clumsy, overbearing, self-deluded, and obnoxious—a veritable personification of the seven dullest sins."
—**MaryAnn Johanson,** *Flickfilosopher*

"The sort of movie that goes beyond mere mediocrity to offer possible evidence of a civilization in decline."
—**Justin Chang,** *Variety*

"So glacially paced that at times it achieves an almost zen-like level of anti-comedy."
—**Tom Huddleston,** *Time Out London*

"Blart is a stereotype of a stereotype; a half-remembered punchline; a stomach with a moustache and wheels."
—**Robbie Collin,** *The Telegraph* (UK)

"Despite the fact that she's featured prominently in the credits, two-time Oscar nominee Shirley Knight disappears within the first few minutes, her character unceremoniously run over by a milk truck. Lucky her."
—**Frank Scheck,** *The Hollywood Reporter*

"The film is so mordantly witless that it takes on the quality of a bleak art-house tragedy."
—**Donald Clarke,** *Irish Times*

"When a family pet accidentally swallows a lighter."
—**from "20 Things That Aren't Quite as Bad as *Paul Blart: Mall Cop 2*" by David Jenkins,** *Little White Lies*

"If aliens invaded our planet and found out that mankind had spent $30 million on such a colossal waste of time and resources, they'd have every right to immediately enslave us all without complaint."
—**Gregory Wakeman,** *CinemaBlend*

"Imagine Inspector Clouseau, only husky, not French, and not funny."
—**Alonso Duralde,** *The Wrap*

"Think of the worst movie you've ever seen—a movie that didn't make you laugh or cry, didn't move you or change you in any way besides giving you the desperate urge to flee the theater. Hold that title in your mind. *Paul Blart: Mall Cop 2* is worse than that."
—**Christy Lemire,** *RogerEbert.com*

They come from the same plant, but it takes 400 lb. of nutmegs to produce 1 lb. of the spice mace.

Message in a Bottle

*According to the insurance company Lloyd's of London, most
messages found in bottles are fakes. These, however, are not.*

LAST WORDS

On April 11, 1912, 19-year-old Jeremiah Burke and his cousin
Nora Hegarty boarded the RMS *Titanic* in Ireland. Two of Burke's
sisters had already immigrated to the U.S., and he and Nora were
planning to join them in Boston. Before Burke left for the ship, his
mother gave him a bottle of holy water for good luck. It didn't work:
neither Burke nor his cousin survived when the *Titanic* sank on April
15. A year later, a man found the bottle washed up on the beach at
Dunkettle, not far from where the Burke family lived. Inside was a note
that read, "From Titanic. Good Bye all. Burke of Glanmire, Cork." The
note remained displayed in the Burke family home for nearly 100 years;
they donated it to a museum in 2011.

MYSTERIOUS WAYS

"Brother" George Phillips, known as the "Whiskey Bottle Evangelist,"
used bottles to preach. In April 1940, the recovering alcoholic was
inspired by driftwood he saw floating along the beach. "God spoke to my
heart there," Phillips said. He started collecting old whiskey bottles from
dumps, placing gospel tracts (religious pamphlets) and return address
cards inside each one and putting the bottles into Puget Sound, near his
home in Tacoma, Washington. Initially he placed them by hand, but by
1941 he'd enlisted sailors on outgoing ships to drop the bottles for him.
Over a period of 20 years, Phillips estimated that he'd sent out around
40,000 bottles and received 2,000 replies from 40 different countries.

GOOD FOR YOU!

In 1954 Guinness Exports Ltd. launched an advertising promotion
called the "Bottle Drop." Fifty thousand Guinness bottles, each with
a card inside asking the finder to mail it back to Guinness to receive a
reply, were dropped from ships around the world. The company received
cards from England, the Bahamas, Tahiti, and Mexico, among other
countries. The promotion—which included the message "Guinness is
Good for You!" in red letters—was so successful that they did it again
in 1959, in celebration of the company's 200th anniversary. This time,
Guinness dropped 150,000 specially made bottles into the Atlantic
Ocean, each containing a scroll from "the Office of King Neptune,"
a booklet with the company history, instructions on how to turn the

bottle into a table lamp, and an ad for Ovaltine. Fifty years after the drop, bottles are still being found. Among the replies: "I was walking along the isolated beach south of the Mundrabilla Road House when I found your bottle. Myself and all the people of Mundrabilla (all five of them) love Guinness." It was signed by Australian Geoff Gibson.

BUILT BY PRISONERS

In 2009 workers renovating a building near the site of the Auschwitz death camp found a bottle bricked into a wall. Inside was a penciled note dated September 20, 1944. It read "Air raid shelter for the T. W. L. personnel. Built by prisoners" and listed the names and hometowns of seven men, ending with "all age 18 to 20." The Auschwitz-Birkenau Museum tracked down some of the men on the list and found that they had been forced to build an aircraft shelter for the Nazis. During construction, the men hurriedly wrote the note, sealed it in a bottle, and placed it inside one of the walls. Survivor Wacław Sobczak told reporters, "The Germans killed the sick and the weak. I didn't think we'd survive. We wanted something of ourselves to remain behind, even if it was only that bottle." Five of the seven men survived the camps. The fates of the other two are unknown.

SAVED BY THE BOTTLE

The *Lennie*, a ship out of Bristol, England, was hijacked by its crew in 1875. The mutineers murdered the captain and the first and second mates and ordered the steward, a Belgian named Van Hoydonck, to pilot the ship to Gibraltar. Under threat of death, Van Hoydonck agreed…but secretly had the cabin boy write 24 notes, which Van Hoydonck put in 24 bottles. Then he steered the ship toward France and tossed the bottles overboard. Amazingly, the French navy found one and sent a warship to investigate. Outgunned, the mutineers surrendered and were arrested and sent to England, where they were tried for murder and hanged. As for Van Hoydonck, he opened a·restaurant in England, got married, and never sailed again.

LOOKING FOR LOVE

While sailing on the open sea in 1955, a young Swedish man named Ake Viking addressed a message in a bottle to "Someone Beautiful and Far Away" and ended the note with, "Write me, whoever you are." Two years later, Viking received a letter from a young Italian woman named Paolina. "I am not beautiful," she wrote, "but it seems so miraculous that this little bottle should have traveled so far and long to reach me that I must send you an answer." The two began a correspondence, and Viking sailed to Sicily to meet Paolina in person. He thought she *was* beautiful, and they were married soon after.

Crunky Ball Nude

Now for some of the most unfortunately named products from around the world.
(If you think these are bad, you should see the ones we couldn't print.)

Tinkle Eyebrow Razor (USA)

Bimbo Bread (Mexico)

Barf Detergent Powder (Iran)

Batmilk Yogurt (Brazil)

666 Allergy and Cold Relief (USA)

PooPoo Smoothie (an iced mango drink sold in Burger Kings in China)

Pee Cola (Ghana)

Plopp Caramel Chocolate (Sweden)

Boudreaux's Butt Paste Diaper Rash Ointment (USA)

Starburst Sucks (Australia, lollipops)

Swiss Army Eau de Toilette Spray (Switzerland)

Cream Collon (Japan, cookies)

Bowel Buddy Bran Wafers (Canada)

Crunky Ball Nude (Japan, crispy chocolate candy balls)

Butter It's Not (USA)

Stupid Child Efficiency Mop (China)

Urinal Hot Drink (Romania, a cranberry juice health drink)

Squeaky Cheeks Foot and Body Powder (USA)

Mushy Peas (a popular English side dish of thick, soupy peas)

PureTouch Tush Wipes (USA)

Barfy Burgers (Argentina)

RetarDEX Oral Rinse (England)

Bum Bum Ice Cream (Germany)

Chubby Kids Soda (Trinidad and Tobago)

Naïve Lady Toilet Paper (Japan)

Salticrax Crackers (South Africa)

Gorilla Snot Hair Gel (Mexico)

Cheese Crack (Netherlands, breaded cheese sticks)

Studies show: The aroma of fresh-baked goods makes customers spend more money.

3-D Printing

Can you really "print" toys, food, and body parts from your desktop? Thanks to 3-D printing, yes you can.

THE LIGHT STUFF

In the early 1980s, Chuck Hull made coatings for a furniture company. Using a process called *stereolithography*, he applied a thin coating of liquid photopolymers—plastic so light-sensitive that UV light made the liquid solidify—to tables and chairs. Hull was also in charge of ordering miniature prototypes of furniture but was frustrated with how long it took to get those prototypes built. So Hull thought that maybe he could make his own prototypes out of the thin layers of the same plastic he used for the veneers...if he stacked them on top of each other thousands of times.

After experimenting with the idea for months, he developed a system in which UV light was shone onto the top of a vat of the liquid photopolymer. Using a software program of his own design, he developed a technique by which he could direct the laser to make the exact shape he wanted, layer by layer. Hull patented "3-D printing" in 1986. Two years later, he was 3-D printing car prototypes in miniature for GM and Mercedes.

Only in the last few years has the technology been embraced. Companies and individuals can use Hull's technology—and printer "ink" made from a variety of materials—to print almost anything they can imagine.

PRINT THIS...

• In 2014 a Texas doctor used a 3-D printer and 3-D imaging software to create a plastic model of the skeleton of a pair of conjoined twins. It was discovered that the twins shared a larger portion of one upper leg bone than X-rays had revealed. Because they had a working model, the surgeons were able to split the leg successfully and separate the twins. After the operation, both were able to walk—something not possible before the 3-D printer revealed the bone.

• A musician and inventor named Scott Summit makes 3-D printed acoustic guitars.

• Defense Distributed offers downloads of plans that can be used to 3-D print semiautomatic rifles out of durable plastics.

• Ultrasound has long been used to create stereoscopic 3-D images of

---

Ringo Starr, the oldest Beatle, was also the last to join the band, making him the "youngest" Beatle.

growing babies. Now those images can be printed as 3-D models. Price for a plastic doll version of your unborn baby: $600 to $1,000.

• The Chinese construction company WinSun used recycled building materials for the "ink" in its 3-D printers. It then assembled thousands of individual pieces of walls, ceilings, and more. The result: a completely 3-D-printed six-story apartment complex.

...AND THIS

• In 2013 Redpath Museum in Montreal, with a team from McGill University, used high-resolution CT scans and 3-D printing to make models of what ancient Egyptian mummies would've looked like.

• Instead of putting liquid plastic in its 3-D printer tanks, the Sugar Lab in Los Angeles uses sugar ink to make edible 3-D cake toppers in the shape of roses, snowflakes, globes, and anything else the bakers can think of.

• As part of its ongoing mission into how to give astronauts food that actually tastes good, NASA has developed 3-D pizza printing. Its printer utilizes multiple cartridges of "ink," containing dough, cheese, and sauce.

• Clothing company Continuum uses a waterproof polymer called Nylon 12. They produce it with 3-D printers to make bikinis.

• Shahid Khan, owner of the Jacksonville Jaguars, hired a company to 3-D print a 6-foot-tall, 13-foot-long metal jaguar. He mounted it on the bow of his yacht.

...AND THIS

• Organovo, a San Diego tech firm that uses 3-D printers to make biological materials, has "printed" human liver tissue, and is developing a way to create an entirely new human liver.

• Pi-Top is a 3-D-printed laptop computer (which can then presumably be hooked up to a 3-D printer to print more laptop computers).

• Artist and educator Heather Dewey-Hagborg makes faces. First she rifles through garbage to find cigarette butts and chewed-up gum, then extracts DNA samples, sequences them in a genetics lab, and uses that information to create a 3-D image of the subject's face. Then she uses a 3-D printer to make a lifelike plastic mask of the person's face.

• The producers of Skyfall used a 3-D printer to make a ⅓ scale model replica of a 1960 Aston Martin and then crashed it. (It was much cheaper than using a real one.)

• You can even print...you. Amazon.com has a 3-D printing store where you can make a three-inch nylon bobblehead of yourself for just $30.

Uncle John's Stall of Shame

Not everyone who makes it into the Stall of Fame is there for a good reason. That's why Uncle John created the "Stall of Shame."

D**ubious Achiever:** Thaddeus Morgan, 24
Claim to Fame: A trip to the can nearly earned him a trip to the can.

True Story: One day in 2014, Morgan used the bathroom...but after he finished, he forgot to put the toilet seat back down. That made his younger sister Cynthia mad, and the two got into a physical confrontation. According to the police report, Thaddeus admitted to pushing Cynthia, breaking her glasses, and slapping her cell phone out of her hand when she tried to call 911. He also claimed that Cynthia threw things at him, but when the police arrived at the scene, he was the only one arrested. He was charged with assault and interfering with an emergency call—a felony, which meant he could have been sent to prison.

Outcome: Rather than risk jail time, Morgan took a plea bargain. He changed his "not guilty" plea to "guilty" and was sentenced to one year of supervised release and mandatory anger management classes. "It was simply a sibling fight that got out of control," Assistant State's Attorney Leah Viste told the *Bismarck Tribune*. (But he probably won't forget to put the seat down again.)

Dubious Achiever: Michelle Ferguson-Montgomery, a sixth-grade teacher at Westbrook Elementary School in Taylorsville, Utah

Claim to Fame: Firing a shot at the schoolhouse pot

True Story: Utah state law allows concealed weapons permit holders like Ferguson-Montgomery to bring loaded handguns to school—and they're not required to notify the school that they're armed. (School administrators aren't allowed to ask teachers if they're carrying a weapon, nor can they forbid teachers from doing so.) Teachers who arm themselves must keep the guns hidden from sight and in their possession at all times. So not only was Ferguson-Montgomery not breaking the law by bringing her 9-mm handgun with her into the faculty bathroom on the morning of September 11, 2014, she was *required by law* to do so. The mistake she made was removing her gun from her hip holster and setting it on the toilet paper dispenser while she did her business—because when she went to put the gun back in its holster, it discharged, firing a round into the front of the toilet, shattering it. "The defendant stated that she did not remember pulling the trigger, but conceded that it is likely what happened," Granite School District police detective Randy Porter wrote in his police report.

Possessing a weapon in an elementary school is one thing; shooting it—even accidentally—is another. Ferguson-Montgomery was charged with "discharging a firearm in a prohibited area within city limits," a misdemeanor punishable by up to six months in jail.

Outcome: Ferguson-Montgomery resigned her teaching position after the charges were filed. She later pled no contest as part of a plea deal. She received no jail time, and the judge agreed to dismiss the case in 12 months if she 1) committed no new crimes, 2) paid the $705 court fee, and 3) completed a course in firearm safety. She also paid $200 to replace the toilet. "There's a lot of debate about guns and where they are appropriate," city prosecutor Tracy Cowdell told the *Salt Lake Tribune*, "but they can't be going off at school. We can all agree on that." It's estimated that as many as 240 teachers in the state may have concealed weapons permits.

Dubious Achiever: The WaterSaver Faucet Company of Chicago, Illinois

Claim to Fame: Not giving employees a break on bathroom breaks

True Story: If you think a company that makes plumbing fixtures would understand the importance of pit stops, think again. WaterSaver Faucet allows its employees just 6 minutes a day for bathroom trips outside of the scheduled 10-minute morning break, 30-minute lunch period, and 15-minute afternoon break. The company tracks its employees' break time by requiring them to swipe their ID cards when they use the bathroom. In one month alone, 19 employees were reprimanded for "excessive use" of the facilities.

Outcome: In July 2014, the union filed a complaint with the National Labor Relations Board, but at last report, the policy was still in place. "Our supposition is that some of the [bathroom] behavior is related to cell phones and texting…although I have no hard evidence," WaterSaver's CEO Steve Kersten told CNN. When CNN asked him if he had to swipe his ID card to use the bathroom, he paused and then answered, "No."

*   *   *

Random Fact: The ancient Greeks thought quartz crystals were made of ice frozen so hard it could never melt.

Honorary U.S. Citizens

Since the United States was founded more than 230 years ago, how many foreigners have been granted honorary citizenship? Answer: only seven. Some honorees are world famous; others aren't nearly as well known.

WINSTON CHURCHILL (1874–1965)

Claim to Fame: Prime minister of the United Kingdom during World War II

Becoming a Citizen: Churchill, who was half-American by blood (his mother was born in New York), became the first-ever honorary citizen of the United States following the passage of a special act of Congress and a proclamation by President John F. Kennedy in April 1963. The honor was purely ceremonial and came with no special rights or privileges whatsoever, not even a U.S. passport. Churchill did, however, receive a special leather-bound "Honorary Citizen's Document" that looked just like a passport. So far he's the only honorary citizen to get one.

Bonus Fact: One honor Churchill refused was Queen Elizabeth's offer to make him the first-ever Duke of London. Churchill declined at the urging of his son Randolph, who would have become ineligible for a seat in the House of Commons when he inherited the dukedom.

RAOUL WALLENBERG (1912–?)

Claim to Fame: Swedish diplomat who saved thousands of Hungarian Jews during the Holocaust

Details: Wallenberg rented 30 buildings in Nazi-occupied Budapest, declared them Swedish territory—and thus protected by diplomatic immunity—and used them to provide refuge to some 10,000 Jews. He saved additional thousands by issuing "protective passports" that prevented them from being deported to Auschwitz. Then, in 1945, during the final days of the Nazi occupation of Hungary, he thwarted the imminent massacre of the 69,000 Jews remaining in the "Big Ghetto" in Budapest by threatening Nazi officials with prosecution for war crimes after the war was over. Four days later, Wallenberg was arrested by the Soviets and was never seen again. According to the best available evidence, he was executed by the KGB in Moscow's infamous Lubyanka prison in 1947.

Becoming a Citizen: One of the Jews who survived the Holocaust by hiding in a Wallenberg safe house was 16-year-old Lantos Tamás Péter, who emigrated to the United States after the war. He anglicized his name to Tom Lantos and in 1980 was elected to the U.S. House of

Representatives in 1980—the only Holocaust survivor ever to serve in Congress. One of his first acts after taking office was to introduce legislation making Wallenberg an honorary citizen of the United States. It passed both houses of Congress and was signed into law by President Ronald Reagan in October 1981.

WILLIAM PENN (1644–1718)

Claim to Fame: English Quaker and Pennsylvania colony founder

Details: In 17th-century England, the Quakers were persecuted for their beliefs. They were eager to find a place where they could practice their religion freely. Penn found one in 1681 when he proposed that King Charles II settle an $80,000 debt owed to Penn's father by granting a charter for a 45,000-square-mile chunk of land in the New World, comprising present-day Pennsylvania ("Penn's Woods") and Delaware. The king, happy to pay the debt and be rid of the Quakers at the same time, agreed.

Penn's "Holy Experiment" had the first written constitution that could be changed by amendment. It also granted the colonists freedom of conscience, freedom of religion, public education, trials by jury, democratic elections, and other rights that are taken for granted today but were radical for their time.

Becoming a Citizen: Penn returned to England in 1701, appointing a deputy to administer the colony in his absence. His growing financial and legal problems and (later) failing health prevented him from ever returning to Pennsylvania. He died in 1718, still the nominal head of the colony, but penniless.

Both Penn and his widow, Hannah, are buried in England. In the mid-1970s the Pennsylvania legislature briefly entertained a plan to exhume their bodies and rebury them in Pennsylvania. Philadelphian Elaine Peden thought that was a terrible idea; she launched a letter-writing campaign for a "more meaningful" gesture of having the Penns named honorary U.S. citizens instead. It took a decade, but in November 1984, a bill doing just that landed on President Ronald Reagan's desk, and he signed it into law.

HANNAH CALLOWHILL PENN (1671–1726)

Claim to Fame: William Penn's widow and successor

Details: From its inception until the mid-1700s, Pennsylvania was the colonial equivalent of a family store: the Penns were personally responsible for running it. When William Penn was incapacitated by a stroke in 1712, Hannah stepped in to oversee the colony in his name. When Penn died in 1718, his will named Hannah as his successor; she administered the colony in her own right for eight more years until her death in 1726. She even fought off an attempt by William Penn Jr. (Penn Sr.'s dissolute son from his first marriage) to have the will thrown out so that he could seize control of the colony for himself.

Becoming a Citizen: Because Hannah played such an important role in the early history of the colony, it was only natural to include her in the campaign for honorary citizenship. Both she and her husband became honorary U.S. citizens on the same day in 1984.

MOTHER TERESA (1910–97)

Claim to Fame: Roman Catholic nun renowned for her charitable works and recipient of the Nobel Peace Prize in 1979

Details: Born in 1910 in what is now Macedonia, Agnes Gonxha Bojaxhiu took the name Teresa after joining the Sisters of Loreto religious order in 1928. The order sent her to India, where she taught school. In 1948 she began her missionary work with the poor and two years later founded her own order, the Missionaries of Charity, dedicated to that work. By the mid-1990s her order had grown to more than 4,000 nuns in 123 countries.

Becoming a Citizen: In 1996 U.S. representative Patrick Flanagan of Illinois introduced a joint resolution naming Mother Teresa an honorary U.S. citizen. It passed unanimously in both houses of Congress and was signed into law by President Bill Clinton in October 1996. (She and Winston Churchill are the only recipients who were honored while still living; the other five were awarded U.S. citizenship posthumously.)

THE MARQUIS DE LAFAYETTE (1757–1834)

Claim to Fame: French soldier and statesman who fought on the side of the 13 colonies in the American Revolution

Details: Lafayette was only 19 when he arrived in the United States in 1777 and volunteered to serve without pay in the Continental Army. He became a member of George Washington's staff and, after demonstrating courage under fire, was given command of a division. He led soldiers in numerous battles, including the British surrender at the siege of Yorktown.

Becoming a Citizen: The fact that Lafayette was a foreigner who had volunteered to fight for American liberty made him popular with Americans of every stripe. After the war, Maryland, Massachusetts, Connecticut, and Virginia all made him honorary citizens of their states. For this reason he's the only honorary U.S. citizen who was already a citizen before being so honored: when the U.S. Constitution was ratified in 1789, the citizens of every state became American citizens by default. No matter—in 2002 President George W. Bush signed legislation making him a U.S. citizen again.

CASIMIR PULASKI (1745–79)

Claim to Fame: Polish nobleman and soldier who, like Lafayette, fought on the side of the 13 colonies in the American Revolution

Details: Pulaski first saw action while serving as an aide to Washington on September 11, 1777, at the Battle of Brandywine in southeastern Pennsylvania. Washington's troops were routed, and two weeks later, Philadelphia, then the capital city, fell to the British. But Pulaski's skill in organizing an orderly retreat at Brandywine saved Washington's life and ensured that the army would live to fight again. Four days later, Washington promoted Pulaski to the rank of brigadier general of the cavalry, which he reformed and reorganized into a more effective fighting force. For this reason he is known as the "father of the American cavalry." In October 1779, he was mortally wounded during the siege of Savannah and died two days later.

Becoming a Citizen: It took two attempts to award honorary citizenship to Pulaski. The first joint resolution made it through the Senate in 2007 but failed to pass in the House of Representatives. The second attempt was passed unanimously by both houses of Congress and signed into law by President Barack Obama in November 2009.

* * *

WHAT DREAMS MAY MEAN

Here are some dream interpretations we found in a fortune-telling book from the 1920s. Read them…and all will be revealed.

• **You are eating candy:** You will be subjected to false flattery.

• **You approach a wall:** If the wall is blocking your path, an embarrassment is just around the corner.

• **You are reading a serious book:** You will attain a high station in life.

• **You are reading a naughty book:** Disgrace is heading your way.

• **You see a candle:** If the candle is lit, it means good luck, and the brighter the candle, the better the luck.

• **You are attending a ball:** Someone will die and leave you money.

• **You have a wooden leg:** Your health is going to get worse.

• **You are choking on your food:** You are overindulgent.

• **You are hunting:** If you're leaving for the hunt, you'll be accused of dishonesty. Returning from a hunt with fresh game means good fortune is coming your way.

• **You are dancing with someone:** That person is in love with you.

If you see stars after you've been hit on the head, you probably have a concussion.

Phoning It In

Apple introduced the iPhone in 2007—the first successful "smartphone." In less than a decade, these sophisticated pocket computers have replaced many common items and services. Result: if you have a phone, you'll probably never again need...

STEREOS. Music can be downloaded directly onto a smartphone or streamed in with services like Spotify or Rdio, and played back on headphones or Bluetooth speakers. Either way, you no longer need CDs or CD players. And most cars now have a jack to plug in a smartphone, eliminating the need for car radios.

CREDIT CARDS. In 2014 Apple debuted its Apple Pay service. Users store digital versions of their debit and credit cards on their iPhone and simply hold the phone up to a special scanner at participating merchants. The money is instantly deducted from the user's bank account.

BANKS. Major banks, such as US Bank and Chase, allow customers to use smartphone apps to pay bills, transfer money between accounts, and, by taking a picture of a check with their phone's camera, deposit checks.

PROOF OF INSURANCE. Several insurance companies have cell phone apps that can serve as a proof of insurance card. If yours has one, you may legally show your phone to a police officer if caught speeding.

KEYS. Several hotel chains have announced plans to let guests use their phones to open new computerized room locks. A company called Lockitron has introduced the technology for residences, too.

MAPS. The days of folding and unfolding maps and trying to read little red and blue lines are over. All smartphones have map apps on them... and with GPS, they even tell you when and where to turn.

BUSINESS CARDS. You can either take a photo of a business card, essentially "scanning" it and keeping it on your phone, or use an app like CardCloud to file and organize them.

WATCHES. Phones display the time, of course, but most also feature timekeeping devices such as stopwatches, alarm clocks, and egg timers.

PHONES. Smartphones have made traditional landlines redundant and an unnecessary cost for many households. Since the arrival of smartphones, 40 percent of Americans have dropped their landlines and—in many cases—talking. Texting overtook voice calls in 2012. More than 300 billion texts are sent each year in the U.S. alone.

When thrown with "optimum effectiveness," a Frisbee spins six times per second.

Grave Errors

Where do you want to be buried when you go to your great reward? It may seem like a grim thought, but many people go to great lengths to plan their eternal resting place. We're dead serious. (Get it? Dead!) Yet despite all that, sometimes those plans go awry.

T OLD YOU SO

Deceased: Edna Lawson, a Houston, Texas, widow who died in July 2014

Details: After Lawson passed away, her son, Bruce, made arrangements with Mabrie Memorial Mortuary to have her laid to rest in the cemetery plot at Houston National Cemetery, where her husband, a World War II veteran, was already buried. But when Bruce dropped by the mortuary to view his mother before the funeral, he sensed that something wasn't quite right. "I said, 'It doesn't look like my mom. Do you think maybe you have the wrong body?'" The funeral director assured him, "We don't make those kinds of mistakes," so Lawson reluctantly gave his consent for the burial to proceed.

Uh-oh! Sure enough, a few days after the funeral, Lawson got a call from the funeral home. There *had* been a mix-up: Edna Lawson's body was still at the mortuary; a woman named Pearlie Jean Deason had been laid to rest—not a very long rest, it turns out—beside Mr. Lawson. Mrs. Deason's body was immediately exhumed so that Edna Lawson could be buried with her husband following a shorter and less-attended second funeral. Deason's one and only funeral was delayed several days. "We deeply regret that the Lawson family had to endure this temporary delay in properly transitioning their loved one," the funeral home said in a statement. Both the Lawson and Deason families are suing Mabrie Memorial Mortuary for gross negligence.

MOTHER NOSE BEST

Deceased: A Philadelphia woman named Sharolyn Jackson

Details: In July 2013, a woman matching Jackson's description collapsed from heat stroke on a street in Philadelphia and was taken to the hospital. The woman wasn't carrying identification and died before she could tell anyone her name. Jackson had been reported missing a few days earlier, so the Philadelphia medical examiner's office showed a photograph of the dead woman to Jackson's son and a social worker assigned to her case. When both identified the woman as Sharolyn Jackson, her body was released to Jackson's family. Following an open-casket funeral

---

Chocolate milk was invented in Jamaica (by an Irishman).

attended by more than 50 of Jackson's friends and loved ones—many of whom commented that her nose "didn't look quite right," something they attributed to the embalming process—the woman was buried in a cemetery in Hamilton, New Jersey, on August 3.

Uh-oh! Two weeks later, the medical examiner's office called the family with good—but troubling—news: Jackson, who struggles with psychological and drug problems, had been found alive and had been admitted to a psychiatric hospital for treatment a few days earlier. The dead woman, it turned out, just happened to look a lot like Jackson (except for her nose).

Update: The mystery woman was exhumed from Jackson's grave; at last report, the medical examiner's office was still unable to identify her. Though the mistake could have been prevented by requiring a positive fingerprint identification before releasing her body to the next of kin, the medical examiner's office says it does not plan to require this in the future. "Our policy is that a visual identification by a family member is the gold standard," a spokesperson told the *Philadelphia Inquirer*. "We deem that enough to release the body…This is probably just a worst-case scenario."

BAD TIMING

Deceased: Bonda Patterson, who died in May 2015

Details: Patterson's funeral was second of two scheduled by the same funeral director, on the same day, in the same cemetery.

Uh-oh! Somehow the funeral director confused the two burial plots and accidentally interred the first decedent in Patterson's grave. The goof wasn't caught until Patterson's family arrived for her funeral later in the day and found a coffin already in her grave. By then the cemetery workers were already filling it in with dirt.

Disinterred: As soon as they realized their mistake, the workers removed the wayward coffin from Patterson's burial plot and reburied it in the proper grave, delaying Patterson's funeral in the process. According to news reports, when "the funeral director contacted the first family…and asked if they wanted to come back out to observe the burial in the proper grave, they declined."

THE PLOT THICKENS

Deceased: Willie Hayes, a Vietnam veteran from New York City who died in 2007 at the age of 59

Details: As an honorably discharged veteran, Hayes was entitled to burial in a national cemetery. But when his family requested that he be buried in Calverton National Cemetery on Long Island, the request was denied. Reason: according to the cemetery's records, Hayes was *already* buried there. That seemed like a simple thing to disprove, so the Hayes family kept pushing.

Uh-oh! After investigating, the cemetery staff concluded that someone had stolen Willie Hayes's name, rank, and social security number and had been buried in his grave under false pretenses. That person turned out to be *William* Hayes, a Vietnam veteran who died in 2003 at the age of 60. He had received an "other than honorable" discharge from the Marine Corps and thus was not eligible for burial in a national cemetery. Investigators believe he stole Willie Hayes's identity so that he could receive the military funeral he wanted but did not deserve. (For several years the impostor had also collected Willie Hayes's social security checks. When the checks stopped coming, Willie "thought maybe they had just run out," his niece Koreen Hayes told the *New York Times* in 2007, and had to prove to the Social Security Administration that he wasn't dead in order to get his benefits restored.)

Reburial: In October 2007, *Willie* Hayes was buried with full military honors in a brand-new grave all his own. A few weeks later, *William* Hayes was dishonorably discharged from the old grave, in what the National Cemetery Administration believes is the only time in American history that a veteran has been thrown out of a national cemetery for occupying a grave that wasn't his. That grave will never be occupied again, and the tombstone that marked it (with Willie Hayes's name, rank, service branch, and birthdate) was smashed to pieces and buried somewhere on the cemetery grounds.

Update: After he was evicted from his first grave, William Hayes seemed destined for Potter's Field, a pauper's graveyard on Hart Island, in Long Island. But Willie Hayes's funeral director, Isaiah Owens, took pity on him and paid the cost to have him reburied at George Washington Memorial Park in Paramus, New Jersey. "I'd rather have this for him than having him to go Potter's Field," Owens told reporters. "I always get a real sad feeling when I leave that place."

*   *   *

SWEET TALK

You might find any of these items on a food ingredients list. What do they have in common? They're all essentially sugar.

Corn syrup, cane juice, dehydrated cane juice, cane sugar, beet sugar, corn sugar, dextrose, galactose, maltose, Diatese, diastatic malt, malto-dextrin, malt sugar, fructose, mannitol, Florida crystals, sucrose, treacle, yellow sugar, lactose, Panocha, rice syrup, castor sugar, Turbinado sugar, barley malt, golden sugar, Muscovado, Barbados sugar, refiner's syrup, glucose, date sugar, ethyl maltol, and dextran.

According to people who know, termites taste like carrots.

"Fishy Goings-On"

In September 2012, Corporal Jim Brown, an officer with the
Collier County Sheriff's Youth Relations Bureau, responded
to a call about an injured teacher at Naples High School
in Naples, Florida. This is his actual police report.

INCIDENT REPORT:
FISHY GOINGS-ON AT HIGH SCHOOL

Date: 09-24-12
Time: 12:10 hours
Suspect: Mackerel
Description: Height 15", weight 16 oz, eyes black, hair none, multi
colored skin, scars multiple, undercut jaw
Victim: (HIPPA-protected) Teacher at school

At approximately 12:10 hours a teacher was standing at an area
called Oasis observing students during lunch when out of nowhere
a flying mackerel came down from the sky and struck her in the
head.

The teacher sustained minor injuries and was escorted to the clinic,
where she was cleaned up. She was complaining of a slight head-
ache and nothing else.

The suspect was later identified as Scomberomorus maculatus
(Atlantic Spanish Mackerel) A.K.A 'Mack.'

He was found lying on the ground possibly attempting to conceal
himself out in the open.

I took control of the suspect without incident and escorted him to
the clinic where he was positively identified by the victim.

While speaking with the victim she advised: 'I was watching
students when all of a sudden I was struck in the head by this
flying fish. I yelled, 'Holy Mackerel, what just happened?'

The victim was not able to advise how 'Mack' got to the school
but theorized that he possibly hitched a ride from an unknown
accomplice/bird possibly named 'Osprey.' She doesn't think it was
'Eagle,' as we are the Eagles at Naples High School.

I made contact with Principal Dr. Graham at Naples High and
showed her the suspect. I advised her at this time he might be
arrested for battery on school employee (Florida Statute 784.081
(2) (c)).

Suspect 'Mack' was escorted back to my office, where I advised him
of Miranda warning.

He 'clammed up' (being from the ocean) and refused to answer any questions or make any statements.

The victim did not fill out a sworn statement or wish to press charges.

She only advised that 'something fishy is going on here.' The suspect was released with further investigation required. The Osprey might be the true suspect for the battery.

We are grateful here that it was not a flying cow, as injuries would be more severe and the teacher might have screamed 'Holy Cow what was that?'

We will still be on the lookout for 'when pigs fly,' though.

Cpl. Jim Brown

*   *   *

WHO ARE THESE GUYS?

All of these guys are named Guy…but what are their last names?

1. This Guy is the English writer and director of comedic crime movies such as *Snatch* and *Lock, Stock and Two Smoking Barrels*.

2. This Guy was a Canadian bandleader and hosted the New Year's Eve broadcast on CBS (radio and TV) from 1928 to 1977.

3. If you "remember, remember the fifth of November," or the 1605 "Gunpowder Plot" to assassinate King James I, you'll know this Guy.

4. This Guy was one of the most successful players in NHL history—he was the first to score 100 points in six straight years.

5. This Muppet Guy hosts game show parodies on *Sesame Street*.

6. This Guy is a TV chef, known for his unique look of flame shirts, bleached hair, and sunglasses on the back of his head.

7. This Guy is a gumshoe played by Garrison Keillor in a sketch on his long-running *A Prairie Home Companion* radio show.

8. This Guy is the main character and primary book burner in Ray Bradbury's 1953 novel *Fahrenheit 451*.

9. Whether in cahoots with the Sheriff of Nottingham or pursuing Maid Marian, this Guy is one of Robin Hood's worst enemies.

10. This Guy was born in Australia, and has starred in films such as *Memento* and *L.A. Confidential*.

Answers

10. Guy Pearce

1. Guy Ritchie; 2. Guy Lombardo; 3. Guy Fawkes; 4. Guy Lafleur; 5. Guy Smiley; 6. Guy Fieri; 7. Guy Noir; 8. Guy Montag; 9. Sir Guy of Gisborne;

The Last Player

It's fun to be the first, but it's also pretty cool to be the last—a living legacy of something that's faded into the sports history books.

LAST ABA PLAYER IN THE NBA

In 1976 the NBA absorbed what was left of the failing American Basketball Association, including four teams and about 60 players. Many became stars, such as Rick Barry, Julius Erving, George Gervin…and Moses Malone. Malone was drafted by the ABA's Utah Stars in 1974, right out of high school. In the NBA, he was a three-time all-star. When he retired in 1995, he was the last ABAer still playing.

LAST "DREAM TEAM" MEMBER IN THE NBA

In 1992 the International Olympic Committee allowed professional basketball players to compete in the Summer Olympics. Team USA was stacked with 11 NBA all-stars (including Michael Jordan, Karl Malone, and Charles Barkley) and one college standout (Christian Laettner of Duke University). They rolled easily into the top position, beating Croatia in the final game 117–85 and winning the gold medal. The last person on the squad to suit up in the NBA: Christian Laettner. He played for six NBA teams after the Olympics, retiring in 2005 after a one-year stint with the Miami Heat.

LAST NHL PLAYER WITHOUT A HELMET

For decades, helmets were optional in the NHL, and those who wore them were derided as not as tough as those who didn't. But when player Bill Masterton suffered head trauma in a 1968 game and died, helmets suddenly became more popular. In 1979 the league made them mandatory but allowed those already in the league to opt out of the rule. Craig MacTavish was one of those who opted out, and by the time he played his final games in 1997, he was the only player on the ice without head protection.

LAST NEGRO LEAGUER TO PLAY IN AN MLB GAME

Minnie Miñoso joined the Negro League's New York Cubans in 1946 (he really was Cuban) and led them to a 1947 Negro World Series championship…the same year that Jackie Robinson integrated Major League Baseball. A year later, Miñoso was signed by the Cleveland Indians. He was a seven-time all-star throughout the 1950s and 1960s and retired from the big leagues in 1963 but played in Mexico for

---

Laundry hung out to dry outside smells better because sunlight bleaches smells as well as colors.

another decade. In 1976 he signed on as a third-base coach for the Chicago White Sox and played in three late-season games. His last hurrah? Nope. Amazingly, the 54-year-old coach was called upon to pinch-hit in two games in 1980. That was the last time a player from the Negro Leagues took the field in a major league game.

LAST AFL PLAYER IN THE NFL

In 1970 the competing National and American Football Leagues merged to become one league, the NFL (with two conferences, the NFC and the AFC). Wide receiver Charlie Joiner joined the Houston Oilers of the AFL in 1969, just as the two leagues were about to be combined. He played a long Hall of Fame career in the NFL after the merger. When he retired from the San Diego Chargers in 1986, he was the last pre-merger player in the league.

LAST BROOKLYN DODGER

Utility infielder Bob Aspromonte was four years into his major league career when his team—the Brooklyn Dodgers—moved to Los Angeles in 1960. He was traded to three more teams before retiring in 1971, the last active player to have played for the Dodgers when they were still in New York.

LAST MONTREAL EXPO

After 30 mostly fruitless seasons in Montreal (they never even made the playoffs, let alone play in a World Series), the Expos were put up for sale in 2004, moved to Washington, D.C., and became the Washington Nationals. The last active player to have worn an Expos uniform is pitcher Bartolo Colón. As of 2015, he's 41 and playing for the New York Mets.

LAST XFL PLAYER IN THE NFL

After NBC lost the rights to air lucrative, popular NFL games in 2000, the network teamed with World Wrestling Entertainment to form a new league to compete against the NFL: the XFL. (The "X" is for "extreme," as the league promised to be more brutal and violent than the NFL.) But the quality of play was poor, and the league folded after its only season, in 2001. A few dozen XFL standouts went on to play in the NFL, including Pittsburgh Steelers quarterback Tommy Maddux. Linebacker Paris Lenon played for the XFL's Memphis Maniacs, and after the league folded, bounced around the NFL, playing for Green Bay, Seattle, Detroit, New England, St. Louis, Arizona, and Denver. Lenon was the last XFL player active in the NFL. Lenon's final game in the NFL was the 2014 Super Bowl, where as a member of the Denver Broncos, he lost to the Seattle Seahawks 43–8.

Augustus Caesar had *achluophobia.* **(He was afraid of the dark.)**

High-Tech Underwear

Who says underwear should only be clean and comfortable?
Here's a look at some skivvies with extra built-in features.

SHREDDIES

What They Are: The latest attempt at flatulence-filtering underwear, this time using military-strength materials

Details: Built into the seat of each pair of Shreddies is a panel of Zorflex, the material used to protect soldiers from poison gas attacks. "Due to Zorflex's highly porous nature, the odor vapors become trapped and neutralized by the cloth, which is then reactivated by simply washing the garment," says the U.K. manufacturer. Thanks to the neutralizing power of Zorflex, Shreddies can trap odors 200 times the strength of a typical toot and will last two to three years. (But how you deal with the *sound* of flatulence is your problem.) Price: £19–24 ($32–40), depending on the style.

OPEDIX LONG UNDERWEAR

What They Are: Underwear that improves your skiing

Details: These waist-to-ankle tights are part of a new generation of "graduated compression garments" that tailor the compression they provide to the specific muscles, tendons, and ligaments they cover. In the process, they reduce muscle fatigue and speed recovery after physical activity. Because these underpants are designed especially for skiers, they provide extra compression around the knees to stabilize them and keep them properly positioned, reducing ski injuries. Price: $225—not cheap, but a lot less expensive than knee surgery.

SNOWBALLS

What They Are: Fertility-enhancing underwear for men who may be having trouble conceiving children

Details: One significant cause of male infertility is a *varicocele* (enlarged) vein in the scrotum. This can cause too much blood—and, therefore, too much heat—to flow into the testicles, inhibiting their ability to produce healthy sperm. That's where Snowballs briefs come in. In place of an ordinary fly, Snowballs feature a built-in pouch that holds a freezable SnowWedge gel pack. "Although testicle icing is never high on anybody's list of things to do, we've designed these wedges to give you the cooling you need without being painful," says the manufacturer. "At least a couple hours of cooling per day is ideal, and we strongly

---

The average novel sells fewer than 250 copies per year.

advise you not to ice for more than an hour at a time." Each $59 "fertility pack" contains two pairs of Snowballs briefs and three SnowWedges.

KNIX WEAR

What They Are: Superabsorbent underwear designed for the 30 percent of women who may experience a light form of "stress incontinence"

Details: Knix Wear contains a special absorbent material in the "gusset," or crotch area of the garment, sandwiched between two layers of ordinary cotton fabric. When incontinence strikes, perhaps when the wearer is exercising, laughing, or sneezing, the top cotton layer wicks the moisture into the absorbent material below. There, a leak-resistant membrane prevents the moisture from traveling any further. Anti-microbial silver fibers in the absorbent material help prevent odors. Price: $24–38, depending on the style.

Note: When the Knix Wear company was launched on the crowdfunding website Indiegogo.com in early 2013, it set a goal of $40,000… but raised more than $60,000 in just over a month.

RADIASHIELD BOXER BRIEFS

What They Are: Men's underwear that protects the wearer's private parts from "harmful cell phone radiation"

Details: There's no evidence that electromagnetic radiation given off by cell phones when they're in use can lower a person's sperm count. (If there was, the phones would probably be marketed as a form of electronic birth control.) But that hasn't stopped Belly Armor, maker of RadiaShield boxer briefs, from promoting the possibility. The crotch panel is made from fabric containing silver threads that the company says blocks 99.9 percent of cell phone radiation, "protecting men's reproductive organs and maintaining fertility health." Price: $49 a pair.

WEARABLE MONITORING SYSTEM UNDERPANTS

What They Are: Underwear that monitors the user's blood pressure

Details: If you get nervous when you have to go to the doctor's office, it can be difficult for your physician to accurately measure your blood pressure. And a typical reading only reveals what your blood pressure is at that moment; your doctor has no way of knowing what it is at other times of day. Wearable Monitoring System underwear addresses these issues by recording your blood pressure around the clock, using sensors in the waistband to track "pulse wave velocity," which is closely correlated to blood pressure. The data is stored in a tiny computer chip, also in the waistband, where it can be retrieved and analyzed by your physician later. The Dutch electronics giant Philips patented the system in 2008, but as of 2014, they had yet to bring the underpants to market.

Duh! *Ultracrepidarianism* means "giving opinions on matters outside of one's knowledge."

I Spy...from the Sky

On page 31 we told you about aerial archaeology, the field of science in which archaeological discoveries are made from above—via airplane, drone, or satellite. Here are some other things that were discovered from above.

A **RIVER OF BLOOD.** In January 2012, a Dallas, Texas, man was flying his small camera-equipped drone over the Columbia Packing Company, a large meatpacking plant, when he spotted what he later told reporters looked like a "river of blood" flowing from the plant. The man, who requested that he not be named, reported it to the Texas Environmental Crimes Task Force. They went to the plant with a search warrant and found a significant amount of pig blood flowing out of the plant into a nearby creek, and from there into the Trinity River, Texas's largest river—a serious violation of environmental laws. The company was immediately shut down; the owners were fined $100,000.

A CROCODILE (IN GREECE). A man on the Greek island of Crete was flying a drone over a small man-made lake in July 2014 when he captured video of a six-foot-long crocodile casually floating on the surface of the lake. Crocodiles aren't native to Greece, so the discovery baffled scientists and frightened locals who swim in the lake. Local wildlife officials fenced off the lake and began capture attempts of the beast. Exactly how a crocodile got into the lake remains unknown, but officials said it had probably been owned by someone who kept the creature as a pet and then released it into the lake once it grew too large to control. Area farmers said the discovery likely explained the disappearances of several animals, including chickens, ducks, and even some sheep. (More footage of the mystery beast has been captured by drones since its initial discovery, but it has so far eluded capture—and is still lurking in the lake today.)

THE MILLENNIUM FALCON. Small-plane pilot Matthew Myatt was flying over an old army base in southern England in 2014 when he saw what looked like a group of experimental aircraft on the grounds of the base. He took photographs of the airships, and when he got home, took a closer look. One of the aircraft looked suspiciously like the *Millennium Falcon*—the spacecraft flown by Harrison Ford's Han Solo character in the *Star Wars* films. Another looked like an X-Wing fighter craft from the films. And that's exactly what they were. Myatt had flown over the secret location of the filming of *Star Wars: The Force Awakens*. "I had to go and grab my son, who's a big *Star Wars* fan,"

Oldest known multiorgan animal: the jellyfish. It has existed for more than 650 million years.

Myatt told the BBC, "and get him to come and look at the picture, and pinch me and make sure I'd seen what I'd seen." The photos created an online sensation among *Star Wars* fans.

A GIANT SWASTIKA. In December 2014, police flying a helicopter over the southern Brazilian town of Pomerode were surprised to see a giant swastika painted on the bottom of a home swimming pool. They snapped a photo of the swastika and posted it online. The photo went viral, causing worldwide outrage—especially among Jewish groups—that increased when police determined that the homeowner hadn't broken any laws because the swastika was on private property. The story was made all the more ominous by its location. Roughly 90 percent of Pomerode's 25,000 inhabitants are of German descent, and most of them still speak German today. Pomerode was a popular destination for Nazis fleeing Germany at the end of World War II.

A MISSING MAN. In July 2014, Guillermo DeVenecia, 82, went missing from his home in the small rural town of Fitchburg, Wisconsin. After three days of fruitless searches by police and rescue workers, DeVenecia, who suffers from dementia, still hadn't been found. David Lesh, 34, of Colorado, happened to be visiting his girlfriend in Fitchburg, and he had his video-equipped drone with him. (Lesh was the owner of a winter outerwear store in Colorado and used the drone to take videos of skiers and snowboarders to make advertisements for his store.) Lesh sent the drone up and, a little while later, spotted a man standing in a remote corner of a 200-acre beanfield. It was DeVenecia. Lesh and his drone had found the lost man—who had somehow been missed by police, along with hundreds of searchers, rescue dogs, and even helicopters, for almost three days—in about 20 minutes. (DeVenecia, rescue workers said, was in remarkably good shape, if a bit confused: he thought he'd been on just a short walk—and wondered what all the fuss was about.)

*   *   *

CONTRONYMS

Words that have two opposite meanings.

• **Sanction** means to "to give approval to" and also "penalize."
• **Seed** means to "to add seeds to" and also "to remove the seeds."
• **Left** means "remaining" and also "departed."
• **Oversight** means "monitoring" and "failure to monitor."
• **Fast** means "quickly" and also "stand still," as in "holding fast."

First Role: Game Show Contestant

Most TV game shows are made in Hollywood, so it makes sense that aspiring actors—a.k.a. Hollywood waitresses and dishwashers—would show up on game shows to get some face time on TV (and maybe win some cash).

JOHN RITTER

Appeared as a contestant on: *The Dating Game*

Story: In 1967 Ritter was a 19-year-old freshman drama student at the University of Southern California when he appeared as "Bachelor Number Three" on *The Dating Game*. He was a hit with the audience and the bubbly blonde bachelorette—and he won. Prize: a trip to a lakeside resort in Arizona. (Ritter went on to become the Emmy-winning star of *Three's Company*, but this was his first time on TV.)

Bonus fact: Years later, Ritter revealed that when he and his date—and their chaperone—got to the resort, it was closed. They had to stay in a nearby motel instead.

AARON PAUL

Appeared as a contestant on: *The Price Is Right*

Story: In January 2000, Bob Barker gave the "Come on down!" call and Paul went absolutely bonkers, making his way to contestants' row, screaming, "You're the man, Bob! You're my idol!" When he guessed the right price on an item, he went even crazier, leaping onto the stage, putting a hand on Barker's shoulder, and screaming to the audience, "I'm touching Bob Barker!" And when Barker told him he had a chance to win a car, Paul fell to the ground, then bounded up and jumped around the stage like a wildman…but he didn't win the car.

Bonus fact: In 2004 Paul, star of the AMC hit *Breaking Bad*, said that right before the show he'd "downed about six cans of Red Bull, because I knew they wanted people with energy. It was not healthy."

PAUL REUBENS

Appeared as a contestant on: *The Gong Show*

Story: Reubens was a 25-year-old unknown in 1977 when he and fellow comic Charlotte McGinnis got a spot on the offbeat game show *The Gong Show*. They performed a goofy routine they called "The Hilarious Betty and Eddie"—and the judges loved it: they received the highest possible score and won the top prize of $500. Reubens was such a hit with the host, Chuck Barris, that he appeared on the show 15 times over the next three years. Reubens later said the appearances helped him survive those lean years, before his Pee-Wee Herman character made him a star.

FARRAH FAWCETT

Appeared as a contestant on: *The Dating Game*

Story: In 1968, the 21-year-old Fawcett dropped out of college in Austin, Texas, and went to Hollywood, hoping to make it as a model and an actress. In March 1969, she took the route that many other aspiring stars took and appeared on *The Dating Game* as a bachelorette. Did it help her career? Maybe: a few months later, she got her first role on a TV series, playing the role of "showgirl #1" on *Mayberry R.F.D.*

Bonus fact: When Fawcett chose "Bachelor Number Two" at the end of that *Dating Game* episode, the other two bachelors became angry and a brawl broke out, with punches thrown and chairs smashed. It was an April Fools' Day gag. (The show aired just a few days before April 1.) All three of the bachelors were professional stuntmen.

KIRSTIE ALLEY

Appeared as a contestant on: *Match Game, Password Plus*

Story: Alley moved from Kansas to L.A. in the 1970s to pursue her interest in the Church of Scientology. While there, she developed an interest in acting. (Her first TV role: an uncredited "handmaiden" on the 1978 science-fiction comedy series *Quark*.) In 1979 Alley, 28, went on *The Match Game*, where she was introduced as an interior designer. And she kicked butt, winning $6,000. (In 1980 she appeared on another game show—*Password Plus*—but only won $800.)

Bonus fact: It took Alley another two years to get her first credited acting job, but it was a doozy: in 1982 she got the part of the Vulcan Saavik in the smash hit *Star Trek II: The Wrath of Khan*.

JON HAMM

Appeared as a contestant on: *The Big Date*

Story: Hamm moved from St. Louis to Hollywood in 1995, at the age of 24, to pursue an acting career—inspired, in part, by the success of his high school friend Paul Rudd. A year later, he appeared as a contestant on *The Big Date*, a dating show that ran for a year on the USA Network. It didn't help his acting career: Hamm got just one paid acting job in his first five years in Hollywood. (When he appeared on *The Big Date*, Hamm was working as a set decorator…for soft-core porn films.)

Bonus fact: During Hamm's *The Big Date* appearance, the future *Mad Men* star was turned down—by two different women.

Odd Animal Studies

*And meow for some fishy animal
research we ferreted out.*

STUDY: "Aging Modulates Cuticular Hydrocarbons and Sexual Attractiveness in *Drosophila melanogaster*" (*Journal of Experimental Biology*, March 2012)

PURPOSE: To find out if fruit flies lose their sex appeal as they age

METHODOLOGY: To test female attractiveness to males, a single male was introduced to a chamber containing two decapitated females, one 8 days old and another 52 days old. (Apparently fruit flies do not lose their sex appeal when they're beheaded.) To test male attractiveness to females, a single female was placed in a chamber with decapitated 8-day-old and 52-day-old males. The lifespan of fruit flies in a lab is two to three months.

FINDINGS: 1) Both males and females showed a marked preference for younger members of the opposite sex.

2) When the experiments were repeated in complete darkness, the males continued to prefer younger females, but the females did not prefer younger males, "suggesting that visual cues are important for *female* preference"—but not for *male* preference, say the scientists.

3) What, then, drives the male fruit fly's preference for younger females? Sexual attractiveness pheromones called *cuticular hydrocarbons*, or CHCs. When the CHCs were washed off one group of female fruit flies, the male fruit flies couldn't distinguish between younger and older females. Similarly, when a special strain of fruit flies that produce no CHCs were "painted" either with CHCs from a young female or with CHCs from an old female, the males were attracted to the flies treated with "young" CHCs even though all the female flies in this experiment were the same age.

STUDY: "Beetles on the Bottle: Male Buprestids Mistake Stubbies for Females" (*Australian Journal of Entomology*, 1983)

PURPOSE: To understand why male *buprestid* beetles "mate" with discarded beer bottles (called "stubbies" in Australia). "We have recently observed this to be quite a common occurrence in the Dongara area of Western Australia," wrote the researchers.

METHODOLOGY: "A short experiment was conducted in which four stubbies were placed on the ground in an open area."

FINDINGS: 1) "Within 30 minutes two bottles had attracted beetles. In total, six male beetles were observed to mount stubbies. Once on the bottles the beetles did not leave unless displaced by us."

2) The beetles continued copulating even when ants attacked and began eating them alive. "A dead male, covered with ants, was located a few centimeters away" from one of the bottles.

3) The brown color of the bottles, combined with rows of bumps, or *tubercles*, at the base of the bottle, caused the beetles to mistake the stubbies for giant females. The tubercles reflected light in a manner similar to the irregular surface of the wings of female beetles, confusing the males and arousing them at the same time.

4) "Improperly disposed of beer bottles not only present a physical and 'visual' hazard in the environment, but also potentially cause great interference with the mating system of a beetle species."

STUDY: "Robotic Squirrel Models: Study of Squirrel-Rattlesnake Interaction in Laboratory and Natural Settings" (*IEEE Robotics and Automation Magazine*, December 2011)

PURPOSE: To understand how squirrels discourage rattlesnakes from attacking (which they're surprisingly good at)

METHODOLOGY: Scientists at San Diego State University and the University of California–Davis converted taxidermy squirrels into robotic squirrels capable of mimicking the behavior squirrels exhibit when they encounter a rattlesnake. Rather than flee from rattlesnakes, squirrels often face off against the rattler head-on, with their tail raised and waving from side to side.

Infrared photography has shown that squirrels increase blood flow to their tail during such encounters, causing it to heat up. But the squirrels only heat their tails when confronting rattlesnakes, which have special organs that allow them to "see" infrared heat. When they challenge gopher snakes, which cannot see infrared heat, squirrels do not heat their tails. The scientists wanted to test whether squirrels communicate a message to rattlesnakes with infrared heat and also whether rattlesnakes "get" the message. That's why they created robosquirrel: they can wave the robot's tail without heating it, and heat the tail without waving it, to test how rattlesnakes respond to such cues.

FINDINGS: 1) When the robosquirrel waved a *heated* tail at a rattlesnake that was preparing to strike, the rattlesnake ceased its predatory behavior and moved away from the robosquirrel.

2) When the robosquirrel waved an *unheated* tail at the rattler, it continued its predatory behavior and attacked, suggesting that the squirrel is indeed communicating with the rattlesnake, and the rattlesnake understands the message. "This is the first example of infrared

communication in the animal world," says Sanjay Joshi, the UC Davis mechanical engineer who designed the robosquirrel.

3) Why would a rattlesnake back down from a confrontation with a squirrel? One theory: to conserve energy. Squirrels are remarkably adept at dodging rattlesnakes, even when ambushed. When a rattlesnake loses the element of surprise—which the squirrel communicates by heating and waving its tail—the odds of killing and eating the squirrel drop so low that it's not worth the effort. The snake abandons its hiding place and goes looking for another one.

STUDY: "Massage Timing Affects Postexercise Muscle Recovery and Inflammation in a Rabbit Model" (*Medicine and Science in Sports and Exercise*, 2013)

PURPOSE: To find out whether massaging rabbits after they exercise speeds "muscle recovery"

METHODOLOGY: The rabbits worked out on special exercise equipment, then were given massages using a "mechanical device that simulates the long, flowing strokes used in Swedish massages." Recovery times were compared with exercising rabbits who received either Swedish massages 48 hours after exercise, or no massages at all.

FINDINGS: The rabbits who received immediate Swedish massages recovered the fastest.

STUDY: "Enhancement of Sexual Motivation" (University of Kentucky, 2011–15)

PURPOSE: To determine how illegal drug use affects the sex drive of Japanese quail

METHODOLOGY: Medicinal cocaine is administered to the birds in varying doses and at different intervals over time. "The overall working hypothesis of this proposal," say the researchers, "is that the magnitude of the sexual response depends on several cocaine pre-exposure parameters including dose, amount of exposure, time between exposures, and the withdrawal period before sexual behavior testing."

FINDINGS: Pending. The experiment was scheduled to run into 2015, with the results being published after they'd been analyzed. Why conduct the experiment in the first place? In the hope that it will shed light on the link between illegal drug use and high-risk sexual behavior in humans. Why Japanese quail? The researchers give three reasons: 1) their "sexual behavior system has been well-studied," 2) the birds "readily engage in reproductive behavior in the laboratory," and 3) "quail provide a convenient and interesting alternative to standard laboratory rats and pigeons."

In the 1400s, narwhal tusks were sold as unicorn horns (Price: four times their weight in gold.)

Oops!

*Everyone loves tales of outrageous blunders, especially
when they happen to someone else. So go ahead
and feel superior for a few minutes.*

HERE COMES TRUFFLE

One Sunday in 2014, a restaurant patron (unnamed in press reports) was having brunch at the Equinox in Washington, D.C., when she saw a complimentary snack on a display plate under a glass dome. She picked it up and took a bite, then put the rest of it on her bread plate and took it to her table. Just then, the restaurant's owner, Ellen Kassoff Gray, walked up and explained to the woman that this was no ordinary snack, nor was it complimentary—it was in fact a rare White Alba truffle. And Gray was charging customers $20 for a single shaving. Estimated cost of the woman's bite: $300. Adding insult to injury, "she didn't like the taste," said Gray, "and suggested the chef salvage the unbitten part." That didn't happen. The woman wasn't charged, but the pricey truffle was a total loss.

NEXT THEY'LL MOVE TO THE TOWN OF HIGHWATER

Several families on the coast of Washington lost their homes to rising tides, battering winds, and a storm surge in late 2014. But they can't say they weren't warned—nearly 200 homes there have washed away into the ocean in the last century. "I knew it was going to happen sooner or later," said unlucky homeowner Ray Miller, "but I had hoped it wasn't this soon." One thing that might have tipped him off: the area's nickname. It's known as Washaway Beach.

PLANTED

Ronald Podlaski is a Portland, Maine, artist who calls himself "RookSye." One night in 2014, he drank a few beers and decided to prank a friend by entering her third-story apartment through the window. The inebriated man went up the fire escape and then climbed into what he thought was his friend's window, but it wasn't even her apartment. Turns out it wasn't even her building. (She was in El Salvador with her fiancé at the time.) The window belonged to a florist shop, and just as Podlaski realized that he was in the wrong place, the burglar alarm went off. He tried to escape but tripped over a "vine-like material" and then toppled out of the third-story window, taking a candelabra with him. When he came to on the ground, he had a sprained wrist…

In Maine, buildings made of round logs are tax-exempt.

and there were two police officers standing over him. At first, Podlaski refused to give his real name, only saying, "I am RookSye." The cops arrested him, believing he'd tried to burgle the shop, but let him go the next day when they realized he wasn't a criminal, but merely—as Podlaski himself described it—"foolish."

ACCIDENTAL TEETOTALERS
The town of Hanover, Manitoba, had been "dry" since the 1800s; the sale of alcohol was illegal there. Then, in 2014, a proposal was submitted to let the townspeople vote to end the prohibition. The first step: town leaders needed to track down the original law…but they couldn't locate it. So they hired a law firm to sift through the town records. They couldn't find it, either. Reason: it turned out that there never was an official alcohol ban in Hanover—everyone had just assumed there was for more than a century.

KEYLESS EXIT
It was Guy Fawkes Night in November 2014, and the people of Alexandra, New Zealand, were celebrating loudly. That's why no one heard Brian and Mollieanne Smith honking their car horn. They were stuck inside their new Mazda3 hatchback, which was parked in their garage. The couple, both in their sixties, didn't have the key fob with them. And the doors were locked. They tried using a car jack to break the window, but that didn't work. So the Smiths sat trapped in their car for 13 hours. When a neighbor discovered and freed them the next morning, they were near death. That's when Brian discovered the manual locking mechanism on the door. "Once I found out how simple it was," he sheepishly admitted, "I kicked myself that I did not find the way out sooner."

KOOKY KAMPAIGN
In 2015 the Krispy Kreme doughnut chain posted an announcement on its U.K. Facebook page for upcoming events at a Krispy Kreme in Hull, England. Shortly after the post went up, hundreds of the page's 200,000 fans commented that it probably wasn't a good idea to abbreviate the "Krispy Kreme Klub." Here's what was posted:

Why not come and join us in our Hull store during the holiday with the children for our fun activities…Funday Monday, Colouring Tuesday, KKK Wednesday, and Face Painting Thursday!

Once company officials realized that "KKK" is the name of the American white supremacist organization, they deleted the post, apologized profusely, and promised to never do it again.

Mind Your Manners

A few tips on how to behave like perfect ladies and proper gentlemen, from the etiquette books of yesteryear.

FASHION

F"As it is bad taste to flaunt the airs of the town among the provincials, who know nothing of them, it is worse taste to display the dress of a city in the quiet haunts of the rustics. The law, that all attempts at distinction by means of dress is vulgar and pretentious, would be sufficient argument against wearing city fashions in the country."

—*The Gentlemen's Book of Etiquette and Manual of Politeness* (1860)

"Tight lacing of corsets is also very unbecoming to those who usually adopt it—women of thirty-eight or forty who are growing a little stout. In thus trussing themselves up they simply get an unbecoming redness of the face, and are not the handsome, comfortable-looking creatures which Heaven intended they should be. Two or three beautiful women well known in society killed themselves last year by tight lacing."

—*Manners and Social Usages* (1887)

PERFORMING IN PUBLIC

"Never exhibit your accomplishments, unless 'by special request,' in the public parlors of hotels, or other places of general gathering. The persons who sing and play the piano make themselves bores and are as reprehensible as window opening and shutting fiends most obnoxious."

—*The Complete Bachelor: Manners for Men* (1896)

SHAKING HANDS

"A man with hands gloved should never shake hands with a woman without an apology for so doing, unless she likewise wears gloves. A sudden meeting, etc., may make a hand-shaking in gloves unavoidable. Unless the other party is also gloved, a man should say: 'Please excuse my glove.'"

—*The Book of Good Manners* (1922)

"Never offer to shake hands with a lady; she will, if she wishes you to do so, offer her hand to you, and it is an impertinence for you to do so first."

—*The Gentlemen's Manual of Politeness* (1860)

The American flags planted on the Moon were made of nylon and cost NASA $5.50 each.

"Inferiors in social position should always wait until their superiors offer the hand, never taking the initiative in this respect. This precaution will sometimes save them the pain of a marked slight."
— *The Manners and Customs of Polite Society* (1896)

UMBRELLAS

"If you have the care of two ladies, let them carry your umbrella between them, and walk outside yourself. Nothing can be more absurd than for a gentleman to walk between two ladies, holding the umbrella himself; while, in this way, he is perfectly protected, the ladies receive upon their dresses and cloaks the little streams of water which run from the points of the umbrella."
— *The Gentlemen's Book of Etiquette and Manual of Politeness* (1860)

"Ladies, what are you doing? Sucking the head of your parasol! Have you not breakfasted? Take that piece of ivory from your mouth! To suck it is unlady-like, and let me tell you, excessively unbecoming. Rosy lips and pearly teeth can be put to a better use."
— *The Ladies' Book of Etiquette and Manual of Politeness* (1860)

REGARDING THE OPPOSITE SEX

"A young lady should not write letters to young men, or send them presents, or take the initiative in any way. A friendly correspondence is very proper if the mother approves, but even this has its dangers. Let a young lady always remember that she is to the young man an angel until she lessens the distance between them and extinguishes respect."
— *Manners and Social Usages* (1887)

"Girls, it is poor policy to call up boys often by telephone, and bad manners to whistle to attract their attention…Boys, you can easily tell what girls would have you sit very close to them, and hold their hands, and put your arms around them. But, be manly. Always protect a girl; protect her from yourself, even from herself. If she does not wish to be so protected, avoid her as you would the plague."
— *Manners and Conduct in School and Out* (1921)

*　　*　　*

UNCANNY FACT

The first tin can was patented in 1810. Can openers weren't invented until 1858.

Gojira ("Godzilla") is a portmanteau of the Japanese words *gorira* ("gorilla") and *kujira* ("whale").

Four Experiments ...of the Paranormal

Many people have conducted paranormal "experiments." (Uncle John spent the entire summer of 1972 trying to prove he became invisible at a Doors concert...but let's not go there.) Every once in a while, though, real scientists take up the challenge. Here are a few notable examples.

THE GOD HELMET EXPERIMENT

In the 1980s, Dr. Michael Persinger, neuroscientist and professor at Laurentian University in Ontario, began a series of experiments with what became known as the "God Helmet." What was that? A modified snowmobile helmet fitted with devices that emitted weak magnetic fields. Those magnetic waves, Persinger said, disturbed normal brain function and disrupted communication between the brain's two temporal lobes. (There's one in each of the brain's two hemispheres.) Result: according to Persinger, 80 percent of the test subjects reported sensations commonly associated with spiritual or religious experiences. Many said they could sense a "spiritual being" near them. This, claimed Persinger, supported his contention that religious experience is not caused by some outside entity but is rooted in our brains. Not everyone agreed with Persinger's conclusion. To publicize the experiment, he invited renowned evolutionary biologist (and atheist) Richard Dawkins to try the God Helmet. Dawkins said he experienced strange sensations in his limbs and that his breathing felt funny at times—but that it felt *nothing* like a religious experience. Persinger responded by saying Dawkins had insensitive temporal lobes.

Update: In 2004 Swedish scientists repeated Persinger's experiment but were unable to reproduce Persinger's results. Persinger's response: the researchers hadn't set the magnetic waves correctly.

THE PHILIP EXPERIMENT

In 1972 Dr. Alan Robert George Owen, a Cambridge-educated British mathematician and founder of the Toronto Society for Psychical Research, devised an experiment to determine whether people could conjure up ghosts...of imaginary people. Eight people were chosen at random from the society's membership. They invented a character named "Philip" and then created a biography for him. He was a 17th-century English aristocrat who lived at Diddington Manor in

Warwickshire. He was married, but when he had an affair, his wife accused the other woman of witchcraft, and she was burned at the stake. Heartbroken, 30-year-old Philip took his own life.

Everyone in the group memorized the details they'd made up for Philip and began having weekly séances around a card table to try to contact his ghost. For a year nothing happened, and then, according to Owen and the team, Philip started revealing himself. When group members asked a question, rapping could be heard and felt on the table. Sometimes the table would move around the room—or even float in the air. (One of the séances was filmed for Canadian TV.)

Ultimately, Dr. Owen and his supporters weren't quite sure what the Philip experiment proved. They were sure they'd conjured up *something*, but exactly what and how they did not know. Perhaps it proved that the phenomena known as ghosts or spirits are actually "projections" created by the people experiencing them. Or maybe the experiment proved that psychokinesis—the ability to move things (like card tables) with your mind—is real. Or maybe a real ghost hijacked the séance and pretended to be Philip. Critics point out that "séances" such as the ones used in the Philip experiment, have been consistently debunked as frauds, which makes any conclusions suspect.

THE SOUL WEIGHT EXPERIMENT

In 1901 Dr. Duncan MacDougall, a physician in Dorchester, Massachusetts, had a specially designed bed built in his office. It was "arranged on a light framework built upon very delicately balanced platform beam scales," which, he said, could weigh a person within 0.2 ounces, or roughly 5.6 grams. The purpose of the bed: to weigh people at the precise moment of their death to determine the weight of the soul leaving the body, thereby proving that the soul is a real, physical thing. For his subjects, MacDougall chose six people dying of tuberculosis. Why tuberculosis victims? Because he wanted subjects "dying with a disease that produces great exhaustion, the death occurring with little or no muscular movement," so as not to upset his delicate bed-scale. Result: according to MacDougall, people lost an average of 0.75 ounce, or 21.3 grams, when they died. He also tried the experiment on 15 dying dogs (the dogs didn't have any diseases—MacDougall simply killed them with drugs), and there was no weight change when they expired. This appeared to prove what Dr. MacDougall undoubtedly believed going into his experiment: that humans have souls, and animals (or at least dogs) do not.

Remarkably, the "results" of MacDougall's studies were published in medical journals and even in the *New York Times*. Skeptics pointed out that an experiment using only six subjects could hardly be called conclusive, and, more important, MacDougall never explained how he

U.S. gymnast George Eyser won six medals in the 1904 Olympics with a wooden leg.

determined the exact point of death, something doctors are unable to agree on even today.

THE AFTERLIFE EXPERIMENTS

In 1993 Gary Schwartz, professor of psychology at the University of Arizona, met and married a fellow psychologist, Dr. Linda Russek. Russek had recently lost her father, and she asked Schwartz, "Do you think it is possible that my father is still alive?" That set off a series of studies—detailed in Schwartz's 2002 book, *The Afterlife Experiments.* Some of the world's best-known "mediums" were asked to provide information about specific dead people; "sitters"—people who had close relationships with those dead people—then noted whether the information the mediums gave was true or false. Outcome: the information provided by the mediums was judged correct a remarkable 77 to 95 percent of the time. The experiment was then repeated, but with students acting as the mediums—and they got an average correct rate of only 36 percent.

This, Schwartz claimed, was "Breakthrough Scientific Evidence of Life After Death"…which was also the subtitle of his book. The experiments received heavy criticism, though, based on a technique used by mentalists and fortune tellers known as "cold reading," in which the "mediums" read the subject's body language more than they read into the subject's soul. That, say critics, is why the mediums did so much better than the students.

*   *   *

UNUSUAL RESTROOM SIGNS

Because anybody can mark the doors "men" and "women."

• "Nuts" *and* "No Nuts"
• "Chickens" *and* "Cats"
• "Marios" *and* "Princess Toadstools"
• "Lagers" *and* "Ales"
• "For Those Who Stand" *and* "For Those Who Sit"
• "Bruffas" *and* "Hula Dancers"
• "Pointers" *and* "Setters"
• "Football" *and* "Shopping"
• "The Men's Room is across the hall" *and* "The Ladies' Room is across the hall"

Like octopuses and chameleons, sea horses can change their color to match their surroundings.

When Audiences Attack

*It's not really funny when comedians and audiences
turn on each other. (Well, sometimes it is.)*

THE PHILADELPHIA EXPERIMENT. In 2006 comedian Bill Burr was part of a stand-up show organized by morning radio shock jocks Opie and Anthony, whose rowdy fans filled Philadelphia's Susquehanna Bank Center amphitheater. By the time it was Burr's turn to go on, the crowd had already booed two comedians off the stage. And these comics, Irish-American tough guy Robert Kelly and Philadelphia native Dom Irrera, were no pushovers. Knowing it was pointless to try to do his usual act, Burr opened with, "F--- all you people! I hope you all f---ing die and I hope those f---ing Eagles never win the Super Bowl!" For the next 12 minutes, Burr dropped an atomic f-bomb on everything holy to Philadelphians: their beloved sports teams, the Liberty Bell, the statue of Rocky. He even called their town so irrelevant that "terrorists will never bomb you." By the end of his set, Burr had laid waste to the City of Brotherly Love…and won them over. Someone in the audience made a cell phone video of the set and uploaded it to YouTube, where it became a viral hit, jumpstarting his career.

KRAMER'S DARK SIDE. Michael Richards isn't a seasoned stand-up comedian—he's the comic actor who starred as Kramer on *Seinfeld*. But in 2006 he decided to give stand-up a try, and his inexperience in handling crowds became national news. During a set at the Laugh Factory in Hollywood, a few people in the audience told Richards they didn't think he was funny. Instead of making fun of their clothes or their need for attention—typical comic responses to heckling—Richards went on an unhinged, racist rant, calling his hecklers the N-word several times. Once cell phone video of the incident spread, Richards had to go into full-on damage control and apologize for his actions. Richards has never done stand-up again.

CHAPELLE'S NO-SHOW. When Funny or Die announced its inaugural Oddball Festival tour in 2013, it created shock waves by landing Dave Chappelle as the headliner. Since abruptly quitting his sketch comedy TV show, *Chappelle's Show*, in 2005, Chappelle popped into a comedy club from time to time but was essentially retired. When the Oddball Festival played Hartford, Connecticut, members of the audience started shouting catchphrases from *Chappelle's Show* as he took the stage, before he could even begin his set. When the crowd ignored his

---

Slow, but they pack a punch: A tsunami typically crashes into a beach at a speed of about 22 mph.

requests to stop yelling, Chappelle took out a pack of cigarettes, stopped doing his set, and told the crowd that when his contractually obligated time was up, he was leaving the stage. Chappelle then proceeded to kill time by reading a book and making fun of the audience until his set was over. While many fans fretted about how audiences would treat Chappelle on the rest of the tour, his other shows went off without a hitch. He said he would never go back to Hartford ("Not even for f--- ing gas"). But he did. He made a surprise return to Hartford for the 2014 edition of the festival. This time, he got a standing ovation.

GIRL TALK. Joe Rogan was performing in a Las Vegas theater in 2006. A table of drunken women began to reply personally to all of his jokes, but the tipping point came after Rogan made fun of the movie *March of the Penguins*. One of the women yelled out, "Aww, I love penguins!" Rogan responded by making fun of her voice, angering the woman enough to yell, "You don't have a girlfriend!" After some more insults back and forth, the woman once again accused Rogan of not having a girlfriend. And that's when Rogan began a minute-long rant. "Don't get confused on your place in the big picture. I'm not saying I'm anything special, but guess what, you're not either. We're all humans. You're pretty now, but you're only, like, what, 24? Talk to me when you're 44, and you're desperate and drunk." The crowd went wild, the heckler backed off, and the woman piped down.

MAKING HIS MARK. One night in the early 2000s comedian Jeff Garlin was performing at Caroline's in New York. His *Curb Your Enthusiasm* co-star Cheryl Hines, and a friend, came in to watch his set. A heckler started talking back to Garlin, derailing his routine. That's when another heckler with a thick Irish accent started yelling at the first heckler to quiet down. The first heckler apologized and quieted himself. "You are no match for this man," Garlin told the initial heckler, revealing that the second heckler was Hines's friend…Robin Williams.

*　　*　　*

PLANET OF THE BABOONS

In 2015 a man driving on a mountain road in Saudi Arabia struck and killed a baboon. According to news reports, the baboons armed themselves with stones and waited for three days on the side of the road. When the same car came driving back the other way, one of the baboons let out a blood-curdling scream, and the angry apes pelted the vehicle with stones. They swarmed the car, ripped out the windshield, and started walloping the driver. He barely escaped with his life.

Wolves make terrible guard dogs—they're more likely to hide from strangers than bark.

Groaners

A good pun is its own reword.

• If you take a laptop computer for a run, you could jog your memory.

• A bicycle can't stand alone; it's just two-tired.

• A dentist and a manicurist had a rough marriage. They fought tooth and nail.

• A plateau is a high form of flattery.

• A thief fell and broke his leg in wet cement. It turned him into a hardened criminal.

• A thief who stole a calendar got 12 months.

• Acupuncture is a jab well done. (That's the point of it.)

• Bakers share bread recipes on a knead-to-know basis.

• Did you hear about the guy whose entire left side was cut off? He's all right now.

• Those who get too big for their britches will be exposed in the end.

• A Local Area Network in Australia is the LAN down under.

• If you don't pay your exorcist, you can get repossessed.

• He broke into song because he couldn't find the key.

• In a democracy, it's your vote that counts; in feudalism, it's your count that votes.

• Police were summoned to a day-care center where a three-year-old was resisting a rest.

• The dead batteries were given away free of charge.

• The guy who fell onto an upholstery machine is now fully recovered.

• The math professor went crazy with the blackboard. He did a number on it.

• The professor discovered that his theory of earthquakes was on shaky ground.

• Thieves who steal corn from a garden could be charged with stalking.

• When fish are in schools, they sometimes take debate.

• He was stuck with his debt. He couldn't budge it.

Every year about 225 Canadian men drown after standing up in a boat to pee.

Who Wants Seconds?

*There are plenty of "famous firsts"—but we wondered
what and who followed up those famous firsts.*

- **2nd video to air on MTV.** It's well known that the first video ever played on MTV in August 1981 was "Video Killed the Radio Star" by the Buggles. The second: "You Better Run" by Pat Benatar.

- **2nd player to break baseball's color barrier.** Eleven weeks after Jackie Robinson integrated Major League Baseball in April 1947 with the Brooklyn Dodgers, the Cleveland Indians signed center fielder Larry Doby.

- **2nd talkie.** Debuting in 1927, Al Jolson's *The Jazz Singer* was the first feature-length film with synchronized dialogue. The second was *Tenderloin* (1928), a romance that featured 15 minutes of sound.

- **2nd state to join the Union.** Delaware is #1 because it was the first to ratify the U.S. Constitution, on December 7, 1787. The second state to join: Pennsylvania, five days later.

- **2nd state to leave the Union.** South Carolina seceded on December 20, 1860, laying the foundation for the Civil War. The second state to secede: Mississippi, on January 9, 1861.

- **2nd pope.** The first pope, or head of the Roman Catholic Church, was Simon Peter (also known as St. Peter), an apostle of Jesus Christ, who served from AD 33 to 67. Next up: Pope Linus, a Tuscan priest. His papacy lasted from 67 to 76.

- **2nd host of *Saturday Night Live*.** George Carlin was the first host of *SNL*. The second episode of the late-night sketch comedy show in October 1975 was hosted by Paul Simon.

- **2nd EGOT.** The first person to win an Emmy, Grammy, Oscar, and Tony was composer Richard Rodgers, who earned his four awards between 1945 and 1962. The second was actress Helen Hayes. She won her first Oscar (for *The Sin of Madelon Claudet*) in 1932, her first Tony (for *Happy Birthday*) in 1947, an Emmy (for *Schlitz Playhouse of Stars*) in 1953, and a Grammy (Best Spoken Word Performance for *Great American Documents*) in 1977.

Makes sense if you've seen them: Not one of Elvis's 31 movies was ever nominated for an Oscar.

- **2nd "Playmate of the Month."** In *Playboy's* second issue (January 1954), a pinup model named Margie Harrison was "Playmate of the Month," succeeding Marilyn Monroe (who was "Sweetheart of the Month") in *Playboy* No. 1.

- **2nd socialist state.** Following the overthrow of the czar and the Russian Revolution, the Soviet Union was formed in December 1922. It was the first socialist country on Earth. The second was Mongolia, which—supported by the Soviets—became a socialist state in 1924 and held on to the form of government until February 1992 (three months after the collapse of the Soviet Union).

- **2nd British Invasion star.** The flood of British artists on American radio began with the Beatles in 1964 and their hits "I Want to Hold Your Hand" and "She Loves You." The first non–Fab Four British artist to get a hit was Dusty Springfield with "I Only Want to Be with You."

- **2nd Miss America.** Ohio's Mary Campbell, competing as Miss Columbus, was named Miss America 1922 in the pageant's second year. She also won the title in 1923, and remains the only woman ever to win the title twice.

- **2nd runner to break the four-minute mile.** British runner Roger Bannister ran a mile in 3 minutes, 59.4 seconds on May 6, 1954, in Oxford. Just two months later, at the Commonwealth Games in Vancouver, British Columbia, Bannister did it again, finishing at 3:58.8. Second place: Australian John Landy, who did the mile in 3:59.6.

- **2nd *The Tonight Show* guest.** When Johnny Carson began his 30-year career as host of *The Tonight Show* on October 1, 1962, his second interview was with Mel Brooks (following Joan Crawford).

- **2nd Queen of England.** The first reigning queen was Mary I (1553–58), known as "Bloody Mary" because of her fondness for executing Protestants. Her successor: Queen Elizabeth I, one of the longest-serving monarchs in English history, who ruled from 1558 to 1603.

- **2nd state with women's suffrage.** The passage of the 19th Amendment in 1920 gave women the right to vote nationwide. Before that, states were allowed to decide for themselves. The first state to allow suffrage for women was Wyoming in 1869. The second was Utah, a year later. (Neither were actually states, though—they were both U.S. territories at the time.)

Sci-fi author Harlan Ellison, employed at Disney for half a day, was fired for telling a dirty joke.

He-Men

Some manly quotes by manly men on what it means to be a man.

"The wussiest thing a guy can do is drive a clean truck. Dents, scratches, and mud— that's manly."
—**Blake Shelton**

"Masculinity is not something given to you, but something you gain. And you gain it by winning small battles with honor."
—**Norman Mailer**

"The real man smiles in trouble, gathers strength from distress, and grows brave by reflection."
—**Thomas Paine**

"Wear what you want to wear. Do what you want to do. Be who you are. Be a man. And if that's too much to ask, as it almost always is for me, think of someone you consider to be a man and pretend to be like him. I pretend to be like my dad."
—**Lyle Lovett**

"I would rather be beaten, and be a man, than to be elected and be a little puppy dog."
—**Davy Crockett**

"Everybody pities the weak. Jealousy you have to earn."
—**Arnold Schwarzenegger**

"The true man wants two things: danger and play. For that reason he wants woman, as the most dangerous plaything."
—**Frederich Nietzsche**

"Men are like steel. When they lose their temper, they lose their worth."
—**Chuck Norris**

"To be a man is, precisely, to be responsible."
—**Antoine de Saint-Exupéry**

"A man who deliberately and intelligently takes a pledge and then breaks it, forfeits his manhood."
—**Mahatma Gandhi**

"Life is too short to be little. Man is never so manly as when he feels deeply, acts boldly, and expresses himself with frankness and with fervor."
—**Benjamin Disraeli**

"To be a man requires that you accept everything life has to give you, beginning with your name."
—**Burl Ives**

"Waste no more time arguing what a good man should be. Be one."
—**Marcus Aurelius**

Wonder Women

"Women are the real architects of society." —Cher

"I declare to you that woman must not depend upon the protection of man, but must be taught to protect herself, and there I take my stand."
—**Susan B. Anthony**

"Some of us are becoming the men we wanted to marry."
—**Gloria Steinem**

"Women must try to do things as men have tried. When they fail, their failure must be but a challenge to others."
—**Amelia Earhart**

"I demanded more rights for women because I know what women have to put up with."
—**Eva Perón**

"Give a girl the right shoes, and she can conquer the world."
—**Marilyn Monroe**

"Don't be fooled. You're not in competition with other women. You're in competition with *everyone*."
—**Tina Fey**

"Why do you have to choose what kind of woman you are? Why do you have to label yourself anything?"
—**Beyoncé**

"I don't care what you think about me. I don't think about you at all."
—**Coco Chanel**

"My advice to women in general: Even if you're doing a nine-to-five job, treat yourself like a boss. Not arrogant, but be sure of what you want—and don't allow people to run anything for you without your knowledge."
—**Nicki Minaj**

"A dame that knows the ropes isn't likely to get tied up."
—**Mae West**

"Some women choose to follow men, and some women choose to follow their dreams. If you're wondering which way to go, remember that your career will never wake up and tell you that it doesn't love you anymore."
—**Lady Gaga**

"The question isn't who's going to let me; it's who is going to stop me."
—**Ayn Rand**

"Whether women are better than men I cannot say—but I can say they are certainly no worse."
—**Golda Meir**

Tiny Bangladesh is 1/50th the size of Russia but has 13 million more people.

The Henley-on-Todd

It's just like any other boat race, minus one important thing: water.

IN THE MIDDLE OF NOWHERE

Located nearly 1,000 miles from the nearest ocean, the small Australian town of Alice Springs, New South Wales, is about as landlocked as it gets: it's in the desert. Even the Todd River, which cuts through the center of town, is bone-dry. Yet, amazingly, every year 20,000 tourists flock to Alice Springs for a boat race.

The idea for the race was hatched in 1962 when a local meteorologist named Reg Smith and his friends were brainstorming ideas for charity events that would draw visitors to the small desert town. Mocking stuffy English rowing races like the Henley-on-Thames (between Cambridge and Oxford Universities), Smith suggested they hold a boat race on the dry river. "What about the boats?" asked one of Smith's friends. "Do we tow them or push them?"

"Neither," replied Smith, "we cut the bottoms out and carry them." The race, dubbed the Henley-on-Todd Regatta, has taken place in the third week of August ever since (except in 1993, when, ironically, the races were canceled because of heavy rains that flooded the dry river).

AND THEY'RE OFF!

The main event is called Bring Your Own Boat, and it's just as Smith described: teams bring a bottomless boat and then hold it up from the inside as they race "Fred Flintstone style" around the sandy riverbed. In 2014 a family calling themselves the "Fab Four" brought the first ever "submarine" to the event. (It was yellow.) Other events include the Bathtub Derby, in which contestants are carried around the course in bathtubs, and Sand-Skiing, which is exactly what it sounds like.

The final event is called Battle of the Boats. A pirate ship, Viking ship, and navy ship (built over the frames of four-wheel-drive trucks) race each other through the sandy riverbed. As the name implies, this is more of a battle than a race. Pirates, Vikings, and sailors bombard each other with flour cannons, confetti, and water balloons…and usually end up drenching the spectators.

What do the winners receive (other than a good night's sleep)? Not a whole lot. There are prizes supplied by sponsors, as well as a "cash prize lucky draw" for $500. But the main reason that thousands of people flock to the Henley-on-Todd Regatta every year is to have fun in the sun and not take life too seriously.

During traditional Balkan dancing, men put hankies under their...

(B)ad Campaigns

Companies are always trying to generate positive attention for their products. But judging by what happened to these companies, things don't always turn out the way they were intended.

Brilliant marketing idea: In 2013 Campbell Soup, maker of SpaghettiOs, decided to generate some patriotic attention for its canned pasta product by sending out a tweet to its 11,000+ Twitter followers commemorating December 7, Pearl Harbor Day. "Take a moment to remember Pearl Harbor with us," it read. The message also included a picture of the brand's mascot: a smiling, sneaker-wearing O-shaped cartoon character standing with one hand on its hip and the other holding the American flag, licking its upper lip.

One small problem: A lot of Twitter followers considered the image an inappropriate commemoration of a surprise attack that killed more than 2,400 Americans and precipitated the U.S. entry into World War II. "Genuinely afraid to scroll back and see what you tweeted on the 50th Anniversary of JFK's assassination," one person tweeted in reply; others responded by photoshopping the SpaghettiO mascot onto iconic photos of the Hindenburg disaster, the 9/11 attacks and other tragedies.

Damage Control: By 11:00 a.m. on Pearl Harbor Day, the tweet had been deleted. "We apologize for our recent tweet in remembrance of Pearl Harbor Day," Campbell Soup officials said in a subsequent tweet. "We meant to pay respect, not to offend."

Brilliant marketing idea: In 2014 the Urban Outfitters retail chain began selling a line of Vintage Collection college sweatshirts on its website. By "vintage" the company meant that the sweatshirts were so worn out and sun-faded that they appeared to be genuine artifacts from the 1960s and 1970s. Each tattered sweatshirt had its own unique pattern of wear, adding to its "authenticity." Price: $129 each.

One small problem: One of the college sweatshirts was, in the minds of some visitors to the website, a little *too* authentic: it was red, faded, and worn to the point that it had small holes on the chest and the waistline. And because they exposed inner fibers that were not as sun-damaged, the holes were bright red and contrasted markedly with the rest of the faded sweatshirt. So what's the problem? That particular sweatshirt happened to be from Kent State University, the site of an infamous shooting in 1970—when National Guard soldiers opened fire on a Vietnam War demonstration, killing four students and wounding nine others. The name "Kent State" has become synonymous with the tragedy, and some visitors to the Urban Outfitters website assumed the sweatshirt was intended to evoke memories of that terrible day. "Blood splatters and all. Nothing says 'hip' like murder," one angry visitor tweeted. Even Kent State officials assumed the association was deliberate: "This item is beyond poor taste and trivializes a loss of life that still hurts the Kent State community today," the university said in a press release. "We take great offense to a company using our pain for publicity and profit."

Damage Control: Urban Outfitters pulled the sweatshirt from the website and promised it would be destroyed rather than sold. "It was never our intention to allude to the tragic events that took place at Kent State," the company tweeted. "We are extremely saddened that this item was perceived as such."

Brilliant marketing idea: In January 2011, the Thalia Surf Shop in Laguna Beach, California, held a Martin Luther King Day sale. Selected items would be marked down 20 percent.

One small problem: Lots of stores have Martin Luther King Day sales, but few are as poorly planned as this one. "RESPECT. MLK Sale," read the online ad promoting the sale. "20% Off All Black Products." (They also had a digitally altered image of Dr. King wearing one of the black wetsuits on sale.)

Damage Control: Was store owner Nick Cocores tone deaf? Racist? Or just stupid? Whatever the case, he received a quick education in public relations: Within hours he pulled the ad from his website. "It's our slow time of year, so we're always getting creative," he told reporters. "We're definitely not trying to bum anybody out."

Brilliant marketing idea: In May 2015 the athletic apparel maker Under Armour began selling a T-shirt that commemorated the Battle of Iwo Jima during World War II. The battle, which raged from February to April 1945, was the bloodiest in the history of the United States Marine Corps.

One small problem: The company decided that the T-shirt should also celebrate basketball. So it named it "Band of Ballers" and printed an image on the front of the shirt that showed basketball players raising a basketball hoop in a way that mimicked the famous photo of the flag-raising on Iwo Jima's Mount Suribachi. Many Marines were offended by the image; more than a few let their feelings be known on Twitter. "Under Armour, this is disgusting and a slap in the face to my fellow marines. 'Band of Ballers' shirt? Such a shame," one wrote.

Damage Control: Under Armour pulled the shirt from store shelves as soon as company execs recognized how poorly the product was being received. "We deeply regret and apologize [for] the release of a shirt that is not reflective of our commitment and support & honor our country's heroes," said a company spokesperson.

Brilliant marketing Idea: In 2013 the Tumbledown Trails Golf Course in Verona, Wisconsin, commemorated the 12th anniversary of the 9/11 attacks with a special offer for golfers. And to promote it, Tumbledown's general manager, Marc Watts, placed an ad in the *Wisconsin State Journal*: "We are offering 9 holes with cart for only $9.11 per person or 18 holes with cart for only $19.11! 9/11/13 Only!"

One small problem: The ad also told readers to "'Like' us on Facebook." Lots of people went to Facebook all right, but not to click the "Like" button: "You're awful people," one Facebook user wrote. "The tastelessness of offering a 9/11 'sale' on golf is sickening. Who sinks that low?" another said. (Those were some of the *nice* posts.)

Damage Control: So many hostile comments (and even death threats) were posted online or phoned in to the golf course that Watts considered shutting down on 9/11 for his own safety. He eventually decided to stay open, with a sheriff's deputy on hand in case any trouble broke out. (None did.) Rather than continue to accept reservations at the advertised sale price, Watts charged the standard rate and donated the difference to the 9/11 Memorial in New York City. "We're a little hurt that people are putting such a negative context on this," he told reporters. "We'll do something next year. I guarantee you it won't be this, but we will not stop trying to remind people of 9/11."

*　　　*　　　*

MORE FLUBBED HEADLINES

Efforts Meant to Help
Workers Batter
South Africa's Poor

On Veterans Day, Killeen
Thinks of Shooting Victims

CHINESE GOVERNMENT
CRACKS DOWN ON
QUALITY

MacLean Finally Gets Shot

*Kayaking Is Hard When
the Water Is Frozen*

Homicide Victims
Rarely Talk to Police

FBI TO LOOK CLOSELY AT NAKED
SCARLETT JOHANSSON SHOTS

Governor: Innocent Man
Freed After 18 Years Shows
Justice System Works

Nature's sundae: Brazilian cupuaçu fruit tastes like a combination of chocolate, pineapple, and bananas.

Tunnel Vision

A "tunnel" is a horizontal underground passageway. But you knew that already. Here are more tunnel facts you may not be familiar with.

London's subway system is called the Underground, but only 45 percent of the system actually runs through tunnels.

• According to *Guinness World Records*, the world's oldest subway tunnel is New York's Atlantic Avenue Tunnel, built in 1844 as part of the Long Island Railroad. It was abandoned (and sealed off) in 1861 and rediscovered in 1980.

• In 17th-century battles, military engineers dug tunnels under fort walls and then caved them in so the walls would collapse. The tunnels became known as "sappers," from the French *saper*, or "to undermine," and are still a part of modern warfare today.

• China plans to build a 76-mile underwater tunnel between the cities of Dalian and Yantai. To do it, Chinese workers will need to dig 100 feet below the seabed and bore through two major earthquake fault lines.

• Modern tunnels are cut with tunnel-boring machines. A TBM can grind a 60-foot tunnel through rock at a rate of 250 feet per day.

• Western Massachusetts's Hoosac Tunnel, built in the mid-1800s, is said to be haunted by the ghosts of the 195 miners killed during its construction.

• One of the worst tunnel disasters in history occurred in Balvano, Italy, on March 2, 1944. A train carrying 650 passengers stalled inside a tunnel, and as the train idled, the tunnel filled with carbon monoxide from its engines. Result: 520 people on board suffocated to death.

• The Zambian mole rat digs the longest tunnels of any (nonhuman) mammal on earth. Colony tunnels can extend for over a mile—a lot of digging for a creature that's only nine inches long.

• In early 2015, Toronto police discovered a 33-foot-long tunnel under some woods. It had electricity and a sump-pump, and officials feared it might be a terrorist hideout. But it was actually a "man cave" that 22-year-old construction worker Elton McDonald was building. "I was hoping to put in a TV," he said. "It was a place to hang out."

The "friendship paradox" states that, on average, most people have fewer friends than their friends do.

The First Wish

*To date, the Make-A-Wish Foundation has fulfilled the wishes
of more than 250,000 kids with life-threatening illnesses.
Here's the story of the wish that started it all.*

D IAGNOSIS

In 1977 an Illinois woman named Linda Greicius made a trip to Phoenix, Arizona, to spend time with her mother, who had recently been widowed. Greicius brought her five-year-old son Chris with her. As soon as they arrived, the grandmother insisted that Chris didn't look well and should see a doctor. Greicius obliged, and that's when she got the kind of news that all parents pray they will never get: Chris had stage-four leukemia and had less than three years to live.

Greicius believed Chris would receive better care in Phoenix, so she made plans to stay there indefinitely. She also decided that she and Chris would squeeze as much life as they could out of whatever time he had left.

POLICE STORY

Chris was a big fan of *CHiPs*, the TV show about California Highway Patrol motorcycle officers. He wanted to be a police officer when he grew up, illness or no illness, so many of his playtime adventures had a police theme. Greicius bought him a battery-powered highway patrol motorcycle that Chris could ride for fun and also use in place of a wheelchair when he was too fatigued to get about on his own.

A family friend named Tommy Austin was an officer with the U.S. Customs Service, and Chris was always talking about wanting to help him catch bad guys. Austin really wanted to oblige, but bureaucratic hurdles within the agency made it difficult for him to do much. One day in the spring of 1980, Austin shared his frustration with Ron Cox, an Arizona Department of Public Safety (DPS) officer, while the two men were on a stakeout. Austin also expressed his concern that Chris might not live much longer.

Cox said he would check with his DPS superiors to see if his agency could help. The DPS director, a man named Ralph Milstead, was moved by Chris's story and gave Cox free rein to do whatever he wanted. That was all Cox needed to hear. There was no time to spare, so he got to work: since Chris was so determined to become a police officer—why not make him a member of the force?

Random horse facts: Horses see in color, dream, and get nervous when they smell blood.

THE ROOKIE

Cox and some colleagues quickly planned a special day for the DPS's newest recruit: On April 29 a police helicopter arrived at the hospital where Chris was being treated and whisked him off for an aerial tour of Phoenix. Afterward it landed at DPS headquarters, where Chris was welcomed by three state troopers in their cruisers, plus a motorcycle officer named Frank Shankwitz. Chris and his parents then toured the headquarters. Afterward, Chris was presented with a real Smokey the Bear–style state trooper's hat and badge and was sworn in as the agency's first—and to date its only—honorary police officer.

The day was an emotional one not just for Chris and his parents but also for Cox and his colleagues. Why stop there? Cox contacted the company that supplied DPS uniforms and ordered one in Chris's size. (The store owner and two employees stayed up all night working on the uniform so that it would be ready by morning.) On May 1, officers brought the uniform to Chris's house. After he changed into it they set up cones in the driveway so that Chris could qualify for his motorcycle officer's wings by driving his electric motorcycle through an obstacle course.

FLY AWAY

Chris passed the test and was awarded a real police motorcycle helmet for his efforts; his wings were on order and due to arrive following day. But that evening he took a turn for the worse and had to be admitted to the hospital. By the time Frank Shankwitz brought the wings to his hospital room on May 2, Chris had slipped into a coma and was not expected to live more than a day or two. So Shankwitz pinned the wings on Chris's uniform, which his parents had hung next to the hospital bed where he could see it.

"Just as I pin the wings on his uniform he comes out of the coma," Shankwitz told the *Arizona Republic* in 2010. "He looks around. He looks at his mom. He just starts smiling. Giggling. Laughing. He's just as happy as can be. 'Am I an official officer?' he asked. 'Yes, you are, Chris.' Unfortunately, he passed away that evening. But his wish had come true."

AN END, AND A BEGINNING

Chris's body was returned home to Illinois, where he received a full "fallen officer" police funeral. He was buried in his uniform, and the words "Arizona Trooper" were inscribed on his headstone. The Arizona DPS sent Frank Shankwitz and another officer, Scott Stahl, to Illinois to attend the service.

On the flight back to Arizona, Shankwitz and Stahl marveled at how Chris and his family had been able to forget his illness for a few hours, even as sick as he was. Why shouldn't other kids and their families facing the same challenges have the same opportunity? When they got back to Arizona, Shankwitz, Stahl, and Greicius decided to start a fund to help other terminally ill kids realize their dreams, just as Chris had. Five people chipped in $37.76 to get the Chris Greicius Make-A-Wish Memorial off the ground. The first outside donation came from a local grocer who contributed $15.

WISHING WELL

By March 1981 the organization had raised more than $2,000, enough to grant its first wish to seven-year-old Frank "Bopsy" Salazar who, like Chris, had terminal leukemia. Bopsy wanted to be a firefighter, so this time it was the Phoenix Fire Department that stepped up. The department hosted a lunch for Bopsy at Station 1, made him an honorary member of the Engine 9 crew—complete with his own firefighting suit—and let him operate the siren when the crew responded to fires. Between calls, Bopsy got to turn the water hose on some cars parked in an alley behind the station. The memorial fund also arranged for the boy and his family to take a trip to Disneyland; when they arrived in Los Angeles, they were escorted to and from the park in a fire engine, courtesy of the Anaheim Fire Department.

When Bopsy's illness worsened a month later and he was admitted to the hospital, his friends at Station 1 drove to the hospital in the ladder truck and used it to climb through the window of his third-floor hospital room. The excitement of his visitors coming in through the window caused Bopsy to rally, and he was able to go down and see the ladder truck. He passed away before morning.

THE IDEA SPREADS

The Chris Greicius Make-A-Wish Memorial might well have remained a local charity administered by Arizona DPS officers in their spare time had NBC not learned of the charity and profiled it on a news show in the spring of 1982. After the show aired, the DPS was deluged with calls from people all over the country who wanted to start similar organizations in their communities. In May 1983, the charity reorganized itself into the national Make-A-Wish Foundation to help them do just that. By the end of the year, six chapters had opened around the country; in 1984 the number grew to 28. And as of 2015 there are more than 62 chapters in the United States, plus affiliates in 47 other countries. Together they grant more than 14,000 wishes a year—an average of one wish every 38 minutes.

WISH FULFILLED

Another thing that's changed about the Make-A-Wish Foundation since its founding more than 30 years ago is that it no longer grants wishes just to terminally ill children. Advances in medical care have made survival of many diseases more likely, including the one that claimed both Chris Greicius and Bopsy Salazar: where once leukemia was a virtual death sentence for a child, today 70 percent of children diagnosed with acute lymphocytic leukemia, the most common form of childhood cancer, will be cured of the disease. Add to this the fact that the Make-A-Wish Foundation raises tens of millions of dollars every year and that companies like Disney are happy to donate their services, and it becomes possible for Make-A-Wish to serve *any* child with a life-threatening illness, not just those who have received a terminal diagnosis.

And yet for all their changes over the years, Make-A-Wish hasn't strayed from its original mission, says Linda Greicius (now Linda Pauling): "They have kept it true to the original goal. Just grant wishes to children," she told the *Arizona Republic* in 2005. "That force has stayed there, and that makes me very happy."

*   *   *

FAMILIAR PHRASES

Phrase: "Shoo-in"

Meaning: One that has a sure chance of winning a contest or being chosen for a position

Origin: "This term comes from horse racing and originally, from about 1900 on, meant a horse that was sure to win, because the race had been fixed beforehand by the jockeys (who of course bet on the winner). The phrase alludes to the fact that the winner is "shooed in"—that is, chased in—by the other jockeys. By about 1930 the term had been transferred to other events in which the outcome was a certainty." (From *Southpaws & Sunday Punches*, by Christine Ammer)

Phrase: "Getting into a scrape"

Meaning: Getting into a fight or any other difficult situation

Origin: "When England was a huge primeval forest, early settlers had to grapple with large herds of wild deer. Well acquainted with the art of hiding when pursued, the deer used their hooves to scrape deep gullies between huge trees and avoid capture. If a settler fell into such a gully, it was difficult to get out. Early inhabitants knew these gullies as 'scrapes.'" (From *Common Phrases: And Where They Come From*, by Myron Korach and John Mordock)

Weird Science

Breaking wind news, an exciting new kind of boredom, cereal attraction, and more in our latest report from the freaky world of science.

BACK TALK

In 2012 researchers in Sydney, Australia, studied 993 people who suffered from intense lower-back pain, comparing the times they experienced the pain with weather conditions in the regions in which they lived. The researchers had expected to find a relationship between cold, wet weather and back pain—but found no relationship between those conditions at all. What they found instead was that people are more prone to experience intense lower-back pain when it's especially windy. The researchers could find no explanation for the result and said more research was needed to understand it.

THE MYSTERIES OF LIFE

In 2013 Japanese scientists reported findings of a study in which they observed 108 pairs of sea slugs having sex. The researchers, from Osaka City University and Tokyo's Nihon University, reported that after mating, a male sea slug wanders off—and its penis falls off…and another penis grows back in just 24 hours. The findings also showed that the sea slugs being studied—*Chromodoris reticulata*, native to the western Pacific Ocean—are hermaphrodites, meaning they have both female and male sex organs and can impregnate another sea slug and be impregnated simultaneously.

HAPPY FEET?

The *Journal of Sexual Medicine* published a report in June 2013 by Dr. Marcel D. Waldinger, a neuropsychiatry professor at Utrecht University in the Netherlands, about a patient who had been experiencing spontaneous "orgasms" in her left foot. The 55-year-old woman said the sensations weren't related to any sexual thoughts, but she'd been experiencing them five or six times a day for several months. Waldinger reported that he could induce the sensations by applying an electrical current to the woman's foot and that he was able to stop them by injecting anesthetic into a nerve in her spine. Waldinger claims it's the first known case of what he dubbed "Foot Orgasm Syndrome (FOS)" and that it was likely caused by some kind of neurological mix-up in the woman's brain.

Lamb-sylvania: Ancient Greeks believed eating a lamb killed by a wolf could turn you into a vampire.

WHO CARES?

German psychologist Thomas Goetz of the University of Konstanz concluded a study in 2013 that showed there aren't four types of boredom, as previously believed—but five. (Goetz also conducted the study that concluded there were four types of boredom.) The five types: *indifferent* boredom; *calibrating* boredom; *searching* boredom; *reactant* boredom; and, the latest, *apathetic* boredom. "We did not except this type of boredom at all," Goetz said of his latest boring discovery.

JUST PLANE AWFUL

In 2014 the *New Zealand Medical Journal* published the results of study by a team of gastroenterologists from Denmark and Great Britain. The question the study sought to answer: Which is better—to go ahead and fart while on an airplane or to try to hold it in? The researchers compared the negative effects of both farting and not farting on a plane. Some negative effects of farting: it can make people around you less friendly and flight attendants more likely to ignore you. Of *not* farting: bloating, discomfort, pain, and stress caused by worrying that you may not be able to hold it in. The researchers concluded that overall, it's probably better to let it go than it is to hold it in. They added that (we're not making this up) it might be a good idea to walk around the plane's aisles while slowly letting the fart go, to increase the area into which the fart is dispersed, a practice known as "crop dusting." The study recommended that airlines install charcoal-lined seat cushions, which limit the escape of sulfurous gases into the air, and offer higher-fiber meals to reduce passengers' gas production.

DIRTY TRIX

The Trix Rabbit is trying to brainwash your children. And so is Cap'n Crunch, Toucan Sam, and dozens of other cereal box cartoon characters. That's what a team of researchers at Cornell University concluded in 2014. They discovered that on cereals marketed to kids, the characters' eyes are shifted down 9.6 degrees…directly at kid level in the cereal aisle. That way, the eyes "follow kids around" (much like a museum painting). Test subjects were shown one of two similar boxes of Trix—one with the silly rabbit looking down, the other altered so he's looking straight ahead. The subjects who were met by the rabbit's gaze "increased feelings of connection to the brand by 28 percent." The study concluded with two recommendations:

- If you are a cereal company looking to market healthy cereals to kids, use spokes-characters that make eye contact with children.

- If you are a parent who does not want your kids to go "cuckoo for Cocoa Puffs," avoid taking them down the cereal aisle.

The network of trenches dug during World War I stretched about 25,000 miles.

Thinking On-side the Box

You probably grew up eating some of these "classic" comfort food dishes, the recipes of which were printed on food packaging or promoted in magazine ads. If you're like us, your feelings range from "Did we really eat like that?" to "I wish I had some right now!"

COCA-COLA JELL-O SALAD
Ingredients:
- One 6-ounce packet of cherry-flavored Jell-O
- 1 cup of boiling water
- 10 fluid ounces of Coca-Cola
- One 14.5- to 16-ounce can of tart pitted cherries in water
- One 8-ounce can of crushed pineapple
- 1 cup chopped raw or toasted pecans

Directions:
Pour the contents of the Jell-O packet into a large ovenproof bowl; add boiling water and stir until the Jell-O crystals are completely dissolved. Stir in the Coca-Cola and refrigerate until the mixture begins to thicken but hasn't set (about 30 minutes). Lightly chop the cherries in a blender or food processor, then add the cherries and their water to the Jell-O mixture, along with the pineapple and pecans. Pour it into a Jell-O mold if you have one, or refrigerate it in the bowl until the Jell-O has completely set. Serve cold with Coca-Cola.

TUNA POTATO CHIP CASSEROLE
Ingredients:
- One 12-ounce package of egg noodles
- ¼ cup chopped onion
- 2 cups shredded cheddar cheese
- 1 cup frozen green peas
- Two 6-ounce cans of tuna, drained
- Two 10.75-ounce cans of condensed cream of mushroom soup
- Half a 4.5-ounce can of sliced mushrooms
- 1 cup crushed potato chips

Directions:
Preheat the oven to 425°F. Cook the egg noodles in lightly salted

---

The first insane asylum in the U.S. opened in 1773 in Williamsburg, Virginia.

boiling water until they're *al dente*—about 8 to 10 minutes. Drain the noodles. In a large bowl, mix the noodles with the onion, 1 cup of the cheese, the frozen peas, tuna, soup, and mushrooms. Pour into a 9 x 13-inch baking dish and top with the remaining 1 cup of cheese and the potato chips. Bake for 15–20 minutes, until the cheese is bubbly.

VELVEETA QUESO DIP

Ingredients:
- One 16-ounce package of Velveeta cheese
- One 10-ounce can diced tomatoes and green chilies

Directions:
Cut the Velveeta into ½-inch cubes. Combine it with the tomatoes and green chilies in a medium saucepan and cook over medium heat, stirring frequently until the cheese is completely melted. Serve warm with tortilla chips, crackers, or vegetables.

FRITOS CHILI PIE

Ingredients:
- One large bag Fritos corn chips
- One 15-ounce can of chili with or without beans, heated in a microwave or on the stovetop according to the instructions on the label
- Chopped onions, tomatoes, lettuce, and jalapeño peppers, as desired
- One 8-ounce bag shredded cheese

Directions:
Preheat the oven to 350°F. Pour the corn chips into a baking dish and spread them out evenly. Then pour the heated chili evenly over the chips. Add the onions, tomatoes, lettuce, and jalapeño peppers, then sprinkle the cheese on top. Bake until the cheese begins to melt. Serve immediately.

GARBANZO HOT POT

Ingredients:
- 1 cup chopped onion
- ¼ cup diced green chilies
- Two 15-ounce cans of chickpeas
- One 15-ounce can tomato sauce
- ½–¾ cup chicken broth
- 2 tablespoons butter
- ¼ teaspoon marjoram
- ½ teaspoon salt
- ⅛ teaspoon pepper
- 1 bay leaf

Directions:
In a saucepan, sauté the onions in butter until soft. Add the rest of the ingredients to the pot and cook, uncovered, for 15 minutes.

Good news for the rest of us: 98% of the U.S. grizzly bear population lives in Alaska.

Sign the Petition!

We, the Bathroom Readers' Institute, love We the People, a government website on which anyone can start a petition. Everyone has a voice—some of them very weird...and some very funny. Here are some real petitions we found.

"Change the national anthem to R. Kelly's 2003 hit 'Ignition (Remix)'"

"Convert at least one National Park into a dinosaur clone park"

"Establish new legal system of motorcycle riding 'judges' who serve as police, judge, jury, and executioner all in one"

"Transfer funds from the drug war to fund the research and development of the genetic engineering of domestic cat girls"

"Deport Justin Bieber and revoke his green card"

"Require Congressmen and Senators to wear logos of their financial backers on their clothing, like NASCAR drivers do"

"Join America and Australia to form Ameristralia"

"Consolidate the Department of Defense and the Census Bureau into a single Department of Kicking A** and Taking Names"

"Mandate states to have state Pokémon"

"Repeal the Second Law of Thermodynamics for a more perfect heat transfer"

"Deport CNN host Piers Morgan"

"Officially recognize the Sasquatch as an indigenous species and have them lawfully protected by laws banning any hunting"

"Make Batman Secretary of Defense"

"Help make United Healthcare pay for my mother's treatment to save her life!"

"Give everyone a unicorn and a lollipop for Boxing Day"

"Ban hammers and baseball bats"

"Allow the state of Canada to withdraw from the United States of America and create its own new government"

"Issue an executive order forcing NFL Commissioner Roger Goodell to return the New Orleans Saints' second round draft pick"

"Nuke everything"

There were women gladiators in ancient Rome. Some emperors liked to watch them fight dwarves.

I Divorce You!

Married couples get divorced for many reasons—lack of trust, finances, and religious differences, to name a few. And then there are strange reasons…like these.

REASON: Not closing the car door

DETAILS: In September 2014, a couple in Riyadh, Saudi Arabia, got into a dispute in their driveway about who should close one of the car doors after they returned home from an outing. The husband insisted the wife should do it because she was the one who'd opened it when she went to get their young son out of the car. The wife said the husband should do it because by the time he asked her to close the door, he was closer to the car. After she repeatedly refused her husband's commands to close the car door, the incensed man threw his wife out of his house and later divorced her.

REASON: Too much cake

DETAILS: A 31-year-old Chinese man divorced his 27-year-old wife in 2009 because she made him eat cake with every meal. "Egg cake, fruit cake, chocolate cake," the man told reporters. "I felt like a bakery dustbin." News reports added that the man said he actually liked having cake so often…at first…but now the mere mention of the word "cake" makes him sick.

REASON: Too much mother-in-law

DETAILS: An Italian couple identified only as Stefano, 39, and Marianna, 36, were married in Rome in December 2010 and set off on a romantic three-week honeymoon stay at a five-star hotel in Paris. When they got to the airport, Marianna got a surprise: Without asking Marianna, Stefano had invited his mother to spend the honeymoon with them. Marianna filed for divorce less than a week after they returned home.

REASON: Irreconcilable house cleaning

DETAILS: In March 2009, a woman in the central German town of Sonderhausen filed for divorce from her husband…because of his incessant need to clean up around the house. "When he wasn't at work, he spent all his time doing housework," 42-year-old Lea Moeller told the divorce court about her husband Sven. "It went on for fifteen years and I had just had enough." She added: "The final straw was when I went away on holiday—to have a break from his constant cleaning—and when I got back I found he had repainted and replastered the entire house." (Because it was dirty.)

REASON: Getting out of prison

DETAILS: When Aying Wu's husband, Ahua Lin, was sentenced to five years in prison in Quanzhou, China, in 2007, she visited him regularly, sent letters, and vowed that she would be there for him when he was freed. When he was freed five years later, Aying discovered that she didn't actually like having her husband around and filed for divorce just a few weeks later. "Somehow it seemed very romantic while he was away," she told the divorce court, but once back home, "he was always in the way and criticizing me." The unhappy husband told the judge he was only trying to be helpful.

REASON: Eating peas the wrong way

DETAILS: A Kuwaiti woman filed for divorce one week after getting married in December 2013 when she discovered that her new husband ate peas by picking them up with a piece of bread rather than with a spoon or fork. The woman said the "shocking sight" was too much for her, and there was no way she could spend the rest of her life with a man who ate peas in such a manner. (No word on whether the divorce went through—or if her husband was able to appease her in some way.)

REASON: He didn't like *Frozen*.

DETAILS: A brokenhearted Japanese man posted his story to the website *Kikonsha no Hakaba* ("The Gravesite of Married People"). He said that he and his wife had enjoyed a happy marriage without any strife or financial hardships…until she saw the Disney movie *Frozen*. She liked it so much she saw it again, and again, and again. And when she finally took him to see it, his response was, "It's okay." She angrily replied, "If you can't understand what makes this movie great, there's something wrong with you as a human being." She left him that day and later filed for divorce.

REASON: No underwear

DETAILS: In 2011 Emese Nagy, 24, of Lemnia, Romania, divorced her husband, Tamas Nagy (age unknown), because he refused to wear underwear. Emese told the judge overseeing the couple's divorce proceedings that she put up with her husband's lack of undergarments for one year of marriage, but then it became too much: women in their town had started staring at her husband, she told the judge, because they knew he wasn't wearing underpants. Tamas told the judge that he loved his wife but that he refused to change his behavior, even if it meant divorce. "Underwear simply makes me feel very uncomfortable," he said.

A woodpecker's tongue can be up to 4 inches long, or two-thirds the length of its entire body.

"Calling Dick Tracy"

*The comic strip Dick Tracy has been running for more than 70 years. During that
time, the square-jawed detective faced dozens of criminals, many with odd
names and physical quirks or deformities to match. Reason: "Because,"
Tracy's creator, Chester Gould, once said, "crime is ugly."*

• **Ugly Christine** had long black hair that covered her face, which presumably was not very attractive.

• **Pruneface** had a wrinkled face.

• **Little Face** had an abnormally large head, and on it a tiny little face.

• **Flattop** had a flat head.

• **B. D. Eyes** had tiny little "beady" eyes.

• **Shaky** shook a lot because he was addicted to nerve tonic.

• **The Mole** was hairy, with a pointy face. He also liked to dig.

• **Piggy Butcher** had a snoutlike nose.

• **Flyface** always had flies buzzing around his face.

• **Lips Manlis** had huge lips.

• **Pucker Puss** wore a set of false teeth, which caused his mouth to stretch and pucker.

• **Itchy Oliver** had a chronic itching problem due to a skin condition.

• **Rughead** wore a bad toupee.

• **Empty Williams** was kind of dumb, which could be attributed to the large chunk missing from his head.

• **Open-Mind Monty** had a knife blade permanently stuck into his forehead—removing it would kill him.

• **Oodles** weighed 469 pounds.

• **Pear-Shape** was pear-shaped.

• **Coffyhead** had a head shaped like a coffee pot.

• **Haf-and-Haf** looked normal on one side of his face, but the other half was deformed and disfigured from a chemical spill.

• **B. O. Plenty** had terrible body odor.

• **Spots** had a blank space on his face where his eyes should have been, and a bunch of black spots constantly hovering in front of his face.

• **Miss Egghead** had a large, oval-shaped head. That, along with a receding hairline, made her head look very egglike.

• **Normal Jones** had an unremarkable appearance.

Penguins & Land Mines

Nature sometimes exhibits a surprising resilience to the terrible things we do to it. Despite land mines, bombs, and radioactivity, animals occasionally have the last laugh, not only surviving…but thriving.

DISASTER: In 1982 Argentina invaded the Malvinas—778 frigid islands 300 miles off its coast. Unfortunately, England was already occupying the islands (they'd claimed them 150 years earlier)—which they called the Falklands—and considered the 1,813 residents and 400,000 sheep there to be solidly British. In response, British prime minister Margaret Thatcher sent 127 ships 8,000 miles across the Atlantic, and after a 74-day war, retook the islands from Argentina with great glory and 907 human fatalities.

AFTERMATH: When the Falkland sheep farmers went back to their fields, they found them full of bomb craters…but that wasn't the biggest problem. The two sides had buried 25,000 land mines in coastal regions all over the islands—a weapon that is very easy to deploy in large numbers but very difficult to un-deploy. Because the mines can maim and kill for many decades afterward, vast swaths of land were suddenly too dangerous to use.

NATURE'S VICTORY: The Falklands' original inhabitants had been several varieties of penguin. With the incursion of people and sheep, though, their population of 10 million had declined to a few hundred thousand. The land mines changed everything. The mines were designed to explode with pressure of about 13 pounds. Since most penguins weigh less than that, the mine fields have become theirs again—safe from people, sheep, or dogs—and the penguins' numbers have rebounded to more than a million.

DISASTER: In 1942, as World War II was raging, the U.S. Navy needed a place to practice dropping bombs. They found a suitable island three miles southwest of Martha's Vineyard in Massachusetts, and over the next 54 years, the aptly named Nomans Land Island was repeatedly pounded with megatons of live ordnance.

AFTERMATH: In 1996 the bombing stopped. For two years, the navy attempted to clear out the massive amounts of unexploded (and buried) ordnance that had accumulated over a half century, but finally gave up in

---

Sweetest fruit: Figs (they're 55% sugar).

1998 and donated the island to the U.S. Fish and Wildlife Service.

NATURE'S VICTORY: Because of the safety risks associated with the unexploded devices, the island and waters surrounding it are closed to the public. Without humans, the wildlife have taken over and the island wetlands have become a safe zone for fish, shorebirds, waterbirds, turtles, reptiles, and even migrating monarch butterflies.

DISASTER: From 1950 to 1953, three million people died in a bloody war between North and South Korea. The two sides eventually ended up in a stalemate, facing each other across a booming battle front that neither could move across.

AFTERMATH: In 1953 the China-backed North Koreans and the U.S.-backed South Koreans negotiated an end to the active shooting by marking the center line of the battle front. From there, each side agreed to back up 2,000 meters, creating a demilitarized zone between the two armies, 2.5 miles across.

NATURE'S VICTORY: Although there have been occasional small skirmishes between the soldiers of the two sides, the uneasy peace has mostly held. Since the 160-mile demilitarized zone is risky for humans to enter, it has become much safer for wildlife. Several endangered species have been sighted, including the seldom-seen red-crowned crane, Korean tiger, Amur leopard, and Asiatic black bear.

DISASTER: In 1986 a nuclear reactor in Chernobyl, Ukraine, melted down, killing more than 100 workers and releasing a plume of radioactivity equivalent to 20 Hiroshima explosions. Result: the accident required permanent evacuation of residents for 1,100 square miles, an area twice the size of Rhode Island.

AFTERMATH: Everything in the Chernobyl Exclusion Zone is highly radioactive, and the land won't be suitable for human habitation for at least 20,000 years. Although residents have been permanently evacuated, thousands have died prematurely, or will, because of their exposure.

NATURE'S VICTORY (SORT OF): Rare wildlife such as roe deer, wild boar, wolves, and once-missing lynxes, now unmolested by humans, have returned, increasing their numbers in the radioactive zone. But it has come at a cost: some have tumors, mutations, and other physical abnormalities. And then there's the Przewalski's horse, the only never-domesticated breed that was nearly extinct (only 12 animals remained, all in zoos). A cooperative breeding program brought that number up to 1,500 by the early 1990s, and a small group introduced into the Chernobyl area reached a peak of 200...but in recent years, poachers have brought that number down to just 60.

About two-thirds of shark attacks on humans have taken place in water less than six feet deep.

Mistaken Identities

Like a lot of kids in the 1970s, Uncle John wore an ID bracelet so that in an emergency, people would know who he was and how to contact his parents. (After reading about these folks, he wishes he still had it.)

STICK FIGURE

In October 2012, police in the town of Chorley, Lancashire, in northwest England responded to a report of a man walking through the town center brandishing a ninja sword. When Constable Stuart Wright came up behind a man carrying a long, slender object, he drew his taser gun and fired 50,000 volts of electricity, dropping the "suspect" to the ground. Only after handcuffing the man, who was still facedown on the ground, did Constable Wright realize he was 64-year-old Colin Farmer, a blind man. The long, slender object: his white cane.

A police investigation found that 1) Farmer was walking away from the constable when he was tasered and thus posed no threat; 2) Wright used "disproportionate force" to subdue Farmer after failing to take "reasonable steps" to confirm that he really was the man with the sword; and 3) Wright compounded his error by handcuffing Farmer even though it should have been obvious by then that he was not the suspect.

Wright was not criminally charged for his actions, nor was he even suspended—a decision that left Farmer, who now suffers from post-traumatic stress disorder, gobsmacked. "I've not had any justice," he told the BBC. "It nearly killed me…for what? Being blind and having a stick."

OUT PATIENT

In 2010 a retired sheriff's corporal named Joseph Wheeler was involved in a car accident and airlifted to Prince George's Hospital in Upper Marlboro, Maryland. He spent the night there, and when he woke up the next morning and asked for food, the nurse told him that he couldn't eat anything because of his scheduled cancer surgery. *Cancer surgery? But he didn't have cancer!* Only then did Wheeler discover that he'd been given the wrong hospital ID bracelet. The one on his wrist was for a *woman* 13 years his junior; she was the one scheduled for the surgery.

At this point, according to legal documents, Wheeler and his wife "decided that it was in their best interest to seek medical care for Mr. Wheeler elsewhere." But when they tried to leave, the nurses wouldn't let them. Two security guards physically restrained Wheeler and, he alleges, assaulted him repeatedly and called him a bad name that rhymes

---

The Easter egg and Easter bunny were introduced to America by the Pennsylvania Dutch.

with "witch." It took three administrators to straighten out the mess and finally allow Wheeler to leave; he then went to another county and checked himself into a hospital there. They diagnosed him with four broken ribs, a sprained shoulder, a ruptured spleen, and a concussion. At last report he was suing Prince George's Hospital and their security company for $12 million.

DEFLATED

In July 2012, eighteen police officers in China's Shandong province responded to a report of a woman drowning in a river. The woman was floating 50 yards offshore, and it took the officers 40 minutes to reach her. That's when they (and about 1,000 spectators standing on the shore) discovered that the "drowning woman" was actually an inflatable sex doll.

GETTING THE CHAIR

In August 1999, a dentist in Auburn, California, pulled two front teeth from the mouth of an eight-year-old boy (not named in news reports) who didn't have an appointment and was only accompanying his teenage sisters to *their* appointments. Here's how it happened: another boy with the same name *was* scheduled to have his teeth pulled, and when the dental assistant called his name, the wrong boy followed her to the dentist's chair. "It wasn't until he emerged from the back room, crying and without two front teeth, that the mistake was discovered," the Scripps-Howard news service reported.

Not that it was any consolation to the boy (or his parents, who sued Dr. Richard Smith for "professional and general negligence, battery and intentional infliction of emotional distress"), but the pulled teeth were baby teeth and would have fallen out in a few years anyway. "We assumed we had the right boy. It was just a basic mix-up—an error on my part for not making sure the right patient was in the chair," Dr. Smith said afterward.

(N)OBITUARY

In May 2006, a man named Terry L. Fergerson, 59, of West Monroe, New York, was killed in a head-on collision while driving his red Chevy pickup truck. Colleagues and students at the Central Technical Vocational Center in Syracuse were shocked to learn of his death, but that was nothing compared to the shock they got when Fergerson showed up for work the following morning as usual, quite surprised to learn that he was dead. It turned out that the man who'd been killed was actually Terry L. Ferguson, 58, who lived in nearby Hannibal, New York, and also drove a red Chevy pickup. "I don't know what the percentages are, but it's pretty far out," Fergerson told the *Syracuse Post-Standard*.

Behind the Hits

Another edition of a longtime Bathroom Reader favorite—the secret stories and hidden factoids behind popular songs.

The Song: "I Shot the Sheriff" (1973)
The Artist: Bob Marley
The Story: Reggae superstar Marley had an international hit with this song about a man and his feud with a sheriff (but not the deputy). But according to Jamaican filmmaker Esther Anderson, who played a big part in Marley's early success—and who was having an affair with Marley at the time he wrote the song—the song has a secret meaning few people would ever suspect. In her award-winning 2011 documentary *Bob Marley: The Making of a Legend*, Anderson claims Marley wanted her to have his child and was unhappy that she was using birth control. According to Anderson, the "sheriff" in the song was the doctor who prescribed birth control, which would explain the song's cryptic "seed" lyric: "Sheriff John Brown always hated me / For what, I don't know / Every time I plant a seed / He said kill it before it grow." Whether or not Anderson's claim is true is anyone's guess. (Marley, it should be noted, had eleven kids with seven different women.)

The Song: "The Way" (1998)
The Artist: Fastball
The Story: The Austin, Texas, rockers hit Billboard's #1 spot in 1998 with this song about an elderly couple who find happiness by leaving their home and possessions behind and hitting the road. "They wanted the highway," the song's refrain says, "they're happier there today." Lead singer Tony Scalzo got the idea for the song from a story in the *Austin American-Statesman* about Lela and Raymond Howard, who left their Salado, Texas, home in June 1997 to drive to a nearby music festival… and disappeared. It was later reported that the Howards, both in their 80s, were suffering from cognitive disabilities due to medical conditions. The song—with its happy ending—was finished before the couple was finally discovered, two weeks later, dead in their car at the bottom of a ravine near Hot Springs, Arkansas—more than 400 miles off their planned course. Exactly how or why they ended up there is unknown.

The Song: "Ticket to Ride" (1965)
The Artist: The Beatles
The Story: What's a "ticket to ride"? According to Barry Miles's

authorized biography of Paul McCartney, *Many Years from Now*, it had to do with the town of Ryde, on the Isle of Wight, just off England's south coast. McCartney had a cousin who owned a pub in Ryde, and he and John Lennon had hitchhiked there in 1960. The inspiration for the song came from that trip to Ryde. But according to the book *A Hard Day's Write* by Steve Turner, "ticket to ride" has a much less family-friendly meaning. Turner quotes British journalist Don Short:

> The girls who worked the streets in Hamburg had to have a clean bill of health, so the medical authorities would give them a card saying that they didn't have a dose of anything. I was with the Beatles when they went back to Hamburg in June 1966 and it was then that John told me that he had coined the phrase "a ticket to ride" to describe these cards. He could have been joking—you always had to be careful with John like that—but I certainly remember him telling me that.

The Song: "Just the Way You Are" (1977)

The Artist: Billy Joel

The Story: Joel wrote this song for his first wife, Elizabeth Weber. "I dreamt the melody," he told *USA Today* in a 2008 interview. "I remember waking up in the middle of the night and going, 'This is a great idea for a song.' A couple of weeks later, I'm in a business meeting and the dream recurs to me right at that moment, because my mind had drifted off from hearing numbers and legal jargon." He left the meeting immediately, went home, and wrote the song, "all in one sitting."

Bonus: Joel almost didn't release it. He thought it wasn't rock-and-roll enough, dismissing it as "a gloppy ballad" and "a chick song." Luckily, he changed his mind. It won the 1979 Grammy for Song of the Year.

The Song: "Save the Last Dance for Me" (1960)

The Artist: Doc Pomus

The Story: Songwriter Pomus and his partner, Mort Shuman, wrote dozens of hits from the 1950s until the 1970s, including Elvis Presley's "Little Sister," "Surrender," and "Viva Las Vegas." But the song "Save the Last Dance for Me," which was a huge success for the Drifters in 1960, probably has the most "aw"-inspiring backstory. In the song, a couple is at a dance, and the singer tells his sweetie she's free to dance with other guys as long as she saves the last dance for him. Pomus wrote the song after his own wedding, where he watched his brother, as well as other guests, dance with his new wife—something Pomus himself could not do: he had polio and used a wheelchair.

Bonus: Besides the Drifters #1 hit version, the song has been recorded by Emmylou Harris, Ike and Tina Turner, Dolly Parton, Buck Owens, Michael Bublé, the Beatles, Jay and the Americans, Harry Nilsson, the Walkmen, Bruce Willis (yes, Bruce Willis), and many others.

Name That Disease

Good news: you're getting something named after you! Bad news: it's a disease.

PARKINSON'S DISEASE. James Parkinson was a successful pharmacist and surgeon in 19th-century London, as well as an amateur paleontologist (he published many scientific studies on fossils) and a political activist (he was connected with a plot to assassinate King George III). But his prime achievement was writing the landmark essay that earned him a namesake disease—"An Essay on the Shaking Palsy," published in 1817. While Parkinson's understanding of the illness was inexact—he thought it was caused by lesions in the cervical spinal cord, not the gradual degradation of brain cells—he was the first person to write a systematic description of its symptoms, which include shaking and loss of motor functions. In 1877 French neurologist Jean-Martin Charcot wrote more precisely of the disease and acknowledged his predecessor by naming it Parkinson's disease.

TOURETTE'S SYNDROME. Jean-Martin Charcot is also responsible for naming this condition. While it was 27-year-old physician George Gilles de la Tourette who was responsible for identifying the syndrome's traits, describing them in 1884 among nine patients he diagnosed with what he referred to as *maladie des tics* ("sickness of tics"), it was his mentor, Charcot, who named it. Nine years later, one of Tourette's former patients shot him in the head, under the mistaken impression that he'd hypnotized her against her will. Although Tourette lived for years after suffering the injury, he was never the same and was only 46 when he died in a Swiss psychiatric hospital in 1904.

CROHN'S DISEASE. In 1932 three gastroenterologists, Dr. Burrill B. Crohn, Dr. Leon Ginzburg, and Dr. Gordon Oppenheimer, collaborated on an academic paper laying out the symptoms of a newly observed disease characterized by intestinal inflammation. Alphabetical order being what it is, Crohn's name went first on the paper and ended up being attached to the disease. Ginzburg and Oppenheimer may have lost credit in the annals of history, but "Crohn's disease" is still catchier than Crohn's own two suggestions for the condition: "regional illeitus" and "regional enteritis."

ASPERGER'S SYNDROME. Austrian pediatrician Hans Asperger started his career under Nazi occupation during World War II. His first major project, a school for special-needs children, was wiped out in an

---

Leonardo da Vinci frequently bought caged birds. Reason: to set them free.

Allied bombing raid in 1944. The bombing raid also claimed his medical partner and destroyed most of his research. That same year, Asperger published a study observing what he called "autistic psychopathy" in children. Asperger called his subjects "little professors," because while they were often highly knowledgeable in a single subject, they lacked social skills, such as empathy and the ability to relate to other children. And yet Asperger's research remained on the fringes of medicine; children who fit the symptoms were misdiagnosed with other mental conditions. Asperger died in 1980 at the age of 74, not quite living long enough to see his work take root in the international medical community after finally being translated from German.

ALZHEIMER'S DISEASE. After graduating from medical school in Würzburg, Germany, in 1886, Dr. Alois Alzheimer started his pioneering career in mental health by making the first of several fortuitous acquaintances: Franz Nissl, a German neurologist whose method of tissue staining eventually proved a crucial component in Alzheimer's own research. In 1901 Alzheimer came across a patient in Frankfurt named Auguste Deter. Her memory loss symptoms at the relatively young age of 51 piqued his interest to such an extent that he requested her medical records—and her brain—to be sent to his lab in Munich after she died. Using Nissl's techniques, he studied Deter's brain and discovered some of the first signs of what he termed *presenile dementia*. Alzheimer lived long enough to see other doctors use his work (and credit him with the disease's discovery), but he died of heart failure at a young age—51.

MUNCHHAUSEN SYNDROME. Baron Hieronymis von Munchhausen was a German nobleman who fought for Russia in a war against the Turks from 1763 to 1772. He isn't notable for any exceptional acts of valor or bravery on the battlefield, but that didn't stop him from telling tall tales about his adventures when he returned home. He had so many stories that in 1785 a German writer named Erich Raspe collected them and published them as *Baron Munchhausen's Narratives of His Marvelous Travels and Campaigns in Russia*. It became a smash hit and was translated into many languages, to the point where the name "Munchhausen" became associated with telling wildly embellished stories. More than 70 years later, British scientist Richard Asher diagnosed a mental disorder characterized by a desperate need for attention, and making up stories about oneself to get it. Other symptoms: hurting oneself, hypochondria, and tampering with medical results. Asher called it "Munchhausen syndrome." (A variant on the disease: Munchhausen syndrome by proxy, in which a parent will hurt their child in seeking attention and sympathy.)

As a Matter of Fact

Some thoughts on the nature of facts.

"If you get all the facts, your judgment can be right; if you don't get all the facts, it can't."
—**Bernard M. Baruch, American financier**

"Yesterday's fairy tale is today's fact. The magician is only one step ahead of his audience."
—**Anne Morrow Lindbergh**

"Facts are like cows. If you look them in the face hard enough they generally run away."
—**Dorothy L. Sayers**

"Facts are stubborn things; and whatever may be our wishes, our inclinations, or the dictates of our passions, they cannot alter the state of facts and evidence."
—**John Adams**

"Facts are stupid things."
—**Ronald Reagan, misquoting John Adams**

"There's no such thing as useless information. Learn something new and your world becomes a little bit bigger."
—**Uncle John**

"Get your facts first, and then you can distort them as much as you please."
—**Mark Twain**

"If a man will kick a fact out of the window, when he comes back he finds it again in the chimney corner."
—**Ralph Waldo Emerson**

"It is not the facts which guide the conduct of men, but their opinions about facts…which may be entirely wrong."
—**Norman Angell**

"Comment is free, but facts are sacred."
—**Charles Prestwich Scott, British newspaper editor**

"There is nothing more deceptive than an obvious fact."
—**Sir Arthur Conan Doyle**

"Facts don't cease to exist just because they are ignored."
—**Aldous Huxley**

"A fact is like a sack—it won't stand up if it's empty."
—**Luigi Pirandello**

"You can spend your whole life building a wall of facts between you and anything real."
—**Chuck Palahniuk**

"If the facts don't fit the theory, change the facts."
—**Albert Einstein**

Ba-a-a-d news? Sheep's milk contains twice as much fat as cow's milk.

Their Nine Lives Are Almost Up

We've all heard the expression that "cats have nine lives," and we all know that it's just that: an expression. Maybe so…but it's a good thing no one told these remarkable—and remarkably resilient—cats.

Fortunate Feline: An unidentified two-year-old female cat living in the village of Norton in South Yorkshire, England

Unfortunate Event: In September 2014, this cat sought shelter beneath the hood of a parked Nissan Primera sedan. She was still there when the owner hopped in and drove to Rufforth, about 30 miles away. Cats in such situations are often badly injured, or killed. Amazingly, this cat suffered no harm, but she did get stuck, and she was still stuck a *week* later. By then the owner of the Primera had driven the 30 miles back to Norton, and the car's fuel pump had failed (no word on whether the cat had something to do with that). Result: the car had to be towed to a garage for repairs. "When I opened up the bonnet," mechanic Ian Brindle told the *Northern Echo* newspaper, "I saw the cat staring back at me, wedged between the steering rack and the gear cables. I had to take half the car to bits to pull it out."

What Happened: The cat was hungry, thirsty, and dirty, but was otherwise unscathed. "We had to shampoo it, and that was all it needed apart from a little bit of TLC.…It was very lucky not to get any injuries," said Dr. Edward Button, the veterinarian who treated her. At last report the cat was being cared for at an animal shelter until her owner could be found.

Fortunate Feline: Bart, a black and white cat owned by Ellis Hutson of Tampa, Florida

Unfortunate Event: In January 2015, Bart was struck by a car and injured so badly that Hutson thought the cat was dead. He was so distraught that he asked a friend, David Liss, to bury Bart for him.

What Happened: Luckily for Hutson and especially for Bart, Liss is a better friend than he is a gravedigger. He buried Bart in a hole that was barely large enough to contain the cat. It's believed that Bart revived soon afterward and either dug himself out of his own grave or (as Hutson suspects) was aided by Hutson's other cat, who may have gone looking for Bart when he wasn't around to play with. Bart returned home five days later. Hutson didn't have money for a veterinarian, so

Sound familiar? Studies indicate that male bats with bigger testicles have smaller brains.

the Humane Society of Tampa Bay paid for the surgery. Their vet was unable to save Bart's right eye but did repair his fractured jaw and other injuries.

Update: The Humane Society initially planned to return Bart to Hutson as soon as he was well enough go to home, but they later decided that the cat would be better off living elsewhere. Bart now has to live inside and away from small children; Hutson has kids, and his cats are outside most of the time. (That, and the fact that he had Bart *buried alive* instead of taking him to a vet.) "Very neglectful," Humane Society director Sherry Silk told the *Washington Post*. "I don't know if it was purposeful, but we just are not going to return the cat to him." At last report, Hutson was suing the Humane Society to get Bart back.

Fortunate Feline: Cleo, an eight-month-old savannah cat (a cross between a domestic cat and a wild African cat known as a serval)

Unfortunate Event: Cleo lives with her owner, Joel Isfeld, on the 17th floor of an apartment building in New Westminster, British Columbia. Like a lot of cat owners in high-rises, Isfeld lived in fear of Cleo jumping out a window or over the balcony to her death far below. That fear became reality one evening in September 2014, when Cleo hopped onto the balcony railing and, before Isfeld could stop her, took a flying leap into the great beyond. "It was like, all of a sudden she was gone," he told Canada's Global News website. "I looked over and said, 'did that really happen?'"

But there was no cat-shaped splat on the ground below, so Isfeld asked every resident in all 16 apartments below his to check their balconies for Cleo. She wasn't on any of them. Nor was she on the commuter train platform below, or anyplace else Isfeld looked. He took the next day off from work and spent the entire day looking for her, but she was nowhere to be found.

What Happened: That night the building security guard called Isfeld and told him Cleo had been found on the ninth-floor roof garden of the building next door. Other than a scratch on her nose and a small cut on her mouth, she was unharmed. "Somehow she landed the fall," Isfeld told the *Vancouver Sun*. (He's keeping the door to the balcony shut from now on.)

Fortunate Felines: Py and Smudgie, two cats belonging to Carlton Smith, a retired high school teacher in Townshend, Vermont

Unfortunate Event: Smith was away on vacation in July 2012; her neighbors, Lorrie and Rick Snow, were looking in on her cats. One day at about 3:00 in the morning, a leaky propane tank caused an explosion that demolished Smith's three-story house. Both Py and Smudgie were inside at the time, and it was assumed that both had been killed by the explosion.

What Happened: The next day the Snows spotted Py peeking out of the pile of debris, all that was left of Smith's house. They were unable to catch him, but the following evening a sheriff's deputy told them that Smudgie had also been spotted. They were able to coax Smudgie out of the rubble, but Py, who'd moved to the basement, refused to leave. "He'd sit on the broken wood and the broken shutters and talk to us. Then he'd go back to the basement," Lorrie Snow told the *Brattleboro Reformer*. Finally, two weeks after the explosion, Py allowed Rick Snow to pick him up and take him to safety. Both cats, though frightened by the experience, were unharmed, except for "superficial singeing on their coats and whiskers," said veterinarian Dr. Heidi Winot.

Fortunate Feline: Stig, a six-week-old black kitten found at a recycling center east of London, England, in 2015

Unfortunate Event: Workers at the center first realized there was a kitten around when they heard terrified meows coming from inside a piece of industrial machinery that sorts recyclable materials by the ton.

What Happened: The powerful machinery could easily have killed Stig, but before the workers could shut it off, the kitten popped out of the machine on a conveyor belt, completely unharmed. "I can't believe he survived. What a lucky escape," supervisor Daniel Corker told the *London Evening Standard*. Stig has since been adopted.

Fortunate Feline: Nigel, a six-year-old cat who belongs to Kathy Howells and Rob Nunner

Unfortunate Event: In March 2013, Howells and Nunner decided to visit relatives for a few days while the bathroom in their apartment was being renovated. A neighbor dropped by once a day to feed Nigel and another cat named Lily, but one morning (after the new tub was installed), Nigel was nowhere to be found. Howells and Nunner spent a week searching the neighborhood for the cat, but it wasn't until their neighbor on the floor below them heard scratching sounds in her apartment, "as if an animal was climbing up the wall," that they realized what had happened.

What Happened: Four days and several holes cut into the ceilings and walls of both apartments later, Nunner was able to grab Nigel by the tail and pull him to safety. Nigel made a quick recovery from his 11 days in the wall; Howells and Nunner took a little longer. "It was the most grueling experience of my whole life," said Howells.

"OW!"

More weird, baffling—and sometimes funny—stories of other people's pain.

VICTIM: Los Angeles Angels first baseman Kendrys Morales hit a bottom-of-the-ninth game-winning grand slam in a game against the Seattle Mariners in April 2010. An elated Morales jogged around the bases, bounding toward home, where a throng of his teammates awaited him. He then jumped into the air to land on home plate and score the winning run.

OW! He landed on home plate…and broke his leg. (More specifically, he broke his fibula, the long thin bone that runs along the outside of the lower leg.) The injury required major surgery, which caused the no-longer-elated Morales to miss the remainder of the 2010 season. (Because of complications from the injury, he missed the entire 2011 season as well.)

VICTIM: In 2008 a young couple, described in news reports as "twenty-somethings," in the city of Zhuhai, on China's southern coast, were kissing.

OW! As the man kissed the woman, he sucked so hard on her mouth that he ruptured her left eardrum, leaving her unable to hear out of that ear. "The inner ear is connected to the mouth via a tube," a Dr. Li told the *China Daily* newspaper. "The kiss reduced pressure in the mouth, pulled the eardrum out and caused the breakdown." The doctor added that the condition was probably temporary, and the woman should have her hearing back in a month or two. The newspaper added: "While kissing is normally very safe, doctors advise people to proceed with caution."

VICTIM: In March 2015, an Australian woman (her name wasn't released to the press) took a trip around the world and made a stop to see some friends in rural Saskatchewan, Canada. The woman and her friends got really drunk one night and she passed out.

OW! The woman passed out…outside. In Canada. In the winter. She awoke to a serious case of frostbite affecting nearly all of her fingers (she wasn't wearing gloves). She documented her medical treatment on the image-sharing website Imgur, under the name TheBassistsMuse. By the time she reached the hospital, her fingers were covered in huge yellow blisters that made her fingers swell to about four times their normal size, all the while burning and painfully pulsating. Her doctor (his name, ironically, was Dr. Frieson) drained the blisters, and the woman's fingers returned to normal size, although they looked like crispy bacon. She's almost fully recovered…although there's a chance that a portion of one of the more severely burned fingers may need to be amputated. "Don't mistake this for a sob story," she wrote on Imgur. "There's no complaining here. Just pure unadulterated idiocy."

VICTIMS: In May 2012, two teenage boys were hanging out in front of an abandoned school in Detroit, Michigan, when they started arguing. What were they arguing about? Who made the best Kool-Aid. **OW!** Both boys pulled out guns and started shooting at each other. Luckily, they missed each other. Not so luckily, they accidentally shot two bystanders. (One was hit in the wrist, the other got it in the butt.) Both victims were treated at local hospitals and released that day. The two Kool-Aid gunslingers were later arrested.

VICTIM: In July 2012, a 31-year-old father was having a day of fun with his kids at a theme park near the town of Gävle, in eastern Sweden. When his four-year-old daughter was unable to operate one of the park's bright yellow motorized mini trucks, the father picked her up and positioned her in front of him on the car's seat while he sat on a small platform just behind her. **OW!** Jutting up from the small platform: an eight-inch-long metal spike meant to serve as a tow hitch. The father didn't see it when he plopped himself down, and, well, let's just say the spike injured him…internally. Amazingly, the park's staff didn't call for an ambulance after they helped free the man from the spike even though he was bleeding profusely. Instead, they gave him a pair of spare pants—and treated him to lunch. Even more amazingly, the man then made a one-and-a-half hour drive back to his home. By the time he got home, he was in such bad shape that he called an ambulance to take him to the hospital, where he was treated for internal injuries and for the blood infection he contracted after to waiting too long to get treatment. Fortunately, he eventually made a full recovery. (The tow hitch, theme park officials told newspapers, was removed from the mini truck.)

*   *   *

ZEN HUMOR
Q: Why don't Buddhists vacuum in the corners?
A: Because they have no attachments.

Inventive Minds

Words of inspiration from some of the world's great inventors.

"There is no thrill that can go through the human heart like that felt by the inventor as he sees some creation of the brain unfolding to success. Such emotions make a man forget food, sleep, friends, love, everything."
—**Nikola Tesla**

"Inventing is a combination of brains and materials. The more brains you use, the less material you need."
—**Charles Kettering (inventor of the electric car engine)**

"The most dangerous notion a young man can acquire is that there is no more room for originality."
—**Henry Ford**

"A new gadget that lasts only five minutes is worth more than an immortal work that bores everyone."
—**Francis Picabia (Surrealist painter)**

"The test of an invention is the power of an inventor to push it through in the face of staunch—not opposition, but indifference."
—**Edwin Land (inventor of the Polaroid camera)**

"Isn't it astonishing that all these secrets have been preserved for so many years just so we could discover them?"
—**Orville Wright**

"An invention has to make sense in the world it finishes in, not in the world it started."
—**Tim O'Reilly (software developer)**

"An inventor is one who can see the applicability of means to supply demand five years before it is obvious to those skilled in the art."
—**Reginald Fessenden (radio pioneer)**

"To invent, you need a good imagination and a pile of junk."
—**Thomas Edison**

"If it's a dumb idea, you'll find out. You'll smack into that brick wall...and then you'll stagger back and see another opportunity that you wouldn't have seen otherwise."
—**Richard Drew (inventor of masking tape)**

"The best way to predict the future is to invent it."
—**Alan Kay (computer scientist)**

130,000 years ago, horses were much smaller than they are today. Some were as small as house cats.

Babyfaces and Gas

Professional wrestling is full of over-the-top characters,
cartoon violence…and some really weird jargon.

KAYFABE. The basis of professional wrestling—scripting out matches ahead of time but presenting them as real and spontaneous. (Possibly from a variation of "be fake" in pig Latin.)

THE BUSINESS. People in the professional wrestling world don't call it a "sport"— they call it "the business."

DARK MATCH. On a night of matches taped for TV, this is a match that doesn't get televised, generally used to warm up the audience.

RING RATS. Groupies.

SPOTS. Holds or blows that are carefully planned out before a match. A "blown spot" is one that either misses wildly or lands too hard.

DIRT SHEETS. Internal wrestling industry memos detailing storylines and match instructions.

STRAP. A championship belt. Also called "the Gold."

BABYFACES. Heroic "good guy" wrestlers (like Hulk Hogan).

HOSS. A physically large but unskilled wrestler.

MONSTER. An unbeatable wrestler.

VISUAL FALL. A carefully choreographed bit in which a wrestler knocks his opponent down in full view of the crowd, but where the referee can't see.

MARK. What people in "the business" call fans who believe wrestling is real.

SMARK. A combination of "smart" and "mark"—a fan who knows wrestling is fake.

SQUASH. A short, one-sided match.

SANDBAG. To defend against a hit by making the body go limp.

CALL. Pre-match instructions to wrestlers on how the match should play out.

GAS. Steroids.

BUST OPEN. When a wrestler starts to bleed after a bad hit.

COLOR. If there was a lot of "color" in a match, there was a lot of busting open.

Tiny country, tiny song: The Qatari national anthem is only 32 seconds long.

Dig It

You only live once. And you only die once. But that doesn't necessarily mean that you'll only be buried once.

BY ANY OTHER NAME

Deceased: Frederick Brown, 83, a retired bank manager who lived in northwest England

Details: Brown died in 1990 and was laid to rest in the churchyard of Holy Trinity Church in the village of Freckleton in Lancashire. He'd still be there, too, if not for the fact that his family wanted his gravestone to read:

> A DEVOTED AND MUCH-LOVED
> HUSBAND, DAD AND GRANDAD

The vicar, Stephen Brian, refused to allow the use of the familiar "Dad" and "Grandad," citing Church of England guidelines that state "Nicknames or pet names (Mum, Dad, Ginger) inscribed in stone would carry overtones of the dog cemetery."

The guidelines are not etched in stone (so to speak), and Brian's predecessors—previous vicars of the Freckleton parish—permitted the use of familiar terms, as older gravestones in the churchyard attest. But Brian was determined that there be no "Mums" or "Dads" in the Holy Trinity Churchyard on *his* watch, and though the Browns fought the decision for four years, they lost. "The use of Father/Grandfather does not indicate cool or unaffectionate feelings," an Anglican court ruled in 1994.

Disinterred: In the summer of 1995, Brown was exhumed from his still-unmarked grave and reburied in a public cemetery five miles away. "He was Dad and Grandad," says his daughter-in-law, Wendy Brown. "He never liked to be called anything else."

YOU WIN SOME...

Deceased: Urooj Khan, 46, an Indian immigrant who owned a chain of dry-cleaning stores in Chicago

Details: After making a pilgrimage to Mecca in 2010, Khan swore off all forms of gambling, including lottery tickets. But in July 2012, in a moment of weakness, he bought two $30 scratch-off tickets at a 7-Eleven store...and one of them was a $1 million winner. After taking the lump-sum payout, Khan found himself $424,000 richer.

But several hours after collecting the money, Khan suffered a seizure

---

In 300 BC, the Carthaginians drove off Roman ships by catapulting live snakes at them.

and died. Was it divine retribution? There was no apparent evidence of foul play, so the Cook County medical examiner decided to take a blood sample rather than conduct a full autopsy. Result: when the blood tested negative for carbon monoxide, opiate, and alcohol poisoning, the medical examiner ruled the cause of death to be heart disease.

Khan's brother ImTiaz wasn't so sure that his brother had died from natural causes, and after he shared his suspicions with the medical examiner's office, they performed additional blood tests. When those revealed lethal levels of cyanide, the cause of death was changed to homicide.

Disinterred: In January 2013, Khan's body was exhumed so that a full autopsy could be performed…and then reburied. No further evidence of poisoning was found—not necessarily because it hadn't happened, but because cyanide decomposes even faster than human remains. Khan's death is still considered a homicide, but as of January 2015, no one has been charged with his murder.

THE TOOTH HURTS

Deceased: Kenneth Manis, 76, of Chattanooga, Tennessee

Details: When Manis passed away in Chattanooga's Parkridge Medical Center in June 2011, hospital staff gathered up his personal effects and gave them to the family. Among those personal effects were Manis's dentures, which were later placed in a case with other personal items and buried with him in his coffin.

At least it was *assumed* they were his dentures…until Mrs. Manis went through the bag of personal effects a few days after the funeral and found her husband's dentures still in the bag, along with another man's wallet and keys. The man who owned the wallet and keys was also a patient at the hospital. He was still alive—and his dentures were missing.

Disinterred: Eight days after Kenneth Manis was laid to rest the first time, he was exhumed and the offending dentures removed at the request of Mrs. Manis, who didn't think her husband "would want to be buried with something that didn't belong to him." Parkridge Medical Center paid for the disinterment and even bought a new set of dentures for the man who owned the wallet. "I know my husband is going to be resting a lot easier and so is our family," Mrs. Manis told ABC News after her husband was laid to rest…again.

*　　*　　*

"Life would be tragic if it weren't funny." —**Stephen Hawking**

Slavery was legal in Saudi Arabia until 1962.

How to Perform C.P.R. on Your P.E.T.

Most people who take courses in cardiopulmonary resuscitation (CPR) will never need to use it. It's even less likely that a pet owner will need to save a pet, but you never know...

BEFORE THE NEED ARISES
It's not the most common occurrence, but it could happen to any dog or cat owner: You hear a yelp in the next room and you discover your pet has collapsed and is unconscious. Is it still breathing? Does it have a heartbeat? Did it have a heart attack? What do I do next? Here are a few things you can learn to do in advance so you'll be better prepared in an emergency:

• **Know where and how to find your pet's pulse.** One good place on both dogs and cats is the area of the chest where the "elbow" of the left foreleg touches it. Feel for the pulse by pressing gently on this part of the chest with your index and middle fingers. The inner thigh of the hind leg is another good place to find a pulse. On larger dogs you should also be able to feel the pulse on the foreleg just above the wrist joint or on the hind leg just above the ankle joint.

• **Know how to tell whether your pet is breathing.** The obvious way is to simply look and see if its chest is rising and falling. But if its breathing is shallow, it may be difficult to see the chest moving. In that case you can cup your hand over its nose and feel for its breath, or place a mirror next to the nose. If your pet is breathing, its breath will fog the mirror.

IN AN EMERGENCY: KNOW THE ABC'S
• **Airway.** If your animal is unresponsive and not breathing, the first thing to do is check the airway to see if it's obscured. Extend the neck (sometimes this is enough to get breathing started) and gently open the animal's mouth. Pull the tongue forward and check to see if anything is obstructing the airway. If there is, remove the object. If it appears to be stuck or wedged in place, you may want to attempt to remove it using the Heimlich maneuver: depending on the size of the animal, wrap your hands, or, in the case of large dogs, your arms, around your pet just below the rib cage and give five quick thrusts to the abdomen. This forces air out of the animal's lungs and will (hopefully) dislodge any foreign objects from its throat.

Ben & Jerry's cows receive massages.

- **Breathing.** If the animal still isn't breathing, perform mouth-to-snout resuscitation. Hold the animal's mouth closed with your hand and place your mouth over its nose. Blow gently into the nostrils until you feel resistance or you see the animal's chest begin to rise. Remove your mouth from the animal's nose and allow the chest to deflate. Repeat three to five times, then check to see if the animal is breathing on its own. If not, check for a heartbeat.

- **Compressions.** If the heart is not beating, you will need to begin chest compressions. With medium and large dogs, lay the dog on its right side. Place one palm on the chest where it meets the dog's elbow, and place your other palm on top of it. Apply compression by pressing downward without bending your elbows. Compress the chest 1–3 inches, depending on the size of the dog: the larger the dog, the deeper the compression.

  With cats and smaller dogs, lay the animal on its right side, then place the fingers and the palm of one hand on its chest. Applying pressure with this hand, compress the chest about half an inch, then release. Some vets recommend picking small animals up and providing compression by squeezing the chest gently with both hands.

  NOTE: Practicing CPR chest compressions on a healthy dog or cat is *never* a good idea. It can cause injury, so it should only be attempted if the animal's life is in danger.

- **Repeat.** Dogs weighing over 90 pounds should receive 10 chest compressions for every breath of air. Cats and smaller dogs should be given five compressions for every breath of air. Check for a pulse after one minute and every few minutes after that. Once a steady pulse is restored, stop the compressions, but continue checking the pulse to make certain the heart doesn't stop again. As soon as the pet is revived, take it to the vet for further medical attention.

- If the animal hasn't responded after 10 minutes, stop the CPR.

GET SOME HELP

- The real key to saving a pet's life is to get it to the veterinarian *before* it needs to be revived. If its heartbeat is irregular or it's having difficulty breathing, get your pet to the vet immediately.

*　　*　　*

"A well-trained dog will make no attempt to share your lunch. He'll just make you feel so guilty that you cannot enjoy it."

—**Helen Thompson**

Oops! Until they competed against each other in the 1936 Olympics, Liechtenstein and Haiti...

Royal Beddings

William and Kate, Grace and Rainier, Uncle John and Mrs. Uncle John.
History provides us with many examples of royalty breaking with
tradition and marrying members of the common, unwashed
riff-raff. (And in Uncle John's case, the uncommonly
unwashed) Here are a few more notable examples
for your royal (flush) reading pleasure.

JAMES, DUKE OF YORK, AND ANNE HYDE

In 1660 James, younger brother of King Charles II of England, Scotland, and Ireland—and a notorious philanderer—got his commoner mistress, Anne Hyde, pregnant. And, to the shock of his family, he announced he was going to *marry* her. This was considered so outrageous that the king forbade James from marrying Anne. Not only that, several noblemen came forward to say *they* were the father of Anne's baby, thereby relieving the royal family of the disgrace James had brought upon them. To James's credit, he would have none of it. He and Anne were married in 1660 and remained married until Anne's death in 1671. And not only was the commoner Anne Hyde made an official "royal," with the title of Duchess of York, two of her daughters with James went on to become British queens: Queen Mary II (1689–94) and Queen Anne (1702–14).

Bonus Fact: Historians say that Anne was devoted to her husband even though James continued his philandering ways throughout their marriage, having numerous affairs and many illegitimate children.

DUKE LUDWIG AND HENRIETTE MENDEL

Duke Ludwig Wilhelm, born in 1831, was the eldest son and first in line to succeed Duke Maximilian Joseph in Bavaria, of the powerful German house of Wittelsbach. Ludwig was destined for a position among the elite of European royalty—his younger sister Elisabeth went on to become empress of Austria and queen of Hungary, and his still younger sister Marie Sophie became queen of the Two Sicilies (at the time the most powerful state in Italy). But Ludwig met an actress, Henriette Mendel, and fell in love. He renounced his rights as firstborn son and married Henriette in 1859—just before the birth of their second child. The couple remained happily married until Henriette's death in 1891.

Bonus Fact: Ludwig's sister, Elisabeth, became empress of Austria and queen of Hungary when she married Emperor Franz Joseph—who had his own rebellious heir. (See next entry.)

ARCHDUKE FERDINAND AND COUNTESS SOPHIE

Archduke Franz Ferdinand was nephew and heir to Emperor Franz Joseph of the Austro-Hungarian Empire. In 1894, at the age of 29, he fell in love with 26-year-old Countess Sophie Chotek. And though she was no commoner—she was from an aristocratic family in Bohemia (in modern-day Czech Republic)—she was not of sufficient royal rank to marry into the house of Hapsburg, one of the most powerful European royal families in history. Franz Joseph refused to allow the union, prompting the love-stricken—and famously stubborn—Ferdinand to refuse the emperor's refusal. After months of bickering and negotiating, the emperor finally relented, but only after Ferdinand signed a contract stating that Sophie would never be recognized as empress and that their children would not inherit the throne. They married in 1900; Franz Joseph did not attend the wedding.

Bonus Fact: Ferdinand and Sophie's story ended in tragedy. While driving through the city of Sarajevo, in Bosnia and Herzegovina, in 1914, they were assassinated, an event that led directly to the start of World War I.

LOUIS II AND GHISLAINE DOMMANGET

Ghislaine Dommanget was a fairly well-known French comedy actress when, in 1946, she met Prince Louis II, ruler of the tiny island principality of Monaco. The two fell in love and became engaged. Prince Louis's family opposed the engagement: it wasn't simply that Dommanget wasn't royalty, or that she was a lowly *actress*—she was also 30 years younger than the 76-year-old Louis and was seen as a gold digger. Louis gave his family's concerns careful thought—just kidding—he didn't care what his family thought, and he married Ghislaine anyway. The two lovebirds rarely went to Monaco after that, spending most of their time in Paris, until Louis's death three years later in 1949. Ghislaine became Dowager Princess of Monaco upon Louis's death, a title she held until her own death in 1991.

Bonus Fact: Louis II had fathered a daughter—out of wedlock—with a French woman he met when he was a soldier in Algeria all the way back in 1898. His daughter had a son, and the son became Louis's successor. That son, Prince Rainier III, went on to marry his own commoner-actress bride, Princess Grace Kelly, in 1956.

CROWN-PRINCE AKIHITO AND MICHIKO SHODA

In 1957 Akihito, 24, the eldest son of Emperor Hirohito of Japan, met Michiko Shoda, the 23-year-old daughter of the president of a Tokyo flour milling company, at a tennis match. The two were soon a couple, and in 1958 they became engaged. This was a *very* big deal in Japan. The Yamato dynasty is the world's oldest continuous hereditary

Opal, or hydrated silica, has been discovered on Mars (suggesting that water was once present).

monarchy, and in its 1,500-year history, a commoner had never married into it. The engagement became an even bigger deal when it was approved by the royal house and by the Japanese government (as required by law), because upon being married, Michiko became an official member of Japanese royal family. And upon the death of Hirohito in 1989, the royal/nonroyal couple became Emperor Akihito and Empress Michiko of Japan, positions they have held ever since.

Bonus Fact: Japanese tradition holds that a royal couple's children are separated from their parents early and raised by nannies and tutors. Continuing their nontraditional ways, Akihito and Michiko raised their three children at home, and Michiko did the unthinkable—she breast-fed the kids.

SAYAKO AND YOSHIKI

Emperor Akihito and Empress Michiko got a royal taste of their own medicine when each of their three royal children—Crown Prince Naruhito, his younger brother Prince Akishino, and the youngest, Sayako, officially known as Princess Nori—married nonroyals. For the sons, it was no big deal, as their commoner spouses were officially welcomed into the royal family as princesses. That was not the case for Princess Nori, who married 40-year-old Tokyo urban planner Yoshiki Kuroda in 2005. Sayako was forced to relinquish her royal status and went from being Princess Nori...to Mrs. Sayako Kuroda. Her parents and her brothers, however, supported the marriage and were among those in attendance at the small ceremony in a Tokyo hotel.

Bonus Fact: Shortly after the wedding, Japanese tabloid newspapers reported that Sayako had asked a friend, "If one shops at the supermarket, how does one carry all the food?" Sayako, who was 36 when she was married, had never learned "normal" skills and suddenly had to learn to do things like drive, keep track of household finances—and use a shopping cart.

EXTRAS

Two more marriages between royals and commoners:

Prince Felipe and Letizia Ortiz Rocasolano: Crown Prince Felipe of Spain married Rocasolano, a Madrid television anchor, in 2004. In 2014, upon the abdication of King Juan Carlos, Felipe became King Felipe VI—and Letizia became Queen Letizia of Spain. She's the first commoner queen in the history of the Spanish monarchy.

Prince Johan Friso and Mabel Wisse Smit: In 2003 Prince Friso, son of Queen Beatrix of the Netherlands, married Mabel Smit, a Dutch diplomat. And because Smit, while in her 20s in the late 1980s, had been in a relationship with a notorious Dutch drug kingpin, Friso lost his royal status.

Simp-Signs

Over 25+ seasons, The Simpsons *has featured hundreds of quick sight gags—such as these funny signs outside stores, businesses, and offices.*

Child Psychiatrist
Where imaginary
friends come to die

SPRINGFIELD SAVINGS
Safe From 1890–1986, 1988–

Springfield Dental Complex
No matter how you brush,
you're doing it wrong

**SPRINGFIELD
PSYCHIATRIC CENTER**
Because there may not
be bugs on you

Adult Education Annex
We take the "dolt" out of
a-dolt education

Plastic Surgery Center
Correcting God's mistakes

Springfield Dog Park
Where dogs meet to sniff
each other and bark

SLOT CAR HEAVEN
¹⁄₂₄ the size, ⅜ the fun

Wild Animal Kingdom
Born free, then caged

**SPRINGFIELD
HISTORICAL SOCIETY**
Where the dead come alive
(metaphorically)

Mom & Pop Hardware
A subsidiary of Global
Dynamics, Inc.

SPRINGFIELD HOSPITAL
Quality care or your
autopsy is free

Springfield Hall of Records
Not the good kind of records,
historical ones

BEER GARDEN
Proof of age or exact
change required

Houseware Warehouse
Your super super-store store!

**SPRINGFIELD
LITTLE LEAGUE
PARK**
Warning: Your child is not as
good as you think he is

Springfield Dog Track
Think of them as little horses

In 'n' Out Ear Piercing
If it dangles, we'll
punch a hole in it

COMMUNITY CENTER
Welcome Candy Convention
Room 1! Also Candy-Shaped
Rat Poison Convention
Room 11

Some archaeologists believe Egypt's Great Sphinx was once painted with a red face and blue beard.

Ad Men

In ancient Greece, they had heroes like Hercules and Pegasus. Today we have new "heroes," like the San Diego Chicken and the GEICO Gecko.

JOE CAMEL

In 1974 an R.J. Reynolds Tobacco executive overseeing Camel cigarettes wrote a company memo about the concept of creating lifetime brand loyalty by attracting teenage smokers. "I wonder whether comic strip–type copy might get a much higher readership among younger people than any other type of copy," he wrote. In 1988, as part of a 75th-anniversary promotion for the Camel brand, RJR introduced a new mascot in the United States, Joe Camel—a hip, sunglasses-clad camel who drove classic muscle cars, wore leather jackets, and hung out with gorgeous human women. (Also, he had no hump, walked on two legs, and always wore shoes.) The character quickly became the target of antismoking groups, which criticized RJR for targeting preteen and teenage boys. In fact, a study by the *Journal of the American Medical Association* found that the two most recognizable cartoon characters to six-year-olds were Mickey Mouse and Joe Camel. Under immense pressure from Congress, the Federal Trade Commission, and impending lawsuits, RJR ended the campaign in 1997 and replaced Joe Camel in their advertising with humans and the old non-anthropomorphized camel logo, whose nickname is "Old Joe."

SONIC THE HEDGEHOG

The Nintendo Entertainment System revived the dormant home video game industry in the late 1980s and made a fortune thanks to games that featured recognizable, kid-friendly characters such as Mario, Donkey Kong, Link (*The Legend of Zelda*), and Samus Aran (*Metroid*). The same could not be said of its direct competitor, the Sega Master System, which foundered in the United States. So when Sega launched the Genesis system to compete with the new Super Nintendo console in 1991, executives knew they needed to come up with a mascot. Fast. Under new CEO Tom Kalinske, who had rebuilt the Barbie and Hot Wheels brands at Mattel, Sega of America came up with Sonic the Hedgehog, a spunky Disney-like character with attitude, who starred in games in which he zoomed across the screen at speeds never before seen (or possible) in a video game. Sega even made up the term "blast processing" to describe how the Sega Genesis handled Sonic's speed in a way Super Nintendo couldn't, leading to commercials featuring the slogan "Genesis Does What Nintendon't." While Sonic helped

Sega stay in the console business for the next decade, the company was bleeding money and eventually restructured operations in 2001. It got out of the game console business and focused instead on developing games—including games that starred Sonic—for other systems: Microsoft, Sony…and Nintendo.

THE MOST INTERESTING MAN IN THE WORLD

In 2006 Dos Equis was a fairly obscure imported Mexican beer sold mainly in Texas and California. Cuauhtemoc Moctezuma Brewery wanted to differentiate the brand from the rest of the crowded marketplace and hired advertising firm Euro RSCG to design an ad campaign. Their market research showed that, contrary to ads that associated the brands with exotic locations and beautiful people, beer customers wanted to be seen as interesting. That inspired brand director Paul Smailes to create an ad mascot called "The Most Interesting Man in the World." The character would tell tales of his accomplishments but be portrayed by an older actor, so that young consumers wouldn't find him threatening. He'd be aspirational. Each commercial followed the same script: old-looking film clips of The Man fighting bears or surfing 80-foot waves are played under a humorous voice-over (read by *Frontline* narrator Will Lyman) before transitioning to a nightclub. There, The Man is surrounded by gorgeous women in a corner booth before he spots the camera and says, "I don't always drink beer. But when I do, I prefer Dos Equis. Stay thirsty, my friends." (Actor Jonathan Goldsmith based his portrayal of The Man on 1950s actor Fernando Lamas.) Eight years after its debut, Dos Equis is now the sixth best-selling imported beer in the United States.

THE GEICO CAVEMEN

In 2004 GEICO Insurance asked the Martin Agency, an advertising agency in Richmond, Virginia, to come up with an ad campaign to raise awareness for its website, where people could sign up for car insurance. Instead of an assigning it to an ad executive, the agency brought in screenwriter Joe Lawson. His campaign: the website is so easy to use, "even a caveman could do it." That line fueled more than 20 commercials featuring cavemen in the modern-day world, with the catch being that the cavemen are fussy, sophisticated yuppies. The ad campaign worked so well that in 2007, ABC commissioned a sitcom based on the fish-out-of-water premise. *Cavemen* lasted half a season.

*   *   *

"If people make fun of you, you must be doing something right."
—**Amy Lee**

Fish out of water: Guam's leaping blenny fish live on rocks by the sea.

Toxic Animals

*From Uncle John's "Wild and Woolly" file, here are a
few odd animals that you've probably never heard
of and certainly don't want to touch.*

JAPANESE GRASS SNAKE

Lots of snakes produce toxic chemical substances, but most of them are *venomous*, not *poisonous*. The difference: Venomous animals inject the toxins into their victims, using specialized equipment such as fangs or stingers. Poisonous animals, on the other hand, have toxic substances in their bodies, which makes them dangerous to touch or eat. The Japanese grass snake is possibly the only poisonous snake in the world. When threatened by a predator, it arches its neck, causing two specialized glands on the back of its neck to bulge and secrete poisonous chemicals called *bufadienolides*. If the predator attacks—and the neck is the most common location a predator will bite a snake—it will get a mouthful of poison, which can result in anything from a nasty stinging sensation in its mouth to prolonged sickness and even death via respiratory and heart failure. (And if it does survive, it's unlikely to try to eat one of those snakes again!) In 2007 researchers discovered that Japanese grass snakes don't actually produce their own poison: they get it by eating poisonous toads and storing the toxin from the toads in their neck glands.

AFRICAN CRESTED RAT

The African crested rat is a large rodent—they're not true rats, and they look sort of like grayish skunks—found in eastern Africa. They've been known to be poisonous for centuries, but the science behind the crested rat's poison wasn't discovered until 2011, when a group of British researchers finally figured it out. African crested rats regularly chew the bark and roots of the *Antiaris toxicaria* tree, also called the poison arrow tree, an extremely toxic tree that native peoples use to produce poison hunting arrows. (Arrowheads dipped in the tree's resin are reportedly powerful enough to kill elephants.) The crested rat smears the chewed-up tree paste onto short, specialized hairs on its sides. When threatened, the creature bristles up the long fur on its back—looking sort of like a porcupine—exposing those short, poison-soaked hairs. If a predator is unlucky enough to take a bite of those exposed sides, it will become violently ill, start frothing at the mouth, lose coordination, and, in the worst cases, suffer heart failure and death. Unfortunately, there are many well-documented accounts of domestic dogs, which often

Some wealthy Chinese criminals have hired "body doubles" to serve their prison time.

haven't learned to steer clear, becoming sick and dying after encounters with these animals. Professor Jonathan Kingdon of the University of Oxford and head of the study that made the discovery called the African crested rat's toxic trickery "one of the most extraordinary defenses known in the animal kingdom."

PFEFFER'S FLAMBOYANT CUTTLEFISH

There are more than 120 species of cuttlefish, marine animals that are in the same family as the octopus and squid. One of the cuttlefish's main features is its internal shell, called the *cuttlebone*, which the creatures use to regulate their buoyancy in the water by filling or emptying it of gases. The Pfeffer's flamboyant cuttlefish is one of the most unique of these unique creatures, for several reasons. First, it generates outrageous "light shows," during which it sends bright, vibrant colors pulsing around its body (hence its "flamboyant" name). Second, it has a very small cuttle-bone, which means it has a hard time maintaining buoyancy. And that means that it spends most of its time crawling around on the surface of the seafloor, rather than swimming through the water. Normally, that would make it easy prey for cuttlefish-eaters, such as sharks, seals, and humans. But you'll never find this critter on a restaurant menu. Reason: the meat of the Pfeffer's flamboyant cuttlefish contains a toxin that scientists still don't fully understand, except that it's at least as powerful as the toxin found in its cousin, the blue-ringed octopus. What they do know is that eating a Pfeffer's flamboyant cuttlefish can cause nausea, respiratory failure, heart failure, paralysis, blindness, and death in humans…in a matter of just a few minutes.

SLOW LORIS

Slow lorises are small, big-eyed tree-dwelling lemurlike primates found across South and Southeast Asia. They have glands on their inner elbows that secrete a clear, strong-smelling substance, which they regularly lick from their elbows and onto their bodies. Why they do this is unknown; scientists say it has no deterrent effect on predators. But that substance *might* act as a kind of "venom." According to legend—and at least one scientific report (from 1972)—people have died after being bitten by slow lorises, reportedly due to a severe reaction to the secretion. This is disputed by other scientists, who point to chemical studies that show the substance to be similar to, and no more toxic than, the allergen in cat saliva. And there are documented cases of people, mostly zookeepers, being bitten by slow lorises and living to tell the tale. But those people *did* suffer from pain, redness, and swelling in the area of the bites, so maybe… (It's probably best, in any case, to just avoid being bitten by one of these creatures in the first place.)

In 1991 the voice actor for Mickey Mouse married the actress who voiced Minnie Mouse.

"Angela Lansbury's Power Loaf"

Celebrity recipes like these were once a common feature in magazines. (Note: If you don't recognize all the names, take our word for it—these folks used to be famous.)

"Barbara Eden's
Crab Stuffed Mushrooms"

"John Ritter's
Favorite Fudge"

"Liberace's Meatball Soup"

"Annette Funicello's
Steak in a Bag"

"Ronald Reagan's
Hamburger Soup"

"Natalie Wood's
Eggs Ranchero"

"Jean Stapleton's
Lobster Quiche"

"Betty Ford's
Curried Tuna Casserole"

"Ann Landers'
Meatloaf"

"Angela Lansbury's
Power Loaf"

"Marlo Thomas's
Lamb Chops Creole"

"Dr. Ruth's
Almost as Good as Sex
Cheesecake"

"Jean Harlow's
Cottage Meat Pies"

"Aretha Franklin's
Queen of Soul Ham"

"Rock Hudson's
Chicken Casserole"

"Tennessee Ernie Ford's
Pea-Picking Cake"

"Bette Davis's
Mustard Gelatin Ring"

"Richard Simmons'
Royal Trifle"

"Merle Haggard's
Rainbow Stew"

"Walt Disney's Chili & Beans"

"Maya Angelou's
Banana Meringue Pudding"

"Bob Hope's
Tuna Macaroni Loaf"

"Arthur Murray's
Hamburger Chops"

"Barbara Walters'
Western Casserole"

"Ed Asner's
Cucumber Olive Mold"

"Cher's
Hawaiian Meatballs
American Style"

According to Pepperidge Farm, the first ingredient in their Goldfish crackers is "smiles."

Great White Hunter

While researching an article on taxidermy recently, we discovered Carl Akeley, a man widely considered to be a pioneer in the field because of his artistic approach to the craft. But that's not all Akeley did: he also changed the way museums are designed, innovated nature photography, and founded Africa's first nature preserve. And it all started the day he killed a leopard with his bare hands.

THINK FAST!

Carl Akeley wasn't planning to hunt big game in Africa bare-handed—it just happened that way. The incident occurred during his first trip to Somaliland in 1896, when he was hunting and observing wildlife for Chicago's Field Museum of Natural History. Akeley and some companions were hunting ostriches at dusk when they heard a rustle in the bush. Akeley fired into it, heard a yowl, and before he could blink, 80 pounds of spotted fur, pointy teeth, and sharp claws was hurtling through the air at him. The leopard caught Akeley's left hand in its powerful jaws and started shredding his right arm and body with its claws and feet. Unable to pull his hand out of the predator's mouth, Akeley punched the leopard's throat as hard as he could. The animal choked, and Akeley slammed it to the ground, crushing its trachea. Then he jumped onto its rib cage with both knees and suffocated the beast. The photo of the bearded he-man posed in front of his tent with the leopard's body hanging from a rope has become the iconic image of the "great white hunter."

CURIOUS CARL

Born in upstate New York in 1864, Akeley grew up on a farm but had a strong interest in sketching wildlife. At the age of 12, a visit to an exhibit of 50 small animals and birds by a local taxidermist named David Bruce changed Akeley's life—he became obsessed with taxidermy. (His first try at preserving an animal: he stuffed a friend's dead canary as a gift to her.) At 18, he apprenticed with Bruce, who was impressed by the young man's artistic skill and advised him to apply for a job at Professor Henry Ward's Natural Science Establishment in Rochester. Akeley hated the conventional "upholstery" method of taxidermy—stuffing the animals with sawdust, cotton, or straw and propping them up on legs that contained the bones. He thought it was crude and lacked artistic vision. Aiming for a more realistic presentation, Akeley worked late at night perfecting his own style.

Texas horned lizards squirt blood from their eyes as a defense mechanism.

BODY BY AKELEY

Akeley's technique started with making an armature of wood, wire, or the animal's skeleton. Then he applied modeling clay or plaster to sculpt the animal's muscles and tendons. Akeley took great care in attaching the fur and stitching it so the seams never showed. His artistry and attention to detail soon caught the attention of Professor Ward, who, in 1885, assigned Akeley to work with veteran taxidermist William Critchley on the mammoth task of preserving the much-loved Barnum and Bailey circus elephant, Jumbo. (Jumbo had died in a head-on collision with a train a few months earlier.) The elephant took five months to mount, but that job established Akeley's reputation as an artist to be respected. He soon moved to the Milwaukee Public Museum in Wisconsin and designed and built the very first museum habitat diorama, displaying local birds and mammals in realistic surroundings. In 1896 Chicago's prestigious Field Museum offered the young wizard a job and a chance to go to Africa. Thus began Akeley's transformation from mild-mannered taxidermist to swashbuckling big game hunter.

ELEPHANTS AND GATORS AND RHINOS, OH MY!

Between 1896 and 1926, Akeley made five expeditions to British Somaliland, British East Africa, and the Belgian Congo. Each time, he returned with harrowing stories of his adventures. He contracted malaria and jungle fever. While resting on the Serengeti Plain, he was charged by three rhinos at once. In Uganda he shot a giant crocodile on the opposite bank of the Nile River. As he swam across to retrieve the body, he found that the river was infested with crocodiles; one grabbed and killed his porter. Finding himself stranded on the wrong side of the river, with no desire to swim back, Akeley used the dead croc as a raft and his rifle as a paddle to float back to safety.

He wasn't always that lucky. On Mount Kenya, a 13-foot-tall bull elephant burst out of the trees and charged him. The enraged beast tried to impale him with its tusks, but Akeley wedged himself between the six-foot-long ivory daggers and held on for dear life. The elephant fought by doing a headstand on the explorer, burying him in the mud. Akeley passed out; the beast ran off, and so did Akeley's native guides, leaving him for dead. He came to hours later and spent the next three months in the hospital. The elephant had broken over half of his ribs, piercing his lung in the process.

GORILLAS IN THE MIDST

Like most naturalists of his day, Akeley considered killing, photograph-ing, and stuffing wild animals to be the best way to preserve Africa's quickly disappearing wildlife. His thinking changed in 1921 while leading an expedition to "collect" mountain gorillas in the Virunga

Mountains of the Belgian Congo. He was the first to observe and film these rare gorillas, and he found them fascinating. Upon dubbing one silverback male "the Old Man of Mikeno," he said, "I am fonder of him than I am of myself." Still, he shot the gorilla and stuffed it for a museum exhibit. The animal's death haunted Akeley, and he turned away from taxidermy to create sanctuaries for the fast-disappearing animals. He talked King Albert I of Belgium into founding the first African national park as a safe haven for the mountain gorilla. Today, solely because of Akeley's efforts, Virunga National Park is home to approximately 400 gorillas.

BIG FINISH

During his lifetime, Akeley hunted with Teddy Roosevelt, served as president of the prestigious Explorers Club, and was a respected author and nature photographer, for which he invented the Akeley Motion Picture Camera—a Hollywood staple in the 1920s and 1930s. He also invented a "cement gun" that shot concrete into his taxidermy molds. Now called "shotcrete," it was adapted for use in building the Panama Canal and is still used by construction workers to build pools, walls, and anything formed with cement.

While working for the American Museum of Natural History in New York City from 1909 to 1926, Akeley meticulously designed the Akeley Hall of African Mammals, considered one of the greatest museum exhibits in the world. It contains 28 habitat dioramas depicting life on the Serengeti Plain, the Upper Nile, and the mountains of the Belgian Congo, all in minute detail. In 1926 the 62-year-old Akeley died of a fever while visiting his beloved mountain gorillas. His burial place is pictured in the mountain gorillas diorama in the Akeley Hall of African Mammals.

* * *

JEDI TOLD YOU SO

One night in September 1955, British actor Alec Guinness (who would later play Obi-Wan Kenobi in *Star Wars*) happened to meet rising star James Dean outside of a Hollywood restaurant. Guinness invited him to dinner. "Okay," said Dean, "but first I gotta show you my new car!" Guinness followed Dean out back to a brand-new silver Porsche Spyder. "Some strange thing came over me," Guinness later recalled. "In almost a different voice than mine, I said, 'Do not get in this car.' I looked at my watch. 'It is now 10:00 on Thursday. If you get in this car, you will be found dead in it by 10:00 next Thursday.'" Dean ignored the warning. A week later, on Thursday afternoon, Dean was driving 85 mph down a California highway and collided with a truck…killing him.

Writer's Fuel

Writing is hard work, but it can also be glamorous and romantic…all of which could explain why many classic writers are associated with a particular signature cocktail.

CARSON McCULLERS. The author of *The Heart Is a Lonely Hunter* and *The Ballad of the Sad Café* liked a drink called a Sonnie Boy. It's equal parts hot tea and sherry. McCullers drank them while writing but didn't like people to know she was drinking. The steaming mugs looked innocuous.

ANTHONY BURGESS. Author Richard Hughes invented a drink called the Hangman's Blood for his 1929 novel *A High Wind in Jamaica*, but Burgess (*A Clockwork Orange*) adapted the recipe to be even stronger. It's a pint glass filled with double shots of gin, whisky, rum, port, brandy, and a small bottle of stout, and topped with champagne.

TRUMAN CAPOTE. The writer of *In Cold Blood* liked to start the day with a screwdriver—vodka and orange juice, with a few orange slices as garnish. Capote called it "my orange drink."

ERNEST HEMINGWAY. While the mojito didn't catch on in the United States until the 2000s, Hemingway discovered the drink—white rum, lime juice, sugar, club soda, and muddled mint—in the 1930s at the La Bodeguita del Medio in Havana, Cuba, where the drink was invented.

WILLIAM FAULKNER. America's quintessential Southern author (*The Sound and the Fury*, *As I Day Lying*) favored the quintessential Southern cocktail: the mint julep—bourbon, water, ice, and fresh mint—served in a metal cup.

JACK KEROUAC. The hard-drinking Beat poet and author of *On the Road* discovered margaritas while traveling through Mexico. But Kerouac didn't drink the sweet, slushy, tequila-based margaritas served by your neighborhood Mexican restaurant. He liked authentic margaritas, slightly tart, served on the rocks, and made with mezcal, not tequila.

RAYMOND CARVER. The prolific short story writer was also a prolific drinker; according to some accounts, he drank two bottles of vodka a day. As far as mixed drinks go, he always ordered a Bloody Mary because he thought the tomato juice in the cocktail provided the drinker (him) with a fair amount of nutrition.

Some castles in Europe sell for less than apartments in New York City.

DOROTHY PARKER. The humorist and newspaper writer joked about drinking a lot. ("I like to have a martini, two at the very most. Three, I'm under the table, four I'm under my host!") Her favorite cocktail was something called a Clover Club. Named for a Philadelphia men's club, it's a frothy, pink, milkshake-like concoction of gin, sugar, egg whites, raspberries, and lemon juice.

RAYMOND CHANDLER. The detective novelist drank gimlets, a simple cocktail consisting of gin and lime juice. It was also the preferred tipple of his main character, Philip Marlowe; when Marlowe became popular in the United States in the 1950s, so did the gimlet.

IAN FLEMING. In Fleming's first James Bond novel, *Casino Royale* (1953), the superspy orders a "dry martini" consisting of "three measures of Gordon's [gin], one of vodka, half a measure of Kina Lillet [a medium-dry aperitif wine]. Shake it very well until it's ice-cold, then add a large thin slice of lemon peel." Later in the book, Bond names the drink a Vesper, after femme fatale Vesper Lynd. The drink was Ian Fleming's personal cocktail of choice.

J. D. SALINGER. Like his character Holden Caulfield in his novel *The Catcher in the Rye*, the reclusive author reportedly liked a simple scotch and soda.

EDNA ST. VINCENT MILLAY. The Pulitzer Prize–winning poet liked a drink of her own invention called a "Between the Sheets." It's a variation on the classic Sidecar, consisting of orange liqueur, lemon juice, and rum instead of the original's cognac.

TENNESSEE WILLIAMS. The New Orleans playwright behind *A Streetcar Named Desire* and *The Glass Menagerie* often included references to his favorite drink—the Ramos Gin Fizz—in his plays. It's still a minor custom in New Orleans to drink one in honor of Williams during Mardi Gras, although bartenders probably hate making them because they require egg whites, cream, lemon juice, lime juice, sugar, gin, and orange flower–flavored soda water.

A FEW MORE:

• **F. Scott Fitzgerald** (*The Great Gatsby*): gin rickey, which is gin, lime juice, and club soda

• **Hunter S. Thompson** (*Fear and Loathing in Las Vegas*): Wild Turkey bourbon on the rocks

• **J. K. Rowling** (*Harry Potter*): gin and tonic

Burned your tongue? Putting sugar or honey on it will soothe it. So will eating yogurt.

Looney Laws

Believe it or not, these laws are real.

In Carmel, New York, it's illegal for a man to appear in public in pants and a jacket that don't match.

• Women in Owensboro, Kentucky, may not buy hats without their husbands' permission.

• It's illegal to ride a bicycle on a tennis court in Eagle, Idaho.

• Kansas law prohibits shooting rabbits from a motorboat. (California law prohibits shooting any game from a moving vehicle…except whales.)

• It's against the law to sell Limburger cheese in Houston on Sundays.

• Hairdressers in Waterbury, Connecticut, may not whistle or hum while cutting hair.

• You're breaking the law if you honk your horn at a Little Rock, Arkansas, sandwich shop.

• Women must have a permit to wear cosmetics in Morrisville, Pennsylvania.

• Pet flamingos are barred from entering barbershops in Juneau, Alaska.

• In Alamosa, Colorado, it's illegal to throw missiles at cars.

• In Detroit, it's illegal to let your pet pig run wild unless it has a ring in its nose.

• In Jefferson Parish, Louisiana, it's against the law to pour a drink on the ground at a drive-in movie theater.

• Launching a catapult at a building is illegal in Aspen, Colorado.

• It's legal to throw bricks onto a highway in Mount Vernon, Iowa, provided you've received written permission from the city council.

• It's against the law in Alabama to wear a fake mustache in church "with the intent of creating laughter."

• Don't throw an old hoop skirt onto the sidewalk in Grand Haven, Michigan, unless you're prepared to pay a $5 fine.

• It's against the law to walk on top of a water tank in Zebulon, North Carolina.

• Between January and April, you need a permit in Wyoming to take a picture of a rabbit.

• It's against the law in Louisiana to tie an alligator to a fire hydrant.

Viking Proverbs

The seafaring Vikings terrorized coastal Europe for 300 years. It stands to reason that their philosophy would be violent and direct, as these "tough guy" proverbs attest.

Never walk away from home
ahead of your sword and axe.

The foolish man lies awake
thinking of his problems.
When the morning rises he
is worn out, and his trouble
is just as it was.

Better a humble house
than none. A pair of goats
and a patched roof is
better than begging.

A head stuck on a pike
no longer conspires.

The lame will run if he has to.

To be without silver is better
than to be without honor.

Be your friend's true friend.
Return gift for gift. Repay
laughter with laughter, but
repay betrayal with treachery.

False peace with bad friends
burns faster than fire.

What's good is often forgotten,
what's bad is often hidden.

You don't have to put out
the fire when all is ash.

At every doorway, before one
enters, one should spy round.

Brawl with a pig and you
go away with his stink.

Two heads cut off and
thrown high into the tree
have only the winds with
which to scheme.

A dead man gathers no goods.

No man should call himself
clever, but manage his mind.

It is fortunate to be favored
with praise and popularity, but
it is dire luck to be dependent
on the feelings of a fellow man.

No friend is he who but flatters.

Eat your fill before a feast. If
you're hungry, you have no
time to talk at the table.

Beware of befriending the
friend of an enemy.

Only your kin will proudly
carve a memorial.

Though the spear spares them,
old age promises no peace.

Deceit sleeps with greed.

Fear the reckoning of those
you have wronged.

The Mad Potter of Biloxi, Part II

On page 110 we told you about a nutty potter who flopped in his profession in the early 1900s and was largely forgotten by the time he died. So how'd he become famous decades later? Believe it or not, he owes it all to auto parts.

ROAD WARRIOR

When George Ohr died at the age of 60 in 1918, he hadn't made a pot in nearly a decade. The thousands that he'd made but never sold were locked away in a shed behind the Ohr Boys Auto Repairing Shop. There they sat for half a century, and they might still be sitting there (or, more likely, they would have been thrown away) had a New York antiques dealer named James Carpenter not passed through town in the winter of 1968. One of Carpenter's areas of expertise was antique automobiles, and every winter he drove through the Gulf Coast states in search of old cars and old car parts, especially Cadillacs and Ford Model Ts. On this trip his wife came with him.

The Ohr Boys shop was the oldest auto repair place in Biloxi, and looked it. Carpenter stopped in and asked Ojo Ohr, still running the place with his brothers Leo and Geo, whether they had any old parts lying around. Ojo invited Carpenter to have a look and then asked Mrs. Carpenter, "Would y'all like to see some of my daddy's pottery?"

"Sure," she replied.

POT LUCK

James Carpenter wasn't interested in looking at pots. Perhaps only to humor his wife, he followed her out to the shed. But as Ojo held one pot after another up to the light—"*Nobody* touches Daddy's pottery!" he barked when Carpenter tried to pick one up himself—the New Yorker was astonished by the beauty and artistry of the pieces. They were similar to the ceramics of the Abstract Expressionist movement of the 1940s and 1950s, but decades older.

TOUGH SELL

Carpenter offered to buy the entire collection, on the spot, for $15,000, or about $2 a pot—the equivalent of around $8.50 a pot today. Ojo refused, but each winter, when Carpenter passed through the area looking for car parts, he dropped by the Ohr Boys Auto Repairing Shop

---

If you're a night owl, just one week of camping can reset your biological clock to daylight hours.

and repeated his offer to buy the pots. Finally in 1972, the brothers agreed to sell the collection for an undisclosed sum estimated to be in the neighborhood of $50,000, or just over $7.00 a pot—about $225,000, or $31.50 a pot today.

In 1901 George Ohr had told an interviewer that he wanted to sell all of his pots to a single buyer so that the collection would remain intact. Seventy years later, Carpenter had indeed bought all the pots… but for the purpose of breaking up the collection and selling pots to individual collectors. In so doing, however, he helped to realize one of Ohr's other dreams: it established Ohr's reputation as a potter of serious artistic merit.

MAD ABOUT YOU

Carpenter sold some of the pots for as little as $40, others for as much as $1,200. Soon the pots began appearing in some of Manhattan's most prestigious art galleries, where they fetched still higher prices. Celebrities like Jack Nicholson and Steven Spielberg collected the pots, and influential artists like Andy Warhol and the painter Jasper Johns began depicting them in their paintings. Prices for the pots climbed even higher.

During his lifetime Ohr had repeatedly tried to interest museums in his work by sending them samples, but he'd had very little success. Now, as the buzz surrounding his work continued to build, many of those same museums began acquiring Ohr's pots for their collections—spending big money to acquire pots they'd refused to accept when Ohr offered to give them the pieces for free. The Smithsonian Institution still had its box of eight pots that Ohr sent them in 1899, but it wasn't until 1986, nearly 90 years after receiving them, that it formally *accessioned* ("added") Ohr's work to its collection of American pottery.

MERRY POTTER

Even the citizens of Biloxi, who laughed at Ohr while he was alive, eventually came around to recognizing the genius of the Mad Potter who'd lived in their midst. In 1994 fans of his work opened the George E. Ohr Arts & Cultural Center to showcase his artistry, the only museum in America dedicated to the work of a single potter. In 2010 the center moved into a new $25 million facility designed by the architect Frank Gehry. Some 450 of Ohr's pots are on display there, of which only about 100 are actually owned by the museum. Why so few? Partly because they don't come on the market that often, and partly because when they do, they sell for very high prices. Today the pots that George Ohr couldn't sell for $25 apiece in the early 1900s, and that James Carpenter paid $7 for in the early 1970s, sell for upwards of $60,000 when they come up for auction. The prices continue to climb.

There's a town in northern France called Y. Alaska has one, too. (We don't know why.)

"GET A BILOXI SOUVENIR, BEFORE THE POTTER DIES, OR GETS A REPUTATION," read one of the many signs on George Ohr's studio at the turn of the 20th century. The locals probably laughed at the idea at the time, but nobody's laughing anymore. More than a few people in Biloxi today wish their grandparents had heeded the Mad Potter's warning and ponied up the $25 for a pot or two (or ten) before he "got a reputation."

HIDING IN PLAIN $IGHT

George Ohr didn't sell many pots during his lifetime, but he did sell some. Precisely how many is not known; estimates run as high as 500, not including the ones he buried in the woods in a fit of despair. Those, apparently, have never been found.

Many of the pots Ohr sold are likely collecting dust on their owners' shelves, as unrecognized for their artistic (and now, financial) value as they were during the Mad Potter's lifetime. Take a look in your attic. Are there any old clay pots that have been in the family for years—perhaps acquired by a grandparent during a swing through Mississippi? Do the pots look melted, crumpled, or squashed? Here's a tip from Uncle John: no matter how ugly you think they are, *don't* throw them away.

* * *

AN IMITATION OF LIFE™

The names of some real copycat store-brand cereals.

- **Crispy Hexagons** (Crispix)
- **Pranks** (Trix)
- **Live It Up!** (Life)
- **Marshmallow Magic** (Lucky Charms)
- **Apple Yo's** (Apple Jacks)
- **Square Shaped Corn** (Corn Chex)
- **Active Lifestyle** (Special K)
- **Freaky Fruits** (Frooty Pebbles)
- **Nutty Nuggets** (Grape Nuts)
- **Wheat Flakes** (Wheaties)
- **Choco Kiddo Balls** (Cocoa Puffs)
- **Cocoa Nuggets** (Cocoa Pebbles)
- **Crisp Crunch** (Cap'n Crunch)
- **Fruit Spins** (Froot Loops)
- **Crispy Rice** (Rice Krispies)
- **Honey Nut Scooters** (Honey Nut Cheerios)

Makes sense: Baby back ribs get their name because they're shorter than spareribs.

More Roll Models

Here's another story about people who found their 15 minutes of fame thanks to good deeds performed with…toilet paper.

ROLL MODEL: THE DEANES

Not long after Matthew and Eliza Deane and their three kids moved to Oakley, Utah, from New Hampshire in August 2014, some teenagers "TP'd" their new house and front yard with toilet paper. It wasn't the kind of welcome they hoped for, but it wasn't entirely unexpected: "We both lived here as kids and we both did it," Matthew Deane told the *Deseret News*. "It's part of the culture."

What *wasn't* part of the culture—at least when the Deanes were younger—was for the pranksters to do it over and over again. Every Friday and Saturday night for weeks after the Deane family moved in, a dozen or more kids at a time pelted the house with toilet paper. The mess they made was only the beginning: the troublemakers also took apart the Deanes' lawn furniture, rang the doorbell, and pounded on the doors and windows at all hours of the night. Sometimes they drove past the house without stopping, honking their horns and screaming as they went by.

Paper Chase

The Deanes' 15-year-old daughter was so upset by the harassment that she dropped out of high school and had to be homeschooled. Matthew Deane lost more than a few nights of sleep lying in wait for the pranksters to show up so that he could chase after them in his car. Once he cornered a carload of teenagers in a cul-de-sac and told them how upsetting their behavior was to his family. He thought the kids got the message, but the next Friday his house was TP'd again.

Finally, after four months of torment, a sheriff's deputy caught some of the teenagers in the act and took them into custody. Deane could have pressed charges, and perhaps even sued the parents for damages. But he didn't: "It sort of came to me that I should ask these people to bring toilet paper to our house and bring it *into* the house and come to know us," he says.

Roll on Over

Deane figured that if the troublemakers knew his family as people, they'd be less likely to TP the house again. (He was right.) And he thought all that toilet paper could be put to much better use if it was donated to a local charity that works with the poor—that's why he told

---

A California plant breeder has created a variety of grapes that tastes like cotton candy.

the kids and their parents to bring some with them.

Even if Deane had only collected toilet paper from those teenagers and their parents, he would have amassed a considerable haul. But when friends and neighbors found out what they were doing, many of them wanted to contribute some toilet paper as well. It wasn't long before the story found its way to the Internet, thanks to Facebook, Twitter, and Matthew Deane's own blog, and soon strangers began sending them packages of toilet paper from all over the country.

On a Roll

The Deanes set an initial goal of collecting 500 rolls of toilet paper by the end of December, then doubled it to 1,000 when their pile grew past 600 rolls. At first they piled the packages of toilet paper in front of the Christmas tree, but so much came in that they had to move it all behind the couch. By New Year's Day 2015 they'd collected more than 1,000 rolls in all, with more arriving daily.

The Deanes had planned to stop collecting toilet paper on New Year's Day, but stopping the donations will probably be as tricky as stopping the TP'ers in the first place. All in all, it's not a bad problem to have. "We just wanted to prove that good will win over all," Deane told the *Deseret News*. "It has become a happy, positive experience. I never thought it would…but it really has."

ROLL MODEL: LEO HILL

Hill, a retired maintenance worker in Denver, Colorado, started on his mission back in 2006 when his wife noticed that rolls of toilet paper sold in packs of four lasted four days, but the same rolls sold in packs of twelve-packs were used up in only three. So Hill started counting the individual sheets of toilet paper he used at every "pit stop," and tallied the figures on flattened toilet paper tubes. After using nine rolls, he found that on average each roll contained 156.75 squares even though the packaging claimed the rolls contained 198 squares—a shortage of 41.25 rolls, or just over 20 percent.

Hill shared his findings with Georgia-Pacific, the company that makes his brand of toilet paper. They thanked him and sent him a coupon for a dozen rolls of toilet paper. When those rolls came up short too, he reported the company to the Denver Business Bureau. No word on whether Hill deserves the credit, but by the time the *Denver Post* repeated his experiment a few years later, all the rolls they tested had as many sheets of toilet paper as advertised, and some had up to 10 percent extra. "I'm sure glad you got a good roll," he told the newspaper. "It's really only important when you run out."

What's the Word?

On page 83 we gave you the stories behind some old words. Here are more!

JENTACULAR

Meaning: Pertaining to breakfast

Details: Derived from *jenatculum*, the Latin word for a very early breakfast consisting of foods like bread, cheese, dried fruits, honey, milk—and even wine. Exactly when it came into use as the English adjective *jentacular* is unknown, but it was commonly used in the 18th and 19th centuries. An example of its use can be found in the *New Family Receipt Book* (*receipt*, in this case, means "recipe"), published in London in 1819. Its authorship was attributed to "A Lady," but it is known to have been written by Maria Eliza Rundell, author of the most popular cookbooks of the era in both England and the United States. Rundell writes that "coffee for breakfast is earnestly recommended as a most wholesome and pleasant *jentacular* beverage." The word is basically obsolete, but it is still used, mostly stylistically, by some writers today.

YARBOROUGH

Meaning: In the card game bridge, a hand containing no ace and no card higher than a nine

Details: Charles Anderson Worsley was the second Earl of Yarborough, an earldom in east-central England, from 1846 until his death in 1862. He is best known for having a standing offer to his bridge-playing friends: a 1,000-to-1 bet against them being dealt the hand described above. (If someone took the bet and won, he would pay them £1,000. If they lost, they had to pay him £1.) The legend of that bet lived on after the earl's death, and in the late 1890s, that hand started being called a "Yarborough" after him, and bridge players still use that term today. (It is also commonly used to refer to any very weak hand.) Actual odds against being dealt a 13-card hand with no ace, and no cards higher than a nine, from a standard 52-card deck of cards: approximately 1,827 to 1. So it was actually a pretty smart bet for the Earl of Yarborough to make.

WHIFFLER

Meaning: According to older versions of the *Oxford English Dictionary*, "A guard armed with a javelin, battle-axe, sword, or staff, and who wears a chain and keeps the way clear for a procession or public spectacle"

Details: Whifflers were soldiers hired by royalty or the very wealthy to get them safely through the throngs of people at public events. It goes back to the early 16th century and was most famously used by William Shakespeare in his 1599 play *Henry V*, in which he describes the sea acting as a whiffler:

> "The deep-mouth'd Sea, Which like a mightie Whiffler 'fore the King, Seemes to prepare his way."

In those days whiffling was serious business, but over the centuries it became more stylized and by the 1800s was used mostly just for show. From English philologist (language scholar) Robert Forby, in 1830:

> ...the whifflers are two active men very lightly equipped...bearing swords of lath or latten, which they keep in perpetual motion, "whiffing" the air on either side, and now and then giving an unlucky boy a slap on the shoulders or posteriors with the flat side of their weapons.

Whifflers were gone by the mid-19th century, after which use of the word dwindled.

MORE WEIRD WORDS

• **Apricity:** The warmth of the sun during winter or on a particularly cold day. From the Latin *apricus*, meaning "warmed by the sun." Sample use: "Despite the icy temperature, she was able to enjoy a moment of *apricity* as the sun emerged from behind a cloud."

• **Brabble:** To squabble or argue noisily about inconsequential things. The word is believed to come from 16th-century Middle Dutch *brabbelen*, meaning "to quarrel or jabber." Sample use: "The school bus driver's attempts to stop the children's brabbling was in vain."

• **Twattle:** To talk idly or chatter. It's from the 1550s, but its origin is unknown. Sample use: "Stop your twattling and get back to work!" Note: *Twattle* is believed to be the root of *twaddle*, which came along in the 1780s and means "drivel."

• **Jargogle:** To confuse or jumble. The earliest known use dates to the 1680s; its origin is uncertain. Sample use: "Thinking about infinity jargogles my brain."

• **Spizzerinctum:** Ambition, pep, the will to succeed. From the early 1900s, possibly earlier, and of unknown origin. An example of its use, from a 1913 story in the *Washington Herald* newspaper: "It is pleasant to fancy that 'endowed with spizzerinktum' may very well take the place of our much-liked 'full of pep'.")

• **Gorgonize:** To have a *mesmerizing* effect on someone. Taken from the mythological Greek sisters known as *Gorgons*, who had hair made of venomous snakes and caused anyone who looked at them to turn into stone. Sample use: "Brian found Megan so alluring that every time he looked at her, he was gorgonized."

Vinyl Gold

"Mighty John" Marshall is one of the nation's premier experts on rock-and-roll record collecting. We all have a few old records stored in the basement or the garage, so we asked Mighty John which ones are the most valuable, and this is what he told us. One thing to note before you go wild about your vinyl treasures, though: prices listed are for original copies in mint condition. There aren't too many of those around, which is what makes them rare …and valuable. Still, you'll probably want to check out what's stored away in your parents' attic because, well, you never know.

THE KING OF 'EM ALL

If you own any Elvis Presley records, you have money. But what's the most valuable Elvis record? In 1962 RCA released the single "Good Luck Charm." It quickly hit #1 on the Billboard Hot 100, selling more than a million copies. The common 45 (with its picture sleeve) can be worth up to $40. But RCA also issued the single as a 7-inch 33⅓, which means it's the same size as a 45 but plays at the speed of an album. If you have a copy of that version—with its picture sleeve—then you have a real "Good Luck Charm." It's worth up to $24,000.

BERRY BERRY GOOD

Frank Wilson is an important name in rock 'n' roll—not because he was famous (he wasn't), but because collectors consider his one and only 45, "Do I Love You (Indeed I Do)," the most valuable record of all time. In 1966 Berry Gordy, the founder of Motown, let Frank Wilson, a Motown record producer, record the song. Wilson made the record but had no interest in becoming a "star." He didn't like the spotlight and refused to promote his own song. That irked Gordy, who wasn't all that crazy about the record anyway, so he demanded that all 250 "promo" copies be destroyed. But some survived. Originals on the Soul label can sell for $40,000 today. Before you start scouring eBay, here's a word of warning: beware of counterfeits and reissues. All originals have "Promotional Not For Sale" printed on the labels.

WHAT CAN A POOR BOY DO?

In 1968 the Rolling Stones single "Street Fighting Man" was banned by some Chicago radio stations because demonstrators were rioting in the streets outside the Democratic Convention being held there. Though the song wasn't about the outbreak of violence in Chicago, many felt its politically charged lyrics could cause more trouble. The picture sleeve, which showed cops fighting with protesters, was issued in limited numbers. The record is worth no more than $20, but one of the picture sleeves is worth up to $18,000 today.

I PROTEST!

In May 1963, Bob Dylan was scheduled to appear on *The Ed Sullivan Show* and perform "Talkin' John Birch Society Blues" from his upcoming album, *The Freewheelin' Bob Dylan*. But the protest song's controversial lyrics made the show's producers nervous. They called Columbia Records and expressed their concern that the song could be libelous. Columbia execs agreed and took their concern a step further: they ordered the song off the album. Too late. Presses were already rolling, and a few copies of the album *with* the song got out before changes could be made. If you have the album, the label on the record might list "Talkin' John Birch Society Blues" as being on the record, but you have to play it to make sure it is. If it is, you have an album worth up to $20,000.

SURF'S UP

It was a case of love and who you know that makes one record by an obscure girl-group of the 1960s so valuable today. The group was known as the Honeys and they had little success until one member of the group—Marilyn Rovell—started dating Beach Boy Brian Wilson. Their good vibrations led to a regular gig for the group (Marilyn, her sister Diane, and their cousin Ginger Blake) as backup singers on Beach Boys records. It wasn't long before Marilyn became Mrs. Brian Wilson. The couple had two daughters, Wendy and Carnie, who found fame in the 1990s with Chynna Phillips as the trio Wilson Phillips. Their 1990 hit "Hold On" led to four Grammy nominations and a Billboard Music Award for the "Hot 100 Single of the Year." But what interests collectors is the 1963 single by the Honeys called "Surfin' Down the Swanee River." With the picture sleeve, its worth up to $1,800 today. (And there are no Beach Boys singles that come anywhere near it in value.)

BEAT IT

In 1962 Decca records released a single called "My Bonnie" by Tony Sheridan and the Beat Brothers. Sheridan was an up-and-coming singer; the Beat Brothers were a pickup band he'd met in Hamburg. The record was a minor hit in Europe and a complete bomb in the United States. But when the Beat Brothers became the Beatles, the record became a huge collectible. Original copies are on Decca's black label with silver print and a multicolored stripe across the center of the label. Black and silver labels without the other colors are relatively worthless bootlegs. Original copies are worth up to $12,000 today.

Asian taste treat: In Bali, dragonflies are boiled in coconut milk with ginger and garlic.

Uncle John's Page of Lists

More random bits from the BRI's bottomless trivia files.

7 People Who Died in the Bathroom

1. Elvis Presley
2. Jim Morrison
3. King George II
4. Whitney Houston
5. Brittany Murphy
6. Judy Garland
7. Orville Redenbacher

7 Things Made with Tallow (Cow Fat)

1. Paint
2. Crayons
3. Candles
4. Wax paper
5. Soap
6. Shaving cream
7. Lipstick

4 Novels by U.S. Politicians

1. *I, Che Guevara,* by Gary Hart
2. *The Hornet's Nest,* by Jimmy Carter
3. *1945,* by Newt Gingrich
4. *Why Not Me?,* by Al Franken

10 Animals That Kill the Most People Per Year

1. Mosquitoes (500,000+)
2. Snakes (94,000)
3. Scorpions (3,000)
4. Crocodiles (1,000)
5. Elephants (500)
6. Hippopotamuses (300)
7. Lions (250)
8. Cape buffalo (200)
9. Tigers (85)
10. Bees (50–100)

6 Internal Investigations Conducted by the U.S. Defense Department

1. Operation Treasure Trolls
2. Operation Shrinkwrap
3. Operation Hack in the Box
4. Operation Kaboom
5. Project Back Orifice 2000
6. Operation Bad Gas

11 "Lyrically Questionable" Songs Pulled from Clear Channel's Radio Playlist after 9/11

1. "Highway to Hell" (AC/DC)
2. "Lucy in the Sky with Diamonds" (The Beatles)
3. "Hit Me with Your Best Shot" (Pat Benatar)
4. "Smokin'" (Boston)
5. "Walk Like an Egyptian" (The Bangles)
6. "You Dropped a Bomb on Me" (Gap Band)
7. "Burnin' for You" (Blue Öyster Cult)
8. "America" (Neil Diamond)
9. "Sunday Bloody Sunday" (U2)
10. "Fire and Rain" (James Taylor)
11. "What a Wonderful World" (Louis Armstrong)

British Medical Journal study: Vegetarians are more intelligent than meat eaters.

It's a Weird, Weird World

Here's proof that truth is stranger than fiction.

THE NEXT BEST MAN

Jugal Kishore's wedding day was supposed to be the biggest day of his life. He was getting married! But during the ceremony at a Hindu temple in New Delhi, Kishore, 25, suffered an epileptic seizure. He was rushed to the hospital for observation. Once he was cleared to leave, he rushed back to the temple to complete his nuptials. But when he got there, he was dismayed to discover that his bride-to-be, Indira, had just married someone else. She was upset that Kishore had kept his epilepsy a secret, so she asked one of the guests—blue-jean-wearing Harpal Singh, a member of her brother-in-law's family—to take Kishore's place. Singh accepted, and the wedding continued. Kishore and his family were furious. They pleaded with Indira to reconsider, but she refused. According to reports, several dishes were thrown and a brawl nearly broke out, but cooler heads prevailed. And Jugal Kishore remained single.

GREGORY THE EGGMAN

West African street performer Gregory da Silva holds an odd world record: "Most Eggs Carried on a Hat" (642, to be exact). The hat is huge. It looks like a big round beehive, around four feet high, and it's the centerpiece of his act. He's performed at festivals throughout Europe and Africa and appeared on international TV, but while performing in Germany on a hot summer day in 2011, da Silva suffered heat stroke and passed out. When he woke up, he was in the hospital, and his hat was gone. "I know Germans are honest people," da Silva told reporters. "I am sure someone will hand it in. I must get it back because it is my whole way of life." But no one came forward to return the hat. Its whereabouts remain unknown. (Da Silva has since built a new egg hat that holds 1,000 eggs.)

THE POWER OF SPRAYER

Churches have long been sanctuaries for the poor and downtrodden, but Saint Mary's Cathedral in San Francisco has had enough of the poor and downtrodden sleeping in the alcove underneath their large doorway—right next to the "No Trespassing" signs. Solution: in 2014 church

---

Viennese university study: Meat eaters are happier and have fewer allergies than vegetarians.

leaders installed a sprinkler system that sprays water on the homeless people for about 75 seconds at random times during the night. After receiving complaints that the showers are inhumane (and a waste of water during a record drought), archdiocese spokesperson Chris Lyford said that it's the only way to keep their doorway clear. "We do the best we can to support the dignity of each person, but there is only so much you can do."

BITING THE HAND THAT SAVES YOU

In 2013 Courtney Schael, 50, was arrested for interfering with firefighters who were trying to do their job—saving her house. She had recently purchased the historic home in Westfield, New Jersey—described as a "whimsical interpretation of a medieval fairy tale"—for $750,000…only to have it catch fire before she had a chance to move in. (The cause was later determined to be faulty wiring in a light switch.) Schael apparently didn't think firefighters were trying hard enough. According to police, she "put herself in harm's way" while yelling at the firefighters. A police officer ordered Schael to move back; she shouted profanities and pushed him, so he arrested her, at which point she bit him on the thumb. Then she kicked two other cops as they were trying to put her in the police cruiser. For what it's worth, the firefighters did save her house.

THAT SUCKS

In 2015 a 52-year-old South Korean woman (name withheld from news reports) was cleaning her house when she decided to take a nap on the floor—not an uncommon practice in Korea. But danger was lurking. As she was snoozing, she felt like someone or something was trying to pull out all of her hair. She woke up in agony and screamed as she fought back the whatever-it-was. What was it? Her robot vacuum. And it wasn't letting go. The woman managed to get to her phone and call for help. Firefighters soon arrived and freed her.

BAD DOG!

The press has called Buddy, a pitbull-lab mix, the "world's worst guard dog." On a Saturday evening in April 2013, a couple returned to their home in East Wenatchee, Washington, to find a mysterious man in the kitchen "standing there with the refrigerator door open," said a police spokesperson, "and feeding their dog some pudding." The couple asked the man what we was doing; he told them his name was Jason McDaniel, and he was "looking for a man to kill." Then he walked into the living room, sat on a rocking chair, rocked for a few moments, and then got up to leave. As McDaniel walked out, he called for Buddy… and the dog trotted out the door with him. McDaniel was arrested later that night at his home. At last report, Buddy was still missing.

Why Did They Name It *That*?

Filmmakers often give their movies weird, ambiguous titles, probably to enhance the film's overall mystique. Often the title's meaning remains a mystery even after seeing the film. We got tired of feeling stupid, so we did some research and came up with these explanations. (Warning: some spoilers!)

ZERO DARK THIRTY (2012). This critically acclaimed film about the U.S. military's hunt for Osama bin Laden originally went by the working title *For God and Country*. Director Kathryn Bigelow told *Entertainment Weekly* that the final title—*Zero Dark Thirty*—is "a military term for thirty minutes after midnight. It refers to the darkness and secrecy that cloaked the entire decade-long mission."

APOCALYPSE NOW (1979). Screenwriter John Milius came up with the idea for Francis Ford Coppola's surreal Vietnam War film in the late 1960s, and explained the title's dark origins in a 1982 interview. "At the time," Milius said, "hippies had these buttons that said 'Nirvana Now,' and I loved the idea of a guy having a button with a mushroom cloud on it that said 'Apocalypse Now.' You know, let's bring it on, full nuke…That's the spirit that it started in right there'."

AMERICAN GRAFFITI (1973). George Lucas directed and co-wrote this homage to the rock-and-roll culture of the early 1960s, largely based on Lucas's own upbringing in Modesto, California. Original title: *Another Quiet Night in Modesto*. Producers wanted something with wider appeal, so Lucas came up with *American Graffiti*. "Everybody has a different way of checking out a culture," Lucas told *Seventeen* magazine in 1973, explaining the film's title. "Some look at clothing, others study cars. My way is to examine rock radio, which is an American form of graffiti."

DJANGO UNCHAINED (2012). The significance of the title of this Quentin Tarantino film may seem obvious at first: the title character, a slave named Django (Jamie Foxx), is freed, or "unchained." But there's more to it. In a 2012 *New York Times* interview, Tarantino explained that he took the name from Italian director Sergio Corbucci's 1966 spaghetti Western, *Django*. (The actor who played Django in that film, Franco Nero, had a cameo role in *Django Unchained*.) The title, said Tarantino, was also "a throwback" to another Italian film—*Hercules Unchained* (1959), in which the mythical hero Hercules is captured by Omphale, the queen of Lydia, but escapes.

MEATBALLS (1979). In 2012 movie reviewer Adam Pockross asked *Meatballs* director Ivan Reitman about the title of this comedy classic, starring Bill Murray in his first big role, as wacky camp counselor Tripper Harrison. "Having watched the film a few times now," Pockross said, "I still have no idea why it's called *Meatballs*." Reitman's response: "Neither do I. It seemed to be one of the staples that was part of camp food: spaghetti and meatballs. And 'meatball' also has a secondary connotation, as in goofy. We couldn't call it 'Summer Camp' because there was going to be another summer camp movie, so it was just a name I came up with." Note: The word "meatball" is used only once in the entire film.

SEVEN POUNDS (2008). (Spoilers alert!) This film centers around lead character Tim Thomas, played by Will Smith, and his attempt to atone for the deaths of seven people in a car accident he caused by texting while driving. His plan: to commit suicide and leave seven of his vital organs to seven "good" people who are awaiting organ transplants. Though it's never explained in the film, Smith told a reporter around the time of the film's release that the title was a reference to the saying "a pound of flesh," originally found in Shakespeare's *The Merchant of Venice*, meant as the metaphorical payment of a huge debt. Smith's character is therefore paying "seven pounds of flesh" with the seven donated organs to atone for causing seven deaths.

BRAZIL (1985). According to filmmaker Terry Gilliam, he got the inspiration for the title of this surreal look at a world gone bureaucratically wrong while sitting on a beach in the town of Port Talbot, Wales. In his 1987 book *The Battle of Brazil*, Jack Matthews quotes Gilliam:

> Port Talbot is a steel town, where everything is covered with gray iron ore dust. Even the beach is completely littered with dust, it's just black. I had this image of a guy sitting there on this dingy beach with a portable radio, tuning in these strange Latin escapist songs like "Brazil." The music transported him somehow and made his world less gray.

The song Gilliam referred to is a famous samba written in 1939 that can be heard playing in the background of the film several times.

Bonus Fact: Universal Studios chief Sid Sheinberg hated the title *Brazil*, so he had the studio staff come up with other ideas, including *If Osmosis, Who Are You?*; *Explanada Fortunata Is Not My Real Name*; *Lords of the Files*; and *Nude Descending Bathroom Scale*.

When Dining at the White House

Tips on table etiquette from The White House Cookbook *(1887), co-authored by renowned chef F. L. Gillette and Hugo Ziemann, White House steward during the Grover Cleveland administration.*

HOLDING YOUR NAPKIN. "When seating yourself at the table, unfold your napkin and lay it across your lap in such a manner that it will not slide off upon the floor; a gentleman should place it across his right knee. Do not tuck it into your neck like a child's bib. For an old person, however, it is well to attach the napkin to a napkin hook and slip it into the vest or dress buttonholes, to protect their garments, or sew a broad tape at two places on the napkin, and pass it over the head."

SITTING AT TABLE. "One must not lie or lean along the table, nor rest one's arms upon it. Nor is one to touch any of the dishes; if a member of the family, one can exercise all the duties of hospitality through servants, and wherever there are servants, neither family nor guests are to pass or help from any dish."

DRINKING. "Don't, when you drink, elevate your glass as if you were going to stand it inverted on your nose. Bring the glass perpendicularly to the lips, and then lift it to a slight angle…Drink gently; do not pour it down your throat like water turned out of a pitcher."

HOLDING THE KNIFE. "Ladies have frequently an affected way of holding the knife half-way down its length, as if it were too big for their little hands; but this is as awkward a way as it is weak; the knife should be grasped freely by the handle only, the forefinger being the only one to touch the blade, and that only along the back of the blade at its root, and no further down."

USING THE KNIFE. "The knife should never be used to carry food to the mouth, but only to cut it up into small mouthfuls."

BREAD AND BUTTER. "Another generally neglected obligation is that of spreading butter on one's bread as it lies in one's plate, or slightly lifted at one end of the plate; it is very frequently buttered in the air,

---

WWII general George S. Patton believed he was the Carthaginian general Hannibal reincarnated.

bitten in gouges, and still held in the face and eyes of the table with the marks of the teeth on it; this is certainly not altogether pleasant, and it is better to cut it, a bit at a time, after buttering it, and put piece by piece in the mouth with one's finger and thumb."

SPOONS. "Spoons are sometimes used with firm puddings; forks are better. A spoon should never be turned over in the mouth."

CHEWING. "Be careful to keep the mouth shut closely while masticating the food. It is the opening of the lips which causes the smacking which seems very disgusting."

TEETH. "One's teeth are not to be picked at table; but if it is impossible to hinder it, it should be done behind the napkin."

SOUP. "Never ask to be helped to soup a second time. The hostess may ask you to take a second plate, but you will politely decline."

PLATES. "Two kinds of animal food, or two kinds of dessert, should not be eaten off of one plate."

COOLING THE FOOD. "The reason why one does not blow a thing to cool it, is not only that it is an inelegant and vulgar action intrinsically, but because it may be offensive to others—cannot help being so, indeed; and it moreover implies haste, which, whether from greediness or a desire to get away, is equally objectionable."

BONES. "One may pick a bone at the table, but, as with corn, only one hand is allowed to touch it; yet one can easily get enough from it with knife and fork, which is certainly the more elegant way of doing; and to take her teeth to it gives a lady the look of caring a little too much for the pleasures of the table; one is, however, on no account to suck one's finger after it."

AT THE END OF A COURSE. "When both knife and fork have been used finally, they should be laid diagonally across the plate, with both handles toward the right hand...but never crossed; the old custom of crossing them was in obedience to an ancient religious formula. A knife and fork laid diagonally across the plate is understood by well-trained waiters to be the signal for removing them, along with the plate."

WHEN IN DOUBT. "Whenever there is any question as to the best way to do a thing, it is wise to follow that which is the most rational, and that will almost invariably be found to be proper etiquette."

Blood Sports

"Blood sport" refers to any form of entertainment that involves injuring or killing animals. Such activities have been practiced in various parts of the world for thousands of years. Today they're banned in most places, but some, including bullfighting, cockfighting, and dogfighting, are still practiced, and in many countries around the globe, they are completely legal. Here are a few unusual examples of blood sports from yesteryear. (Warning: Get out the smelling salts—these are not for the squeamish.)

GANDER PULLING

History: From the 17th to the 19th centuries, gander pulling was popular at festivals and fairs around Europe, as well as in colonial and post-colonial America, especially in the wilder frontier regions. It was associated with the centuries-old (and often raucous) festivities held on Shrove Tuesday—also known as Fat Tuesday, Mardi Gras, and Pancake Day—the day before the start of the Christian period of abstinence known as Lent.

Description: A live male goose was hung by its feet from a horizontal pole suspended over a flat patch of ground. A rider on horseback would then attempt to pull the gander's head off while riding by at full gallop—a very difficult feat. The frightened goose would be thrashing around, and to make grasping it even more difficult, its head would be covered in oil. The rider who was able to pull off the goose's head won a prize—usually the goose. (Gander pulls are still held in Holland, Belgium, and Germany, but they use dead geese, not live ones.)

BEAR BAITING

History: Especially popular in England from the 16th century—both King Henry VIII and Queen Elizabeth I were big fans—until the late 18th century, bear baiting was also popular in parts of the United States, primarily during its colonial era.

Description: A captive bear was chained by one leg to a pole or confined in a pen. Teams of dogs were then released to attack the bear. In a common form of the gruesome sport, different teams of dogs, usually five or six per team, were released at different intervals. Prizes were awarded to the owner of the dogs that put up the best fight. These events were often fatal to both the bears and the dogs, but some bears had long and gory careers as bear baiting champions. A similar sport of the same era: *bull baiting*, with a bull in the place of a bear. (Bear baiting continues to

A Lone Star tick bite can leave the victim allergic to red meat.

take place in Pakistan…and the United States. A 2010 investigation revealed that some people in remote regions of South Carolina were still practicing bear baiting under the guise of "training" hunting dogs.)

COCK THROWING

History: Like gander pulling, cock throwing, or *throwing the cock*, was particularly popular during Shrove Tuesday festivities in cities and towns across England, starting at least as early as the 15th century.

Description: In the most common variation of this "sport," a rooster's leg was tied with string to a short post. People then paid a small fee to take turns throwing *coksteles*—two- or three-foot-long wooden clubs—at the rooster from a set distance, usually around 20 yards. The person whose throw finally killed the rooster won the bird as a prize. Cock throwing remained popular—especially among schoolboys—until it was outlawed in the late 18th century.

FOX TOSSING

History: This bizarre blood sport was popular among European aristocracy in the 17th and 18th centuries.

Description: A team of two men stood about 20 feet apart, each man holding one end of a long sling made from netting or stiff fabric. Most of the sling lay loosely on the ground. Several such teams would be positioned inside a large fenced arena—and several foxes would be released into the arena. When a startled fox ran over a team's sling, they would yank on the ends, tossing the fox into the air. The team that tossed a fox the highest was the winner. (Fox tossing heights of more than 20 feet were recorded.) And not just foxes—other animals could be included in such events. A written account of a royal tossing event in Dresden, Germany, in the early 18th century, for example, recorded the tossing of "687 foxes, 533 hares, 34 badgers, 21 wild cats, and at the end 34 young wild boar and 3 wolves." Most of the animals involved were killed either during or after such events. Fox tossing died out in the 1850s.

RAT BAITING

History: Popular in England in the 18th and 19th centuries.

Description: A dog was released into a pit or small arena with a set number of rats—often 50 or 100. The dog that killed the most rats in the shortest amount of time was the winner. Some dogs became rat-baiting legends: a bulldog-terrier mix named Billy set a record in 1822, killing 100 rats in 5 minutes 30 seconds. A bull terrier named Jacko set a different record in 1867, killing 1,000 rats in less than 100 minutes in 100-rat sessions held over a 10-week period.

Banyan trees, which are native to India, can span areas larger than a Walmart.

"I Hate My Movie!"

*You may love these movies…but apparently
the actors who starred in them do not.*

• "I can't look at this movie and be proud of what I've done. It's just impossible for me to connect to it emotionally."
—**Nicole Kidman,** *Australia* **(2008)**

• "It was so awful and sentimental and gooey. You had to work terribly hard to try to infuse some minuscule bit of humor into it."
—**Christopher Plummer,** *The Sound of Music* **(1965)**

• "It was the most irresponsible bit of filmmaking—if you can even call it that—that I've ever seen. I couldn't believe it."
—**Brad Pitt,** *The Devil's Own* **(1997)**

• "That was a bad, bad, bad movie."
—**Charlize Theron,** *Reindeer Games* **(2000)**

• "I gotta be a bit better when I'm looking through my scripts."
—**Sam Worthington,** *Terminator: Salvation* **(2009)**

• "It paints the women as shrews, as humorless and uptight, and it paints the men as lovable, goofy, fun-loving guys."
—**Katherine Heigl,** *Knocked Up* **(2007)**

• "It is what it is. F****** trees, man. The plants. You can't blame me for wanting to try to play a science teacher."
—**Mark Wahlberg,** *The Happening* **(2008)**

• "I'd just bought a castle. I had to pay for it somehow."
—**Jeremy Irons,** *Dungeons and Dragons* **(2000)**

• "It completely changed my career, even if it was weak and I was weak in it. It was a difficult film to be good in. I don't know what I could have done differently."
—**George Clooney,** *Batman and Robin* **(1997)**

• "That's a piece of s*** movie. It's an unbelievably bad movie; just bad from the bottom. It was maybe the only time I've known something was just bad and there was nothing I could do about it."
—**Jamie Lee Curtis,** *Virus* **(1999)**

In 1989 Ted Nugent offered to buy Muzak for $10 million so he could put the company out of business.

Out of Line

It seems like common sense: If you're trying to call attention to environmental issues, find a way to do it that doesn't harm the environment. But maybe not.

IT SEEMED LIKE A GOOD IDEA AT THE TIME

In December 2014 Greenpeace hit upon an idea to attract the attention of international delegates who were flying into Lima, Peru, for a conference on climate change. Several activists went out into the Peruvian desert and unfurled giant cloth letters on the sand spelling out the message:

TIME

FOR A CHANGE!

THE FUTURE IS RENEWABLE

GREENPEACE

ON SECOND THOUGHT...

The activists unfurled the letters in the part of the desert that contains the Nazca lines, ancient markings made on the desert floor by the Nazca people some 1,400 years ago. The lines and figures, which are so large that they are best seen from the air, are a precious—and extremely fragile—cultural treasure, protected by UNESCO as a World Heritage Site. They are off-limits to unescorted visitors. Those few people who are allowed anywhere near them must wear special footwear to avoid damaging the lines. Only problem: the Greenpeace activists didn't have permission to enter the area, and they were not wearing the special footwear when they laid out the giant letters right next to the giant figure of a hummingbird. According to Peru's deputy culture minister Luis Jaime Castillo, the footprints the activists left at the site are "a true slap in the face at everything Peruvians consider sacred" and will likely be visible for "hundreds or thousands of years."

"We are deeply sorry for this. We fully understand that this looks bad," Greenpeace said in an apology after the publicity stunt blew up in its face. The group promised to cooperate with investigators and pay for any of the damage activists may have caused, but at last report it was still refusing to give the names of the activists to the prosecutors. "It is the personal choice of individual participants whether they offer their names to the prosecutor," said a spokesperson. If the activists are identified and convicted of "attacking an archaeological monument," they could spend up to six years in prison.

Jellyfish have no hearts—but they don't know it, because they don't have any brains, either.

Not Coming to a Future Near You

One of the points of science-fiction is to speculate about the future. Sometimes they get it right—the Tricorders of Star Trek are very similar to today's smartphones, for example. Here are some sci-fi movies that tried to predict the future…and were way, way off.

Movie: *Red Dawn* (1984)
Set In: The late 1980s
Plot: World War III has begun, but not with a nuclear attack. Soviet paratroopers have invaded the United States and taken over using conventional warfare. The Red Menace is put down, however, thanks to a group of courageous teenagers (including Patrick Swayze, C. Thomas Howell, Lea Thompson, and Charlie Sheen) from a small town in Colorado, who fight off the Soviets and their Cuban allies with primitive weapons…and save democracy.

Movie: *Alien Nation* (1988)
Set In: 1991
Plot: There's a whole new kind of racism in the world—alien racism. Hundreds of thousands of humanoid aliens have landed on Earth (in the Mojave Desert). They're bipedal and have two eyes and scaly faces, but other than that, they look and act human. Nevertheless, most humans don't trust the "Newcomers." They are quarantined at first but after a year or so start to assimilate into human society. One Newcomer (named "Sam Francisco," portrayed by Mandy Patinkin) becomes a Los Angeles police detective and proves that when push comes to shove, aliens can be trusted.

Movie: *The Apple* (1980)
Set In: 1994
Plot: Alphie and Bibi are two teenagers (George Gilmour and Catherine Mary Stewart) from Moose Jaw, Saskatchewan, who travel to the United States to compete in the Worldvision Song Festival. Their syrupy folk rock wins over the crowd, but they lose to the robotic disco of BIM, an act that, like the contest itself, is controlled by the mysterious music executive "Mr. Boogaloo" (Vladek Sheybal) who also happens to be the devil. Boogaloo has brainwashed the country into following his "National BIM Hour," a daily period of mandatory exercise. Alphie

---

Why do astronauts eat tortillas instead of bread? No crumbs.

and Bibi sign with Mr. Boogaloo and fall into a neverending orgy of rock 'n' roll hedonism. Ultimately, though, they escape Boogaloo's clutches, join a hippie cult, and ascend to heaven in a space car.

Movie: *Escape from New York* (1981)

Set In: 1997

Plot: The crime rate has gotten so bad in the United States that the prison system has reached its capacity. The government's response: convert the island of Manhattan into a maximum-security prison colony where the most violent offenders are dropped off and left to fend for themselves. It's bad news for the president (Donald Pleasence), then, when his plane crashes into the penal colony and he has to rely on a thug named Snake Plissken (Kurt Russell) to rescue him—and a cassette tape of a vital speech. Snake succeeds, of course, but by 1997, cassette tapes were on the way out.

Movie: *Death Race 2000* (1975)

Set In: 2000

Plot: Financial disasters and rule under martial law have turned the United States into a fascist wasteland. The populace is distracted by the annual "death race," a gladiatorial sport in which drivers race cross-country and earn points for hitting civilians. A resistance movement plans to overthrow the government by kidnapping the best driver (named "Frankenstein") and sabotaging the death race. The government discovers the plot and blames it on the French. Frankenstein (David Carradine) escapes, wins the race, and becomes president.

Movie: *Timecop* (1994)

Set In: 2004

Plot: Time-travel technology has been perfected. The U.S. government forms the Time Enforcement Commission to make sure that the technology isn't misused and history all mixed up…which is exactly what happens when a rogue agent goes back to 1929 to profit from the stock market crash. It's up to a timecop (Jean-Claude Van Damme) to undo all the "mistakes" that have been made to history. Bad news: he can't restore the original timeline. Good news: he makes it even better.

*   *   *

"Prediction is very difficult, especially if it's about the future."
—**Nils Bohr**

Hello! White-faced capuchin monkeys greet one another by sticking their fingers up each other's noses.

Slinging the Bat

More colorful wartime slang you're unlikely to find in the history books.

Chief Cook and Bottle Washer (Civil War): Someone skilled at a variety of things; a jack of all trades

Cheap Charlie (Vietnam): A soldier who is very careful with his money

Plenty Cheap Charlie (Vietnam): Someone who's even tighter with a buck than a Cheap Charlie

Burp Gun (WWII): A German MP38 submachine gun

Groundhog Day (Afghanistan/Iraq): Refers to the Bill Murray movie—when one day is indistinguishable from the next

Grayback (Civil War): A Confederate soldier

Bombaconda/Mortaritaville (Iraq): Nicknames for LSA Anaconda, a base near the city of Balad that came under frequent mortar attack

Sling the Bat (WWI): To speak in slang

Blueleg (Vietnam): An infantryman

Big Bugs (Civil War): VIPs

Going Over the Hill (WWII): Deserting

Diggers (WWI): Australian infantry soldiers

Mickey Mouse Movies (WWII): Personal hygiene films

Conchie (WWI): A conscientious objector

Goober Grabbers (Civil War): Soldiers from Georgia

Quartermaster Hunter (Civil War): A shell that passes safely overhead and toward the rear, where the quartermasters are

Billjim (WWI): An Australian soldier—many were named either Bill or Jim.

Lifer Juice (Afghanistan/Iraq): Coffee

Bedpan Commando (WWII): Medical corpsman

Bark Juice/Knock-Knee/ Old Red Eye/Bust Head/Pop Skull/Mother (Civil War): Liquor

Jack Tar (Revolutionary War): A sailor

"Ass Antlers"

Every language has idioms—expressions whose meanings are different from the literal meanings of the words, such as "beat around the bush" or "raining cats and dogs." Here are some translations of actual German words and phrases you might find handy someday.

DREIKÄSEHOCH

Translation: "Three cheeses high"

Meaning: A playful term to describe small children in general (roughly equivalent to "nipper" or "whippersnapper"). The origin is uncertain, but it is believed to reference cheese wheels, as in a small child is only as tall as three stacked wheels of cheese.

SCHATTENPARKER

Translation: "Shade parker"

Meaning: A derogatory phrase, akin to "wimp" or "sissy"—although most often used in fun and not as a serious insult. The idea is that a guy who goes out of his way to park his car in the shade is less manly than one who parks in the hot sun.

DIE SAU RAUSLASSEN

Translation: "Let the pig out" (literally the *sow*, or *female* pig)

Meaning: To celebrate wildly—often translated as "letting it all hang out," or "painting the town red."

ESELSBRÜCKE

Translation: "Donkey bridge"

Meaning: A mnemonic device, a mental technique used to help remember something. (A well-known English mnemonic device: the rhyme used to remember which months have 30 days and which have 31, starting with, "Thirty days hath September...") According to legend, the German phrase was invented in the days when donkeys were regularly used to transport goods. Because donkeys dislike walking through water—and are famously stubborn about not doing things they don't want to do—people built bridges across streams and rivers just for their donkeys in order to reduce travel time. Thus, donkey bridges were shortcuts, much the way mnemonic devices are.

ARSCHGEWEIH

Translation: "Ass antlers"

Meaning: You've probably seen women who have tattoos on their lower

---

Nature study: Hospital patients who have a view of nature from their window heal faster.

backs, often designed so that the tattoo can be seen emerging from the pants line above their butts. The Germans call them *arschgeweih*, or "ass antlers," because, depending on the design, they can look sort of like painted-on antlers emerging from the woman's butt. (English equivalent: "tramp stamps.")

TORSCHLUSSPANIK

Translation: "Gate-shut panic"

Meaning: It's the fear that time is running out. For example, a woman who feels her biological clock ticking, meaning she fears the time for her to have children is nearly over, could be said to be feeling *torschlusspanik*. Another English approximation: "midlife crisis."

SCHROTTWICHTELN

Translation: "Scrap exchange" (or "crap exchange")

Meaning: The German equivalent of "secret Santa" or "white elephant," in which groups of people, often workmates, agree to buy each other inexpensive gifts for Christmas—with the understanding that they will be intentionally trashy.

ARSCHGEIGE

Translation: "Ass violin" or "ass fiddle"

Meaning: An insult that is not family-friendly, roughly equivalent to "jerk" or "idiot"—but actually closer to words we can't use in this book. An example of how you might use it: if someone steals your parking spot just before you're about to pull into it, you might angrily yell, "Du Arschgeige!" or "You ass violin!" The origin of this insult is unknown.

EXTRAS

• A turtle in German is a *schildkröte*. It means "shield toad."

• What's a *warmduscher*? The word translates to "warm shower," meaning a wimp—someone who is too timid to take a cold shower, or too frightened to leave their comfort zone.

• A lightbulb is a *glühbirne*. It means "glow pear."

• Your *innerer schweinehund* is your "inner pig dog." It's the lazy slob inside you that keeps you on the couch eating potato chips when you should be doing something constructive.

• *Brustwarze* literally translates to "breast wart." Nonliteral: it's the German word for "nipple."

• *Drachenfutter* means "dragon's food." It's the gift you bring your wife when you know she's mad at you.

The World's Most Valuable Eggs

Unless you happen to be a Russian history buff, you probably don't know much about Czar Alexander III. But if you're a fan of Fabergé eggs, you have him (and Carl Fabergé, of course) to thank for them.

HOW EGGS-CITING

In 1885 the emperor, or *czar*, of Russia, Alexander III, placed an order with his jeweler for a decorative Easter egg for his wife, the czarina Marie Feodorovna. Alexander had given his wife jeweled Easter eggs before: Easter was the most important holiday on the Russian Orthodox calendar, and eggs were traditionally given as gifts. But this year's egg would be different, because Alexander placed his order with a new jeweler: 38-year-old Carl Fabergé.

Fabergé differed from other jewelers who served the Imperial court in that he was more interested in clever design and exquisite craftsmanship than in merely festooning his creations with gold and precious gems (though his eggs would have plenty of those) without showing much imagination. "Expensive things interest me little if the value is merely in so many diamonds and pearls," he said.

NEST EGG

That first Imperial Easter egg was very plain indeed, but only on the surface: known today simply as the *1885 Hen Egg*, it was 2½ inches long and made of gold but had a plain white enamel shell to give it the appearance of an ordinary duck egg. When the two halves of the egg were pulled apart, they revealed a golden yolk that in turn opened to reveal a golden hen "surprise" sitting on a nest of golden straw. The hen was hinged at its tail feathers and split open to reveal a small golden replica of the Imperial crown; hanging from the crown was a tiny ruby pendant that Marie Feodorovna could wear around her neck on a gold chain that came with the egg.

Marie Feodorovna loved the egg, and for the rest of his life, Czar Alexander bought all of her Easter eggs from Fabergé. Alexander gave the jeweler great latitude in designing the eggs and set only three requirements: 1) the eggs had to be egg-shaped; 2) they had to contain a surprise; and 3) Fabergé's designs could not repeat themselves. Those three requirements aside, Fabergé was free to do whatever he wanted. The jeweler made a point of not revealing anything to Alexander about each egg until he delivered it a few days before Easter so that the czar could enjoy the suspense as well. "Your Majesty will be content," was all he'd say.

BY THE DOZEN

Not much is known about the second egg, *Hen with Sapphire Pendant*, which Fabergé made for 1886; it disappeared in 1922. For his third egg, in 1887 Fabergé made a golden egg not much larger than a hen's egg. It sat on a gold pedestal with three lion's paw feet. Pressing a diamond on the front of the egg caused its lid to pop open, revealing a ladies' watch face inside. The watch was mounted on a hinge and could be tilted upright, allowing the egg to be used as a clock. (For more on this egg, which was missing for 90 years, see page 451.)

In the years that followed, the eggs produced in Fabergé's workshop became larger and more elaborate as teams of craftsmen worked the entire year, sometimes longer, to complete the eggs. The *Danish Palaces Egg* for 1890 contained a folding screen comprising 10 miniature paintings of the palaces and royal yachts that Marie Feodorovna, a Danish princess, remembered from her childhood. The *1891 Memory of Azov Egg* contained a gold and platinum model of an Imperial Navy ship of the same name, which had taken the future czar Nicholas II and his brother George on a tour of the Far East in 1890. The egg was carved from solid *bloodstone* (green quartz speckled with red), and the model inside was an exact replica of the *Memory of Azov* and floated on a blue sea of aquamarine. The ship was accurate down to its diamond portholes, movable deck guns, and tiny gold anchor chain.

TWO OF A KIND

If Fabergé feared losing his best customer when Alexander III died in 1894 at the age of 49, he needn't have worried. When Alexander's son Nicholas II came to the throne in November 1894, he doubled the order to two eggs each year: one for his mother, Marie Feodorovna, and one for his wife, the czarina Alexandra. He bought them every year except 1904 and 1905, when the purchases were suspended during the Russo-Japanese War.

Nicholas didn't let the outbreak of World War I in 1914 stop him from buying Easter eggs, though the wartime eggs were more modest and subdued in design. Both eggs for 1915, for example, had Red Cross themes. He bought two each year until he was forced to abdicate his throne during the Russian Revolution of 1917. By then Fabergé's workshop had produced 50 Easter eggs for the two czarinas (plus another 15 for other wealthy customers, including England's Duchess of Marlborough and the Rothschild banking family).

SCRAMBLED

Czarina Marie Feodorovna managed to escape to England, but Nicholas, Alexandra, and their children were not as lucky. They were executed by revolutionaries in the summer of 1918. Carl Fabergé escaped to Switzerland, where he died in 1920. In the chaos of the revolution and the civil war that followed, the royal palaces were ransacked, and any property not looted by mobs was seized by the provisional government and, when it fell, by the Bolsheviks led by Vladimir Lenin. The Fabergé eggs disappeared in the turmoil, some of them never to be seen again.

In 1922 about 40 of the eggs were rediscovered in a government warehouse in Moscow. At the time the government of what had become the Soviet Union needed to raise foreign currency, and over the next decade, all but 10 of the eggs were sold abroad.

CRACKED

Considering how much Fabergé eggs sell for today, it's remarkable how little they fetched when they first hit the market. But in an age when people like Pablo Picasso and Henri Matisse were stirring up artistic revolutions of their own, the eggs were seen as gaudy, old-fashioned, and vulgar. Museums and most "serious" collectors weren't interested in them, and for this reason, the earliest buyers were able to snap them up for very little money—in some cases paying only a fraction of what it had cost Fabergé to make them in the first place.

Alexander Schaffer, an American dealer of prerevolutionary Russian artwork, bought the 1903 *Peter the Great Egg* (a gift from Nicholas II to his wife, Alexandra) from the U.S. Customs Service for about $1,000 ($13,500 today), after the original buyer balked at having to pay import duties. Other dealers thought Schaffer was nuts to pay even that much. In 1930 American businessman Armand Hammer bought 10 eggs for prices ranging from $240 ($3,200) for the 1915 *Red Cross Egg* to $3,900 ($53,000) for the 1912 *Czarevich Egg*, both gifts from Nicholas II to Alexandra.

EGG-CEPTIONAL COLLECTIONS

If Hammer hoped to sell his eggs for a quick profit, he was soon disappointed. It took him more than a decade to sell them all, though he did make a bundle. He, Schaffer, and other dealers unloaded their wares on *nouveau riche* collectors with more money than taste—people like Lillian Thomas Pratt, the wife of a General Motors executive, who bought the first of five Fabergé eggs in 1933. She probably would have bought even more than that had her husband not threatened Armand Hammer with a lawsuit if he sold her any more.

The Post breakfast cereal heiress Marjorie Merriweather Post bought two Fabergé eggs: the *1896 Alexander III Portraits Egg* and the *1914 Catherine the Great Egg*, both of which were gifts from Nicholas II to his mother. In the 1950s, the Swingline stapler tycoons, Jack and Belle Linsky, amassed a huge collection of Fabergé objects that included the *1893 Caucasus Egg* and the *1894 Renaissance Egg*, both gifts from Czar Alexander III to his wife, Marie Feodorovna. But when the Linskys showed their prized collection to the director of New York's Metropolitan Museum of Art, he dismissed the objects as "turn of the century trinkets" and suggested that the couple direct their energy toward "more serious collecting." The Linskys took his advice and sold every piece of Fabergé they owned.

I AM THE EGG MAN

That the Linskys and other early collectors would come to regret selling their Fabergé eggs too soon and for too little money was due almost entirely to the buying habits of one man: *Forbes* magazine publisher Malcolm Forbes. He bought his first Fabergé egg, the *1902 Pink Serpent Clock Egg*, in 1965. (The egg, then thought to have been one of the Russian Imperial eggs, is now understood to have been commissioned by the Duchess of Marlborough, Consuelo Vanderbilt.) Forbes paid $50,000 for the egg, triple the preauction estimate and a record for a Fabergé egg. He bought his second egg, the *1894 Renaissance Egg*, later that same afternoon. In the 15 years that followed, just about every time a Fabergé egg came up for sale, Forbes paid whatever was necessary to add it to his collection. By 1985 he'd pushed the price to nearly $2 million per egg, when he paid $1.7 million for the *1900 Cuckoo Clock Egg*.

EGGING ON

In February 1990, Forbes died from a heart attack at the age of 70. By then he'd acquired nine Russian Imperial eggs plus three eggs that Fabergé made for other wealthy clients, along with another 180 smaller objects produced in Fabergé's workshop. The publisher's death raised an interesting question: Would the eggs hold their value now that he wasn't there to outbid every other buyer?

In 1992 Forbes's children passed on the chance to add a tenth Russian Imperial egg to the family collection when the *1907 Love Trophies Egg* came up for auction and they didn't even bid on it. The egg sold for $3.2 million anyway. When the *1913 Winter Egg* came up for auction in 1996, they passed again. It sold for $5.6 million…and then for $9.6 million when the new owner put it up for auction in 2002. When the Forbes children decided to auction off their father's Fabergé collection at Sotheby's in 2004, a Russian billionaire named Victor Vekselberg swooped in before the auction could be held and bought the entire collection for an undisclosed price estimated to be well over $100 million, pushing the price per egg to around $10 million. Could the value possibly go any higher? Of course. When a Fabergé egg made for the Rothschild banking family went up for auction in 2007, it sold for $18.5 million.

EGG-STRAORDINARY

As of 2015, 43 of the 50 Russian Imperial Easter eggs have been found; the other seven are missing. Some may be casualties of either the Russian Revolution, the civil war that followed, or World War II. But others are almost certainly out there. The *Third Imperial Egg* of 1887, for example, only surfaced in 2004, when a scrap dealer in the American Midwest bought it at an antique sale. Nearly a decade passed before he even realized what it was.

That story, and a description of the still-missing eggs to keep an eye out for, is on page 451.

*   *   *

DANCING WITH(OUT) THE STARS

Celebrities who didn't appear on Dancing with the Stars.

• Shortly after John McCain lost the 2008 presidential election, *DWTS* producers signed up his wife, Cindy McCain. John nixed the idea.

• *The Sopranos* co-star Vincent Pastore, who once appeared on the weight-loss reality show *Celebrity Fit Club*, had to drop out during rehearsals because he weighed too much.

• Lindsay Lohan was offered $550,000 to dance, but said: "I'd never do reality TV."

• Suffering from a career slump, Sylvester Stallone wanted to be on the show…until *The Expendables* (2010) restored his movie star status.

• In 2012, after Mitt Romney lost the presidential election, his wife Ann was offered a spot. She "seriously considered it," but declined.

• Pop singer Jewel quit during rehearsals after fracturing bones in both of her legs.

• Facebook founder Mark Zuckerberg was asked to be on the show, but he said didn't "like" it.

• Number-one fan request? Jennifer Aniston. But she's not interested.

• After losing the Democratic presidential primary in 2008, Hillary Clinton seriously thought about competing on *DWTS*, but accepted the position of Secretary of State instead. (Bill Clinton was also offered a spot, but he said no. Reason: "It's too much work.")

In Cairo, Egypt, the pyramids at Giza can be seen from inside the Pizza Hut.

Ol' Jay's Brain Teasers

Time to test your mental fortitude with these tricky conundrums. (Answers are on page 509.)

1. How can you hold an egg above a concrete floor and drop it four feet without it breaking? (And it's a raw egg, not hard-boiled.)

2. A snail is stuck at the bottom of a well that's 16 feet deep. He crawls up four feet each day but slips back down three feet each night. How long will it take the snail to reach the top?

3. Only one letter does not appear in any of the 50 U.S. state names. Which letter?

4. A princess fell in love with a peasant. They wanted to get married, but the king was against it. So he told the peasant he would write "yes" on one card and "no" on another card. "Come before my court tomorrow," said the king. "If you pick the 'yes' card, you may marry my daughter." That night, the peasant found out that the king wrote "no" on both cards…but the peasant knew he could win. How?

5. Two people were in a car speeding down the road. When they arrived at their destination, there were three people in the car. No one got in or out, so how can this be?

6. Only six words end in *-dous*. Two are the little-used *jeopardous* and *palladous*, but the other four are quite common. Can you name them?

7. How can you arrange four 5's to be 4 less than twelve 5's?

8. The missing words each contain the same seven letters, but in a different order. Can you figure them out?

> *Writing Bathroom Readers can be very* _ _ _ _ _ _ _, *so we like to go* _ _ _ _ _ _ _ *every now and then to relax.*

9. What's your relationship to your father's only brother's wife's only brother-in-law?

10. Before you can figure out the final date in the sequence below, you'll have to figure out the secret word:

> *October 2nd, March 2nd, April 5th, June 4th, January 3rd, December 1st, May 2nd, November ?*

11. You're sitting at a keyboard. How can you spell DEFLATE by only hitting three keys?

Easter chicken? Araucana chickens, which originated in Chile, lay pastel blue eggs.

Oh, That's So Sweet

Tasty tidbits about dessert, candy, and all things sweet to eat.

"Vegetables are a must on a diet. I suggest carrot cake, zucchini bread, and pumpkin pie."
—**Jim Davis**

"Life is uncertain. Eat dessert first."
—**Ernestine Ulmer**

"Pie is the food of the heroic. No pie-eating people can ever be vanquished."
—*NY Times* **editorial**

"There are two kinds of people in the world: those who love chocolate, and communists."
—**Leslie Moak Murray**

"Seize the moment. Remember all those women on the *Titanic* who waved off the dessert cart."
—**Erma Bombeck**

"Strength is the capacity to break a chocolate bar into four pieces with your bare hands and then eat just one of the pieces."
—**Judith Viorst**

"I lied on my Weight Watchers list. I put down that I had three eggs…but they were Cadbury chocolate eggs."
—**Caroline Rhea**

"Desserts are like mistresses. They are bad for you. So if you are having one, you might as well have two."
—**Alain Ducasse**

"Sometimes I think that the thing I love most about being an adult is the right to buy candy whenever I want."
—**Ryan Gosling**

"I prefer Hostess fruit pies to pop-up toaster tarts because they don't require so much cooking."
—**Carrie Snow**

"Whoever thought a tiny candy bar should be called fun size was a moron."
—**Glenn Beck**

"A party without cake is just a meeting."
—**Julia Child**

"Carob works on the principle that, when mixed with the right combination of sugar and fat, it can duplicate chocolate in color and texture. Of course, the same can be said of dirt."
—**Sandra Boynton**

"We must have a pie. Stress cannot exist in the presence of a pie."
—**David Mamet**

Games People Play

Here are three strange-but-fun game fads that took off in the 2010s.

ESCAPE GAMES. Picture this: you and your teammates are locked in a dingy basement room. The only way to escape is to work together to solve a series of obscure clues. You have one hour. Strewn about the room are strange diagrams, baby doll parts, half a car stuck in a wall, and other odd puzzles to decipher. Meanwhile, the game master taunts you over a loudspeaker. That's the description of ParaPark, the escape game that started this fad. A social worker named Attila Gyurkovics created it in 2011 as a team-building exercise in Budapest, Hungary, but soon realized that tourists might pay money to try it...and he was right: since then, more than 50 other escape games have popped up in Budapest (and elsewhere) with colorful names like Mindquest, Da Vinci's Secret, and Claustrophilia.

SPORTHOCKING. This fad combines skateboarding and sitting down. Seriously. Instead of a board, players have a plastic stool—called a *hocker* in German—that resembles a big spool. "Hockers" perform complicated tricks—they juggle the hocker with their feet, ride it down railings like a skateboard, do acrobatic flips and twists, and whatever else they can think of. When each trick is complete, they sit on the hocker and "strike a pose." Sporthocking was invented by German brothers Michael and Stephen Landschütz as a project in their industrial design master's program. Their motto: "Hock and roll!"

BUBBLE SOCCER. A soccer ball is placed in the center of a field. Two five-person teams—all wearing inflated clear-plastic bubbles over their upper bodies—line up at their own goals. The whistle blows. The bubble players run as fast as they can toward the ball. The first one to get there kicks it...and the rest of the players collide, bounce off each other, and fall down. That's how a bubble soccer match begins. Otherwise, it's just like regular soccer, except that it's legal to plow directly into the opposing players. In fact, that's the main draw. In 2011 Norwegian talk show hosts Henrik Elvestad and Johan Golden created the game as a joke on their comedy show *Golden Goal*. A YouTube clip of the match amassed so many views that the sport took on a life of its own, and now there are bubble soccer leagues in several countries, including the United States. The best thing about the sport: it doesn't matter how often you watch the bubble players knock each other over—it's funny every time.

Only one U.S. coin can be picked up by a magnet: the steel penny produced during WWII.

Rags to Riches

Life sure is funny—one day you're living on the street wondering where your next meal is coming from and the next you're living in the lap of luxury. It happened to these people.

JOE ROBERTS

Rags: Roberts was born in Midland, Ontario, in 1966. He left home and his abusive stepfather at 15, went to jail on drug charges at 16, and took a bus to Vancouver at 17—where he became addicted to heroin. He spent a good part of the next seven years pushing a shopping cart around, collecting cans for refund money by day and sleeping under bridges (mostly under the Georgia Street viaduct in downtown Vancouver) at night. In 1991, at the age of 25, Roberts finally sought help. He went back to Midland, reunited with his mother, enrolled in a rehab program, and went back to school. In 1996 he returned to Vancouver, where he got a job with a website design company.

Riches: Within four years, Roberts was president and CEO of the company, and by 2001, at the age of 35—and just 10 years from being a homeless heroin addict—he had made his first million dollars. Today Roberts, who bills himself as "the Skid Row CEO," is a best-selling author and one of the most sought-after motivational speakers in Canada, with a special focus on helping teens—especially those with substance-abuse problems.

JOHN WOO

Rags: Woo was born to a Catholic family in Guangzhou, China, in 1946. During the purges that came after the Communist Revolution of 1949, his family—along with hundreds of thousands of other Chinese refugees—fled to nearby Hong Kong. Woo's father contracted tuberculosis, and the impoverished family ended up living in a wooden shed in a shantytown slum. On Christmas Day 1953, the entire shantytown was destroyed in a fire, making its 53,000 inhabitants instantly homeless. Woo and his family remained on the streets of Hong Kong for a year before they finally got a unit in a public housing project.

Riches: Even though they remained poor for years, Woo's parents made sure he got an education (he didn't start school until he was nine)—and his mother regularly took him to the movies, where he developed a love for films. He started making experimental films in his 20s, made his major directorial debut in 1974, and by the 1980s, he was one of Hong Kong's most successful filmmakers. He went on to make several

Ancient Japanese beauty custom: Ohaguro—the practice of dying teeth black.

Hollywood blockbusters, including *Hard Target, Face/Off,* and *Mission: Impossible II,* and is considered one of the most influential action-film directors of all time.

FRANK O'DEA

Rags: O'Dea was born into a middle-class family in Montreal in 1945, but after developing a drinking problem while still in his teens, he was thrown out of the house. He ended up in Toronto, and by the time he was 20, he was homeless, panhandling for drinking money, and sleeping in parks, alleyways, or flophouses in the city's seedy bowery district. In 1971 O'Dea responded to a radio ad for an alcohol treatment program. He got help, got a job, saved some money, and, in 1975, he and a friend opened a coffee shop in a Toronto mall.

Riches: Over the next 10 years, the two partners' Second Cup coffee shop expanded to 70 outlets across the country and, as Canada's biggest gourmet coffee business, was worth several million dollars. O'Dea sold his share of the company to his partner in 1985 and then went on to found or co-found several other successful businesses—becoming a multimillionaire in the process—and several philanthropic organizations. In 2004 O'Dea was made an officer of the Order of Canada, the nation's second-highest honor for meritorious service to the country.

ELLA FITZGERALD

Rags: Ella Fitzgerald was raised by her mother in Yonkers, New York. When her mother died in 1932, 15-year-old Ella went to live with an aunt in Harlem. Formerly a good student, Ella allowed her grades to slip, and she started skipping school. Her truancy led to her being sent to the New York State Training School for Girls in Hudson, New York, in 1933. (Among other harrowing features, the reform school had "punishment cottages" where the girls were shackled to the floor and beaten by male staff members.) Fitzgerald escaped the school in late 1933 and spent the next year homeless, living on the streets of Harlem, and singing and dancing on sidewalks for change, often earning just barely enough to survive.

Riches: In November 1934, Ella, 17 and still homeless, got an opportunity to perform at an amateur night contest at Harlem's Apollo Theater. Originally planning to do a dance routine, she became too nervous and decided to sing a song instead. (She sang Hoagy Carmichael's "Judy.") The song brought down the house. Ella won the contest…and the rest is jazz history. She was hired by band leader Chick Webb in early 1935, took over the band when Webb died in 1939, and by the 1940s was an international star. The once-homeless street waif went on to record more than 70 albums, sell more than 40 million copies, and win 13 Grammys. She is considered one of the greatest jazz singers in history.

The History of U.S. Intelligence Agencies

Question: How many intelligence agencies does the U.S. have? Let's see...there's the CIA, the FBI, the NSA, and maybe...the DEA—that's four, right? Wrong. How many do we really have? NONE OF YOUR BUSINESS! Just kidding. Correct answer: 17. Here's the history of the whole—mostly secret—business.

SPY STORY

In January 1790, President George Washington, in his first State of the Union address, asked Congress for funding for foreign intelligence gathering. The president wanted to ward off any foreign threats against the new nation by learning about them before they could come to fruition. Congress approved Washington's request and established the Contingent Fund of Foreign Intercourse, more commonly known as the Secret Service Fund. Amount of money appropriated for the fund: $40,000 per year, which the president could use at his own discretion with virtually no oversight. (That set the foundation for future problems between the executive and legislative branches of the U.S. government over intelligence matters—problems that have existed ever since.) Within just three years, the fund had grown to $1 million a year. Funding for U.S. intelligence operations today is about $70 *billion* a year. (That we know of, anyway.)

Here's a brief look at how we got here.

EARLY OPERATIONS

For the first 70 years of the country's existence, the Secret Service Fund was the closest thing the United States had to an "intelligence agency"—although it was just a fund, not an agency. And use of the fund quickly expanded from simply intelligence gathering to...*other* areas. Some of the fund's more memorable uses during this time:

• In 1801 President Thomas Jefferson used the fund in America's first-ever covert attempt to overthrow the head of a foreign government—Yusuf Karamanli, pasha of Tripoli, one of North Africa's Barbary pirate states. The operation, which involved U.S. Marines and Greek and Arab mercenaries, was intended to replace the pasha with his more U.S.-friendly brother. It failed.

• Between 1810 and 1812, President James Madison used the fund to back covert paramilitary and propaganda operations aimed at taking over Spanish-controlled regions of Florida. Those operations failed as well. (Although the U.S. did acquire Florida just a few years later, in 1819.) Madison repeatedly lied to Congress about the operations in the course of these events.

• In the early 1840s, President John Tyler and Secretary of State Daniel Webster used money from the Secret Service Fund in support of propaganda efforts that they hoped would help settle a U.S.-Canadian border dispute. They bribed newspaper editors and reporters to run stories favorable to the U.S. position, and this time America was successful. Only thing: the government was lobbying *against* Maine and in support of Great Britain. (More on that on page 499.)

UN-CIVIL INTELLIGENCE

The first formal intelligence *agency* in the United States was organized in early 1863, about two years into the Civil War, when the Union army established the Bureau of Military Information (BMI). Both sides had engaged in intelligence activities, especially the use of scouts and spies, from the start of the war to gather information on enemy troop movements. But those efforts were poorly organized and had inconsistent results.

The BMI changed all that. Under the leadership of its first chief, George H. Sharpe, a New York lawyer, linguist, diplomat, and volunteer army colonel, it became a true, almost modern, intelligence-gathering unit. The agency employed roughly 70 full-time scouts (both military and civilian), ran spy rings, intercepted mail and other communications, developed code-writing and code-breaking operations, and ran interrogation programs. Perhaps most important, Sharpe set up units to organize gathered information into promptly delivered reports for military commanders in the field, as situations unfolded around them.

Through such actions, the BMI is credited with improving the Union army's intelligence operations and in playing an important part in several key Civil War battle victories. The unit was, however, still a temporary wartime program and was disbanded at the war's end in 1865.

THE POSTWAR LULL

In the years after the Civil War, the attentions of war-weary Americans turned toward rebuilding the country and away from things involving the military. Result: the size of both the army and navy diminished drastically. (How drastically? In 1865 the U.S. Navy had a force of more than 700 ships and 50,000 sailors. By 1880 that number had decreased to about 50 operable ships, almost all of them Civil War relics, and 6,000 sailors. The army was similarly affected, and much of the remaining force was serving in the remote American West, engaged in the ongoing Indian wars.) Then, in the early 1880s, people began to notice a disturbing trend. While the size and state of the U.S. military had declined, other nations—particularly Great Britain, France, Russia, and Japan—had been building, modernizing, and improving their armies. This presented obvious potential dangers to the United States. What's worse, the U.S. government was unable to reliably track these developments because its intelligence-gathering operations were once again decentralized, unorganized, and impossible to make sense of.

But that was about to change.

ONI AND MID

In 1881 President James Garfield appointed William H. Hunt Secretary of the Navy, and the state of the U.S. Navy—and U.S. intelligence operations—would never be the same. Hunt pushed Congress to provide funding for a long-term expansion and modernization program for the navy. The following year Hunt ordered the formation of what became known as the Office of Naval Intelligence (ONI)—the first permanent, official intelligence agency in American history. It was a far cry from agencies of the future: for the first 10 years of its existence, it averaged only 10 employees. (Two notable Naval Intelligence officers: former Supreme Court justice John Paul Stevens and *Washington Post* reporter Bob Woodward, famous for his role in exposing the Watergate scandal.)

In 1885 the U.S. Army followed the navy's lead and formed its own intelligence unit—the Military Information Division (MID). And over the next few years the two branches developed the attaché system, wherein navy and army attachés were stationed in American embassies in foreign capitals, ostensibly as representatives of the U.S. military. But in reality, they were ONI or MID officers, and they were there to gather intelligence on the militaries of the nations in which they were stationed. The attaché system continues today.

Both the ONI and MID grew quite slowly over the next several years. Then, as the century drew to a close, everything changed again. What happened? War.

For Part II of the story, slither over to page 499.

*   *   *

"What all the wise men promised has not happened, and what all the damned fools said would happen has come to pass."

—**Lord Melbourne**

Ole Evinrude had the idea for the outboard motor while rowing a boat to a picnic.

More from the Department of Silly Measurements

Didn't get enough on page 145? Here are a few more bizarre units of measurement.

THE ALTUVE (pronounced al-TOO-vay)

Description: A unit of length, meant to be used for baseball statistics, equal to 5.417 feet.

Explanation: In 2012 Houston Astros fan Bryan Trostel was watching a game when he heard the announcers joke about how many "altuves" a home run had traveled. They were referring to Astros second baseman Jose Altuve, who, at 5 feet 5 inches (or 5.417 feet) tall, is the shortest active player in Major League Baseball. That inspired Trostel to create a website—*www.howmanyaltuves.com*—where you can calculate how many altuves something is. (A 450-foot home run? That's 83.07 altuves. A 98-mile-per-hour fastball? A blistering 26.55 altuves per second. And so on.) The website went viral, and the altuve has been jokingly used by Major League Baseball announcers ever since.

THE FRIEDMAN UNIT

Description: A unit of time equal to six months—or, more specifically, the *next* six months—referring primarily to the war in Iraq.

Explanation: In May 2006, the media watchdog group Fairness and Accuracy in Reporting did a study in which they counted the number of times *New York Times* columnist Thomas Friedman predicted that the Iraq War, which Friedman supported, would be resolved "in the next six months." Their finding: over a period of two and a half years, he made the prediction 14 times. That led liberal blogger Duncan Black, an outspoken opponent of the war, to coin the term "Friedman Unit"—or the "F.U."—in honor of Friedman's repeated (and repeatedly wrong) predictions. The F.U. became so well known in press circles that Friedman was asked about it directly a number of times, including by comedian Stephen Colbert on a 2007 episode of *The Colbert Report*. Friedman responded to Colbert's question by saying, "I'm afraid we've run out of six months. It's really time to set a deadline."

World's priciest chess set: the Jewel Royale ($9.8 million), made of gem-encrusted gold and silver.

THE BEARD-SECOND

Description: The distance a beard grows in one second—about five nanometers, or five billionths of a meter.

Explanation: The inventor of the beard-second is unknown, but it's been around since at least the mid-2000s. In *This Book Warps Time and Space*, a 2008 collection of witty essays by scientists, physicist Kemp Bennet Kolb explained that the beard-second came about because scientists wanted a unit similar to a light-year—the enormous distance light travels in a single year—except they wanted it for extremely short distances. "The proposed unit," Kolb explained, "is the *beard-second*: the distance a standard beard grows in one second." He added that "a standard beard is defined as growing on a standard face."

THE SMOOT

Description: A unit of length equal to 67 inches.

Explanation: In October 1958, Oliver Smoot, 18, was pledging to become a member of the Lambda Chi Alpha fraternity at the Massachusetts Institute of Technology (MIT). For a hazing prank, his fraternity brothers had him measure the length of the Harvard Bridge—in *smoots*. (Harvard Bridge spans the Charles River, between Cambridge and Boston.) Smoot—who is 5' 7", or 67 inches tall—was used like a yardstick. He laid down at the start of the bridge; his fraternity brothers made a chalk mark at the top of his head. Then Smoot scooted ahead so that he was lying with his feet at the chalk mark, while the top of his head was marked again. And every 10 smoots was marked with paint. (How long is the Harvard Bridge? It's 364.4 smoots "and one ear" long.) The prank became an MIT legend—and it remains so today. When the bridge was renovated in the 1990s, officials had lines scored in the new concrete at 67-inch intervals, in honor of the smoot.

Bonus Fact: In 2011 the *American Heritage Dictionary* added "smoot" to its list of official new words.

MORE SILLY MEASUREMENTS

• A *dirac* is a unit of talkativeness. One dirac equals one word per hour. It was coined by colleagues of renowned physicist Paul Dirac, who was famously *untalkative*.

• A *wheaton* is a measurement of followers on the social media site Twitter. One wheaton equals 500,000 followers. The term was coined by English cartoonist John Kovalic in honor of actor Wil Wheaton (best known for playing Wesley Crusher on *Star Trek: The Next Generation*), one of the earliest celebrities to embrace Twitter. As of publication time, Wil Wheaton has more than 2.75 million—or 5.5 wheatons of Twitter followers.

Cockroach Science

Cockroaches may be gross, but scientists can't stop studying them. Reason: they're fascinating (the roaches, not the scientists). For example, did you know that...

• **Cockroaches succumb to peer pressure.** Researchers in Belgium discovered that when cockroaches were placed in a test area, "shy" ones ran underneath a shelter right away, while "bold" ones explored their surroundings. However, when the shy and bold cockroaches were put in the test area as a group, they all ran under the shelter. In other words, the insects may display individuality when they're alone, but if they're with others, there are no rebels—they do what the majority does.

• **Cockroaches have a good sense of direction.** How do cockroaches know where their nest is? They remember the location in much the same way you know where you live. It's a type of spatial learning called *place memory*. You recognize the streets that lead to your house, and cockroaches similarly notice visual cues around their nests, remember them, and use them to navigate home.

• **Cockroaches teach robots how to walk.** We humans use our legs to walk, but it's our complex brains that help us keep our balance. Because robots lack complex brains, it's tough for them to keep their balance. Researchers have discovered that tiny hairs on cockroaches' legs react to changes in terrain so quickly that almost nothing they encounter slows them down. Engineers adapted this feature in Rhex, a six-legged robot whose insectlike movements let it cross uneven ground easily.

• **Cockroaches can be trained like dogs.** Researchers have re-created an experiment made famous by Russian scientist Ivan Pavlov, who trained dogs to salivate on cue: when the dogs heard a bell before feeding time, they learned that the bell meant food and salivated whenever it was rung. In 2007 Japanese scientists trained cockroaches to react in a similar way. Instead of a bell, the bugs were exposed to the scents of peppermint and vanilla just before they were fed. The roaches learned that the scents equaled food and salivated, even if no food was in sight.

• **Cockroaches are not morning bugs.** Researchers at Vanderbilt University also tried teaching cockroaches to salivate at the scent of strawberries. Interestingly, the bugs that learned at nighttime did fine. But the bugs that were taught in the morning had a much tougher time remembering the lesson. The scientists couldn't explain why cockroaches can't learn in the morning. (Maybe they need some coffee first.)

MIT scientists can eavesdrop on conversations by videotaping the vibrations of a potato chip bag.

Weird Tumblrs

Tumblr is a blog service where people can post any multimedia or short-form content they want. Result: some users post really weird things...like these.

If **Babies Had Puppy Heads.** Baby pictures with the heads of dogs superimposed on them. (There's also a tumblr called If Puppies Had Baby Heads.)

Women Laughing Alone While Eating Salad. Stock images and advertisements of women laughing while eating a salad.

Hotties from History. Photos and portraits of historical figures the user says are attractive. Examples: Dylan Thomas and Joan of Arc.

Ugly Renaissance Babies. Closeups of unattractive babies and children from Italian Renaissance paintings.

Law & Order & Food. Stills of the long-running TV crime drama that show people eating.

Turds of Portland. Pictures of dog poop not picked up by dog owners in Portland, Oregon.

Lindsay NoHands. Images of Lindsay Lohan with her hands digitally removed. (There's also a tumblr called Actresses Without Teeth, featuring photos of actresses with all their teeth digitally removed.)

Chicks With Steve Buscemi Eyes. Pictures of beautiful movie stars and singers with actor Steve Buscemi's eyes in place of their own.

Brides Throwing Cats. Photos of the traditional post-wedding bouquet toss, but with the flowers taken out and a cat inserted.

Breaded Cats. Cats with a slice of bread around their faces or necks.

Hungover Owls. Pictures of owls that, to the site's author, look like they had too much to drink the night before.

Lonely Cheetos. Photos of single Cheetos laying on the ground.

Auto Buds. Pictures of two cars of identical make or model, or nearly identical, parked next to each other.

Paula Deen Riding Things. Photos of the celebrity chef superimposed over animals and dinosaurs to make it appear that she's riding them.

Only three mammals go through menopause: elephants, humpback whales, and humans.

A Pirate's Life for Shih

"Ching Shih" isn't a name that springs to mind when most people think of pirates. Nevertheless, this powerful buccaneer could have taught Blackbeard a thing or two.

VAST! THAR BE LADY PIRATES!

If you think the high seas have always been the domain of men, think again. There have been several female pirates over the centuries. Teuta of Illyria terrorized the Roman Empire in the third century BC, and, more recently, Anne Bonny, the world's best-known lady pirate, helped herself to plenty of British mercantile ships during her short career in the 1700s. But odds are you've never heard of Ching Shih, the most successful female pirate of all.

HARD START

Ching was born in China in 1775. She was sold into prostitution at an early age and worked at a brothel in Canton well into adulthood. Zheng Yi, a second-generation pirate and head of the small but powerful Red Flag band of buccaneers, was a frequent visitor to Ching's brothel. He became so smitten with her that, in 1800, he ordered a group of his men to raid the brothel, kidnap Ching, and bring her to him.

Madly in love, Zheng proposed marriage. Ching quickly realized that she had her pirate suitor wrapped around her finger, so she came up with a plan. She accepted Zheng's proposal...but under one condition: he had to bring her on not only as his partner in marriage but also as his partner in crime. Zheng agreed and offered to share his plunder with her, 50/50, to seal the deal.

The happy couple spent the next few years raiding merchant ships up and down the South China Sea. And they had help: Nguyen Quang Toan, the emperor of Vietnam, gave Zheng and his bride financial support and free rein to pillage. In return, the Red Flag fleet attacked and plundered the ships of Toan's enemies.

By 1804 Zheng and Ching had managed to build a massive coalition of pirate fleets, organized by colored flags. Their Red Flag fleet remained at the forefront of the growing armada; their subsidiaries sailed variously under black, white, blue, and green flags. By one estimate, Zheng and Ching now controlled an astounding 400 ships and 70,000 pirates.

Their immense criminal navy established a lucrative blockade around Portugal's trading post in Macau. Every merchant ship in East Asia was terrified of the Red Flag fleet, and they had two options: pay the pirates' huge "protection fees" or surrender their cargo.

THE TURNING OF THE TIDE

In 1807 Ching and Zheng adopted a promising young pirate who had quickly risen through their ranks. The young man, Chang Pao, was so skilled and so trusted that they made him their second-in-command (as they were equally first-in-command).

The exact cause is unclear, but in late 1807, Zheng died. (He may have disappeared while in Vietnam, or his ship may have been lost at sea during a typhoon.) This left the widow Ching the difficult task of managing 70,000 pirates. Without missing a beat, Ching quickly seized power and started calling the shots all on her own.

Needless to say, many of her "employees" weren't happy about taking orders from a woman. To prevent them from staging a coup, Ching asked for help from two of Zheng's relatives, both of whom were pirate captains themselves. With their support, and the sworn loyalty of other captains in the fleet, Ching retained control of the coalition. Still, she feared that her femininity might be her undoing. If Ching was going to stay in power, she was going to need a strong—and loyal—man by her side. She knew the perfect pirate for the job: Chang Pao. Despite being his adopted mother, the two became lovers and soon married.

OFF WITH THEIR HEADS!

Part of Ching's ability to keep order was a strict code of conduct for the Red Flag fleet. Among the stipulations:

• Any pirate caught disobeying orders would be immediately beheaded.

• Any pirate found guilty of stealing booty received a whipping for his first offense and the death penalty for his second.

• Deserters had their ears chopped off and were then paraded in front of their fellow pirates and sent back to work.

• Ching's rules concerning female captives were revolutionary at the time. "Ugly" captives had to be returned, unharmed, to shore. The more lovely among them were auctioned off. However, if a pirate bought a captive, he had to marry her and remain faithful to his new bride, because sex out of wedlock—even if it was consensual—was forbidden. Failure to comply could result in the pirate being beheaded and the wife being thrown into the sea with cannonballs tied to her legs.

Despite her iron-fisted approach to employee relations, Ching kept her crews happy by generously sharing plunder, providing every pirate with a larger share than they'd get from her competitors. This generosity further cemented her control of the fleet.

"THE TERROR OF THE SOUTH CHINA SEA"

In the years that followed, Chang Pao conducted the actual raids; Ching did the planning and strategizing. With an armada larger than most nations' official navies, Ching earned the nickname "the Terror of the South China Sea." When her empire reached its peak around 1810, she controlled 1,800 ships and somewhere between 80,000 and 100,000 pirates and other underlings.

Her control over the sea meant that any merchant fleet that wanted to sail through "her" waters came to her for permission rather than going to government officials. She typically made them pay a toll. Those who refused were considered fair game for the pirates. And to make it easier for them to pay the tolls, Ching set up convenient collection offices in various ports so that merchants wouldn't have to go too far out of their way to pay up.

EXPANDING HORIZONS

But Ching didn't just rule the sea—her coalition used smaller boats to raid villages along various rivers. Besides piracy, her operations also extended to include blackmail, extortion, and protection. With this intricate network—and landlubber allies that included merchants and farmers, paid well to keep the massive fleet fed—Ching became the de facto ruler of the Guangdong province. She grew so powerful that her forces were soon collecting taxes from Chinese coastal villages, which, needless to say, infuriated Emperor Jiaqing. He had no choice but to move against her.

NEVER UNDERESTIMATE A LADY

Jiaqing assembled a massive armada to take down Ching's pirate empire. He appointed Kwo Lang, a cunning admiral, to lead the attack. Unfortunately for the emperor, Ching and her pirates were one step ahead of him. Rather than wait for the armada to come to her, Ching went after Jiaqing's ships. She even decided to personally command the attack herself.

Her forces hunted down the armada and made short work of it. After Ching sank dozens of the emperor's ships, the rest of his fleet surrendered. Terrified of what was going to happen if Ching captured him, Kwo opted to commit suicide before she reached his ship.

To send a clear message to anyone considering further defiance, Ching appropriated the 63 ships her pirates hadn't sunk. Then she gave the surviving members of the emperor's armada a choice: join her fleet or face the consequences. Those who refused to join her had their feet nailed to the decks of their own ships before her pirates beat them to death.

Undaunted, Jiaqing came up with another plan. He enlisted the help of the British and Portuguese. Both governments were fed up with Ching's raids on their merchant ships, but both had been unwilling to deal with Ching themselves—officially, at least: they'd sent bounty hunters after her, but to no avail. Now, as the emperor paid them handsomely to send warships from Europe, the combined powers of China, England, and Portugal declared war on Ching…to no avail. Ching's pirates won battle after battle in a conflict that dragged on for two years.

NEVER SURRENDER

By this point, Jiaqing was desperate to end Ching's reign. Since trying to take her down with armadas and European warships was getting him nowhere, the emperor decided to try another tactic: negotiation. In exchange for her immediate retirement, Jiaqing offered Ching amnesty. She wouldn't be put to death for her crimes, or even punished. Instead, Ching would keep all of her amassed wealth as well as a small fleet of ships. She would also become a "Lady by Imperial Decree," entitling her to numerous legal protections as a member of China's aristocracy. Ching took the deal.

FINAL VOYAGE

In addition, Jiaqing agreed to prosecute only the absolute worst pirates in her ranks. In all, about 300 of Ching's men were punished. The rest were allowed to leave the operation in peace with their share of the plunder. In an ironic turn of events, several of them joined the emperor's navy and became pirate *hunters*. Among them: Chang Pao, who was given command of 20 ships.

Still only in her mid-30s (and a former pirate lord), retirement didn't suit Ching. She ran a successful gambling house and was happy for the remainder of her years—she even became a grandmother. Unlike most of history's notorious pirate captains, she enjoyed a long life and a peaceful death. "The Terror of the South China Sea" died in 1844 at the age of 69… of natural causes.

*　　*　　*

"Better to be strong than pretty and useless."

—**Lilith Saintcrow**

You Stole *What*?

Some people will steal your heart, but your skin? Eww!
Here are some weird items that have gone missing.

UNABRIDGED

Who would steal a bridge? It happens more often than you might think. For example, in 2011 thieves made off with a 50-foot-long steel bridge in Pennsylvania and sold it for scrap. In 2012 a bridge in the Czech Republic was stolen by men pretending to be railroad workers. For Michigan resident Robert Cortis, losing his bridge was especially heartbreaking because he had helped his father build it over a creek on their property in suburban Detroit in 1989. But in 2014, when Cortis went to check on the 40-foot, 5,000-pound steel bridge…it was gone. He saw ruts in the dirt, suggesting that heavy equipment was used. His neighbors said they heard the removal and figured he'd authorized it. But Cortis insisted to police that he had neither sold the bridge nor authorized its removal. He was planning on relocating it to his catering company, where it would be used for wedding photos, but now his plans had to be put on hold. "That bridge had sentimental value," he said.

Update: A few weeks later, police found the bridge in a lot about 30 miles away. Intact. But they still have no idea who stole it or why.

DID THEY PUT IT IN THE TRUNK?

A 400-pound bronze elephant statue named "Bon Bon Babar" was stolen from Gene and Beverly Darnell's front porch in Garland, Texas, in 2012. The heist was pulled off in the middle of the day, while Beverly was home. Baffled police could find no tire or dolly tracks—it would have required at least four people to carry it. The couple is "heartbroken" about losing Bon Bon Babar. (Beverly had given the statue to Gene as a gift many years ago.) They are offering a $500 reward for Bon Bon's safe return. "We'd really like our elephant back," said Gene.

THE SKINNY

Gary Dudek, 54, of Wallingford, Pennsylvania, was arrested in May 2014 for stealing skin…human skin. Working as a sales rep for a regenerative medicine firm called Organogenesis, he managed all the accounts of Mercy Hospital's biomedical department. When the hospital's accountants ran a routine audit, they discovered that Dudek had ordered more than 200 unauthorized skin grafts at a cost of $357,000. But auditors were unable to locate the skin (or the money), even though surveillance video shows Dudek loading boxes of what authorities believe are the skin grafts into his car. At last report, he was standing trial for the crime. His lawyer claims that he is "not a Frankenstein" and that the whole thing is just a "big misunderstanding."

IGOR IN TRAINING

Of all the weird things that could happen in a Dairy Queen parking lot, a police sting operation to catch a brain thief may be the weirdest. The culprit: a 21-year-old Indianapolis man named David Charles. On several occasions in 2013, Charles broke into the Indiana Medical History Museum (a former psychiatric hospital) and stole jars of brain tissue that had been extracted from dead mental patients. Then he sold the brains on eBay. When a San Diego buyer received some tissue (he paid $600 plus $70 shipping), he noticed the museum's labels on the jars…and realized he may have bought stolen brains. So he called the museum, and someone there called the police. Undercover officers arranged a sale and nabbed Charles—with brains in hand—at the DQ.

SHORE LEAVE

An entire beach was stolen from Jamaica in 2008. The theft took place in Trelawny (on the island nation's north coast) while a new resort was being constructed there. Truck drivers simply showed up with forged work orders and began hauling the fine white sand away. By the time they were finished, an estimated 500 truckloads of sand were gone—leaving nearly 1,300 feet of beach bare. The theft went unsolved and became a major scandal in Jamaica—with citizens protesting that the police were either completely oblivious or took bribes to look the other way. The sand's fate? Unknown, but it was most likely sold to rival beach resorts in the Caribbean.

HOME AWAY FROM HOME

Leah Watson, a 24-year-old single mom from Newport, Washington, was living in a travel trailer parked on a friend's property. One day in 2013, Watson and her daughter returned to the property…and the trailer was gone. Lots of trailers get stolen, but in this case, the crooks took everything Watson owned, including her pets—a dog, a cat, and a turtle. In order to tow away the 30-foot-long trailer, the culprits had to cut the lock off the trailer hitch, inflate the two rear tires (they were flat), and push some cars out of the way. The bad news: as of last report, the police had no leads. The good news: Watson's family and friends pitched in to help them get back on their feet. But the theft is still tough for Watson to fathom, and even tougher for her little girl. "She keeps telling me she just wants to go home and keeps asking me about all of her stuff," says Watson. "I have to just say, 'I'm sorry babe, it's gone.'"

Nudes and Prudes

Nudity can be shocking....and so can prudery.
Which side of the fence do you fall on?

NUDE: February 22, 2015, was the final day of "The Naked Life," an exhibition at the LWL Museum for Art and Culture in Muenster, Germany. Patrons that day saw more than nudes on the walls. They saw a Swiss performance artist—a woman named Milo Moiré, 32—walking through the museum naked except for high heels, looking at the art while carrying a baby (also naked). Most of the patrons were unimpressed; one called it "ridiculous." But Moiré, who is strikingly beautiful and has created several other nude pieces, explained (as only a true performance artist can), "This direct confrontation with live nude art challenges others to reflect on familiar forms of perception."

PRUDE: In 2015 portrait photographer Jade Beall, who specializes in "truthful images of women," posted an image to her Facebook page of several naked women breast-feeding their babies. Per Facebook's policy, Beall blurred out all the naughty bits...but she accidentally missed a nipple. Result: someone flagged the picture as "pornography," and Facebook deleted it. By that time, however, the image had received 9,000 "Likes." Hundreds of Beall's 80,000+ Facebook fans complained to the social media site, but all Beall could do was blur out the offending breast and repost the image. She told *Cosmo* magazine, "Do I think it's silly that men can have exposed nipples but women cannot as a rule for this platform? Sure, but that's a cultural thing, not simply a Facebook thing."

NUDE: One night in 2011, while vacationing in the Florida Keys, a 43-year-old Pennsylvania man named Richard Gervasi took some LSD. A few hours later, he was running around naked in traffic yelling, "I'm king of the world!" When a deputy ordered him to stop, he refused, so she Tasered him. Undeterred, Gervasi pulled the prongs out of his skin and kept running around and yelling. After two more Taserings, the naked king was finally subdued and arrested.

PRUDE: The Lingerie Football League (now the Legends Football League) features scantily clad women playing competitive football. In 2009 Lingerie Bowl VI was going to be shown live on pay-per-view during the Super Bowl halftime, but the event was canceled. Reason: it was going to be held at the Caliente Resort in Land O' Lakes, Florida, which is clothing-optional. Just days before the game, LFL officials realized they didn't want a bunch of naked spectators watching their scantily clad women play football. LFL spokesman Stephon McMillen said, "It is in the best interest of the Lingerie Football League not to place ourselves in what some would consider a potentially negative environment."

NUDE: In 2013 in Crossville, Tennessee, a young married couple knocked on 54-year-old Stephen Amaral's door and told him they were his neighbors. The woman asked if she could skinny-dip in his pool. Amaral said yes. So he took them to his backyard, where the wife took off her clothes and jumped in. Then her husband left to "get some cigarettes." But while Amaral was distracted by the skinny-dipper, the husband went into the house and stole nearly $2,000 worth of jewelry, guns, and medicine. When the young woman finally left 20 minutes later, Amaral invited her to church (she declined). Only later did he realize that he'd been robbed. At last report, police still hadn't found the couple.

PRUDE: Hundreds of parents were horrified on Christmas morning 2014 when their kids opened up their new Play-Doh Sweet Shoppe Cake Mountain Playsets. Why? The "extruder tool"—which squirts fake icing onto the fake cake—happens to closely resemble a certain part of the male anatomy (it even has "veins"). After several moms complained that the toy "ruined Christmas," Hasbro officials went into damage control mode: they removed all images of the toy from their Facebook page, deleted all the angry comments, and recalled the extruder tool. Some commenters thought the whole thing was overblown. Said one: "Next they'll want toy companies to change the shape of balls."

NUDE *AND* PRUDE: In 2014 a 28-year-old runway model named Jessie Nizewitz was a contestant on the VH1 reality show *Dating Naked*. At the request of producers, she agreed to naked-wrestle a male contestant on a beach. "I'm extremely comfortable in my own skin," she said. "Honestly, being naked to me means absolutely nothing." But after the show aired, Nizewitz changed her tune and sued VH1 for $10 million because for a brief moment during the action, a blur that was *supposed* to cover up her private parts…failed to cover up her private parts. "I felt lied to, manipulated, and used," she said. The worst part: "My grandma saw it."

The U.S. male prison population is 15 times the size of the female prison population.

Start Your Own Country

Ever wonder what it would be like to be the founder and ruler of your own country and/or empire? These people found out…sort of.

THE NATION OF CELESTIAL SPACE

Comprising: "The Entire Universe (excluding Earth)"

Founding Father: James T. Mangan, 52, a Chicago publicity agent and industrial designer in the late 1940s

History: At midnight on December 20, 1948, Mangan declared all of outer space to be part of his nation; then he waited nine minutes for Earth to move out of the space it had just occupied and claimed that as well. Acting as "First Representative" of the new nation, he registered it with the Cook County Recorder and sent letters to 74 countries requesting official recognition. (They ignored him.) He applied for admission to the United Nations. (They turned him down.) Undeterred, he began issuing stamps and passports, minted silver and gold coins, and announced plans to sell Earth-sized "plots" of outer space for $1.00 apiece. Then he banned atmospheric nuclear testing (it went on anyway), and when the space race got under way in the late 1950s, he wrote letters to the United States and the Soviet Union accusing them of "trespassing." (They ignored him again.)

What Happened: The universe is still out there, but the Nation of Celestial Space is not—it became defunct when Mangan died in 1970, and his three grandsons, Glen (Duke of Selenia), Dean (Duke of Mars), and Todd (Duke of the Milky Way), showed little interest in carrying on the dynasty. Today the stamps, passports, and coins issued by the Nation of Celestial Space are valuable collector's items; some of the gold coins sell for $1,000 apiece.

THE COPEMAN EMPIRE

Comprising: A rundown travel trailer on the English seaside

Founding Father: Nick Copeman, 26, a chronically unemployed university dropout from Sheringham, Norfolk, England

History: In 2003 Copeman was broke and living with his parents. When a friend dared him to apply to the local job center on horseback and wearing a crown, he did. Why stop there? Copeman changed his name to HM King Nicholas I, moved into a run-down travel trailer, and

---

The German word *kummerspeck,* meaning "emotional overeating," literally translates to "grief bacon."

declared "Copeman Palace" the seat of his empire.

What Happened: After spending just £29 (about $50) to change his name, His Majesty started selling lordships over the Internet for £2,000 ($3,300). Even Copeman admitted they were fake, but people bought them anyway, earning him more money than he would have made through the job center. His 2005 autobiography was also successful; his attempt to marry Queen Elizabeth's granddaughter Zara Phillips was not. She married a rugby star named Mike Tindall in 2011. Not that King Nicholas is complaining: "We seem to have struck gold with something that is basically stupid," he told the *Eastern Daily Press* in 2005.

THE DOMINION OF BRITISH WEST FLORIDA

Comprising: A strip of territory occupying a portion of the Florida panhandle as well as parts of Alabama, Mississippi, and Louisiana. It belonged to England from 1762 until 1781, when they surrendered it to Spain during the American Revolution.

Founding Father: Some guy who calls himself "Robert VII, Duke of Florida"

History: Spain ceded West Florida to the United States in 1819, but the duke (whoever he is) claims the transfer of ownership was invalid. He says the territory should have reverted to England in 1808, when Napoleon Bonaparte removed King Ferdinand VII from the Spanish throne and made his own brother, Joseph Bonaparte, the new king. West Florida, says Duke Robert, still belongs to England. He wants it recognized as a *dominion*, or self-governing territory, of the British Commonwealth, and has appointed himself its governor-general.

What Happened: Nothing. Neither Spain, nor England, nor the United States have ever heard of Robert VII, nor do they recognize his claims. (In 2009 the duke was succeeded as governor-general by someone called "Bo Register, Marquess of Mobile.")

FREEDONIA

Comprising: A couple of houses in Houston, Texas, and later a dorm room "embassy" at Babson College in Boston, Massachusetts

Founding Father: John Kyle, a Houston high school freshman

History: In 1992 Kyle and some friends declared their parents' homes to be a single country founded on libertarian principles, with power shared by two presidents and a cabinet. They chose the name Freedonia, not realizing it was the name of a fictional country in the 1933 Marx Brothers film *Duck Soup*. And as might be expected in a utopia founded by teenage boys, recreational drugs were legalized, the drinking age was lowered to 15, and there were no speed limits or restrictions on gun ownership.

If Brussels sprouts taste bitter, blame your parents—you have the "bitter" gene.

Kyle's friends outgrew the project, but he never did. When he went off to college, he replaced the existing government with a constitutional monarchy headed by himself—Prince John I. The following year he set about looking for more territory. After rejecting artificial islands and cruise ships anchored in international waters (too expensive), he hit on the idea of minting and selling Freedonian coins and using the money to buy a small plot of land in Somaliland, which had broken away from the East African nation of Somalia in 1991.

What Happened: Having just won their struggle for independence, the people of Somaliland weren't about to hand over a piece of their hard-won territory to a foreigner. "There is no deal…We never support these types of groups," a spokesperson told the *Australian* newspaper in 2000. Freedonia struggled on for a few more years until Prince John pulled the plug in 2004.

THE RUSSIAN EMPIRE

Comprising: Suwarrow, an uninhabited atoll that's part of the Cook Islands in the South Pacific, plus 16 other "possessions" (including Antarctica)

Founding Father: Anton Bakov, a Russian politician and head of the Russian Monarchist Party

History: Bakov proclaimed the new Russian Empire in June 2011, appointed himself prime minister to run it, and started looking for a member of Russia's former royal family who was willing to sit on the throne. (The old Russian Empire became defunct following the Russian Revolution of 1917; the last czar, Nicholas II, and his immediate family were assassinated by revolutionaries in 1918.)

In October 2011, Bakov announced he'd purchased Suwarrow from the Cook Islands. He also claimed 15 other islands for his empire, plus Antarctica, all of which he said had been discovered by Russian explorers but abandoned by the original Russian Empire.

What Happened: Suwarrow is a national park; the government of the Cook Islands denied that it had ever been for sale and denounced Bakov as a con man. Not that it really mattered: when Bakov sailed out to "his" island, he became so seasick that he had to turn back before reaching it. He abandoned his plan to make Suwarrow the capital, moving it instead to a 200-acre parcel of land in Montenegro, in eastern Europe. Even there the Russian royal family refused to have anything to do with him, so in 2014 he installed one of their distant German cousins, Prince Karl Emich of Leiningen, as Emperor Nicholas III. At last report, Bakov, his emperor, and their empire were still seeking official recognition from the Montenegrins. (Don't hold your breath.)

In 15th-century Bavaria, selling adulterated saffron (a rare spice) was punishable by burning at the stake.

"New" Old Shows

Coming up with an idea for a TV show must be difficult. That would explain why producers sometimes just revive old shows with the word "New" in the titles, hoping success will follow. As these examples prove, it rarely works.

THE NEW LASSIE. *Lassie*, the TV show about a heroic collie, changed formats several times during its 19-year run (1954–73). First she was the companion of a boy named Jeff, then one named Timmy, then she helped out a forest ranger, then she wandered around, and then she worked on a ranch. In the 1980s, reruns of the Timmy and Lassie episodes on Nick at Nite performed so well that in 1989 producers revived the concept for *The New Lassie*. This time, Lassie lived with a boy named Will in a Southern California suburb. (Confusingly, Jon Provost, who played Timmy on the original show, plays Will's Uncle Steve but later reveals that his real name is... Timmy.) *The New Lassie* ran in syndication for three years.

THE NEW ODD COUPLE. Neil Simon's 1965 hit play about mismatched roommates (one is a slob, the other is compulsively neat) has been adapted for television several times. The most famous TV series was the 1970–75 version starring Jack Klugman and Tony Randall (which is technically an adaptation of the 1968 film version with Jack Lemmon and Walter Matthau). Then in the late 1970s, ABC aired a Saturday morning cartoon called *The Oddball Couple*—the roommates were a dog and a cat. ABC brought back the live-action version for 16 little-watched episodes in 1982 as *The New Odd Couple*, only this time the roommates (Ron Glass and Demond Wilson) were African American. In 2015 CBS revived *The Odd Couple* once more with Matthew Perry and Thomas Lennon...but under its original name (and not, as its name should have been, *The New New Odd Couple*).

THE NEW PERRY MASON. *Perry Mason* was one of the most popular drama series of all time. Based on Erle Stanley Gardner's courtroom novels, the show is closely associated with the actor who played the title role, Raymond Burr. The show wrapped up a nine-year run in 1966. But just seven years later, CBS debuted *The New Perry Mason*. Lacking the imposing presence of Burr as the unbeatable lawyer Perry Mason—actor Monte Markham had to fill those shoes—the revival ran for only 15 episodes in 1973. More than a decade later, it was revived again. In 1985 NBC bought the rights to the character and produced a series of top-rated made-for-TV Perry Mason movies. They wisely got

Yes, it's dangerous: the fatality rate for Blue Angels pilots is about 1 in 10.

Raymond Burr to reprise his role, and he starred in 26 Mason movies between 1985 and 1993. (They probably would've made more…except that Burr died.)

NEW MONKEES. In 1986 *The Monkees* marked its 20th anniversary with record ratings of reruns of the 1960s series on MTV, as well as a successful reunion tour and a new album. One thing the members of the Monkees would not do, however, was revive their manic sitcom. So some TV producers auditioned hundreds of musicians, picked four of them, and dubbed them the New Monkees—the same way the original Monkees had been created. Then they shot a new sitcom for syndicated TV that reflected the flavor of the original. Example: at the end of each episode of *New Monkees*, the group played a song (critics compared their synth pop sound to Mr. Mister). Both the show and the band flopped hard. *New Monkees* was canceled after 13 episodes in the fall of 1987, and the New Monkees didn't manage a single hit on the pop charts.

THE NEW ANDY GRIFFITH SHOW. Andy Griffith left *The Andy Griffith Show* in 1968, while it was still the #1 show on TV. Reason: he was worried that any more time as Sheriff Andy in Mayberry would typecast him as a country bumpkin. In 1970 he won the title role on *Headmaster*, a CBS sitcom about a prestigious California private school. That flopped (it aired against ABC's *The Partridge Family*), but before CBS canceled it, they lined up Griffith for another show and had it ready to replace *Headmaster* at midseason: *The New Andy Griffith Show*. Griffith didn't get to stretch his acting muscles much. This show took place in a small town in North Carolina (like the old *Andy Griffith*), although this time he played the mayor, not the sheriff. It lasted just 10 episodes.

THE NEW DICK VAN DYKE SHOW. CBS was so eager to get Dick Van Dyke to return to TV and repeat the success of *The Dick Van Dyke Show* (1961–66) that it was willing to do anything. Van Dyke made some steep demands. He wanted a guarantee that the show would air for three years, he wanted full creative control, and he wanted to tape it at a studio in Arizona, where he was living. The network met them all. *The New Dick Van Dyke Show* ended up being very similar to the old *Dick Van Dyke Show*: it was a mixture of the lead character's work life (backstage at a TV show—this time a local TV talk show) and his family life. In 1971 CBS put it on Saturday night, sandwiched between top-10 hits *All in the Family*, *Funny Face*, and *The Mary Tyler Moore Show*. Ratings were middling, and CBS wanted to cancel the show but couldn't; it had given Van Dyke a three-year contract. Result: *The New Dick Van Dyke Show* stayed on the air until 1974.

In one study, 28% of TV news directors said they'd dropped info from a story to avoid a lawsuit.

More Tech Name Origins

On page 94 we Binged your bluetooth right up to your Etsy. Now enjoy a few more tech name origin stories.

KINDLE. Amazon's e-book reader was named by San Francisco graphic designers Michael Cronan and Karin Hibma. According to Hibma, the name referred to *kindling*, in the sense of "starting a fire," and it was inspired in part by the 18th century French philosopher Voltaire, who once wrote, "The instruction we find in books is like fire. We fetch it from our neighbors, kindle it at home, communicate it to others and it becomes the property of all." (Cronan and Hibma also named TiVo.)

ANDROID. The company that developed the Android operating system—designed especially with mobile devices like smartphones in mind—was headed by computer engineer Andy Rubin. Andy's nickname was "Android." Reason: He's a robot fanatic—and his name is Andy! So Rubin named the company (Android, Inc.) and the operating system after himself.

GARMIN. The Global Positioning System device maker founded in 1989 was named after its founders: **Gar**y Burrell and **Min** Kao.

ASUS. The name of this Taiwanese computer manufacturer, best known for its low-cost laptops, was derived from the winged horse of ancient Greek mythology—Pegasus. According to its marketing department, the company "embodies the strength, purity, and adventurous spirit of this fantastic creature." Why did it use only the last four letters in Pegasus? So it would start with the letter "A"—and therefore show up earlier in alphabetical lists.

WOOT. The online retailer specializing in one-day deals took its name from "w00t"—the exclamation "woot," expressing excitement or joy, but spelled with zeroes instead of O's. (Example use: "Just got a great deal on a camera - w00t!") The term originated in the 1990s with gamers, who used it as an abbreviation for "Wow! Loot!"

CISCO. Computer networking colossus Cisco Systems was founded in 2004 by Stanford University computer techs Leonard Bosack and

---

Elephants walk on their toes.

Sandy Lerner. They named the company after the last five letters of San Francisco. Bosack and Lerner claim they got the idea while driving across the famed Golden Gate Bridge—which is why a likeness of the bridge is the company's logo.

TUMBLR. This social network was started in 2007 by 20-year-old New York City high school dropout (and computer whiz) David Karp. Tumblr is a micro-blogging platform, meaning it's an online blogging site designed to accommodate very short, often mixed-media postings. Another name for a multimedia-blog: a "tumblelog," a term coined in 2005 by influential Internet writer and programmer Jonathan Gillette. Karp simply took "tumblelog" and shortened it to "Tumblr." (In 2013 Karp, at the ripe old age of 26, sold his little blogging platform to Yahoo!…for $1.1 billion.)

REDDIT. According to the founders of this popular news aggregator/bulletin board website, the name is a play on the phrase "I read it on reddit." An interesting coincidence discovered by Reddit users: *reddit* is Latin for "render," which can mean "to furnish for consideration, approval," which is pretty much exactly how Reddit works—users submit news or other items to the site, and other users vote on them.

SAFARI. In 2003 Apple engineer Don Melton was the team leader on the secret development of the Apple browser that eventually became Safari, but claims nobody can remember exactly who came up with the name. Melton says that when he was first told that Apple CEO Steve Jobs had finalized the name choice—about a month before the browser's launch—he was less than impressed. Melton's first words about it: "It doesn't suck." (He does admit that he eventually came around, and grew to love the name.)

Wii. At the 2005 Electronic Entertainment Expo in Los Angeles, gaming giant Nintendo revealed a prototype for a new gaming system they were working on. They called it "Revolution" because it was a *revolutionary* new system. So when the new system was released under the name "Wii" a year later, their fans were pretty confused. Nintendo's explanation: "Wii sounds like 'we,' which emphasizes this console is for everyone." When gaming fans responded with a lot of "wee" jokes, Nintendo exec Reggie Fils-Aime explained that "revolution" was hard to pronounce in some cultures, so they decided to go with something "short, to the point, easy to pronounce, and distinctive." They probably don't care much about the mocking. Consumers have taken more than 100 million Wiis—er, have *bought* more than 100 million Wii units—since the product hit the market in 2006.

Bizarre Baseball Bits

Strange stats, facts, and oddities from Major League Baseball.

• In 1950 Pete Castiglione of the Pittsburgh Pirates made one error as a first baseman, two as a second baseman, and three as a third baseman.

• When the U.S. Army designed hand grenades for World War II soldiers, they made them the size and weight of a baseball. Reason: "Any young American should be able to throw it."

• Only two MLB pitchers have struck out their age in a single game: In a 1936 game, the Cleveland Indians' 17-year-old ace Bob Feller struck out 17 batters. And in 1998 the Chicago Cubs' Kerry Wood, age 20, struck out a record-tying 20 batters.

• Speaking of Bob Feller, the only time his mother came to the park to see him play in his 18-year big league career, she was hit in the head by a foul ball...from a pitch he threw.

• After the Chicago Cubs won the 1908 World Series, their second in a row, they were hailed as "baseball's first dynasty." They haven't won a championship since.

• In the first game ever played at New York's Shea Stadium in 1964, Pittsburgh Pirates slugger Willie Stargell hit a home run. In the first game ever played at Atlanta-Fulton County Stadium in 1966, Stargell hit a home run. In the first game ever played at Pittsburgh's Three Rivers Stadium in 1970, Stargell hit a home run.

• In the 1994 season Jeff Bagwell won the MVP award for the National League, and Frank Thomas won the MVP for the American League. Both players were born on May 27, 1968.

• For 50 years, Hall of Famer Hank Aaron was the first player listed alphabetically in the *Baseball Encyclopedia*...until 2004, when San Francisco Giants pitcher Dave Aardsma made his MLB debut.

• What do the Mets, Astros, A's, Yankees, Royals, Braves, White Sox, Pirates, Dodgers, Rockies, Blue Jays, Cardinals, and Tigers have in common? Octavio Dotel pitched for all of them, making him the only person to ever play for 13 major league teams.

Small Worlds: the Dwarf Planets

In 2006 the International Astronomical Union, which names planets and other objects in the solar system, created a new category of celestial body: the dwarf planet. Five have been recognized so far, and there are likely many more in the outer solar system waiting to be discovered.

DISCOVERED

From the time the "planet" Pluto was discovered in 1930, astronomers have wondered whether it was the only object of that size in the outer reaches of the solar system, beyond Neptune. Just as Saturn has rings, scientists speculated that our entire solar system might have a ring or "belt" of debris circling it, some 30 to 50 times farther from the Sun than Earth is. The question wasn't answered until August 1992, when astronomers from the Massachusetts Institute of Technology discovered the first Pluto-sized objects in what would become known as the *Kuiper belt,* named for astronomer Gerard Kuiper, who theorized its existence.

More than 1,300 Kuiper belt objects, or KBOs, have been discovered since then; billions more are thought to exist. Most are far smaller than Pluto—which is 1430 miles in diameter—but some rival it in size, and at least one (so far) has an even greater mass. That created a quandary for astronomers. Should the Pluto-sized objects be classified as planets?

ORBIT-UARY

In 2006 the International Astronomical Union opted for a different approach: it created a new category of celestial body called "dwarf planets" to accommodate the new objects. Like an ordinary planet, a dwarf planet orbits the Sun and is large enough that its gravitational field squashes it into a spherical shape. But unlike an ordinary planet, a dwarf planet's gravitational field is *not* large enough to clear other similarly sized objects from its orbit. And because Pluto itself fits the definition of a dwarf planet, the IAU removed it from the list of planets in the solar system. Result: today schoolkids are taught that there are eight planets orbiting the Sun, not nine. Pluto is a planet no more—it's a dwarf planet.

The IAU recognizes four other space objects as dwarf planets:

WWII field rations were called K-rations. Why? They were named after the developer, Ancel B. Keys.

CERES

Named For: The Roman goddess of grain and agriculture (cereal also gets its name from Ceres)

Location: Orbiting the Sun between Mars and Jupiter

Size: 590 miles in diameter, with a surface area about the size of India. It orbits the Sun every 4.6 (Earth) years.

Details: Does this story sound familiar? When this ball of rock and ice was discovered in 1801, it was categorized as a planet and was considered one for more than 50 years. But when many more objects were found in the same area, they were all reclassified as a new kind of object called an *asteroid* (which means "star-like"), and areas that were full of such objects became known as asteroid *belts*. Today it's thought that there may be millions of asteroids in the "Main Belt" between Mars and Jupiter; Ceres, which constitutes as much as one-third the mass of the entire belt, is the largest of them all. Because it's large enough to be round in shape, in 2006 Ceres was recategorized as a dwarf planet.

Bonus Fact: Ceres may contain more fresh water than is found on Earth—and where there's water, life may be present as well. NASA's *Dawn* space probe became the first craft ever to orbit a dwarf planet when it arrived in March 2015 for a 16-month visit. The probe is equipped with instruments that will look for evidence of a liquid ocean beneath Ceres' icy surface.

ERIS

Named For: The Greek goddess of chaos and strife. When Eris was first discovered by Caltech astronomer Mike Brown in 2005, he nicknamed it "Xena" after the lead character in the TV series *Xena: Warrior Princess* and nicknamed its moon "Gabrielle" after her sidekick. The following year, when "Xena" received the official designation *Eris*, "Gabrielle" became *Dysnomia*, daughter of Eris and the Greek goddess of lawlessness.

Location: In an area beyond the Kuiper belt called the "scattered disc". (Some astronomers consider the scattered disc part of the Kuiper belt, but others do not.)

Size: Roughly 1,445 miles in diameter, about the same size as Pluto, which is about one-third the size of our Moon. Eris has a surface area nearly as large as South America. It orbits the Sun every 557 years. Pluto, by comparison, completes one orbit every 248 years.

Details: If you're one of the people who's sad that Pluto isn't considered a planet anymore, you can blame Eris for your misfortune. Eris is the troublemaker that got Pluto demoted from planetary status. It was one of *three* such objects whose discovery was announced in July 2005. Because it was the largest—and initially thought to be larger than Pluto—Ceres was briefly classified as the tenth planet in our solar system. By then, however, it was clear that there were likely to be many more similarly sized objects in the Kuiper belt, so Eris, Pluto, and the other two newly discovered objects, *Haumea* and *Makemake*, were recategorized as dwarf planets. Because it is made of denser material than Pluto, Eris has 27 percent more mass, even though they're roughly the same size.

HAUMEA

Named For: The Hawaiian goddess of fertility and childbirth. (Because it was discovered a few days after Christmas in 2004, the Caltech team that discovered it gave it the nickname "Santa.")

Location: In the Kuiper belt

Size: About 1,200 miles in diameter, with a mass equal to about 30 percent of Pluto's. It orbits the Sun every 283 years.

Details: Haumea (pronounced "how-MAY-ah") is large enough for its own gravitational field to squash it into a spherical shape, and 4.5 billion years ago it was that shape. But at some point early in its history, another object of similar size smashed into it, causing it to begin tumbling end over end. The spinning caused it to elongate into a shape that its discoverer, Mike Brown, likens to a football or an M&M candy (plain, not peanut).

Brown, whose team is also credited with discovering Eris, Makemake, and more than a dozen other dwarf planets awaiting official recognition by the IAU, says that Haumea's composition is also analogous to an M&M: it has a core of solid rock with a thin coating of water ice on the surface. Because it spins so rapidly, a Haumean day is less than four hours long. It has two moons, Hi'iaka and Namaka, and is followed by a "swarm" of smaller bodies, all of which are believed to be remnants of the collision that started Haumea tumbling in the first place.

MAKEMAKE

Named For: The Rapanui (Easter Island) goddess of fertility. Why an Easter Island goddess? The object was discovered four days after Easter in 2005. For a time it was nicknamed "Easter Bunny."

Location: In the Kuiper belt

Size: Uncertain. One of the ways astronomers calculate the size and mass of a dwarf planet is by studying the orbit of the moon or moons around it. However, to date, no moons of Makemake (pronounced "mah-kee-mah-kee") have been found, and its precise size is unknown. Best guess: about two-thirds the size of Pluto. It orbits the Sun every 310 years.

Details: Makemake is the second-brightest object in the Kuiper belt after Pluto. It reflects nearly 80 percent of the sunlight that strikes it, which makes it about as reflective as dirty snow—in this case, snow made from frozen nitrogen and methane ice, thought to cover much of its surface.

SOMEWHERE OUT THERE

Mike Brown says that as of early 2015, he and the other astronomers who are looking for dwarf planets have found 10 more objects that are "nearly certainly dwarf planets," 22 that are "highly likely," and 42 that are "likely." Brown says another 75 objects are "probably" and 359 are "possibly" dwarf planets. That's 508 potential dwarf planets in all...and the numbers continue to grow.

Two of the most interesting objects discovered so far are Sedna and 2012 VP113, nicknamed "Biden" after Vice President Joe Biden. (Get it? VP!) Both Sedna and 2012 VP113 are believed to have originated far beyond the Kuiper belt, in a comet-filled debris field called the inner Oort cloud, which is theorized to surround the solar system at a distance of 2,000 to 20,000 times the distance of Earth from the Sun. If you're still mourning the demotion of Pluto to a dwarf planet, cheer up: analysis of the orbits of both Sedna and 2012 VP113 indicate that they may have been influenced by the gravitational field of an as-yet-undiscovered ninth and perhaps even a *tenth* planet in the solar system, both several times the size of Earth and hundreds of times farther away from the Sun.

Stay tuned…

*   *   *

THAT EXPLAINS IT!

In shocking world news (that somehow failed to shock the world), the Iranian news agency Fars News reported in 2013 that the U.S. government has been under the control of Nazi space aliens since World War II. The revelations, said the paper, were brought to light by Russia's defense minister. His source: leaked memos obtained by NSA-whistleblower Edward Snowden. They reportedly contained pages of top-secret documents that laid the whole thing out: In 1945, just prior to their defeat in Europe, the Nazi "tall white aliens" took control of the U.S. government and have been secretly driving American domestic and foreign policy from a secret base in Nevada ever since. But before you rush out to buy a tin-foil helmet, you should also know that Fars News, which bills itself as "Iran's leading independent news agency," previously reported that an Iranian scientist has invented a time machine and that the British royal family is Jewish.

"Never Call Me Needle Nose!"

Remember when you did that thing with the guy at the place near the spot by the thing? If your memory isn't what it used to be, read on.

YOU MUST REMEMBER THIS
Medical students have to memorize a lot of lists: symptoms, nerves, bones, medications, procedures, and more. How do they do it? One technique they use is *mnemonics*—memorable words or sentences that remind them of what they need to remember and in what order. So if your doctor starts mumbling something that sounds like a bunch of nonsense words, don't worry that it's a sign of insanity. It may be their favorite mnemonic reminder about what to ask you, how to treat you, or how to put you back together again.

Mnemonic phrase: Really **N**eed **B**ooze **T**o **B**e **A**t **M**y **N**icest
To remember: The parts inside your elbow (cubital fossa)
Stands for: Radial Nerve, Biceps Tendon, Brachial Artery, Median Nerve

Mnemonic phrase: TV CRAP CUBES
To remember: Signs of shock
Stands for: Thirst, Vomiting, Coolness, Respiration (shallow and rapid), Anxiety, Pulse (weak), Cyanosis (bluish skin or lips), Unconsciousness, Blood pressure (low), Eye blankness, Sweating

Mnemonic phrase: Play **G**olf **O**r **G**o **O**n **Q**uaaludes
To remember: The hip muscles that rotate your leg's femur bone
Stands for: Piriformis, Gemellus superior, Obturator internus, Gemellus inferior, Obturator externus, Quadratus femoris

Mnemonic phrase: Virgil **C**an **N**ot **M**ake **M**y **P**et **Z**ebra **L**augh!
To remember: Facial bones
Stands for: Vomer, Conchae, Nasal, Maxilla, Mandible, Palatine, Zygomatic, Lacrimal

Mnemonic phrase: AC/DC Rocker **K**ids **P**arty **D**own
To remember: Major retroperitoneal organs

Stands for: Ascending Colon, Descending Colon, Rectum, Kidneys, Pancreas, Duodenum

Mnemonic acronym: SCALP
To remember: Layers of the scalp
Stands for: Skin, Connective tissue, Aponeurosis, Loose areolar tissue, Pericranium

Mnemonic phrase: Never Call Me Needle Nose!
To remember: Nasal cavity components
Stands for: Nares (external), Conchae, Meatuses, Nares (internal), Nasopharynx

Mnemonic phrase: Stop Letting Those People Touch The Cadaver's Hand!
To remember: Carpal (wrist) bones
Stands for: Scaphoid, Lunate, Triquetrum, Pisiform, Trapezium, Trapezoid, Capitate, Hamate

Mnemonic phrase: Old People From Texas Eat Spiders
To remember: Cranium bones
Stands for: Occipital, Parietal, Frontal, Temporal, Ethmoid, Sphenoid

Mnemonic phrase: Screw The Lawyer, Save A Patient
To remember: Branches of the axillary artery (shoulder to hand)
Stands for: Superior thoracic, Thoracoacromiol, Lateral thoracic, Subscapular, Anterior circumflex humeral, Posterior circumflex humeral

Mnemonic phrase: O SPIT!
To remember: Treatment for managing severe asthma
Stands for: Oxygen, Salbutamol, Prednisolone, Ipratropium bromide (if life-threatening), Theophylline (if life-threatening)
NOTE: Hydrocortisone can substitute for Prednisolone…which will make a slightly different mnemonic.

*   *   *

WHO HAD THE MOST TOP 10 HITS BY DECADE?

1940s: Bing Crosby (54)
1950s: Perry Como (20)
1960s: The Beatles (30)
1970s: Elton John (16)
1980s: Madonna (17)
1990s: Mariah Carey (19)
2000s: Beyoncé (12)
2010s: Taylor Swift (12…so far)

1,000 Ways to Die

Can you match each term for murder to its definition? (Answers on page 510.)

1) Lupicide	**a.** Killing an uncle
2) Ceticide	**b.** Killing a bishop
3) Episcopicide	**c.** Killing a prophet
4) Uxoricide	**d.** Killing a whale
5) Senicide	**e.** Killing a fox
6) Ecocide	**f.** Killing a deer
7) Matricide	**g.** Killing a sister
8) Mariticide	**h.** Killing a nephew
9) Amicicide	**i.** Killing a friend
10) Sororicide	**j.** Killing an elderly person
11) Avunculicide	**k.** Killing a god
12) Deicide	**l.** Killing a wolf
13) Vulpecide	**m.** Killing the environment
14) Tauricide	**n.** Killing a husband
15) Vaticide	**o.** Killing a ram
16) Patricide	**p.** Killing a steer
17) Nepoticide	**q.** Killing a father
18) Cervicide	**r.** Killing a mother
19) Ariecide	**s.** Killing a wife
20) Omnicide	**t.** Killing all humans

In one study, more than a third of Americans admit they have eaten pie in bed.

Govern-Mental

Strange but true tales from the public sector.

NAME RECOGNITION

In a January 2015 story in Maryland's *Frederick News-Post*, journalist Bethany Rodgers wrote, "Councilman Kirby Delauter has joined [former Commissioner Billy] Shreve in concern over parking for elected officials." After reading the article, Delauter went on his Facebook page to condemn Rodgers and her "unauthorized use" of his name. (Three months earlier, Rodgers had written an article about strained relations between Delauter and town officials, which the conservative councilman referred to as a "hit piece.") Rodgers replied that it was not only within the newspaper's rights to mention names of elected public officials—it was their responsibility. Delauter's response: "Use my name again unauthorized and you'll be paying for an Attorney. Your rights stop where mine start." Terry Headlee, the *Frederick News-Post's* managing editor, called the threat a "misguided attempt to intimidate and bully the press," with "an astonishing lack of understanding of the role of a public servant." The next day, the newspaper published an editorial titled "Kirby Delauter, Kirby Delauter, Kirby Delauter" that mentioned Delauter's name 30 times. After both the editorial and the Facebook post went viral, Delauter apologized: "I thought I had long ago learned the lesson of waiting 24 hours before I hit the send key."

THE ~~17TH~~ 48TH STATE

In 1953, while Ohio state officials were making preparations to celebrate the state's 150th anniversary, they made an alarming discovery: Ohio wasn't actually a state. The measure to declare it the nation's 17th state was submitted to Congress in 1803, but for reasons unknown, the lawmakers never got around to making it official. Once the error was discovered, Congress quickly passed a resolution making Ohio a state (and they backdated it to 1803).

STATE OF THE YAWNION

The president's annual State of the Union address can be an animated affair. Every time he says something even mildly inspirational, half the lawmakers—the ones in the president's party—stand up and cheer while the other half scowl from their seats. But that's not the case for members of the U.S. Supreme Court, who also attend but show no party affiliation. Traditionally, the nine robed justices sit stone-faced, showing no emotion at all. During the 2015 State of the Union address, Justice Ruth Bader Ginsburg showed even less emotion…because she fell asleep during President Barack Obama's speech. When asked about her nationally televised nap, Ginsburg, 81, explained that she would have stayed awake but, "I wasn't 100 percent sober."

WAS HE HIGH?

"States have their own official soft drinks and desserts," explained Missouri Rep. Courtney Allen Curtis (D). "Missouri even has an official dinosaur. But we do not have an official form of the most basic human interaction: greeting each other." So in January 2014, Allen submitted a bill that would make the high-five Missouri's official state greeting. "It's a form of celebration and promotes positivity among our citizens," he said. Unfortunately for Curtis, the reaction to his bill was not positive. It was derided by his fellow politicians, the media, and his constituents—many of whom complained that lawmakers should focus on the more pressing issues facing the state, like child poverty and racial tension. (And some people were concerned that all that high-fiving would spread germs.) The bill never even made it to a vote.

DR. POPE

During an interview on Fox News in 2015, Republican presidential candidate Rick Santorum criticized Pope Francis for saying that climate change is primarily caused by humans. The politician complained that "the pope should leave science to the scientists." At that point, host Chris Wallace pointed out that Santorum is *not* a scientist…and that Pope Francis actually has a degree in chemistry.

TREE-MAIL

As part of its goal to be "the most livable city in the world," the Australian city of Melbourne has given an ID number to every one of its 70,000 trees. Residents can now go to the city's website, choose a tree from an online map, and send an e-mail to it. And the tree will write back! (Obviously, trees can neither read nor type—City of Melbourne staffers write the replies.) Critics have accused the city of wasting taxpayer money that could be better spent actually trying to protect the trees from extended droughts, but Melbourne city councillor Arron Wood (that's really his name) defended the program: "The trees were always going to have individual ID numbers anyway. So it was only logical we'd assign the ID numbers to an e-mail which connects these trees to the community." A reporter at the *Guardian* newspaper decided to send a complimentary e-mail to a ginkgo tree near the city center. The reply: "Thank you for your lovely words. I am very well. Enjoy your day. Yours sincerely, Tree 1441724."

(These Aren't) Needed

Music publishers often add parentheses to song titles to make them more identifiable to the casual listener. These songs probably didn't need them.

"I Wanna Dance with Somebody (Who Loves Me)"
—**Whitney Houston**

"(It) Feels So Good"
—**Sonique**

"(I Know) I'm Losing You"
—**Rod Stewart**

"All Night Long (All Night)"
—**Lionel Richie**

"There's a Moon in the Sky (Called the Moon)"
—**The B-52s**

"P.Y.T. (Pretty Young Thing)"
—**Michael Jackson**

"(Sittin' On) The Dock of the Bay"
—**Otis Redding**

"(Shake, Shake, Shake) Shake Your Booty"
—**KC and the Sunshine Band**

"(You Gotta) Fight for Your Right (To Party)"
—**Beastie Boys**

"Same Ol' Situation (S.O.S.)"
—**Mötley Crüe**

"Dude (Looks Like a Lady)"
—**Aerosmith**

"(Nice Dream)"
—**Radiohead**

"Rock Me Again and Again and Again and Again and Again and Again (Six Times)"
—**The Human League**

"(A) Face in the Crowd"
—**The Kinks**

"(I Can't Get No) Satisfaction"
—**The Rolling Stones**

"Sad Songs (Say So Much)"
—**Elton John**

"Clones (We're All)"
—**Alice Cooper**

"Forever Afternoon (Tuesday?)"
—**The Moody Blues**

"You're Pretty Good Looking (For a Girl)"
—**The White Stripes**

"Na Na Na (Na Na Na Na Na Na Na Na Na)"
—**My Chemical Romance**

Squirrel Barking

Even if you're not a hunter, you may find this bit of American frontier history fascinating. (If you're a vegetarian…maybe not.)

BARK-GROUND

In the decades after the American Revolution, an odd hunting fad spread around the wild frontier region that became the state of Kentucky in 1792. The fad was known as "squirrel barking," and it grew as a combination of two popular frontier pastimes. The first was mass squirrel hunts. In those days, squirrels were hunted not only for their meat and pelts, but also because they were considered pests—they could do considerable damage to people's gardens—hence these hunts, which often took place in the form of contests. Hundreds of people would take part, with prizes given to the hunters who bagged the most squirrels. Also popular at the time were marksmanship contests. These included "candle snuffing," in which marksmen competed to see who could extinguish a lit candle from a distance of 40 paces or more with a shot from a muzzle-loading long rifle (the most common type of weapon used on the American frontier). Another contest favorite: "nail-driving," in which nails were partially hammered into targets, and shooters would attempt to drive them into the targets with rifle shots.

THE BOONE BOON

Squirrel barking, or "barking off squirrels," combined these two pastimes. A hunter would shoot the bark of a tree next to a squirrel, rather than at the squirrel itself, thereby killing the squirrel by the concussive force of the exploding bark alone. This not only required great skill, but it also had the added benefit of keeping the squirrel's body completely intact, making its meat and pelt more useful to hunters than if it were blown to pieces by the ball of an old muzzle-loader. By the 1790s, squirrel barking was a frontier pastime of its own, especially in Kentucky, where famed frontiersman Daniel Boone had taken up the odd sport. Naturalist John James Audubon, who accompanied Boone on a hunt, wrote, "I was astounded to find that the ball had hit the piece of the bark immediately beneath the squirrel, and shivered it to splinters; the concussion produced by which had killed the animal, and sent it whirling in the air, as if it had been blown up."

Squirrel barking contests remained popular in Kentucky until the 1810s. And there are still squirrel hunters who practice the technique today—complete with old-fashioned muzzle-loaders.

Bumming a ride: Crabs have been known to hitchhike on jellyfish.

Don't Wash That Chicken!

We all know standard food safety rules—wash your hands after serving food, sneeze only on other people's dishes, and don't eat raw cookie dough—but we can all use a…wait…did we just say "don't eat raw cookie dough"?

AN ILLNESS IS BORNE
According to the U.S. Centers for Disease Control (CDC), roughly 48 million Americans get sick every year because of food-borne illnesses. Of those, around 128,000 are hospitalized…and more than 3,000 die. The overwhelming majority of these incidents are caused by just a few pathogens, including the well-known *Salmonella* and *E. coli* bacteria. In most cases, those pathogens make their way into unlucky diners' systems because someone—in a restaurant or in a home kitchen—practiced unsafe food-preparation methods. In the hopes of lowering these numbers, every year the CDC, along with other health organizations like the Food and Drug Administration (FDA), publishes lists of common food safety errors, along with tips on how to avoid them. We thought we'd pass along some of those tips, with some added details, for your bathroom (and kitchen) reading pleasure. Bon—and safe—appétit!

Common Mistake: Washing raw poultry

Background: Surveys show that most home cooks regularly rinse raw chicken before cooking, believing they are washing away germs or bad-tasting elements. The same is true—though to a lesser degree—with meats, such as steak and pork, and with fish.

Why It's Bad: It may sound creepy, but there's a very good chance that the poultry, meat, or fish you buy at the store carries some sort of pathogens—they're simply very common today. Unfortunately, washing or rinsing those foods does almost nothing to remove those pathogens. It does, however, do a lot to help spread them onto your sink, countertops, utensils, and other things in your kitchen. Studies have found that people who wash raw chicken are actually *more* likely to become infected with a pathogen than those who do not.

Solution: Simple—don't wash your poultry, meat, or fish! (Or eggs. The CDC and the FDA both recommend against washing or rinsing eggs—meaning eggs in their shells, of course.)

Forgotten first: George Richmann, the first person killed while experimenting with electricity (1753).

Common Mistake: Undercooking poultry, meat, seafood, and eggs

Background: Does that mean it's unsafe to eat a rare steak? Read on.

Why It's Bad: When it comes to pathogens, poultry, meat, seafood, and eggs are among the riskiest foods. The single most effective way to kill pathogens in those foods is to cook them properly. If you don't, you're increasing their chances of survival.

Solution: Cook foods to the temperatures recommended by the experts. Your best way to go is to get a food thermometer—and use it. Chicken, for example, needs to reach an internal temperature of at least 165°F. Ground beef: 160°F. Steaks, pork chops, and roasts: 145°F—with three minutes of rest time, during which the internal temperature of such foods actually rises a bit, killing off any germs that survived the cooking process.

Steak-Based Bonus: Cooking a steak to 145°F means it will be about medium. If you like your steak medium-rare, which means it will have reached an internal temperature of only 125–135°F—a temperature that does not kill all pathogens—eat at your own risk.

Common Mistake: Putting cooked poultry, meat, or fish on the same plate you used to hold it while it was raw

Background: You might see this one at a barbecue. Someone brings out a plate of raw hamburgers and chicken breasts, someone else cooks them up…and right back onto the same plate they go.

Why It's Bad: This one should be obvious. When you let cooked meat come in contact with raw meat juices, you are reversing all the good you did by cooking it in the first place.

Solution: Designate any cutting board or plate used to hold or prepare raw meat as for that use only, and wash it (and your hands) in warm, soapy water immediately after using.

Common Mistake: Tasting questionable food to see if it's edible

Background: We've all done it—we warily take a sip out of the milk carton, or a bite of that old pizza, to find out if it's okay to eat.

Why It's Bad: It takes just the tiniest sip or nibble of infected food to become sick—even very sick. And taste-testing is unreliable, anyway: contaminated foods often don't taste or smell any different from safe food.

Solution: Throw questionable foods away—it's not worth the potential consequences of testing them. And if you're not sure how long is too long to keep food, the FDA's website has a food and freezer storage-time chart that's easy to download or print. Examples of safe refrigerator storage times: whole chicken—1 to 2 days; steak—3 to 5 days; bacon—7 days; Spam—until the sun burns out. (Just kidding. It'll last for about a week.)

America's oldest living cultivated grapevine: a 400-year-old Scuppernong on Roanoke Island, NC.

Common Mistake: Thawing food on your countertop

Background: The "Danger Zone" for food temperatures is between 40°F and 140°F. Between those two temperatures, food-borne pathogens thrive. The reason we cook food: to get it *above* the 140°F mark—to kill pathogens. The reason we refrigerate food: to get it below the 40°F mark (average refrigerator temperature is about 35°F)—because pathogens can't thrive at those low temperatures.

Why It's Bad: If you thaw food on your countertop—leaving it in that temperature "danger zone" for several hours—you're inviting a pathogen supercolony to grow on it.

Solution: Plan ahead. Put frozen food in the refrigerator the day before you plan to eat it. And if you must speed up thawing time, submerge the frozen food in cold water—in a leakproof plastic bag, so that airborne bacteria can't be introduced through the water—and change the water every 30 minutes.

Common Mistake: Cleaning up with a filthy sponge

Background: If your sponge were a housing development, it would be called "Bacteria Estates."

Why It's Bad: Sponges and dish clothes are designed to absorb—that's how they get your surfaces so clean. But once they harbor food-borne pathogens, it can be tougher than you think to rid them of it.

Solution: Don't be frugal with sponges. Replace them regularly and disinfect them every day or two. The most effective method: heat your sponge in the microwave for one minute; that will kill 99 percent of the bacteria. You can also wash it in your dishwasher or clothes washer, but in each case, make sure you dry it on high heat. And don't use the sponge to wipe up raw meat, or scoop up that sauce you dropped on the floor. That's what paper towels are for.

Common Mistake: Eating raw cookie dough

Background: You've done it, Uncle John has done it, probably everyone at the CDC and the FDA has done it. But it's just wrong!

Why It's Bad: Raw cookie dough commonly contains raw eggs—and raw eggs are susceptible to bacterial infestations, especially *Salmonella*—which can cause serious illness. In 2009, 77 people in 30 states became ill after eating the raw dough of an *E. coli*–infested batch of Nestlé Toll House cookies. (The *E. coli* were traced to the flour in the dough. *E. coli* comes from poop. How the *E. coli* got in the flour—nobody knows for sure.)

Solution: Continue eating raw cookie dough—and live in a state of dangerous denial! Or…just start cooking your cookie dough. (It's pretty tasty when it's cooked, too!)

Saved from the Trash

At the BRI, we love tales of treasures that narrowly escape being tossed out with the garbage. It isn't often that we come across a story about enough treasures to fill an entire Dumpster.

FLIP!

In December 2006, two real estate investors named Larry Joseph and Thomas Schultz made an offer to buy a rundown two-bedroom cottage in the village of Bellport, New York, on the South Shore of Long Island. If the sale went through, they planned to "flip" it by fixing it up and reselling it for a quick profit. Joseph, who lived in Los Angeles, would put up the money, and Schultz, who lived in Bellport, would provide the sweat equity. They offered $300,000 for the place and hoped to sell it for $400,000.

The cottage had been owned by an elderly woman named Armen Pinajian, who had lived there since the 1970s. She died in 2005, and her relatives were selling the house "as is." That meant that whoever bought it was stuck with the contents of the detached one-car garage: more than 3,000 paintings, drawings, and other artwork created by Pinajian's brother Arthur, a onetime comic book illustrator and failed artist who had lived with her until his death in 1999.

CANNED!

The garage wasn't much more than a drafty, oversized shack with a dirt floor, and the oldest paintings had been sitting there since 1973. Decades of exposure to the elements had left much of Arthur Pinajian's artwork damp, mildewed, and rotting. The garage *had* contained more than 7,000 paintings, but half were so badly damaged that they had already been thrown away. Rather than tackle the rest of the job, Pinajian's relatives rented a Dumpster, apologized for the mess, and told Joseph and Schultz that if the sale went through they'd have to clean it up themselves.

Neither man knew much about art, and since this artist was a nobody, they must have suspected that his work was mediocre and almost certainly worthless. Schultz couldn't have examined much of it if he had wanted to: hundreds of the canvases had been removed from their wooden stretchers and rolled up for more compact storage, and the rest of the art was stacked in great moldering piles. Even so, Schultz couldn't bring himself to "throw a man's life's work into a Dumpster," as he put it. After talking it over with Joseph, who was still in Los Angeles and hadn't seen the cottage or the artwork, the partners decided to hang onto it at least for the time being. Joseph renegotiated the terms of the real estate deal to include clear legal title to the art, just in case they did decide to keep it. He even upped the offer on the cottage by about $2,000, or roughly 70¢ per painting. That was 70¢ more per painting than Pinajian's relatives ever thought they'd get, and they happily accepted the offer.

POW!

Back in the 1930s and early 1940s. Arthur Pinajian (who went by the nickname Archie) had earned a pretty good living as an illustrator for Marvel and other comic book companies. He created a few characters of his own, including the Invisible Hood and Madam Fatal, the first cross-dressing superhero. He served in the U.S. Army during World War II, fought in the Battle of the Bulge in 1944, and was awarded a Bronze Star for valor.

Pinajian's wartime experiences may have changed his outlook on life, because he returned home with a determination to make it as an abstract expressionist painter. He gave up his paying gigs, went to art school on the GI Bill, then moved in with his sister, Armen, who worked as a secretary. She agreed to support him on her modest salary until he made it big as an artist, after which they would live on the proceeds from the sale of his artwork.

FLOP!

Pinajian never did find success as an artist. Instead, he and his sister lived out the rest their lives in the tiny cottage. Pinajian may have eventually abandoned the idea of becoming a famous artist, but he never stopped painting. Relatives remember him as an amiable flop: "Cousin Archie, who painted all the time and never tried to find a job after the war," Schultz says.

Pinajian's tiny 8 x 8-foot bedroom in the cottage doubled as his studio. There, in addition to his abstract expressionist pieces, he painted portraits, still lifes, and landscapes and drew sketches in pencil, ink, and even crayon. He rarely showed his work to anyone: as soon as a piece was finished, he carried it out to the garage and tossed it on the pile, then went back into his bedroom and started another one. He painted every day for the rest of his life, and when he died in 1999 at the age of 85, he left instructions in his will for all of his artwork to be disposed of in the town dump. It very nearly was, but at the last minute, a cousin of Pinajian's, also an artist, refused to let the dump truck haul it all away. The artwork was still sitting in the garage when Armen Pinajian died in 2005.

BUZZ!

After the sale of the cottage went through, Schultz loaded the artwork into a moving van and hauled it to some rented office space in a neighboring town. There he began unrolling the canvases and flipping through sketchbooks pulled from the piles to see just what he and Joseph had gotten for their $2,000. He was impressed by what he saw, but what did he know? He'd taken some art classes in college, that was it. By chance, he was close friends with the brother-in-law of William Innes Homer, a respected art historian and a prominent authority on American contemporary art. The brother-in-law invited Homer to have a look at Pinajian's artwork. Perhaps only to humor him, Homer agreed.

What should have been a cursory glance at a few paintings turned into much more than that. Homer was astonished by both the quantity and the quality of the work. It was, as he put it, "an exhilarating discovery rarely made available to scholars of any stripe"—thousands of works of art by a painter no one had ever heard of and who should, Homer believed, "be ranked among the best artists of his era." (To date no one has been able to find even a single article published in Pinajian's lifetime that mentions him or his work. But it wasn't that he'd been ignored by the fine art world—he was completely unknown to it.)

SPEND!

Homer studied Pinajian's artwork for several months; then he asked another respected art historian named Peter Hastings Falk for his opinion. Falk too concluded that Pinajian was an artist of exceptional merit. Based on both men's assessments, Larry Joseph decided to invest more of his money not just in cleaning and restoring the paintings but also in raising Pinajian's public profile.

There must have been times when Joseph wished he'd thrown the artwork into the Dumpster when he still had the chance. He burned through hundreds of thousands of dollars and spent six years trying to talk prestigious New York galleries into showing Pinajian's art, but none of them were interested. Then, when his cash was nearly gone, he sold his house in Los Angeles and used the money to rent his own gallery space on Madison Avenue in a last-ditch effort to generate some buzz.

By March 2013, Joseph had just a few days to go on his lease, with few sales to show for it. That's when he finally got a break, in the form of an unusually slow news day. With nothing else going on, New York's *Newsday* newspaper ran a story on Arthur Pinajian on the front page. That got some attention: when the Madison Avenue lease was up, a gallery in Manhattan's artsy SoHo neighborhood offered to show Pinajian's work. There Joseph sold more than $500,000 worth, recouping his entire investment in just a few days.

...skirmish" in Texas on May 13, 1865, one month after the South surrendered).

KA-CHING!

If you're hoping to pick up a Pinajian on the cheap, you're already too late. The paintings that were destined for the Dumpster on more than one occasion now sell for as "little" as $4,000 for an 11-inch acrylic or as much as $125,000 for one of Pinajian's larger abstract expressionist works—not a bad return on the initial 70¢ per painting investment. Even at those prices, collectors and art museums are eager to buy because the expectation is that the Pinajians will triple or quadruple in value in the years to come and will probably keep rising after that. (Estimated value of the entire hoard: $30 million.)

Today Arthur Pinajian's reputation as a 20th-century painter is growing. Career-wise, he has something in common with Vincent van Gogh, who sold only one painting in his lifetime before dying a "failure" in 1890. Will his fame ever equal van Gogh's? Probably not—but thanks to two real estate flippers who knew nothing about art yet couldn't bring themselves to "throw a man's life's work into a Dumpster," we're going to find out. Either way, Pinajian is finally getting the recognition that he never lived to see.

* * *

YOU'RE MY INSPIRATION

• **Aladdin.** Disney filmmakers originally based the look and persona of Aladdin on Michael J. Fox, specifically his *Back to the Future* character. But Disney president Jeffrey Katzenberg scrapped that plan in favor of someone more "masculine." Result: Aladdin was rewritten so he had the "looks of Tom Cruise and the swagger of Indiana Jones."

• **The Seattle Seahawks Logo.** Sometime in the 19th century, a Pacific Northwest native of the Kwakwaka'wakw nation carved a "transformation mask" depicting an eagle with a long beak that hooked down at the end. The beak opened to reveal the face of a human within. In 1975, after Seattle's expansion team decided on the name "Seahawks," the NFL's logo designers found a photograph of that mask in a book called *Art of the Northwest Coast Indians.* The Seahawks logo is almost a direct copy of that eagle mask.

• *Celebrity Jeopardy!* The *Saturday Night Live* skit starring Will Ferrell as a frustrated Alex Trebek dealing with brain-dead celebrities was taken directly from a 1980s skit called *Half-Wits,* written by Eugene Levy for the Canadian show SCTV. *SNL's* Norm MacDonald (who played Burt Reynolds in the skits) asked SCTV alum Martin Short to get permission from Levy to use the idea. Short agreed and even played Jerry Lewis in the first *Celebrity Jeopardy!* sketch, which aired in 1996.

Dumb Crooks

Here's proof that crime doesn't pay.

HEADING DOWN THE HIGHWAY

Zhen Yin, 32, was wanted by Chinese police for dealing drugs but managed to evade arrest—until November 2014. Just before going to meet a contact, he loaded thousands of dollars' worth of cocaine and methamphetamines into the trunk of his car and then ingested a bunch of the drugs himself. Bad idea: he got on the freeway… and promptly passed out behind the wheel. His $150,000 Porsche rear-ended a semi and got stuck under the trailer. The truck driver had no idea what had happened and kept driving, as other motorists frantically tried to get his attention. Finally, six miles later, the truck pulled over with the Porsche still stuck to it. Police arrived soon after, woke up Zhen, and took him to jail.

SHEET HAPPENS

Eric Frey, 29, scribbled a robbery note onto a sheet of toilet paper: "I have a gun. Give me $300." Then he took it to Michael Maria's Pizza in Uniontown, Pennsylvania, and showed it to the cashier. Sensing Frey wasn't that dangerous (the toilet paper was a dead giveaway), the cashier refused to give him any money and hit a panic button instead, which locked Frey inside. When officers arrived on the scene, Frey told them that a "big, bearded man" in an alley forced him at gunpoint to rob the restaurant. The police searched the alley but found no one, so they searched Frey's home, where they discovered the roll of TP with the writing indentations still visible on the top sheet. (He was arrested.)

SOFT MONEY

One night in 2014, two serial burglars from Hartlepool, England— Michael Hogg, 33, and Andrew Wood, 28—were cruising a neighborhood looking for an easy score. Then they found it: a wad of cash sitting on a windowsill. While Wood acted as a lookout, Hogg tiptoed up to the house and smashed the window, but the cash fell on the floor. The noise woke up the homeowner and a neighbor, who called the police. Hogg and Wood tried to escape, but officers got there quickly and apprehended them. Here's the dumb part: the cash wasn't even real—it was a stack of novelty tissue paper made to look like £50 notes. Even though they didn't technically steal anything, both men's rap sheets were so long that each was sentenced to three years in prison.

Surely you can't be serious: *Airplane!* actor Leslie Nielsen's brother was a member of Canada's parliament.

FOUR ON THE FLOOR

First rule of shoplifting from a convenience store: before you start, make sure there aren't four uniformed sheriff's deputies in the store. Ignoring that rule, Jacob Wallace, 29, and Robert Martin, 19, entered a Chevron Food Mart near Los Angeles at 4:00 a.m. and proceeded to steal some snacks and a six-pack of beer. Seconds after they left, the four cops gave chase and quickly captured them.

STING OPERATION

Jamie Brown of Leeds, England, broke into a local furniture store, stole a fish tank, and ran out. The break-in set off the store's alarm, alerting police, who swarmed the area—but it looked like the thief had gotten away. Suddenly, Brown burst out from some nearby bushes and ran straight toward the police, screaming for help. He'd been hiding in the bushes when he had to answer the call of nature…and peed on a wasps' nest. (Oops.) Brown received so many stings that he had to spend several hours in the hospital. Then he spent a few minutes in front of a judge, who sentenced him to six months in jail.

THAT'S JUST COLD

On a freezing night in February 2015, Brian Byers of Sparta, New Jersey, had too much to drink and then tried to drive a relative's BMW home. But less than a mile from his house, he ran a stop sign and hit a guard rail. Apparently aware that he would have some explaining to do, Byers drove the wrecked car home and then convinced his friend Alexander Zambenedetti—also drunk—to help cover up the accident. The men, both 20, filled two big buckets with water, loaded them into Zambenedetti's car, drove back to the scene, and poured the water onto the road. Their plan: blame the accident on black ice. But the jig was up when a police officer caught them red-handed. (The officer noted in his report that Zambenedetti wasn't wearing a shirt, and it was –1°F.) The two friends were charged with drunk driving, disorderly conduct, and "creating a dangerous condition by purposely icing the intersection."

HERE I AM COPS LOL

In 2015 Eddie Smith, 22, of Mineral Wells, Texas, posted a status on his Facebook page:

> So, I have 16 warrants out right now. Lol they know where I'm at tho so, it must not be TOO bad.

It was TOO bad, however, because a "concerned citizen" shared the status with cops, who tracked Smith down that same day and arrested him. "You can poke fun at a lot of things," warned Detective Nick Wells, "but don't poke fun at us."

BIC has sold more than 50 pens every second of every day since 1950.

Icy Language

Antarctic research stations are so isolated that they have a lingo all their own.

DIRT TOWN/McMUDHOLE: McMurdo Station, the largest research station in Antarctica. Summer temperatures there occasionally rise above freezing, exposing dirt and mud. Stations in colder locations seldom get muddy.

BEAKER: A scientist. Everyone who works in Antarctica is either a beaker or support staff.

AOD: Airport of Departure—the place you came from. (The preferred term used to be Point of Origin, but the acronym for that is POO.)

POPPIES: Alcoholic drinks made with Antarctic ice cubes. The ice, formed under intense pressure, contains compressed air bubbles that pop in the drinker's face as they melt.

ON THE ICE: In Antarctica.

BOLO: Someone who's been on the ice too long.

GREENOUT: The wave of emotions a person experiences when they return home from Antarctica and see plants for the first time in months.

ANTARCTIC 10: Someone who might be sexually attractive by Antarctica standards but would be less so back home.

CHING: A "Dear John" letter from a boyfriend or girlfriend back home, ending the relationship.

CHING CLUB: People who've been chinged.

300 CLUB: People who have rolled naked on the ice, then dashed inside to the sauna, exposing themselves to a 300°F temperature change.

FRESHIES: Fresh food and vegetables, available only during the short Antarctic summer, when conditions are good enough for supply ships to deliver them.

SAWDUST: Dehydrated cabbage—eaten when freshies are unavailable.

BOOMERANG: A flight bound for Antarctica that has to turn back due to extreme weather or mechanical problems.

HERO SHOT: A naked picture taken at the South Pole in temperatures lower than –40°F. (Boots are permitted.)

In ancient Persia, you could get a ticket for parking your chariot on the king's road. Fine: death.

Behind the Cameras

We've written about the origins of Kodak, Polaroid, and other famous camera brands in previous Bathroom Readers. Here are the backstories of a few more familiar camera names. (And they're all true—because we Canon tell a Leica!)

NIKON

Nikon was founded in 1917 as Nippon Kogaku Kogyo Kabushikigaisha, meaning "Japanese Optical Corporation." In 1948 the company released its first camera, called the "Nikon." At first glance Nikon looks like a take on the company name, but there's more to the story: the German optics manufacturer Zeiss had a popular camera at the time called the "Ikon," and many people—including the owners of Zeiss—believed "Nikon" infringed on the Ikon trademark. Zeiss sued Nippon Kogaku, and the issue became so contentious that during the 1960s, Nikon cameras were sold in Germany under the name "Nikkor." The Japanese eventually won the court battle and in 1969 switched back to Nikon for the German market. Nippon Kogaku officially changed its name to the Nikon Corporation in 1988.

LEICA

The Ernst Leitz Optische Werke, a lens and microscope manufacturer, was founded in 1869 by Ernst Leitz in Wetzlar, Germany. In 1913 one of their engineers, Oskar Barnack, developed a compact 35-mm camera— the first of its kind. Eleven years later, in 1924, Ernst Leitz II, the head of the company, went against his advisors' recommendation and decided to market Barnack's camera. He called it the "Leica"—for **Lei**tz **ca**mera. It popularized 35-mm photography and changed the history of cameras forever. Leica is still one of the world's leading camera brands today. (And Barnack is known as the father of 35-mm photography.)

KONICA

In 1873 pharmacist Sugiura Rokuemon, an early proponent of home photography in Japan, got permission to use the well-known name of his employer, the Konishiya apothecary in Tokyo, to begin selling photographic equipment. (The store was named after someone with the common Japanese surname "Konishi"—who exactly is not known. The "ya" ending means "store or "company.") Rokuemon later started his own company, called "Konishiroku," a combination of his name and the pharmacy's, and in 1903 started making cameras. In 1948 the company introduced its first 35-mm camera, the "Konica"—from **Koni**shiroku and **ca**mera. (Konica made 35-mm cameras for more than 50 years but stopped production in 2006. See "Minolta" on page 363 for more.)

OLYMPUS

This company was founded in Tokyo in 1919 under the name Takachiho Seisakusho. "Takachiho" came from Mt. Takachiho, a mountain that in ancient Japanese mythology was the home of the gods; "Seisakusho" simply means "factory" or "plant." The company introduced its first "Olympus" brand product—a microscope—in 1921. Why "Olympus"? Because Mt. Olympus, like Mt. Takachiho, was the mythical home of the gods—in this case from ancient Greek mythology, which made the name more appropriate for a European-based market. The company introduced the first cameras under the Olympus brand in 1936, and it's still one of the world's most respected camera brands today.

MINOLTA

Japanese businessman Kazuo Tashima founded this company in Osaka in 1928. In 1931 the company was incorporated under the name "Molta," and in 1933, the similar-sounding "Minolta" was trademarked. Both of these names are believed to have been derived from the phrase **M**echanism, **In**struments, **O**ptics, and **L**enses by **Ta**shima. But many sources say Tashima chose "Minolta" because it had a double meaning. Minolta, as pronounced in Japan, sounds like *minoru-ta*, Japanese for "mature rice field." Tashima chose the name because of that connection, this story goes, and because it reminded him of a proverb his mother taught him: "The ripest ears of rice bow their heads lowest," referring to humility. (Note: in 2003 Minolta merged with Konica to form Konica Minolta. In 2006 the company announced that it was getting out of the camera business and sold all its camera technology to Sony. Today Konica Minolta makes copiers, printers, and related imaging devices… but no cameras.)

CANON

In 1933 Goro Yoshida, a former camera repairman, founded Precision Optical Instruments Laboratory. Yoshida's mission: to "conduct research into quality cameras." What did that entail? He bought a German-made Leica II 35-mm camera and then, as he explained years later, took it apart:

> I just disassembled the camera without any specific plan, but simply to take a look at each part. I found there were no special items like diamonds inside the camera. The parts were made from brass, aluminum, iron and rubber. I was surprised that when these inexpensive materials were put together into a camera, it demanded an exorbitant price. This made me angry.

Pres. William H. Harrison's term was so short (32 days) that his wife never moved to Washington, D.C.

Yoshida set out to make his own camera, based on the Leica II but cheaper. In 1934 the first prototype was finished, and Yoshida, a devout Buddhist, named it the "Kwanon," after the Buddhist goddess of mercy. Yoshida left the company that year because of internal disagreements, but his partners carried on and in 1935 released the first Canon, based on Yoshida's prototype. Canon, of course, went on to become one of the world's most popular camera brands.

MINOX

In the 1969 film *On Her Majesty's Secret Service*, James Bond, played by George Lazenby, uses a tiny camera—not much larger than a pack of chewing gum—to surreptitiously take photos in the lair of the bad guy, Blofeld. That camera was a Minox. The "subminiature" camera brand was developed in 1936 by Walter Zapp, a 31-year-old undereducated German-Latvian photographer's apprentice—and part-time inventor. Origin of the name: in 1935, while Zapp was still working on the prototype, one of his friends jokingly suggested he call the camera a "Minox"—"min" was short for "miniature," and the suffix "-ox" was popular for cameras of the era. Zapp liked the sound of it...and that was that. (The tiny cameras were used in dozens of spy movies over the years. And for good reason: they were used by real spies, too—by both sides in World War II, throughout the Cold War, and well into the 1980s.)

*   *   *

WHY ARE PEOPLE...?

Thanks to the autofill feature, Google allows us to see what everyone else wants to know. We typed "Why are people" into Google and these options showed up, based on what people were asking in 2015. Why are people...

...racist

...homeless

...gay

...so mean

...ticklish

...so stupid

...joining ISIS

...left-handed

...against vaccines

...so rude

Beekeeping News

Can beekeeping stories bee weird? Yes, we beelieve they can.

MELT IN YOUR MOUTH

Beekeepers in the region around the town of Ribeauville in northeastern France were baffled in the fall of 2012 when their bees started producing blue, green, and even red honey. The beekeepers launched an investigation and after several days finally figured it out: instead of focusing on flowers in their search for sweet nectar, the bees were feeding on leftover M&M candies that were being processed in a nearby waste-processing plant, and the colorful candies, it turned out, were the source of the colorful honey. Unfortunately for the beekeepers, this was not a good thing: France's food purity standards do not allow the sale of honey not derived from plant nectar. Result: all the honey had to be thrown out. (The waste-treatment plant promised to keep their M&M waste covered in the future.)

SUITING UP

In 2015 a Chinese beekeeper named Gao Bingguo set the world record for "wearing bees." Gao, 55, stood there in his underwear while other beekeepers placed 12 queens onto his body and then dumped several boxes of worker bees at his feet. He smoked cigarettes to keep the bees off his face, and got stung an estimated 2,000 times. His record-setting suit weighed 240 pounds and totaled more than 1.1 million bees.

MEET MY ASS-OCIATE

Manuel Juraci, a beekeeper in the town of Itatira in western Brazil, decided in early 2012 that he needed a helper in his beekeeping business, so he enlisted his donkey, Boneco. But he couldn't take Boneco out on his honey-collecting rounds without some protection: the bees in the region are Africanized, or "killer," honeybees, notorious for their swarming attacks on people and animals. So he made a full-body bee-keeper suit for Boneco, complete with a mesh helmet not unlike the one he wears himself. And it worked: with Boneco to help carry the honey, within a year Juraci was the most successful of the region's roughly 120 beekeepers. Boneco remains the world's only known beekeeping donkey. And if you ever find yourself in the Itatira region, you might get a glimpse of Juraci and Boneco making their rounds through the area's dusty, desert landscape, looking like a pair of white-suited and helmeted astronauts…one of them is strangely donkey-shaped.

1st dog to earn a rank in the U.S. Army: Sgt. Stubby, for alerting his unit to a gas attack (WWI).

Where Did "CEO" Come From?

Uncle John is the CEO…of his mind. (Mrs. Uncle John is the CEO of everything else.) Now, here's the story behind those corporate officer acronyms we constantly hear about. (For more on corporations, go to page 469.)

ALPHABET SOUP

Corporations didn't have CEOs, CFOs, CIOs, and all the other acronym titles until fairly recently. Then, starting in the 1970s, there were suddenly CEOs and CFOs everywhere. Why the change? They were a result of changes in the internal structure of corporations in the booming post–World War II years. In the old days, companies were typically *vertically* oriented: they had a president at the top, then a vice president, and beneath that varying levels of managerial positions. In the 1960s, when corporations started to evolve into the sprawling, multinational behemoths they are today, that changed—corporations became more decentralized and more *horizontally* oriented with multiple departments. This led to the creation of more high-level positions—and eventually to the modern corporate officer system. (Plus: they probably just thought the "officer" names sounded cool.)

Now, a look at what some of those "C-suite" titles, as they're known, and what the people who hold them do.

Chairman. This isn't one of the "officer" titles, but it's still part of the story of corporate officer ranks. By law, a corporation must have a board of directors. This is a body of people, usually between seven and fifteen members, elected by the corporation's shareholders. The board's job: to represent those shareholders and to ensure that the company is doing all it can to maximize profits. A company's board is made up of a combination of employees—most often from top management—and people from outside the company. Board members elect a chairman, who is technically the most powerful person in a corporation since the board has the power to fire and hire the CEO and to override the CEO's decisions. In practice, however, the CEO often has the most power because CEOs are often also the company's owner or principal shareholder—and, in many corporations, the chairman.

CEO (Chief Executive Officer). The highest-ranking employee of a corporation. The CEO oversees management of the entire company and all its departments and is usually a company's visionary and leading strategist, as well as its public face. The CEO answers to the company's board of directors; all other corporate officers answer to the CEO. Famous CEOs: Lee Iacocca (Chrysler), Ken Lay (Enron), Steve Jobs (Apple), Meg Whitman (Hewlett-Packard), Mark Zuckerberg (Facebook), and Warren Buffett (Berkshire Hathaway).

COO (Chief Operating Officer). Not all corporations choose to have a COO—only around 40 percent of major corporations do. But in those companies, this person is seen as second in command, performing some of the duties of the CEO, and overseeing a firm's day-to-day operations. COOs are commonly considered the CEO's heir-apparent. (Tim Cook, for example, was Apple's COO under Steve Jobs and became CEO when Jobs resigned in 2011.)

CFO (Chief Financial Officer). As the title implies, this is the person in charge of a company's finances, including payroll, record keeping, reporting to financial watchdog agencies, financial planning regarding pensions and investments, and the overall maintenance of a company's financial health. This very high-ranking position usually reports directly to the CEO. (And it is becoming more common for CFOs to move up the ladder to become CEOs themselves.)

CIO (Chief Information Officer). It used to be that a company's IT person—the person who handles the company's information technology (basically everything that has to do with a company's computer and related systems)—was a lowly geek with very little power within a company. But starting in the mid-1980s, computers became such an important part of how companies do business that IT geeks started getting kicked upstairs—to the high corporate officer rank of CIO. Now nearly all major corporations have them. And while computer expertise is necessary for this position, over the decades, it has evolved into a much larger role. CIOs are now expected to be integral to a company's overall management team, with skills outside of technology. (However, CIOs seldom move up to become CEOs.) One of the first people to hold the title of CIO was Al Zipf, a pioneer in the field of electronic banking who became the first CIO of Bank of America in 1986.

CHO (Chief Happiness Officer). We're not joking—this is a real corporate officer title...although it's pretty rare. The term was first used—jokingly—in 2003, when McDonald's dubbed their mascot, Ronald McDonald, the company's "Chief Happiness Officer." About that time, corporations started focusing more on their employees' emotional well-being—the idea being that happy employees are more productive. By 2010 that had evolved into actual CHOs, with varied job

---

According to one estimate, Americans are sitting on $44 billion worth of unredeemed gift cards.

descriptions, but basically all focused on the satisfaction of employees and customers. They include Ginni Chen, who was the CHO of Silicon Valley tech startup iDoneThis from 2011 to 2014, and Tony Hsieh, who holds both CEO and CHO titles for the online shoe store Zappos.com.

EXTRA HELPING OF ALPHABET SOUP

There are literally dozens more corporate officer titles in use around the world today. Here are just some of them. (And none of them are made up...except one.)

CAO (Chief Accounting Officer)

CAO (Chief Analytics Officer)

CBDO (Chief Business Development Officer)

CBO (Chief Brand Officer)

CCO (Chief Customer Officer)

CDO (Chief Diversity Officer)

CDO (Chief Design Officer)

CHRO (Chief Human Resources Officer)

CISO (Chief Information Security Officer)

CIO (Chief Innovation Officer)

CIO (Chief Insurance Officer)

CIO (Chief Inspiration Officer)

CKO (Chief Knowledge Officer)

CLO (Chief Legal Officer)

CLO (Chief Learning Officer)

CLO (Chief Listening Officer)

CMO (Chief Medical Officer)

CMO (Chief Motivation Officer)

COO (Chief Observance Officer)

CPO (Chief People Officer)

CPO (Chief Privacy Officer)

CQO (Chief Quality Officer)

CRO (Chief Research Officer)

CRO (Chief Risk Officer)

CSO (Chief Science Officer)

CSO (Chief Security Officer)

CVO (Chief Visionary Officer)

CXO (Chief Experience Officer)

C3PO (Chief...um...wait...)

* * *

Celebrity Irony: The first song Kim Kardashian and Kris Humphries danced to at their wedding in 2011 was "Let's Stay Together" by Al Green. The marriage lasted 72 days.

Blue Language

Colorful law-enforcement lingo used by the boys (and girls) in blue.

Road Ninja: A car driving down the road without its lights on

Knock and Talk: Questioning a suspect or witness to a crime at his or her residence

J.D.L.R.: When something Just Doesn't Look Right

Fish Eye: What a "perp" does when he watches a cop out of the corner of his eye while pretending to look straight ahead

Warrant Wagon: A suspicious car that a cop thinks is likely to contain wanted criminals

Swivel Head: What the occupants of a warrant wagon often do when they realize a police car is following them

Sidewalk Inspector: A drunk passed out facedown on the pavement. (If they've passed out on the grass, they're "lawn ornaments.")

Ramp Rooster: A patrol car parked at a highway on- or off-ramp watching for speeders

Road Soda: An open container of alcohol in a vehicle

Edison Medicine: A Taser

Ride the Lightning: Get Tasered

Liquid Jesus: Pepper spray. (Combative suspects quickly "get religion.")

Squirrel Day: A day when all the nuts are out and about

Pumpkin Patch: The area where newly incarcerated inmates wait after changing into their orange jumpsuits

Litter Critter: Someone who serves community service time picking up trash along the side of the highway

Land Shark: A vicious dog guarding a prison yard

F.I.A.: A juvenile delinquent too young to go to jail ("Future Inmate of America")

Break Leather: To draw a gun from its holster

Yard Bird: A suspect who's caught while hiding in bushes

Organ Donor: A motorcyclist who isn't wearing a helmet

Donorcycle: Any motorcycle

In Egypt, a 3,000-year-old mummy was found with an artificial big toe.

Bad Words

You may use these words on a daily basis, but in certain parts of the world, they could land you in a whole lot of trouble.

HOOLIGAN. It's used to describe someone who is behaving badly. In Europe, it's also become synonymous with soccer fans who tend to become violent when they get a few beers in them. Where did the word come from? Some scholars think that it was inspired by an 1880s music hall song called "The O'Hooligan Boys." When the song was turned into a newspaper comic, "O'Hooligan" was shortened to just "hooligan." Others think it was inspired by Hooley's Gang, a group of thugs who caused trouble in London around the same time. Eventually, however, "hooligan" became an ethnic slur for any Irish immigrant living in England.

GYP. Typically used to refer to a rip-off or deception during a business transaction, it's thought to be short for "gypsy," a term for the Roma ethnic group of eastern Europe. Linguists believe "gypsy" comes from "Egyptian." The word "gypsy" dates back to at least the early 16th century. In those days, many northern Europeans used it to describe anyone with a dark complexion because it was thought that if the person wasn't pale-skinned, they *had* to be from Egypt. The use of "gyp" for "rip-off" developed from the belief that the Roma people were devious con artists.

BLOODY. The British use of "bloody" as a rude adjective dates back to the mid-17th century, and it was still considered offensive in the U.K. well into the 20th century. In 1914 an actress in the first performance of George Bernard Shaw's play *Pygmalion* improvised the line "not bloody likely," causing a scandal. Nowadays, "bloody" isn't considered all that offensive, and even characters in the Harry Potter films have uttered it a time or two. Nevertheless, many British publications still censor the word in their pages and use "b___y" when they absolutely must print it.

FANNY PACK. These zippered belt pouches were a big fad in the early 1990s (and are still used by tacky tourists everywhere). In North America, "fanny" is an innocuous euphemism for "buttocks," and the packs were supposed to be worn hanging over that part of the body. But don't call them "fanny packs" in the U.K., Australia, or Ireland. In those countries "fanny" is a fairly crass slang term for a woman's private parts, and the zippered pouch is called a "bum bag."

The first American foreign-aid bill provided relief to Venezuela after an earthquake in 1812.

Superfans

Sure, you support your favorite sports team. You wear the team ball cap, have a team logo decal in your car window, maybe even drink out of an official team mug. But do you love it enough to dress up in team colors and dance around in public?

CLIPPER DARRELL

Darrell Bailey loves the Los Angeles Clippers. In the 1990s, he was fired from his job as an electrician. He went home and turned on a Clippers game, only to hear the announcers talking about what losers the Clippers were—that the team was a lost cause and was never going anywhere. Bailey could relate—his boss had told him similar things that day. That's the moment Bailey decided to devote himself to being a die-hard Clippers fan. He eventually got another job, affording him the season tickets that would make him "Clipper Darrell." Since 2001, he's been at every Clippers home game wearing a tailored suit in Clippers colors (red and blue). In 2010 the Clippers briefly lost Darrell's support when they asked him not to use the word "Clipper" when making paid appearances. Darrell's renunciation of his fandom made national headlines and drew support from star Clippers players Blake Griffin and Chris Paul. The two sides eventually came to a compromise: Clipper Darrell would notify the organization whenever he was hired to appear at an event. He's now back in the stands at every game.

RONNIE "WOO WOO" WICKERS

There are two constants for the Chicago Cubs: waiting till next year (their last World Series win was in 1908), and Woo Woo Wickers. Born and raised on Chicago's South Side, Wickers has been going to Cubs games and yelling his signature cheer of "Cubs! Woo! Cubs! Woo!" at the top of his lungs since the late 1950s. Wickers has had a hard life: he spent much of the 1980s homeless and, unable to hold down a job, earned money by washing windows and making personal appearances at Cubs-centric events. And not everybody loves him—some people find his loud cheers disruptive and annoying. But for most Cubs fans, Woo Woo's unwavering optimism, even in the face of such criticism, makes him a living embodiment of baseball's lovable losers.

FIREMAN ED

New York City firefighter Edwin Anzalone started regularly attending New York Jets games at the Meadowlands in 1986. At every game, Ed's brother, Frank, would hoist him up on his shoulders while Ed (wearing his fireman's helmet) led the crowd in a chant of "J-E-T-S! JETS! JETS! JETS!" Dubbed "Fireman Ed" by local sports radio shows, he became one of the NFL's most famous cheerleaders and was even featured in a Football Hall of Fame exhibit about fandom in 1999. But it all came to an end on Thanksgiving in 2012. During a sold-out, nationally televised game, Jets quarterback Mark Sanchez ran into a teammate's backside and fumbled the ball, and an opposing team's player ran it back for a touchdown. Anzalone was so embarrassed by how Jets fans booed and taunted Sanchez that he left the game during halftime. Fireman Ed still goes to Jets games, but he sits in a different section and no longer wears his fireman's helmet.

ROBIN FICKER

The Washington Bullets of the 1980s never contended for an NBA championship. Despite the Bullets' losing ways, their arena was among opposing teams' least favorite places to play. Reason: Robin Ficker. For 12 years, the season-ticket holder heckled Michael Jordan, Patrick Ewing, Charles Barkley, and other NBA stars from his seats directly behind the visiting team's bench. Barkley was so impressed by his jeering that he even flew Ficker out to sit behind the Chicago Bulls bench during a playoff game against Barkley's Phoenix Suns. But Ficker's reign as the NBA's top heckler ended in 1997 when the Bullets (now called the Wizards) moved to their new arena, the MCI Center. For reasons unknown, Ficker's seat was relocated from behind the opposing bench to underneath the basket, robbing him of his ability to distract the other team's players and coaches. Ficker immediately canceled his season tickets and didn't attend another Wizards game until the 2014 playoffs.

WILD BILL HAGY

Except for maybe Cal Ripken Jr. (and his streak of 2,632 consecutive games played), the most consistent presence at Baltimore Orioles games in the 1970s and 1980s was Wild Bill Hagy. This superfan would stand on top of the home team's dugout and lead fans in chants of "O-R-I-O-L-E-S!" But in 1985 Memorial Stadium banned fans from bringing outside alcohol into the stands with them, and that made Hagy go wild. He staged a protest against the new rule by tossing his cooler onto the field. When police arrested Hagy for disorderly conduct, he vowed never to attend another Orioles game. But after the Orioles were sold and moved to a new stadium—Camden Yards—in 1992, Hagy agreed to return on special occasions to lead the "O-R-I-O-L-E-S!" chant... such as the night Ripken broke Lou Gehrig's consecutive game streak in 1995. Hagy died in 2007 and has since been inducted into the Orioles Hall of Fame.

Your abdominal muscles relax in space. That's one of the reasons why astronauts fart. (A lot.)

Under Pressure

Save this page of powerful quotations for when you're having "one of those days."

"You have power over your mind, not outside events. Realize this, and you will find strength."
—**Marcus Aurelius**

"Look at a day when you are supremely satisfied at the end. It's not a day when you lounge around doing nothing; it's when you've had everything to do, and you've done it."
—**Margaret Thatcher**

"The weak fall, but the strong will remain and never go under!"
—**Anne Frank**

"In the depth of winter, I finally learned that within me there lay an invincible summer."
—**Albert Camus**

"The strongest people are not those who show strength in front of us but those who win battles we know nothing about."
—**Unknown**

"If they hadn't told me I was ugly, I never would have searched for my beauty. And if they hadn't tried to break me down, I wouldn't know that I'm unbreakable."
—**Gabourey Sidibe**

"The difference between perseverance and obstinacy is that one comes from a strong will, and the other from a strong won't."
—**Henry Ward Beecher**

"Hardships often prepare ordinary people for an extraordinary destiny."
—**C. S. Lewis**

"You were given this life, because you are strong enough to live it."
—**Robin Sharma**

"I ask not for a lighter burden, but for broader shoulders."
—**Jewish Proverb**

"Big shots are only little shots who keep shooting."
—**Christopher Morley**

"Never be ashamed of a scar. It means you were stronger than whatever tried to hurt you."
—**Evan Carmichael**

"When you reach the end of your rope, tie a knot in it and hang on."
—**Franklin D. Roosevelt**

"A diamond is just a piece of charcoal that handled stress exceptionally well."
—**Unknown**

A newborn panda weighs less than a cup of coffee.

Wacky World Championships

We humans are so competitive that we can turn just about any mundane activity into a contest. But it takes real dedication to turn something like a drinking game or memorizing things into a "world championship."

THE WORLD SERIES OF BEER PONG

Where They Do It: Las Vegas

Details: If your idea of a sport is yelling, "You suck, bro!" as your inebriated opponent tries to throw a Ping-Pong ball into your beer, then beer pong is for you. The rules are simple: two teams of two face off from opposite ends of an eight-foot table. Each team sets up ten 16-ounce plastic cups of beer in a triangle (like bowling pins) on their end of the table. When a player successfully tosses a Ping-Pong ball into one of his opponent's cups, an opposing player chugs the beer and tosses the cup. The first team to clear the other side's cups is the winner.

History: Not surprisingly, beer pong (also called Beirut) originated on U.S. college campuses. In 2001 a student at Pittsburgh's Carnegie Mellon University named Billy Gaines had the idea to turn it into an organized sport. "I remember beating a few of the upperclassmen one night and thinking, wow, this is really fun," he said. "Beer pong doesn't require much setup, and even if you're not that good, you can still have the thrill of beating someone in a competition." A few years after graduating, Gaines quit his job as a patent attorney to start the World Series of Beer Pong. The first WSOBP took place in Las Vegas in 2006. The tournament lasts for four days and draws more than 1,000 entrants. **Top prize:** $50,000.

WORLD BATHTUBBING CHAMPIONSHIPS

Where They Do It: Llanwrtyd Wells, Wales, and Christchurch, New Zealand

Details: In this sport—not to be confused with "bathtub racing," which features speedboats that resemble bathtubs—"bathtubbers" drop an actual bathtub into a river, paddle it like a kayak, and hope it doesn't sink. (Many do sink, which is why each tub is outfitted with a big rubber ducky attached to a rope so it can be located at the bottom of the river.) Adding to the silliness, contestants wear "fancy dress" costumes, so you might see "Captain Jack Sparrow" trying to paddle a bathtub past

"Doctor Who" down the Avon River in New Zealand. That's where one round of the Bathtubbing World Championship takes place; the other is held in Wales.

In addition to the races, the festivities include a 100-meter individual speed dash, as well as "synchronized bathtubbing," in which two people face each other in a bathtub while one rows forward and the other rows backward in an attempt (often in vain) to get anywhere.

History: The annual event has been hosted by Green Dragon Activities, a Wales-based "adventure activity provider," since 2010, and draws in hundreds of bathtubbers from all over the world.

Top Prize: "The highest accolade—the prestigious Bath Tap."

MOBILE PHONE THROWING WORLD CHAMPIONSHIPS

Where They Do It: Savonlinna, Finland

Details: There are four categories—distance, junior, team, and freestyle (for "aesthetic creativity"). Examples of freestyle: throwing your phone while riding a unicycle or acting out a "breakup" with your phone before tossing it aside. But the biggest thrills come from the long-distance, over-the-shoulder throws. The strongest competitors can chuck their phone more than the length of a football field.

History: "This is the only sport where you can pay back all the frustrations and disappointments," says Christine Lund, who created mobile phone throwing in 2000. Her inspiration: recycling. Finns are among the world's highest per-capita cell phone users, and Lund was troubled to learn that most people weren't disposing of their old phones correctly; many ended up at the bottom of Finnish lakes. So she founded the contest to raise awareness of recycling. Several other mobile phone throwing competitions have since popped up around the world, including one in the United States, but the world championships still take place each August in Finland.

Top Prize: A new phone.

WORLD MEMORY CHAMPIONSHIPS

Where They Do It: In a different country each year

Details: The other games are played mostly for laughs. Not the World Memory Championships. This is one of the most intense contests you'll ever witness. Hundreds of "mental athletes" from dozens of countries compete in the three-day competition each year. The concept is simple: contestants are shown a series of things—playing cards, random words, historic dates, binary numbers, etc.—and then they must repeat as many as they can in the allotted time (usually one or five minutes). In 2013 Germany's Johannes Mallow set a new world record by recalling 501 digits (in order) in five minutes. The winner is whoever scores the most combined points in all 10 events.

History: The WMC was started in 1991 by author Tony Buzan, the inventor of the memory trick "mind mapping," along with chess grandmaster Raymond Keene. Reason: they thought that feats of memory should be included in the *Guinness World Records*, but there was no formal method to test memory, so they set up the WMC. "The great thing about memory sports is that everyone can compete in them," said Buzan. "All of us, no matter how appalling we might think our memories are, can—with the correct formulae and a little bit of practice—train our brains and memories to function ever more efficiently and effectively."

Top Prize: There is no prize money—just the title "World Memory Champion," and for the best of the best, a coveted spot in *Guinness World Records*.

WORLD SIGN SPINNING CHAMPIONSHIPS

Where They Do It: Las Vegas

Details: You've probably seen them spinning arrow-shaped signs on city sidewalks. They perform dance moves, toss their signs in the air, and do whatever it takes to alert you to the fact that Verizon is having a sale on Blackberries or that McDonald's now serves lattes. They're all employed by AArrow Advertising, and each January the most talented spinners from around the world—one from as far away as Croatia—convene in Las Vegas to compete for the title of champion spinner. Contestants are judged on "performance and showmanship, style and originality, and technicality of trick knowledge and execution." Prizes are given for trick of the year, best smile, most creativity, and best rookie. "It's definitely an art," said the 2015 winner, Laramie Rosenfield of Phoenix, Arizona, who added that, along with strength and technical skill, you need "personality." And a thick skin, too: "I've taken plenty of signs to the face."

History: In 2002 a group of sign spinners from Ocean Beach, California, formed AArrow Advertising. Their employees can be seen on street corners all over the world, spinning and twirling their arrow-shaped signs. "It's about getting attention and delivering the message—not just being another sign," said Mike Kenny, one of AArrow's cofounders. "More complicated moves attract more business." AArrow held the first WSSC in 2008.

Top Prize: $1,000.

THE SWAMP SOCCER WORLD CUP

Where They Do It: Scotland originally, but now it's held in a different country each year (the 2015 event was held in Turkey)

Details: Have you ever tried running as fast as you can through knee-high mud? Probably not, but now imagine trying to dribble a soccer ball

---

As many as 15% of adults sleepwalk or will at some point in their lives.

through that same mud and then kicking it. That's exactly what swamp soccer is. Naturally, there's a lot of falling down, but that's part of the fun that attracts dozens of teams from all over the world to the SSWC. Each team fields six players at a time, and they're encouraged to wear costumes. (In 2012 one team came dressed up as Smurfs, complete with blue body makeup.) But all competitors quickly become muddy-brown once they hit the field.

History: The sport was created in the 1990s by Jyrki "the Swamp Baron" Väänänen. His inspiration: Finnish cross-country skiers. They train by playing soccer in swamps, so Väänänen turned it into an organized sport. The first matches were held in actual swamps, but today the fields are made artificially. Heavy machinery tills the area, then it's filled with water. As the day goes on, the goop gets soupier and soupier, and the games get harder to play. It's quite tiring, so teams get as many substitutions as they want, but one of the rules is: "Boots cannot be changed during the game." Playing dirty is encouraged.

Top Prize: According to Swamp Soccer UK Ltd. director Stewart Miller, "The winners receive a hand-crafted trophy made from copper—the same skills used to design and manufacture whisky stills!"

THE AIR SEX WORLD CHAMPIONSHIPS

Where They "Do It": This barroom sport is played throughout the United States. The championships take place in different cities each year.

Details: Just like air guitar contests, in which people are judged on their ability to pretend to play an invisible guitar, at the World Air Sex Championships, contestants pretend to, well, you know. But first, they have to pretend to meet a partner, pretend to talk to him or her, and then pretend to get down to business. One rule: no nudity.

History: Comedian and pro wrestling manager Chris Trew got the idea after watching a 2006 YouTube video of people playing "air sex" at a Japanese karaoke bar. Noticing how much fun both the contestants and the crowd were having, Trew decided to bring the sport to America. "Sex is a big part of life," he explains, "and framing it in a way that allows us to laugh at it is a very powerful thing. We're making a difference in the world. We hope to one day make air sex an official sport at the Olympics." (Not likely.)

Top Prize: A championship belt along with "undying respect."

*   *   *

"Flops are part of life's menu." —**Rosalind Russell**

Dustbin of History: $am Upham

During the U.S. Civil War, New York printer $am Upham crippled the Confederacy's economy and hindered its ability to fight the war. Yet he was never officially honored, and is all but forgotten now.

LIKE PRINTING MONEY

Samuel C. Upham never intended to be the most prolific counterfeiter in modern history. In fact, some people insist he wasn't a counterfeiter at all, but a mere trafficker in souvenirs. In 1850 Upham opened a small patent medicine shop in Philadelphia, selling his own "Upham's Freckles, Tan & Pimple Banisher" and "Japanese Hair Stain," as well as newspapers, stationery, toiletries, sheet music, patriotic cards, and other self-published printed goods. He made a modest living for a decade, but then he got lucky: Abraham Lincoln was elected, the southern states seceded from the Union, and soon the Civil War was on. At first, Upham exploited patriotic sentiment by printing novelty cards—for example, caricatures with Confederate president Jefferson Davis's head on the body of a jackass. They sold modestly well, but it wasn't like he was printing money.

On February 24, 1862, though, opportunity struck. On that day, he was mystified when all of his copies of the *Philadelphia Enquirer* quickly sold out and people were clamoring for more. The reason, he discovered, was that the paper had printed a full-size facsimile of a five-dollar Confederate note on its front cover. Most Philadelphians, many with sons in the war, had never seen Confederate money before and were anxious to have a copy as a curiosity and keepsake.

EASILY IMPRESSED

Inspired, Upham ran to the *Enquirer* office and convinced someone to sell him the copper electroplate of the bill. With it, he printed 3,000 copies on high quality French paper. Upham wasn't sure if it was legal to print copies of money, even money of a "country" that wasn't officially recognized by the U.S. government. So to avoid confusion with the real thing (and get some advertising) Upham printed an inscription below the image: "Fac-simile Confederate Note—Sold Wholesale and Retail, by S. C. Upham, 403 Chestnut Street, Philadelphia."

The bills sold out quickly, so Upham bought some real banknote paper to print his "fac-similes" on. He also began advertising that

---

United Arab Emirates law requires mothers to breastfeed their newborns for two full years.

he'd pay good money for more examples of Confederate money and postage stamps to copy. Within months, he was offering 28 varieties, with denominations from 5 cents to $100, and selling them in his shop for a nickel each. However, his customer base was shifting from local Philadelphians buying souvenirs to mail-order buyers from all over the country, taking advantage of his bulk rate of 50 cents for 100 bills of assorted denominations, with even deeper discounts for larger quantities. One of his many ads, appearing in *Harper's Weekly*, read

CONFEDERATE MONEY $20,000! - TWENTY THOUSAND DOLLARS in fac-simile REBEL NOTES of different denominations sent, postpaid, to any address, receipt of $5 by S. C. Upham, 403 Chestnut Street, Philadelphia.

BILLS, BILLS, BILLS

Upham believed the inscription protected him from prosecution, since he wasn't fooling any of his customers into thinking they were getting the real thing. However, at some point he must have become aware that nothing stopped *them* from cutting the inscription off the bottom and passing the "fac-similes" as real. Upham's bills, with the inscription removed, became very popular with cotton smugglers who bought their wares in Confederate states and illegally shipped them north. (Ironically, because paper shortages in the South had forced the Confederate government to print on flimsy rice paper, Upham's money, printed on good-quality currency paper, was often preferred to the real thing.)

By April 1962, large quantities of Upham's bills had been discovered in Richmond, Virginia, the capital of the Confederacy, causing a great deal of alarm in the Confederate Treasury Department. The *Richmond Daily Dispatch* accused the United States government of sanctioning counterfeiting, and warned its readers against "Yankee scoundrelism…of the most depraved and despicable sort."

PAPER HANGING

The Confederate Congress responded to Upham and copycat counterfeiters by making counterfeiting a capital crime. One senator denounced Upham as having done more harm to the Confederacy than Union general George McClellan's army. But the renegade country had no extradition treaty with the United States, so Upham—who later bragged that the Confederacy government had offered a $10,000 reward for his capture or death—didn't feel particularly endangered. In fact, he claimed that he was doing his patriotic duty by sabotaging the country's enemy and shortening the war.

Some on both sides of the Mason-Dixon line believed that the U.S. government was behind Upham's operation, possibly even providing the banknote paper. But in reality, Upham's counterfeit bills were causing consternation in the U.S. Treasury as well. Some government officials feared that the Confederates would start counterfeiting American money in retaliation and wanted to close down Upham's printing business. There were already signs that the influx of bad bills was devaluing Confederate currency and destabilizing its economy—what if the same thing happened in the United States?

There was, however, a legal loophole: Since the United States did not recognize the Confederacy as a legitimate country, copying its banknotes—especially with Upham's disclaimer attached—wasn't actually illegal. Or at least that was the excuse U.S. Secretary of War Edwin Stanton gave for not interfering with Upham's business.

While cotton smugglers and others transported the notes into the Confederacy, Union soldiers also routinely carried a king's ransom of counterfeits for when they pushed into enemy territory. One private stationed in Virginia wrote to his brother back home in Pennsylvania, asking him to send more fake $10 bills: "The boys buy a good many of them around camp for ten cents apiece and after steeping them in coffee to give them color they would take them to the Farmers and pass them for good Confederate Money."

OUT OF THE MONEY AND INTO THE DUSTBIN

After 18 months, Upham retired from making his "fac-similes," having printed in the neighborhood of 1,564,050 various bills, totaling nearly $15 million worth of fake Confederacy currency (nearly a half billion dollars in today's money).

Why did he stop? He was a victim of his own success. First of all, he inspired too many counterfeiting competitors. His counterfeits made up 1–3 percent of the Confederacy's total money supply, triggering widespread inflation and a deep suspicion about the rebel currency. By August 1863, when he quit his counterfeiting, a Confederate dollar's buying power was so low that it took $10 to buy what once sold for $1. When Confederate cotton merchants began accepting only U.S. greenbacks for payment, Upham decided the money simply wasn't worth counterfeiting.

CRIME DID PAY...EVENTUALLY

Upham died in relative obscurity in 1885, leaving an estate of $4,889.97—nothing like the millions he'd printed, but still quite a bit of money at the time. And if your heirloom family cache of Confederate dollars turns out to contain only Upham fakes, should you be disappointed? Nope. Among collectors, his counterfeits often sell for more than the real thing.

Art Now, Pay Later

It's a truism that many great artists are never fully appreciated (or well paid) in their own lifetimes. Don't believe it? Here are some examples.

The Artist: Amedeo Modigliani was born in 1884 to a poor family in Italy; his childhood was fraught with battles against tuberculosis and typhoid fever. But Modigliani survived into adulthood and became a painter, apprenticing under the Italian master Guglielmo Micheli. Following a move to Paris in 1906, where he became friends with members of the burgeoning Modernist art movement, Modigliani honed his skills and developed his painting style of portraits with "long faces." Still, his life would end tragically. His tuberculosis returned, made worse by the drugs and alcohol he used to deal with his physical pain, and he died at age 35. His wife, art student Jeanne Hébuterne, eight months pregnant and overcome with grief, committed suicide.

The Painting: In 2010 Sotheby's auction house sold the 1917 painting *Nude Sitting on a Divan* for $68.9 million.

The Artist: Wang Meng was a 14th-century Chinese painter, known as one of the Four Masters of the Yuan Dynasty. All four men were widely recognized for their intricately rich and detailed ink drawings of Chinese landscapes. But after the fall of the ruling Mongols to the Ming Dynasty in 1368, intellectuals like Meng were persecuted by the new rulers. Meng was accused of conspiring against the new government, and was imprisoned for the final years of his life. Most of his art was destroyed; only a few dozen works survive.

The Painting: In 2011 his 650-year-old painting, *Zhichuan Resettlement*, sold for just over $62 million.

The Artist: If Paul Cézanne's father knew how much his son's work would one day sell for, he might have been more accepting of his career choice. The Post-Impressionist painter never won the respect of his father or of the established art world, but he did earn the praise of up-and-coming artists like Henri Matisse and Pablo Picasso, who once called Cézanne "my one and only master." The artist lived off the small inheritance left to him by his estranged father until he died from pneumonia in 1906 at age 67.

The Painting: Cézanne's *The Card Players* holds the record for fetching the largest sum for an individual painting at auction. The sultan of Qatar paid a staggering $250 million for it.

Is That Jerry Garcia?

It's easy to understand how the spiritually inclined might interpret the face of Jesus on a pierogi as a sign from above (see page 24)…but Jerry Garcia in a chunk of horseradish?

RINGO STARR IN A DROP OF WATER

R**Seen by:** James Dacey of *Physics World* magazine

Details: In 2009 Dacey was reporting on a Duke University study of the water-repelling properties of leaves. He noticed that some high-speed photos of a droplet bouncing off a leaf bore a striking resemblance to the Beatles drummer, mop top and all.

What Happened: Dacey posted the pictures on the *Physics World* website, prompting a flurry of comments, some from people who thought the droplet looked more like George Harrison. Either way, "this is the first time I have seen the image of a Beatle in a physics experiment," he told London's *Daily Telegraph* newspaper.

JERRY GARCIA IN A JAR OF HORSERADISH

Seen by: Tom Haupert, 50, of Naples, Florida

Details: Haupert bought a jar of Good-N-Hot Fresh Ground Horseradish in the summer of 2012 and a few weeks later noticed that one chunk, visible through the transparent plastic jar, was the spitting image of Grateful Dead guitarist Jerry Garcia.

What Happened: Haupert, a "Dead Head" who saw the band 43 times before Garcia's death in 1995, converted a corner of his refrigerator (next to the Bud Light) into a shrine to the dead Dead guitarist.

Update: At last report Haupert was looking for a more permanent home for his treasure to protect it from hurricanes. "I don't know what would happen if I lost power to the refrigerator," he said.

MICHAEL JACKSON ON A SONOGRAM

Seen by: Dawn Kelley and her partner, William Hickman, who live in Sunderland in the north of England

Details: When Kelley was about five months pregnant with her seventh child in late 2009, she went to the hospital for her 20-week sonogram appointment. One of the images produced looked like the King of Pop, complete with his famous single white glove. "We were looking at the pictures and I just saw Jacko there with his sunglasses and his hair," Hickman told the *Sunderland Echo*. "I showed my daughter Ami, who's six, and she saw it straight away, so I thought, 'well, if she can see it too, it's not just me.'"

What Happened: In March 2010, Kelley gave birth to a healthy baby girl named Lilly May...who (to both parents' relief) looks nothing like Jackson. "None of us are really Michael Jackson fans," said Hickman. "I mean I like him, but we're not crazy about him or anything."

OSAMA BIN LADEN ON A CRAB

Seen by: The Canfield family of Everett, Washington

Details: In the summer of 2012, the Canfields went crab fishing off Hat Island, near Everett. When it was time to pull the crab pots out of the water, someone videotaped them as they sorted through their haul. It wasn't until the Canfields got back home with their catch and watched the video that someone noticed that the markings on the underside of one of the crabs bore a striking resemblance to the infamous planner of the 9/11 attacks.

What Happened: The crab was a female, and state law requires that females be thrown back into the water. By the time the Canfields saw the video, the crab was already back on the bottom of Puget Sound.

LORD VOLDEMORT ON A HEAD OF GARLIC

Seen by: Anwar Siddiqui of Coventry, England

Details: Siddiqui picked a head of garlic from her garden in July 2011. When she washed off the dirt, she saw an evil face staring back at her. "The garlic is in the shape of a head, with eyes, eyebrows, ears and a nose," she told the *Coventry Telegraph* newspaper. She wasn't sure who it was, but when she showed it to her son, he said it was the *Harry Potter* villain Lord Voldemort.

What Happened: Siddiqui's keeping the garlic, just like she kept the heart-shaped potato she found on Valentines Day. "I don't know what we'll have next," she said. "There's plenty more shoots in my back garden, so who knows what will turn up."

ILLINOIS IN A PLATE OF SCRAMBLED EGGS

Seen by: Al Pattarozzi, 77, a retiree living in Paragould, Arkansas

Details: In the summer of 2013, Meals on Wheels delivered a breakfast of oatmeal, scrambled eggs, sausage, gravy, and toast to Pattarozzi. It wasn't his first such breakfast, but this one was special: "I'm cutting away at it and I look down and there it is. It's the state of Illinois!" Pattarozzi told the Springfield (IL) *State Journal-Register*. Sure enough, the eggs were shaped just like his home state.

What Happened: If you're hoping to buy the eggy Land of Lincoln on eBay, you're out of luck: Pattarozzi took a picture for posterity, then ate the state. "It was awful good," he said.

Familiar Phrases

Now for the origins of some common phrases. Let 'er rip!

PONY UP

Meaning: To pay someone what they are owed

Origin: *"Pony* has meant 'a small amount of money' in England since the late 18th century, when it specifically meant 'the sum of twenty-five pounds sterling' (which was actually a hefty chunk, but go figure). To pony up thus meant 'to settle a small debt.'" (From *The Word Detective*, by Evan Morris)

LET 'ER RIP!

Meaning: Get started, get going

Origin: "*Oxford English Dictionary* reports 'Let 'er rip!' as early as 1853. That this phrase comes from St. Louis strengthens the belief that the engine of a steamboat, or the boat herself, was the 'female' encouraged to 'rip' along at her topmost speed. Perhaps the imminent danger of being ripped open by a sunken tree added to the appropriateness of the cry, but it is unlikely that the R.I.P. found on tombstones played a part in this phrase's history." (From *Phrase and Word Origins*, by Alfred H. Holt)

GOT IT FOR A SONG

Meaning: When a product or service was much less expensive than its perceived value

Origin: "The 'song' was a long poem called 'The Faerie Queene,' presented to Queen Elizabeth I by Edmund Spenser in 1590. When Lord Burleigh heard that the Queen intended to pay Spenser £100 for it, he exclaimed, 'What! All this for a song?' The incident was widely reported and the phrase became English slang." (From *Red Herrings & White Elephants*, by Albert Jack)

PORK BARREL

Meaning: Legislation that includes several of the politician's "pet" projects that can add up to a lot of money

Origin: "It was once the custom in county stores to keep available an open barrel of salt pork. Certain persons of the community would, at times, dip into the pork barrel and help themselves. And so we came to use the term 'pork barrel' to indicate a common fund of money into which our legislators dip for their own personal projects." (From *Why Do We Say It?*, by Frank Oppel)

The Eskimo Pie was originally called the I-Scream-Bar.

Typo's Happpen

Enjoy these spelling goofs big and small from present and passed.

• An ad displayed in shopping malls for Creative Kids Software read: "So Fun, They Won't Even Know Their Learning."

• An ad for a Pentax Optio M60 Compact Digital Camera made it sound more like a laxative: "Powered by lithium batteries, you'll always be ready for a sh*t." (That asterisked letter was not an "o").

• John Barge's 2014 gubernatorial campaign got off to a bad start. The front page of his official website featured a photo of the smiling candidate next to the words "John Barge: Georgia's Next Govenor." (It's supposed to be "Gover̲nor.") Barge, a former teacher, was the Georgia state school superintendent. His explanation: "It's just a typo. Typos happen." (He lost.)

• WNDU, a local NBC affiliate in South Bend, Indiana, answered its own question when it displayed this question on the screen: "School Two Easy For Kids?"

• In 1940 the *Washington Post* ran this headline about President Franklin Delano Roosevelt: "FDR IN BED WITH COED." He was actually in bed…with a cold. (The president thought the goof was so funny that he called the *Post* and asked for 100 copies.)

• Former New York City mayor Ed Koch died in 2013 at 88 years old, but according to his tombstone, he was only 70. That's because the carver put "1942" as Koch's birth year. He was born in 1924.

• A billboard for the fast food chain Hardee's advertised its burgers as having "100% Anus Beef."

• In a 2013 school yearbook was a picture of a baseball player with the caption "Congrats to our Home Run Hitler!" (It caused quite a Führer.)

• In 1904 a malted milk drink called Ovomaltine was released in Switzerland. When it was exported to Britain five years later, a typo on the trademark application misspelled it as "Ovaltine." That's what it's been called in English-speaking countries ever since.

• Seen on a sign in a parking lot: "Illegally Parked Cars Will Be Fine." (That's nice.)

The Dog Ate My...

More stories of what happens when good dogs eat bad.

Dog: Tucker, a four-year-old Rottweiler mix owned by Lois Matykowski of Stevens Point, Wisconsin

Details: When Matykowski's wedding band went missing in 2008, she suspected that Tucker, her resident "food bandit," might have eaten it. She followed him for more than a week, checking every time he did his business to see if the ring was in it, but it never appeared.

Six years later, on a hot June afternoon, Matykowski and her granddaughter were sitting in her yard eating Popsicles. As Matykowski got up to get some water for Tucker, now 10, the dog wolfed down her granddaughter's Popsicle, stick and all. The veterinarian told her that feeding the dog some Vaseline smeared between slices of bread would bring the stick back up, and a few hours later it did. Two days after that, Tucker barfed again, and as Matykowski cleaned up the mess, she saw that it had brought up something else: "I look in the paper towel and here is my wedding ring. I kid you not, it was in Tucker's puke!" she told a reporter. (The vet suspects the Popsicle stick dislodged the ring from wherever it had been stuck for six years.) "My friends have been telling me, 'I want a dog that throws up diamonds.' Who wouldn't, right?"

Dog: Charlie, a Newfoundland owned by Terry Morgan, a retired pub owner in Cockwood, Devon, in southwest England

Details: When Morgan owned his pub, he used the alarm on his Casio wristwatch to remind him when it was time to announce last call. After he retired, he never turned off the alarm, and one night in July 2014 he heard it go off right on schedule at 10:55 p.m., near where Charlie was laying. But the sound was muffled. "I thought he was lying on it," he told reporters. "Only when I rolled him over did I realize it was inside him." Morgan rushed Charlie to the vet, who informed him that the watch would have to be removed surgically. It probably wasn't the dog's first visit to the doctor, because as soon as he saw the vet's hypodermic needle, he let out a terrified howl and barfed up the watch, saving Morgan the price of the £1,000 surgery (about $1,600).

Dog: Jack, a 13-year-old Jack Russell terrier owned by Tim Kelleher, who lives New York City

Details: In March 2013, Kelleher finished eating a bagel and left the crumpled-up bag on his desk. That's where Jack found it a short time

---

Marrying younger than age 25 dramatically raises the odds that the marriage will end in divorce.

later. As the dog was ripping the bag apart, he knocked it and a jar of pennies onto the floor. Chasing the bag, he licked the last of the crumbs from the floor—and also swallowed some of the pennies, though how many (if any) did not become apparent until after he started vomiting and Kelleher took him to the veterinarian. (Because pennies are made mostly of zinc, which is toxic to dogs, swallowing even one can be fatal if it is not removed in time.) An X-ray revealed that the pennies were still in Jack's stomach and fortunately had not yet made their way to his intestines. That was good news: rather than having to remove the pennies surgically, the vet attached a small net to a medical instrument called an endoscope, inserted it into Jack's throat, and over the next two hours removed five pennies at a time until 111 had been recovered. Jack made a full recovery; Kelleher got to keep the change.

Dog: Augie, a two-year-old greater Swiss mountain dog owned by Kelley Davis of Apex, North Carolina

Details: When a dog swallows pennies, it's painful to the dog. When a dog swallows paper currency, it's painful to the owner. That's the lesson Kelley Davis learned in 2009 when she went to deposit five $20 bills and three $100 bills, only to realize after she got to the bank that the $400 was not in her pocket. The last time she'd seen the money was when she counted it out on her dresser while Augie was with her. Suspecting the worst, she went back home and took Augie for a long walk. Sure enough, the dog started paying doo-vidends...with *interest*: though Davis was sure she was missing only $400, over the next day and a half, Augie pooped out the chewed, torn, and partially digested remains of $420 worth of bills. (Davis figures she must have miscounted the money.) "We're going to send it to the U.S. Treasurer to see if they can reimburse the cash," she said after the last remnants of dog dough were recovered.

Dog: Liza, an 18-month-old Labrador retriever owned by Mark Meltz and his fiancée, Hillary Feinberg, of Ipswich, Massachusetts

Details: Liza swallowed her owner's wedding ring too, and she couldn't have done it at a worse time: the day before Meltz and Feinberg were to be married in September 2000. The day before the wedding, Liza had a coughing fit when Feinberg took her for a walk. But it wasn't until the following morning, just a few hours before the wedding, when Meltz couldn't find Feinberg's ring that he realized what must have happened. He rushed Liza to the veterinarian to have the dog X-rayed (diagnosis confirmed), then raced to his wedding. When the time came to present the ring to his wife, he gave her the X-ray instead—the ring was still inside the dog. "I explained it and the guests exploded with laughter," Meltz said afterward. Bonus: Liza barfed up the ring, saving the risk and expense of having it surgically removed.

Nothing to sneeze at: Americans use more than 112 million pounds of black pepper per year.

What's the Pointe?

These ballet facts will keep you on your toes.

When a ballerina dances on her toes, it's called going *en pointe*. A 2011 science fair project tested the amount of force on a dancer's toe while en pointe. It measured 40.81501 Newtons per square centimeter—the equivalent of over 8,000 pounds per square foot of pressure.

• The dancers of the New York City Ballet go through around 350 Band-Aids every week.

• Ballet terms such as *pirouette* are in French because King Louis XIV founded the first ballet academy in France in 1661, and the classic steps, turns, and leaps were all developed there.

• One tutu requires around 10 yards of tulle (a netlike fabric) and takes about 40 hours to sew.

• On a ship traveling to America in 1840, a "stocky sailor" tried to rob Austrian ballerina Fanny Elssler. She kicked him so hard that he died a few days later.

• In 2013 Pittsburgh Steelers nose tackle Steve McLendon attended a weekly class at Pittsburgh's Ballet Theatre and credited it with strengthening his feet and ankles.

• The first production of *The Nutcracker* in 1892 was a flop: neither the St. Petersburg critics nor the audience liked it. It was actually choreographer George Balanchine's 1954 production at the New York City Ballet that established it as a Christmas tradition.

• Dancers learn the technique of "spotting" to be able to turn without becoming dizzy. As they spin, they fix their eyes on one object, and that focus helps them maintain their balance.

• The shoes that ballerinas wear are called *pointe* shoes. It's a common misconception that wood is used in the shoe's toe, but it's really more like papier-mâché. The toe, called the "box," is made from layers of paper, fabric, and/or cardboard hardened with coats of glue.

• The male equivalent for the term "ballerina" is "danseur."

• In 2013 Sergei Filin, artistic director of Moscow's Bolshoi Ballet, suffered permanent eye damage after someone threw acid in his face. Dancer Pavel Dmitrichenko arranged the attack. Reason: "Personal hostile relations linked to their professional activities."

It's Taking Over My Brain!

As you may recall from your eighth-grade biology class, protozoa are single-celled creatures. Here's something your teacher probably didn't cover: There's a protozoan that can alter what you think, feel, and do. It may sound like science fiction...but it's not.

INVASION!

Imagine this plot for a movie: A trusted pet helps a race of microscopic invaders enter your body. Once inside, they affect your brain. You might start taking more risks and become more outgoing, or you might become paranoid. Strange smells, repugnant to most people, might suddenly give you great pleasure. And there's a chance of blindness, insanity, and death.

Fairly ordinary science fiction, right? Nope. Because the invaders, protozoa known as *Toxoplasma gondii*, are real. What's worse, they've already infected billions of people—maybe even some of your friends, neighbors, family members...and you.

HERE, KITTY KITTY

Ironically, all that *T. gondii* want is to find their way inside a susceptible cat so they can wake up from suspended animation, break out of their protective shells, and start to reproduce. They can only do this in the lining of a cat's intestines, but when they do, they launch huge quantities of their spawn with each load of cat poop. And time is urgent, because they have only a few weeks before the cat's immune system surrounds and neutralizes them.

Once outside of their host, the newly encapsulated protozoa go into a state of suspended animation. They can remain that way for weeks, months, or years—alive and ready, no matter how much the cat poop gets trampled, turned into compost, spread on crops, or eaten by scavengers. They wait patiently, hoping to get inside another cat.

They have evolved certain strategies to do that: one is by packaging themselves inside a slow, easy-to-catch mouse. (Seriously.) But mice are rarely that slow—they're usually fast, smart, and very cautious about avoiding cats. The protozoa make them easier for cats to catch by a kind of mind control, which not only affects mice, but other unsuspecting mammals as well...including humans.

During WWII, the U.S. military commandeered 40% of all pickle production.

ROBOMOUSE

Of course there's no guarantee that a cat will see, chase, or catch a toxo-plasma-laden mouse. So *T. gondii* have evolved to tilt the balance to the cat's favor. They do that by altering the mouse's body chemistry. After the protozoa invade a mouse's body, they migrate to its muscles and into its brain. After a short sickness, the mouse's immune system combats the invaders by permanently encasing them in cysts throughout the mouse's body, where they go into suspended animation again.

Here's how the protozoa fight back: they produce certain chemicals from inside the cysts, notably dopamine and a brain messenger called GABA. When those powerful chemicals are released by protozoa trapped in or near the brain, they cause the mice to act in ways that greatly increase their chance of being eaten by cats. For one, the mice, which usually avoid anything that smells like cat urine, suddenly become attracted to it, so they seek it out. Infected mice also act less fearful, move around in a way that makes them more visible to cats, and hang out in open spaces instead of creeping around its dark corners. All of these behaviors are essentially a huge "EAT ME" sign for cats on the prowl. The mice do get eaten, and the protozoa, released from their cysts during digestion, find themselves exactly where they want to be.

OF MICE AND MEN

It's not just mice and cats. Some other mammals—including humans—and some birds can be infected, too. They experience the short, flulike sickness, the migrating of the protozoa into muscles and brain, and the surprising changes in the way the brain acts and reacts.

Studies have found that people infected with toxoplasma exhibit slower response times and have higher rates of schizophrenia, OCD, mood disorders, and depression, but a reduced level of fear, anxiety, and sexual arousal. Strangely, there's also a gender difference: infected men are somewhat more likely to be rule-breakers, introverted, oblivious to fashion and social cues, suspicious, and attracted to the scent of cat urine. Infected women, by contrast, are more likely to be rule-followers, extroverted, stylish, promiscuous, sensitive to others' opinions, trusting, and *repulsed* by the smell of cat urine. Infected men and women are both more likely to be neurotic—prone to guilt, self-doubt, and insecurity—and more accident-prone: infected drivers and pedestrians were found to be almost three times more likely to be involved in a traffic accident.

Another odd effect: latent toxoplasmosis may also have contributed to wine and perfume production. It's estimated that 45 percent of the French are infected, and two of France's trademark products unwittingly exploit the fact that infected men are attracted to the scent of cat urine. One is Chanel No. 5, which reportedly mixes floral scents with those of peelike sexual hormones from the African civet. The other is sauvignon blanc wine, which contains a chemical byproduct that's similar to a pheromone in cat urine. (Believe it or not, "cat pee" is a common, and usually favorable, description in wine reviews.)

PARASITE LOST

Most people who get infected don't even know it, or at most feel vaguely sick for a week or two before their immune systems kick in. Afterward, when the infection goes into its latent stage, victims will likely exhibit only a few fairly subtle behavioral changes. However, people who are most vulnerable to the condition—babies and people with suppressed immune systems—can get seriously ill when first infected, with damage to their internal organs, brain, and eyes.

However, your best bet is to avoid getting infected in the first place. You can get toxoplasmosis from undercooked meat, unwashed vegetables, and contaminated water, or from being born to a mother who is in the two-week active infection stage, before her immune system neutralizes the protozoa. In North America, toxoplasmosis often comes in on little cat feet and is contracted through handling cat feces, which is why doctors recommend that pregnant women and people with compromised immune systems avoid contact with cat litter boxes.

Does this mean you should give away your cat? No. Indoor cats don't usually get the parasite; outdoor cats can pass it along for only about three weeks of their lives, usually just to the point when they're old enough to begin hunting. Then, as with humans, they become permanently immune to getting an active case of toxoplasmosis again.

It does, however, mean that you should wash vegetables and cook meat well to kill the parasite. And one more word of warning: don't flush cat poop down the toilet. Marine birds and mammals can get toxoplasmosis from sewage and rain runoff. A study of dead sea otters in California found that 13 percent were killed by *T. gondii* protozoa.

'TIL DEATH DO YOU PART

There is no cure for the dormant stage of infection yet. If the protozoa are inside you now, they'll likely stay there until you die. The good news is that the effects, if any, are usually pretty subtle. It might be possible to manage even the mental effects that are more troublesome: experiments in infected mice found that dopamine-blocking drugs brought their behavior back to normal. And if there's any comfort in knowing that you've got company, studies estimate that 10–20 percent of Americans, and up to half of all people on Earth, have it. In fact, more people worldwide are infected with toxoplasma than are connected to the Internet.

Dining with the Stars

Lots of movie and TV stars invest their fortunes in restaurants…ignoring the fact that restaurants are a notoriously risky investment with razor-thin profit margins. Here are some celebrities who learned that the hard way.

STEVEN SPIELBERG. In front of the Century City Shopping Center in Beverly Hills sat a gigantic bright yellow submarine. It was Dive!, a 300-seat restaurant that served gourmet submarine sandwiches. Spielberg opened it in 1994 (with film producer Jeffrey Katzenberg) because he claimed he couldn't find anyplace in Los Angeles that made sandwiches he liked. The inside of Dive! was just as stunning as the outside, with monitors displaying underwater special effects and submarine control panels, gauges, and throttles. Every half hour the sub would "dive"—the building would shake as sirens blared and lights flashed. It was pretty successful…until Spielberg expanded, opening locations in Las Vegas and Barcelona. The whole enterprise went under for good in 1999.

FLAVOR FLAV. After a series of VH1 reality shows revitalized his career, in 2011 the Public Enemy rapper invested in a restaurant—Flav's Fried Chicken in Clinton, Iowa, the 18th-largest city in the state. After checks to employees bounced numerous times, the restaurant shut down, only four months into its existence.

PETER FONDA. Fonda is probably best known for his role in the classic biker movie *Easy Rider*. In 1993 he opened Thunder Roadhouse, a restaurant on the Sunset Strip inspired by dingy biker bars—only cleaner, and catering to "RUBs" ("rich urban bikers"). In fact, there wasn't a single motorcycle worth less than $30,000 in the parking lot on the day in 1997 when a fire destroyed Thunder Roadhouse.

HULK HOGAN. During his 1980s "Hulkamania!" heyday, Hogan was one of the most famous and best-paid athletes on earth, but he made a lot of bad business decisions after his retirement. For one, he turned down the chance to be the face of a tabletop grill (manufacturers went with boxer George Foreman instead). Not wanting to lose out on millions again, Hogan jumped on the celebrity restaurant bandwagon in 1995 as the face of (and an investor in) Pastamania, a quick-serve spaghetti restaurant in Minnesota's Mall of America. Customers evidently couldn't make the connection between wrestling and noodles, and Pastamania went out of business in less than a year.

Most fish can see you peering at them in a fish tank.

EVA LONGORIA. Shortly after her Los Angeles restaurant Beso filed for bankruptcy in 2011, Longoria (*Desperate Housewives*) opened another restaurant—this time in Las Vegas—called SHe. The one thing stranger than the odd capitalization in the restaurant's name: its concept. It was a "female-focused" steakhouse, which meant that it served small steaks. That's it—they cut the meat into smaller portions. SHortly after a health department inspector cited the restaurant for 32 health code violations in 2014, SHe SHut down.

THE BALDWIN BROTHERS. The two most famous Baldwins who aren't Alec—Stephen and William—joined forces (and funds) in 1999 to open Alaia, named for Stephen's six-year-old daughter. Located on New York City's Fifth Avenue, the two-story restaurant had a bar upstairs and a Mediterranean restaurant downstairs. After opening to great fanfare and then languishing for a few months, the restaurant changed its name to Luahn and became a lounge. When that didn't bring in business either, Stephen Baldwin dropped out, and Luahn became Society 5. By 2001, it was closed.

TOM BERENGER. In 1994 the macho character actor (*Platoon, Major League*) became the chief investor in a restaurant on New York's Upper East Side called Twins. And that was the theme: 37 pairs of identical twins worked as the restaurant's hostesses, bartenders, and waitstaff. The food was twin-themed, too, such as "Twin Burgers" and the Paté Duke (although on *The Patty Duke Show*, the characters were identical cousins, not twins). Twins who came in to Twins enjoyed two-for-one drink specials. By the time Twins closed in 2000, more than 100,000 identical twins had patronized the restaurant. (Fun fact: Tom Berenger doesn't have a twin.)

*　　*　　*

STRETCHING THE TRUTH: THE RUBBER CHICKEN

Rubber chickens became a fad during the French Revolution (1789–1799), when soldiers dangled them from their muskets for luck. Why? It's unclear. But it doesn't matter. The French soldier story was actually spread by Loftus International, a Utah-based novelty company founded in 1939…which also happens to be the world's largest manufacturer of rubber chickens. The true origin: Somebody at Loftus came up with it. The company invented the French myth because it's more interesting (and funnier) than the truth.

Odd but true: Ducks walk pigeon-toed.

YouTube U.

We all use YouTube to look up household tips like how to fix a dishwasher or how to tie a tie. But it turns out there are millions of odd "instructional" YouTube clips out there. For example, you can learn…

- How to trick people into thinking you're good looking

- How to make balloon chocolate bowls

- How to make a paper crossbow

- How to chair dance to Christmas music

- How to give a possum a pedicure

- How to make slime goo

- How to make pickle pancakes

- How to turn on a light

- How to make your nose look smaller

- How to pop bubble wrap

- How to give medication to goats

- How to pronounce "Frappuccino"

- How to make a dog sling out of a shirt

- How to fall on a snowboard

- How to see in the dark

- How to peel potatoes

- How to make your hair grow faster

- How to fold a T-shirt in two seconds

- How to mildly annoy your dog

- How to make your own lipstick

- How to do cat yoga

- How to know your body is aroused

- How to give a good hug

- How to survive a lightning strike

- How to make an igloo house

- How to never lose in Tic-Tac-Toe when you start

- How to draw a perfect circle

- How to cut the sleeves off your T-shirt

- How to use a daddy saddle

- How to manage tattoo pain

- How to make your own natural colon cleanser

- How to be awake when you dream

China produces two-thirds of the world's garlic—over 13 billion pounds annually.

Three Weird Deaths

If you gotta go, you might as well make your final act one to remember.

TOUCHY SUBJECT

Queen Sunandha Kumariratana was one of the four wives of King Chulalongkorn of Siam (present-day Thailand). In 1880, when she was just 19 (and pregnant), she was being transported by barge to the royal family's summer residence, the Bang Pa-In Royal Palace, north of Bangkok. The barge capsized, and even though there was a crowd of onlookers that by all accounts could have saved her, no one dared. Reason: it was against the law for a commoner to touch a member of royalty. And while the story goes that at least some of those watching were willing to break that law to save the young queen, a royal guard on the scene ordered them away.

NEVER LET GO

In 2003 Emma Blackwell of Devon, England, was riding on a ferry in the south of France. After a long night of drinking, the 31-year-old woman decided to re-create Kate Winslet and Leonardo DiCaprio's iconic scene from *Titanic*. Only problem: DiCaprio wasn't there to hold her. Blackwell went to the bow of the ship, stretched out her arms, and yelled, "I'm king of the world!" Then she lost her balance, fell into the ocean, and drowned.

HOLE-Y COW

David Douglas was a renowned Scottish botanist best known for his explorations of the American Northwest. (The Douglas fir tree is named after him.) He also spent time in the Hawaiian Islands, and in 1834, the 35-year-old scientist was exploring the region around Mauna Kea volcano, on Hawaii's Big Island. The area was home to thousands of wild cattle, descendants of a few bulls and cows that had been intro-duced by English explorers in the 1790s. It was common for locals to dig pit traps—deep holes concealed by branches and brush—to capture the cattle. Unfortunately for Douglas, he fell into one of the pits. And at some point (no one knows exactly when) a bull fell in there, too. On July 12, 1834, two Hawaiian men discovered Douglas's mangled corpse at the bottom of the pit…along with the bull, which was still alive. Douglas's backpack and his terrier dog, Billy, were found not far away. In 1934, on the 100-year anniversary of his death, a stone monument to Douglas was installed at the location of the pit. It's still there today.

The first mechanical dough mixer was invented in the 1st century AD. It was powered by a donkey.

Why Did They Title It *That?*

On page 295 we told you the backstories of some mysterious movie titles. For the more literary-minded, here are the stories behind a few famous book titles (some of which—for the less literary-minded—were also made into films).

WHO'S AFRAID OF VIRGINIA WOOLF? (1966)

Allusions to celebrated author Virginia Woolf are made in Edward Albee's award-winning play, and the entire phrase "Who's afraid of Virginia Woolf?" is even used a couple of times. But none of this explains the significance of the title, so where did Albee get the idea for it? "I saw 'Who's Afraid of Virginia Woolf?' scrawled in soap, I suppose, on this mirror," Albee told the *Paris Review* in 1966. The mirror he was referring to was on the wall of a Greenwich Village saloon he frequented in the 1950s. "When I started to write the play, it cropped up in my mind again," he said. "And of course, who's afraid of Virginia Woolf means 'who's afraid of the big bad wolf'—who's afraid of living life without false illusions?"

A CLOCKWORK ORANGE (1962)

British author Anthony Burgess's science-fiction novella, set in England at an unspecified time in the future, revolves around Alex—the leader of an incredibly violent gang of teens—and how he gets "cured" of his violent tendencies via a bizarre aversion therapy. (He's forced to watch extremely violent films while experiencing the negative effects of drugs he is forced to take.) The title is mentioned only once in the book, after Alex's gang assaults a writer and his wife, and Alex finds a manuscript the writer's working on. Alex says, "Then I looked at its top sheet, and there was the name—A CLOCKWORK ORANGE—and I said: 'That's a fair gloopy title.'" (That scene does not appear in Stanley Kubrick's 1971 film adaptation.) The exact meaning of the title remained a mystery until 1987, when Burgess wrote in the preface to the 25th-anniversary edition of the book:

> …a human being is endowed with free will. He can use this to choose between good and evil. If he can only perform good or only perform evil, then he is a clockwork orange—meaning that he has the appearance of an organism lovely with colour and juice but is in fact only a clockwork toy…

Note: Earlier, in a 1972 interview, Burgess gave a different explanation. He claimed the phrase "queer as a clockwork orange" was old Cockney

---

In the U.K., you must have a license to watch TV.

slang and that he'd always liked it and always wanted to use it as a title. Linguists who have investigated the phrase could find no reference to it ever being used before Burgess's book.

THE GOOD SOLDIER (1915)

In 2014 the U.K.'s *Guardian* newspaper ranked this novel by English author Ford Madox Ford at #41 on its list of "100 best novels written in English" and told the story behind the title—and why Ford hated it. The novel centers on a retired British army soldier who regularly cheats on his wife and causes a great deal of misery to many people. Ford didn't mean to give the book an ironic title: he wanted to call it *The Saddest Story*, after its first line, "This is the saddest story I have ever heard." But Ford's publisher felt the title was too bleak for the public, especially since World War I had just broken out. He wrote to Ford, who had just enlisted in the army, asking him to come up with a new title. An angry Ford wrote back with the sarcastic suggestion, "Why not *The Good Soldier?*"

"To my horror," said Ford, "six months later the book appeared under that title."

THE POSTMAN ALWAYS RINGS TWICE (1934)

There's no postman and no doorbell in this best-selling James M. Cain crime novel. So why the title? There are two possible explanations. The first one is from Cain himself:

Explanation #1: Cain wrote in the preface to one of his later novels that the title was born during a conversation with a friend, screenwriter Vincent Lawrence. Lawrence was recalling the first time he'd mailed a screenplay to a producer and how nervous he was waiting for the postman to bring him a reply. Cain wrote that Lawrence remarked, "How I'd know it was the postman was that he'd always ring twice"—and Cain thought "The Postman Always Rings Twice" would make a great title for his book.

Explanation #2: The second explanation is unverified…but makes a great story. Cain based the book on the 1927 real-life murder case of Ruth Snyder, who had conspired with her lover to kill her husband after taking out a life insurance policy on him without his knowledge—just as happens in the book. Snyder had kept her husband in the dark about the insurance policy by making an arrangement with her postman. He was to give any letters related to the policy only to her. If he had any such letters, the postman would give Snyder a secret signal. Whether or not the signal involved a doorbell is unknown, but given that Cain based his book on the Snyder case—which he had covered as a journalist in New York—it's hard to believe he didn't know about the postman's secret signal and that it didn't have at least *something* to do with the book's title.

Bonus fact: Other titles Cain considered include *Bar-B-Que*, *Black Puma*, and *The Devil's Checkbook*. Cain's publisher rejected them all.

TO KILL A MOCKINGBIRD (1960) and *GO SET A WATCHMAN* (2015)

It was one of the biggest literary stories of 2015—Harper Lee's long-lost follow-up to *To Kill a Mockingbird*, written in the 1950s, would finally be published. But even though it's a sequel, Lee wrote *Go Set a Watchman* first. It follows the grown-up protagonist Scout as she travels from New York to her hometown of Maycomb, Alabama, during which she tells the story of a Depression-era trial that rocked her small town: a black man was wrongly accused of rape, and Scout's lawyer father, Atticus Finch, bravely defends him. The title was inspired by the *Book of the Prophet Isaiah* in the King James Bible: "For thus hath the Lord said unto me, Go, set a watchman, let him declare what he seeth." In Lee's book, the "watchman" looking over the town is Atticus Finch. But Lee's editor rejected the manuscript and urged her to write the story over from the point of view of six-year-old Scout. So Lee spent two years rewriting it, and she also wanted to call the new manuscript *Go Set a Watchman*… but her editor rejected that as well. He thought a Biblical title would turn off readers outside of the South. Lee renamed it *Atticus*, but that was turned down, too. So Lee took a line from the book, where Atticus tells his two kids, "It's a sin to kill a mockingbird." The title is symbolic of the destruction of innocence, a major theme throughout both novels.

TREASURE ISLAND (1883)

The title of this influential adventure story by Scottish author Robert Louis Stevenson doesn't seem to need explanation—it's about the search for buried pirate treasure on a deserted island. But few people would guess that the title came from a painting. Stevenson wrote years after the book was published that he had spent the summer of 1881 in Scotland with his family and had spent many rainy summer days entertaining his 12-year-old stepson by painting pictures with him. Stevenson wrote: "On one of these occasions, I made the map of an island; it was elaborately and (I thought) beautifully coloured; the shape of it took my fancy beyond expression." Stevenson became so enamored of his island painting, he said, that as he stared at it, "the future characters of the book began to appear there visibly among imaginary woods. The next thing I knew I had some papers before me and was writing out a list of chapters." His original title for the book was *The Sea Cook: A Story for Boys*. But he later decided to use the same title he had given the painting: *Treasure Island*.

If you're average, you'll consume almost your entire body weight in food additives this year.

Whiz Kids

"Whiz kid" is used to describe any exceptionally smart or successful young person. Here at the BRI, we use it to describe folks who are not only smart—but also use their brilliance for...well, read on and see for yourself.

WHIZ KIDS: Randy Hurd, Kip Hacking, Benjamin Haymore, and Tad Truscott, four physicists at Brigham Young University's "Splash Lab"

CONTRIBUTION TO HUMANITY: Studying the physics of urinal "splash-back" and devising a way to prevent it. (For anyone who's never used a urinal, splash-back is exactly what it sounds like: when you pee into a urinal, some droplets hit the back wall and splash back onto the floor...or onto your pants.)

DETAILS: BYU's Splash Lab studies the physical properties of liquids in motion, an area of physics known as fluid dynamics. Because they receive a lot of funding from the Office of Naval Research, they usually study water. But late one night in 2012, while driving back from a conference in San Diego (a 700-mile trip that must have included plenty of pit stops), Hurd and Truscott came up with the idea of using the lab to study another kind of fluid dynamics.

Using a 3-D printer, the team created a simulated *urethra* (the duct by which urine leaves the body), then rigged some equipment to squirt a stream of blue-dyed water through it at a rate of 21 ml (about 1½ tablespoons) per second, the pressure and flow rate of a healthy adult male. They aimed the device at an improvised "urinal-like environment" and let it flow, filming the results with a high-speed camera. They placed sheets of white paper below the fake urinal to show how much liquid splashed out and where.

Findings:

• One of the main culprits in creating splash-back is a phenomenon known as the *Plateau-Rayleigh instability*—the tendency of a stream of liquid to break into droplets after traveling a short distance. The researchers found that their stream broke into droplets six inches after exiting the simulated urethra, and those droplets created more splash-back than that of a single unbroken stream.

• When the droplets splashed into water, such as that pooled at the bottom of a urinal, the impact created a momentary cavity or "hole" in the surface of the water. (If a second drop struck the same spot, it made the hole even deeper.) When the hole collapsed a fraction of a second later, it created its own splash, adding to the size and volume of the splash-back.

Recommendations:

• **Stand closer to the urinal.** You want to stand close enough to the urinal to allow your stream to remain a stream. And since the Plateau-Rayleigh instability comes into effect six inches after the stream leaves your body, you want to close the gap to less than six inches. The Splash Lab researchers found that standing 15 inches back from the urinal sprayed droplets over a 150-square-inch area, but standing five inches away reduced the spray to almost nothing.

• **Aim for a vertical surface.** Aim for the back wall of the urinal but not straight on. If the stream strikes the back of the urinal at a 90° angle, the droplets will splash back the same way they came—toward *you*. Aim sideways, down, or both and try to reduce the angle of attack to less than 30°. That helps contain any splash-back within the urinal, reducing the amount sprayed back toward you by as much as 90 percent.

• **Stay out of the water.** Aiming for the water at the bottom of the urinal or toilet bowl (even if it's being flushed) will only increase the amount of splash.

WHIZ KIDS: Nate Rhodes, James Allen, Mitch Barneck, Martin de La Presa, and Ahrash Poursaid, bioengineering students at the University of Utah

CONTRIBUTION TO HUMANITY: Finding a way to prevent the most common—and dangerous—hospital-acquired infections

DETAILS: Rhodes's aunt works as a primary care nurse, and she taught him more than he probably ever wanted to know about infections caused by catheters, the tubes that are used to drain urine and other fluids from the body. They're responsible for 40 percent of all hospital-acquired infections, including four million urinary tract infections each year. Infections caused by catheters can be deadly, but they're notoriously difficult to prevent because once a catheter is in place, it's hard to keep it sterile and free of infections caused by bacteria...or at least it used to be.

After researching different ways to fight infection, Rhodes and his classmates developed a catheter that can be sterilized *in vivo* (while it's still inside the patient's body), using nothing more than light. The technology they devised is similar to fiber-optic cables, which use light to transmit telephone calls or cable television signals. But instead of transmitting TV shows, the catheter glows with light of a wavelength that's 99.9% effective at killing bacteria without harming the surrounding human tissue. It is the first catheter capable of sterilizing *itself* while still inside the patient.

Results:

• If you think their idea is a good one, you're not alone: The students have already won more than $95,000 in academic prizes for their invention. They are using their winnings to fund further development of the catheter.

• The students have filed for a patent for the device and have founded their own startup company, Veritas Medical LLC, to bring their LIGHT LINE Catheter to market. Clinical trials are scheduled to begin in 2015. If successful, the LIGHT LINE Catheter could be saving lives as early as 2016.

WHIZ KIDS: Georgia Institute of Technology assistant professor David Hu and the undergraduates in his fluid dynamics course

CONTRIBUTION TO HUMANITY: Discovering a new "Law of Urination" for mammals

DETAILS: One afternoon a few years back, Hu was changing his kid's wet diaper, and it occurred to him that he was lucky the child wasn't an elephant. That thought turned into a problem for his fluid dynamics class: given that an adult elephant has a bladder as large as an oil drum and a urethra "comparable to a drain beneath a sink," as Hu puts it, how long does it take the animal to relieve itself? Answer: an average of 21 seconds. We know this because some of Hu's students went to Zoo Atlanta and filmed the elephants peeing.

What about other animals? The undergraduates filmed mice, rats, a bat, a dog, two goats, and two cows. They also found 29 YouTube videos of mammals answering nature's call—including a gorilla, a panda, three horses, a rhino, and a house cat—and timed them all to see how long it took them to pee. That's when they noticed something that apparently no one had noticed before: every one of the animals that weighed more than 3 kilograms (6.6 pounds) took, on average, 21 seconds to relieve itself. It didn't matter if the animal was male or female, or whether the bladder held half a cup of liquid, as in the case of a 20-pound dog, or 42 gallons, as in the case of the elephant. They all emptied their bladders in the same amount of time. "This constancy of emptying time is quite a feat upon consideration of the substantial bladders of larger animals," Hu wrote in "Law of Urination," his academic paper describing the phenomenon.

Findings:

• To find out what was responsible for the pit stop parity, Hu and his students researched the "urethra geometries" of the animals and concluded that they were remarkably consistent: no matter what the animal's size (even if it was too small for the Law of Urination to apply), the length of its urethra was always 20 times the diameter. A rat weighing half a pound had a urethra 1 millimeter (0.03 inch) in diameter and 2 centimeters long, for example, and an elephant weighing 11,000 pounds had one that was 5 centimeters (about 2 inches) in diameter and 1 meter (39.3 inches) long. Bladder capacity was also consistent. Regardless of the animal's size, its bladder, when full, made up 5 percent of its total body weight.

• Why are the animals able to relieve themselves so quickly? According to Hu, it's all in the urethra:

> By providing a water-tight pipe to direct urine downward, the urethra increases the gravitational force acting on urine….Larger animals have longer urethras, and so greater gravitational force driving flow…enabling them to empty their substantial bladders over approximately the same duration. Our findings reveal that the urethra evolved as a flow-enhancing device, allowing the urinary system to scale up by a factor of 3,600 without compromising its function.

So does Hu plan to delve deeper into the subject in the future? No, he says. "I think this is all I wanted to say about urine."

HONORABLE MENTION: Adam Natusch

"CONTRIBUTION": Inventing a device that aids people who can't wait in long lines to use public restrooms

DETAILS: Natush invented the Whizdom "personal urinary device," mankind's latest attempt to provide males with a discreet way to pee anywhere, anytime. The design of the device is simple: it's a 40-inch narrow latex tube that's open at both ends and worn underneath pants. Roll one end of the tube up to adjust for length, so that the end pokes out of your pant leg about ½ inch above the ground, then roll the other end onto your you-know-what. Now anytime nature calls, simply stroll over to some grass or step onto the grate of a storm drain and go with the flow.

The Whizdom isn't for everyone, but if you think it isn't for *anyone*, you'll be surprised to learn that Natusch has managed to find some buyers. "Guys, if you are in an occupation that makes it inconvenient to get to a bathroom when it is an absolute emergency, then make sure you are equipped with this high quality and reliable survival tool," one "verified purchaser" writes on Amazon.com. Still, just because you can pee anywhere, that doesn't mean you should, Natusch cautions. "Always try to be respectful and discreet. Please pee responsible!"

*　　*　　*

"The first half of our life is ruined by our parents and the second half by our children."

—**Clarence Darrow**

Disorder on the Court (and Field)

The sports world is pretty conservative—play is governed by strict rules, and it rarely recognizes political controversy. But when it does—such as when two athletes gave the "Black Power" salute at the 1968 Olympics—it's big news. There are few ways players (or referees) can make their voices heard, so when they want to say something, they sometimes just use the shirts off their backs.

Athletes: Los Angeles Clippers players

Protest: At the tail end of the 2013–14 NBA season, the league was hit by a scandal involving Los Angeles Clippers owner Donald Sterling. Sterling's fiancée leaked his phone conversations, which contained racial slurs, and suddenly a litany of Sterling's other racist behaviors came to light. One example: he had to pay multiple million-dollar settlements after being sued by both the L.A. Housing Rights Center and the U.S. Department of Justice for refusing to rent apartments he owned to blacks and Latinos. Pundits and politicians called for the NBA to oust Sterling. Prior to a playoff game against the Golden State Warriors, Clippers players dumped their warm-up jackets at center court to reveal that their shirts were inside-out—a silent protest against Sterling. The following night, Miami Heat players, including the NBA's biggest star, LeBron James, did the same thing in solidarity. "The NBA has no room for Donald Sterling," James told reporters.

Outcome: After these protests and a threat by the remaining play-off teams to boycott their next games, commissioner Adam Silver announced Sterling's punishment: a $2.5 million fine and a lifetime ban from the NBA that forced the sale of his team. The Clippers returned from losing game 4 to win an emotional game 5 on their home court and eventually take the series in seven games.

Athletes: Phoenix Suns players and executives

Protest: In 2010 Arizona passed SB 1070, one of the harshest immigration laws in the nation. It allowed police officers to ask the citizenship status of anyone if they had a "reasonable suspicion" the person was an illegal alien. Critics took this to mean anyone who looked Latino. The law didn't sit well with players on the Phoenix Suns, including Brazilian-born Leandro Barbosa, Slovenian Goran Dragic, and two-time

---

China's chairman Mao Zedong had a barber named Big Beard Wang.

MVP (and Canadian) Steve Nash. It also struck a chord with Suns owner Robert Sarver and general manager Steve Kerr, who publicly spoke out against SB 1070 in the press. With both the players and the front office against the law, the team decided to wear their "Los Suns" jerseys. (The jerseys were a marketing program the Suns used to honor Arizona's Latin-American community.)

Outcome: The NBA and the players union supported the protests. The NBA Players Association released a statement criticizing the law and praising the Suns: "We applaud the actions of Phoenix Suns players and management and join them in taking a stand against the misguided efforts of Arizona lawmakers." Commissioner David Stern told reporters that the Suns' actions were "appropriate." Nevertheless, SB 1070 remains in effect.

Athletes: NBA referees

Protest: NBA rules state that if a missed shot hits the rim, the 24-second shot clock must be reset. But during a 2004 game between the Denver Nuggets and the Los Angeles Lakers, referee Michael Henderson mistakenly blew his whistle for a 24-second violation after the Nuggets' Carmelo Anthony rebounded his teammate's missed shot off the rim. After the play was ruled an inadvertent whistle, the Lakers won the ensuing jump ball and hit a game-winning shot. The league dealt with Henderson's mistake by suspending him for three games. Shocked by the harsh punishment, 28 of his fellow refs officiated their games that week while wearing inside-out jerseys with Henderson's number Sharpied on the back.

Outcome: Henderson lasted only two more seasons before being fired. Later, during the NBA referee strike of 2009, he repaid his former colleagues by crossing their picket line to officiate preseason games.

*   *   *

"HELP! FIRE!"

Firefighters in Middleton, Ohio, arrived at a house fire one night in 2015. Before they began to battle the blaze, they heard what sounded like an elderly woman crying, "Help! Fire!" over and over. The crew used thermal imaging equipment to try to locate the woman, but she wasn't detectable. The brave firefighters went into the burning structure to perform a search. "Help! Fire!" they heard coming from a room, so they burst in…and found two parrots, one of them sitting on a table saying "Help! Fire!" The birds were scooped up and carried to safety. No one else was in the house, which the firefighters were able to save.

Ripping Off the Band Aid

It's no surprise that Band-aids are part of the healthcare system. But aiding bands?
Say hello to HealthSouth CEO Richard Scrushy.

HOLD THE LINE

In 1997 a Birmingham, Alabama, country music band called Dallas County Line got a taste of national exposure when the group was invited to perform on the United Cerebral Palsy Telethon (hosted by John Ritter and Henry Winkler). The band was hugely popular in Birmingham; local radio stations received dozens of requests for Dallas County Line songs every day. Though the band never gained national prominence, it did play a slew of corporate gigs and company conventions across the South.

The band's leader, Richard Scrushy, also had a day job: he was the founder, chairman, and CEO of HealthSouth Corporation, an Alabama-based company that ran a chain of more than 1,300 hospitals, outpatient surgery clinics, and physical rehabilitation facilities. But what he really wanted was to be a country singer, and Dallas County Line was his attempt to make that dream become reality. And he made free use of HealthSouth's resources to help. The band, comprising HealthSouth execs plus some seasoned Nashville studio musicians, used the company jet to get to gigs, which were mostly HealthSouth corporate events, and those Nashville veterans (probably hired to offset Scrushy's lack of talent) were put on the HealthSouth payroll. More help from the company: HealthSouth employees were "asked" to call radio stations and request Dallas County Line's songs.

But this wouldn't be Scrushy's only attempt to break into the music business, nor would it be the only time he siphoned off company funds or committed fraud to do so.

SICK OF IT ALL

In the late 1990s and early 2000s, the music world was dominated by teen pop—slickly produced songs marketed to teens and preteens, performed by the Backstreet Boys, Spice Girls, *NSYNC, Christina Aguilera, Hanson, Britney Spears, and dozens more solo singers, girl groups, and boy bands. Around the same time, Richard Scrushy was overseeing Go For It!, a public service roadshow sponsored by HealthSouth that traveled around the country to deliver messages about

---

Van Gogh painted *The Starry Night* while a patient in an insane asylum.

healthy eating and exercise to kids and teenagers. Music producer Tim Coons, who had helped create the Backstreet Boys, heard about Go For It! and thought it would be a good platform for a teen-pop girl group he'd created called Real. He approached Scrushy with the idea, and Scrushy agreed to put Real on the bill in Salt Lake City. Response: the crowd loved it.

They loved it so much, in fact, that Scrushy wanted to make teen-pop music a permanent fixture of the stage show. But he didn't want Real; he wanted his own girl group—one that could cross over into mainstream music and make him millions…with HealthSouth footing the bill.

Scrushy left the details of creating and developing the group to Coons. Atlantic Hill Music—Coons's tiny production company, not to be confused with Atlantic Records—signed a five-year deal with Scrushy, and Coons immediately went on the HealthSouth payroll (at a weekly rate of $1,650).

FAZE ONE

Coons auditioned dozens of singers before recruiting three women in their early twenties: Halie Clark, Minia Corominas, and Sara Marie Rauch. While training them to sing and dance, Coons named the group 3rd Faze, after the three phases of life: birth, life, and death—a subtle reference to the health-care corporation that employed them, along with the fact that there were three women in the group.

In April 2001, just six months after forming, the trio secured a deal with GFI Productions which turned out to be a shell company—a subsidiary of HealthSouth, run by Scrushy. And the health-care executive gave himself veto power over anything 3rd Faze did, including album cover art and song selection.

While Coons earned about $85,000 a year from HealthSouth, the singers in the group stood to earn a lot less. Under the GFI contract, Clark, Corominas, and Rauch would receive $9,000 each for their first year in the group, $12,000 for the second, and $15,000 for the third, fourth, fifth, sixth, and seventh years of the contract, plus small advances for recording albums. After that, there was a chance of earning royalties.

FAZE TWO

But it's not as if the members of 3rd Faze were starving or wanting for much of anything.

• They were flown to concerts, radio shows, and HealthSouth corporate events in jets owned by HealthSouth.

• When a private jet wasn't available, they used three tour buses (secured by HealthSouth). Outfitted with two big-screen TVs and eight extra-large sleeping spaces with their own TVs, the buses had previously belonged to the rock band Aerosmith.

• On the road, they stayed in luxury suites in high-end hotels, all paid for by GFI Productions.

• Scrushy once sent a private helicopter to whisk 3rd Faze away for a weekend at his multimillion-dollar vacation home on Lake Martin in Alabama.

• When not on the road, the women in 3rd Faze lived in a huge Orlando apartment paid for by GFI Productions.

• Shopping sprees were frequent, and paid for by GFI.

• Their bodyguards and security staff: HealthSouth's security team.

• They received full medical benefits…as HealthSouth employees.

GFI was spending so much money on them that the members of 3rd Faze began to worry. Having a basic understanding of the music industry, they knew that the money spent to promote the band—including recording costs, music video costs, and touring costs—would come out of their cut of any future profits. According to Clark, Scrushy told her, "I'm honestly not keeping track of it all."

THE BIG TIME

When the group's self-titled album arrived in September 2001, released on the small Edeltone Records label, it sold only a few hundred copies. One reason: teen-pop's critical mass had been reached—sales were falling and the fad was dying. But 3rd Faze was still getting bigger…or it least it seemed that way. A few days before they attended the 2002 Grammys (via the HealthSouth jet), 3rd Faze moved from Edeltone to Sony-owned Columbia Records. That was around the same time that Sony CEO Tommy Mottola came to possess 250,000 shares of HealthSouth stock.

A lucrative future seemed all but certain for 3rd Faze. Scrushy bought out Coons and brought in a new manager for the group: HealthSouth vice president of marketing Jason Hervey. Is it odd for a health-care company executive to manage a major-label pop group? Yes, but according to Scrushy, that was specifically why he was hired. It's also notable that Hervey is a former child star—he played the obnoxious older brother on the ABC sitcom *The Wonder Years*.

Hervey landed the group high-profile gigs opening for boy band O-Town and Britney Spears on their 2002 tours. Mottola recruited Desmond Child, one of the biggest producers in pop music (Bon Jovi, KISS, Ricky Martin), to put together 3rd Faze's next album, its first with Columbia.

Only four songs were ever completed.

EX-SCRUSHY-ATING

HealthSouth was spending millions it had earned from expensive health care, surgeries, and rehabilitation programs on a girl group for a pop music world that no longer cared about girl groups. But remarkably, neither Scrushy, nor GFI Productions, nor HealthSouth were concealing their activities; 3rd Faze continued to appear frequently at HealthSouth corporate events and Go For It! tour stops. A *New York Times* account of a Grammy afterparty included a photo of Scrushy, 3rd Faze, and Mottola together, with Scrushy identified as "the manager of 3rd Faze and chief executive of HealthSouth."

In January 2003, Sony's Japanese board of directors forced Mottola to resign. It wasn't because of his sketchy involvement with HealthSouth—it was because he'd alienated two of Columbia's biggest stars: Michael Jackson and Mariah Carey (who happened to be Mottola's ex-wife) and let them defect to other labels. With Mottola gone, the 3rd Faze album deal was off.

FAZE THREE

That March, the FBI raided HealthSouth's Birmingham, Alabama, headquarters in the first step of a massive federal accounting probe. At the center of the probe were charges that HealthSouth executives, particularly Scrushy, had falsified $2.5 billion in profits, doctored financial statements, and committed many other irregularities (including covering up the 3rd Faze debacle).

A few days later, Hervey flew to Orlando and went to the apartment where the members of 3rd Faze lived. He told them that in addition to having their album canceled, the accounting scandal meant HealthSouth was pulling the plug on the band, effective immediately. The three women were dropped from the company payroll and evicted from their apartment. Now 3rd Faze was in its final phase: death.

POP WILL EAT ITSELF

A yearlong investigation of HealthSouth by the FBI and the Securities and Exchange Commission ensued. Scrushy and 10 other company executives pled guilty to fraud. Scrushy faced 85 counts and was tried for 36 of them. In June 2005, a jury acquitted him of all charges...but he wasn't out of the woods. A month before the end of the trial, federal prosecutors filed 30 new counts against Scrushy, including money laundering, obstruction of justice, and racketeering. This time he was convicted.

By 2006, more than 1,200 books had been published on the subject of 9/11.

Three years into his 82-month prison sentence, Scrushy was sued by HealthSouth shareholders seeking financial damages for his crimes. The judge found him liable, ordering him to pay $2.87 billion. He was released from prison in 2012.

Although 3rd Faze never reunited, all three continued in show business. Minia Corominas did some solo singing, and now runs a company called Makeup by Minia, doing makeup for brides. Halie Clark and Sara Marie Rauch wrote songs together for a while. Rauch now lives in Florida and recently sang with a local electronic music group called Violentfingers. Clark went back to college in Florida and now lives in Los Angeles, where she does occasional backup vocal work, mostly for Christian pop bands. She says that if she ever gets the chance to sign another record deal, she's going to "be careful."

*　　　*　　　*

4 DUMB JOKES

Man: "Doc, you gotta help me, I think I'm a chicken!"
Doctor: "How long have you felt this way?"
Man: "Ever since I was an egg."

Two drunks were walking home from a bar one night when one of them passed out cold on the sidewalk. His friend tried and tried but couldn't wake him up, so he called 911: "You gotta get someone here fast!"

"Where are you?" asked the 911 operator.

"On Eucalyptus Street!"

"Could you spell that?"

"Uhh…" said the drunk, "let me drag him over to Main Street and I'll call you back."

Teacher: "Johnny, name two pronouns."
Johnny: "Who, me?"

A waitress brought an Englishman his soup du jour. "Good heavens," said the Englishman, "what *is* this?"

"Why, it's bean soup," the waitress replied.

"I don't care what it's been," he grumbled. "What is it now?"

Most popular name for pets in Britain: Molly.

Those '70s Shows

The music-and-comedy variety show was a television mainstay until the 1980s. Why did the format die out? Probably because of shows like these.

JOEY AND DAD. After Sonny and Cher got divorced, Allan Blye, producer of *The Sonny & Cher Comedy Hour*, attempted to create another variety show duo: sultry singer-dancer Joey Heatherton...and her father, Ray Heatherton, star of the 1950s children's TV show *The Merry Mailman*. Most of the sketches and banter were about the Generation Gap. The show ran for just four weeks in 1975.

THE KEANE BROTHERS SHOW. In 1976 a former record executive named Bob Keane started promoting a bubblegum pop duo called the Keane Brothers—consisting of his sons Tom (on piano) and John (on drums). They had just one minor hit ("Sherry," which reached #84), but CBS still hired them for a summer 1977 variety show. At ages 12 and 13, the Keane brothers became the youngest people ever to host a prime-time variety series.

THE HARLEM GLOBETROTTERS POPCORN MACHINE. In 1974 Curly Neal, Meadowlark Lemon, and the other Harlem Globetrotters moved from the basketball court to a Saturday morning TV variety show. The Globetrotters sang, danced, and did sketches with comedian Avery Schreiber (as "Dr. Evil") and child star Rodney Allen Rippy (as himself). The show was created by John Aylesworth, who also created *Hee Haw*. It lasted one season.

SHIELDS AND YARNELL. If you think variety shows are too loud and exciting, this was the show for you. Shields and Yarnell were a married mime duo who had appeared more than 400 times on other variety shows by the time they got this short-lived series in 1977. In addition to hosting bands and comedians, Shields and Yarnell frequently performed the Clinkers, their signature mime routine about married robots.

VAN DYKE AND COMPANY. At a press conference announcing the show in 1976, Dick Van Dyke told reporters that he wanted to do a variety show strictly because it was "fun" and he didn't care if it succeeded because he was "too old to care about ratings." Good thing, too: Despite appearances by Andy Kaufman, the Los Angeles Mime Company, and Dick Van Dyke singing and dancing, the show was canceled after 11 episodes.

You Swallowed *What*?

More stories about people eating things they shouldn't.

I'M SOY SORRY

In March 2013, John Paul Boldrick, a 19-year-old student at the University of Virginia, was going through an initiation ritual with his Zeta Psi fraternity brothers when they dared him to drink a quart of soy sauce. Did he do it? Of course he did! Bad idea: a short time later, Boldrick started foaming at the mouth and having seizures. By the time his frat brothers got him to a hospital, he was in a coma. Doctors diagnosed Boldrick with *hypernatremia*, a condition caused by an excess of salt in the body. (A quart of soy sauce contains about one-third of a pound of salt.) The condition causes the brain to dehydrate and shrink, often resulting in brain damage and even death. Doctors immediately started flushing Boldrick's system by pumping more than a gallon of sugar-water into his body via a nasal tube to get his salt levels down to normal—and, fortunately, it worked. Boldrick woke from the coma after three days and quickly made a full recovery. Doctors said Boldrick was the first person known to science to have ingested such a large amount of salt without suffering any lasting neurological effects.

I'M VERY HAIRNGRY!

Ayperi Alekseeva, 18, was admitted to a hospital in Bishkek, Kyrgyzstan, in September 2014, suffering from malnourishment and dehydration. Reason for the condition: Alekseeva got sick nearly every time she tried to eat or drink. As she was near death, doctors performed emergency surgery on the young woman …and found a nine-pound hairball, about 15 inches long and 5 inches thick, in her stomach. Alekseeva, it turned out, suffered from a compulsive hair-eating disorder known as *trichophagia* and had been eating her own hair—and hair she found on the floor or ground—for years. The young woman stayed in the hospital for a week but was finally sent home in good shape. She promised that she would try not to eat hair anymore. (The medical reports on Alekseeva's case noted that if trichophagia is allowed to continue without treatment, it can lead to a rare condition called "Rapunzel syndrome," in which the hairball in the victim's stomach develops a tail of sorts that grows from the stomach down into the intestine.)

I WIN!

In July 2010, Zaver Rathod, a 35-year-old farmworker in the western

---

Never can say good-bye: 70% of all Land Rovers and 60% of all Porsches ever built are still on the road.

Indian city of Surat, killed a highly venomous snake by throwing stones at it after it bit one of his friends. Later that day, Rathod ate the snake. All of it. Raw. From its head to its tail, very quickly. Reason: one of his friends had bet him he couldn't do it. Within minutes, Rathod began vomiting and was rushed to a hospital. Luckily for him, doctors were able to remove the contents of his stomach before too much of the snake's venom made it into his bloodstream, and he was soon released from the hospital. How much had Rathod bet his friend that he could eat the venomous snake? One hundred rupees—or about $2.40.

THE HUMAN OSTRICH

An 1894 *British Medical Journal* article tells the tragic tale of a patient whom doctors called the "Human Ostrich" because he'd eat anything anyone gave him…for a price. One morning the man showed up at the London Hospital complaining of extreme abdominal pain. Because X-ray machines were still years away, Dr. Frederic Eve (who wrote the article) had to cut him open to investigate. It didn't take long to find the problem. The 42-year-old man's innards had been twisted and mangled by various odd objects he'd eaten, including a metal hook…

> so bent upon itself as to clamp the intestinal wall. It could not be freed until bent open with a pair of pliers. Attached to this hook was a narrow strip of leather; this was firmly pulled upon but could not be detached. Its opposite end was evidently fixed in some portion of the bowel.

Dr. Eve painstakingly removed all of the objects, but his patient—who'd been awake throughout the procedure—wasn't doing well. He was, however, able to explain how all that stuff got there: "He confessed to me that to gain a livelihood he would swallow penny pieces, halfpence, pieces of tin, paper, cork, swivels, watch chains, keys, tintacks, nails, pieces of indian-rubber, and purses." The "Human Ostrich" (his real name has been lost to history) was under the impression that it all had passed out of him. He was mistaken. His condition deteriorated throughout the afternoon, and by nightfall he was dead.

NATAL ATTRACTION

A mom in Russia walked into her kitchen and noticed something odd—all of the refrigerator magnets were missing. Nearby was her 16-month old baby boy…who didn't look very well. She rushed him to the hospital, where an ultrasound proved her suspicions correct: several marble-sized magnets had reconnected inside the baby. He needed emergency surgery. "Over the years," said surgeon Nikolay Rostovtsev, "I have had to take a variety of foreign bodies, including magnets, from young patients. Once I removed about 20 of them, but this incident of our little patient has broken all records." Final total: 42 magnets.

Do they taste familiar? SweeTarts are Pixy Stix powder in solid form.

Butchers & Croakers

Here's hoping you never find yourself in prison, where you could put these real terms and expressions to use.

G**randma's House:** The cell belonging to the leader of a prison gang

Public Pretender: The public defender

Four-Piece Suit: A full set of restraints (handcuffs, leg irons, waist chain, plus "security boxes" covering the keyholes on the restraints)

Life on the Installment Plan: Serving one prison sentence after another, which in effect amounts to a life sentence

Buck Rogers Time: A sentence whose parole date is many, many years in the future

Flat: A ground-level cell

Hot Box or Cold Storage: Solitary confinement

Snitch Box: A metal detector

Butcher: The captain of the guards

Topped Out: An inmate who has completed parole and has no further restrictions or obligations to the state

Cadillac: An enjoyable work assignment

Croaker: The prison doctor or medical officer

Brake Fluid: Psychiatric medication for mentally ill inmates

Chin Check: Punching an inmate in the jaw to see if they'll fight back

Real Man: A con who fights back when chin checked

Cell Warrior: An inmate who is menacing when they are safely locked in their cell, but meek when around other inmates

Boneyard: A trailer used for conjugal visits

Take It to the Stall: Settle a dispute with another con by fighting it out in the shower area

Bowlegged: A con serving his sentences consecutively (more time) instead of concurrently (less time)

Rain Check: Parole

Coming-Out Party: Discharge or release from prison

Back-Door Parole: Dying in prison

Fart sniffing is a career in China. (It's done to diagnose illness.) Sniffers can earn $50,000 a year.

Variety Is the Spice of Life

Have you ever been in the supermarket and wondered why there are dozens of different options for seemingly every product? The answer: Howard Moskowitz.

READY TO EAT

Howard Moskowitz got his doctorate from Harvard in behavioral psychology in 1969; he did his dissertation on the emerging subject of *psychophysics*—the relationship between physical stimuli and the sensations they create in the brain. Moskowitz's understanding of how the brain perceives flavor—and how it reacts almost euphorically to salt, sugar, and fat—made him a pioneer in the field of market research.

Moskowitz's first job was with the U.S. Army. He worked to improve the taste of soldiers' MREs ("meals ready to eat"). The army wanted him to the make the notoriously bland meals taste better so soldiers would get enough calories to perform their duties. Moskowitz introduced new flavor profiles and changed the formulation for dozens of meals, but his main trick was increasing the salt, sugar, and fat content, which his research showed tricked the brain into wanting to eat more. He called this the "bliss point."

In 1975 Moskowitz left the army to apply his research to the civilian world. He started a consulting firm in White Plains, New York, then spoke at conferences and wrote articles for research journals about how the tongue and brain unite to taste food. However, he couldn't attract enough clients to put his theories to practical use.

THE DIET PEPSI PROBLEM

In 1980 executives at Pepsi Cola heard that the FDA was about to approve a new artificial sweetener called aspartame. It was hoped that the substance would replace saccharine—unlike saccharine, aspartame was not linked to cancer in lab rats…and it was much, much sweeter. It was so sweet—approximately 200 times sweeter than sugar—that it created a problem for food scientists at Pepsi. They had been tasked with trying to reformulate Diet Pepsi with aspartame but couldn't come with anything satisfactory, so Pepsi called in Moskowitz.

Moskowitz was set up in a test kitchen with certain parameters: internal testing had shown that a serving of Diet Pepsi with less than 8 percent aspartame was too bitter, but more than 12 percent was too sweet. So Moskowitz and a group of Pepsi employees set about brewing dozens of different batches of Diet Pepsi, each with a slightly different level of sweetness. One batch had 8.1 percent aspartame, another had 8.2 percent…all the way up to 12 percent. He was looking for the bliss point—the level of sweetness that pleased the tongue so much that it made the brain ask for more and more.

Next, Moskowitz convened focus groups. He asked hundreds of men and women of different races and ages to test different formulations of Diet Pepsi, and then he graphed the ones people liked best. Only problem: there was no pattern for preference. In other words, some people liked the 8.3 percent batch, but just as many liked a 10 percent batch. Moskowitz showed his results to Pepsi execs and, unable to find a bliss point, they parted ways.

COFFEE BREAK

In 1985 Moskowitz was hired by Nestlé to consult on how to improve the flavor (and increase the sales) of Nescafé instant coffee, which was losing popularity. While drinking a cup of coffee in a diner one morning, he considered how coffee was one of the few foods or drinks that people openly customized. For example, some people like it black, others take cream, or cream and sugar, or just sugar. It was strictly a matter of personal preference, and no one version was objectively any better than the other.

Moskowitz thought back to Diet Pepsi and had an epiphany: just as people prefer their coffee in a variety of ways, it was equally logical that some would prefer a sort-of-sweet Diet Pepsi, and others would like an extra-sweet Diet Pepsi. The bliss point, he reasoned, was not just one bliss point—there could be dozens of bliss points. To Moskowitz, this meant that food companies should provide a variety of products to capture the bliss point—and dollars—of as many people as possible.

HITTING THE SAUCE

Moskowitz's next big client was Campbell's Soup. In the 1980s, technicians at the company devised a way to produce and package large quantities of tomato sauce without the water separating from the solids. Bottled spaghetti sauces like Ragu and Hunt's got around the problem by packaging tomato purees with lots of starch powder to keep the ingredients together and saucelike. But Campbell's technology allowed them to create a new kind of spaghetti sauce, which the company marketed under the name Prego, with ads touting how it was "more like homemade" because it contained visible chunks of tomato.

Prego soon overtook Ragu and Hunt's as the #1 bottled spaghetti sauce on the market, but by 1986 sales had flattened, so Campbell's hired Moskowitz. Working with Campbell's test kitchens, Moskowitz created 45 different test varieties of spaghetti sauce. Each was slightly different, with varying levels of spiciness, tartness, aroma, mouth feel, creaminess, even ingredient cost. (One thing they all had in common: the top two ingredients were tomatoes and sugar.) Then Moskowitz hired professional food tasters to try the varieties and describe their feelings for each. Moskowitz then narrowed down his samples to the 10 most popular and did taste tests in New York, Chicago, Los Angeles, and Florida. In each test, groups of 25 people ate the 10 bowls over a two-hour period and rated them on a scale from 1 to 100.

Once again, Moskowitz graphed the results, and this time, patterns emerged. The preferred taste was plain marinara, but there was a different favorite for texture: extra-chunky sauce. Moskowitz's sample was chunkier than any sauce on the market—including Prego—and that's what got a strong response. In 1989 Prego passed Ragu in market share (again) by introducing "Extra Chunky" spaghetti sauce. Number of Prego varieties available today: 19. Number of Ragu varieties: 29…which could be because Moskowitz was hired to revitalize that product, too.

TO MARKET TO MARKET

Moskowitz, now in his 70s and still in demand by food companies, has helped dozens of companies create not only new products but also new product lines designed to capture every possible consumer. He's worked with Sara Lee, Subway, Dunkin' Donuts, McDonald's, and Kraft. And through an experiment similar to what he did with tomato sauce, Moskowitz revitalized the Vlasic Pickles line and created Vlasic's "Zesty" style—the best-selling pickle of all time.

*   *   *

WHO COINED THE TERM "COINED THE TERM"?

The first known use of *coined* comes from George Puttenham, an Elizabethan writer who wrote in his 1589 book *The Arte of English Poesie*: "Young schollers not halfe well studied…seeme to coigne fine wordes out of the Latin." Puttenham drew from the original meaning of the word *coine*—a verb that described the act of stamping a metal disk with a die. Although those flat metal disks later became the monetary "coins" we still use today, the verb survives in the form of "to coin" a word or a phrase. It was popularized in large part by William Shakespeare, who wrote in his 1607 play *Coriolanus*: "So shall my lungs coine words till their decay."

State secret: The ancient Chinese kept the method of making silk a secret for 3,000 years.

An Unfamiliar Face

Ever hear the expression "I never forget a face"? Well, there are some people who never remember a face, and there's a reason for it—a loose connection in the brain.

BRAIN POWER

There's a part of your brain that processes faces. It's located, according to MIT scientist Nancy Kanwisher, in the area "just behind and underneath, and a bit from your right ear." It's called the *fusiform gyrus*. (The *gyrus* is a ridge in the brain, and *fusiform* describes its shape—elongated and tapered at both ends.) Whenever you see someone you know, the fusiform gyrus tells you, "That's Bob." It also sends out messages to other parts of the body that add emotions to the information, such as "I like Bob. He's my friend." But what happens when an accident, illness, or hereditary gene disconnects the wiring between the fusiform gyrus and other parts of the brain?

There are people who may see a particular person's face every day of their lives and still not recognize it. They see a nose, teeth, and cheeks, but when the features are put together, they cannot retain a memory of it. The medical term for this condition is *prosopagnosia* (from the Greek *prosopon*, for "face," and *agnosia*, for "ignorance"), but it's more commonly called *face blindness*. Researchers say that as many as 1 in 50 people suffer from some form of the condition.

YOU KNOW THEM, BUT THEY DON'T KNOW YOU

Jane Goodall, the world's foremost expert on chimpanzees, has it. So do Swedish Crown Princess Victoria and Markos Moulitsas, founder of the popular news blog *Daily Kos*. The artist Chuck Close, whose portrait of President Bill Clinton hangs in the National Gallery, didn't recognize the woman he lived with for two years when he saw her a year after they broke up. Probably the best known sufferer of prosopagnosia is the neurologist and psychiatrist Dr. Oliver Sacks, renowned author of the best-selling books *The Man Who Mistook His Wife for a Hat* and *Awakenings*, which was made into the 1990 Oscar-nominated film starring Robin Williams. A lifelong sufferer of extreme face blindness, Sacks has said that his condition is so severe he often doesn't recognize his own face.

Sufferers of face blindness must develop alternate ways of identifying coworkers, friends, and family, so they remember single features—a mole, a specific style of clothing, or an extra toothy smile. Says Jane

Goodall, "I usually make up for it by pretending to recognize everybody. And then, if they say, 'But we haven't met before,' I say, 'Well, you look just like somebody I know.'" Oliver Sacks has extremely large ears, so when he sees those ears in a mirror, he knows he's looking at a reflection of himself. Prosopagnosia also makes watching movies or TV very confusing for a sufferer. When a viewer can't identify faces, he or she can't follow the story.

IMPOSTOR!

Face blindness alone is hard enough to live with, but it can be even worse. When the brain receives visual information about a face, it connects with the *amygdalae*, which is the emotional-response part of the brain. That connection creates a reaction, such as, "I know you. I like you." But if the connection between the two areas gets damaged, the brain may recognize the face but not have the emotional response that tells it, "This is a person I know." The brain is convinced it is looking at an impostor. This condition is called *Capgras syndrome*, after French psychiatrist Jean Marie Joseph Capgras, who in 1923 treated a patient called "Madame M." who insisted that her family members had been replaced by strangers who looked identical to them. The unusual part of this syndrome is that the sufferer can talk to a family member on the phone and recognize him or her because there is no damage in the link between the emotional and audio part of the brain. But the second the person appears, the sufferer will believe that same "family member" is an impostor.

DOUBLE INDEMNITY

Scientists have likened Capgras syndrome to the science-fiction film *Invasion of the Body Snatchers*, where aliens take over human bodies. But Capgras can expand beyond people to animals and objects. One man believed his pet poodle was an impostor. Another was convinced that his running shoes had been switched. Capgras syndrome is most often caused by damage to the brain, but it can also be a delusional result of schizophrenia. It is particularly dangerous if the sufferer is a violent person and is afraid of the "intruder" in his home.

In 2009 a student from New Zealand named Blazej Kot murdered his 28-year-old wife in Ithaca, New York, claiming she was an impostor. The jury didn't buy his Capgras syndrome defense, and Kot was convicted of murder and sentenced to 25 years to life. Ironically, there is a population of New Zealanders who have a very high incidence of Capgras syndrome—the Maori. Studies show that it is actually a common side effect of psychotic illnesses within this group. (Kot, however, is a New Zealander of Polish descent.)

First person to "swagger": William Shakespeare. (He invented the word.)

Barn Burners

Need a euphemism for "breaking wind" or "passing gas"? Try one of these.

Trouser trumpet	Beeping your horn
Duck call	Hot wind
Back draft	Butt cheek screech
Air biscuit	Fluffy
Booty cough	Message from the interior
Butt salute	Human hydrogen bomb
Anus applause	Thunder from down under
Panty burp	Bean fumes
Crack concert	Pop tart
Back-end blowout	Belching clown
Frump	One-cheek sneak
Cheek squeak	Nether belch
Fanny beep	Benchwarmer
Heinie hiccup	Fizzler
One-gun salute	Bull snort
Prison break	Gurgler
Quack	Power puff
Bottom blast	Blampf
Rectal turbulence	Putt-putt
Barn burner	Cushion creeper
Crack splitter	Stepping on a duck

The first mass-marketed disposable diapers, introduced in 1948, won't finish biodegrading until 2500.

The History of U.S. Intelligence Agencies, Part II

That's odd—after researching the FBI and the NSA for Part I of the story (page 318), all of a sudden there's a black van parked out front that says "Flowers by Irene." Wonder what it's doing there.

THE BOOM YEARS

In the 33 years between 1865 (the end of the Civil War) and 1898, the United States took part in just one military conflict outside North America. And that was the one-day overthrow of the Kingdom of Hawaii in 1893, which resulted in one wounded person. Over the next 50 years there were only about five years in which the U.S. was *not* involved in at least one conflict around the world. These conflicts included the Spanish-American War in the Caribbean and the Philippines (1898), the "Banana Wars" in Central America (1898–1934), the Boxer Rebellion in China (1899–1901), and World War I (1917–1918) and World War II (1941–1945) in Europe, Africa, the Middle East, Asia, and other locations.

Along with more wars and new (and unknown) enemies came a greater need for intelligence gathering. As U.S. military operations expanded, the size and scope of U.S. intelligence agencies expanded, too. Not only that—they aimed inward, with the founding of the nation's first *domestic* intelligence agencies.

TACTICS

The turn of the 20th century was when the modern intelligence agency came into being. Here's what their chief duties were and still are.

Collection: The agency's first job is the collection of *intelligence*—information about an enemy or any information deemed useful to the country's security. There are many different kinds of intelligence, including *communications intelligence* (COMINT), meaning information gleaned from communications, such as through phone wiretaps or intercepted mail, and *human intelligence* (HUMINT), meaning information gathered from human sources, such as captured enemy soldiers, double agents, or simply informants.

Rock music: Capuchin monkeys bang stones together to warn each other of approaching predators.

Analysis: The process through which "raw" intelligence is studied and organized or developed into usable form. (Code-breaking falls under the duties of intelligence analysts.)

Counterintelligence: Any activity designed to protect against the intelligence operations of foreign governments, including spying, covert actions, assassination attempts, and more. (It can also mean actions to protect against domestic threats: the FBI, for example, has its own counterintelligence unit.)

Covert Action: Secret activity performed in a way that prevents it from being traced back to the government that ordered it. There are several types, such as political, economic, propaganda, and paramilitary. (See page 499 for more about the CIA's covert ops.)

Espionage: Spying and all it entails, including the use of secret agents, the development of foreign agents, and the development and use of spy gadgetry (as popularized in James Bond movies), all with the express purpose of collecting intelligence.

NEW AGENCIES

In the early 20th century, U.S. intelligence activity grew enormously, and by the end of World War II the government employed tens of thousands of people across numerous organizations. Key events from this period:

• In 1908 the Bureau of Investigation—precursor to the FBI—was formed as a part of the Justice Department. Created as a federal criminal investigation unit, it was soon doubling as a domestic intelligence agency, charged with gathering intelligence (and spying) on Americans.

• In 1919 the U.S. State Department and the U.S. Army combined to form what became known as the Black Chamber—a code-breaking unit...but not for the military. The Black Chamber broke codes used in the diplomatic cables of foreign nations. It was the first peacetime, nonmilitary intelligence agency in U.S. history. It was closed down in 1929 but is seen today as the precursor to the NSA—the National Security Agency—which was formed in 1952.

• In 1942 the Office of Strategic Services (OSS) was formed as a unified intelligence service for all the branches of the U.S. armed forces during World War II. By war's end, the OSS employed more than 24,000 people.

POSTWAR YEARS

Unlike what happened at the end of previous wars, intelligence agencies did not shrink at the end of World War II. The U.S. immediately found itself enmeshed in the Cold War with the Soviet Union, which included the Korean War (1950–1953) and the Vietnam War (1955–1975).

Humankind almost went extinct from climate change 150,000 years ago.

Result: the size and the scope of American intelligence agencies (along with those of the Soviet Union and other nations) expanded again. Most significantly, the OSS was broken into two different agencies—the Bureau of Intelligence and Research, which served the State Department and still exists today, founded in 1945, and the Central Intelligence Agency (CIA), founded in 1947.

This era was also marked by increasing—and, critics claim, excessive—secrecy around anything having to do with these agencies. One such agency, the National Reconnaissance Office, was created in 1960 but wasn't officially acknowledged as even existing until 1992.

THE SCANDAL ERA

It's important to note that even at this time, the president still had control of U.S. intelligence activities. Congress, although granted its first nominal oversight duties upon the creation of the CIA in 1947, had only one real function in regard to America's intelligence agencies: signing off on the secret budgets that funded them. This led to problems.

Starting in the early 1970s, the intelligence agencies were rocked by a series of revelations about how they'd abused their power. It was reported that the FBI had conducted widespread illegal spying and infiltration operations against domestic political organizations since the 1950s; that the NSA had spied on civil rights leaders, including Martin Luther King Jr. and boxer Muhammad Ali; and that the CIA had been secretly opening and reading Americans' mail on a massive scale and on a regular basis since the 1950s. The reports also revealed that the CIA had taken part in the violent overthrows of foreign governments and had assassinated or attempted to assassinate foreign leaders.

The fallout from the revelations led to a string of congressional investigations and the passage of several laws restricting the actions of intelligence agencies. In the mid-1970s, both the U.S. House of Representatives and the Senate formed permanent committees dedicated to the oversight of intelligence activities. This was the first time in the nation's 200-year history that Congress got a real foothold in the American intelligence world.

TO THE PRESENT

But that didn't slow down the agencies. From the 1970s onward, they continued to grow, both in size and number, despite continued tension with Congress. (The CIA's torture program under President George W. Bush and domestic surveillance practices under Presidents Bush and Obama are just a few of the latest of such controversies.)

Today there are 17 separate U.S. intelligence agencies, all united under one umbrella organization called the U.S. Intelligence

Community, or IC for short. They are overseen by the Director of National Intelligence, who reports directly to the president. The 17 agencies include several you've probably never heard of, such as the CGI—Coast Guard Intelligence (they've been around since 1915 and have intelligence duties revolving around the nation's maritime systems); the previously mentioned NRO—the National Reconnaissance Office (their work involves the use of spy satellites); and the United States Cyber Command, or USCYBERCOM (formed in 2009 to handle cyberspace security issues, such as protecting against hacking by foreign governments).

FACTS AND FIGURES

• Among the many thousands of pieces of information leaked by NSA whistleblower Edward Snowden in 2013: the so-called Black Budget—the top-secret budget detailing the funds allocated to U.S. intelligence agencies. After consultations with government officials about what should remain secret for national security reasons, parts of it were published in newspapers. It was the first time the budget had been revealed to the public.

• Black Budget for 2013: $52.6 billion. The CIA got the largest share with $14.7 billion. Second: the NSA, with $10.8 billion. The Black Budget numbers don't include the budget for military intelligence agencies, though—they get around $23 billion annually, which brings the total to about $75 billion. (Sound like a lot? It is…but in 2010, the total was closer to $80 billion.)

• The leaked budget also revealed the number of people employed by U.S. intelligence agencies that year: about 107,000.

• The number of CIA agents killed in the line of duty in history: 111. They are honored at the Memorial Wall at CIA headquarters in Langley, Virginia, each with a single star. The names of many of the agents are public, while some remain classified. (More than 30 of those deaths are just since 2001.) The NSA has a similar memorial at its headquarters in Fort Meade, Maryland, honoring the lives of both military and civilian code-breakers killed in the line of duty over the years. Number killed: 173.

*   *   *

"The crisis of today is the joke of tomorrow."

—**H. G. Wells**

Blind people in the U.S. "watch" an average of 24 hours of TV per week.

Stars Living in Cars

The road to success can be a rocky one—and sometimes it literally is a road. Don't believe it? Take a look at how these celebrities rode out the early days of their careers…and made it to the big time.

STEVE HARVEY

On the Street: In the late 1980s, comedian Steve Harvey could be found washing his armpits and underwear in gas station restrooms, and sleeping in his car in parking lots and on roadsides, in any number of American cities.

Story: Harvey debuted as a professional comedian in a Cleveland, Ohio, comedy club in 1985. Freshly separated from his first wife, and flat broke, he spent the next several years intermittently homeless, including a three-year stretch in which he lived in his 1976 Ford Tempo, traveling from gig to gig, relying on public restrooms to get cleaned up. (He had an Igloo cooler in the back seat, he said years later, that he used as a refrigerator.)

Breakthrough: Harvey got his big break in 1992, when he was made host of the TV comedy show *Showtime at the Apollo*—and it's been pretty much uphill ever since. Today he has his own talk show on NBC, he's the host of the game show *Family Feud*, and his best-selling book, *Act Like a Lady, Think Like a Man*, was made into the 2012 film *Think Like a Man*—which earned more than $100 million worldwide. Today the formerly homeless, struggling comedian is worth in the neighborhood of $85 million.

WILLIAM SHATNER

On the Street: He lived out of his truck after starring in the original *Star Trek*.

Story: *Star Trek* has been so popular for so long, it's easy to forget that the original TV show didn't do very well: its ratings were so low that Shatner, who starred as Captain Kirk, didn't expect it to last through its second season, and the show was in fact canceled after just its third season in 1969. Shortly after *Trek*'s demise, Shatner not only found it hard to find work—he went broke. But he refused to give up, and hit the road…in his pickup truck. According to the Shat himself, in a 2014 interview with *Details* magazine:

> It was the early 1970s and I was recently divorced. I had three kids and was totally broke. I managed to find work back east on the straw-hat circuit—summer stock—but couldn't afford hotels, so I lived out of the back of my

Fidel Castro named three of his sons for Alexander the Great: Alexis, Alexander, and Alejandro.

truck, under a hard shell. It had a little stove, a toilet, and I'd drive from theater to theater. The only comfort came from my dog, who sat in the passenger seat and gave me perspective on everything.

Breakthrough: Shatner spent almost all of the 1970s playing bit parts in TV series, along with a few more prominent roles in (really bad) B-movies. He didn't hit the jackpot until 1979—when he reprised his role as Captain Kirk, this time in *Star Trek: The Motion Picture*. That led to his own TV show, *T.J. Hooker*, in 1982; a total of six more Star Trek films; and, more recently, his critically acclaimed role as Denny Crane in the ABC series *Boston Legal*. Today the once pickup-truck-living Shatner is an internationally famous star, and is worth somewhere around $100 million.

SAM WORTHINGTON

On the Street: He was living in his car just weeks before getting a call from his agent about a big audition.

Story: Worthington got into acting in Sydney, Australia, in 1995, when he was 19 years old. Over the next decade he became fairly well known in Australia, acting in some critically acclaimed films, as well as in some TV shows, but he couldn't break into Hollywood. At the age of 30, in 2006, after reassessing his life and deciding he needed a major shaking up, he sold all his belongings and bought a car. He lived out of that car, in the mountains southwest of Sydney, for the next several weeks. What ended his homeless stretch? He got a call from his agent: he wanted Worthington to get back to Sydney and audition for a role that had just come up.

Breakthrough: The audition was for the lead role in James Cameron's *Avatar*. Worthington didn't get the role right away: it was a grueling eight-month process, which meant flying back and forth from Sydney to Los Angeles several times, but Cameron finally made up his mind in mid-2007. What this meant: Worthington went from living in his car… to starring in the most successful film ever (*Avatar* grossed more than $2.7 *billion*) in a matter of months. Worthington has appeared in several more Hollywood films since then, and today has a net worth of about $12 million.

TYLER PERRY

On the Street: Perry spent a good part of six years broke and living in his car in Atlanta, Georgia.

Story: In 1990 Perry, then 21, moved from his childhood home in New Orleans to Atlanta, where he developed an interest in writing. In 1992 Perry spent his life savings—about $12,000—producing a musical play he had written. It bombed. He spent the next six years trying to make

Americans spend about 9% of their income on food; people in India spend 53%.

it as a playwright, repeatedly failing—and mostly homeless and living in his car. (Although occasionally, he later said in an interview on the *Oprah Winfrey Show*, he stayed in a "pay-by-the-week hotel that was full of crackheads.")

Breakthrough: In 1998 Perry's musical, *I Know I've Been Changed*, became a hit in Atlanta. He has since written and/or produced several more hit plays, films, TV shows, and books, and he owns his own TV and film production studio. In 2011 *Forbes* magazine named him the highest-paid man in entertainment, earning $110 million that year alone. The formerly homeless and penniless Perry is now worth around $400 million.

MICHAEL PITT

On the Street: The *Boardwalk Empire* star didn't live in a car. Why not? He couldn't afford one. He was homeless and panhandling while he was trying to break into the acting business when he was still a teenager.

Story: Pitt left his New Jersey home in 1997—when he was 16—determined to make it as an actor in New York City. Over the next two years, in between the odd independent film role, Pitt was regularly without a home, "just kind of panhandling and stuff, ya know?" He added that he was "sleeping behind the NYU [New York University, Manhattan] recreational building, with a bunch of other kids who had no place to go." During that time Pitt was arrested and fined a number of times for being homeless. In 1999 he landed a role in an off-Broadway play. One night after a performance a casting agent was waiting for him—and Pitt almost ran away: he was afraid the agent was a cop, and he still owed money on the fines accrued from those earlier arrests.

Breakthrough: The casting agent helped Pitt land a recurring role in the TV show *Dawson's Creek*, which led to his breakout role as Tommy Gnosis in the 2001 cult hit *Hedwig and the Angry Inch*. By 2006, when he turned 25, Pitt was an international star, with several films on his résumé, including Bernardo Bertolucci's *The Dreamers* (2003), M. Night Shyamalan's *The Village* (2004), and *Delirious* (2006)—in which he played a homeless young man in New York City (not too hard for Pitt!). Today he's best known for his award-winning role as Jimmy Darmody in the HBO series *Boardwalk Empire*. (Pitt is worth around $4 million today, and owns his own brownstone in New York City—so no more sleeping behind NYU—unless he wants to.)

*　　*　　*

"In preparing for battle I have always found that plans are useless, but planning is indispensable."

—**Dwight D. Eisenhower**

When old books disintegrate, a chemical breakdown gives them a vanilla flower–almond aroma.

Two Monkeys Go into a Bar

Primates are our closest relatives in the animal kingdom. How close? According to some unconventional scientific research, we may have more in common with them than we thought.

RAISING CANE

About 250 miles east of Puerto Rico is an island in the Caribbean called Saint Kitts. Today it's a popular tourist destination, but for more than 300 years it was best known as a producer of both sugarcane and rum, the liquor made from sugarcane. The first cane plantations were established in the 1640s by England and France, which both had settlements on the island.

In those days, France also had colonies in Africa, and when French colonists from West Africa came to Saint Kitts, they often brought monkeys called *vervets* with them as pets. Many of these monkeys escaped into the wild, where they thrived in the tropical paradise, free from predators and disease. The vervet population exploded in the years that followed. There were plenty of mangoes for them to eat, and when mangoes weren't in season, the vervets happily devoured the sugarcane, as an English visitor named Lady Andrews observed in 1774:

> They are the torment of the planters, they destroy whole cane pieces in a few hours and come in troops from the mountains, whose trees afford them shelter…When pursued, they fly to the mountain and laugh at their pursuers, as they are as little ashamed of a defeat as a French general.

MONKEY SEE

And just as vervets—like humans—acquired a taste for cane sugar, they also developed a taste for the rum produced from it. The monkeys probably got their first taste of alcohol by eating naturally fermenting cane stalks in the fields, then graduated to stealing rum whenever the opportunity presented itself. Islanders soon learned that an easy way to catch a vervet was to set out some rum in a bowl, then wait for one to come along and drink itself into insensibility.

As the years passed and Saint Kitts's economy evolved from sugar and rum production to tourism, the vervets may have had an easier transition than the islanders did—at least as far as imbibing was concerned. Instead of heading out to the cane fields or into town in search of rum, the monkeys simply staked out the vacation resorts and stole drinks from tourists whenever their backs were turned. Some visitors found this annoying, of course, but for others, watching vervets steal drinks was—and still is—part of the experience of visiting Saint Kitts.

BIRDS OF A FEATHER

Vervets are one of few primate species (other than humans) that *choose* to drink alcohol. Though they're covered in gray fur, have long tails, stand only two feet tall, and weigh less than 20 pounds, they share 90 percent of their DNA with humans. That has prompted scientists to study their drinking habits in the hopes of developing insights into the drinking behavior of humans.

Frank Ervin, a professor of psychiatry at McGill University in Montreal, has been observing the behavior of a colony of vervets in Saint Kitts since the 1970s. Earlier in his career he ran a rehabilitation clinic for alcoholics in Boston, Massachusetts, and after witnessing the ravages of alcoholism firsthand, he began studying vervets to "understand more about alcoholism so that the damage can be reduced."

MONKEY BARS

Ervin has conducted numerous studies over the years. Many have a similar structure. Vervets are given access to three kinds of liquids:

1. Plain water
2. Water mixed with fruit juice or some other sweetener
3. Alcoholic beverages ranging in potency from 7.5 percent alcohol, about as strong as malt liquor, to 25 percent, which is stronger than wine but not as strong as the rum the vervets drink "in the wild"

The vervets select what they want to drink and in what quantities. In some studies, the alcohol is available all the time; in others, it is only available at certain times of day. Sometimes the vervets choose between alcohol served straight, diluted with water, or mixed with fruit juice. Whatever the case, the vervets decide for themselves what to drink.

GROUP DYNAMICS

"The parallels between the vervets' behavior and human behavior is striking," Ervin says. He divides vervets into four categories:

1. Teetotalers

• Fifteen percent of the vervets studied drink little or no alcohol at all. That's a larger proportion than is found in those human societies where alcohol consumption is not forbidden for religious or other reasons.

• The teetotalers prefer sweetened, nonalcoholic "soft" drinks over water. This distinguishes them from the vervets who do drink alcohol: all categories of those drinkers prefer water over soft drinks when they aren't drinking alcohol.

2. Social Drinkers

• Sixty-five percent of vervets drink small to moderate quantities of alcohol, and only when other monkeys are around.

• Social drinkers prefer alcohol mixed with fruit juice or other sweeteners and rarely drink before noon.

• Social drinkers are more likely to be female than male, and older males rather than young males.

3. Abusive Binge Drinkers

• Five percent of vervets will drink until they pass out in an alcoholic coma, "sometimes repeatedly within a 24-hour period," if the alcohol isn't allowed to run out or isn't taken away. "They will stand at the alcohol bottle," Ervin writes, "and will drink continuously, blocking access for all other monkeys."

• Binge drinkers prefer their alcohol straight or mixed with water rather than mixed with fruit juice or other sweeteners. They drink more in the morning than they do in the afternoon.

• If access to alcohol is restricted to certain times of day, the binge drinkers can consume an entire day's worth of alcohol in as little as an hour. They will not drink water as long as alcohol is available.

• Left to their own devices, abusive binge drinkers can drink themselves to death in a matter of months or even weeks.

• Most abusive binge drinkers are young males.

4. Heavy Steady Drinkers

• Fifteen percent of vervets drink as much as abusive binge drinkers but do so gradually, sipping it over time instead of drinking it all at once.

• Heavy steady drinkers prefer their alcohol either straight or diluted with water, not sweetened with juice.

• They tend to be dominant, sociable animals with strong leadership skills.

• Males who drink heavily as adolescents, either as binge drinkers or heavy steady drinkers, are likely to continue drinking heavily into adulthood. Their offspring will, on average, drink twice as much as the offspring of social drinkers.

OTHER FINDINGS

Behavior

• In vervet studies where access to alcohol is restricted to a certain time of day, in the hour before that time, the monkeys show "significant attention to the external environment" and "anxious attention to

---

According to a Fox News poll, more than a third of Americans under age 35 have at least one tattoo.

stimuli." After the alcohol is made available, this heightened attentiveness and anxiety diminish considerably.

• As with humans, how vervets respond while under the influence of alcohol varies from one individual to the next. Some become more social; others are playful but keep to themselves and interact little with others in the group. Still other monkeys become withdrawn and remove themselves from the group, often retreating to a corner or sitting next to the alcohol bottle so that they can continue drinking. If approached by other vervets, they will either ignore the overture or respond aggressively.

• For the group as a whole, when the monkeys are drinking, the total number of social interactions increases...but the number of friendly or "affiliative" behaviors such as grooming and huddling decreases. "The increase was accounted for by fragmentary and inappropriate behaviors...There were many 'aggressive' overtures, including threats and slapping...which were neither responded to nor followed up by the initiator," Ervin writes.

• Play sessions between males who have been drinking are more likely to end in fights than play sessions between sober males.

Miscellaneous

• Adolescent vervets of both sexes, and adult females who have low social status in the group, Ervin writes, are both "over-represented among drinkers."

• Young vervets showed a greater preference for sweetened alcoholic drinks than did older vervets.

• In one study, alcohol was available in unlimited quantities for three weeks and then suddenly taken away. The result: "abrupt withdrawal led to restlessness, cage pacing, voluminous consumption of [sweetened water], hyperirritability to sound or observer intrusion, tremulousness... and repeated approaches to the drinking bottle together with handling, rattling and banging of the drinking bottle."

* * *

AMAZING LUCK

In 2014 German police were making a routine sweep of a casino when they came across a gambler who had an outstanding warrant for resisting arrest. They informed him that he had to pay a fine of 710 euros ($910) or go to jail. Only problem: the man didn't have the money. Then, just as they were about to arrest him, his slot machine hit the jackpot, and he won 1,000 euros. The man paid the cops on the spot, in cash.

News Correcshuns

Just because it's the job of journalists to get they're facts strait,
that doesn't mean there write all the thyme.

"Due to a production error, a quote was altered to change its meaning. Colonel Ghulam Shafiq did not say: 'It's not like 25 years ago. I was killing everybody.' In fact, he said: 'It's not like 25 years ago I was killing everybody.'"

—*The Australian*

"Correction: The Jumble puzzle, which appeared on page D1 of Thursday's edition, actually was the puzzle scheduled to appear today. The Jumble originally scheduled to appear Thursday as well as the answer to Wednesday's puzzle are on page E1 today. The answers to the puzzle published today appeared Thursday, and the answers to the puzzle published Thursday will appear Saturday."

—*The Arizona Republic*

"Correction: The earth orbits the sun, not the moon."

—*The Ottawa Citizen*

"Due to an error in transcription, Danielle Brisebois was misrepresented discussing the demands of the acting profession, Brisebois was misquoted as saying, 'You have to know how to run, you have to be in shape, you have to know how to do sex acts.' She actually said, 'You have to know how to do circus acts.'"

—*US* magazine

"We wish to apologize for our apology to Mark Steyn, published Oct. 22. In correcting the incorrect statements about Mr. Steyn published Oct. 15, we incorrectly published the incorrect correction. We accept and regret that our initial regrets were unacceptable and we apologize to Mr. Steyn for any distress caused by our previous apology."

—*The Ottawa Citizen*

"ERROR! ERROR! We mistakenly gave you the wrong dates for July FLy-In at the Arlington Airport. The correct dates for this annual event are: July 5th through the 9th; NOT July 5th to the 9th, as was reported. We regret any problems this misinformation may have caused."

—*Seattle Times*

Studies show: Women are more likely than men to notice (and be annoyed by) a dripping faucet.

Six Famous Illegitimate Kids

The fascinating stories of six people who were born in situations deemed less than ideal…and made it to the top anyway.

WHO'S YOUR DADDY?

For a long time—until very recently, in fact—children born out of wedlock were treated as second-class citizens, both socially and legally. England's Statute of Merton (1235), for example, stated, "He is a bastard that is born before the marriage of his parents" and prohibited these "illegitimate" children from inheriting the estates of their birth parents. Such laws were common throughout the world for centuries. Amazingly, they weren't fully overturned in the UK until 1969—and not in the United States until 1977. But throughout the ages, there are examples of kids who overcame the odds stacked so unfairly against them—and achieved greatness. Here are a few famous ones.

WILLIAM THE CONQUEROR

Born around 1028 to Robert I, Duke of Normandy (a region of northern France) and his mistress, a young peasant woman known only as Herleva. William was lucky, though—he was raised by his father. (His mother married one of Robert's friends.) When William was named Duke of Normandy upon Robert's death in 1035, a contingent of Norman barons objected. They believed "William the Bastard," as they called him, should have been ineligible. A power struggle ensued, and William eventually came out on top. In 1066 he cemented his place in history when he led Norman forces to defeat the English at the Battle of Hastings and became King William I of England, a seat he held until his death in 1087. With a few exceptions, every British monarch since then is a descendant of "William the Bastard."

ALEXANDER HAMILTON

Born on the British Caribbean island of Nevis sometime around 1755, the second son of Scottish businessman James Hamilton and Rachel Faucette Buck, an island woman of French descent—who was married to another man. (She would divorce that husband a few years later.) Because his parents weren't married, Alexander wasn't allowed to go to school, so he received private tutoring and taught himself by reading

In 1988 BIC launched a line of perfume. (It flopped, but you can still buy it in Iran.)

anything he could get his hands on. James abandoned the family in 1765; Rachel died in 1768. Around 1771 Alexander and his brother, James Jr., were adopted by a cousin, but he committed suicide a year later. The boys were then split up, and Alexander came under the care of a merchant named Thomas Stevens. The following year, he was sent to the American colonies, where he attended schools in New Jersey and New York. In 1774 he published his first political writings, in 1775 he joined the New York militia, in 1776 he joined General George Washington's staff, in 1789 President George Washington named him the first U.S. Secretary of the Treasury, and today the face of Alexander Hamilton, a seemingly luckless kid from the West Indies, can be seen on millions of American $10 bills.

SOPHIA LOREN

Appropriately enough, Loren's story sounds like something from a Hollywood movie. She was born Sofia Scicolone in 1934 in a ward for unwed mothers in Rome, Italy. Her mother was Romilda Villani, a 20-year-old piano teacher. Her father, 36-year-old Riccardo Scicolone, was married to someone else and refused to help raise Sofia, although he did grant her the use of his last name. (He did not do the same when he and Villani had a second daughter, Sofia's younger sister Anna Maria, four years later.) The young family lived with Villani's mother in the slums of Nazi-occupied Naples during World War II, subsisting on meager rations, often close to starvation. Things began to look up in 1948, when 14-year-old Sofia became a finalist in a Naples beauty contest. Her mother encouraged her to model and try out for films—and in less than a decade she was a Hollywood star. She won an Academy Award for Best Actress in 1962 and received an Honorary Oscar in 1991 for being "one of world cinema's greatest treasures." Bonus fact: After she made it big, Loren paid her father a million lire (about $1,500) for the right for her sister to use his last name so that Anna Maria would no longer be considered illegitimate.

THOMAS EDWARD LAWRENCE

In 1885 Thomas Robert Tighe Chapman, 39, a wealthy Irishman and the married father of four young girls, got his daughters' governess, 24-year-old Sarah Lawrence, pregnant. He eventually left his wife for his young mistress, and they went on to have several more children. One, born in Wales in 1888, was a son named Thomas Edward Lawrence. Why Lawrence and not Chapman? Because Chapman had taken Sarah's last name to hide the fact that he was the already-married Thomas Chapman. The family moved several times over the years, finally settling in Oxford, England, where, while living as Mr. and Mrs. Lawrence, they were able to get their children decent educations. Young Thomas

Israel Bissell rode a horse 350 miles to warn of the British invasion in 1775; Paul Revere rode 20.

eventually graduated from Jesus College in Oxford, made his way to the Middle East, and became an archaeologist, then a British Army officer, then a prolific writer, and, finally, the man still known around the world as "Lawrence of Arabia." And very few people knew that the "Lawrence" in his name came from his mother…because he was born out of wedlock.

LEONARDO DA VINCI

Born in 1452 in the Italian region of Tuscany to a 25-year-old lawyer named Piero Fruosino di Antonio da Vinci and a poor peasant (possibly a slave) named Caterina. (Her age and last name—if she had one—are unknown.) At that time in Tuscany, illegitimacy was treated differently by different families: the boy could have been left to his impoverished mother. Luckily for Leonardo, his father took him in. He was raised in his father's house and, according to many records, looked after by an uncle or possibly a grandfather. When Leonardo was 14, his genius was already obvious, and his father apprenticed him to a Florentine artist, beginning the career of one of the most influential painters, architects, engineers, inventors, and writers in history.

GEORGE FOREMAN

Born in 1949 in Marshall, Texas, to Nancy Ree and Leroy Moorehead. Except he didn't know that. He *thought* his father was J. D. Foreman, whom his mother married when he was a baby. (He didn't find out the truth until years later.) The elder Foreman was a hard drinker and was seldom home. Young George grew up angry and violent and, by his own account, "became a mugger and brawler on the streets of Houston by age 15." At 16, after seeing an ad on TV, Foreman joined the Job Corps, a program for troubled kids, and then moved to California, where he met boxing coach Doc Broaddus. Just two years later, at the 1968 Olympics in Mexico City, Foreman won the heavyweight gold medal. He turned pro in 1969 and went on to become one of the best boxers in sports history, winning the heavyweight championship twice, once at the age of 45—still the record for the oldest champ. Foreman retired in 1997 with a record of 76–5, including 68 knockouts. (Muhammad Ali's record, by comparison: 56–5, with 37 knockouts.) And if all that wasn't enough of a rags-to-riches story, Foreman is probably better known for his successful second act: in 1994 he became the namesake and smiling TV pitchman for the George Foreman Grill. It's estimated that Foreman has earned more than $250 million from that enterprise—more than three times his total earnings in the ring. He's going to need every penny: Foreman has 11 children, including 5 sons…all named George.

Junk food wisdom: Dunked cookies are best when immersed in a hot drink for 3.5 seconds.

The Life and Times of Oney Judge

George and Martha Washington owned hundreds of slaves over the course of their lives. The names of many are known, but most of the details of their lives have been lost to history. Here's the story of one woman who hasn't been forgotten.

BORN INTO SLAVERY

In the early 1770s an English tailor named Andrew Judge signed a contract to work as an indentured servant at Mount Vernon, George Washington's plantation in Virginia. Indentured servitude was a common way for Europeans with no money to pay their way to the American colonies. By signing the contract, Judge agreed to work for Washington for a set period of years in exchange for his passage to Virginia, plus his room and board for the length of the contract.

At Mount Vernon, Judge made military uniforms and other clothing for Washington. He also taught his tailoring skills to Washington's slaves so that when his term as an indentured servant was up, they would be able to do the tailoring themselves.

Around 1773 Judge fathered a baby girl with an African American slave named Betty, who worked as a seamstress at Mount Vernon. They named their child Oney, but though Judge was white and free, Oney was born a slave because her mother was a slave. In the eyes of the law, she was "property" and belonged to the Washingtons; neither Betty nor Andrew had any parental rights over their child whatsoever.

LADY'S MAID

Oney became a favorite of Martha Washington's and served as her personal attendant, helping her wash and dress, and accompanying her on social calls. Judge was one of eight slaves who accompanied the Washingtons to New York City, then the nation's capital, when Washington was elected president in April 1789, and then to Philadelphia when the capital moved there in 1790.

In Philadelphia, Judge enjoyed a measure of freedom unheard of at Mount Vernon. She ran errands around the city unsupervised, and in her limited free time, she explored on her own. President Washington even gave her and other slaves of the household money for the theater, the circus, and other entertainments in the city.

What is a *duodecillion*? A 1 followed by 39 zeroes. (We'd show you, but we're out of room.)

FREEDOM ALL AROUND

There was something else in Philadelphia that Judge had never encountered before: a thriving community of *free* African Americans, the largest such community in the United States at the time. Slavery was still legal in Pennsylvania, but the state's Gradual Abolition Act, passed in 1780, was phasing it out, and the number of free blacks in the city was growing. There were so many, in fact, that Washington and other slave owners worried about bringing their slaves to live among them in Philadelphia. They feared the slaves would be "tainted" by exposure to free African Americans and abolitionists living in the city. Washington was concerned that even if his slaves didn't try to escape, they'd become, as he put it, "insolent in a state of slavery."

As the president soon learned from his attorney general, Edmund Randolph, the slaves had the law on their side. Under the terms of the Gradual Abolition Act, slaves who'd been brought into the state by nonresidents (including Washington and Randolph) and who lived there for six consecutive months became free citizens automatically. Slaves owned by members of Congress were specifically exempted from the law, and Washington and Randolph had assumed that their slaves were also exempt. They were wrong. Randolph learned as much in 1791 when his slaves demanded their freedom when the six months were up—and got it.

IN ROTATION

To prevent the same thing from happening to Washington's slaves, the attorney general advised the president to rotate his slaves out of state for a few days every six months before the deadline was up. Moving slaves out of state for the purpose of denying them their freedom was illegal, but Washington did it anyway. He kept it up for the rest of his presidency, instructing his secretary that he wished "to have it accomplished under the pretext that may deceive both them [the slaves] and the public." Accordingly, when the president's slaves were sent back to Mount Vernon for brief visits ahead of the six-month deadline, they were told they were being sent home to spend time with their families.

Martha Washington did her part by taking her slaves across the state line into New Jersey for short overnight trips. In this way she denied Judge her chance at freedom in May of 1791.

Judge knew that if she returned to Mount Vernon when Washington retired, what little freedom she'd had in Philadelphia would be gone forever. But it wasn't until 1796, when Washington was nearing the end of his presidency, that she decided to escape. She did so after learning that Martha Washington was planning to give her away as a wedding present to her granddaughter, Elizabeth Custis, whom Judge knew to be a moody and vindictive woman.

Judge detested Elizabeth Custis and was, as she put it, "determined not to be her slave." In May 1796, she used an upcoming trip the Washingtons were taking to Mount Vernon as cover for her escape. "Whilst they were packing up to go to Virginia, I was packing to go," she told an interviewer in 1845. "I had friends among the colored people of Philadelphia, had my things carried there beforehand, and left Washington's house while they were eating dinner."

HEADING NORTH

Judge hid out somewhere in Philadelphia; she never revealed where or for how long. She had to lay low because of an advertisement in the *Pennsylvania Gazette* giving her physical description ("...a light mulatto girl, much freckled, with very black eyes and bushy hair...of middle stature, slender, and delicately formed, about 20 years of age"), offering a $10 reward for her capture. When she felt safe enough to venture out, she made her way to the Philadelphia waterfront and boarded a ship called the *Nancy*, whose captain, a man named John Bowles, was known to be sympathetic to escaping slaves and who may have had "Black Jacks"—free African American sailors—on his crew. Judge sailed to Portsmouth, New Hampshire, and disappeared into the free black community there. That probably would have been the end of her story had a family friend of the Washingtons, Elizabeth Langdon, not spotted her walking on the street in Portsmouth a few months later.

THE RESCUERS

Word soon got back to George and Martha Washington that Judge was in Portsmouth. As odd as it may sound to modern ears, the Washingtons were actually stunned and hurt that one of their favorite slaves—"more like [our] child than a servant," as Washington put it—had escaped. They could not bring themselves to accept that she'd done so out of a genuine desire for freedom. Instead, they convinced themselves that she'd been "seduced and enticed off by a Frenchman" (a recent visitor) and tricked into escaping against her own best interest. There's no evidence that the man in question had anything to do with the escape, but the Washingtons feared that he'd gotten her pregnant and abandoned her. They were determined not just to recover their "property" but also to return Judge to the safety, as they saw it, of home.

Once again Washington was willing to flout the law where his slaves were concerned. Under the terms of the Fugitive Slave Act, which he himself had signed into law in 1793, slave owners were required to go into open court and provide proof of ownership of an escaped slave before crossing into another state to capture them. But Washington wanted to avoid publicity. So he ignored the law and instead asked his

---

...kissing everyone who bought $50,000 worth of WWII bonds.

treasury secretary, Oliver Wolcott Jr., to order the customs collector in Portsmouth, a man named Joseph Whipple, to capture Judge and put her on a boat back home.

HE SAID, SHE SAID

Whipple had no reason to doubt Washington's pregnant damsel-in-distress story—he was the president, after all—and was more than happy to aid in rescuing Judge from the harm she'd supposedly fallen into. After discovering where Judge was living, Whipple secretly booked passage for her on a ship to Philadelphia. He waited until the day the ship was due to sail, then he approached her, introduced himself, and made a phony offer of a job with his own family. He hoped either to grab her and drag her onto the ship or trick her into coming aboard voluntarily. But as Whipple talked to Judge, he realized that she hadn't been seduced by a Frenchman, wasn't pregnant, wasn't in distress, and in fact was in Portsmouth of her own free will. "She had not been decoyed away as had been apprehended, but that a thirst for compleat freedom... had been her only motive for absconding," Whipple explained in a letter to Wolcott.

THE OFFER

Satisfied that Judge was happy where she was, Whipple abandoned his plans to take her back to Philadelphia. If Washington wanted to bring Judge back against her will, he suggested that the president go through proper legal channels as described in the Fugitive Slave Act. But was that even necessary? As Whipple reported to Wolcott, Judge was willing to return to the Washingtons voluntarily, on one condition:

> She expressed great affection and reverence for her Master & Mistress, and without hesitation declared her willingness to return and to serve with fidelity during the lives of the President and his Lady if she could be freed on their decease, should she outlive them; but that she should rather suffer death that return to slavery and [be] liable to be sold or given to other persons.

Wolcott forwarded Judge's offer to Washington. So was the president happy to learn that Judge was willing to return? Hardly—he was furious that Whipple had accepted a slave's version of events over his own. And he angrily rejected the notion that a master would ever negotiate with a slave over any matter, let alone negotiate with a slave who had shown disloyalty by running away:

> To enter into a such a compromise with her, as she suggested to you, is totally inadmissible...It would neither be politic or just to reward unfaithfulness with a premature preference; and thereby discontent beforehand the minds of all her fellow servants who by their steady attachments are far more deserving than herself of favor.

Holi-day: In India, people celebrate the spring festival of Holi by throwing paint on each other.

STAYING PUT

Her offer having been rejected, Judge remained in New Hampshire. But Washington refused to give up, at least not if he could get Judge back without attracting negative publicity. He told Whipple to use "compulsory means" to seize Judge if possible, provided that he didn't "excite a mob or a riot…or even uneasy sensations in the minds of well disposed citizens." If that couldn't be avoided, he wrote, "I would forgo her services altogether."

Whipple made no further attempt to capture Judge. But Washington did. When he heard that Martha Washington's nephew, Burwell Bassett Jr., was planning a trip to Portsmouth in the fall of 1799, Washington asked him to try to get Judge back. Bassett agreed, and paid a visit to Judge, who by now was married to a free African American sailor named John Staines and already had the first of three children by him. (Staines was away at sea when Bassett dropped by.) Bassett asked Judge to return to Mount Vernon. She refused, telling him, "I am free and choose to remain so."

Bassett was the guest of Senator John Langdon while visiting Portsmouth, and after the first visit to Judge, he confided to Langdon that he'd been instructed to seize both Judge and her daughter by force if necessary and would do so in the coming days. Langdon, a longtime friend of the Washingtons, was nonetheless so disturbed by what he heard that he slipped out of the house while Bassett was eating dinner and warned Judge of the danger. She fled to Greenland, New Hampshire, and hid there with friends.

FREE AT LAST

George Washington died a few months later, on December 14, 1799; Martha Washington followed in May 1802. Ownership of Oney Judge and her three children now passed to relatives on Martha's side of the family, but there's no evidence that they ever tried to reclaim Judge under the Fugitive Slave Act.

Judge didn't take any chances, though. She laid low for the next 40 years. It wasn't until she was in her 70s and too old and sick to work—and therefore no longer worth the expense of capturing her and bringing her back to Virginia—that she began telling her story to abolitionist newspapers in the mid-1840s. By then her husband and all three of her children had died, and she had been living in abject poverty for many years. One of the reporters asked her if she ever regretted leaving the Washingtons and Mount Vernon, where, if she had stayed, she might have lived an easier life. "No," she replied, "I am free and have, I trust, been made a child of God by the means."

Amazing Geoglyphs

Quick answer to the question, "What the heck is a geoglyph?" Do you know what the Nazca lines are? Then you know what a geoglyph is!

PICTURE PERFECT

A *geoglyph*, meaning "land picture," is a large—sometimes huge—image formed on or carved into the surface of the earth. The most famous are probably the Nazca lines, the enormous figures of people, animals, plants, and geometric shapes scribed into the ground in southern Peru by the ancient Nazca people roughly 1,500 years ago. (Editor's note: we told you about the Nazca lines and the German woman who made it her life's work to protect them in *Uncle John's Unstoppable Bathroom Reader*.)

But the Nazca lines aren't the only ones. Geoglyphs can be found all over the world, including in North America. Here are the stories of a few you might want to see for yourself someday.

THE UFFINGTON WHITE HORSE

Located on a hillside in the parish of Uffington, in south-central England, this geoglyph is so big (about 374 feet across) that from up close it's impossible to make out what it is. But from a distance—as far as 20 miles on a clear day—it comes to life. It's the stylized figure of a running horse. It was made by digging trenches up to 10 feet wide in places and filling them with crushed white chalk, making the image stand out starkly against the lush green hillside. And it's very, very old: archaeologists say it dates to between 1400 and 600 BC. Who made it—and why—is unknown. And some people say it's not a horse but a cat or perhaps a dragon, although written descriptions of the ancient work going back to the 11th century AD refer to it as a horse.

Note: Similar chalk "hill figures," as this type of geoglyph is known, can be found all over southern England. Some, like this one, are made by filling trenches with chalk taken from nearby quarries, and others are made by simply stripping away the turf and exposing chalk already deposited below the surface.

THE CERNE ABBAS GIANT

This figure is similar to the Uffington White Horse in that it's a chalk figure, but this one has a human shape…and it's naughtier. It's the figure of a man cut into a steep hillside in the village of Cerne Abbas, not far from England's southern coast. The figure is 180 feet long—so it can be seen from very far away—and depicts a man standing with outstretched arms, carrying a long knotted club in his right hand. It has facial features (eyebrows, eyes, nose, and mouth), two circles for nipples, lines on the midsection that appear to be ribs, and below the waist it is (ahem) anatomically correct. (That area of the figure explains the site's alternate name: "The Rude Man of Cerne.")

The Cerne Abbas Giant was long thought to be an ancient geoglyph, but more recent investigations suggest that may not be the case. One reason: unlike other chalk figures in the region, it was not written about in ancient times. The earliest known reference to it only dates to the late 17th century, which leads some experts to believe it was made around that time, possibly as some kind of political parody.

THE SAJAMA LINES

If you look at aerial or satellite photographs of the region around Mount Sajama, in the high desert plateau land of western Bolivia, it appears as if someone took a giant ruler and scribed thousands of very straight, crisscrossing lines into the land. These are the Sajama lines. Archaeologists say they were made by scraping away surface layers of dark topsoil and rock, thereby exposing the light-colored rock below. They range from 3 to 10 feet in width, with the longest stretch about 12 miles. And each of the lines somehow maintains its very straight course over the rugged, uneven landscape—evidence, experts say, that the lines weren't built as simple footpaths, as such paths wouldn't need to be so straight. Many of the lines radiate from a center point, over the region's hills and peaks, like spokes emanating from the hub of a wheel; this has led some to conclude that the lines carry some kind of religious significance, perhaps as paths used in ritual pilgrimages. Sources vary as to their age: some say they are hundreds of years old, others say thousands. In any case, exactly who made them—and why they made them—remains a mystery.

THE BLYTHE GEOGLYPHS

These six huge figures—three depicting humans; two of animals, possibly horses or pumas; and one spiral shape—are scribed into the earth in the Sonoran Desert, not far from the town of Blythe in remote southeast California. The largest, the figure of a man with outstretched arms, measures 171 feet from head to toe. Archaeologists theorize that the drawings were made much the way the Sajama lines were made—by scraping away dark layers of pebbles and sediment, revealing lighter-colored soil below—and that they were likely made by ancestors of the native Mojave and Quechan peoples who still live in the region today. They are at least 450 years old—and possibly much older. They were completely unknown to science or the general public until 1931, when

U.S. Army Air Corps pilot George A. Palmer saw them from his small airplane and alerted scientists to their existence. (For more on discoveries from the sky, go to page 31.) Since Palmer's discovery, hundreds of other ancient geoglyphs have been discovered in the region.

THE ATACAMA GIANT

The Atacama Giant is one of more than 5,000 geoglyphs that can be found on the Atacama Desert in northern Chile, home to the largest collection of geoglyphs in the world. But this is one of the most spectacular. It's the depiction of a humanlike figure scraped into the side of a steep, rocky hill. It's a towering 393 feet tall and more than 100 feet wide. It has a large, wide, rectangular head with large square eyes and a single square hole that could be either a nose or a mouth. Straight, parallel lines emanate from the top and sides of the head. The figure has a long, rectangular body; the arms are bent, with hands held up at shoulder height; and it has long, thin, straight legs—giving it a vaguely robotic (even Lego-ish) look overall. There are several other images drawn into the earth nearby, including circles and lines, and some archaeologists believe they may have all been used together for some kind of astronomical purpose. Most experts assume the figure represents a deity of some importance to whoever made the giant image, while others believe the Atacama Giant is a drawing of an alien in a space suit. (Which is a lot more fun.)

*   *   *

REAL TATTOO TYPOS

"Exreme"

"I'm Awsome"

"East Cost"

"BELIVE"

"Nolege Is Power"

"To Cool for Scool"

"Only God Can Juge Me"

"TOMARROW NEVER KNOWS"

"Keep Smileing"

"IT'S GET BETTER"

"Babby Girl"

"ARE YOU JALOUS"

"ITS GONNA BE ALRIGTH"

"Regret Nohing"

Secret Spaces in Legendary Places

Many well-known buildings all around the world contain secret chambers and passageways. Why are they there? What is their purpose? How are they used today?

Building: Palais Garnier (Paris Opera House)
Location: Paris
Secret: If you've seen a stage or screen version of *The Phantom of the Opera*, you know about the hidden rooms and passageways in the Paris Opera House that the Phantom uses to avoid detection. One of those rooms contains an underground lake that's connected to the Seine River. Unlike the other passages in *The Phantom of the Opera*, the lake is real. Architect Charles Garnier and his crew had a difficult time laying the foundation for the opera house back in the 1860s. Accidentally digging into an arm of the Seine only made matters worse—the foundation was quickly flooded. The crew tried various ways to pump the water out, and each failed. Garnier finally resorted to dumping it all into an artificial lagoon. It's still there today, helping to keep the groundwater from rising and destroying the opera house's interior. Fish from the Seine make their way into the lagoon on occasion, and it's also used for training drills by the Paris Fire Department's dive squad.

Building: The Mansion on O Street
Location: Washington, D.C.
Secret: This odd hotel is located in the capital's historic Dupont Circle district. Originally built in the 1890s as a row of connected townhouses for the family of acclaimed architect Edward Clark (designer of the Capitol Building), the property was later converted into rooming houses for the FBI and, in 1980, a hotel. (Among the hotel's unusual features: everything in it, from the furniture to the fixtures, may be purchased by guests.) The Mansion's hallways have been described as "mazelike," and it boasts more than a few secret passages and hidden rooms. It also has 70 "secret doors" hidden behind pantries, mirrors, panels, and bookcases. What's behind them? More hotel rooms, some with original Tiffany stained-glass windows and other historic decor. The hotel also has a "hidden" log cabin and a secluded Art Deco penthouse with a private elevator. According to local lore, these features were installed when the Mansion was converted into a hotel to provide a place for

---

First dinosaur to be named: *Megalosaurus,* in 1824 by the paleontologist Rev. William Buckland.

the district's politicians and bureaucrats to "unwind" without attracting unwanted attention. Throughout the 1980s and early 1990s, the Mansion reportedly hosted many private parties for D.C.'s elite…and more than a few illicit affairs.

Building: Wolf's Lair Castle
Location: Los Angeles
Secret: Architect L. Milton Wolf designed dozens of homes in the Hollywood Hills in the 1920s, but he saved his grandest ideas for himself. In 1928 he built Wolf's Lair Castle, an elaborate mansion with a heart-shaped swimming pool and a fantastic view of the Hollywood hills. Wolf's luxurious home also included a secret "miniature turret" room for his pet gibbon, a hidden lounge where he hosted booze-filled Prohibition-era parties, and an apartment under the gatehouse, with hidden hallways connecting them all. The architect was said to have used the lounge to romance young starlets while his wife was asleep upstairs in the master bedroom—it even had a mechanical couch that turned into a bed at the push of a button. The castle's most recent owner was electronic musician Moby, who spent millions renovating the estate and then, in 2014, put it on the market for $12.4 million.

Building: Passetto di Borgo
Location: Vatican City
Secret: Commissioned by Pope Nicholas III in 1277, this elevated 2,600-foot passageway was originally built to serve as a convenient route between Saint Peter's Basilica and the Castel Sant'Angelo—Roman emperor Hadrian's mausoleum, built in 138, which was later converted into a fortress and is now a museum. The Passetto di Borgo has helped save many clergy over the centuries. As the armies of Charles VIII of France stormed through the city's gates in 1494, Pope Alexander VI fled across the Passetto to hole up in the Castel Sant'Angelo. Pope Clement VII used it to escape to safety during the sack of Rome in 1527 (by Holy Roman Emperor Charles V) while his guards were being slaughtered on the steps of St. Peter's. More recently, it was featured in Dan Brown's *Angels & Demons*: a nefarious member of the Illuminati uses the walkway to kidnap a few cardinals. It also appears in the video game *Assassin's Creed II*, where it can be used by players to sneak from the Castel Sant'Angelo to the Sistine Chapel.

*   *   *

"Man is not what he thinks he is, he is what he hides." —**André Malraux**

Women didn't shave their armpits until sleeveless dresses were introduced in the 1910s.

Cat Food

This article falls into the "train wreck" category: You really don't want to read it…but somehow you just can't stop yourself. Warning to cat lovers (and vegetarians): you might just want to skip this page.

MEOW MIX

In November 2014, animal-rights activists in Switzerland made international headlines when they presented a petition with thousands of signatures to their parliament. The goal: to convince the government to pass a law making it illegal to eat cats. *Eat cats?* It seems unfathomable to pet-loving Americans, but lots of people around the world actually do dine on felines. In fact, it's something of a holiday tradition in Switzerland. Reports indicate that about 3 percent of the country's population—roughly 240,000 people—regularly consume cats (and dogs), often at Christmas cooked the way rabbits are cooked—with thyme, garlic, and wine.

With that in mind, here is a real cat recipe (we're not joking) from one of Spain's oldest cookbooks, *Libre del Coch*, or "Book of Cookery," first published in 1520. It was written by one Ruperto de Nola, who claimed to have once been the royal cook for King Ferdinand I of Naples, in southern Italy. The book, which contains 243 recipes, was a huge success: it was republished at least a dozen times in the decades following its initial release. Among its many recipes for desserts, sauces, vegetables, fish, fowl, and meat was this one. These instructions are quite graphic, but in our ongoing mission to bring you bizarre facts and information, we couldn't *not* include it.

GATO ASADO COMO SE QUIERE COMER
(Roast cat as you like to eat it)

You take a fat cat, and cut its throat, and after it is dead, cut off the head and throw it away, because it is not something to be eaten, because it is said that those who eat the brains will lose their minds and lack judgment. After cleanly skinning the cat and gutting it and washing it well, wrap the carcass in a clean linen cloth and bury it in the ground, leaving it for a day and night, then take it out of the ground and roast it on a spit over a fire, and when it begins to cook, rub it with garlic and olive oil; once it is smeared well with the garlic and oil, take a green branch, and hit the meat until it is well roasted, continuing to smear it with oil. And when the meat is done, cut it up as if it were a rabbit or goat, and put the meat on a large plate, taking garlic and oil boiled in thin broth, and pour this over the cat. And you can eat this because it is a good dish.

Male funnel-web spiders use pheromone "knockout drops" to stun females before mating.

How D'ya Like Them Apples?

There are more than 7,500 known varieties, or cultivars, of apples. Luckily for us, a lot of them have amusing names.

Bloody Ploughman	Beauty of Bath	Chiver's Delight
Nickajack	Zestar	Topaz
Pound Sweet	Winter Banana	Cripp's Pink
Mother	Sheep's Nose	Wealthy
Nanny	Early Joe	Shell of Alabama
Marriage Maker	Burr Knot Monks	Pigeon de Jerusalem
Smokehouse	Cissy	Sergeant Peggy
Rev. W. Wilks	Byfleet Seedling	Laxton's Epicure
Arkansas Black	Dudley Winter	Coconut Crunch
Brown Snout	King of the Pippins	Crow Egg
Foxwhelp	Hollow Log	Greasy Jack
Aunt Rachel	Prairie Spy	Queen Cox
Striped Beefing	Stump	Sops in Wine
Tower of Glamis	Champion	Duck's Bill
Knobbed Russet	Old Fred	Voyager
Maiden's Blush	Lemon Square	Ten Commandments
Suntan	Catshead	Cornish Tiger
Gragg	Hunge	Sir Isaac Newton's Tree
Green Cheese	Cockpit	Orange
Ashmead's Kernel	Dr. Hogg	

A lion's roar is 25 times louder than a lawn mower.

OW!, *Extreme Edition*

On pages 17 and 259 we told you some stories about people's bizarre injuries. Good news: we saved the best for last. (Warning: These cringe-worthy tales are NOT for the squeamish…but every one of them has a happy ending.)

NOSY KID

Scary Beginning: In September 2014, a man in the eastern Chinese city of Wuhan was looking after his two-year-old son when he turned away for a moment to do some chores. Suddenly, he later told reporters, he heard the boy scream. When he turned back, he saw his son…with a chopstick stuck up his nose. (It is believed that the boy fell while holding the chopstick.) Sounds funny, but it's not: a CT scan revealed that the chopstick had penetrated almost three inches into the boy's brain.

Happy Ending: Surgeons removed the wooden utensil in a four-hour operation. They reported that the chopstick had somehow avoided any major arteries and nerves in the boy's brain, and he was expected to make a complete recovery.

LOOSE SCREW

Scary Beginning: A 25-year-old man in Bialystok, Poland, was working in his garden one day in March 2013 when he lost his balance and fell. The man, who did not want to be identified, blacked out for a while, and when he came to, a screwdriver was sticking out of his forehead (just above the inner end of his right eyebrow). His next move: "I smoked a cigarette to calm down," he said. Then he asked a neighbor to take him to a hospital.

Happy Ending: Scans showed that the screwdriver (a Phillips head) had punctured the man's skull and penetrated two inches into his head but thankfully had stopped just short of the right frontal lobe of his brain. Doctors were able to remove the screwdriver and said the man was not likely to suffer any lasting harm from his head-puncturing accident.

OW ARE YOU?

Scary Beginning: Dante Autullo, 32, of Orland Park, Illinois, was building a shed in his yard in January 2012 when the nail gun he was using—above his head, while standing on a ladder—slipped, hit the back of his head, and fired a 3.25-inch nail through his skull and into the center of his brain. But he didn't even notice. He thought the nail gun had simply hit his head, leaving a little cut. His girlfriend put some peroxide on the wound, and he went back to work. The next day he started feeling nauseous, so he went to the hospital. When a doctor showed him an X-ray of his brain—with the nail eerily suspended in the center of it—Autullo thought it was a joke. Doctors finally convinced him that he really did have a nail in his brain, and Autullo underwent surgery to have it removed. (Before he went into surgery—and while he still had the nail in his brain—Autullo took a few moments to post a picture of the X-ray on his Facebook page.)

Happy Ending: Doctors said the nail had inexplicably missed vital areas of Autullo's brain—although only by a few millimeters—and he suffered no debilitating effects from the injury.

WE'RE GONNA NEED A HARDER HAT

Scary Beginning: Eduardo Leite, a 24-year-old construction worker in Rio de Janeiro, Brazil, was on the ground floor of a job site in 2012 when a six-foot metal bar fell from the fifth floor above him—and went straight through his skull. The bar, about ¾ inch in diameter, penetrated Leite's hardhat, then entered the top right portion of his skull and ended up sticking several inches out of his face, between his eyes. Astonishingly, Leite remained lucid even though he had a metal bar stuck in his brain. When he got to the hospital, he calmly told the doctors what had happened to him.

Happy Ending: Doctors spent five hours removing the bar. They said afterward that the bar had passed through what they called a "non-eloquent" region of the brain, not known to have any major motor, sensory, or cognitive functions. Leite hadn't suffered any neurological effects from the incident, they said, nor was he likely to. Leite will have to be monitored for years for any lingering or delayed effects from the injury, but so far he's fine.

SHE'S EX-SPEAR-IENCED

Scary Beginning: On May 6, 2013, Elisangela Rosa, 28, was in her kitchen in the Brazilian coastal city of Arraial do Cabo when her husband, Adriano Goulart, accidentally shot her in the face with a spear gun. (Goulart, who regularly uses the spear gun to fish, had been tinkering with it while Rosa was in the kitchen.) The gun's 10-inch harpoon shot through Rosa's mouth and came out the back of her neck, damaging two of her teeth, puncturing her pharynx, and penetrating the top vertebrae in her spine. Rushed to an emergency room, she was not expected to survive.

Happy Ending: Unbelievably, even though the harpoon had penetrated Rosa's vertebrae, it somehow just missed her spinal cord. "If the object hit only one centimeter to one side, the patient would have become a quadriplegic," said neurosurgeon Allan da Costa. "If it had hit one centimeter to the other side, or reached one artery to the brain, she would have been dead." A team of surgeons was able to remove the harpoon—and less than three weeks later, Rosa walked out of the hospital, smiling for news cameras. Doctors expected her to make a complete recovery. (Note: Police investigated the shooting and were convinced it really was an accident.)

BRANCHING IN

Scary Beginning: Michelle and Daniel Childers, 20 and 22, were driving their truck down a narrow, deeply forested wilderness road in northern Idaho on Labor Day 2009 when, while taking a sharp curve, the branch of a spruce tree unexpectedly came through the passenger side window...and impaled Michelle's neck. The branch snapped off before Daniel could stop the truck, leaving a foot-long piece in his wife's neck. Michelle was conscious and felt no pain, only "pressure" in her neck, but she was terrified. Fortunately, the branch was preventing any blood loss. Unfortunately, they were out of cell phone range. Daniel had to drive more than an hour on the bumpy dirt road before they were able to find a phone at a hunting lodge. Michelle was airlifted to a hospital in Missoula, Montana, where she underwent a six-hour surgery.

Happy Ending: Doctors told Michelle she would require several more surgeries and would have to spend months in the hospital. They were wrong. Michelle left the hospital a week later and hasn't required another surgery since. Two weeks after that, Michelle and Daniel appeared on the *Today* show to talk about her remarkable recovery. Since then she has experienced no lasting effects from the injury, although she says she's still a bit wary around trees...

*   *   *

A SPORTS FLOP: TWO-RACKET TENNIS

It's like regular tennis, except that you hold two rackets—one in each hand. Invented in 2006 by Don "Professor Tennis" Mueller, a physics teacher at Concordia College in Bronxville, New York, the sport hasn't become the sensation he hoped it would. "Everyone I asked, including some teaching pros, saw no redeeming value in it. They basically thought it was a ludicrous idea." That hasn't deterred Mueller, though. "If enough people try this, then maybe one day we could have tournaments."

ace 1989, more than 300 convicted "criminals" in the U.S. have been exonerated based on DNA evidence.

Who's on First?

Ever wonder who was on the very first cover of your favorite magazine?

ROLLING STONE: John Lennon (November 9, 1967)

TIME: Speaker of the House Joseph G. Cannon (March 3, 1923)

PEOPLE: Mia Farrow (March 4, 1974)

WIRED: Science-fiction author Bruce Sterling (March/April 1993)

SPORTS ILLUSTRATED: Milwaukee Braves slugger Eddie Mathews, mid-swing (August 16, 1954)

NINTENDO POWER: Mario and his nemesis, King Koopa (July/August 1988)

THE NEW YORKER: The magazine's mascot: tophatted, monocled dandy Eustace Tilley (February 21, 1925)

ESQUIRE: An illustration of three men in a canoe repairing a downed hydroplane (Autumn 1933)

NEWSWEEK: Nazi troops carrying swastika flags (February 17, 1933)

TV GUIDE: Lucille Ball and Desi Arnaz Jr. (April 4, 1953)

LIFE: Fort Peck Dam in Montana (November 23, 1936)

TIGER BEAT: The Righteous Brothers (September 1965)

EBONY: Children in a newly integrated classroom (November 1, 1945)

SPIN: Madonna (May 1985)

ENTERTAINMENT WEEKLY: kd lang (February 16, 1990)

GUNS & AMMO: A .44-caliber 1860 Colt Army revolver (Summer 1958)

ELLE: The American version of the long-running French fashion magazine depicted model Yasmin Le Bon (September 1985)

FORTUNE: An illustration of Fortuna, the Roman goddess of fortune, with her "Wheel of Fortune" (February 1930)

MAXIM: TV star Christa Miller…billed as "*The Drew Carey Show* girl" (Spring 1997)

POPULAR MECHANICS: Three men working inside a submarine (January 11, 1902)

CAT FANCY: An orange cat (May 1965)

O: The Oprah Magazine: Oprah Winfrey (May 2000)

The Great Easter Egg Hunt

As we told you on page 308, there may be as many as seven Russian Imperial Fabergé eggs out there somewhere, hiding in plain sight. Do you have an antique egg lying around? It may be worth a lot.

EGG-CEPTIONAL

E Not so long ago, an American scrap dealer who insists on remaining anonymous bought an antique golden egg at a flea market in a midwestern state that he refuses to identify. He paid $14,000 for it—that much he will say.

The egg was an exquisite example of the jeweler's art: it was a ridged egg of yellow-gold that sat on its own three-legged, jewel-studded golden pedestal with lion's-paw feet. When you pressed a diamond on the front of the egg, the top opened up, revealing a surprise: a ladies' watch with gold hands. The watch had been removed from its case and mounted on a hinge so that it could swivel into an upright position, allowing the egg to be used as a table clock. The egg itself was about the same size as a hen's egg; when seated on its pedestal, it was just 3¼ inches tall.

NO YOLK

As beautiful as the egg was, the scrap dealer bought the egg in order to destroy it. He wanted to resell it to a buyer who would melt it down for the scrap gold. But (lucky for him) he must have guessed incorrectly about how much gold was in the egg, because not even one of the potential buyers he approached thought the egg was worth his asking price.

The man had a lot of money tied up in the egg. But he didn't want to sell it for a loss, so he set it aside in the hope that the price of gold would rise enough for him to make a profit. Finally, in about 2013 (he won't say exactly when), despairing of ever getting his money back, he went on the Internet and Googled the words "egg" and "Vacheron Constantin," the name of the watchmaker inscribed on the back of the watch. The first search result that popped up was a 2011 article in London's *Daily Telegraph* that read "Is This £20 Million ($33 million) Nest Egg on Your Mantelpiece?"

A picture of the man's egg was included in the article.

Robin Williams's daughter Zelda is named after the video game *The Legend of Zelda.*

EGG-STRA! EGG-STRA!

According to the article, the egg was the long-lost *Third Imperial Egg*, one of eight missing Fabergé Easter eggs made for the Russian Imperial family between 1885 and the Russian Revolution of 1917. Czar Alexander III had given it to his wife, Marie Feodorovna, as an Easter gift in 1887. Most of the 50 Imperial Fabergé eggs were seized during the revolution, including this one. It disappeared in the 1920s and hadn't been seen—or at least recognized—since then. No one even knew what it looked like until 2007, when researchers poring over photographs taken during an exhibition of the Russian Imperial eggs in 1902 saw the egg sitting on a shelf next to other Fabergé eggs. Through process of elimination, they were able to identify it as the *Third Imperial Egg*.

Then in 2011, another picture of the egg was discovered in an auction catalog from 1964, proving that it had survived the Russian Revolution and made its way to New York City, where it was sold to a woman named Rena Clark for $2,450. Neither the auction house nor Mrs. Clark had known that the object was one of the Imperial eggs.

EGG-CELLENT

The egg wasn't seen again until the scrap dealer bought it at the flea market. After realizing that the egg sitting on his kitchen counter was worth a lot more than the $14,000 he paid for it, he flew to London with photographs of his egg and showed them to the experts at Wartski, a London antiques dealer that specializes in Fabergé objects. They were impressed enough to fly back to the man's house to see the egg in person, where they confirmed it was genuine. In 2014 Wartski negotiated the sale of the egg to an undisclosed buyer. No word on how much the new buyer paid for it, but it could easily have fetched the $33 million price that the *Daily Telegraph* article predicted for it.

The bad news, at least as far as you are concerned, is that this egg has already been found, and you aren't the person who found it. The good news: there may be as many as seven more Russian Imperial eggs still out there, waiting to be discovered, each worth many millions of dollars. Here's what is known about them:

EGG WITH HEN IN BASKET (1886)

Given To: The czarina Marie Feodorovna, by her husband Czar Alexander III

Description: No drawings or photographs of the egg survive, so it's difficult to know for certain what it looks like. All egg hunters have to go on are a few descriptions of it in the Russian archives, such as "hen picking a sapphire egg out of a basket" and "one silver hen, speckled with rose-cut diamonds, on gold stand." It may be only about three

---

Popular snack for Japanese teenagers: Dried sardines mixed with slivered almonds.

inches tall, making it one of the smaller Fabergé eggs. And that may explain why it has not yet been recognized for what it is, if indeed it has survived at all. Since so little is known about the egg, even if it is found, it may be difficult to authenticate.

Last Seen: In 1922, when it was transferred to the Sovnarkom, the government agency that sold off confiscated property to raise foreign currency for the Soviet state. Whether it was sold—and if so, to whom—is unknown.

CHERUB WITH CHARIOT (1888)

Given To: Marie Feodorovna, by Alexander III

Description: One grainy photograph of the egg sitting in a display case in 1902 survives, but there's a catch. The image of the egg is almost entirely obscured by the 1893 *Caucasus Egg*, which is sitting in front of it in the photo. However, a blurry *reflection* of the egg can be seen in the glass of the display case. Only the wheel of the chariot and what appears to be the head of the angel can be seen directly because they stick out past the *Caucasus Egg*. Fabergé researchers have used this information to draw a sketch of what they think the egg looks like: a single cupid-like angel pulling a large egg in a two-wheeled chariot that resembles a wheelbarrow.

Last Seen: The last confirmed sighting of the egg was in 1922, but it may have been purchased by Armand Hammer in the 1930s. If so, even he probably didn't realize that it was one of the Imperial Easter eggs because he never advertised it as such. In 1934 he did put up for sale a "miniature silver amour holding wheelbarrow with Easter egg, made by Fabergé" at the Lord and Taylor department store in New York City. It's possible that by "amour," Hammer meant an angel and that he mistook the chariot for a wheelbarrow. Who bought that egg and where it is now remain a mystery.

NÉCESSAIRE EGG, LOUIS XV STYLE (1889)

Given To: Marie Feodorovna, by Alexander III

Description: This is Uncle John's favorite Fabergé egg. Reason: it's an *étui* ("small case") for 13 "diamond-encrusted toilet articles." They are the egg's surprise. One photo of the egg survives (it was taken in 1949), but like the one of *Cherub with Chariot*, it provides very little information. The egg appears to be lying on its side on the bottom shelf of a display case and is almost entirely concealed behind folds of a fabric.

Last Seen: In 1952, when Wartski, the same London firm that sold the *Third Imperial Egg* in 2013, sold it for £1,200 (around $43,000 today) to someone listed in company records only as "A Stranger." At the time of sale, no one realized the *Nécessaire* was one of the Russian Imperial eggs,

---

It would take a train stretching from Colorado to Maine to hold Kansas's annual wheat crop.

so it's certainly possible that the current owner, whoever and wherever he or she may be, has no idea either.

MAUVE EGG (1897)

Given To: Marie Feodorovna, by her son Czar Nicholas II

Description: The *Mauve Egg* is another egg for which no pictures and few good descriptions survive. In the original invoice, Carl Fabergé describes it as simply, "mauve [pale purple] enamel egg with three miniatures." The miniatures are the surprise contained inside the egg. They're in a heart-shaped frame that opens into a three-leaf clover, with portraits of Nicholas, Alexandra, and their newborn daughter, Olga, on the leaves.

Last Seen: The *Mauve Egg* has been missing since 1917, but there's a good chance that it has survived, because in 1978 Malcolm Forbes bought a small heart-shaped picture frame that opens into a three-leaf clover with portraits of Nicholas, Alexandra, and baby Olga. On the outside of the frame, the year 1897 is set in diamonds, so there's little doubt that it's the surprise for the *Mauve Egg*. How it came to be separated from the egg, and where the egg is now, is unknown.

EMPIRE NEPHRITE EGG (1902)

Given To: Marie Feodorovna, from Nicholas II

Description: In Carl Fabergé's original invoice, the egg is described as an "Egg in 'Empire' style, of nephrite [a pale or green form of jade] with gold, two diamonds and miniature." The miniature, a portrait of Czar Alexander III, is the egg's surprise.

Last Seen: In 1917, when the egg was sent from St. Petersburg to Moscow because of the threat of advancing German troops. After that it disappeared.

The surprise may have been exhibited in London in 1935; a catalog from the show describes a "miniature Alexander III…in a nephrite frame, let by Her Imperial Highness the Grand Duchess Xenia of Russia." Xenia was Nicholas II's younger sister. If she had the miniature, she may also have had the egg. But the egg did not surface following her death in 1960. If any of her seven children (or their descendants) inherited it, they aren't talking.

ROYAL DANISH EGG (1903)

Given To: Marie Feodorovna, from Nicholas II

Description: A single photograph of this egg has survived in the Fabergé archives. The blue-and-white egg seated on its pedestal stands over nine inches tall, making it one of the largest Fabergé eggs. The surprise is a double-sided picture frame on a stand, with a portrait of

Marie Feodorovna's father, King Christian IX of Denmark, on one side, and her mother, Queen Louise, on the other.

Last Seen: In 1903 in Copenhagen, where Marie Feodorovna had gone to celebrate Easter and her father's 40th anniversary as king. Nicholas II mailed the egg to her there. It's possible that Marie Feodorovna left the *Royal Danish* egg in Denmark. If so, it could be lost somewhere in the Danish royal archives or sitting on a shelf somewhere in Copenhagen's Amalienborg Palace.

ALEXANDER COMMEMORATIVE EGG (1909)

Given To: Marie Feodorovna, by Nicholas II

Description: One black-and-white photograph of the egg survives, as does Fabergé's original invoice to the czar. The invoice describes it as an "egg of white enamel with gold stripes, decorated with two diamonds and 3,467 rose-cut diamonds. Inside is a gold bust of Alexander III on a lapis lazuli [bright blue stone] pediment decorated with rose-cut diamonds." No photograph of the Alexander III bust has survived.

Last Seen: 1917. Unlike some of the other missing eggs, there is no record of this one being transported to Moscow for safekeeping during the Russian Revolution. This may mean that the egg was either destroyed or stolen before it could be protected from looters.

*   *   *

4 OLD JOKES

Zookeeper: "Did you hear about the baby that was fed elephant's milk and gained 20 pounds in a week?"
Man: "That's impossible—whose baby?"
Zookeeper: "The elephant's."

Kid 1: "Meet my baby sister!"
Kid 2: "Oh, she's so cute! What's her name?"
Kid 1: "I don't know—I can't understand a word she says."

A pirate walks into a bar and the bartender says, "Hey, is that a steering wheel in your pants?" The pirate replies, "Yarr, it's drivin' me nuts!"

A woman gets on a bus with her baby. The bus driver says, "That's the ugliest baby I've ever seen!"

Angry, the woman sits down in her seat and says to the man next to her, "Did you hear that? That driver just insulted me!"

"Well then," replies the man, "you should go right back up there and tell him off. I'll hold your monkey for you."

When baby Eurasian roller birds sense danger, they vomit orange barf to warn their parents to stay away.

Medical Fictionary

We found these silly definitions of medical terms while doing "research."

Artery: The study of paintings

Cesarean section: An old neighborhood in Rome

Recovery room: Place where furniture is upholstered

Benign: What you be after eight

Postoperative: Mailman

Carpal: When two or more people drive to work together

Enema: Opposite of friend

Congenital: Friendly

Nitrates: What hotels charge after 6:00 p.m.

D&C: Where Washington is

Terminal illness: sickness contracted at an airport

Node: Understanded

Dilate: Live long

Electrolytes: Low-calorie electricity

Medical staff: A doctor's cane

Bacteria: Back door to the cafeteria

Diarrhea: What a daily journal is called in Italy

Barium: What doctors do when patients die

Red blood count: Dracula

Fibula: Small lie

Fistula: Small punch someone gives you for telling a fibula

Hangnail: Where you hang your coat

Outpatient: A patient who has fainted

Malady: What a bad song has

Cardiology: The study of poker playing

Catscan: What happens when kitty goes missing

G.I. Series: World Series of military baseball

Seizure: Roman emperor

Tumor: Food ordering phrase, e.g., "Tumor tater tots, please"

Ultrasound: What awesome stereo systems have

Fester: Quicker

Varicose: Not far away

Asphyxia: Cosmetic surgery involving the buttocks

In late 17th-century London, the mail was delivered 10 to 12 times a day.

Herbivores No More

What has fleece as white as snow…and a taste for blood? Read on.

NIGHT OF THE UNGULATES

An odd experiment took place in North Dakota in 1998. Biologists wanted to find out what was eating all the songbird hatchlings in the area, so they set up video cameras next to the ground nests. As expected, several squirrels raided the nests, as well as a few foxes—but what they saw next astonished them: in the middle of the night, a herd of white-tailed deer roamed through and gobbled up the little hatchlings like they were hors d'oeuvres.

But wait, aren't deer supposed to be *herbivores*—animals that only eat plants? It turns out that a lot of these so-called vegetarians aren't really that strict about their diets.

FOOD GROUPS

The group of mammals known as *ungulates* ("hoofed mammals" in Latin) includes cattle, deer, pigs, horses, sheep, goats, giraffes, hippos, elephants, and, according to some classifications, dolphins and whales. Despite the common perception that all ungulates are strict herbivores, they're not. For example, wild boars will hunt small mammals and reptiles, and some farm pigs have developed a taste for cats—which makes pigs (like humans and bears) *omnivores*.

Grazing animals known as *ruminants*—which include cattle, deer, sheep, and giraffes—have specially adapted teeth for chewing grass and a four-chambered stomach to help them digest it. So what could make them suddenly turn into meat eaters? There are a lot of factors involved—some natural, some not. Here are some ruminants, the meat they eat, and why they eat it.

• **Deer:** On the Scottish island of Rum, the red deer supplement their grassy diet with the legs, heads, and wings of Manx shearwater chicks. What are they supplementing? Calcium. The island's soil has a low mineral content, and over time, the deer have figured out that they can get calcium from bird bones. It helps their antlers grow (even though it's very difficult for ruminants to digest bones). And not just birds: deer have been witnessed eating dead fish that wash up on shore.

• **Cows:** There have been many scattered reports of cows eating birds. In India, for example, a cow named Lal ate dozens of baby chicks before she was caught in the act and separated from the chicken coop. This odd diet made her something of a celebrity in India (we even wrote

First woman elected to the US Senate: Hattie Caraway, 1932. First ladies' room in the US Senate: 1992.

about Lal in our *Triumphant 20th Anniversary Bathroom Reader*). Her owner believes she was a tiger in a previous life, but biologists can't explain why a well-fed cow would suddenly develop a taste for chicken nuggets.

• **Sheep:** A seabird ecologist named Bob Furness has documented wild sheep eating arctic terns in the Shetland Islands north of Scotland. Just as with the red deer, the sheep are only interested in the birds' bones, not their bodies.

• **Giraffes:** On the African savanna, it's not uncommon to see the world's tallest ruminant chewing on an impala skull. Giraffes don't eat the whole head, they just gnaw on the bone to suck out the calcium. It may be a grisly thing to witness, but not as grisly as the habit that a giraffe named Tony recently took up at a zoo in Australia. "It just ruins your talk," lamented tour guide Goldie Pergl. "You'd explain to visitors how giraffes are herbivores…and then Tony would eat a dead rabbit."

OTHER UNGULATES

Though not technically ruminants, these "herbivores" have also been known to skip the salad from time to time.

• **Horses:** As most horse owners know, horses will eat almost anything they're given, including meat. But in the book *Deadly Equines: The Shocking True Story of Meat-Eating and Murderous Horses*, Irish journalist CuChullaine O'Reilly alleges that meat was once a staple of the equine diet and that there is evidence that horses have "slain lions, tigers, pumas, wolves, hyenas, and humans." Could it be true? Yes. Although it's not considered part of their normal diet, horses can and will eat meat. Animal behaviorist Sue M. McDonnell, PhD, polled her readers on thehorse.com to see what kind of meats their equines ate. The responses: "hot dogs, hamburgers, steak, bologna, ham, and fried chicken."

• **Hippos:** They may look serene floating along in a river, but hippos have a well-earned reputation as killers; they're responsible for at least 500 human deaths every year. That's usually for defense, though—hippos don't eat people. But they will eat each other. (Look up "hippo cannibalism" online to see the gruesome acts.) Hippos are also known to scavenge carrion, and there were reports from Ethiopia in 2002 that a pod of hippos hunted down and ate small farm animals.

• **Camels:** There isn't a lot to feed on in the desert, so over time camels' digestive systems have adapted to eat and drink all sorts of things, including thorny plants and brackish water. And birds. One quite disturbing YouTube video shows a camel nonchalantly devouring a full-grown dove. And unlike the deer and the sheep, the camel doesn't stop at the wings.

Ironically, goats, which are known for eating *everything*, are one of the few ungulates that won't eat meat (unless you count leather boots). Another strict vegetarian: the elephant. They may strip a forest bare to obtain all the nutrients they need, but (except for any unfortunate insects that don't get out of the way in time) elephants won't eat other animals.

And there's one ungulate—a domesticated ruminant, in fact—that has become a meat eater without even knowing it.

WHY U MAD, COW?

It turns out that some cows are fed…cows. Reason: grass is difficult to digest, even for ruminants and their specially adapted digestive systems, so nearly half of what they eat is excreted as waste (as anyone who's stepped in a fresh cow patty no doubt knows). So in the 1980s, to cut down on high feeding costs, some ranchers and dairy farmers started giving their cattle protein-rich "food pellets." The pellets have been made out of everything from dead farm animals, to leftover restaurant food, to expired pet food. This new diet made big news when cattle that had been fed the brains, eyes, spinal cords, and intestines of older cattle came down with *bovine spongiform encephalopathy* (BSE), also known as "mad cow disease."

This progressive neurological disorder has mostly been eradicated, thanks to improved farming techniques. However, the practice does still exist, even in the United States. Thankfully, the USDA requires that all "brain and spinal cord materials be removed from high-risk cattle—older cattle, animals that are unable to walk, and any animal that shows any signs of a neurological problem." However, according to the Humane Society, "Cattle remains are still fed to chickens, and the poultry litter (floor wastes that include the feces and spilled feed) is fed back to cows."

TIME TO HOOF IT ON OUT OF HERE

Now that you'll never look at Bambi (or a steak) the same way again, it's important to note that—in the wild, at least—animals are opportunists. Even if their systems have adapted to specialize in flora or fauna, in the battle for survival, nutrients are nutrients. And hungry animals will get them wherever they can. Does that mean that a cow might one day try to hunt *you* down for dinner? Probably not…for now.

*   *   *

"For me, vegetarianism is about saying yes to things…even meat."

—Jane, *Coupling*

What's a "sugarplum"? Chopped dried fruit, nuts, and spices rolled into a ball and coated with sugar.

The Ten Longest Wars in History

*Historians often disagree on whether certain wars should be considered
one continuing conflict or a series of separate wars. But that
doesn't stop them from compiling lists of the longest wars
ever fought. Here is the most popular version.*

10 THE VIETNAM WAR
Length: 19 years (1955–1975)
Details: Although there was no official declaration of war,
the Vietnam War began on November 1, 1955, when the United States
began providing military support to the newly created nation of South
Vietnam in their war against communist-controlled—and Soviet- and
Chinese-supported—North Vietnam. Major fighting didn't really begin
until 1963 (total number of U.S. troops killed in Vietnam prior to 1962:
fewer than 100), when the war was escalated, first by President John F.
Kennedy and then by President Lyndon B. Johnson. The war officially
ended on April 30, 1975, when the last American forces left Saigon and
North Vietnam took control of the entire country, reunifying the North
and South into the Socialist Republic of Vietnam.
Estimated deaths: 2.4 million

9 THE GREAT NORTHERN WAR
Length: 21 years (1700–1721)
Details: This war's two main adversaries were Russia, under
Peter the Great, and the Swedish Empire, under Charles XII, with
various allies fighting on either side at different points—including
Denmark-Norway, Poland-Lithuania, the Ottoman Empire, and Great
Britain (which actually fought on both sides at different times over the
course of the war). Winner: Russia. The outcome drastically reshaped
the power structure of Europe, reducing what was then a very powerful
Swedish Empire to a minor player in European affairs. Russia, in turn,
was officially renamed the Russian Empire, with Peter the Great as its
first emperor. The victory marked Russia's emergence as a major world
power.
Estimated deaths: Historians believe the number of battle deaths,
along with deaths due to disease and famine brought on by the war, was
more than 300,000.

8 FIRST PUNIC WAR

Length: 23 years (264–241 BC)

Details: This was the first of three wars between the powerful North African city-state of Carthage (now Tunisia), and the Roman Republic over control of the lucrative trade routes in and around the Mediterranean Sea. The First Punic War was the longest of the three and was fought primarily over control of the island of Sicily, where much of the fighting took place. In one notable battle near the city of Panormus (now Palermo), the Romans not only killed an estimated 20,000 Carthaginian soldiers in one day but also captured 100 elephants, which the Carthaginians famously used in battle. The elephants were sent back to Rome, where they are believed to have been killed in the games in the Coliseum. The First Punic War ended in 241 BC, with the Romans emerging as victors, gaining control of most of Sicily. (Rome won the Second Punic War as well, when Roman general Scipio defeated Carthaginian general Hannibal in 201 BC. By the end of the Third Punic War in 146 BC, the Romans had demolished the Carthaginian army; destroyed the city of Carthage; enslaved, sold, or killed all its inhabitants; and annexed every last inch of Carthaginian territory.)

Estimated deaths: Around 250,000

7 THE ACHINESE WAR

Length: 31 years (1873–1904)

Details: This war was the result of an effort by the Dutch to consolidate their rule in the Dutch East Indies, the former colony that is the nation of Indonesia today. In 1873 the Dutch attacked the Sultanate of Aceh (pronounced *ah*-che), an independent kingdom on the Indonesian island of Sumatra, in order to take control of the region's lucrative black pepper industry. The Dutch captured the capital of Kutaraja in 1874 and declared victory. But they badly underestimated the Acehnese, who took to using guerrilla tactics, and the war dragged on for a total of 31 years, with territory changing hands several times over that period. In the late 1890s, the frustrated Dutch began a scorched-earth campaign that led to the destruction of Aceh villages and the slaughter of thousands of civilians, including women and children. By 1903 the war was basically won (by the Dutch), but fighting continued in some pockets of the region until 1914. Today Aceh is a province of Indonesia, which gained its independence from the Netherlands in 1949.

Estimated deaths: 90,000

6 THE PELOPONNESIAN WAR

Length: 27 years (431–404 BC)

Details: Remember the Greek city-states that banded together

Some cowboy cooks took their sourdough starter to bed with them to keep the yeast warm (and alive).

and beat the mighty Persians in the Greco-Persian War? Well, once that was settled, the Greeks got back to what they did best—fighting each other. In this war, Athens, which had grown into a powerful empire, fought the Peloponnesian League, a coalition of allied city-states led by Athens' archrivals, the Spartans. (Sparta is located on the Peloponnese Peninsula, a large landmass that makes up much of southern Greece.) Fighting raged throughout southern Greece and as far away as western Turkey and southern Italy. This included massive sea battles, the last of which, the Battle of Aegospotami, off Turkey's Mediterranean coast, saw the Spartans decimate the mighty Athenian fleet, sinking approximately 150 ships and executing more than 3,000 sailors. Athens surrendered some months later, and by 404 BC, the war—and Athens's superiority over the region—was history.

Estimated deaths: Unknown

5 THE WARS OF THE ROSES

Length: 30 years (1455–1485)

Details: This war for the right to the English throne was fought by supporters of two royal houses: the House of Lancaster, whose heraldic symbol was a red rose, and the House of York, whose symbol was a white rose—hence this war's name. Over the course of the war, the throne changed hands three times. One king was killed in battle; another king was executed after being captured; two more kings died of natural causes; and scores of lords, dukes, earls, and other royal figures lost their lives—after which many had their heads put on pikes for public display. When it was all over, the House of Lancaster had won: Henry Tudor, the Lancastrian claimant to the throne, defeated the Yorkist claimant, Richard III, at the Battle of Bosworth Field in 1485 and became King Henry VII. The following year, he strengthened his position by marrying Elizabeth of York and started a new house, the House of Tudor, which ruled England for the next century.

Estimated deaths: Around 100,000

4 THE THIRTY YEARS' WAR

Length: 30 years (1618–1648)

Details: On May 23, 1618, a crowd of angry Protestants stormed the royal castle in the city of Prague, in the Kingdom of Bohemia, and threw three members of the newly appointed Catholic government out of a castle window. (All three somehow survived the 70-foot plunge.) That event, known as the Defenestration of Prague, ignited Protestant rebellions all across the region. That eventually escalated into an all-out—and incredibly destructive—war between the great powers of Europe. The main belligerents: the powerful Holy Roman Empire, comprising all of the German states and several neighboring regions,

allied with the Spanish Empire against France, Sweden, and Denmark. The losers: the Holy Roman Empire and Spain, both of which lost huge amounts of territory and influence. The big winners: France and Sweden, which emerged as major powers, although Sweden was unable to sustain that position for very long. (See entry number 9.)
Estimated deaths: 8 million

3 THE GUATEMALAN CIVIL WAR
Length: 36 years (1960–1996)
Details: In 1954 a right-wing army colonel, Carlos Castillo Armas, led a successful coup d'état against the democratically elected leftist government of Guatemala. The coup was engineered by the U.S. State Department and the CIA. In 1960 a group of left-wing army officers led a coup of their own—but failed to take power. What followed was 36 years of war between the Guatemalan military, which eventually took control of the country, and various leftist guerrilla groups. Fighting didn't stop until 1996, with the signing of a peace treaty between the rebel groups and the government; concessions were made on both sides, but it was largely deemed a win for the rebel groups. The conflict is one of the first in which a terror tactic known as *forced disappearance* was used: the Guatemalan army and National Police forces kidnapped, tortured, and murdered between 40,000 and 50,000 people, primarily civilian activists. Most were native people, especially Mayans, and their bodies were dumped into mass graves or dropped into the sea from helicopters. (The fate of most of those victims remains unknown today.)
Estimated deaths: 200,000

2 THE GRECO-PERSIAN WARS
Length: 38 years (between 499–449 BC)
Details: This was actually three conflicts, fought over a period of 50 years, that historians bundle into one major war. The fighting was between a coalition of several ancient Greek city-states led primarily by Athens and Sparta, and the Persian Empire—at the time the largest and most powerful empire on Earth. (Think that's an exaggeration? At its peak—including the period during which this war was fought—the Persian Empire encompassed approximately 50 million people, or about 44 percent of the world's population.) The war began with a series of revolts by Greeks in territories that the Persians had conquered decades earlier, followed by full-scale invasion attempts by the Persians, and counterattacks by the Greeks—all with varying degrees of success and failure. Finally, after 50 years, the winner: the Greeks, who successfully repelled the Persians and won back their territories.
Estimated deaths: Unknown

Do their big, floppy ears help? A dog can locate the source of a sound in 1/600th of a second.

1 THE HUNDRED YEARS' WAR

Length: 116 years (1337–1453)

Details: Fought primarily between England and France, the Hundred Years' War is usually divided into three main component wars—one of which raged for 38 years: the Lancastrian War (1415–1453). The fight was over English-controlled territory in France and control of the French throne. (The rulers of England and France had been related for centuries, so the English claim to the French throne actually had some merit.) The war ended with the surrender of the English in 1453, after more than a century of bloodshed. The winners: the French, who took back almost all of England's holdings in France, beginning a long era during which England was left mostly isolated from European affairs. And within two years, the English were engulfed in yet another long conflagration. (See #5.)

Estimated deaths: Possibly as high as 3.5 million

Bonus: Several of William Shakespeare's best-known plays center on events that occurred during the Hundred Years' War, including *Richard II*, *Henry IV*, and *Henry V*, all of which detail the lives of English kings who ruled during the war. Another famous character from the Hundred Years' War: Joan of Arc, who, at the age of 18, led the French to several victories before being captured by the English and burned at the stake in 1431.

* * *

LISTEN TO YOUR WIFE

You've probably never heard of Carolyn Hopkins, but if you travel a lot by train or plane, you've definitely heard her voice. From her home in Maine, Hopkins has recorded thousands of airport and train station announcements since the 1990s. Some of her greatest hits: "Welcome to New York Kennedy International Airport." "This is a special security announcement." And of course, "The moving sidewalk is about to end."

In a 2012 interview with NPR, Hopkins admitted that her odd career has created a few surreal moments—like when she hears her own voice tell her (and everyone else) not to leave any bags unattended. One time, her husband was picking her up at the airport, and a security officer told him, "Buddy, you gotta move. You hear that voice up there? You gotta move."

His reply, "Well I don't pay attention to that voice at home, why should I do it now?"

As food, or as customers? Worldwide, restaurants serve about 1 billion snails annually.

Who Stole the Yeti's Finger?

Anyone who doesn't believe in cryptids can kiss our unicorn. Cryptids are mythological creatures that many people believe actually exist—bunyips, chupacabras, hoop snakes, and the like. Our favorite: the Yeti.

YETI OR NOT

The Yeti (or "Abominable Snowman") is a legend of the Himalayan Mountains. The hairy apelike creature is said to stand more than six feet tall and walk on two legs like a human. From the 1920s on, as more and more Westerners tried climbing Mount Everest, they heard more and more stories about the Yeti. Sherpa guides insisted Yeti were real, telling the climbers about sightings and attacks. Even Tibet's Buddhist monks told tales of the creatures. And they kept Yeti bones and scalps as holy relics in their monasteries. Fascination with the Abominable Snowman led, inevitably, to expeditions to locate the elusive beast.

One of the most famous was mounted in 1958 by Texas oil millionaires F. Kirk Johnson and Tom Slick, who had an avid interest in *cryptozoology*—the study of creatures whose existence is disputed or unsubstantiated. (Slick once bought a "hoat," the purported offspring of a hog and a goat.) As the expedition scoured the Himalayas for signs of the Yeti, some members visited the Pangboche monastery in Nepal where they saw—and were permitted to photograph—a Yeti scalp and hand that the monks kept in a glass case. The hand looked human...sort of. It had humanlike digits, but the fingers ended in long curved nails, and the skin was blackened as if frozen. The photographs stirred up a lot of excitement in the Yeti-hunter community. When a second expedition was mounted in 1959, its leader, Peter Byrne, went to Pangboche for a look at the fabled hand.

SCIENCE GETS THE FINGER

Before Byrne left for Nepal in 1959, the expedition's financial backer, Tom Slick, and British primatologist William Charles Osman Hill told him that they wanted the hand brought back to London so it could be examined scientifically. Byrne asked the monks if he could borrow the hand for that purpose. Their response: No. Apparently they believed that if the hand left the building, bad luck would befall the monastery.

Hill had another idea: if Byrne could talk the monks into giving him a close look at the hand, he could then "borrow" a single finger to bring back to London. Byrne balked. Surely the monks would notice a missing digit on their prized Yeti hand. Not a problem, at least according to Hill. Byrne could simply replace that finger with a mummified human finger Hill would supply. (Byrne never asked where Hill planned to get a mummified human finger.)

HAVE FINGER, WILL TRAVEL

Byrne finally agreed and traveled to London to get the fake finger. On his return to Pangboche, the monks generously allowed him to examine the hand in private. But once alone with the relic, he not-so-generously removed some of the bones and rewired the finger Hill had given him in their place. (Byrne later claimed he'd given the monks a donation in exchange for the finger. However, author Loren Coleman's biography of Tom Slick, *True Life Encounters in Cryptozoology*, quotes a letter in which Byrne wrote to Slick, "I shall not go into details here of how we got the thumb and phalanx of the Pangboche hand. The important thing is that we have them, and that the lamas of the monastery do not know that we have them.")

Now Byrne had a real problem: How was he going to get the relic back to London? He decided to hide the finger in a backpack and smuggle it from Nepal into India. That part of his plan worked, but passing it through Indian customs and onto an airplane would be an even greater challenge. Tom Slick described the dilemma to his partner, F. Kirk Johnson, and Johnson came up with a solution. Customs officials sometimes gave preferential treatment to celebrities that they would not give to an explorer like Byrne. Johnson's buddy, actor Jimmy Stewart (*It's a Wonderful Life*), happened to be vacationing in Calcutta with his wife Gloria. So Johnson contacted Stewart to ask for help, and the Stewarts, who seemed amused by the whole thing, agreed.

THE PLOT THICKENS

Byrne met the Stewarts in Calcutta's Grand Hotel and handed off the relic to them. The Stewarts hid the finger under the undies in Gloria's lingerie case, checked their bags, and flew to London. But when they tried to claim their bags in London, they discovered that Gloria's case had been separated from the rest of their luggage. Several nail-biting days later, the Stewarts got a call from customs. The case had been located, and the couple would have to come to the airport to collect it in person. The Stewarts were nervous when they went to collect the case. Had it been searched? Were they about to be arrested? No, customs officers assured them, they would *never* rummage through a lady's lingerie. After the airport scare, Stewart turned the finger over to Johnson, who gave it to Hill.

Male pandas—don't hesitate! Female pandas are only fertile for two or three days in a year.

TESTING...TESTING...TESTING

At last, Hill had the finger. The primatologist carefully examined the Pangboche relic and declared the bones to be...human (although tests performed on the skin were inconclusive). Four more experts analyzed the finger and were divided as to whether it was human, ape, or Yeti. Despite this, Hill added the finger to his private collection of specimens. And there it remained until 1975, when Hill's collection was donated to the Royal College of Surgeons Hunterian Museum in London. It took another 33 years until the collection was cataloged and the museum staff found a box labeled "Yeti's finger." Notes in the box stated that the finger came from the Pangboche temple in Nepal and had been given to Hill by explorer Peter Byrne.

But that's not the end of the Yeti tale. In 2011 BBC journalist Matthew Hill (no relation to William Charles Osman Hill) stumbled upon the finger while touring the College of Surgeons museum. He contacted Peter Byrne, who was 88 at the time, and interviewed him for a radio documentary. Next, Hill enlisted a Royal College professor of surgical anatomy to examine the finger without being told where it came from—he had no clue about the Yeti connection. Based on the shape of the joints, the professor concluded that the finger was... human. Just to be certain, the museum allowed the BBC to take a small fragment to the Zoological Society of Scotland in Edinburgh for DNA testing. The Edinburgh tests proved that the finger was...human. Its genetic profile was a match to known human DNA sequences from China and the surrounding region (i.e., Nepal).

THE FINGER POINTS HOME

In 1991 the TV show *Unsolved Mysteries* broadcast an episode that featured tests on a skin sample from the Pangboche hand. Shortly after the broadcast, the Yeti hand and scalp were stolen from the temple. Because the monks charged visitors admission to see the Yeti relics, the theft was a financial blow to the monastery. In 2005 New Zealand mountaineer Mike Allsop visited Pangboche and learned about the stolen relics. He wanted to help. Deciding to "replace" the missing artifacts, Allsop contacted Weta Workshop, the New Zealand special effects company that created the props for the *Lord of the Rings* movies. Working from photographs, Weta Workshop reproduced the Yeti hand and scalp. In 2011 Allsop took the replicas to Pangboche and presented them to the monks. As for the finger that Byrne removed in 1959? It's still on display at the Royal College of Surgeons museum, but the museum would be happy to return the finger to the monastery if the monks request it.

Actress Melanie Griffith slept with a pet lion as a kid. Her mom admits it was "stupid beyond belief."

Cheesy Does It

These facts are so gouda we had to share them.

Cheese's exact origin is unclear, but archaeological evidence reveals that people have been eating it for nearly 8,000 years.

• According to Greek mythology, cheese was invented by Aristaeus, a demigod who was the son of Apollo.

• According to an Arab legend, thousands of years ago a merchant named Kanana was traveling through the desert. When he stopped to eat, he poured milk out of a bottle made from a calf's stomach and found that the milk had turned into cheese.

• First known book about cheese: *Summa Lacticiniorum*, by Pantaleone da Confienza, published in Turin in 1477. It was an encyclopaedia of European cheeses.

• When Queen Victoria and Prince Albert were married in 1840, one of their wedding gifts was a giant wheel of cheddar cheese. It weighed over 1,250 pounds. Victoria didn't know what to do with it, so she sent it on a tour of England.

• Why is cheese made in the shape of a wheel? So it can be rolled from place to place.

• The largest hunk of cheese ever made (in 1995) was 4½ feet wide, 32 feet long, and weighed more than 28 tons.

• Colby—a soft, mild form of cheddar—is named after Colby, Wisconsin (population: 1,100), where it was invented in 1874.

• The state of Wisconsin uses the salty brine water left over from the cheese-making process to de-ice the roads.

• Cheese can help prevent tooth decay. How? By promoting saliva, which washes sugars and acids off of your teeth.

• Most popular cheese dish in the U.S.: macaroni and cheese.

• The holes in Swiss cheese were long thought to be made by bacteria that emitted carbon dioxide, but in the early 2000s, the holes mysteriously started disappearing. In 2015 researchers at a Swiss agricultural institute discovered why: The cheese was no longer made by hand-milking the cows. Automated machines had taken over, which removed one crucial ingredient: tiny particles of hay. Once the hay was added back into the mixture, the holes reappeared.

The Corporation

To some people, the word "corporation" has negative connotations, and not without reason—names like Enron and Lehman Brothers come to mind. But it's also one of the greatest tools for economic growth ever invented. Here's a brief history of the corporation.

BACKGROUND

Most of us have a simple understanding of corporations as large businesses, such as Coca-Cola, Microsoft, or GE. But there's more to it than that: a corporation is a company or group of people acting as a single entity—often, but not always, a business—legally recognized as separate from the people who own it. That last part is crucial. One of the fundamental aspects of a corporation is that it is legally permitted to take on risks that do not personally affect its individual owners beyond their financial investment in it. If, for example, you and some friends wanted to invest money in an expedition, wherein you'd sail a fleet of ships across the ocean to a strange, unknown land, conquer or kill the people there, and take over that land for yourself, you'd probably want to form a corporation to legally protect yourselves against any trouble—financial or otherwise—that such a risky adventure might bring about. (That, of course, is exactly what happened in some of the earliest forms of the modern corporation…but more on that later.)

CORPORATE HISTORY

The word *corporation* was derived from the Latin *corpus*, meaning "body" or "body of people." The ancient Romans had what could be seen as an early form of the corporation—legally recognized groups as diverse as religious organizations, schools, and even cities—but those groups did not have the same legal status or structure as today's corporations. A more direct precursor to the modern corporation came in the 16th and 17th centuries, the heyday of the Age of Discovery, when the nations of Europe were competing for the opportunities for vast wealth being discovered around the world. Western European monarchies began granting royal charters to groups of investors, authorizing them to act as legal entities for purposes of foreign trade and conquest, with mutual benefits for both the government and the investors. (Royal charters had already been in use for centuries, but only to found institutions such as hospitals, universities, and cities.) Two notable examples of early royal charter–based corporations:

• In 1600 Queen Elizabeth I granted a group of wealthy investors a royal charter forming the British East India Company. It gave the company a monopoly on all trade in the East Indies—basically everything from India to China—and in return the English government got to tax the enormous profits the company made.

• In 1606 the Virginia Company was granted a charter by King James I, with the goal of establishing colonies in North America. In 1607 the company founded Jamestown, in present-day Virginia—the first permanent English settlement in North America.

THANKS FOR SHARING

Both the East India and Virginia Companies were early examples of *joint-stock corporations*: businesses that are jointly owned by a group of investors who own differing percentages of the company's total value in the form of *shares* or *stock* in the company. (These shares are what's sold on "stock markets" or "stock exchanges.") The roots of such share-divided organizations go back to the 1200s, but they didn't evolve into this more modern form until the British government started chartering joint-stock corporations in the late 1500s.

That was a huge development in the history of corporations. It allowed them to raise enormous amounts of cash and attract a wider portion of the public into the investment game—a big part of why joint-stock corporations are so common today. After the Virginia Company got its charter in 1606, the founders launched an advertising campaign aimed at selling stock throughout England. More than 1,600 people bought shares in the company—netting the company the equivalent of several million dollars in today's money. They used the money to pay for the ships and provisions needed to found the first successful English colony in North America.

The history of corporations for most of the next 200 years revolved primarily around the chartering of corporations by various European powers for purposes of overseas trade and colonization.

BUBBLE AND CRASH

In the midst of all this, another event occurred: in 1720 the principal shareholders of a British overseas trade corporation called the South Sea Company, in collusion with members of the British government, used a rumor campaign to make the company appear much more successful than it actually was. This set off a national frenzy to buy the company's stock, which sent the stock price soaring. This was the first stock market "bubble."

But the South Sea Company was a sham; it was making almost no profits at all. In late 1720, the bubble burst, the company collapsed, and the price of its stock plummeted, sending thousands of shareholders

One species of jellyfish has tentacles as long as two blue whales end-to-end.

(individuals and companies) into bankruptcy and almost ruining the entire British economy. This was history's first "stock market crash." Public outrage stemming from the event led to some of the first laws regulating corporations. Such scandals, and subsequent government reactions, have played a major part in shaping the course of corporate history ever since.

SEPARATE ENTITIES

It was also during this time that one of the most important legal concepts regarding corporations came into being: *limited liability*. That means that if a corporation in which you own stock fails or is sued and ends up owing millions of dollars, you're not personally responsible for the debt. The debtors can't come and take your home or any other personal belongings. You and all the other shareholders in the corporation can lose only what you invested when you bought the company's stock. Your liability, in other words, is limited to the amount you paid for your shares.

Limited liability was devised as a way to encourage people to invest in risky business ventures they might otherwise be wary of, thereby encouraging entrepreneurship. The concept is credited with being a major reason for the enormous success of corporations worldwide. (The first U.S. laws granting corporations limited liability protection weren't passed until the early 1800s, but earlier corporations had some forms of these protections going all the way back to the early 1600s.)

CORPORATE REVOLUTIONS

The next great leap in the history of corporations came just after the American Revolution. No longer subject to British laws, the new United States suddenly had the power to charter corporations themselves, and in order to encourage business in the fledgling nation, they made it relatively easy to do. And the Industrial Revolution, which was in full swing at this time, only added fuel to the growing corporate fire. By 1800 there were about 300 corporations in the United States. By 1840 there were an estimated 10,000—by far the most of any country in the world. Some examples:

• The Second Bank of the United States was chartered by Congress in 1816 as a private corporation jointly owned by the government and a group of private investors. By the 1830s, it was worth about $35 million (almost $900 million today's money) and was the single largest corporation in the country.

• The Northern Pacific Railway Company was incorporated by congressional charter in 1856 and was worth roughly $100 million (about $2.7 billion today). Railroad companies remained among the largest

---

In 2013 a tunnel in Norway was closed for five days due to 29 tons of burning goat cheese.

companies for the rest of the century, creating the enormous wealth of such American "robber barons" as Jay Gould and Cornelius Vanderbilt.

• In 1892 the State of New Jersey, known at the time as the most business-friendly state—charging low corporation fees, levying low taxes on corporations, and so on—granted Andrew Carnegie a charter of corporation for his steel empire, marking the official founding of the Carnegie Steel Company. Nine years later, in 1901, Carnegie sold the company to J. P. Morgan for $480 million (more than $13 billion today). It was at the time the largest commercial transaction in history.

UP TO DATE

Since the beginning of the 20th century, corporations have continued to grow in size, number, and complexity. This was the start of the era of *conglomerates* (massive combinations of different corporations under a single ownership) and *multinationals* (corporations that operate in more than one country). And it is almost impossible to overestimate the status that corporations have in the world today. In the United States alone, there are more than 6 million active corporations. America's largest (and the world's second largest): Wal-Mart. It's worth roughly $476 billion—and it has 2.2 million employees.

Large corporations have also been guilty of rampant abuse and subsequent attempts to rein in those abuses through the law. A 1911 Supreme Court decision, for example, declared Standard Oil Company an illegal monopoly that engaged in unfair business practices, and it broke the company into 33 smaller companies. Similar breakups have occurred several times since. More recently, a string of scandals has once again changed the corporate landscape. These include the fraud-caused collapses of Enron (2001), WorldCom (2002), and financial giant Lehman Brothers (during the much larger 2008 global financial crisis)— which alone caused the loss of a mind-boggling $691 billion.

WHAT ARE YOUR TERMS?

A few terms that are helpful in understanding corporations:

"Corporation" versus "company." Most of us use the words *corporation* and *company* interchangeably, but for legal purposes, there are basic differences. A *corporation* must have more than one owner, and the business is legally a separate entity from its individual owners. Businesses that do not fit these definitions: a *sole proprietorship*, a company owned by one person, and a *general partnership*, a company owned by two or more people. Neither of these types of companies are legally separate from their owners, and their owners are not protected by limited liability. (Most small businesses fall into these categories.)

"Private" versus "public". Corporations can be classified as *private* or *public.* Private corporations are normally owned by just a few share-holders, often family members, and those shares cannot be publicly traded. (Koch Industries, Dell, and LEGO are examples of privately held corporations.) Public corporations are owned by many people who buy shares of such companies on stock exchanges or in other stock-selling businesses. (Apple, Facebook, and banking giant Wells Fargo are all publicly held corporations.)

Conglomerate. This type of corporate arrangement, in which huge parent corporations own collections of unrelated corporations, came into fashion in the 1960s. Example: Warren Buffett's Berkshire Hathaway Inc. owns insurance companies, food production companies, restaurant chains, credit card companies, and all or portions of hundreds of other companies all over the world. (Berkshire Hathaway is worth about $182 billion.)

RANDOM CORPORATE FACTS

• Another characteristic of corporations, and another advantage they have as entities separate from their investors: they continue to exist even after their original owners die—making corporations basically immortal as long as they don't fail, get sold, or simply close up shop for one reason or another. (This is a legal concept known as *perpetual succession.*)

• There are types of corporations that are not businesses—including nonprofit corporations—and many towns and cities are in fact types of corporations, because they're incorporated by charters they receive from their respective states.

• The largest corporation in the world as of 2015: Sinopec Group, a Chinese oil and gas conglomerate. It has about 401,000 employees—and is worth roughly $486 billion.

*   *   *

REAL PUNNY BAND NAMES

• Japancakes
• Alcoholocaust
• Pabst Smear
• Furious George
• JFKFC
• Cerebral Ballsy
• The Dictatortots

• Hostile Comb-Over
• Kathleen Turner Overdrive
• Harmonica Lewinsky
• Mary Tyler Morphine
• John Cougar Concentration Camp
• Ringo Deathstarr

Sacre bleu! **It's not legal to advertise wine on TV in France.**

Obamacare? Try Cleveland-O-Care

The White House Cookbook, *written by Mrs. F. L. Gillette, noted expert on "cookery and house-keeping," and Mr. Hugo Ziemann, Steward of the White House, was first published in 1887, during Grover Cleveland's first term as U.S. president. It contained household recipes, menus, rules of etiquette…and these health tips, which should make you realize how far medical science has advanced since then.*

FOR A TOOTHACHE. "The worst toothache, or neuralgia, coming from the teeth may be speedily and delightfully ended by the application of a bit of clean cotton saturated in a solution of ammonia to the defective tooth. Sometimes the late sufferer is prompted to momentary laughter by the application, but the pain will disappear."

TO CURE EARACHE. "Take a bit of cotton batting, put on it a pinch of black pepper, gather it up and tie it, dip it in sweet oil, and insert it in the ear; put a flannel bandage over the head to keep it warm; it often gives immediate relief. Tobacco smoke, puffed into the ear, has often been effectual. Another remedy: Take equal parts of tincture of opium and glycerine. Mix, and from a warm teaspoon drop two or three drops into the ear, stop the ear tight with cotton, and repeat every hour or two."

FOR CUTS. "For a slight cut there is nothing better to control the hemorrhage than common unglazed brown wrapping paper, such as is used by marketmen and grocers; a piece to be bound over the wound. A handful of flour bound on the cut. Cobwebs and brown sugar can be pressed on like lint."

FOR RELIEF FROM ASTHMA. "Sufferers from asthma should get a muskrat skin and wear it over their lungs with the fur side next to the body. It will bring certain relief."

FOR CHOKING. "A piece of food lodged in the throat may sometimes be pushed down with the finger, or removed with a hair-pin quickly straightened and hooked at the end, or by two or three vigorous blows on the back between the shoulders."

TO REMOVE WARTS. "Wash with water saturated with common

Time to move into an assisted-living facility? Consider a cruise ship instead—they cost about the same.

washing-soda, and let it dry without wiping; repeat frequently until they disappear. Or pass a pin through the wart and hold one end of it over the flame of a candle or lamp until the wart fires by the heat, and it will disappear."

HOW COLDS ARE CAUGHT. "A great many cannot see why it is they do not take a cold when exposed to cold winds and rain. The fact is, and ought to be more generally understood, that nearly every cold is contracted indoors, and is not directly due to the cold outside, but to the heat inside. A man will go to bed at night feeling as well as usual and get up in the morning with a royal cold. He goes peeking around in search of cracks and keyholes and tiny drafts. Weather-strips are procured, and the house made as tight as a fruit can. In a few days more the whole family have colds. Let a man go home, tired or exhausted, eat a full supper of starchy and vegetable food, occupy his mind intently for a while, go to bed in a warm, close room, and if he doesn't have a cold in the morning it will be a wonder. A drink of whisky or a glass or two of beer before supper will facilitate matters very much."

FOR A COLD IN THE HEAD. "Nothing is better than powdered borax, sniffed up the nostrils."

FOR A SORE THROAT. "Everybody has a cure for this trouble, but simple remedies appear to be most effectual. Cut slices of salt pork or fat bacon, simmer a few minutes in hot vinegar, and apply to throat as hot as possible. When this is taken off as the throat is relieved, put around a bandage of soft flannel."

FOR HEMORRHAGES OF THE LUNGS OR STOMACH. "They are promptly checked by small doses of salt. The patient should be kept as quiet as possible."

A CURE FOR HICCOUGH. "Sit erect and inflate the lungs fully. Then, retaining the breath, bend forward slowly until the chest meets the knees. After slowly arising again to the erect position, slowly exhale the breath. Repeat this process a second time, and the nerves will be found to have received an access of energy that will enable them to perform their natural functions."

A CURE FOR LOCKJAW, SAID TO BE POSITIVE. "Let anyone who has an attack of lockjaw [tetanus] take a small quantity of spirits of turpentine, warm it, and pour it in the wound—no matter where the wound is or what its nature is—and relief will follow in less than one minute."

ENTERING A SICKROOM. "One should be cautious about entering a sickroom in a state of perspiration, as the moment you become cool your pores absorb. Do not approach contagious diseases with an empty stomach, nor sit between the sick and the fire, because the heat attracts the vapor."

FEEDING AN INVALID. "Dishes for invalids should be served in the daintiest and most attractive way; never send more than a supply for one meal; the same dish too frequently set before an invalid often causes a distaste, when perhaps a change would tempt the appetite."

TO VENTILATE A ROOM. "Place a pitcher of cold water on a table in your room and it will absorb all the gases with which the room is filled from the respiration of those eating or sleeping in the apartment. Very few realize how important such purification is for the health of the family, or, indeed, understand or realize that there can be any impurity in the rooms; yet in a few hours a pitcher or pail of cold water—the colder the more effective—will make the air of a room pure, but the water will be entirely unfit for use."

DRINKING WATER. "Never use water which has stood in a lead pipe over night. Not less than a wooden bucketful should be allowed to run [before drinking]."

COD-LIVER OIL. "The flavor may be changed to the delightful one of fresh oyster, if the patient will drink a large glass of water poured from a vessel in which nails have been allowed to rust."

TO SOFTEN THE HANDS. "Mutton tallow [rendered sheep fat] is considered excellent to soften the hands. It may be rubbed on at any time when the hands are perfectly dry, but the best time is when retiring, and an old pair of soft, large gloves thoroughly covered on the inside with the tallow and glycerine in equal parts, melted together, can be worn during the night with the most satisfactory results. Another good rule is to rub well in dry oatmeal after every washing."

*　　　*　　　*

OLD-TIME SLANG FOR THE BATHROOM

- The leaky
- The dubby
- The temple
- The excuse me
- Where the Queen goes on foot
- Gutter alley
- The closet of decency
- The growler
- Mrs. Jones's place
- The poet's corner
- House of Lords

Duct tape was invented during WWII as a waterproof sealing tape for ammunition boxes.

Turtle Recall

Three odd stories about the world's most resilient reptile.

YOU CALL THAT ART? In August 2014, an installation at Colorado's Aspen Art Museum had animal lovers up in arms. "Moving Ghost Town" by contemporary artist Cai Guo-Qiang featured three African sulcata tortoises wandering around the museum's rooftop garden. Glued to each of their shells were two Apple iPads playing videos of local ghost towns "filmed by the creatures themselves." Shortly after the show opened, complaints of animal abuse started pouring in. "These creatures were not designed to carry two-pound iPads," said Lisabeth Odén, who started an online petition to shut down the exhibit. "I can see them doing this in some Third World country, but not in Aspen." Museum officials insisted that the tortoises were well taken care of, and that the iPads "don't weigh that much"…but closed the installation.

THAT TURTLE WAS SOOOO FAT… How fat was it? It was so fat that none of the ponds at the Forever Wild Exotic Animal Sanctuary were big enough to hold it, so staffers had to build a new one. This common snapping turtle, which weighed a whopping 70 pounds—more than twice its natural weight—was found loafing by a pond at the La Cañada Flintridge Country Club in Los Angeles. Because snappers are native to the eastern United States, it's a good bet that it was an escaped pet. "The turtle appears healthy," said Joel Almquist of the sanctuary. "Maybe *too* healthy. It's quite obese." He added, "They're very detrimental to the native wildlife. They eat everything that they can fit in their mouths, and apparently by the size of this one, it has."

HIDE AND SEEK. In 1982 the Almeida family was having their home renovated in Realengo, Brazil, when their red-footed tortoise, Manuela, went missing. A worker had left the gate open, so they searched the nearby woods but couldn't find Manuela anywhere. Thirty years later, in 2013, the now grown-up Almeida kids went to the house after their father died to clean out the upstairs storage room. It was stuffed so full of boxes and furniture that no one had been in there for ages. Except Manuela. They found her alive and well. "At that moment I was white and did not believe it," said Leandro Almeida. The tortoise had survived alone in the dark attic for three decades, sustaining herself with bugs. The family said she seemed "happy" to have human contact again.

In 1980 a wrench fell into an Arkansas missile silo. The missile exploded. (The warhead didn't.)

Capital Punishment

If you don't read these facts about the death penalty, you will be sentenced to...nothing, really. Have a nice day.

From 1851 to 1888, beheading was a legal execution method in the Utah Territory. (In Utah the condemned chose their method of execution and no one ever chose beheading.)

• The death penalty was banned in Japan from the 9th to the 12th century. It's legal today.

• Since 1700, there have been more than 15,700 executions in the United States: 9,183 by hanging; 4,439 by electrocution; 1,211 by lethal injection; 593 by gas chamber; 130 by firing squad; and 65 by burning.

• Number of pirates executed in U.S. history: 68.

• Crushing or dismemberment by elephant was a commonly used execution method in parts of South and Southeast Asia until the 19th century.

• First U.S. state to abolish the death penalty: Michigan, in 1846, upon becoming a state.

• Crimes punishable by death in the American colonies included witchcraft, adultery, trading with Indians, and stealing grapes.

• Number of condemned Americans since the 1970s who were later exonerated based on evidence of innocence: 150 (so far).

• Youngest person executed in U.S. history: Hannah Ocuish, a 12-year-old Pequot girl. She was hanged in 1786 for the murder of a 6-year-old girl.

• 98 countries have abolished the death penalty; 58 still have it. Canada officially abolished the death penalty in 1976. Mexico abolished it in 2005.

• Last person executed in the United States for a crime other than murder: James Coburn, who was executed for robbery in Alabama (1964).

• State with the most executions in the modern era (since 1977): Texas, with 515. Second: Oklahoma, with 111.

• The British used "blowing from a gun" for executions in India until the mid-1800s. The condemned was tied to the front of a cannon, and then the cannon was fired.

Poll result: One in four British women claims to prefer gardening to sex.

The Myth-Adventures of King Richard III

According to Shakespeare, Richard III (1452–1485) was one of England's most villainous kings. He was also the only English monarch whose final resting place had been lost to history—until some history buffs went looking for the grave…and found some answers.

FAMOUS LAST WORDS

Even if you're not a Shakespeare fan, you've probably heard the lines "My horse! My horse! My kingdom for a horse!" King Richard III shouts them near the end of the play that bears his name. In the next scene he is slain by Henry Tudor, who is then crowned King Henry VII with the crown that fell from Richard's head.

Richard III is one of Shakespeare's most popular characters. Actors love to play him because he's such a great villain. He's King Quasimodo, a "foule hunch-backt toade" with a withered arm and so ugly that dogs bark at him as he limps past in the street. Richard III is also a cruel schemer who steals the throne from his 12-year-old nephew, Edward V, and locks both Edward and his younger brother Richard away in the Tower of London. According to Shakespeare's version of events, Richard has both boys murdered.

BASED ON A TRUE STORY

The plot of the play hews fairly closely to English history. In 1483 Richard did indeed become king by locking his nephews, the sons and heirs of his dead brother King Edward IV, in the Tower of London. They were never seen again. Even in Richard's lifetime it was widely assumed that he'd had them killed. But there's no evidence to prove that the boys were murdered or that Richard had anything do with their deaths.

As Shakespeare's play relates, in August 1485, Richard met his rival, Henry Tudor, in battle at Bosworth Field, near the city of Leicester in the English Midlands. When Richard's horse got bogged down in marshy ground, he was set upon by Tudor's men (not, as in the play, by Tudor himself) and killed. Tudor was then crowned Henry VII with the same crown that Richard had worn.

Shakespeare may have gotten his history right, but his portrayal of Richard III the *man* is another matter. The Bard was born some 80 years after Richard's death. When he wrote *Richard III* in the 1590s, he relied on descriptions provided by Tudor historians, some of whom were hired by Henry VII himself. Henry had an interest in painting his vanquished foe in a negative light because it legitimized his seizure of the throne.

His historians were happy to comply. If anything, their depictions of Richard III were even less flattering than Shakespeare's: John Rous, for example, writes in his *History of the Kings of England* that before Richard was born he was "retained within his mother's womb for two years, emerging with teeth and hair to his shoulders." (In an earlier work—written before Henry VII became king—Rous had described Richard as a "good lord" with "a kind heart.")

GOT A HUNCH?

Doubts about the Tudor/Shakespeare portrayal of Richard III were raised as early as 1619, and questions have been asked ever since. Was Richard really a hunchback? Such a deformity, combined with the claim that he had a withered arm, doesn't exactly mesh with historical accounts of his skill in battle. How can a hunchback with only one good arm ride a horse and fight with a sword at the same time?

The earliest claim that Richard was hunchbacked dates to 1491, six years after his death. During his lifetime not even his enemies claimed he had a hump, though a few contemporary accounts did say that his right shoulder was higher than the left. That led historians to speculate that he may have suffered from *scoliosis*, an abnormal curvature of the spine that could have given him uneven shoulders without making him a hunchback.

MISSING PERSON

The questions about Richard III's deformities might have been answered long ago if it had been possible to examine his remains. But no one knew where he was buried or whether his grave had survived. After Richard was killed at the Battle of Bosworth Field, his body was stripped naked and slung over the back of a horse, then paraded through the streets of Leicester, where it remained on display for two days. What happened after that was unknown. Richard might have been buried in any of four nearby churches, including the church of the Franciscan friars, who had a monastery in Leicester known as Greyfriars.

Another story claimed he was buried "in a dyke like a dogge." A third said that his remains were dug up in the 1530s and reburied beneath Leicester's Bow Bridge, or perhaps thrown off the bridge into the river Soar. Afterward his stone coffin was said to have found use as "a drinking trough for horses at a common inn." Whichever story you believed, by 1700 the location of his grave (assuming there really was one) had long been forgotten.

THE KING AND US

Luckily for Richard III—and in spite of all his bad press—he still had admirers, or at least skeptics who questioned the portrait painted by the Tudors. In 1924 a group of them formed what became known as the Richard III Society, founded to engage in scholarly research that might shed a more accurate light on the man and his times.

Society members have been burrowing away in libraries, universities, museums, and the British national archives ever since, more than 90 years in all. One of the topics they tackled from the beginning was the question of where Richard III was buried. As the years passed and more information came to light, one by one, the unsubstantiated burial stories fell away until a single site emerged as the most likely location of his grave: the church at the Greyfriars monastery in Leicester. Then in 2008, a historian and society member named Dr. John Ashdown Hill found a document in the National Archives dating to 1494, just nine years after Richard's death, that stated definitively that he had been buried "in the Church of Friers in the town of Leycestr."

That created a new problem: figuring out where the church had stood, because it too was long gone. When King Henry VIII (the son of Henry VII) ordered the dissolution of hundreds of monasteries, convents, and friaries in the late 1530s, the Greyfriars monastery was abandoned, and the buildings were later torn down. The stone foundation of the church could have survived, but if so, it was buried somewhere on the nearly seven-acre site (about 1½ football fields in size), and no one knew precisely where it might be.

Making finding it even more difficult, over the centuries the entire site had been built over—in some places more than once—and was now entirely covered by buildings, streets, and paved parking lots. Simply poking around in the dirt looking for the old church's foundations was not an option, since there was hardly any exposed dirt left to poke.

P(ARK) MARKS THE SPOT

The best available evidence pointed to a part of the site that now served as the parking lot of the Leicester City Council's Social Services building. But this was only an educated guess, and not enough to get permission from the city to start digging up parking lots. It wasn't until 2008 that another society member named Philippa Langley found what she describes as the "smoking gun": a copy of a medieval map of Leicester that showed the church being located directly beneath what is now the Social Services parking lot.

It took more than three years to raise the £32,000 (about $48,000) needed to pay for an exploratory dig and to get the permission of the city to do it. Finally, on August 25, 2012, a team of University of

Random weird fact: Some seeds will not sprout unless they have passed through a bat's digestive tract.

Leicester archaeologists began excavating the first of three exploratory trenches in and around the parking lot.

RETURN OF THE KING

So how good was the Richard III Society's guesswork? Just a couple of hours into the excavation on the first day, the archaeologists unearthed the skeleton of a man in the first trench they dug. Not just any man, either: this one had an irregular S-shaped curve in his spine, indicating that he'd had a severe case of scoliosis. There was also evidence of multiple combat wounds inflicted at or near the time of death, suggesting that the man had died in battle. That certainly fit the description of Richard III, but whatever doubts remained were dispelled when DNA extracted from the skeleton was compared to DNA samples taken from the living descendants of Richard's sister. They were a 99.999% match.

BODY OF EVIDENCE

Analysis of Richard's skeleton and the grave it was in revealed more details about how he died and how his body was treated afterward:

• Eleven *perimortem* (inflicted near the time of death) battle wounds were found on the skeleton. Nine of these were on the skull, suggesting that Richard either lost or took off the helmet to his suit of armor in the moments before he was killed. No defensive wounds were found on his hands and arms, indicating that he was probably still wearing the rest of his armor at the time of death.

• Two of the head wounds were serious enough to be fatal. One was caused by a bladed weapon, perhaps a sword, that cleaved off a portion of the rear of the skull near the neck. The other was a stab wound that entered the right rear of the base of the skull, passed through the brain, then impacted the inner surface of the left side of the skull. Both injuries were likely to have been inflicted when Richard was kneeling or lying facedown on the ground; either would have caused his death.

• There was evidence of *postmortem* (after death) "humiliation injuries" to the back and buttocks, areas of Richard's body that would have been exposed when he was slung over the horse.

• Richard was not buried in a coffin, nor was there any evidence that his body had even been wrapped in a burial shroud. No remnants of clothing (buttons, buckles, etc.) were found with the body either, suggesting that he was still naked when placed in the grave.

• The skeleton's head was propped up at an odd angle in the grave, indicating that the grave was too small for the body. That could mean that the body was buried in a hurry, with no time to enlarge the hole once the diggers realized it was too small.

• Richard's hands were crossed when they were found, strongly suggesting that they were still tied together when he was buried. No traces of rope were found, but those would have decomposed long ago. It's possible that the rope had been used to tie Richard's body to the horse when it was paraded through the streets of Leicester.

SPEAKING ILL OF THE DEAD

• Analysis of the abnormal curvature of the spine indicated that Richard's scoliosis would have made his right shoulder higher than the left, just as contemporary accounts had described. However, it would not have made him a hunchback, nor would he have walked with a limp. There was no evidence that either of his arms was withered.

• The difference in shoulder height would have been difficult to detect when he was wearing clothing or a suit of armor. That may explain why the condition attracted so little notice during his lifetime. After Richard was killed and his naked body was slung across the horse, his severely curved spine would have been obvious to anyone who saw his body when it was paraded through Leicester, causing tales of his being a hunchback to circulate after his death.

REST IN PEACE

It's the custom in the Church of England that when a body is exhumed in an archaeological dig, it is reburied in the nearest consecrated ground. In this case, it would be Leicester Cathedral, just one block from where Richard's body was discovered. Usually, however, the body 1) cannot be identified, and 2) doesn't belong to a former king of England. Richard III was certainly a special case, but the decision was nonetheless made to inter him in Leicester Cathedral in a tomb inside a simple English oak coffin made by London cabinetmaker Michael Ibsen—who is Richard's great-nephew 17 generations removed.

In March 2015, Richard III was given what was a state funeral in all but name, complete with a procession from Bosworth Field through the Leicestershire countryside to Leicester Cathedral. He made the last part of the journey on a gun carriage drawn by four horses—more than 520 years later, the king best known by William Shakespeare's line "My horse! My horse! My kingdom for a horse!" had finally gotten his wish.

Richard's bones may have been laid to rest, but the campaign to repair his image and better understand his life and times continues. If anything, it has been reenergized by the discovery of his remains. "Now," Richard III Society member Philippa Langley told the *New York Times*, "perhaps we can finally get to the real Richard III—to the truth that lies behind the Tudor lies."

Australian wombats are about the size of dogs; in prehistoric times they were as large as rhinos.

A Forgotten Hero

*Here's the story of a World War II bomber pilot who survived
being shot down over the English Channel, saved most of
his crew in doing so, and later vanished without a trace.*

TOP GUN

Leon Robert Vance Jr., was born in Enid, Oklahoma, in 1916, and graduated from the U.S. Military Academy at West Point in 1939. The day after graduation, he married his girlfriend, Georgette Brown. He then joined the Army Air Forces (predecessor of the U.S. Air Force), where he trained to become a pilot.

Vance quickly earned a reputation as an exceptionally disciplined pilot, and by the time the United States entered World War II in December 1941, he held the rank of captain. In 1943, after less than four years in the service, he was promoted to lieutenant colonel. By 1944, having spent the first three years of the war stateside, primarily as a flight instructor, and having seen many of the pilots he'd trained killed in the war, Vance was itching to get into the action.

BOMBS AWAY

In April 1944, Vance got his chance. He was sent to a Royal Air Force station near the town of Halesworth, in the southeast of England. From there he was to lead bombing raids on Nazi-occupied France, designed to help the Allies gain air superiority in that part of Europe in preparation for the D-Day landings. On June 5, 1944, the day before those landings, General Dwight D. Eisenhower ordered a massive air assault on Nazi positions all along the French coastline. Vance, on just his second mission, had command of the 44th Bombardment Group, a group of B-24 Liberator heavy bombers (meaning they carried an especially large load of bombs). The 44th's mission was to raid Nazi targets near Wimereux, a town on the far northern coast of France, just across the English Channel. Each of the six bombers carried ten 500-pound bombs.

Vance was in the lead plane. He allowed the regular pilot and copilot to fly the plane, and stood behind them to observe. The other nine men in the 12-man crew included the navigator, radio operator, bombardier, and several gunners. They took off at 9:00 a.m., climbing as they crossed the Channel, finally reaching the recommended altitude of 22,500 feet. They flew directly over their target, passed it, then turned around and headed back. This had a dual purpose: it gave German antiaircraft batteries on the ground the impression that the bombers had aborted their mission, and also allowed the bombers to approach their target from the south, so that once they'd dropped their bombs, they could fly straight over the Channel and back to base. But when Vance's plane reached the target area, the release mechanism jammed. The bombs failed to drop.

LET'S TRY IT AGAIN

Because the lead plane's bomb-drop was supposed to be the signal for the other planes to drop *their* bombs, not a single plane in the group released its bombs. Now over the Channel, they all prepared to drop their bombs in the water. This was standard practice for bombers that had been unable to complete their missions, as it was too dangerous to fly back to base loaded with powerful ordnance. But Vance wouldn't have it: he ordered the group to turn back toward their targets. They were going to make another pass.

If they'd fooled the antiaircraft batteries the first time, they didn't this time. As soon as they reached the coast, Vance's plane was hit by a barrage of shells from the Nazis' "eighty-eights," German antiaircraft weapons that fired huge shells—about 3.5 inches in diameter (8.8 centimeters, hence the nickname) and almost 2 feet long—at a rate of one every three seconds. And the shells were explosive: they exploded on impact...or without impact. Their fuse mechanisms activated upon being fired so that the shell would explode when it was in the air. (Fire from such weapons was called "flak," from the German name for this type of weapon, *Flugzeugabwehrkanone*, meaning "aircraft defense cannon.")

HIT

Within seconds, the radio operator, Technical Sergeant Quentin Skufca, was badly hit in both legs by flak that tore through the floor. Another strike ruptured fuel lines, and gas began to spray around the plane. Then Lieutenant Nathaniel Glickman, manning two machine guns in the "ball turret" (a gun turret mounted on the belly of the plane), was hit in the head and lower back. Finally, they reached the target. The lead plane released its bombs, the other five bombers did the same, and they made a direct hit. The other five bombers flew on safely, but the cockpit of Vance's plane was taking fire. The pilot, Captain Louis Mazure, was killed, and the copilot, Lieutenant Earl Carper, was badly injured.

Carper struggled to keep the plane level. Three of the engines had been shot out. The last one had to be shut down to prevent sending the plane into a spiraling dive. More shots flew up through the floor. Vance tried to dive forward to shut down the last engine, but he couldn't move. He looked down and saw that he'd been hit: his foot was nearly severed from his leg, attached only by the Achilles tendon. The foot was also stuck in the mangled metal of the plane's floor. Ignoring the pain, Vance stretched out his body to its full length—stretching that tendon near to breaking point—and shut down the last engine. Then he discovered that one of the bombs hadn't dropped—it was stuck in its bay. And gas was still spraying all over the inside of the plane.

GOING DOWN

Somehow, from a nearly prone position on the floor between the pilot and copilot seats, Vance managed to help Carper steady the plane… but it was losing altitude fast. Lieutenant Bernard Bail, the radar navigator, managed to free Vance's foot and applied a tourniquet to stop the bleeding. A short time later, as they passed over the English coast, Vance ordered the men to bail out. After most of them had jumped, Vance turned the plane around and headed for the Channel: there was no way to land safely, and a crash on English soil—carrying an armed 500-pound bomb—would be disastrous.

The last crewman out was Carper, the copilot. Logically, Vance should then have bailed out, parachuted over the water, and let the plane crash. But for some reason, possibly because he was suffering from shock, Vance believed that one of the men had been too badly injured to jump from the plane. Unwilling to let that crewman die without trying to save him, Vance decided to land the plane—on the water—in the hope that they'd both survive the crash.

IMPACT!

Some accounts say Vance managed to take Carper's copilot seat, others say he was too injured to do this and had to guide the aircraft from an almost-prone position. In any case, the B-24 landed very hard. The nose of the plane slammed into a cresting wave, forcing the turret on top of the aircraft into the cockpit and pinning Vance to the floor. The plane started sinking; Vance couldn't move. He was certain it was the end. "I was honestly past the point of being frightened," he recounted later. He was thinking, he said, of his wife and their two-year-old daughter. Then something exploded.

Vance was suddenly blown free of the aircraft and, bewildered, found himself at the surface of the water. (It is believed that the oxygen tanks exploded, not the 500-pound bomb.) Then Vance dove back down into the plane to locate his injured crewman. When he didn't find anyone (except the dead Captain Mazure), he returned to the surface, found a life vest, and started swimming. And while he'd lost a lot of blood, and the water was very cold (less than 60°F)—and even though his right foot was close to falling off—Vance managed to swim more than two miles until he was finally picked up by a rescue boat.

Who doesn't? President Rutherford B. Hayes reportedly suffered from *lyssophobia*, the fear of going insan

ONE LAST FLIGHT

All the crewmen who'd bailed from the plane survived. Most landed on land, a couple of them breaking their legs in the process. Vance lost his right foot. He remained in the hospital for the next seven weeks. Then, in late July, he was scheduled to return to America, where he hoped to be fitted with a prosthetic foot so he could get back to flying bombers. Sadly, that was not to be.

On July 26, 1944, Vance, along with several other men who'd been wounded in action, boarded a military transport plane. They took off from England, stopped to refuel in Iceland, then took off again, heading for Newfoundland. The pilot made radio contact about three hours later, and the plane, Vance, the crew, and the other wounded men—26 people in all—were never heard from again. It is assumed the plane crashed into the North Atlantic somewhere south of Greenland. A search found no wreckage.

On January 5, 1945, Lieutenant Colonel Leon Vance was posthumously awarded the nation's highest military award, the Medal of Honor. In 1949 Enid Air Army Base, in Vance's hometown of Enid, Oklahoma, was renamed Vance Air Force Base in his honor. At the time of his death, Leon Vance was 27 years old.

*   *   *

WE ALL MAKE MISTAKES

"It is very easy to forgive others their mistakes. It takes more grit to forgive them for having witnessed yours."

—**Jessamyn West, author**

"The fellow who never makes a mistake takes his orders from one who does."

—**Herbert Prochnow, banker**

"The greatest mistake you can make in life is to continually fear that you will make one."

—**Elbert Hubbard, author**

"We have not passed that subtle line between childhood and adulthood until we have stopped saying, 'It got lost,' and say, 'I lost it.'"

—**Sydney Harris, journalist**

"I may have my faults, but being wrong ain't one of them."

—**Jimmy Hoffa**

George de Mestral, inventor of Velcro, received his first patent at age 12 (for a toy plane).

Wild, Man!

Hurry! Hurry! Step right up to Uncle John's Amazing Freak Show. For 10¢, only one thin dime, see Jay Jay the Dog-Faced Mermaid! See Patrinka the Tasmanian Giant. And the most terrifying attraction of all: Norto the Wild Man of Borneo!

FREAKING OUT

A hundred years ago, any freak show worth its bearded lady also had a Wild Man of Borneo. Sometimes more than one…and maybe even a Wild Woman, too. Even now, in pop culture sources ranging from professional wrestling to episodes of *Downton Abbey*, you still hear references to Wild Men of Borneo. Who were they, and where exactly in Borneo did they come from? Answer: there's no evidence that *any* of them actually came from the island of Borneo. In fact, if the first of them was any indication, they were more like the Wild Men of Toledo.

In 1852 Catherine Davis of Mount Vernon, Ohio, had a surprise visitor: a circus sideshow promoter named Lyman Warner. She didn't know it, but he was there on business. He'd heard that Davis had twin sons and that they were little people, were mentally challenged, had long blond hair, and spoke their own language to each other. All that turned out to be true. Warner was intrigued to find that the twins, named Hiram and Barney, were nearly identical, in their 20s, and *very* little—40 inches tall, weighing only about 45 pounds each. He told her that he wanted them for his freak show. At that, Mrs. Davis's warm midwestern cordiality turned cold. She angrily ordered Warner out of her house.

MONEY TALKS

But then Davis started thinking about her children's bleak future. She wasn't getting any younger—what would they do when she wasn't around? Hiram and Barney were severely mentally challenged, and while they were well behaved and hardworking, how were they going to survive in the world without her to take care of them? What really were the options?

Warner made the decision easier for her. He didn't stay away along, returning with a tub full of cash to show the kind of money that a popular attraction could bring in. Davis was shocked. She needed the money, and maybe her sons would be better off in a freak show than in an institution. Assured that Warner would take good care of them, she signed away all rights to the young men in exchange for the cash. The lives of Hiram and Barney Davis were about to get a lot wilder.

The last Labrador duck was shot in 1875; it was the first North American bird hunted to extinction.

WHERE THE WILD THINGS AREN'T

On their way back to the circus, Warner tried to figure out what to do with the twins. They had a peculiar look that he liked, but he couldn't exhibit people just because they looked unusual. The public would only feel sorry for them. He needed a gimmick so that people didn't feel that they were just gawking, but somehow being elevated with new knowledge.

Suddenly it came to him. Their exotic look, small stature, and invented language reminded him of an old sideshow act called "The Wild Children of Australia." Those kids, supposedly "raised in the Australian wilds," had also come from Ohio. He considered presenting these odd-looking, yellow-haired, blue-eyed twins as natives of some remote part of the world. But where? He thought of places Americans would have heard of but wouldn't know enough about to picture what the natives looked like. Africa and Asia were out, because Americans knew what people there looked like. Suddenly, a name came to him: "The Wild Men of Borneo."

And why not? At the time, Borneo, an island in Southeast Asia, was in the news because England and the Netherlands were both trying to dominate the Malaysian region. Some Americans might have heard tales of fierce tribes in Borneo's rain forest that still occasionally made shrunken heads, but they'd never seen them. So why couldn't Americans be convinced that these short, pale-skinned, blond twins came from Borneo?

CREATIVE LICENSE

Warner immediately began working on the Davis twins' new and completely fictitious biography. First of all, the farm boy names had to go: Hiram became "Waino," and Barney "Plutano."

Warner claimed that they were of a bloodthirsty nature "with the force of four stout men" and were only captured in Borneo after fighting off a dozen sailors armed with guns, knives, and nets. In their early years, they were exhibited in chains to underscore how dangerous they were.

The next problem was their personalities. Quiet, polite, and shy, the brothers halfheartedly brandished spears and growled at audiences, but it was clear their hearts weren't in it, so Warner tried a new approach. Playing off their disproportionate strength, he had them lift huge weights and wrestle each other, bringing out a fierceness that only sibling rivalry could inspire. He even invited members of the audience to wrestle or be lifted into the air. Newspaper ads screamed:

"THOUGH DWARFS IN SIZE THEY EXHIBIT GREAT STRENGTH, LIFTING MANY HUNDRED POUNDS IN WEIGHT, Throwing the most scientific Six-foot Athlete with Ease."

UNDER THE BIG TOP

After 30 years of appearing in traveling shows and "museums," in 1882 the twins finally hit the big time: they joined up with P. T. Barnum's famous circus and became one of his most popular exhibits.

By that time, Charles Darwin's theories of evolution were well known, and Barnum's publicists jumped on the opportunity to suggest that the brothers might be a "missing link" between apes and humans. "Borneo is an island so large that England, Ireland, and Scotland might be set down in the middle of it," said a pamphlet offered for sale. "The interior of this vast island is a dense forest, inhabited by a race of humanity very little different from the animal creation…If you examine their little fingers, you will find conformation such as to afford them astonishing prehensile power. Either of them can lift his entire body by his little finger, and so swing to and fro, in the manner of a Borneo gorilla."

The act changed, too. The twins had been coached to use their soft-spoken natures to good effect. They were now presented as "civilized wild men," dressed in identical eccentric American kid's clothes, their long hair tamed and sometimes braided. Waino would read poetry aloud. Plutano offered comic relief, playing tricks on his brother and members of the audience.

When Hiram died of natural causes at age 80 in 1905, Barney left the business for good. He could afford to retire: the brothers had lived frugally and in their Barnum years alone made about $200,000, more than $4 million in today's money. Barney died in 1912, and the two were returned to their hometown of Mount Vernon, where they are buried under a gravestone marked "Little Men."

BORN TO BE WILD

The success of the Davis brothers made "Wild Men of Borneo" a circus staple. There were scores of them, populating freak shows all over the country, though only a few made an impression as memorable as the originals. Here are a few:

Oofty Goofty: Leon Borchardt arrived from Germany as a stowaway in 1876, at the age of 14. He roamed from city to city for a few years, then joined the U.S. Cavalry in 1883, but didn't like it, so he deserted and joined a sideshow act. In 1884 he appeared in a San Francisco freak show, billed as the "Wild Man of Borneo". His act: he appeared in a cage, covered with tar and horsehair, eating raw meat thrown to him by his "keeper." As he devoured the meat, he shouted "Oofty goofty!" which is how he got his name. A few years later, Oofty Goofty—a heavy drinker—branched out into a new act when he discovered, after being tossed into the street, that he didn't feel much pain. He took to wandering the San Francisco streets with a baseball bat, inviting people to beat him with it for 25¢. (Hitting him with a walking stick cost 15¢, and kicking him, 5¢.) Oofty's greatest "theatrical" triumph: starring in *Romeo and Juliet* opposite Big Bertha, a circus fat lady who had became a star of sorts because she couldn't act, sing, or dance but did anyway. Because of Bertha's girth, it wasn't safe to allow her on the traditional Juliet balcony; instead she stayed on the ground, and Oofty Goofty, playing Romeo as the Wild Man of Borneo, howled out his lines from the balcony…but reportedly performed his love scenes so roughly that Bertha quit after a week.

Mingo the Mudeater: This ad hoc wild man was created out of desperation. Ray Daley and a partner were stranded in Pawhuska, Oklahoma, after the circus they were traveling with went under. Deciding that a Wild Man show was the only thing they could trick up quickly to raise money, Daley advertised the appearance of "Mingo the Mudeater." To avoid having to eat real mud, he concocted a mix of Grape Nuts, chocolate, and milk. The plan was for Daley to appear in front a pen of wood and cloth as Mingo's "trainer" and announce what they were about to see. His partner would sell tickets and stall the crowd until Daley could change into his homemade costume and wig. Instead, the audience pushed inside, catching him halfway through his transformation. Daley quickly smeared his "mud" over his face and started eating it, but it was too late. One of the spectators grabbed his wig and pulled it off. On hearing the uproar inside, Daley's quick-thinking partner pushed over the enclosure and the two escaped in the confusion with $40, enough to get out of town and join up with another circus.

The REAL Wild Men: By the 1920s, the "Wild Man of Borneo" acts had become something of a cliché, but clever operators like Coney Island freak show entrepreneur Sam Gumpertz knew they still brought people in. That gave Gumpertz a novel idea. Instead of just slapping the "Wild Man" label on a sideshow performer, he recruited a group of real natives from Borneo and billed them as the "Authentic Wild Men from Borneo." Exactly how many Wild Men he imported and what became of them is unknown, but legend has it that Gumpertz convinced their chief to send them to New York by giving him 200 bags of salt.

*   *   *

STAYIN' ALIVE

Barry Gibb of the Bee Gees survived several major accidents as a child. He was severely burned, was hit by a car, fell through a roof, was hit by a car again, and accidentally shot himself in the face with a BB gun.

Animals Famous for 15 Minutes

Andy Warhol didn't mention animals when he said "in the future everyone will be famous for 15 minutes" but he should have. Here are five critters who briefly reigned over the news.

BUMMER AND LAZARUS

Background: San Francisco in the 1860s was a rough-and-tumble city where rat infestations were common and stray dogs roamed the streets. Two strays, though, became the talk of the town: Bummer—so called because he was a "bum," begging from passersby—and his buddy, Lazarus. Their friendship began in 1861 when Lazarus, a scruffy yellow/black terrier mix, was attacked by a larger dog. Bummer, described as a cross between a bull terrier and a Newfoundland, raced to Lazarus's aid, fought off the other dog, and then brought his new friend scraps of food until he recovered.

What Happened: From then on the two dogs were inseparable and became known around town for their rat-killing prowess. (The *San Francisco Bulletin* once reported that the pair had killed 400 rats at a local fruit market.) The dogs' hijinks became a regular feature in the city's newspapers, prompting the San Francisco Board of Supervisors to declare them official "wards of the city," and exempt from leash laws—important because strays were routinely caught and killed at the time.

Aftermath: The friendship came to an end in 1863 when Lazarus was poisoned, reportedly by a man who claimed the dog had bitten his son. Newspapers covered the dog's death—the *Daily Evening Bulletin* published an article called "Lament for Lazarus"—and a funeral procession followed. The dog's final resting place: he was stuffed and put on display in a saloon. Bummer rarely left the neighborhood where his buddy had died after that. His passed away in 1865, two months after a drunk kicked him down a flight of stairs. Mark Twain wrote the dog's obituary in the *Virginia City Enterprise*:

> The old vagrant "Bummer" is really dead at last; and although he was always more respected than his obsequious vassal, the dog "Lazarus," his exit has not made half as much stir in the newspaper world as signalized the departure of the latter.

Bummer was also taxidermied, and both dogs were displayed in the Golden Gate Park Museum until 1910, when their musty old carcasses were discarded. In 1992 a plaque in their honor was placed in a park near the Transamerica Pyramid, where it remains today.

PUFFY THE PERSIAN CAT

Background: One night in 1944, while sitting in a nightclub, Arthur Newman "discovered" that Puffy, his cream-colored Persian cat, possessed amazing powers of hypnosis. Newman had settled the cat on the end of the bar, and a woman was petting him when suddenly, as Newman put it, "Well, sir, that girl was simply out on her feet. It wasn't from drinking, either. I'm something of a hypnotist myself and I quickly realized that she was in a real hypnotic trance, brought on by Puffy staring into her eyes." With that, Puffy's career as a hypnotist was born.

What Happened: Newman trained Puffy to look longer and more steadily into people's eyes. The cat would hold his subject's stare while Newman counted, and within 10 seconds the person would go into a trance. A few months later the duo was touring military hospitals, where, according to Newman, some 300 people were hypnotized by Puffy. (Besides having entertainment value, Newman claimed Puffy's trances also cured headaches.) The cat also appeared at war bond drives, "autographing" photos with his paw print in exchange for the purchase of a war bond. Puffy became so famous that the American Feline Society made him their honorary president and officially declared Puffy to be "king of all cats." The society's president, Robert Lothar, said, "We believe you to be the greatest living feline…with powers never before possessed by a cat, or, so far as we can learn, by any living creature other than a human being."

ROSIE THE BEAR

Background: In the mid-1940s, Rosie, a 250-pound bear, was probably one of the most unusual pedestrians on the streets of New York City. A performer on radio, on TV, and in movies, Rosie and her owner, Stanley Beebe, often walked arm-in-paw down the city streets on their way to her gigs. Rosie's parents were born in Russia but came to America in 1917 as cubs. By 1945 they were living—along with Rosie and her two siblings—in a converted bus in Stanley Beebe's Brooklyn backyard.

What Happened: Beebe trained and managed the performing bear family, booking them into theaters, carnivals, and hospitals. When they performed together, the bears ice-skated, roller-skated, or acted out comic skits where they pretended to be in love or drunk. Rosie, though, was the breakout star. She was an accomplished voice actress, appearing on radio shows where she'd growl or snort on cue, and she was a popular guest on game shows. (On one, a blindfolded man had been told to waltz with a partner, who was wearing a fur coat. The "partner," of course, was Rosie.)

2008 an artist created a hybrid tree that grows 40 different fruits, including cherries, peaches, and plums.

Rosie had a part in the 1946 movie *Road to Utopia* starring Bob Hope and Bing Crosby. That same year, *Life* magazine ran an article on Rosie that featured photos of her in a cab, walking down the city streets, and at work. She was well compensated for her jobs, as *Life* noted: "Rosie makes as much as $100 an appearance, which is a lot of money for a 10-year-old bear."

HUBERTA THE HIPPO

Background: Hippos aren't migratory, which is why it was newsworthy when one began wandering along the South African coast in 1928. The hippo was probably born near St. Lucia Bay in Zululand, but rather than stay with the herd, she headed south. She was first noticed in an area with no indigenous hippos, and when reporters realized she was on the move, they followed her. (She was first called "Bill," then "Hubert," and then, when she was discovered to be female, "Huberta.")

What Happened: Huberta traveled for more than two years, covered close to 1,000 miles, and crossed more than 120 rivers. She preferred to stay concealed, traveling at night and hiding in bushes and swamps, although she did occasionally stir up excitement by wandering into town squares and markets. Crowds followed her, and the international press detailed her journey, calling her "South Africa's National Pet." The Natal Provincial Council declared Huberta "Royal Game" to protect her from hunters. Some Zulu believed she was the reincarnation of their leader, Shaka.

Nobody knew why the hippo was traveling: some thought she was returning to ancestral hippo lands in the south; others thought she was on the run after having seen her mother killed; still others said she was looking for her lost mate. Whatever her reasons, Huberta traveled ever southward, never staying in one place for more than a few months.

Aftermath: On April 23, 1931, tragedy struck: Huberta's body was found floating in the Keiskamma River, near King William's Town. Despite her protected status, she'd been shot in the head six times. The international outcry was immediate. As the South African parliament ordered the police to find her killers, people sent sympathy cards, flowers, and donations to have her taxidermied. On May 27, four farmers were tried and convicted of Huberta's death (and fined £25 each). Huberta was skinned, mounted, and put on display at the Durban museum, where more than 20,000 people came to see her in a single month. Death didn't end Huberta's travels: she was shipped off to London for a special exhibition and then returned to her final resting place at the Amathole Museum in King William's Town. She remains on display there to this day.

Secret History: Covert Operations

On page 318 we told you the origins of U.S. intelligence agencies such as the CIA and the NSA. Almost from the start, those agencies were involved in what are now known as covert operations—secret activities done in a such a way that, if discovered, the president can deny them. Here's a look at some notable covert operations ordered by presidents from different eras in U.S. history—right up to the (mostly secret) present.

MAINE BORDER DISPUTE

Background: In 1841 the U.S. was mired in an increasingly volatile dispute with Great Britain over the location of the border with Canada, most notably in Maine, where the situation threatened to break out into open war. President John Tyler wanted to negotiate a deal—even if the deal meant that Maine would lose territory—because he believed that resolving the issue would be a major foreign policy coup for his administration. But most citizens of Maine were adamantly against making concessions to the British.

Covert Operation: Through his secretary of state, Daniel Webster, Tyler secretly paid Francis O. J. Smith, a Maine politician and former newspaper publisher, to embark on a secret yearlong propaganda mission to bribe newspaper editors and reporters all over Maine to publish stories that were favorable to compromise. (Smith also bribed leading citizens in Maine to speak in support of compromise.)

Outcome: It worked. Opposition to a compromise steadily decreased over the months, and in 1842 political leaders in Maine agreed to concede the contested territory to the British. That allowed for the passage of a treaty—and Tyler was lauded in the press for what was called a historic foreign policy accomplishment.

Bonus Fact: Four years later, someone leaked documents about the operation to Congress, and it became one of the biggest scandals of the era. But Tyler was out of office by then, and the outcry went nowhere.

THE MEXICAN SPY COMPANY

Background: In 1847, one year into the Mexican–American War, the U.S. Army began a push from the Atlantic coastal city of Veracruz, west toward Mexico City. Problems: 1) the Americans had little knowledge of the terrain, and 2) not only did they have to contend with the Mexican army—the area was teeming with bandits.

Covert Operation: When the army captured a bandit chief named Manuel Dominguez, President James Polk approved a scheme proposed by an army intelligence officer. They offered to pay Dominguez and each of his men $20 a month—a *lot* of money at the time—to serve as spies, couriers, and scouts, and guide the Americans through the hostile terrain. Dominguez, whom army journals described as "portly" and "bold as a lion," agreed.

Outcome: The Mexican Spy Company, as it became known—and which grew to more than 100 men—served as the U.S. Army's Mexican intelligence unit for the remainder of the war. It played a significant role in the taking of Mexico City, which led to the end of the war in February 1848. Dominguez and many of his fellow bandits even settled down in the United States after the war ended.

Bonus Fact: Dominguez's company had uniforms by which members could be easily recognized—bright green jackets with scarlet cuffs, and red bandanas on black sombreros.

OVERTHROW IN PANAMA

Background: In 1902 President Teddy Roosevelt persuaded Congress to take over the failed French attempt to construct a canal across the isthmus of Panama, in what was then part of Colombia. The United States would pay the French company that had abandoned the canal project $40 million, but the deal would only go through if Colombia agreed to a treaty on the issue. The Colombian senate refused.

Covert Operation: In October 1903, Roosevelt secretly collaborated with Phillippe Bunau-Varilla—one of the shareholders in the French company—in a plan to take advantage of unrest in Panama. Just weeks later, Panamanian rebels—with a fresh infusion of cash from Bunau-Varilla—stormed government buildings in Panama City and the port city of Colón. When a Colombian navy vessel arrived at Colón to put down the revolt, a U.S. Navy gunship, conveniently sent to the region by Roosevelt, "persuaded" them to leave without firing a shot.

Outcome: Within days, the independent nation of Panama was created. And just days after that, the new country agreed to a treaty granting the canal region to the United States, and work soon commenced on the Panama Canal.

Bonus Fact: The Frenchman, Bunau-Varilla, not only received his share of the $40 million—he actually negotiated the canal treaty on behalf of Panama. Not a single Panamanian signed it.

ELECTIONS IN ITALY

Background: After World War II ended, U.S. leaders feared that communists might be victorious in upcoming Italian national elections.

Eulachon, a kind of fish, are so oily that Native Americans added wicks and used them as candles.

This was in the early years of the Cold War and at the beginning of the decades-long competition between American and Soviet intelligence agencies to influence events around the world.

Covert Op: In early 1948, President Harry Truman approved a CIA plan to sway the Italian election. Agents were sent to Italy with what were described as "bagloads of cash" to bolster the campaigns of candidates of the anti-communist Christian Democratic Party. Agents also engaged in a countrywide propaganda campaign, sending letters to millions of Italian citizens, warning of the dangers of communism, and paying for placement of newspaper articles on the subject as well.

Outcome: The Christian Democratic Party won the election by a large margin, and the operation—the newly formed CIA's first covert action—was considered a great success.

Bonus Fact: The CIA ran covert actions to influence every Italian election for the next 24 years until the operations were exposed in the early 1970s.

THE CIA AND THE DALAI LAMA

Background: In 1949 communist forces led by Mao Zedong won China's civil war, marking the founding of the People's Republic of China. In 1950 Mao's Red Army invaded Tibet. A Tibetan resistance movement quickly formed but was severely outmatched.

Covert Operation: On orders from President Truman, the CIA began covert operations in Tibet in 1951. This included the training of about 300 Tibetan soldiers—near the town of Leadville, Colorado. (The idea was that the Rocky Mountain region provided a good match for the terrain in Tibet.) Over the next several years, with direct CIA support, those fighters helped lead a guerrilla war against Chinese forces in Tibet.

Outcome: The CIA's operations in Tibet continued until the early 1970s, but were unsuccessful. Tibet remains under Chinese control today. The agency was, however, directly and successfully involved in the escape of Tibet's leader, the 14th Dalai Lama, and several of his followers to India. (The Dalai Lama still leads Tibet's government-in-exile in Dharamsala, in northern India.)

THE BAY OF PIGS

Background: In 1959 Fidel Castro's communist revolutionaries defeated the Cuban army and took control of the island nation. The following year, Castro cut off all ties to the United States and nationalized U.S. assets in Cuba.

Covert Operation: In 1960 President Dwight Eisenhower approved a CIA plan to overthrow the Castro government. When John F. Kennedy took office in early 1961, he gave his consent to move the operation

New Year's Eve tradition: in Italy and Spain, people wear red undies for good luck. (Venezuela: yellow.)

forward. The CIA trained about 1,400 anti-Castro Cuban exiles for 10 months at a secret CIA base in Guatemala. In April 1961, the makeshift army attacked, landing boats at the Bay of Pigs, on Cuba's southern coast, with support from a handful of U.S. fighter planes and B-26 bombers.

Outcome: The "Bay of Pigs" operation, as it has become known, was a disaster. The exiles were crushed by Castro's much larger and better-equipped forces in just three days, with 118 exiles killed and 1,200 captured. In addition, two of the B-26s were shot down, killing four Americans. The blundered attack strengthened Castro's popularity in Cuba and around the world and was a huge embarrassment for the Kennedy administration.

Bonus Fact: Details of the CIA's involvement were not declassified until 2011. Among the facts revealed, CIA leaders apparently didn't believe the operation would work…but didn't share that information with Kennedy.

ARMS TO AFGHANISTAN

Background: In 1978 a Soviet-backed coup saw communists take power in Afghanistan. A few months later, *Mujahideen* fighters—Afghan Muslims opposed to the communists—staged an uprising that turned into a civil war.

Covert Operation: In July 1979, President Jimmy Carter authorized Operation Cyclone, a CIA plan to funnel arms and money through Pakistani intelligence agencies to Mujahideen fighters in Afghanistan. In December 1979, the Soviet Union invaded Afghanistan, marking the beginning of a full-scale international war. When Ronald Reagan became president in 1981, he expanded the CIA operation exponentially, and by 1987 it was costing more than $600 million a year.

Outcome: American arms and funds helped the Mujahideen take power back from the communists in Afghanistan; the war ended in a stalemate in 1989, when the last Soviet forces left the country. This was seen as a win for the U.S., especially because it was done without the use of American troops—important in the aftermath of the Vietnam War. But Operation Cyclone has been the target of a lot of criticism over the years because it cost as much as $3 billion of American taxpayer money. In addition, it was from the U.S.-backed Mujahideen fighters that the Muslim terrorist organizations Al Qaeda and the Taliban both emerged.

THE DRONE WARS

Background: In 2001 the United States began using *unmanned aerial vehicles*—or drones—armed with missiles in its war with Afghanistan. Two years later, drones were being used in the war with Iraq.

Covert Op: In 2004 President George W. Bush gave the go-ahead for a secret CIA program targeting terrorists with drone missile strikes—in Pakistan, which was not a U.S. war zone. When Barack Obama became president in 2009, he expanded the program, adding targets in Yemen and, later, in Somalia, two more countries not officially at war with the United States.

Outcome: The existence of the CIA drone program has been widely reported almost since its start, but many of its details remain secret. And while supporters hail the program's success in eliminating several known terrorists, it has been controversial from the start, especially because the strikes have killed hundreds of civilians, including women and children. In 2013 a U.N. report found that the program's lack of transparency regarding civilian deaths may mean it is in violation of international law. The number of confirmed CIA drone strikes under President Bush: 52. Under President Obama: 456 (so far).

A FEW MORE TOP SECRET FACTS

• The CIA has its own paramilitary division, known as SAD/SOG—Special Activities Division/Special Operations Group. (A paramilitary is an army-like organization that is not officially aligned with a country's armed forces.) SAD/SOG fighters engage in the blackest of "black ops"—the most secretive and dangerous covert operations, including sabotage, kidnappings, and targeted killings behind enemy lines. Very few details of the organization are known. SAD/SOG paramilitary operatives, along with Pakistani forces, captured Khalid Sheikh Mohammed, one of the architects of the 9/11 attacks, in Rawalpindi, Pakistan, in 2003.

• In 1960 the CIA ordered Larry Devlin, station chief in the central African nation of Congo, to assassinate the country's first elected prime minister, Patrice Lumumba. Devlin wrote in a 2007 memoir that he received a tube of poison-laced toothpaste, created by a CIA chemist, with which he was supposed to carry out the plot. Devlin claims he disagreed with the order and stalled. Three months later, in September 1960, Lumumba was deposed in a CIA-backed coup. A few months later he was captured and subsequently tortured and executed by a rival Congolese faction.

• The CIA admitted in a 2000 report that it was deeply involved in the events leading to the 1973 coup that ended in the overthrow and death of Chilean president Salvador Allende. (Allende's death during the coup was officially declared a suicide, but many believe he was assassinated.) The report also admitted that the CIA had actively supported the brutal military dictatorship of Augusto Pinochet that ruled the nation for 17 years after Allende's death.

According to the USDA, a "fresh" chicken can be frozen as long as it's never been chilled below 26°F.

Behind the Lines

Every screenwriter dreams of writing a line of dialogue that achieves TV or movie immortality. But it takes more than good writing; it also takes good direction, great acting—and more than a little good luck. Here are the stories behind some of film and TV's most enduring quotes.

Famous Line: "Fasten your seat belts, it's going to be a bumpy night."

Said By: Margo Channing (Bette Davis) in *All About Eve* (1950)

Story: This oft-imitated phrase—usually ending with "ride" instead of "night"—was coined by Oscar-winning screenwriter Joseph L. Mankiewicz in this movie about an aging actress who takes a young starlet under her wing, only to be betrayed by her. (Interestingly, the metaphor is referring to passenger air travel, as most cars didn't have seat belts in 1950.) According to film historian Sam Staggs in the book *Vanity Fair's Tales of Hollywood*, it was Davis's improvisational delivery that elevated the line to iconic status:

> It is in the party scene, Margo takes her cue from Karen, who says, "We know you, we've seen you like this before. Is it over—or is it just the beginning?" Instead of responding immediately as indicated in the script, Margo drains her martini and walks toward the stairs with a shoulder-rolling, hip-swinging swagger. She halts, swerves, regards Karen, Lloyd, and Bill with a scowl, then lets it rip: "Fasten your seat belts, it's going to be a bumpy night."

Mankiewicz came up with the line, but the timing was all Davis's. "Those are things that you should be able to do as an actress that a director wouldn't think of telling you to do," she said. "When Margo holds back like that, it lets you know that she's collecting venom."

Famous Line: "Show me the money!"

Said By: Rod Tidwell (Cuba Gooding Jr.) in *Jerry Maguire* (1996)

Story: Cameron Crowe admitted that while writing the sports agent drama, he was "swinging for the fences" by trying to write a classic movie line. But he also warns screenwriters that this approach rarely works: "Audiences are smart. They smell the typewriter; they feel the studio executives' hands reaching into their pockets. More often than not, they reject the spoon-fed big line with glee." Proving his own point, Crowe actually thought that another of Tidwell's lines—his fake form of currency called "the Kwan"—would resonate with audiences. But it was

---

Nutty fact: There are four towns in the U.S. named Peanut.

"show me the money" that really caught on. (Even presidents have used it.)

Crowe got the line while researching for the movie. He followed around an NFL player named Tim McDonald, who was going through difficult contract negotiations at the time. "He was at an owners' meeting to be paraded through the lobby to get his price up, because he was a free agent," recalled Crowe. "McDonald said, 'I've got a wife and I've got kids, and I've been beaten up for five years here in Phoenix, and now I'm a free agent. Show me the money.'" Crowe said he "turned McDonald's yearning for financial self-worth into Tidwell's war cry." (Gooding later said that the line has "haunted him" ever since. "I can be at a funeral, and in the back you'll hear some jerk go, 'Show me the money.'")

Bonus: Crowe actually wrangled two classic lines from that movie. The other one: Renée Zellweger's "You had me at hello."

Famous Line: "There's no crying in baseball!"
Said By: Jimmy Dugan (Tom Hanks) in *A League of Their Own* (1992)
Story: Screenwriting partners Lowell Ganz and Babaloo Mandel (who also wrote *City Slickers* and *Parenthood*) say they come up with their best lines while conversing as the characters they're writing—and that's how this line was born. It comes in a scene in which washed-up player Dugan is managing an all-women's baseball team during World War II —he berates a player in the dugout, and she starts tearing up. "Are you *crying?*" he asks. She says "no" between sobs, to which Dugan whines, "There's no crying in baseball!" (He then repeats it several times.) Ganz and Mandel knew it was a funny line, but they didn't expect it to become a famous line…until they heard Hanks's delivery.

Famous Line: "I drink your milkshake! I drink it up!"
Said By: Daniel Plainview (Daniel Day-Lewis) in *There Will Be Blood* (2007)
Story: In the final scene of writer-director Paul Thomas Anderson's drama, oilman Plainview drunkenly explains to a preacher, Eli Sunday (Paul Dano), how he had stolen his oil reserves and defeated him: "Here, if you have a milkshake, and I have a milkshake, and I have a straw. There it is, that's the straw, you see? Now my straw reaches across the room, and starts to drink your milkshake. I drink your milkshake! I drink it up!"

Anderson didn't come up with the milkshake metaphor himself, though. He took it from the testimony of Albert Fall, a New Mexico senator who appeared before Congress in 1924 during the Teapot Dome scandal. "He was asked to describe drainage," said Anderson. "And his

the 1500s, English ladies put apple slices under their arms to absorb odors, then gave them to suitors as gifts.

way of describing it was, 'If you have a milkshake and I have a milkshake, and my straw reaches across the room…' I'm sure I embellished it and made it more Plainview. But Fall used the word *milkshake*, and I thought it was so great. I get so happy every time I hear that word."

But wait: a 2013 article in the *Case Western Reserve Law Review* reported that there was no such quote from the Teapot Dome scandal hearings. The article suggests that Anderson's inspiration was much more recent: while debating drilling in the Arctic National Wildlife Refuge in 2003, Senator Pete Domenici (coincidentally, also of New Mexico) said,

> The oil is underground, and it is going to be drilled and come up. Here is a giant reservoir underground. Just like a curved straw, you put it underground and maneuver it, and the "milkshake" is way over there, and your little child wants the milkshake, and they sit over here in their bedroom where they are feeling ill, and they just gobble it up from way down in the kitchen, where you don't even have to move the Mix Master that made the ice cream for them.

(Wherever Anderson got the line, it makes us want a milkshake.)

Famous Line: "I am the one who knocks!"

Said By: Walter White (Bryan Cranston) in *Breaking Bad* (2011)

Story: This chilling line was written by Gennifer Hutchison, who started out as *Breaking Bad* creator Vince Gilligan's assistant on *The X Files*. She has since emerged as one of television's most lauded scripters, thanks in no small part to the "one who knocks" speech. It came in a pivotal episode of the AMC show's fourth season when Walter's transformation from cancer-stricken chemistry teacher to murderous meth manufacturer becomes known to his wife Skyler (Anna Gunn). "It's the first time Walt really owns up to it," explains Cranston, "not only to himself but also to his wife." Skyler tells Walter that she's afraid someone will come knocking on their door and shoot him. "No," he responds coldly, "you clearly don't know who you're talking to, so let me clue you in. I am not *in* danger, Skyler. I *am* the danger. A guy opens his door and gets shot and you think that of me? No. *I am the one who knocks!*"

Hutchison is proud of that speech: "It was always a cool scene, but I didn't realize how big it would become." Not only was it voted *Breaking Bad*'s best line by its fans, but like any iconic quote, it has become the subject of numerous parodies. (Don't believe it? Go online and check out all of the *Breaking Bad* "I am the one who knock-knocks" jokes.)

Famous Line: "I'll be back."

Said By: The Terminator (Arnold Schwarzenegger) in *The Terminator* (1984) and nearly every movie Arnie's made since

Story: Writer-director James Cameron didn't expect this to become the most famous line from the film. In the original script, the Terminator enters the lobby of a police station and queries about the location of Sarah Connor (whom he's hunting), only to be told he can't see her. He then scans the lobby and says to the clerk, "I'll come back." But when it came time to film the scene, Schwarzenegger thought it felt a little flat—that it would be more comedic if he says "I'll be back" instead. Cameron was reluctant, initially telling his star, "I don't tell you how to act; don't tell me how to write." But then he eased up and gave Schwarzenegger 10 takes to say the line. Then came another problem: Schwarzenegger's thick Austrian accent made it difficult for him to say "I'll" clearly (it sounded like "owl"), so he suggested, "I will be back." Cameron didn't like that either, but let Schwarzenegger try it. When it came time to edit the film, Cameron chose the take in which the Terminator says "I'll be back."

The first time Cameron saw the film with an audience, he didn't expect the line to get a reaction because the joke, as he wrote it, isn't complete until a few moments later when the Terminator drives a police van through the lobby. But when Schwarzenegger looks around, leans in, and says, "I'll be back," the audience "erupted with laughter." Right then, Cameron knew that it would become a classic movie quote.

Famous Line: "I am serious, and don't call me Shirley."
Said By: Dr. Rumack (Leslie Nielsen) in *Airplane!* (1980)
Story: One of the reasons *Airplane!* works so well as a comedy is its drollness. In scene after scene, the actors deliver silly lines with straight faces, and the result is one of the funniest movies of all time. That mixture of serious and silly comes from the fact that writer-directors David Zucker, Jim Abrahams, and Jerry Zucker bought the rights to a 1957 disaster film called *Zero Hour!*—which has the same plot and many of the same lines—and added jokes. For example, in *Zero Hour!*, the controller says on the phone, "He's a menace to himself and everything in the air!" That same line is in *Airplane!*, but after a pause, the controller says, "Yes, birds too." Another example, says David Zucker: "A character would say, 'Surely you can't be serious.' That was a straight line right from *Zero Hour*. Then we would put in, 'I am serious—and don't call me Shirley.'"

For actor Leslie Nielsen, that film not only changed him from a dramatic to a comedic actor—which he'd always wanted to be—but the "Shirley" line became indelibly linked to him for the rest of his life (he died in 2010). "I thought it was amusing," he recalled, "but it never occurred to me that it was going to become a trademark." The silly pun actually earned a spot on AFI's "100 Best Movie Quotes" list.

Half of all adult Russians have college degrees—the highest percentage of any country.

Famous Line: "Here's looking at you, kid."

Said By: Rick Blaine (Humphrey Bogart) to Ilsa Lund (Ingrid Bergman) in *Casablanca* (1942)

Story: This Best Picture–winning romance set in a North African nightclub reigns supreme as the movie with the most memorable lines. In fact, six of them have made it onto the AFI's "Top 100" list. And two weren't even in the original script. The final line—"Louis, I think this is the beginning of a beautiful friendship"—was written by producer Hal Wallis after filming had completed. (Bogart was called back in to dub it.) And the movie's most famous line wasn't in the script, either. The story goes that in between takes, Bogart taught Bergman how to play poker, and when he won he'd say, "Here's looking at you, kid." After Bogie ad-libbed it an early scene set in Paris, director Michael Curtiz liked the line—and Bogie's delivery—so much that he had him say it three more times in the film. It's unknown where the line originated, but Bogart had used it eight years earlier in the 1934 movie *Midnight*.

Famous Line: "Live long and prosper."

Said By: Mr. Spock (Leonard Nimoy) in *Star Trek* (1967)

Story: Written by science-fiction great Theodore Sturgeon, the *Star Trek* episode "Amok Time" introduced Mr. Spock's home planet. That's when most of Spock's backstory was written. It's well known among Trekkies that Nimoy invented the Vulcan hand salute himself (borrowed from an ancient Jewish blessing), but he was always quick to point out that it was Sturgeon who came up with "Live long and prosper." Where did Sturgeon get it? Shakespeare. In *Romeo and Juliet*, Romeo says to Balthasar, "Live, and be prosperous." But it's even older than that: The ancient Egyptian blessing *ankh wedja seneb* translates to "May he live, be prosperous, be healthy." Spock and numerous other "Vulcans" have used the line through six Star Trek TV series and 10 Star Trek feature films (so far).

Famous Line: "My mama always said, 'Life was like a box of chocolates—you never know what you're gonna get.'"

Said By: Forrest Gump (Tom Hanks) in *Forrest Gump* (1994)

Story: The line in the original novel by Winston Groom was "Being an idiot is no box of chocolates," but when screenwriter Eric Roth was adapting the story, he decided the line would work better if it sounded like an "aphorism that doesn't particularly make sense." So he changed it to "Life is like a box of chocolates." When *Gump* director Robert Zemeckis read it, he asked Roth, "What the hell does this mean?" Roth's answer: "You never know what you're going to get." So Zemeckis tacked on Roth's explanation, and the rest is movie history.

Someday Their Prince Will Come

North of New Zealand, east of Australia, and west of Fiji there's an island that's home to one of the more unusual religious sects we've ever come across.

D OUBLE TROUBLE

The nation of Vanuatu is independent today, but from 1906 to 1980, this island group in the South Pacific was a colony jointly administered by England and France. Then called New Hebrides, it was perhaps the only territory in the world with two colonial masters instead of one. Relations between the two countries were often strained and remained so as New Hebrides moved toward independence in the 1970s. England backed one political party in a bid to retain their influence; France backed another.

Both countries also worked to sway public opinion in their favor. In this battle, the British had a weapon that France could not counter: the prestige of the British royal family. Portraits of Queen Elizabeth and her husband, Prince Philip, were distributed all over the 65 inhabited islands that made up New Hebrides. In 1974 the couple even paid a visit, steaming into the capital city of Port-Vila, on the island of Efate, aboard the royal yacht *Britannia*.

The royal treatment worked. The British-supported party won a majority in the Vanuatu parliament in the first elections after independence…but victory came at an unusual price: 128 miles south of Efate on the island of Tanna, an aboriginal tribe of some 300 people called the Kastam came to see Prince Philip as a god in human form and began to worship him as their messiah.

TRADITIONAL VALUES

Life in Yaohnanen, the isolated hillside village that is the tribe's home on Tanna, has changed surprisingly little since their ancestors arrived some 2,400 years ago. The villagers live in bamboo huts, and what little traditional clothing they wear—skirts for the women, and *nambas*, genital sheaths resembling whisk brooms, for the men—they make themselves out of plant fibers. There is no electricity in the village, no running water, no radio, no television, no newspapers, and no Internet. Pigs are the only form of currency. Members of the tribe rarely leave the

---

Horses like calming instrumental music but are agitated by rock music.

island, and what little contact they have with the outside world comes from the few visitors willing to make the difficult trek to the village. The language spoken by the Kastam has no written form, and most tribespeople are illiterate. More than a century of contact with missionaries determined to stamp out Kastam culture and traditions has left the tribe wary of change; the few families who desire formal education for their children have to send them outside the village to get it because there are no schools in Yaohnanen.

IN THE BEGINNING

It's a safe bet that all of those royal portraits passed out in the 1970s had something to do with the isolated Kastam coming to see Philip as a living god. Their tribal culture is male-dominated; they have difficulty conceiving of a Great Britain in which Queen Elizabeth is the head of state and her husband has no constitutional role whatsoever. When the tribespeople were presented with portraits of the royal couple and told that the queen was one of the most important women in the world, they naturally assumed, based on their own cultural experience, that the man standing next to her in the picture was even more important than she was.

OUR FATHER, WHO ART IN LONDON

This conclusion dovetailed nicely with the tribe's creation myth: where the Judeo-Christian world has Adam and Eve, the Kastam have the story of two spirits, one dark-skinned and one light-skinned, who emerged from Mt. Yasur, the active volcano that dominates the landscape of Tanna. The dark-skinned spirit remained on the island and founded the Kastam, whose members also have dark skin. The light-skinned spirit traveled far away in search of a queen to marry and fathered the light-skinned races of the world. (Another legend says that the volcano god sent his oldest son to the U.K., both to give spiritual guidance to the British and to prevent their missionaries from converting the Kastam to Christianity.) Exposure to those same missionaries and their teaching about a returning messiah likely put the next piece of the puzzle into place: the idea that someday the light-skinned spirit would return, ushering in Paradise when he arrived.

What was it that finally cemented the notion that the spirit had taken the human form of Prince Philip? When the royal yacht *Britannia* brought him (and the queen) to Vanuatu in 1974, the chief of the Kastam, Jack Naiva, was one of the dignitaries on hand to welcome the royal couple. Like other tribal leaders, he was on the water paddling his canoe when the majestic 412-foot royal yacht sailed into port. It may have been the biggest ship he'd ever seen, and it made quite an impression. So did Prince Philip. "I saw him standing on the deck in his white uniform and I knew that he was the true Messiah," the chief told the London *Daily Mail* in 2006.

ABSENCE MAKES THE HEART GROW FONDER

Chief Jack must have hoped that Prince Philip would come to Tanna Island, but the royal visit to Vanuatu was a short one, and the *Britannia* soon sailed off again. Philip never did visit Tanna, and in the more than 40 years since, he hasn't returned to visit it or any of Vanuatu's other islands.

But that hasn't stopped the Kastam from believing that Philip, who turned 93 in 2014, not only *will* return but has *promised* to do so. When he does return, the Kastam believe that a miraculous age will dawn, much like the one Christians believe will accompany the second coming of Christ. Mature *kava* plants, which the tribe uses to brew a potent drink of the same name, will burst forth from the soil the moment Philip sets foot on Tanna. He will bring a wealth of material goods with him—everything from knives for sticking pigs and shovels for digging up yams, to electric appliances, pickup trucks, and all the cigarettes the Kastam can smoke. They won't have to worry about the adverse health effects of smoking, either, because Philip will banish sickness and death when he arrives. Old people—Philip included—will become young again, shedding their skin like snakes to reveal their rejuvenated selves underneath.

HOME AWAY FROM HOME

To be ready for Prince Philip's arrival, which like the Rapture could come at any moment, the tribe has planted a garden for him and built the hut that he will live in. Like the rest of the dwellings in the village, Philip's hut has a dirt floor and lacks electricity and running water. "I know that in England he had a palace and servants, but here he will just live simply, like us," Jack Naiva's grandson Sikor Natuan said in 2010. There are no closets in the hut, but Philip won't need any: the tribe believes that as soon as he arrives he'll shed his Western clothing for a *namba* genital sheath that is tied around the waist with a cord. Other than that, he'll be completely naked, just like the men of the tribe.

The Kastam expect that Prince Philip will take several wives when he arrives, and the candidates have already been selected. These women have not been prevented from marrying other men and starting families while they wait for Philip, but he can still claim them when he arrives. "Don't worry. Whichever one Prince Philip picks will leave her husband willingly," Chief Jack assured reporters in 2008. Bonus: if Queen Elizabeth becomes lonely after Philip returns to Tanna, the tribe has offered to dispatch a warrior to London to keep her company.

Study: Men dream about other men 70% of the time; women dream of men and women equally.

STILL WAITING

So what does Prince Philip think of all this? He's aware of the Kastam and their interest in him, and he met with five members of the tribe who visited the U.K. in 2007 as part of a documentary film project. But at last report he still had no plans to visit Tanna. His daughter, Princess Anne, visited Vanuatu in 2014 but did not go to Tanna.

Philip has exchanged letters and gifts with the Kastam over the years. When the tribe sent him a pig-killing club called a *nal-nal* in the 1970s, he reciprocated with a framed photograph of himself holding the club. This and other photos and letters he has sent the tribe are among their most treasured possessions; they are kept in a special hut that serves as a shrine.

The Kastam have enough contact with the outside world to understand that their beliefs appear odd to others, but it doesn't faze them. "Christians have been waiting 2,000 years for a sign from Jesus, but our Philip sends us photographs!" Chief Jack Naiva told a reporter in 2005. "And one day he will come."

*　　*　　*

FACTS THAT ROCK

• Sulfur smells like rotten eggs, but it's not the only mineral with an odor. When crushed, arsenopyrite smells like garlic, and when heated, selenium smells like horseradish.

• The minerals aluminum oxide, limestone, phosphate, silica, and titanium dioxide all show up on the list of ingredients for toothpaste.

• Three percent of the carbon found in meteorites is pure diamond. It's pointless to look for them. They're a hundred-millionths of an inch wide and invisible to the human eye.

• Tough as steel yet soft enough to carve, jade's been used for thousands of years for everything from Chinese vases to Mayan axes to Maori tikis.

• Rubies and sapphires are rare forms of corundum, but small grains of this hard mineral make up a much more common material: sandpaper.

• What do pencils and nuclear reactors have in common? They both contain graphite rods.

• The popping noise a barbecue lighter makes comes from a spring-loaded hammer hitting a crystal. Thousands of volts shoot across the faces of the crystal, causing the spark that lights the gas in the grill.

• Of the more than 4,000 minerals on Earth, salt is the only one that humans eat on purpose, but it's not the only one with an interesting taste. Borax tastes sweet, epsomite bitter, and halite tastes salty. Warning: Some minerals are poisonous, so try not to lick any strange rocks.

In Tunisia, new buildings often have fish bones embedded in them as a good-luck charm.

Answers

AUNT GLADYS THE GREAT
Answers from page 166

One...Two...Three: Whichever number of matches I picked up, Aunt Gladys made sure to pick the number of matches that made our picks add up to *four*. For example, when I picked up one match, she picked up three. When I picked up two matches, she picked up two. When I picked up three matches, she picked up one. By doing this, she was able to pick up the 24th match every time, forcing me to pick up the 25th.

Multiplication: Aunt Gladys picked up the first two matches and made an X with them, creating the symbol XIII, the Roman numeral for 13.

Subtraction: Aunt Gladys used the napkin to cover the lower half of the XIII, creating VIII, the Roman numeral for eight.

Connecting the Dots: When Aunt Gladys turned the dominoes facedown on the table and mixed them around with her hands, she also palmed one of them and put it in her pocket without me noticing. She knew that if you take one domino away from a complete set and match the remaining 27 dominoes together in a single row, the dots at each end of the row will match those on the missing 28th domino.

Aunt Gladys brought the pilfered domino with her into the next room. After she closed the door, she took it out of her pocket and looked at it for the first time. She saw that it had one dot on one end, and four dots on the other end. That meant that when I finished putting the remaining dominoes together in a row, it too would have one dot at one end, and four dots at the other end. (Aunt Gladys repeated the trick four times, pocketing a different domino each time. I didn't figure out how she did it until she explained it to me.)

MOCK 'N' ROLL
Answers from page 181

1. f), **2.** m), **3.** n), **4.** d), **5.** j), **6.** e), **7.** p), **8.** q), **9.** a), **10.** r), **11.** h), **12.** s), **13.** b), **14.** i), **15.** c), **16.** l), **17.** g), **18.** k), **19.** t), **20.** o)

OL' JAY'S BRAIN TEASERS
Answers from page 313

1. Hold the egg five feet above the floor and let it go. It won't break until after it falls the first four feet.

Elvis Presley's last words: "I'm going to the bathroom to read."

2. Each word's letters are in alphabetical order.

3. 13 days. The snail gains one foot per day, so at the end of the 12th day, he is 12 feet from the bottom. The next day, he crawls up the last four feet to freedom.

4. The letter Q.

5. When the peasant drew the first card, he proclaimed that he'd picked the "yes" card and then tore it up into little pieces. "Hold up your card," he said to the king, who was left holding the "no" card.

6. The woman was pregnant; her baby was born on the way to the hospital.

7. The four words are "tremendous", "horrendous", "hazardous", and "stupendous".

8. Arrange them as: 55 5/5. That equals 56—four less than 12 x 5, which equals 60.

9. The missing words are "tedious" and "outside".

10. He's your father.

11. November 8th. The secret word is "calendar." (Each number represents the letter in the month. So, for October second, the second letter is "c"; for March second, the second letter is "a"; for April fifth, the fifth letter is "l", and so on until you spell "calendar.")

12. You're sitting at a piano keyboard, so press D, E-flat, E.

13. The last word is "zoos." That's because the first letters of each word are the only letters that rhyme with "e."

1,000 WAYS TO DIE

Answers from page 347

1. l), **2.** d), **3.** b), **4.** s), **5.** j), **6.** m), **7.** r), **8.** n), **9.** i), **10.** g.) **11.** a), **12.** k), **13.** e), **14.** p), **15.** c), **16.** q), **17.** h), **18.** f), **19.** o), **20.** t)

*   *   *

A NUMBERS GAME

The first—and probably the only—National Sheep Counting Championship took place in New South Wales, Australia, in 2002. It was inspired by sheep auctioneers who often have to count up to 100,000 sheep in a single day. So they decided to make a game out of it. The rules: several hundred sheep run past 10 competitors, who must accurately count them. The winner was Pete Desailly, who correctly counted 277 sheep. His prize: an official entry in *Guinness World Records*. (And we assume he also got a good night's sleep.)

More UNCLE JOHN than you can shake a stick at!

Log onto our online store at www.bathroomreader.com for dozens more great titles in the Bathroom Reader line. You'll find puzzle books, regional-interest books, big books, little books, and even—e-books! Great reading no matter where you are!

The Last Page

FELLOW BATHROOM READERS:
The fight for good bathroom reading should never be taken loosely—we must do our duty and sit firmly for what we believe in, even while the rest of the world is taking potshots at us.

We'll be brief. Now that we've proven we're not simply a flush-in-the-pan, we invite you to take the plunge: Sit Down and Be Counted! Log on to *www.bathroomreader.com* and earn a permanent spot on the BRI honor roll!

If you like reading our books…

VISIT THE BRI'S WEBSITE!

www.bathroomreader.com

- Receive our irregular newsletters via e-mail
- Order additional Bathroom Readers
- Find us on Facebook
- Tweet us on Twitter
- Blog us on our blog

Well, we're out of space, and when you've gotta go, you've gotta go. Tanks for all your support. Hope to hear from you soon.

Meanwhile, remember…

Keep on flushin'!